THE AUTHOR

William Empson was born in Yokefleet, in the East Riding of Yorkshire, in 1906. He was educated at Winchester College, then at Magdalene College, Cambridge, where he graduated in Mathematics and subsequently gained a first-class degree in English Literature. While Empson was still at Cambridge, his supervisor, I. A. Richards, encouraged him to develop the brilliant and original ideas which were published in *Seven Types of Ambiguity* (1930) when Empson was only twenty-four. This was followed, in 1935, by *Poems*, and although he produced only one more collection of Poetry – *The Gathering Storm*, in 1940 – he is widely regarded as one of the most important poets of his distinguished generation. His influence has been confirmed and extended by his other critical writings, notably *Some Versions of Pastoral* (1935), *The Structure of Complex Words* (1951) and *Milton's God* (1961), all of which have achieved the status of classics. His *Collected Poems* was published in 1955, and a new collection of essays, *Using Biography*, in 1984.

Empson's long teaching career began at the national university in Tokyo, where he lectured in English from 1931–34, and continued, from 1937–39, in Peking. During the Second World War he returned to England to work for the BBC, first in the Monitoring Department and then as Chinese Editor. He was married, to Hetta Crouse, in 1941, and they had two sons. In 1947 Empson returned to Peking, and in 1953 was appointed to the Chair of English Literature at Sheffield University, which he held until his retirement in 1971. He was knighted in 1979, and died in London in 1984.

The Hogarth Press also publishes *Seven Types of Ambiguity* and *Collected Poems*. *Some Versions of Pastoral* follows shortly.

THE
STRUCTURE OF
COMPLEX WORDS

William Empson

THE HOGARTH PRESS
LONDON

For
I. A. RICHARDS
Who is the source of all ideas
in this book, even the minor ones
arrived at by disagreeing with him

Published in 1985 by
The Hogarth Press
40 William IV Street, London WC2N 4DF

First published in Great Britain by Chatto & Windus 1951
Hogarth edition offset from the original British edition
Copyright The Estate of Sir William Empson

British Library Cataloguing in Publication Data

Empson, William
The structure of complex words.
1. Ambiguity in literature
I. Title
809'.91   PR56.A5
ISBN 0 7012 1006 0

Printed in Great Britain by
Cox & Wyman Ltd
Reading, Berkshire

Contents

Acknowledgements

Some of this material appeared as articles in *The Criterion*, *Psyche*, *The Southern Review*, *The Kenyon Review*, *The Sewanee Review*, *Life and Letters*, and a pamphlet called 'Shakespeare Survey' sponsored by *Life and Letters:* to whom permission to reprint is gratefully acknowledged

Chapter 1

FEELINGS IN WORDS

EMOTIONS, as is well known, are frequently expressed by language; this does not seem one of the ultimate mysteries; but it is extremely hard to get a consistent and usable theory about their mode of action. What an Emotive use of language may be, where it crops up, and whether it should be praised there, is not so much one question as a protean confusion, harmful in a variety of fields and particularly rampant in literary criticism. It is not hard to see why there is a puzzle here. Much of our thinking has to be done in a summary practical way, trusting to a general sense of the whole situation in the background; we get a feeling that the rest of the situation is within call, so that we can concentrate our attention on one aspect of it, and this feeling is often trustworthy. But we also know that our judgement is often misled by our emotions, and there seems to be nothing in the feeling itself, at any rate before we give it attention (perhaps at the expense of something else which also needs attention) to show whether it is Emotive or Cognitive, whether we have adequate reasons for it in the background or not. This is the basis in experience of the question, and it is then developed into philosophical or psychological issues about what an adequate reason would be, or about what an emotion is.

A man writing on the borderland of linguistics and literary criticism cannot expect to solve such a problem, but he must try to clear an area where it will not do harm. I may be told that I would do better to stick to literary criticism, and keep away from the intellectual buzz-saws; and I could answer that I am trying to, but that I cannot do it unless I know where they are. To be sure, this would be a false answer, because I think that even a moderate step forward in our understanding of language would do a good deal to improve literary criticism, and in any case to improve our general reading capacity. I think that Professor I. A. Richards has already done so much in this field that it only needs to be clarified and worked out in detail before it can be found useful on a serious scale. But as regards what might be called the simple Emotive theory this answer would at least suit my feelings; such a theory does I think merely need clearing away before an adequate one can be developed.

I had better then try to say at once where I think it goes wrong, or in other words how the buzz-saws came to impinge upon me as a literary critic. Theorists on language, it seemed clear, were threatening to affect the ordinary practice of criticism when they claimed that literary metaphors are Essentially Emotive, or decided that some particular passage was a case of Pure Emotive Language, and therefore that the Sense need not be considered. On the face of it, if this state of things were to be praised, it would make most literary criticism irrelevant, let alone the sort of verbal analysis that most interested me. But I could only answer such a theory by a fairly elaborate account of what is in the background of the mind, or in the subconsciousness, when such uses of language are invented or absorbed ; and to give the answer in a clear-cut form, I think, requires the use of symbols. Some uses of language are actually hard to understand, but some you clearly get to know a good deal about, and yet when faced with an obviously inadequate theory you feel that this knowledge cannot be put into words. A reason which is at any rate plausible is that there are merely too many ill-defined things in view at once. What is done in other branches of study, when this kind of difficulty arises, is to give symbols to a few elements that seem essential, avoid refining on the definitions till the examples make it necessary, and try how far the symbols will go.

I am sorry that so many of the resulting pages are so tedious, and feel I had better give a warning about what to expect. (Or rather, sometimes in going over this text I have not thought any of it at all tedious, but at other times I have glimpsed the possibility of the other point of view.) Owing to a tug between two interests the book has turned out like a sandwich. The reader interested in literary criticism will find his meat only in a central area, from chapter III " Wit in the Essay on Criticism " to chapter XIV " Sense in the Prelude ", and even there will not want the chapters called " Honest Numbers " and " Sense and Sensibility ". I hope he will turn to the literary parts rather than abandon the whole book in disgust at the first two chapters. But I shall have failed if he does not then turn back and read the first two chapters, feeling that the conclusions drawn from them are worth looking into. On the other hand, the chapters from XV on are more or less theoretical, an attempt to consolidate the results from the point of view of linguistic theory ; such a reader need not bother about them. And I will not be depressed at all if he ignores my Appendices, which are merely rather amateur attempts to push some problems from Philosophy out of the way.

But in any case most literary critics will regard this as an offensive way to deal with literature, and I don't deny that the symbols might be used stupidly. It is an important rule, I think, that when the reader is being asked to exercise taste, to decide whether he agrees with the critic or not on the exact shade of meaning a passage is meant to carry, he should not be teased with symbols at the same time. Actually I have used the symbols rather little in this book, except in a few large-scale patches, and maybe I ought to have tried them out more continuously. But their other main function, apart from making distinctions clear-cut which can afterwards simply be remembered, is to suggest a fuller technique for making dictionaries ; and this of course is in any case pretty separate from criticism. As the various elements interact a good deal I shall have to introduce a clump of symbols together in this chapter, and not give major examples of their action till enough of them are ready. I hope no reader will object that the symbols are " mathematical " and that he is not a mathematician ; they are no more mathematical than road-signs.

But perhaps I need first to make this plan seem a reasonable one by giving cases where I think the term Emotive has actually led to confusion. It is rather a pity to have to begin the book in an atmosphere of controversy, but the resistance of most readers to mechanisation is I suppose fairly strong, and a decent effort should be made to overcome it. I was made to realise that the Emotive approach could go absurdly wrong through an otherwise excellent treatise *Meaning and Change of Meaning*, by Gustav Stern. He maintains that all literary metaphors are essentially " emotive " though " intentional ", and deals with them in such ways as this :

" . . . Similarity of imaginal elements would be disturbing and ridiculous : *lips like cherries, eyes like almonds, a skin like milk and strawberries, her beauty hangs upon the cheek of night like a rich jewel in an Ethiop's ear*—in every case it is the feeling that is the essential element, not cognitive similarities. The feeling is intensified and expands in fresh, strongly emotive words, in order to reinforce and enhance the original emotion. The poetic figure exists to intensify emotion, not to supply the reader's imagination with more material."

One feels this may mean something true till poor old Imagination is named only to be excluded, and that is clearly going too far. No doubt the seeing of the " image " need not be done by a picture, but you do not even possess the almond simile till you " see " (till you realise) that this eye is *shaped* like an almond ; only in a parrot could the mere thought of an almond " intensify emotion ". As to cherries, the short pouting lips admired when the simile was admired, whether you find them ' disturbing ' or ' ridiculous', were as much like cherries as possible ; the impossibility of the picture is not kept out of sight but claimed as hyperbole ; this woman approaches more nearly than others to the ideal. Indeed Suckling positively labours to make you visualize this lower lip : " some bee had stung it, newly." The idea that one had better not imagine cherries comes when the simile is conventional and there is no longer a fashion for the lip. At both stages, no doubt, there are other ideas at work, which might more easily be called " emotive " ; both lips and cherries are fresh, natural, " sweet " (further metaphor), have dew on them and so forth. These extra ideas may cause Emotions, as may the picture itself. But a conventional reading may take the extra ideas with hardly any emotion, as reasons *why* the simile is thought sensible. It is the extra ideas, apparently, which give Stern his " feeling " which is " fresh ", but they seem to exert a cooling and intellectual influence rather than anything else. So far from finding a distinction here between Emotive and Cognitive Transfer one must go back to the Cognitive use, if that is its name, imagine a lip like a cherry, before the old trope can take effect. It looks as though Stern actually performed this experiment ; what he found " disturbing and ridiculous " may have been a real emotive use of metaphor.

Stern often uses the first lines of the Keats *Grecian Urn* as a clear illustration of his position :

" The far-fetched metaphors are comprehensible to the reader, and thus possible, because the heading of the poem gives its topic : *To a Grecian Urn*."

and in using such metaphors we wish (p. 167):

" not only to present the topic to the listener in an objectively correct way, we wish also to make the hearer take up a definite attitude towards it, to perceive it in a certain colour, and so on."

He shows by these phrases that he does not think the process " merely emotive " in a simple sense ; indeed on p. 296 he remarks that " figures of speech are intentional transfers that include emotive (incl. æsthetic) factors " ; and this " incl.", which might beg a question, seems rather to abandon a claim. With the claim goes the convenience of the term " emotive ". The example of the *Urn* lets one give a quick answer which I think carries the main point. Stern clearly thinks the topic is the pot, and this is all right when he supposes a man reading the first lines for the first time. When you get hold of the poem the topic is some such idea as " brief life becoming long art ", and the pot is only the chief metaphor. While you think the *pot* is called a bride and a foster-child and so on it seems fair to call the metaphors emotive, because they only apply well to feelings about it and mean only to excite them. Then various contradictions (apparently living people tied onto the pot as pictures, for one) send you through a process not unlike allegory, which I shall call Mutual Metaphor, by which you extract the common element of the things compared and make that the topic ; then the metaphors with their new application apply in detail, and are " cognitive ", and make the thought as clear as they can. This shift of topic and metaphor is not complete, and the strength of the metaphors is to work both ways ; also of course in calling them " cognitive " for the new topic I do not mean that they stop giving emotions ; they give large sanctions for emotions which at first seemed simply felt about a pot.

Whether this account is accepted or not, I can hardly think that anybody who liked the poem would agree with Stern's. It is natural to think that he cannot really mean anything as absurd as he seems to be saying here, but there is another passage where the doctrine is very clear-cut and reaches much greater heights of absurdity. He is discussing " abusive words used as endearments ", and quotes a joke from *Punch* as an extreme instance of the case where there is " no connection between the referents but the emotive element ". Certainly the only point of the use is a play with feelings, but that is another thing.

" First Youth : ' Hullo, congenital idiot.'
Second Youth : ' Hullo, you priceless old ass.'
The Damsel : ' I'd no idea you two knew each other so well.'
   " Intense emotion is liable to inhibit other mental processes, and to attract all attention to itself . . . The designations for unpleasant emotions are not only more numerous, they are also of greater intensity . . . "

than those for pleasant ones, so you had best express one intense feeling (love) by expressing another (contempt). It is mistaken here, I submit, to think (1) that the speakers are incoherent with passion of any kind (2) that there is an emotive connection between the referents of the words, that is, on the one side the person addressed and on the other the imbecile or donkey (we gather something about what they feel towards each other, but nothing about what they would feel towards actual imbeciles or donkeys) and (3) that there is no cognitive connection between these referents—the joke, such as it is, says " fools they are, so are imbeciles and donkeys ". Maybe some of these are rather glib debating points, but it seems clear that the trick of speech must be analysed in terms of thought not of emotion. Indeed I think that a crude hearty joke of this type has a fair-sized logical structure, and I must postpone giving my own answer to the puzzle till I have got my symbols into play.

No doubt these lapses might be put right in Stern's book, leaving a reasonable structure as a whole, but they did at least illustrate how liable the Emotive approach was to produce lapses. Stern based his main position on the Ogden-Richards *Meaning of Meaning*, where the doctrine that there are emotive uses of language is prominent but is not given detailed application to literary criticism. But in what might be called the middle period of Professor Richards' books, from *The Principles of Literary Criticism* to *Mencius On The Mind*, a series of literary hints of this sort are dropped which are I think actively misleading. I had been feeling that what was true in them was very hard to separate from what was false, and when I read what was in effect a parody of them in Stern I felt that this ought to be a help in making the separation. The precise doctrine about the Emotive use of language in poetry is hard to isolate in Professor Richards' books, and indeed the part that is wrong with it seems to me a product of confusion ; but there are a series of phrases to the effect that the Emotions given by words in poetry are independent of their Sense. It seems to me that this doctrine, if taken at all simply, would be sure to lead to bad criticism. However on the whole Professor Richards has succeeded in not giving definite examples of this effect ; perhaps this is partly because his most thorough-going speculations about the Emotive functions of language were made in connection with texts by Mencius which have remained obscure even to the Chinese. But I think an example can be found in his defence of the last lines of the *Grecian Urn* (*Mencius*, p. 116) ; as Stern claimed the beginning of the poem, it becomes something of a battlefield, and I shall have to return to it later in the book. Professor Richards says :

" Urns induce states of mind in their beholders ; they do not enunciate philosophical positions—not in this kind of poetry— and *say'st* here is used as a metaphor which should not be overlooked."

I do not think poor Keats would have liked to be told he was writing " this kind of poetry ". Professor Richards goes on to show that the ranges of meaning in Truth and Beauty overlap at three points, so that there are three ways of making " Beauty is Truth " a mere tautology (not a sentence with any meaning). These possibilities, he says :

" account for its power *in the poem* (when, of course, it is not apprehended analytically) to convey that feeling of deep acceptance which is often a chief phase in the æsthetic experience."

Now it may well be that the lines are bad. But it seems to me that Professor Richards is not defending them ; he is merely calling them bad in a complacent manner. And I should have thought, for that matter, that any word other than an exclamation or a swear-word has got to be apprehended as a meaning, giving room for a possible analysis of the meaning, if it is apprehended at all. A poet no doubt is not building an intellectual system ; if you like the phrase, he feels the thoughts which are in the air (and here, I take it, the thoughts of Coleridge were in the air); or he is recording a time when his mind was trying out an application of the thoughts, not proving a doctrine about them. But all the same if he leads up with clear marks of solemnity to saying that Beauty is Truth he does not want to be told, any more than anyone else, that " of course " he meant nothing at all except to excite Emotion. It seems to me that a flat separation of Sense from Emotion would be merely a misreading here.

The question here looks like a verbal one, and yet it clearly brings in much larger issues. Apart from the doctrine that the Emotions of the words in poetry are independent of the Sense, Professor Richards maintains, and I take it is more interested in maintaining, that the function of poetry is to call out an Attitude which is not dependent on any belief open to disproof by facts. The two doctrines seem intimately connected, though I am not sure that they need be ; and in both I think it needs a rather subtle analysis to get at the truth. Certainly I think it would be a worse heresy to maintain that poems are not concerned with Emotion, because they are Pure Art ; but I hope it is clear from these examples that one needs more elaborate machinery to disentangle the Emotive from the Cognitive part of poetical language. Such at least is my excuse for offering my own bits of machinery ; but as the second Richards doctrine is closely connected with the first it seems necessary to look at that as well.

The crucial belief here, which I take it he still holds, is that " awareness of the nature of the world and the development of attitudes which will enable us to live in it finely are almost independent ". (*The Principles of Literary Criticism*, p. 282.) It is clear that *almost* might become important here. The effects of the doctrine are complicated and far-reaching ; he has been attacked for them on different grounds at different times, and indeed to recall them is rather a matter of digging up misunderstandings. Max Eastman wrote a very amusing book, *The Literary Mind*, some while ago, a great quarry for the background of this controversy, in which he attacked nearly everyone else for thinking that poetry ought to teach truths and attacked Professor Richards for thinking that, though not concerned with truth, it ought to convey valuable Attitudes. Max Eastman himself thought that it ought to communicate experience, good or bad (because everyone likes to have plenty of experience); and the effect on him so far as he ventured into literary criticism, it seemed clear to me, was to make him prefer very trivial poems. He found it particularly absurd that the arts should be viewed as a socially important alternative to religion ; on the other hand Dr. F. R. Leavis became angry with Professor Richards for not taking this view seriously enough, because if he did he would obviously support the Leavis projects about the matter. As a writer of verse myself, I felt that

Professor Richards' faith in the poets was a beautiful but rather unrealistic trait ; the question was a more complicated one, about the taste of the public in general. Judging the theories in terms of the criticism they produced, I felt that Professor Richards was clearly less wrong than Max Eastman, but that a wilful inhibition of all the truth-seeking impulses in poetry would make for a kind of bad criticism of its own. For example, the idea comes up again (and this form of it will be relevant later in the present book) when we are told in *The Principles of Literary Criticism* that people who say " How True " when reading Shakespeare are wasting their time ; it is suggested that they are comical old fogies anyway. This is not merely an attack on Bradley and other delvers into " character " ; it is an attack on what almost everyone had felt, on what was most strikingly witnessed, with a sort of unwillingness, by Dr. Johnson, that in spite of all their faults the plays are somehow unescapably " like life ". I do not think one can write any useful criticism of Shakespeare if one has succeeded in repressing this sentiment. Indeed I do not think that Professor Richards seriously meant to recommend that ; the point is that when he claims to illustrate his doctrine he tends to use misleading language.

The reason why Tragedy was held to illustrate especially clearly the separation of Attitudes from Belief, if I follow him, was that a Christian audience has to drop the belief in Heaven, or tacitly confess that this belief is of a peculiar kind, because otherwise the death of the hero would not appear tragic. At least this is what an unbeliever is tempted to suppose ; the believers seem to feel they can drop their habitual prop while seeing a tragedy, since they are being offered an alternative means to strength which will do as well for the moment. I think this does apply to *Lear ;* the attempts to fit Christian sentiments onto it seem to me to falsify the play. But there are a great variety of tragedies, and it is hard to generalise about what Christians feel. *Faustus* is a tragedy which assumes that you believe the hero went to Hell, but it does not depend on that ; indeed the author probably did not believe it himself. We are to envisage Hamlet as sung to his rest by flights of angels ; Heaven appears as a state of peace, which he has been wanting to get to for some time ; you may adopt so Christian a point of view as to wish he had died earlier, and the play is still tragic. Cleopatra says repeatedly that she expects some kind of happiness after her death, though in very metaphorical language (except in " Dido and her Æneas shall want troops. . . .") ; we seem meant to feel that her belief is pathetically untrue but has something profound about it. The atheist and the Christian presumably disbelieve her about equally, because the Christian consigns her to a very hot part of Hell. But on the other hand the pantheistic belief that we are somehow absorbed into Nature seems to have remained so natural to us that people of all opinions can follow the last act of the play without feeling positively that her assertions are wrong. Actually, if one reads straight ahead, I am not sure that she seems to assert anything, but the critics like Mr. Wilson Knight and Mr. Middleton Murry, who have found a great deal in her speeches, do not seem to be misreading them either. As Mr. Eliot pointed out, it is not so much that Shakespeare is really thinking along the lines he has suggested ; he is aware that the character might think along those lines, and leaves room for it. In this play, to use the woolly language of criticism, an " atmosphere of paganism " is what is wanted. Surely the audience is to do the same ; the solution of the " Problem of Belief ", as to how we can enjoy the literary expression of beliefs which we don't hold, is not that we separate them from their consequences but that we imagine some other person who holds them, an author or a character, and thus get a kind of experience of what their consequences (for a given sort of person) really are.

But this whole question, though interesting, is a very minor one compared to the central generalisation of Professor Richards. It seems clear that, even if your views about Heaven are in abeyance while watching *Lear*, you need to feel that the play is a true illustration of some part of human nature and the human situation ; and indeed that you need to feel this about even the most unnaturalistic plays, if they are to be any good. Now there is no reason why Professor Richards should deny this ; in fact the whole point of introducing the Theory of Value into *The Principles of Literary Criticism* was to give a means by which it could be maintained. The sort of truth we are shown, in which we find ourselves believing, is one about our own natures and the natures of the other people we have to deal with ; perhaps it is essentially no more than the truth that to act in some ways would be good, and in others bad. Dr. Johnson, one can suppose, would have been ready to limit it to that. But if this is the truth in question, then according to Professor Richards' own Theory of Value it is a real one and could eventually be tested by experience. No doubt the means by which this sort of truth can be verified or discovered are very different from those of scientific procedure, and this could give a basis for the distinction between emotive and cognitive uses of language. But it is a very different idea from saying that the belief-feelings are attached to nothing, like those induced by drugs (a parallel which he often uses). Indeed there is a curious footnote, on p. 276 of the *Principles*, referring us back from the argument that Poetry does not depend on Belief to the argument that Art is not separate from Life ; and this I think would

9

have been enough to settle the matter if the confusion had not gone on creeping like a fog about the valleys of his later books, which have so much wild scenery.

The main theme of *Science and Poetry*, a moving and impressive pamphlet, is that the arts, especially poetry, can save the world from the disasters which will otherwise follow the general loss of religious and semi-religious belief ; they can do this by making us experience what the higher kinds of attitude feel like, so that we adopt them of our own accord without needing to believe that we are repaid for them in Heaven or that they bring good luck on earth. I would be sorry to treat this as a mere false analysis of poetical language ; the only objection that could be raised, I think, is that the plan is not strong enough for the purpose or is liable to excite an unreasonable expectation of quick results. The point I want to make, on the contrary, is that all this has almost nothing to do with the analysis of poetical language ; when you come down to detail, and find a case where there are alternative ways of interpreting a word's action, of which one can plausibly be called Cognitive and the other Emotive, it is the Cognitive one which is likely to have important effects on sentiment or character, and in general it does not depend on accepting false beliefs. But in general it does involve a belief of some kind, if only the belief that one kind of life is better than another, so that it is no use trying to chase belief-feelings out of the poetry altogether. I am not sure how far to follow Professor Richards in his efforts to shoo them out, such as his plaintive remark that neither Yeats nor D. H. Lawrence " seems to have envisaged the possibility of a poetry which is independent of all beliefs " (whereas they obviously needed to believe that good results would follow from what they were recommending) ; or his claim that :

" A good deal of poetry and even some great poetry exists (e.g. some of Shakespeare's Songs and, in a different way, much of the best of Swinburne) in which the sense of the words can be almost entirely missed or neglected without loss. Never perhaps entirely without effort however; though sometimes with advantage. But the plain fact that the relative importance of grasping the sense of the words may vary (compare Browning's *Before* with his *After*) is enough for our purpose here."

The contrast here seems to me merely one of how far the inter-connections of sense can be handled adequately while left in the subconsciousness, a region from which criticism can fish them up if it chooses. Many quite practical false beliefs can hang about in the dim suggestions of a word, for instance the belief that thirteen is unlucky. In any case, the idea of a puritanical struggle to avoid noticing the Sense of " Hark, hark, the lark ", and still more the idea that if you succeeded in doing this you would have a substitute for puritanism, are I think obvious products of confusion. What I need to emphasize is that rejecting this verbal part of the theory does not involve rejecting the main thesis of the book ; and for that matter when first speaking of the two streams of experience in reading a poem, the intellectual and the active or emotional, Professor Richards remarks " It is only as an expositor's device that we can speak of them as two streams. They have innumerable interconnections and influence one another intimately " (p. 13). Exactly ; this interconnection is what I am trying to follow out ; and my only objection to his other phrases on the subject is that they tend to imply that the interconnection had better be suppressed.

Looking back to the *Meaning of Meaning* (which of course was written earlier, with Mr. C. K. Ogden), I think the confusion there is only present in germ. The book often makes very reasonable admissions about the difficulty of separating the Emotive from the Cognitive parts ; " this subtle interweaving of the two functions is the main reason why recognition of the difference is not universal " (p. 150); and it puts the main emphasis on whole passages not on single Emotive words :

> " Very much poetry consists of statements, symbolic arrangements capable of truth or falsity, which are used not for the sake of their truth or falsity but for the sake of the attitudes which their acceptance will evoke. For this purpose it frequently happens, or rather it is part of the poet's business to make it happen, that the truth or falsity matters not at all to the acceptance."

Put in this way, the doctrine seems so reasonable that I must make a new set of admissions. Indeed it hardly says more than the old line of joke that the poets tell " excellent lies ", or that the truest poetry is the most " faining " ; but we still need to examine what kind of truth the joke enshrines. I do not feel there is much puzzle about pleasant lies (as that the mistress is perfect) ; the puzzle is rather over lies which are unpleasant and yet eagerly absorbed by the fit reader. Such a description, I think, applies to the Housman nettle poem (*More Poems* XXXII) ; after the first sentence (the lads are sowing) every one of the sentences contains an untrue assertion ('Tis little matter What are the sorts they sow, For only one will grow. . . . The charlock on the fallow . . . will not twice arise. The stinging nettle only Will still be sure to stand . . . It peoples towns, and towers About the courts of kings. . .). Apart from the absurdity of the literal meaning, the metaphorical meaning seems to me plainly untrue ; but I also think it is one of his finest poems, which is saying a good deal. Of course you may say that my optimism is naive, and that Housman is uttering the bitter truth which we recognise unconsciously but labour to ignore. It is also naive, I think I can retort, to imagine that in a " pessimistic " poem such as this one the despairing assertions are meant to be accepted quite flatly. The art-works which can be viewed as glorifying death-wishes cover a large field ; T. E. Hulme seemed to regard all Byzantine art as of this type, Otto Ranke argued that the invention of portrait sculpture by the Egyptians derived from a sort of necrophily, Mario Praz in *The Romantic Agony* extended a solemn clinical disapproval over most of nineteenth century literature. It seems to be a general rule, however, that if the effect is beautiful the lust for death is balanced by some impulse or interest which contradicts it. One might argue that the contradiction merely supplies the tension, and does not decide the note on which the string will vibrate—the resultant meaning may have very little to do with the apparent despair. I think the same applies to the nettle poem, so that, even supposing that its assertions are true, they are not really what it means to say.

At any rate, one must not be led aside into supposing that its merit depends on a belief that Housman was sincere. I think it does seem better if you know about Housman (who never published it) but it would still be a good poem if it had been written as a parody of him. But even then, it seems clear, the reader would be in effect asked to imagine a person who *was* in the " mood " expressed by the poem, who did believe these assertions, and who faced them with the pride, calm, and pity which the poem conveys. The point is not that their truth or falsity is irrelevant, but that you are asked to imagine a state of mind in which they would appear true. True perhaps within a particular world of experience, maybe a narrow one, but true somewhere. However, this kind of narrowing of the field might leave the claim still naive. The absurdity of the literal meaning is I think a positive help to the wilful pessimism of the metaphorical one, because (as well as making the supposed painful truth dramatic, astonishing, un-natural) it can suggest a slanging match—the speaker is spitting in the face of the blackguard who made the world, whatever tortures will follow ; he is exaggerating because he thinks the facts deserve it, and perhaps to encourage his disciples. This kind of untruth (which need not be imputed) does not hurt the poem because you still have to imagine a person who is deeply convinced of the general case he is making out. And it seems clear that you can feel invigorated and deepened by the process of imagining this character, without agreeing with him at all.

I don't deny, at the other extreme, that you may simply agree with his assertions, but in that case I think the poems are merely harmful. I remember a Japanese class of mine reading Housman in 1931, when they were liable to be conscripted to fight in Manchuria, indeed a man had already been drafted from the class and killed in Shanghai, and they wrote down pretty consistently " We think Housman is quite right. We will do no good to anyone by being killed as soldiers, but we will be admired, and we all want to be admired, and anyway we are better dead." To do the old gentleman justice, I fancy he would have been rather shocked by these bits of school work. So I think Housman is about as pure a case as you can get of a poet using untruths to excite attitudes, and even here I think it would be a tedious flippancy to say that the truth or untruth of the assertions is simply irrelevant to the poem.*

There is a distinction needed, I think, which becomes clearer if we go back to *Science and Poetry* and examine its idea of a " pseudo-statement ". This is presented as an alternative to the idea that false statements in poetry belong to " a supposed universe of discourse, a world of make-believe, of imagination, of recognised fictions common to the poet and his readers " (p. 57). There is no such separate universe defined by a poem, Professor Richards truly pointed out, and he went on (wrongly, I think) to say that " except occasionally and by accident, logic does not enter at all ". In any case :

" The acceptance which a pseudo-statement receives is entirely governed by its effects upon our feelings and attitudes . . . A pseudo-statement is ' true ' if it suits and serves some attitude or links together attitudes which on other grounds are desirable."

The objection I should want to make is that this account is liable to be misunderstood so as to short-circuit the process. It seems to me that the attitude recommended by the nettle poem, if we regard its pseudo-statements as a series of stimuli imposed on the organism of the reader, is quite clearly a very *un*-desirable one. There is merely a sullen conviction that no effort is worth making, a philosophy for the village idiot ; and the illogicality which we are told to admire (as being typical of poetical language) is not any " freedom " from logic but the active false logic of persecution mania. On this theory the poem is very bad, whereas it seems clear that an adequate theory would be able to admit its merits. It seems enough to say that the experience ought to be " imaginative ", in that we imagine some other person in this frame of mind ; we are not simply worked upon, ourselves, as objects of a psychological experiment. But as soon as you admit this a good deal more

---

*No doubt some critics would say that an Absolute or Essence is being presented, " the Idea of a despair and not as she was ". But it always seems to me that these philosophical terms are only used by metaphor as terms of rhetoric, and cannot alter the literary process they describe ; that is, if you did not feel that a real person might get reasonably near the extreme case, a presentation of that case would be trivial whatever theory of rhetoric you had.

thinking has to go on in the background, and indeed a good deal more logical consistency.

It can no doubt be objected that I am using truth in some peculiar literary sense of the term here, and that scientific truth is obviously not in question. The distinction seems to me extraordinarily hard to draw. The person we are asked to imagine believes that any efforts he makes will be frustrated, and surely this idea (however remote) is entirely in the world of practical experience. The Japanese students, to sum up the meaning of such a poem, said that they would be better dead, a judgement of value, and this I take it could be judged either true or false by applying Professor Richards' Theory of Value to their cases. Of course it is true that the connection of the attitudes with fact is a very remote one, and furthermore that the attitude of the nettle poem needs to be accepted in a peculiar way, neither as completely right nor as inconceivably wrong ; but I do not see that the subtlety of the process detaches it from any connection with fact, any more than the answer has free will if the sum is hard. And in any case, of course, even if the meanings of the sentences were detached in this way, it would not make the meanings of the separate words Purely Emotive.

However, by the time Professor Richards came to write *The Philosophy of Rhetoric* and *Interpretation in Teaching*, he seems to have dropped the idea that a writer of poetry had better not worry about the Sense. I suspect this was because he had subjected himself to so much reading of bad criticism by his students in their " protocols " that his common sense revolted against a doctrine which they illustrated so frequently ; and we now find him at the other extreme, writing as though the " somnial magic " was the natural enemy of " the sunshine comparative power ", so that the only tolerable way to read poetry is to give the full Sense a very sharp control over the Emotion. This indeed had always been more in line with his temperament, so that the earlier doctrine might be regarded as a determined effort to give the emotions their due. Oddly enough the people influenced by him seem to have followed the beckoning of his style rather than his repeated instructions ; the influence seems to me rather too anti-emotional and intellectualistic, without any reference to the doctrine that the Emotion can be practically independent of the Sense.

It may therefore seem unnecessary and disagreeable to write down lengthy objections, here and later in the book, to phrases by Professor Richards which are merely open to misunderstanding, or views which he probably no longer holds. But after all anyone who reads me also reads Richards, or had much better start to, and his books are still very much alive whether he agrees with them or not.

And a mistake made by Richards, it has long seemed to me, is a great deal more illuminating than the successes of other writers in this line of country. I ought also to admit that, as I re-read his books with these complaints in view, I was impressed by how often my own writing had repeated him unawares without acknowledgement, and how far beyond my own range his mind has habitually gone.

II

I shall now put forward my little bits of machinery. The main thing needed, it seems to me, is to give symbols of their own to some elements often called "feelings" in a word, which are not Emotions or even necessarily connected with emotions. We assume that the Sense of the word now in view is already listed, as in the N.E.D., with a number attached to it, which may be generalised as "A." Then "A/1" is its first or main Implication, part of what is sometimes called the "connotation" of the word in this use. Thus many uses of *honest* imply "brave" because honesty often requires courage ; "brave" is not a Sense of the word, but it is often felt to be present as a Sense, not an Emotion, something implied by the logic of the case. It seems natural, to be sure, to say that such an idea can be "translated" into an emotion, so that it is recognised only as an admiring sentiment ; where this process is complete the idea should not be listed with the "/" form. But normally the process will go both ways (Emotion and Implication are tied so that each calls up the other), and then the Implication is the better one to list (for showing connections between uses etc.), though you may need both. The term Implication is not meant to suggest that this meaning follows logically from the Sense of the word now in use ; we say that a man "implied" something precisely when it did not follow logically from his remarks but was somehow present. However the logical meaning need not be cut out ; it is only a special case. For example a quadrilateral necessarily has four angles, but you need not attend to this while mentioning one ; when you do attend to it you can treat "quadriangular" as an Implication of the word *quadrilateral*. For that matter you can treat "quadripedal" as an Implication of the word *cow;* that is, the usual as well as the logically necessary properties of the referent will tend to appear among the Implications of the word. But in the less obvious cases the Implication will come from an habitual context of the word (not from its inherent meaning) and will vaguely remind you of that sort of context. The context is presumed to be usual among some group of people ; a merely private fancy would be called an Association of the word. Of course the *immediate* context of the use of the word now in view may also be felt to " imply " the extra meaning, and indeed will commonly support the habit of giving the word this Implication by providing another example of it. But one case alone would not produce a stock implication. Sometimes the word itself in most of its uses will as it were logically imply the extra meaning ; I should think this is true of *honesty* implying " courage " ; but even so, past experience is what makes the word able to point it out. And we do not necessarily attend to past experience ; nowadays the implication of " courage " in *honesty* is I think rather a remote one, though it would be a strong one if the logical implications from past contexts merely added themselves up. People make words do what seems to be needed, and whether one of the normal uses of a word carries a given Implication is a question of fact, however hard to decide.

Two other symbols for senses are often convenient. It is natural to use brackets " (A) " for a Sense of the word when " at the back of the mind "; normally it will appear in this way beside another Sense which acts as the chief one, so that the full symbol would be " A (B) ". It is thus acting like an Implication, and indeed that usually deserves a bracket too, because it does not get the main attention. But it is quite possible for two senses to get attention at once, and an implication may be heavily emphasized. Commonly it is not important to decide which senses are in brackets ; in ordinary good writing a reader can shift his attention how he likes without knocking the structure down ; but probably there are false arguments which depend on a bracket technique. On the other hand there may be a Sense of the word which is definitely not required, and is deliberately excluded ; for example when a history master speaks of a " bloody battle ". The symbol for this is "−A ", read " not Aye ". It is only listed for a clear performance with the word, not for a mere assumption that irrelevant uses are kept out ; the obvious uses of it are for irony and other jokes, but the example of the history master shows that no joke need be intended. All these symbols may be combined ; thus we may write " (−A) " ; but to have a symbol for a thing is of course no proof that it exists, and I daresay a denial in a bracket never occurs.

The next two symbols perhaps trench a bit on the field of Emotive language, as they stand for Senses which are commonly imposed by a play of feeling. However in themselves they are senses all right, and the phrase written after the symbol in a chart of the word should treat them as such. I write " A+ " and " A− " for the senses reached by what are called Appreciative and Depreciative Pregnancy ; this is taken simply as a process that makes the meaning of the word warmer and fuller or contrariwise less so. As a rule there is no fixed sense of the word corresponding to the ideas put in by pregnancy, so it is convenient to have a separate symbol for this trick. You get a depreciative pregnancy for example when one elderly lady says about another " Really, Maria is getting more and more eccentric. I hardly know what to say. Well, really, it's scarcely honest." A disinterested observer may feel that what Aunt Maria did was quite farcically dishonest, in its petty way, but the suggestion here is that *honest* is such a very elementary virtue that Maria cannot be conceived not to possess it ; if you thought of her as not honest you might next have to envisage her as going to jail, a thing quite outside her style of life. The sense of the word *honest* here, I think, must be given as something like " not a member of the criminal classes ". No doubt the play of feeling is very complex ; the word seems to be a euphemism and yet it is a direct means of expressing astonishment as well as disapproval. But all the same I think one can fix a resulting Sense for the word, independent of the feelings ; the sign " A— " is concerned only with that. What is made narrower than usual, in the definition of " A— ", is the meaning of the word ; it is not necessary that the person or situation described should be viewed coolly, though the speaker may be doing that as well. Indeed the people who said that Shakespeare " wanted art " would turn the accusation into praise if they gave *art* a depreciative pregnancy. By the way, we have now to put full stops between symbols when they are combined, to distinguish between " A.—B " and " A—.B ".

The next symbol is for what I shall call the Moods. These are a mixed class giving the hints of the speaker about his own relations to the person addressed, or the person described, or persons normally in the situation described (or in fact any other person, but these are all he is likely to cover). A Mood is not a Sense but a sentence, and it tends to give the speaker's personal judgement, so I shall use " £ " for it as the only symbol on the typewriter which suggests valuation (American typewriters can use " $ "). The rule is that, while after " A ", in the chart of the word, you list a word or words that are its Sense, after " A£1 ", the first Mood of the Sense " A ", you list a sentence relating " me " to someone else. They are to cover any supposed " me ", if there are more than one, as for example in oratio obliqua or Satan's speeches in Milton, and they can be either statements or orders. I call them Moods to suggest the parallel to the moods of verbs ; thus " fire " for " I command you to fire " has an imperative mood in both senses. They are nearly the same as what Professor Richards has called Tones, but he defines those as expressing only " the speaker's relation to the person addressed ". For purposes of making a chart you do not want to worry about who was addressed, because there are fixed structures which appear as Tones in some sentences but not in others.

This symbol will appear more fantastic than the previous ones and must be defended at greater length. However, the main argument in its favour is sufficiently obvious ; language is essentially a social product, and much concerned with social relations, but we tend to hide this in our forms of speech so as to appear to utter impersonal truths. The Moods are a mixed class, which had better be subdivided, and I want to bring in two symbols for particular sorts of Mood before discussing them in general. One simple type, perhaps hardly recognisable as a Mood but still a way of picking out the Sense intended by a personal hint, is the use of quotation marks. This is done in speech by various tricks, particularly by a slight pause before the word and then an unusually precise enunciation of it. Both this and the written quotation marks can mean either of two things according to context : " What *they* call so-and-so, but I don't " or " What *I* call so-and-so, but they don't ", and " you " can be made to join either party. Thus there are several possible Moods behind a quotation mark, but we can add it to our symbols as it stands, " 'A' ", and use it as required. Also I propose to introduce a symbol for the return of the meaning of the word to the speaker ; this is a definite Mood, and I think a fairly frequent one, though perhaps not of much theoretical importance. A play of this sort may seem far from the speaker's intention, in a straightforward use of language, but most judgements about other people, when you make them public, can be felt to raise a question about how you would be judged in your turn. This is particularly so of inherently shifting moral terms like the miserly-thrifty group ; when one man calls another thrifty he is a little conscious of what people would call him. To call someone else clever is rather to imply that you are not clever yourself. A short man can hardly talk about " a tall man " for fear that people will wonder what he considers tall ; he tends to estimate the height in figures instead. It has become unusual to talk about anybody being chaste, partly because people do not want to imply either that they themselves are or that they aren't, and it is difficult to use the word without one or the other. " Fool " is a clear case, because in some kinds of joke the reflex action is the whole point of it ; the regular function of the Shakespearean clown is to make fools of other people. Proust gives a neat example, when Morel delights Charlus by calling him " mon vieux " and thus implies he is as young as Morel ; the idea is " we are both experienced " rather than " both old", but anyway it can be assumed to be mutual. And on the other hand in calling a man a " Cad " it is usual to imply no less clearly that you are not a cad yourself. The question-mark is the most self-conscious object on the typewriter, and I give " x? " as " the sense 'x' used of oneself under cover of using it about someone else " ; probably the negative " —x? " " I am not like that " is rather the more common performance of the two.

These then are a variety of elements which might be called " feelings " in a word but are not merely Emotions. I set out with the prejudice that there were probably no Emotions in words at all, after everything which might be connected with a Cognitive use had been removed ; but this seemed a rather silly position, even if a logically rigorous one, and I was not unduly distressed to find that there were cases where one could plausibly say that an Emotion still remained. Roughly speaking, then, the Emotion in a word is what is left in the way of " feelings " when these other feelings have been cut out. The first or main one associated with the Sense " A " is written " A!1 " and read " Aye shriek one " ; this reading (for the logical use of the symbol, not for my one) seems to have been invented by F. P. Ramsey. " A/1 " is read " Aye bar one " and "A—" " Aye minus ". The brutality of the intellectualist approach will be recognised in these instructions ; and indeed I think it needs to be made frank. We must not develop tender feelings towards our little bits of machinery ; they need to be kept sharply separate from the delicacy and warmth of the actual cases they are to be used on. There really might be a harmful effect from using this kind of analysis if the two things were liable to get mixed up. Two more symbols will be introduced in the next chapter, but apart from that there are no others in the book.

We can now go on to some examples, and it seems better to do that before trying to get the idea of an Emotion in a word more clear-cut. The main use of the Mood symbol is to explain how a word can express a Feeling which seems to have nothing to do with the Sense concurrent with it. Professor Richards in *Practical Criticism* (p. 213) discussed cases where the Sense rules the Feeling, the Feeling rules the Sense, and thirdly where the two are allied only through their context. The distinction between the first two was rather obscured by his giving the example of a word whose Sense was concerned to describe a Feeling. Often, I think, you turn from one class to the other in moving from speaker to hearer. If the speaker's use of the words is Class I, so that the Sense is what gives him the Feeling, the listener has still to hit on this sense, and the Feeling expressed may guide him to it. If, as in Class II, the feeling of the speaker makes him choose a peculiar Sense of the word, and the context cuts out other possible senses, this will help the hearer to gauge the Feeling. The puzzling case is Class III ; as a rule, I think, and comfortably in the example given, one can explain it by a Mood. The example was from a poem about a cloud :

O sprawling domes, O tottering towers,
O frail steel tissue of the sun.

Professor Richards calls the sense ' absence of symmetry, regularity, poise, and coherence, and stretched or loose disposition of parts ' ; and the feeling (in this context) ' a mixture of good humoured mockery and affected Commiseration '. Yes ; my question is how it gets there. There seems an Emotion normally tied to *sprawl*—though a moderate or negative one such as ordinary language, which makes emotion a serious word, would only call a feeling—that the position (sense ' 1 ') does not excite respect (though negative, this may be called the emotion ' 1! '). As in the other types the emotion has a clear connection with the sense ; the sprawler has not ' pulled himself together '. It does not lead to contempt if you are prepared to sprawl too ; you then view an equal with ' good humour '. But till now the cloud has been miraculous, heavenly, and so forth, so if we now view him as an equal the contrast brings in ' mockery or pity '. Of course there is also an idea that a building is breaking up, but *sprawling* lays weight on these more social ideas to keep the thing from melodrama, and can put some of them into *tottering*. It is curious that so strong a sound effect as ' sprawling ' does not impose an ' emotive colour ', but the movements of your mouth seem only to make you feel the sense of the word vividly ; this will add its weight either to contempt or to undignified sympathy. Now the change from the slight tied Emotion of the word to its feeling here must go through you, who view the cloud as an equal ; it is fair then to write the feeling as a Mood—' I view him with a mixture of etc.' This way of writing it serves to insist on the definition but may tend to mislead ; the question is not whether the effect is self-conscious, though it probably is a little, but how the feeling was put in. The example perhaps makes things easy for the ' £ ' form but is at least not of my choosing. By the way, there is room for a puzzle here about Professor Richards' definition of a Tone ; the poet is addressing his readers, but he pretends to be addressing the cloud. For the general usefulness of the Richards set of terms it seems clear that " Tone " should be kept for the real situation, the poet's relation to his readers ; so that this is not an example of a Tone, but it is still an example of a Mood.

We may now observe that the lady who said Aunt Maria was " scarcely honest ", and thus gave *honest* a depreciative pregnancy, did it by imposing a Mood. The idea is " In spite of the evidence before me, I can hardly bring myself to suppose that Maria would do anything dishonest ", and in view of the evidence before her (I am supposing) one must deduce that she would not call anything dishonest short of downright crime. There is another suggestion

FEELINGS IN WORDS

" We are all rigidly upright in the family ; that is why dishonesty in Maria is unthinkable "; and yet the astonishment of the thing also conveys " I find I have to raise a question, about Maria, which I should expect only to have to raise about a servant girl ". It is clear that a Mood may be very complex ; but the complexity need not, and generally does not, get into the meaning of the word. All these three sentences only affect the meaning of *honest* by making it a very elementary virtue, or at least one which can usually be taken for granted about people like Maria.

We may also deal with the young men in *Punch* who called each other fools. The magazine I suppose was merely concerned to report the slang words currently used in this process, for the benefit of retired old gentlemen or what not ; there does not seem any other point or novelty in it. The reason why such an insult is not insulting is that it is somehow mutual—" I am rather like that too "; the Sense " fool " could carry a " ? " sign. Then the presumption " We can afford to talk like this to each other " implies " We are free, natural, safe ". These can be classed as Moods, though the usual opposition in a Mood between me and the other man collapses. Probably also the apparent insult, once admitted to be mutual, carries positive praise for us both—here " not one of the clever people I dislike, self-centred, ill-tempered, cranky, unreliable ". These are rather remote Implications from the Sense " fool ", but are called out by the Mood. Then, so far as the hearty insult itself can be called a joke, the joke is that it pretends to ignore the Implications, by a use of " —A/x ", and be simply rude. The joke in *Punch* (" you know each other so well ") presumably makes them recognise the process which they have already used from habit or convention. Perhaps one should say that the two Moods beginning " We " are merely states of feeling, and should be classed as Emotions, whereas the Implication " not nasty-clever " appears as a Sense, but only " at the back of the mind " so that it requires brackets. However these points are not important for understanding the trick, which is little disturbed by such changes of attention as translate emotions into senses. People understand what they are about in these matters pretty well.*

* I am trying to introduce the idea of a Mood with fairly striking cases, where an analysis of this kind is clearly in order ; there may be a separate puzzle about cases where the extra idea is best analysed as a Mood but does not feel like one. It seems largely a matter of convenience. In actual teaching of the language I think one does need to explain " He knows that, he shows it, he points it out " etc. as " He believes it and I the speaker believe it too ". For example *show* might easily not be in the class of verb implying personal agreement, but nowadays gets firmly taken so ; whereas *apparently* is a tricky word to use because though it most often implies a false show it can sometimes mean " obviously " and imply a true one. No doubt the truth-feeling in itself is not a covert assertion about other people, but I think this kind of intrusion of it into a word is best learned as one ; and a speaker will sometimes use it so, quite intentionally.

21

A firm hold on these different sorts of extra meaning, I think, throws some doubt on what is usually said about Emotive words, as in the following case, also from Stern's *Meaning and Change of Meaning* :

> " Some words possess an emotive colouring as a permanent element of their meaning ; instances are relatively numerous ; compare *horse* and *steed*, *poor young man* and *wretched wight*, *house* and *hovel* ; *bright*, *gaudy*, *gorgeous*, and *flashy*, where different attitudes to identical referents are expressed."

What he wants to say is clearly true, but the shift from " emotive colouring " to " attitudes " leaves it somewhat undefined. Archaic words simply carry an implication about their date and supposed normal context ; the emotion, if any, must be worked from the set of implications '/', and will vary with that. A hovel is 'a small dirty ill-equipped house ' ' 1'; the referents of house and hovel are not identical. The sense gives a normal emotion ' 1! ' of pity or disgust, and you can stretch the word on to what would otherwise be called a ' house ' (new sense ' 2 ') to show you feel the emotion— ' 2£1 ' 'To me, this is a contemptible man's house'. To add the mood blurs the sense ' 1'; thus the word has an ' emotive use ' with the sense of *house* but not simply a ' colour ' added to a 'sense.' The last case contrasts three projective adjectives with a comparative one ; certainly they might all be used about the same thing, and may all excite emotions. *Gorgeous* apparently started from rich-looking dress and got at once to ' rich colours ', colours such as orange and crimson ; there is a field for explanation as to why these colours are rich, but the word has a normal sense not of æsthetic type and different from *bright*. If you stretch it on to something with simply bright colours, either you are making an æsthetic statement, in projectile form, e.g., ' any one with good taste will feel that the effect here is rich ', or, for an ' emotive' use as in *hovel*, you are giving the word an odd Sense with a Mood. No doubt the play of feeling in the word is often rather elaborate ; it tends to hint at satire or at least at satiety. But in all these cases, it seems to me, a foreigner who was taught that the words had the same Sense but different Emotive Colourings would be likely to go wrong. He needs to learn the different Senses and then get used to the tricks that people play with them.

Indeed it seems likely that, if you did find a pair of words identical in Sense but with one carrying a special Emotion, this would be an unstable word. I think this is only true after various qualifications have been made, but it gives the broad intention of the speakers. However some words can be found which are concerned to fix (and if possible transmit) a mere state of feeling, without directly naming it, and without connecting this Feeling to their Sense ; nor are they unstable words. In looking for a clear and worthy case we had best look among minor parts of speech, because nouns and adjectives, feeling responsible for truth, tend to keep their Emotions within reach of Implications or make them the results of specific opinions ; and it is better to choose an inhibitive word rather than a stirring one, because the stirring ones have the simple but confusing habit of repeating their Emotions in their Moods.

While teaching English in Japan I had often to attempt explanations of the word *quite* (it doesn't seem to give so much difficulty in China). A man would write " the death of Lear is quite tragic ", or for that matter " the Fool was quite a nice friend for Lear", and one would find, after some floundering, not that his feelings were all wrong, but that there was nothing in the N.E.D., his constant study, to keep him from thinking that these uses meant " very, completely, in the strictest sense of the term ". There may be a good deal that is wrong in my theory, but I know at least that the current methods do not explain such words.

The N.E.D. makes a bold attempt at controlling *quite* by promoting its suggestion to one of the major divisions marked by Roman numbers, but has then to treat it as such ; and though this is all right for classifying the examples it does not give an explanation.

" I.   In the fullest degree (Subheads 1, 2, 3, . . .)
  II.   Actually, really, truly, positively (implying that the case or circumstances are such as fully to justify the use of the word or phrase thus qualified). (Further Subheads)."

Apart from the peculiar stutter of the great work in its thesaurus aspect this amounts to the phrase in the bracket, but the alternative words have the useful function of showing why the phrase is misleading. They have first a certain warmth—' I insist on this justifiable word '—then this makes an appeal to the reader's sympathy which may easily become a confession—' the word is justifiable here because one ought to speak strongly, though the word is only actually really truly positively true in a broad sense '. They may thus come to moderate the idea of completeness but by a different route from ' quite ', which happens to have no complete synonym. ' Quite II ', like many other parlour tricks of the language, enters literature with Richardson (after a slang use by Pope); the derivation connects *quite* with ' quit ' (free) and ' quiet ', which may do something to explain its habits. The subtle flatness of *quite* is not due to an idea ' certainly so, but in a broad sense of the term ' ; indeed there is a feeling of tidiness and strictness which makes for a narrow sense ; but a word like ' long ', which being essentially comparative has no strict sense, will easily give ' quite a long way ' the sense ' only a moderately long way '.

This is explained if you write :
> I. Completely.
> I.—I! Completely. Not exciting.

I write the main emotive part as negative more for clarity than to leave room for positive excitement ' I! ', which the word hardly ever carries in modern English. Still it is apparently the old use, and the N.E.D. example of an early ' II ' is I think simply ' I.I! ':

> *To my kin a stranger quite,*
> *Quite an alien am I grown.*

In modern English this would suggest a pathetic moderation, but in the context that is little different from the direct intensive use probably intended. The N.E.D. is of course right in listing it with ' II ', for it shows that the growth of ' II ' could be gradual ; the shift of the emotion made little difference ; the real change comes when the new emotion produces moods.

' Oh, yes, *quite* a good day ; we did *everything* ', or take Pope's early use :

> *But something much more our concern*
> *And quite a scandal not to learn.*

The feeling here is ' how cosy '. Now in a direct expression of emotion—' this intolerable scoundrel '—the fact that the speaker feels the emotion is much less in view than the presumption that anybody would feel it ; the emotion is made public like the sense. In the same way the stock emotion of *quite*—' —I! ' ' without excitement '—is somehow a public part of the word. But in the moods of *quite* you contradict ' —I! ', though it is still present, with a word or turn of grammar implying excitement ; the effect brings *you* into prominence as making the clash ; and I fancy you never do this except in view of someone else. So the account of it must involve you and the other man. Still, the use once settled need not be self-conscious ; the sentence defining the mood only gives the process that made and still supports the use. In the clash here you may be felt to confess mixed feelings, and thereby show intimacy, or to pretend either the excitement or the calm ; " I have my feelings, but shall only state the facts with a placid *quite* " (" as we have the same standards I need not insist on what I feel "), or " I make a pretence of excitement about this to show pleasure, decision, etc., though really, as is clear from *quite*, I feel settled and satisfied about it " (" I want you to share what I could feel, or felt at the time "). Thus the main mood, which the others have to evade, brings in the other person by " we agree about this, we who know, don't we ? ". Cosy mood ' I£1 '.

The clash may also be used for insolence " I£2 ", by various methods. ' I maintain bare politeness by this pretence of excitement but mean you to see that it is forced ' or in another context ' I don't ask much of you ; I shan't be grateful ; I only "—I! " want the thing quite right '. The cosy mood must be clearly cut out, but the second sentence is not a direct irony from it.

Uses with *not*—" not quite right " " not quite nice "—tend to borrow the clash from other uses, not make it themselves by a pretence of excitement. " I£3 "—" I speak as moderately as I can about this person's faults, though one could feel strongly. This much can't be denied ". The cosy mood " we shall agree ", when it has become normal, is enough to impose here a context of social convention where not to be quite right is to be all wrong.

Quite used alone for an answer is more independent ; it comes simply from complete agreement ' I ' without excitement ' —I! ' so expressed as briefly as possible : ' I£4 ' ' I knew that already, but you were right to say it '. More cordial uses tend to patronage— ' you deserve praise for saying what I knew already '—more bitter ones to irony—' This is only a trivial part of the truth ', which may amount ' —I ' to denying the completeness of its truth. These have to be shown separately by your voice, and feel apart from ' the word ', but may support themselves on its cosy and insolent moods.

Being ' in ' the word is of course a matter of degree. Thus the nineteenth century developed a trick of changing the place of *quite* and the article—' a quite tragic play ' ; this cut out the cosy and insolent moods but kept the emotion ' —I! ' because that was ' in ' the word in any use. It is then reinforced by a mood deduced from the grammar : " I£5 " " You may notice that, so far from being excited, I am picking my words with somewhat precious care ".

So much detail seemed necessary to show the forms in action. No doubt I have put most of the puzzles into the mood-sign ; the claim is that to explain the word you want a Sense and an Emotion, only one, and that these are the basis for its whole performance of moods. I do not pretend to explain why partial contradiction of the emotion did in fact, at a certain date, resolve itself so firmly into the cosy mood, or (probably the same question) what keeps an unsupported emotion alive in this charming and very English word. There seems to be a sentence like ' This is sober ; it will still be true when the excitement has died down ' which takes the place of the sense-implication which is usually the sanction of a fixed emotion. Still there is a real case here for talking about the Emotive part of a word as something flatly detached from its sense.

The historical change in *quite* has been explained as due to a process of " fading " ; that is to say, persons trying to emphasise their remarks frequently used *quite* in situations which were not really exciting, as the listeners could observe, so the listeners came to feel that the proper use of *quite* was to mark not really exciting situations. This may be true, but if so it illustrates the more general truth that the cause of a sense-change need have nothing to do with the use made of it after it has been pushed through. The modern feeling about *quite* is entirely different from that about a discredited intensifier (*awfully, frightfully*) ; in fact it is the opposite. It is not true to say, as Mr. A. P. Herbert did somewhere, that " quite all right " is like using three blows of a steam hammer to kill a fly, because *quite* acts as a moderator here not as an unnecessary intensifier. The phrase is therefore a polite way of saying " Taken as a whole (*all*) this is good enough (*right*) ; I can put up with it (*quite*)".

It is rather significant, I think, that the " fading " theory is so hard to test from the examples. The difference between the N.E.D. " I " and " II " is not in the Emotion but in the Moods that are produced by it. If you take "−I! " for granted you can read it into nearly all uses of " I " and it will only give an effect of finality—" no use making a fuss ". Very few contexts will show for certain whether the word is used as an intensifier or not. The N.E.D. was therefore right in refusing simply to chatter about the Emotions in the word ; that would not be enough without the Moods as well. For that matter the heading " II " is a good collection of the Moods, with an adequate description if you understand them already. The gap only appears when you try to explain the word to a foreigner who does not, and then, though this may seem a pedantic discussion, you will have to drop into your talk the substance of " −I! " and " I£1 ".

This process had better be compared with the loose " nice " and the absolute " so ", two other cosy forms which came in with Richardson ; they reach the same moods through a different emotion. Like *quite* they have an air of keeping the talk from getting too excited, and yet they were developed to express excitement in a childish form. This is clearest about " I am *so* pleased " (" *that* I " —" forget my manners " left out) which got its emotion while it was thought bad grammar. Writing as " x ", like the N.E.D., not so much the sense here as the grammatical form, we have " x! " " excited, asking sympathy ". The mood appears when you feel that this is common, not merely a mistake caused by feverishness, and yet not your usual standard : " x£1 " " While decently cool, I pretend a burst of excitement so as to ask you to feel as I do, and so as to say I feel sure you will ". To appeal for sympathy and be rebuffed is a shock most people are careful to avoid, so the mood has two parts. In all such attempts to explain a complicated use one must of course consider how it was imposed ; this is imposed simply by accepting a slang form with calm. The cosy effect from the second part, when taken as normal, becomes the strongest element as in *quite* ; " x£2 " " How nice it is that we agree so well ".

With *nice* there is a sense-change to consider.

" 1.   exact, neat.   1/1 (such things are) pleasing.

  1/1! excitement.   2. pleasing.

The symbol for the Emotion had best attach it to the Implication, not to the new Sense, as the emotion is already needed to make the implication appear alone, and thus become a new sense, and once established alone the new sense need not carry the emotion. An evidently placid use absorbs the emotion into a mood " 2£1 " " pretended excitement for cordiality and to presume sympathy " as in *so*. It seems excess of pedantry to write even the mood as " 1/1.£1 ", but probably the mood must be well established before you get the plain sense " 2 ", not needing either mood or emotion to impose it, though tending to carry them. It can now go near to kill " 1 ", as the mild suggestions of the use do not clearly cut out either the sense of " 2 " or its mood. The intriguing thing about *nice*, not needed to explain the shift but I think a reason why the shift was so complete, is that it always returns to the speaker : " While the sort of person who is habitually pleased by neatness, I am so pleased by this not very neat thing that I give it my habitual praise neat " ; she feels she is generally *nice* " I " and now in her excitement *nice* " 2 ". It is thus an example of the peculiar form " ? ", which could be attached to both the Senses ; but the effect does not seem a decisive one.

I said that *quite* had no complete synonym, but *just* is a close parallel. In its history it goes from an idea of completeness to an idea of moderation rather earlier than *quite*, but I think the same process was at work. " Exactly, precisely, closely " (1400) is the early use, according to the N.E.D., and the sense " no more than ; only, merely ; barely " comes in with Hooke : " so cold that it just begins to freeze " (1665). This form was arrived at by shortening ; the older expression would be " but just ". But even this involves a change of feeling ; you would not say " only exactly ". I fancy that the adverb was attracted by the adjective ; " but just " seems to have a connection with judging justly. The new form of " just " has the coolness of the scientist observing Nature and summing her up, and the first use that happens to be listed in the N.E.D. describes his technical operations. There is a development earlier in the seventeenth century of " just " used alone, like the nineteenth century " quite " used alone, where the man agrees with you by saying that your judgement of the case was a just one. Both words get an Emotion " not exciting " from a context of cold truth. The N.E.D. gives a separate group which extends from " I was just ready to expire with grief " (1726) to the modern " isn't that just splendid! ". Here, as in *quite*, the new Mood is a contradication of the negative stock Emotion by pretence of excitement, and what the dictionary gives first in its examples of the group seems to be really a simple emotive use of the word as an intensifier, so that even the negative stock Emotion is not present. It appears that the old warm use, ingeniously defined as " no *less* than ", is mainly Scotch, and the invasion of Scotchmen during the seventeenth and eighteenth centuries may have had a (rather contradictory) influence on the English word. But anyway it is a less interesting case than *quite*, because the idea of moderation comes into the new Sense and not only into the new Emotion. Indeed " no less than " and " no more than " are straightforward cases for the symbols " A+ " and " A—".* Thus the entry of coolness into *quite* is a close parallel to alter the Sense of the word, because you can't have " more than completely ", so that it stands out as an Emotion about the situation in view.

By the way, the same kind of coolness has established itself in various phrases used in arguments, to admit one of the assertions of the opponent while claiming that this does not weaken your case. *No doubt* and *it is true that* and *certainly* all have this effect when used at the beginning of a sentence, whereas *surely* is a tender appeal to the opponent—" even you, though you will want to deny this, can see the truth of it if you try ". The trick in *surely* is I think a Mood, because it needs to be recognised as an appeal, but *certainly* can make its effect merely from the negative Emotion " not exciting ". *Sure* is rather more " intimate ", that is, concerned with immediate feelings, than the more Latin *certain*, and this I think is the only basis for the contrast, which in a context of debate amounts to using them as opposites. But the Emotive difference alone is not enough for the contrast ; indeed *surely* tends to be used with more coolness than *certainly*, not with less, because its function is to bluff the opponent into admitting more than he wants. Here again the effect has to be explained as a slight contradiction of the tied emotion, which produced a Mood.

These words are of a special type, simple in meaning and indeed in emotion but socially complicated, so that analysis with the Mood sign is more obviously relevant here than elsewhere. We need now to consider some words in which the Sense is expected to be more decisive. It seems likely here that the Emotion cannot run off on its own without giving the effect of an obvious mistake ; but there may be a variety of purposes to be served. Thus *lust* has a sense ' A ' " sexual desire of a low kind ", then several possible implications to support " low ", " A/1, 2, 3 etc.", " selfish, brief, cruel,

---

* So for example is the contrasted pair " He was little fond of display " — " He was a little fond of display ".

without marriage in church, etc.", and these are what will decide when the speaker is to use the word. The element " low " in this definition of the word may be listed as its Emotion " A ! " " contempt or disgust ". You may use the word with a new sense " sexual desire in general " " B " whenever you want to show disgust " A ! " about a specimen of that ; and the presumption will be that you have some implication to support you. But if this becomes a general habit, so that desire in general is felt to become the normal sense of the word, people will begin to talk about "jolly lust". This happens in one of H. G. Wells' novels, *The Bulpington of Blup,* and is done by a character designed as a parody of G. K. Chesterton ; it is very unfair to Chesterton, by the way, who might be in that intellectual muddle but would not be in that stylistic one. " Jolly lust " might amount to accepting the new sense, and consequently intending to drop the old Emotion, and indeed might support this plan by claiming to be an archaism and recalling " lusty ". Or it might be a campaign against the mixture " B.A ! " which if successful would wear itself out and let *lust* go back to its normal " A.A ! ". This would involve implied quotation—" what *they* call lust ". This intention may have been somewhere in the mind of H. G. Wells, but it is harder to say what intention he was giving to the character who was to parody Chesterton. Perhaps it is chiefly meant to show that the character made silly paradoxes ; the neo-Catholic, being sure he was not a " Puritan ", claimed to view sex outside marriage without alarm while suggesting that among well-balanced people it never got further than a slap and tickle. The thing is meant to be disingenuous and at the same time naive, and does I think succeed in making the character seem very unpleasant. But the doctrinal background is after all very elaborate, perhaps too much so for what we need here. Regarded simply as an attempt to fix the new Sense without the old Emotion it would still I think feel rather " in bad taste ", but merely because it would show ignorance of what changes in the language are (so to speak) practical politics. We expect people to be conscious of how far they can get others to follow them even when they are fixing their own senses for words, and this I think shows how inadequate it is for a psychological linguist to suppose that the shifts are " merely Emotive ". Talkers are casual and often silly but they are up to something. In the ordinary way, the emotion in a word is backed by a judgement which the speaker would be prepared to maintain, and for that matter a word like " poop ", which obviously expresses mere contempt by sound, has to find for itself an implied sense, here " fool ", to support the emotion. To be sure, if two words for the same thing imply different habitual contexts it is felt that they may have reasons for emotions in reserve, or simply that it is convenient to have two words for the two frames of mind or universes of discourse ; the word " copulate " and its colloquial equivalent are an example of this, and seem clearly a stable pair. Even when there is no such intention behind a contrast the testing of it is a rather dim and clumsy process, and a " merely emotive " word can go on for some time without being found out. But it is no use generalizing to the normal case from an accident felt to be a mistake.

However there is another type of contrast, as in the difference between a miserly man who hoards money out of avarice and a thrifty man who saves money out of prudence. These groups of contrasted terms are evidently very stable, and yet the Senses in each pair appear to be the same, and furthermore there is no difference of " context "—nothing in the type of approach or the " universe of diction " of the speaker—which would make him choose one rather than the other. Probably indeed most people would say that there is a real difference of meaning, which they could expound, and so they could ; the puzzle for the linguist is that different people would expound it quite differently, and yet they can realise this without feeling that the words themselves are made useless by it. The *use* of the words, in fact, is to sum up your own attitude to the practical questions that they raise, and it is their business to be fluid in meaning so that a variety of people can use them. This is widely recognised, I think. " 'E's what I call thrifty ", the charlady will say, with a rich recognition of the possibilities of using the other word. And the way one person uses these words about another is felt to give you information about the first one ; " Tom's not that sort at all ; 'e thinks George awful mean ". There is commonly a shortage of neutral words in this kind of field, because the play of feeling along these lines is so habitual that they all get attracted to one side or the other. On the other hand, I doubt whether this arrangement of the words would be stable if there were a keen controversy in the world of the speakers on the topic the words deal with, so that rival camps held opposed doctrines. The words would probably be re-interpreted to carry the rival doctrines, and to imply that the speaker revered the one and hated the other. But in matters where a large variety of judgement is not only recognised but vaguely approved it would be useless, I think, to look for a definition which would cover all the speakers. A dictionary had better list the meaning common to the two words and then their two Emotions, approval and disapproval ; not because there are no implications, but because they would need a long sociological essay. Incidentally the word " good " itself, which some theories about ethics take as " purely emotive ", is an example of this process taken to an extreme ; it is useful because it is prepared to cover whatever anybody thinks good, or thinks good to be, but this practical piece of information about the word does not in itself constitute a theory about ethics.

We may now pause to take stock of the position. Various objections are likely to be made to the idea of using these symbols, even apart from the question whether they represent elements that really occur. " Do you fancy that this is all one *can* feel about a word ? " : No, I am trying to give the regular working parts ; the over-all impression from a consecutive passage is of course something quite different, and how much of it may echo into a key word one cannot say. " Are all these elements supposed to be conscious and intentional ? " : often very little, and commonly in different degrees for different readers or hearers. But I am trying to write linguistics not psychology ; something *quite* unconscious and unintentional, even if the hearer catches it like an infection, is not part of an act of communication. " Surely you can see that these elements are all blurred together, and that to analyse them is to change them ? " : yes, but everybody analyses a bit when he chooses his words, and commonly does it well ; I am trying to trace the lines which this quick but important process follows. " Why don't you *define* an emotion in a word if you want to be rigid ? " : this is a nastier one. I might say that the only practical difficulty about this phrase, which everyone feels he understands, is that it is used loosely ; to cut out the irrelevant parts may be enough. And in any case, I might go on, the Emotions are very little used as the work develops ; I am only refusing to take the harsh step of denying their existence altogether. But certainly it is time that I tried to consider what they may be.

The general position I have reached is that it would be sensible for a dictionary to recognise the Emotions in a variety of words (it is already done in a timid manner, as by writing a shortened form of " derogatory " after a definition), but that these emotions are usually tied up with more complicated elements. And I introduced the Emotion in a word merely as a term for what was left behind when various other elements, such as Implications, had been separated out. But it might be argued that an Emotion is simply one of the kinds of Implication. The interest of the example *quite*, I should claim, is that it shows a tied Emotion almost at variance with the simple Sense of the word and yet not getting support from any extra implied sense. But the element " not exciting " in *quite* is learned from its normal past contexts, and so is an Implication. Indeed the more behaviourist linguists, if I understand their position, would maintain that a distinction between Emotion and Implication is not even allowable, because it claims to know more about the speakers' minds than can be known. I think this is a wrong point of view, as I try to show in an appendix. But certainly, whichever term we use, the extra element is put in by the same process ; and it does not seem very obviously Emotive, even if it makes a very vague kind of Sense. To be sure, the N.E.D. would have succeeded in defining its main head QUITE II if, instead of " implying that the circumstances fully justify the use of the word qualified ", it had put " implying that the matter is settled or accepted ". I choose this phrase as being in a more decorous dictionary style, having more of the appearance of a sense-implication, than " implying that the matter is not exciting " ; but I think that would be clearer ; and if you were allowed to put " Not exciting ! " with a shriek mark I think that would be clearer still, as well as shorter. Even so the question seems one of style rather than of fundamental theory.

But if it were seriously maintained that the Emotion and the Implication cannot be distinguished, so that to use both of them would be " multiplying entities without necessity ", I should answer that this is a typical case of the linguist pretending not to know what he really does know, on the bad ground that it is hard to see how he comes to know it. The implication " not exciting ", it seems to me, really does appear in the speakers' minds as a tone of feeling, not as something like a covert sense. It has been so completely " translated " into an Emotion (or has not completely always been one), that it is notably hard to translate back ; this I think is the reason why the N.E.D. muddled it. Furthermore I doubt whether the structure of Moods in *quite*, a queerly complicated thing, would arise unless there were an adequate drive behind it, and this required an Emotion rather than an Implication. In the same way, the Moods can only pile up and contradict each other in *Honest* (chapter 9) because of the basic moral weight of the word. This kind of argument from structure, as a reason for postulating two separate entities, is after all considered respectable in the sciences.

I have sometimes talked as if an Emotion in a word could normally be translated into an Implication, which is also the sanction or reason for it. This is only putting in an extra step ; the Sense itself may act as the sanction without more ado. Thus the Emotion " good ! " attached to *trustworthy* reflects the belief that it is good to be trustworthy ; no doubt one could give a large sociological and psychological background, and claim that this is the real reason why the belief is held, but it is not likely to be an Implication within the immediate reach of the speaker. The Emotion that results from calling a lip a cherry may depend on the Implications, but it is likely to be stronger if it depends on the picture itself. And a word which admittedly names an emotional condition, e.g., *fear*, does not leave much room for an opposition between Sense and Emotion ; whether a listener sympathizes with the condition or merely recognises it is largely his own affair. However no doubt there are medical terms for odd fears (*pavor noctis* I believe is one) which would specifically avoid making you feel like the patient does ; the denial of the Emotion would be worth listing in them, rather than its presumable presence in the common word.

In discussing " fading " I admitted that there are some words, such as *frightfully* and *absolutely*, which have been used emotively as intensifiers ; that is, the literal meaning would be fatuous in the context, and the word is used with the Emotion usually due to this literal meaning, without being given any new Sense which would support it. The context is felt to deserve a fairly strong emotion, but the word is dragged in to carry the emotion only. The reason why the Emotion tends to " fade ", or the use as an intensifier to become out of date, is of course that the word in its new Sense (so far as there is one) no longer gives the Emotion any solid support. Swearing is an even better example of this process ; Stern's remarks about metaphors are quite accurate if applied to swear-words. Ingenious ones tend to drop out, because there is no reason except novelty to select them, but " By God " and so on do not fade because the Sense of the word continues to supply the Emotion which is to be thrown about at random. I must not, therefore, deny that a purely Emotive use of words can occur ; it would be beside the point to argue that there is a residual amount of meaning even in intensifiers and swear-words (they at least impose a Mood) ; and it would be still more foolish to erect an unsuccessful linguistic law into a moral one, and say that they ought not to occur. What I maintain is that such uses are ordinarily felt to be trivial and separate from the straightforward uses of language, and that there is no ground for supposing that the same trick is really at work on a large scale without our knowing it. Indeed the standard way of making a word carry more weight, either in poetry or prose, is to make the context bring out one of its Implications to show that its stock Emotion is deserved here. This is the opposite process to that which blurs the Sense to get an effect of Emotion. And for that matter poets often make their work look more nakedly emotive than it really is, because that gives the right basis for the relation of the emotive to the cognitive part. It is rather like a polite pretence of humility, and to take it at its face value misses the point in the same kind of way. On the other hand, if this account seems rather too pure-minded, I do think there is ground for supposing that another trick is at work on a large scale without our noticing it, as I shall try to explain in the next chapter ; but that is not a specifically Emotive one.

It might be objected that all this talk about Emotions comes from a tea-taster's approach to the subject, natural in a *litterateur*, whereas language in real use is "dynamic", so that the important things in a word other than its plain sense are attitudes, tendencies to action. I do not think the distinction would amount to much when you were trying to draw up a chart. *Promisekeeping* would I suppose have an Emotion "Good!" but *promise* an Attitude "Good to keep it!". The difference here seems to be merely one of grammar. One could make a more real distinction in that the speaker is sometimes urging the hearer to feel the emotion, and hence act on it, or sometimes implying that he himself feels it more deeply than his neighbours. Both these I think require an extra performance in pronouncing the word or in the written style, done on a personal basis, so that I could class them as Moods. But the conception of an Attitude certainly needs to be considered in talking about Professor Richards' view of Emotive language. The emotions, in his account, are not important in themselves but as signs of attitudes. Some emotions may be delusive, in that they do not correspond to any important or lasting structure of attitudes, but others are the only way we can learn that we have such a thing. In themselves the emotions are either the consciousness of bodily reactions (sweating and suchlike) or images of them ; but as signs of attitudes they have a peculiar sort of truth-function, very different from that of a Sense. Certainly I don't deny that this is a valuable idea, as giving an insight into which emotions are important. But it seems hard to connect an emotion so conceived with "the emotion in a word", a fixed tendency in reacting to the word, which we are to list in a chart. We do not want it at all unless it is pretty automatic, and then it cannot be telling us anything about the depths of our nature at the moment. The emotion in a word, as I am treating it, is an extremely public object, practically as much so as the Sense ; there is a presumption that anybody would feel it under the circumstances, rather than that the speaker feels it. Indeed most of the obvious emotions in words (many words seem to have none) are moral, marking approval or disapproval only, and it is a regular mark of moral feelings that they claim not to be private ones—if nobody knows what is right except me they still ought to know. It seems clear that a feeling of approval is not a consciousness of a bodily reaction such as sweating, and I am not sure that it need be a tendency to action by the person who feels it either. I am putting in an appendix a discussion of the view that ethical judgements are Emotive uses of language; it is an important branch of the imbroglio about emotions but seems a side-issue here. Whether Approval is an emotion or not, and from Professor Richards' account of emotions I should think it is not, it certainly needs to be counted as one of the emotions " in words ", otherwise there would be no convenience in supposing that such a class existed.

Such is the best light I can find on the matter, and I cannot pretend that it puts the emotion in a word on a very solid theoretical foundation. But I hope it is now tolerably clear what kind of function the emotions in words are expected to play ; they are comparatively permanent and simple, and they are used in building structures more elaborate and changeable than themselves. Normally they are dependent on a Sense which is believed to deserve them, and when they are detached from it the process is fairly easily recognised as some kind of playing or cheating.

So far I have tried to give symbols for all the tools of classification used or needed in a dictionary ; but there is another one in common use which I think had better not be symbolised. It is what is called the Range of a given meaning of a word (the range as the whole group of possible meanings for the word is of course a different idea). This kind of Range is illustrated by the subhead under *honest* which reads " Of women : chaste ". In any case, this could not be made shorter ; there would be no immediate convenience in a symbol, because the extra element is not another part of the word. And as soon as you try to symbolise the referents as apart from the reference to them, the class defined as apart from its defining property, the extension as apart from the intension, you get into philosophical questions which only distract you from examining the mind of the speaker. All the same, the Range cannot be ignored. The case of " Of women : chaste " is a delusively simple one, because whatever you think about women there is little doubt about which persons they are. But very often in ordinary language the class supposed to be in view is secretly altered whenever a new property of it is considered. Many cases of Metaphor can be regarded simply as giving an old Sense of the word an unusual Range, " the *leg* of a table " for instance ; they merely assert some of the properties defined by the word about a new class. One can also drag the idea of Range into the puzzle about " thrifty " and " miserly " ; it is clear that the behaviour thought proper for a farm labourer might be given a different name when adopted by the squire. But it would only be useful to put this into the definition if you were dealing with a simple and clear-cut society. And then again, there might be much odder uses of the Range idea about misers. Some people think they can recognise misers by their manner or their smell or something, so that any sign of thriftiness in one of these men will then be called Miserly. In such a case the class is formed independently of the supposed property, and yet is liable to change the speakers' idea of the property itself. You could argue that what this man thought he meant by *miserly* was quite different from what he really meant, but this " real " meaning would still be hard to find. Of course, if he only calls Jews miserly, the work of the lexicographer is simple ; he can put " Of Jews : thrifty (derog.) " ; but there may often be a similar Range process at work when it is impossible to describe the actual range. And I do not want to talk as if an " intuition " about which men are miserly is sure to be wrong ; the man's subconscious judgement may have got hold of some subtle truth, but this would not make it any easier to define the meaning he puts on the word.

In a simple case like " Of women : chaste " the Range tends to be given by the immediate context (e.g., *women* is the noun of the adjective *honest*) and then an eighteenth century listener would have no problem. But the process of arriving at the Range was a gradual one, the hardening of a convention about this Sense ; I think Iago plays with it about Cassio as well as about Desdemona, though it was already considered more suitable to women. In an eighteenth century speaker such a use would have to be called a metaphor, and would need imposing by the context very firmly ; but I think that some of the Augustan moralists did try to revive the sense " chaste " used of men, without success. A complete lexicographer would not only have to give the Range but its degree of vagueness at different dates, and a separate symbol for the Range might be misleading because too definite. Besides, the notion of a Range when taken seriously becomes hard to separate from " the field of discourse ", which needs to be a much vaguer idea ; for example are we to say in " Two and two make four " that the Range of the word *four* excludes drops of water ?

There is a more fundamental problem when the Sense actually reduces itself to the Range. Most critics who talk about " romantic " or " metaphysical " poetry have in mind some defining property of these classes, however dim ; but it is the normal business of a historian of literature to mean the classes only, that is, to describe whatever has been given one of these names, whether rightly or not. It is clear that this movement of thought, from the supposed common property to the things actually grouped under it, is a frequent and necessary one ; I would not be dragging in unnecessary philosophical distinctions if I tried to give symbols for it. You might indeed say that this case is quite different from " Of women : chaste " ; because it is assumed that only the things covered by *some* definition of " romantic poetry " are given that name, whereas women are not defined by " honest " at all. But you have merely to write " having female chastity " to define this use of *honest*, and it will be assumed that only females are normally covered by the definition. The logical problem is trivial here ; but it becomes serious in cases like " romantic poetry ", where all you have is a class of things, vague at the edges, which somehow feel as if they deserved one name, and are in fact given one name of doubtful meaning. A critic may have a kind of skill at putting the right things into this class without being at all clear what he is doing ; his definition of " romantic poetry " is what he is working towards, not a tool he is working with. And these processes of thought are among the most important or decisive uses of language ; they cannot simply be left out. But in such a case one cannot say that the man is only using the Range not the Sense of the word ; his whole skill lies in altering the edges of the Range, for some purpose which is still obscure to him, until the new Range fits a new Sense. I do not think therefore that a symbol for the Range alone would help us to follow his thought ; and so far as he uses the word merely with doubt, so as to convey "what is commonly so called ", the only symbols we need are quotation marks. They also cover the case of the historian, who need not be feeling doubt at all.

I should be willing to agree that there are other important questions which this symbolism does nothing to clarify ; a very relevant one, for example, is raised by *The Meaning of Meaning* when it points out that :

" ' animal ' in current speech and ' mammal ' in zoology stand for almost the same referents, but the references vary very greatly in the definiteness and complexity of the sign chains involved " (p. 128).

and earlier (p. 93) two references may be to the same referent but at

" very different levels of interpretation, in a definite sense in-volving the number of applications of interpretative processes and the complexity of these processes . . . All our usual discussion of subjects of general interest suffers from the uncertainty, difficult even to state, as to the level of interpretation, of reference, at which we are symbolising. All those engaged in education know what ' levels of reference ' stand for. The fuller analysis of the question is of great urgency."

The difference between *animal* and *mammal*, in my set of terms, must be put into their Implications, and it seems to fit there all right. But how far the user of such a word is following up these Implications, along a possible series of " sign chains ", does seem a more mysterious matter ; and I think it must be regarded as a matter of how he interprets the whole passage rather than of how he interprets the single word. We can see this kind of process particularly clearly in metaphor ; an analogy can almost always be followed up in great detail (yielding both likenesses and unlikenesses) though it seems to be accepted without more ado on one ground of likeness. I think we follow up these connections more than we realise, so that they contribute to the immediate effect of the metaphor ; and certainly the same process may be going on when we do not consider that metaphor is in play. No doubt my class of Implications could do with a lot of subdividing. But I do not see that there is any fallacy in lumping together the basic material for these further sign-chains into one class " Implication ", and leaving it to be developed as required.

There is a final point of definition which I want to ask the reader to notice, as it will keep cropping up in the book. I shall use the " head " meaning of a word for a meaning which holds a more or less permanent position as the first one in its structure ; there may be various criteria for this, such as being the most frequent in use or the one supported by derivation, also a word may change from having one meaning as the head to having another, or a writer may impose a head meaning of his own. Thus there are important practical decisions for a critic to take about which is the head meaning ; the term perhaps is merely a convenience which needs subdividing, but anyway it never refers only to the example of a use of the word which is being considered at the moment. On the other hand I shall use the " chief " meaning of a word for the meaning which the user feels to be the first one in play at the moment. It might be argued that there sometimes isn't such a thing, but we generally assume that one word has one meaning, and a speaker if challenged about a rich use would normally pick out one meaning as " what he really meant ". If the " chief meaning " is allowed a suggestion of local or tribal chieftains I think it can easily be remembered as applying only to a local occasion. This contrast seems to be the way the two terms are commonly used, but one can reduce the verbiage of discussion a good deal if it is taken as fixed. And by the way, in case a conscientious reader looked for another distinction, I shall make no difference at all between " sense " and " meaning " but try to pick the one that sounds less ugly. Indeed when talking about the word *sense* I am afraid I have sometimes thrown in the term " interpretation " to make a third synonym, because what I have to avoid is often " the sense ' sense ' of *sense* ", a phrase which can leave no impression on the mind except that of a sordid form of lunacy.

As to the theory of J. P. Sartre in his book *The Emotions*, which I understand to say that the feeling of any emotion is a return to the world of magic, it is surely enough to reply that animals obviously feel emotions whereas magic was invented by primitive man.

Chapter 2

STATEMENTS IN WORDS

THE first chapter tried to separate various entities in the habitual uses of a single word, for example Senses, Implications, Emotions and Moods. But this in itself does show how they work when together; a more adventurous stage of the inquiry is reached when you try to codify the process of combination. A word may become a sort of solid entity, able to direct opinion, thought of as like a person; also it is often said (whether this is the same idea or not) that a word can become a " compacted doctrine ", or even that all words are compacted doctrines inherently. To get some general theory about how this happens would clearly be important; if our language is continually thrusting doctrines on us, perhaps very ill-considered ones, the sooner we understand the process the better. So far as I know the main work on this subject has been done by Professor Richards, and he implies that the process is an interaction between a word's Sense and its Emotion or Gesture. It seems hard to follow out this programme in detail, and I shall mainly follow the alternative programme of keeping to the inter-actions between Senses (including Implications). I do not deny that Emotions and Moods may well be important as calling out and directing the interaction, but it seems clear that the first thing to examine is the result, what may be called the logic of these un-noticed propositions; and I think that all the important cases can be handled in this way.

I propose to distinguish five ways in which a word can carry a doctrine. The most obvious and most irreducible type is the Existence Assertion, which says that what the word names is really there and worth naming. This of course need not be present and may be overtly denied, as in " astrology is false ", but it tends to crop up of its own accord; thus if you go on talking about astrology without positive disclaimers people will begin to say " He talks as if he really believed in it ". Nor is the feeling peculiar to nouns; it can be called out even in unlikely parts of speech, as is witnessed by the proverb " There's allus an If an' a But ". Such an assertion may be very complex. One must read very deeply in Aquinas to know all of what he meant by God, or meant to assert when he claimed to have proved the existence of God (the " five proofs " deal with different parts of the conception); and yet he would claim to mean all this complex idea even in a passing reference to God. Furthermore the same covert assertion may shade off into assertions *about* God, according as your attention is directed to one or other of his properties (there may for example be a suppressed syllogism " But God is good, therefore what I now say is true "). You might say that one of the Implications of the word is being asserted in such a case. But there would be no great advantage in saying this, because it does not matter how much of the thought you suppose to be " in " the word and how much in the whole treatise. Aristotle, for that matter, pointed out that a syllogism might be regarded as a re-definition followed by a tautology. And of course there should be a similar position for the word " electron " in the writings of any one physicist who claimed to put forward a complete atomic theory ; all the properties should somehow be included in the idea. No doubt while you are reading the single consistent author the meaning of his key words will grow in your mind, but once you have got the full meaning it is a fully unified one. The complexity of the word is simply that of the topic, and the linguist cannot pretend to tidy it up. This type is therefore of no interest for my purpose here, except that the feeling it gives of simplicity and irreducibility is often borrowed by the other types, to make themselves stronger, so that they are easily confused with it. An existence assertion, of course, does not require very careful uses of language ; I have appealed to cases like that only to try to isolate the type. It is very common ; most newspaper headlines, for example, not being sentences, must be supposed to make assertions of this sort. No doubt it is often thought to occur when really the mental goings-on are more confused, but then there is often nothing to be gained by looking into this confusion (because it " comes to the same thing in the end "). On the other hand a " verbal fiction " may need a great deal of looking into, and the full analysis of it may be very complex, but so far as a speaker is wholly deceived by it I think we must accept his own view that he is simply using it for an existence assertion. If there is any need of a symbol for existence assertions the obvious one is Russell's " ∃ ".

I think that the same feeling of assertion is carried over to an entirely different case, which I shall call an " equation " and propose to divide into four types. Two senses of the word are used at once, and also (which does not necessarily happen) there is an implied assertion that they naturally belong together, " as the word itself proves ". After numbering the senses as if for a dictionary I write this " A=B " in figures and expect it to make sense when read as " A is B " in words. The English verb " to be ", I take it, is a witness to the same mental process as that which forms the equation, so that " is " here has the same range as in ordinary English, except that some of the uses for more complex grammar would clearly be out of place. I do not think that we interpret " A " clearly as a noun and " B " as an adjective, because they are too much on the same footing (except in quite odd cases as when Mr. Brown is expected to be brown) ; and a relational " is " like " A is (in the relation) B to C ", which might conceivably connect three senses of one word, would also be likely to put one of them on too separate a footing from the others. I do not want to limit the possible interpretations, only to get clear the usual ones so that the work can go ahead. The most frequent are " A is part of B ", " A entails B ", and " A is like B ", and the more peculiar one " A is typical of B " will have to be introduced. By definition an equation always generalises, because if it only said " *This* A is B " the effect would only be a double use of the word (which I symbolise " A.B "), imputing both " A " and " B " to " this ", and there would be no compacted doctrine. However it may presume a limited view of " A ", probably one with vague limits, and one could describe this process as saying " A's *of this sort* are B ". When the sort is clear at the time of speaking the analyst ought to write instead of " A " the narrower definition, but the speaker may be so vague that this would misrepresent him ; for example the sort required may be recognised only as what suits the Emotion or Mood. In particular, you can get equations of the form " a normal A is B ", or " a good A is B ", and I do not know that this last has any important difference from " A ought to be B ". Here we get a case where " A=B " could apparently be the same as " B=A ", using different interpretations for them ; because " a normal A is B " is the same sort of thing as " B is typical of A ". I think however that the two orders have different effects, and so are worth distinguishing ; the first can be taken very lightly, but the second makes you hold a specific doctrine which you are likely to remember.

In any case, an " A is B " assertion, for example " A is part of B ", treats " A " and " B " as two classes, not one as a thing the other as its property ; they are on the same footing ; though the practical effect may be much the same as making " B " an adjective. Nor are they both regarded as groups of properties, because the order is " cats are mammals " ; the class cats is part of the class mammals, whereas the properties which constitute a mammal are part of those which constitute a cat. No doubt our analysis could use either set of terms, but we need to choose one and stick to it ; in any case there is no linguistic tendency to swap over to " mammals are cats ". From " A is part of B " one could deduce " A entails B ", but this is not the only way of getting it ; it could cover " A is the cause of B " and even " A is the effect of B ", though this is less common, if the thought is " We know a case of

A is here so we can presume a case of B is here ". This gives a second way of making the two orders for the terms yield practically the same result, using different interpretations ; but I think it only happens in the peculiar case where each is felt to entail the other. The only third case seems to be " likeness ", but there you start from one term and call the other like it ; some cases of allegory may want you to be prepared to start from either end, but normally the order is fixed. By the " entails " relation " A " and " B " can be equated even if very unlike, whereas we could presume that " A " was " part of B ", after extending the idea of " B ", merely because "A" was " like B ". Thus the three interpretations are connected but no one of them is fundamental to both the others.

The casual interpretation of " A is B " has of course great importance for all kinds of thinking, but one should not say this placidly without adding that it is a great source of delusion, probably much more so than any of the others. Indeed in any organic setting the cause is likely to be the opposite of the effect, because the machinery of an organism is aimed at stabilising it. Scarlet fever and high temperatures go together, but the " fever " is part of Nature's cure ; in general a medical treatment aimed only at removing symptoms is likely to be harmful. In the same way the classical economists claim that the market acts as an organism ; high prices go with inflation (the excess of demand over supply) but ameliorate it. There is quite a wide field in which rules of that sort apply. None of the other interpretations, so far as I can see, lead to paradox in this way, though of course the curious fourth one " A is typical of B " may turn out to be a larger assumption than you have bargained for.

I take it that the relation of false identity is one which we are always first imputing and then interpreting ; it is a fundamental tool in the process by which we classify things. There is a good deal of evidence from psychologists and anthropologists that this process is a fundamental one. I ought to quote some authorities, but they will probably make the range of agreement look narrower than it is. The Freudian complex is mainly a process of " identifying " one situation or person with another ; and it is important to notice that the order of the terms is fixed ; a case who feels during Transference " my psycho-analyst is my father " does not go on to deduce " my father is my psycho-analyst ". Levy-Bruhl was writing too early to be influenced by psycho-analysis, but he treated the imputing of identity between two things known to be different as the distinctive feature of the primitive mind. Piaget's children are doing it all the time. The only definite theory I could find in Pareto is that the mind treats as identical those things which excite the same feelings. It may be said that these are all in their different ways mad-doctors, concerned with the abnormal, though they would deny it. But Spearman has some tests by introspection on people who were to look at a cube, and they wrote down that they felt their visual sensations *were* the cube, even while they were recognising the distinction. Indeed a puzzle about identity feelings (recognising that this is the same cross-road when you come at it down a different street, for instance) is often obvious to commonsense. There is plenty of backing for the idea that we use false identity ; the difficulty is in applying it to verbal analysis in a definite enough way to be useful. I hope I have not suggested that to use an equation is somehow lunatic or savage ; the same process is used in an ordinary metaphor, where critics are accustomed to talk about the " identification " or the " fusion " effected as a way of giving rather extravagant praise. The main thing to be gathered from the various mental experts, I think, is that the order of terms in an equation is likely to be fairly rigid ; given " A is B " you can easily change the interpretation of " is ", but it is much harder to make " A " and " B " change places ; and the differences between my four types of equation turn on which way round they go.

However, the most elementary case is that of simple confusion, and there it need not be assumed that any order has yet been decided on. Proust gave this case a very beautiful image when he was dealing with the thought of Francoise :

> " ' Ay, they're a great family, the Guermantes ! ', she added, in a tone of respect, founding the greatness of the family at once on the number of its branches and the brilliance of its connections . . . For since there was but the single word ' great ' to express both meanings, it seemed to her that they formed a single idea, her vocabulary, like cut stones sometimes, showing thus on certain of its facets a flaw which projected a ray of darkness into the recesses of her mind."

We are not told that Francoise made any deduction from the confusion in this case, but the idea is that she would always be liable to do so. And such a situation is obviously very common. A word has two uses normally separate ; there is a case where they can be used together ; an assertion is added that they normally come together or even are the same. There seems to be a trace of this assertion in the remark of Francoise, because of the " tone of respect " ; she wants the word to mean as much as possible. But this example does not show what argument she would base on the connection under other circumstances ; it is a confusion, which I would symbolise " A+B ", from which some equation " A=B " or " B=A " could arise. What we want to examine is not a speaker accepting extra meanings in a word but a speaker using them to assert a doctrine. However we should recognise that this process will always be somehow near the process of confusion, because he is claiming that the connection is normal since the word is one thing. Also there is commonly an appeal to an outside body of opinion, which adds greatly to the power of this little trick ; the idea is " everybody agrees with me ; language itself agrees with me ; but you the hearer seem not to know it well enough ". Thus the connection may not only assert a doctrine but give it a specially portable or catching form.

A good case of this kind, I think, would be given by the Victorian matron saying " You can't take Amelia for long walks, Mr. Jones ; she's *delicate* ". The word has two senses (to be sure, the N.E.D. gives a dozen, of which only five are obsolete, but there are two groups of senses which make the contrast here) and I suppose the lady to assert a connection between them. " Refined girls are sickly " is the assertion, and this gnomic way of putting it is a way of implying " as you ought to know ". I choose this case partly to point out that a stock equation may be quite temporary ; this combination of meanings in the word seems to be a Victorian one only. You might think the expectation that young ladies will be unfit to walk was enough to produce it, and that the expectation merely followed from tight-lacing ; but the eighteenth-century young ladies also had waists, and would agree that long walks were rather vulgar, and yet this use of the word would be " out of period " if you were writing a pastiche. The reason seems to be that in the eighteenth century the older meaning " fastidious " was still knocking about, and even the meaning " luxurious, self-indulgent " was not yet sufficiently forgotten. For the suggestion of a high moral tone in the Victorian use it has to be entirely forgotten. Now it is clear that *refined* and *sickly* must be given different logical positions in the Victorian use ; all refined girls are sickly, but not all sickly girls are refined. One might think that there was a difference of class ; a servant-girl called *delicate* would be merely sickly, but a young lady so called would also be refined. The distinction would then be one of Range. Certainly an equation can have a Range, just as a special sense of a word can ; this equation was apparently confined to young women, and I have put that idea into the sentence expounding it. But I do not think the idea of high class was enough to call it out ; in the course of gossip the matron could say " I hear Caroline is very delicate ", and this would not suggest that she is " artistic " but that the tight-lacing and the lack of ventilation are giving her incessant headaches. Indeed the sentence about the walks, as it stands, might quite well have meant only that the girl was not strong enough, as it would do nowadays ; I am merely supposing that the majesty of the utterance was sufficient to turn the assertion of sickliness into some kind of moral praise. The immediate verbal context, it is clear, requires the meaning " sickly ", and if the meaning " refined " is to appear it must come from some other source. However talkers have great powers in this direction ; Darwin in *The Expression of Emotion in Men and Animals*, I remember, remarks that he had heard Sydney Smith say placidly " I hear that dear old Lady Cork has been overlooked ", and he made quite clear to everyone that he meant the Devil had forgotten to take her, but how he did it Darwin could not say. Clearly the incident is relevant to the title of the book ; a certain emotion had to be conveyed, however placidly it was done ; and in the same way it is by a tone of moral grandeur that the Victorian matron has to put the meaning " refined " here into her use of *delicate*. Of course we could alter the sentence to make it assert both meanings : " Amelia has been brought up very carefully, Mr. Jones, so you can't take her for long walks ; she's delicate " ; and no doubt the powers of *delicate* came from being used regularly in some such context ; but still the case that needs to be examined is the one in which it makes its point alone. I think it is rather hard to classify. But at any rate the logic of the thing is quite clear ; there is no suggestion of confusion, as in the case of Francoise. No doubt the trick of the thing is to pretend that the two ideas are identical, but they are also recognised as very distinct ; in effect the matron packs in a syllogism ; the relation imputed is " A entails B ", with *refined* as " A " and *sickly* as " B ". Indeed the case of mere confusion between the Senses, which may have been illustrated by Francoise, should not be regarded as an equation at all ; it might assert the existence of a supposed thing, " A+B ", but that would feel different from an equation. Both parts of the phrase " false identity " need to be given their weight ; the equation form asserts identity between things actually known to be distinct, and gets its effect from a sort of contradiction.

However it is not enough merely to assert that the equation is " refined entails sickly ". I did that because it seemed the only thing that made sense, but as we shall see later there is another possible formulation which puts them the other way round. What we need is some kind of criterion for which meaning is to act as subject of the equation ; and I think it can only be that the subject is " what the word really means here " in the mind of the user of it. I also call this the " chief " meaning in the given use. The predicate is the extra idea, which he feels he can add under the circumstances. Of course if he is being very tricky he may be trying to confuse the hearer, but this is abnormal and need not prevent us from trying to understand the ordinary case. There is a more normal difficulty in that we, no less than poor Mr. Jones, may feel a good deal of uncertainty about what the speaker thinks that *delicate* means here. Often the process of decision is rather an elaborate one, both for speech and writing ; but all the same it is a thing which we are commonly able to do. I should not agree that this criterion is metaphysical to the point of being useless.

It has been argued that we have some general tendencies by which we decide which way round to put the terms in an " A is B " sentence, and I shall try to list them here though I am not sure how decisive they are. In general, the subject is what both the parties to the conversation are ready to talk about, whereas the predicate is what the speaker is putting forward. The hearer will more readily accept " A " ; but what the speaker wants to say is " B ". It has also been pointed out that the subject of a sentence gives the stimulus and the predicate gives the reaction to it ; indeed this completing of a process is what makes the sentence feel an experience open to anyone, therefore a truth independent of the speaker. Hence the predicate is likely to carry more Emotion or a greater " tendency to action ". Finally, and rather as a consequence of the other two, the subject is felt to be somehow more concrete, the narrower in range, the more like a noun. These three rules do I think come into play, but they are overshadowed by the necessity of getting the right logical implications. I should think *refined* is a more emotive idea than *sickly*, and at any rate it has to be put in here by a tone of pride and praise, whereas no feeling is required to put in the extra idea " presumably sickly " ; none the less *refined* has to act as subject. On the other hand *sickly* is the idea that carries the tendency to action (no more walks) ; the lady will assume that Mr. Jones knows already that the girl is refined, and only needs to deduce that she is therefore sickly ; and the idea *refined* is the more narrow in range, because though all refined girls are sickly not all sickly girls are refined. The rules do therefore apply to this case so far as they go.

The way I propose to classify these equations, which clearly exist in great variety, turns on both how the two meanings are imposed and which order they are given. We will start the types from the opposite end to that of an existence assertion, in which the word is fully unified ; thus in the first type of equation the word is least unified. It is also the type most easily imagined in theory. Two meanings are to appear together though distinct, and the simplest way will be to make one the head meaning of the word, since that is likely to be called out irrelevantly, and the other the meaning required by the immediate context. Then we will expect that what the context requires will be the subject of the equation, because it is " what you are really talking about ", and the head meaning will act as predicate, since it is a sort of extra idea which happens to be added. Both " immediate context " and " head meaning " can clearly give rise to puzzles. It may be said that, if the use is at all sensible, the context has to require both of these meanings, and the general purport of a passage exists as a whole ; it is absurd to think that you can locate one requirement nearer to the word than another requirement, on the printed page. I should agree that in some kinds of artful writing the distinction breaks down, though this is not necessarily an advantage. But I am chiefly concerned with covert assertions in single words which are liable to crop up of their own accord, so that they seem to direct opinion ; and there the distinction seems fairly definite. Also one can commonly distinguish the phrase-context from some larger unit, and then the phrase-context has a sort of right of way, or is the more automatic. I say the " head " meaning because that has sometimes been defined (e.g. by Professor Bloomfield) as what you would think of first if the context did nothing to define the word. If there is such a thing it seems likely to crop up. But it is probably better to use the more specific term " dominant ", with the proviso that it must not beg any question ; this meaning is dominant merely because it can force its way in. To call it the " intrusive " meaning would be too narrow, implying that it is actually unwanted. I do not know whether any experiments have been done on which meanings people think of first when a word is given without context, but I should expect the results to be very mixed ; the technique seems a psycho-analytic rather than a linguistic one.

In any case, examples can be found which fit this simple formula. Thus when you call a mountain-saddle a *saddle* there is often an idea " Such things are (shaped) like horse-saddles ", but when you use the word about a horse-saddle there is commonly no idea of a mountain-saddle. The horse-saddle is clearly in some sense the " major " meaning of the term, and it acts as a dominant meaning ; and the equation only arises when the immediate context requires the secondary meaning. The secondary meaning was only invented to impute a likeness of shape, and the equation merely serves to remind you of it. No doubt a mountaineer with no experience of horses might feel all this the other way round, but that only illustrates the principle at work ; he would take the other meaning as the major one. The trouble with this example is that it is too simple to illustrate the group as a whole. If the idea of an intrusive meaning is the criterion for it, we must include for instance many uses of the word *sense* by the Elizabethans. They appear to have been so interested in the problems of sensuality, or fond of jokes about it, that this idea often pokes itself forward even when the immediate context requires something quite different. And yet it seems hard to say that "sensuality" was the head meaning of that rich word ; it must have been recognised as only a specialisation. It may be argued that any user of the word who gave it this equation would think of the word as meaning "sensuality" if the context did not decide, so that this is necessarily the head meaning of the word, so far as he is concerned, by Professor Bloomfield's definition. I doubt whether this follows ; they seem to have thrown in "sensuality" as an extra meaning much more often than they gave the word that meaning alone. The first reaction of an Elizabethan to the experiment might well be " This word is the material for a joke, and how can I use it to make a joke about the experiment?". That is, he would feel that "sensuality" had the first claim to be predicate in an equation with the word, but not the first claim to be subject or "what the word really meant ".

It is clear that a variety of ideas might be covered by the term " head sense ", though Professor Bloomfield did not examine them because to do so would not be behaviouristic. One could make the " main " meaning the most frequent one and the " central " meaning the one from which others are felt to branch out ; there are also the " root " meaning, suggested by derivation, and the " primary " meaning which actually came first in history—in an English word derived from Latin this is often not the root one. In connected writing one must suppose that the large context or topic has an effect on which meaning you think of first, and this may drag against the small or phrase context, which none the less has its right of way. Thus the " topical " meaning might become dominant. *Post* seems to me a word with no head meaning of any sort, so that it means nothing without context, but in an article about the Post Office it would acquire one. One might also distinguish the " probable " meaning, as a vaguer object for cases when you can hardly say there is a topic ; it is clear that " mountain-saddle " would be a probable meaning for *saddle* if you were simply on a mountain without a horse (in my example this made it the chief meaning not the extra one). But it would clearly be an endless business to look for technical terms for all the shapes and sizes of context. The dominant meaning, which can act as predicate in an equation of Type I, is likely to have some claim of this sort before it can force its way in, but I do not see how we can lay down more definitely what claim it must have. As to " sensuality ", it appears to be merely the " interesting " meaning of *sense*.

The second main type of equation has for subject a major sense of the word and for predicate one or more of its Implications—as I am calling them ; the more usual way of putting it would be that part of the word's Connotation is called out. Of course, these Implications have previously been put in, by a series of uses of the word in which the immediate context demands or supplies them ; but in such uses, I think, the word is simply given both meanings without asserting an equation between them—the assertion is implied or actually made by the whole sentence. The interesting case is where the immediate context no longer demands the extra idea but it comes up by habit. Thus we can say that in Type II the immediate context demands the major sense of the word, and this acts as subject, and the minor sense or the Implication appears as predicate of its own accord. We are extending the idea of an equation here, because an Implication as such is not a Sense of the word at all ; but it often becomes one later in its career, and our criterion for saying so is I think merely that the word can appear with that meaning alone. It is hard to be sure just when this change occurs, and the change need not affect the equation, so we might be mistaken as well as pedantic if we assumed that we could draw the line in the right place. The group of ideas acts as a unit, so that when one of the Implications is promoted to be a Sense the others can easily be attached to it as predicates. All this of course is quite the other way round from Type I ; the immediate context does not have to demand a subordinate meaning, and the extra idea, so far from having to be a dominant sense, need not be a Sense of the word at all. An equation of this sort can be symbolised " $A=A/x,y$ " ; presumably a case of " $A=B/x,y$ " would be a cross with another type of equation.

A notorious case of this growth of Implications in a word is provided by *native*, in itself able to arouse sturdy local patriotism, which came to be felt as insulting when applied to the natives of (say) India. The empire-builder's use of the word was naturally limited to the persons native where he worked, and acquired stock Emotions (contempt sometimes touched with fear) and Implications such as " inherently subjected ", which could easily become " racially inferior ". So far the word merely does what the speakers want ; their opinion of the natives in view colours the word and may then be asserted as a piece of common knowledge. The equation is " such people are—inherently subjected ", or whatever less stark view the speaker might entertain. The only puzzle is to decide whether there was any memory of history at work. The N.E.D. gives the oldest meaning of the word as " one born in bondage ; a born thrall " ; the first example is no earlier than 1450, but is cognate to an earlier technical term " neif " for persons attached to the soil. A disparaging use for the local residents of an English country town is quoted from 1800, whereas the use for the natives of countries considered savage is found in the late seventeenth century. A tendency to rude suggestions might well go on clinging to the word, as a rival to the suggestions of local patriotism (" that we are native where we walk ") ; so that the empire-builders were not putting any strain on it. On the other hand the seriously rude use of the word does not seem to appear till the historical meaning had been quite forgotten. In any case the meaning presumed from the Latin derivation, " one of the original or usual inhabitants of a country, as distinguished from strangers or foreigners ", dated 1603, was taken through all this development as " what the word really meant ". There was no idea that two meanings of the word were in play, even when the Implications became so strong as to seem actually part of the word's meaning. Nor did the change of feeling in the word involve any change of the referent in view, which continued to be the natives of India (or wherever it might be). There was no puzzle about the referent until the empire-builder's dialect began to affect the talkers at home, and then the meaning of the word had to change ; but I had better finish listing the types before trying to deal with changes of meaning.

In an equation of Type II the various meanings are normally felt to converge on one referent which has complex properties, and I call such a word more " integrated " than those with equations of Type I, where the different meanings are felt to be independent. In Type III the different meanings are felt to be independent but the word is so integrated that the head meaning acts as subject ; the case is similar to Type I in that a major meaning intrudes, but it has the opposite order of terms. As in Type I the immediate context has to demand a secondary meaning (otherwise the head meaning is likely to appear alone) but the head meaning appears as the " essential " meaning of the word, or the " only real " meaning, or something like that, so that the word can only be applied to the referent in view by a kind of metaphor. I am not anxious to claim that straightforward cases of Type III are at all common ; the point is rather to get clear under what conditions the rules of Type I can be broken. It seems to me that many of Shakespeare's uses of the word *fool* are an example of it ; he takes the symbolism of the clown so far (as I find myself reading him) that in effect he treats the word as meaning " clown " and nothing else ; when he uses the word about ordinary people they are not called foolish but described metaphorically as clowns. And the equations of the word have only accidental connections with the person so called ; they are simply the standard doctrine about the Shakespearean clown—that he is foolish, mysteriously wise and so forth. No doubt in any particular case other readers would disagree with me, but this has the advantage of bringing the alternatives clearly into view. To arrive at Type III requires a distinct performance with the word, and if you are interpreting a given case as an example of Type III it is fairly easy to recognise that you are doing so, if only because it gives a feeling of metaphor.

This at least is true of the simple version in which the two senses are easily distinguished ; but the important use of equations of Type III, I think, is for making assertions of a more subtle kind, which would not ordinarily be considered as proceeding from a double meaning of the word at all. To be sure, if the user were completely unconscious of the double meaning, I agree that it should not count as an equation ; but we may suppose that he has some kind of practical knowledge of the process on which his argument depends without supposing that he recognises it clearly. The trick is that one part of the range of the word is treated as the " key " or typical part of it, in terms of which the others are to be viewed. The rest of the meaning indeed seems to be remembered rather by treating it as a Connotation of the selected part, and to that extent Type III is analogous to Type II rather than Type I. My examples must come later in the book ; the chief one is the use of *sense* for pro-sense-ist or plain-man philosophies, in which good judgement of a narrow kind is made the key example of all mental processes, so that others must be viewed in terms of it. I also claim to find Type III in a sophistical argument about " grammar ", already fully examined by Professor Richards ; in fact I think that, in most controversies where both sides agree on using a key word, the word is given two rival equations of Type III. The process of typifying is after all a common and familiar one ; nearly all political propaganda, for instance, depends on trying to establish in the reader's mind your own " type " of Worker or Business Man or what not, the sort of man they are to imagine when they think about the worker or the business man in general. And here again I do not mean that the process is necessarily fallacious ; one really does need to be able to sum up a complex matter briefly. It is for this very central process of thought that the third type of equation is required.

The third type broke the rule for the order of terms in the first type, and the fourth breaks the more fundamental rule that the order is always important. We have now to consider what kind of case can occur in which the terms can go either way round. No doubt cases can easily be found in which " B " is like " A " as well as " A " like " B ", or in which each entails the other (e.g. a quadrangle and a quadrilateral) ; but it is not as easy as one would expect to find cases in which this idea is enshrined in a word. The case where " a normal A is B " and " B is typical of A " has already been rejected from this type, because there is a difference of feeling according as you assert one or the other, and whichever you assert the order of terms is not indifferent. I have an impression that equations of Type IV are to be found in individual theorists and stylists rather than in common use, because if the doctrine that is implied becomes generally accepted it settles down into a more comfortable linguistic form. This type clearly implies a very high degree of integration of the meanings of the word, so that we have nearly worked our way back to the Existence Assertion. I do not think you get examples of it unless the " A " and " B " are in a similar relation to a third meaning of the word, which may be only vaguely conceived. This at any rate makes them symmetrical, so that the two orders do not conflict. To take a logical and clear-cut example, Hooker (as I learn from the N.E.D.) maintained that there is a sense of *law* meaning " both human and divine law ", and undertook to give the conditions which such a law must satisfy. Here he is merely establishing a new sense of the word, which might seem to outface any claim that there is a confusion between the old ones. But in ordinary discourse it will appear that one is discussing either a human or a divine law ; if while discussing a human law Hooker implies that it is also a divine law he can put an equation into the word *law* " Human laws of this sort are also divine laws ", and precisely the same the other way round, and the effect will merely be to say that this law falls into the narrower class which satisfies the conditions for both. A good use of the trope would also serve to remind you what the conditions were. But the same process can be used when we merely have a vague idea that there is such a third concept, and are not worrying for the moment about what it may be ; and I think we can go on like this for a long time. One might indeed suppose that our ordinary idea of *law* is always of this sort, or becomes so whenever we think of its different meanings as being rightly connected in one word. I should have thought that few people took it so seriously, and that the only standard simpleminded equation (between these two meanings of the word) was fixed in order, and of Type I, and said " the laws of this country are underwritten by God ". Indeed to sustain an equation of Type IV, even if it is not fully justified, seems to be a fairly skilled process. I think it is an example of a more general trick of the mind which I propose to call Mutual Metaphor, and though such an equation need not be metaphorical it tends I think to give a feeling of being *like* a metaphor, as does Type III. However the process need not be at all recondite ; a compound word such as " silly-clever " has much the same purpose, but it does not give the same effect of profundity, because it does not use the trick of false identity. In any case, the position is that an equation of Type IV claims to make an Existence

Assertion, but that the claim is not always justified. When a third concept of the type required is firmly in view it should no doubt be given its own symbol "C"; when there is mere confusion the symbol "A + B" can be used, as before; but when, as in the majority of interesting cases, there is room for doubt about the matter we can simply write it as a fourth-type equation. My chief example of this type is the use of *sense* by Wordsworth in *The Prelude*.

The symbols already defined allow of a clear-cut treatment of the paradoxes of the great religions, though I am afraid it will look rather an absurd one. We can write "A = − A", and this I think is always a fourth-type equation, since the function of such a paradox is to hint at some reconciliation otherwise ineffable; it is an extreme case of the obscure existence assertion ("He that saveth his life shall lose it"). No doubt the only use of the thing will come from some actual interpretation, but it is important I think for the analyst to be willing to recognise the paradox as such, because it is often the root from which various doctrines are derived, or from which the incitements to action or judgement branch out. For instance it seems to be one of the main ideas of the Taoist use of " way " that " all men are inherently on the Way; therefore the best men strive unceasingly to get onto it ". Of course I think one should always try to interpret paradoxes, and if a stylist gambles on the chance that they will mean something important the results are likely to be as flat as most of Wilde's; but still if you were trying to chart the uses of the Taoist word you would need to put this paradox in, and it does not seem to be two ideas equated but one idea contradicted.*

I should claim that these four types, together with the existence assertion, cover all the possibilities for a word which is to imply a doctrine. The fourth type deals with the case where the order of terms does not matter. If the terms have an order, there may be a minor sense required by the immediate context and a major one intruding, and here the major sense may act as predicate (Type I) or subject (Type III); or there may be a major sense required by

---

* This in itself is not an uncommon twist of thought. Obviously there is a similar contradiction for people who make democracy a cult instead of a political technique; the good man must try to become what everybody is supposed to be already. The idea crops up again in the cult of Darwinism as a justification for a creed of violence, though this argument requires another fallacy as well : " We cannot possibly disobey a law of Nature. Both lambs and tigers were produced by the Struggle for Existence. We ought therefore to try to behave like tigers." But one must distinguish a " fallacy ", which depends on your not noticing the logical contradiction, from a "paradox", in which it is recognised and viewed as " profound ". It is only the paradox which is apprehended as a contradiction, and could become a candidate for listing as " X = − X ".

the immediate context and a minor one intruding, and here the minor sense may act as predicate (Type II) or as subject, but this last case requires an intentional trick with the context and could not be " taken for granted ".   I am concerned here with the kind of suggestion in a word which seems to cling to it and can affect opinion, so that nonce-equations by jokers and poets are not what I am looking for.   But I can give an illustration, from Pope, of the fifth type which is to be rejected :

> *Where Bentley late tempestuous wont to sport*
> *In troubled waters, but now sleeps in port.*

The drink and the harbour are perhaps simply two words, but if we accept the suggestion of the poet that they are one there seems no doubt that the harbour is the major sense, the drink the minor, and that the only plausible equation is something like " This placid afterdinner drink is like having reached harbour ".   Here the minor sense acts as subject, but the immediate context clearly demands the major sense, so that *port* here has an equation of the aberrant type.   But of course the reason is that the meaning " drink " is intentionally hidden ; you are meant to plume yourself on your cleverness in seeing the joke, or perhaps to feel that the dangerous Master would not be able to see it, so that you could say it to his face tittering behind your hand.   The obstacle to understanding set up by the equation form is part of the effect, and I do not mean that equations of this sort are bad ; only that such an equation is not likely to impose a doctrine on us.

It is easy to give a chart of the arrangement :

		Subject	Predicate
The major sense of the word is the........		Subject	Predicate
The sense demanded by the most immediate context is the........	Subject	II	I
....	Predicate	III	V
The order of the two senses is indifferent :		IV	

A classification, of course, can cover a field without telling us anything important about it ; and I have admitted that there can sometimes be doubt about what the major sense may be and what the immediate context may require.   But it seems to me that this classification is the natural way to go at the matter, and that the four types (or at any rate the normal versions of them) are in a way real objects since they have other properties besides the defining ones.   There is an important question which this treatment tends rather to obscure ; that is, whether the same stock equation (with the same terms, order, and interpretation) may crop up on different occasions in different types.   Which sense is considered the head one can vary too, but I want here to consider the alternatives while that remains fixed. If " B " is the minor sense in " $A = B$ ", this equation would count as Type III when the immediate context demanded " B " but as Type II when it demanded " A ". If " A " is the minor sense there is no corresponding puzzle, because the equation is either of Type I or of the aberrant type suited to jokes. It seems likely that an equation of Type III will also function in another context as Type II, but that many equations of Type II cannot rise to the occasions which would make them Type III. However it can also be argued that a context which makes "$A = B$" a third type equation will call out a different interpretation of it, more serious than that called out by a context which makes it Type II. Thus when Shakespeare uses *fool* about a clown, the equation merely gives his usual assumptions about a clown, but when he uses it about an ordinary person, and the word still seems to mean " clown ", the equation takes on much more grandeur and becomes " the clown is the central type in terms of which all foolish people are to be viewed ". The same thing occurs, though less obviously, in the more subtle cases of Type III where a man is sticking to his own definition of a controversial term. In a use where his definition fits the case he will merely take his opinion for granted, but when the context (as an opponent would say) is crying out against his definition he must stick to his opinion defiantly, and he does it by assuming that his own definition is the *typical* meaning of the term, in terms of which these more plausible meanings are to be viewed. Contrariwise I see no occasion for an equation of Type III unless the speaker wants to make an assertion of this kind. So I think it is a working rule that the interpretation " A is typical of B " is only found in equations of Type III and that all equations of Type III carry it ; but there is an exception, to be discussed later, in the special case of " typifying pregnancies ".

It may be objected that this account has ignored the Emotions, and that they are the deciding factor for these rich uses of words. I do not deny that Emotions or Attitudes supply the driving power, but they are not necessarily " in the words ", and indeed the speaker may be hiding them from the listener. The Emotions which are in the words will normally evoke Senses that correspond to them (except in swear-words, intensifiers, and for that matter in raving), and the structure to be examined is that of the resultant Senses. But we had better examine what happens if you put an Emotion into the equation form. In the simplest case, an underlining of the Stock Emotion " A.A ! " may be assertive, as if saying " A does deserve the emotion commonly given to it ", and we could write this " $A = A$! ". But I think this can be classed as a kind of existence assertion. In the same way the denial of the stock

Emotion " A. — A ! ", as in " jolly lust ", can be viewed as a denial of the reality of the supposed " thing ". Of course the function of " jolly " is to act as a context which kills the stock emotion, and I agree that the first effect is this and nothing more ; but we are at once driven to look for a new Sense of *lust*, whether successfully or not, which will account for such a use ; and people who fail to find one would tend I think to call it a " cynical denial that there *is* any such thing as lust ". In any case there seems no great advantage in extending the equation form to this sort of case. The important type would be " A.B ! ", and I deny that an equation " A = B ! ", without further complications of sense, ever occurs ; at any rate without being a recognisable error of a kind very unlikely in a native speaker of the language.

Here I am running up against views expressed some while ago by Professor Richards, especially in *Mencius on the Mind* ; I am not sure how far he would still maintain them, or indeed how far my difference from him is only a verbal one ; but the point as he puts it there seems to me actively misleading, and I need to try to get the point of difference clear. He has been arguing that the Gesture of a word (in which he includes its emotion, tone and intention) may be wholly separate from its Sense (p. 105) :

> " When a word has been much used with a sense that is naturally associated with a strong and rich emotive reverberation, it frequently carries this gesture over to senses that can give no natural support to any such stirrings. Normally we tend, I think, unless we are on our guard, to expect the rest of a word's meaning to be consonant with and dependent on the sense. It sounds a reasonable expectation, but the analysis of poetry would go very little distance upon this principle. The chief danger, however, is that we may give a word a far more elaborate sense than it really has, in order to justify its gesture, because we have not noticed what other senses it may have on other occasions from which its stirring qualities derive."

Now of course I do not deny that rhetoricians often indulge in a gross throwing about of the emotional resources of words, and that it is emotively very satisfying, because it marks a just irritation, for people like Professor Richards to say that such uses of words are merely emotive. But I do not think the rhetoricians can throw them about quite so frankly as this passage suggests ; they have to do something more to get us confused, or we would see through them pretty easily. The trouble I think is that Professor Richards conceives the Sense of a word in a given use as something single, however " elaborate ", and therefore thinks that anything beyond that Sense has got to be explained in terms of feelings, and feelings of course are Emotions, or Tones. But much of what appears to us as a " feeling " (as is obvious in the case of a complex metaphor) will in fact be quite an elaborate structure of related meanings. The mere fact that we can talk straight ahead and get the grammar in order shows that we must be doing a lot more rational planning about the process of talk than we have to notice in detail. I do not want to make any holy mystery out of the subconscious mind ; a man may think very badly in those regions ; but if he were not thinking there at all he could not even engage in connected speech. Now in any plausible case such as Professor Richards describes there will be something in the context which makes the Gesture relevant, as well as something that makes the Sense relevant (other-wise, in dealing with a piece of writing, he could not tell that they were both present and failing to fit each other). The word comes in to give the Sense " A " relevant at the moment, and the context is so arranged as also to make relevant the Emotion " B ! " which belongs to another sense of the word. No doubt, but the process will not stop there ; the Emotion " B ! " (combined with the word in question) will then call up its Sense " B ", even if only " at the back of the mind ", and what feels like " a more elaborate sense than the word really has " is therefore an equation of the senses " A " and " B ", which may be quite simple ones. I do not imagine that Professor Richards would seriously disagree with this ; in fact he was already making the essential points on the matter in *Practical Criticism*, some time before the Mencius book ; but I feel that only serves to show that a clear-cut equation theory is needed. As soon as the thing is phrased at all loosely it appears to recommend bad criticism, as I think is illustrated by the remark about poetry in this quotation*.

*Perhaps it would be more of a test to wonder whether Coleridge would agree with me, not whether Professor Richards would if in a Coleridgean frame of mind. Coleridge would be likely to despise any equation theory as trying to reduce the absorption of the living water of thought to a manipulation of " fixities and definities." I don't myself think that there is a fundamental difference here. Of course I do not claim that the terms of an equation (as the mind uses it) are always clear-cut ; I give some examples where they aren't, though perhaps not important enough ones. A term of an equation may be adumbrated as the sort of thing that would fit the Emotion, or may itself be the spurious concept suggested by a previous fourth-type equation. And this treatment is not supposed to be explaining the deeper experience by which the work of a writer is absorbed and made part of your own *corpus* of half-conscious feeling and instinctive choice. It is concerned with a more modest and if you like more superficial question—how in the world we come to do such a thing, what intellectual machinery we have to start doing it, to approach the actual words on the page (left us by Coleridge or whoever it is) without merely feeling that they don't fit. I do not see that Coleridge need have objected to such an account ; indeed I think it gives a reasonable basis for some very bold suggestions by Coleridge, to the effect that too much definiteness of terms is a bad thing, wasting " the vital and idea-creating force" and preventing "originality." (*Coleridge and S.T.C.*, Stephen Potter,

However, my innocent desire to speak up for the poets may be intruding into a generalisation which covers very different people. It seems a plausible view that the account given so far applies to tolerable uses of language but does not apply to lying propaganda. I was concerned with enemy propaganda through almost the whole of the last war, working in minor capacities for the B.B.C., and I did not find it so easy to answer as this view would imply. Spoken propaganda is of course particularly likely to be Purely Emotive ; Goebbels is said to have made a rigid distinction between the degrees of effective lying possible in the written and the spoken word. The Germans had a rather surprising tendency, during their early successes, to make philosophical boasts about the process of lying ; as in saying that allied propaganda was merely ridiculous, but " our good German propaganda is subsequently justified by facts " ; and indeed the German claim to have captured a town was at that stage bound to be impressive because it was a prophecy. This kind of thing raises no theoretical problem. One might expect a problem to arise, on the other hand, in the moral words used for selfpraise and abuse of the enemy. The example in the papers as I write seems as good as any other ; the Russians have objected that the Americans are " treacherous " to publish in 1948 captured German state documents about Russo-German agreements reached in 1939. Of course there may be some unmentioned ground for using this term, for instance there may have been a wartime secret agreement about the matter which the Americans have now broken, but the public appeal of the phrase cannot depend on that. Incidentally, it seems to me that no major country has much to boast of in its pre-war dealings with Hitler, so I hope I can view the case with sufficient detachment. There seem to be two ways of taking this accusation ; that the immediate action is treacherous, perhaps only with the sense " showing ill-will towards an ex-ally ", or that it is an example of a general American tendency which would produce acts of real treachery if given a chance (if America were trusted). The second idea is an important part of the general Russian case for non-co-operation, and could easily be felt as relevant here. The trope then amounts to a metaphor, giving the cause the name of the effect. Emotive language, I think, often provides a let-out of this kind, so that a reflective listener could satisfy himself, given the right general approach (or, if you prefer, given the touch of persecution mania which is being encouraged). But, granting this, the first idea taken alone will still

---

p. 200). As to what Coleridge can have meant by "ideas", I do not have to decide but if you read through Professor Muirhead's account of the difficulty of deciding (*Coleridge as Philosopher*, pp. 96-110) it does not seem to make nonsense if you regard them as the Attitudes causing and evoked by a consistent set of Equations.

seem " purely emotive ", a case of using the first rude word that comes to hand. It is not easy to fit the case onto Professor Richards' thesis, because it is not clear that any second meaning of the word " B " is used together with the emotion " A ! " felt for ordinary treachery ; but I suppose we could regard " B " as a generalisation of the word, " any behaviour showing ill-will towards an ex-ally ". And indeed, for people who reject the argument, I do not deny that it is an almost pure case of " B = A ! ". But that is why they reject it ; for that matter, a mere suspicion that the argument is of this sort would make an adherent uneasy ; he must be prepared to overcome it. I do not think that this gives any encouragement to the theory that " B = A ! " is frequently used without being observed. Nor is it difficult to invent other ways of accepting such an argument. One obvious effect of it is to make the speaker seem very highminded (or as the opponent would say selfrighteous) ; he himself has a very pure code of honour in such matters, so that acts which rough men would not call treachery do seem treachery to him. In its new sense, therefore, the word really is held to deserve the old Emotion. Of course the opponent would say that this is absurdly untrue about the Russians ; but the question is now much more remote from the single use of the word. It would seem quite " fair ", as we say, to shift the meaning of *treachery* as much as this if the speaker meant to stick to it ; the real difficulty for a pro-Russian apologist in elaborating this text would be to show that the Kremlin could produce a definition of the word by which its own actions could stand the same scrutiny. And the listener can easily not think of such an objection when he accepts the new use of the word in consecutive speech. The trick of such a trope, so far as it deceives people (no doubt it might be a mere relief of feelings like swearing), is through a breakdown of the reciprocity which we learned as children—the word is to be used in one way about me and in another about you, and this seems to be a matter of practice which cannot be symbolised as being inside one use of the word. No doubt a regular barrage of this kind of talk, lasting for years (as when Isherwood remarks in *Mr. Norris Changes Trains* that the language of German newpapers, through incessant abuse of opposing parties, had come to seem as remote and formal as the Chinese system of politeness), in the end breaks down the senses of such words altogether, so that *treachery* becomes merely a swearword habitually addressed to an opponent, and recognised as such. But by that time, I should have thought, it no longer means its " A " and cannot expect the " A ! " to deceive anyone.

I said in the last chapter that it would be absurd for an unsuccessful linguistic law to try to turn itself into a moral one, by which the examples that break the law are called bad. But the grammarian need not claim that human values are as irrelevant to his work as to a physicist's ; it would be convenient to have a simple rule by which corrupt language could be recognised. However I do not think we can get it. Cases of " B.A ! " do I think occur (supported by a Mood) and need not be bad ; they may be amusing. Cases of " B = A ! ", that is, cases where the false argument actually depends for convincing you on that equation, do not I think occur even in corrupt uses of language.

We might now also consider how the equation process applies to quite simple emotive uses of words, such as appeared in the last chapter. There was a paragraph in an American weekly, some years ago, about the return from Britain of a distinguished foreign visitor ; it appeared that he refused to go unless his mistress was sent with him, and the English comment was supposed to be " How awful for the Foreign Office ". This seemed to me very funny, and rather strong anti-British propaganda. However the propaganda effect merely depends on making this speaker appear typical of the British, so that they all have the peculiar assumptions which the phrase implies. I am concerned to examine the actual speaker, who may well have really said it. She appears as a slave to petty social embarrassments which are entirely unconnected with any moral conviction. The question for me is whether any equation is involved ; it might well seem that she makes a slang use of the word with the sense " embarrassing " and adds the irrelevant Emotion, due to another Sense of the word, " causing awe (also horror and terror) ". However when a word is only employed to define Emotions—when they are its Sense—the distinction becomes a trivial one. I take it the joke turns on the habitual context in which the speaker is imagined to use this word— what *she* feels Awe about. The standard awful thing for this debutante, the Type of awfulness, is something like " not being able to go to the lavatory without positively asking for it ". (This may seem a far-fetched connection, but I think it is why the quotation in question seems so intimately silly.) In itself the use of the word in such a context does not involve any change of meaning ; the persons who use this school-girl slang really do feel awe on the occasion ; they feel the adult world to be cruel about meaningless rules. Afterwards no doubt the meaning is " adequated " to convey extravagant Emotions about the occasion, and one could now call the Sense " embarrassing ". But the effect of the queer little piece of slang is still to convey " I am the sort of speaker who might really find the occasion terrible ". So far as the speaker recognises that she is using slang there is an idea " by putting it in this amusing way I admit that it is really only embarrassing, but still I am . . . " etc. This second stage is what I would call a

Mood ; the first is too unconscious. Even in the first stage it might be said that there are two meanings of the word in play, because there are two situations which presumably excite different feelings, though the feelings are in effect said to be alike. This kind of extension of a word's use might be called Transfer, but I do not think it is worth calling an equation.

There are I think serious difficulties about Emotions in classifying equations under my four types, but they arise in a different kind of case ; the question is about the immediacy of the emotion and whether it appears as cause or effect. Let us go back to the lady who said that Amelia was delicate, which was given as an example before the types were listed. I asked the reader to believe that she said it so as to make her point very clearly. An air of pride and praise gave the word an Emotion which imposed the Sense " refined " ; and, as the chief meaning in this use of the word, " refined " became subject of the equation. " Sickly " is the more usual meaning of the word, and it was demanded by the context ; it became predicate. Now we might suppose that the lady considered " refined " to be the head or the only real meaning of the word, and thus made an equation of Type III. But this would be too elaborate, and besides, the equation would not say what is meant, if it has to be " A is typical of B ". We need a rather *ad hoc* definition for this simple case. From the point of view of the lady, the Emotion appears as called out by the Sense ; to the listener the Sense is defined by the Emotion. From the point of view of the listener, we can define the tone of voice with which the word is uttered as its " most immediate context ". Then " refined " is imposed by the most immediate context, and " sickly ", the more usual meaning, is only demanded by a remoter context, so that the equation is of Type I. This I think is clearly what it ought to be, and in the crude version I have supposed there is no difficulty. But many of the actual versions would be much less crude. Suppose the lady only give a faint touch of this feeling, so that Mr. Jones was baffled to know whether the insinuation had really been dropped. We need a more specific case here. The Duchess of Berwick, in *Lady Windermere's Fan*, has instructed her daughter to pass two dances on the terrace with Mr. Hopper from Australia ; " Mind you take great care of my little chatterbox " she says on releasing the girl, whose part consists wholly of repeating the words " yes, mamma " ; and on their return (she will answer " Yes ; mamma " when asked what she said to him) the Duchess leads off with " Mr. Hopper, I am very, very angry with you. You have taken Agatha out on the terrace, and she is so delicate ". An emphasis on the girl's delicacy of feeling is quite habitual with the Duchess (" And now I must tell you how sorry I am for you,

Margaret. Agatha, darling ! " " Yes, mamma." " Will you go
and look over the photograph album that I see there ? " " Yes,
mamma." " Dear girl ! She is so fond of photographs of
Switzerland. Such a pure taste, I think."). Also of course the
Duchess's whole set of tricks is presented as farcically artificial.
At the same time this use of the word is far too smooth for one to
say that the meaning *refined* is imposed on it ; indeed there is a pride
in her lightness of touch. I think there are two ways of symbolising
it, according as we suppose her consciously tricky with the word
or not. The problem is that we have to make *sickly* " what the
word really means here", and let *refined* come in merely as a predicate,
and yet the equation must not make nonsense. If she does this
naturally, or rather if her tricks can be done almost without thinking,
the equation seems to be " the good kind of sickly girl is a refined
one ". That is, the tone of voice puts in some of the Emotion of
praise, and yet the Sense is allowed to remain the obvious *sickly* ;
we thus start off with Professor Richards' combination " A.B ! " ;
this calls up Sense " B ", which is equated to " A " ; and logic is
then preserved by supposing that a special kind of " A " is now in
view. (I shall call this a qualifying pregnancy, as opposed to a
typifying one.) But I think there is another possible process, when
the thing is more intentional ; so that poor Mr. Hopper is likely
to think afterwards " Was she getting at me ? ". The sense *sickly*
is apparently what is meant " A ", but the other meaning *refined*
" B " is put into the back of his mind ; I gave the symbol " A.(B) "
for such a case. The doubt whether " B " was meant to *carry
anything* now takes the form " A.(B = A) ", so that the equation
if it is there at all is there in the militant form " refined girls are
sickly ". The Victorians, especially these powerful matrons, went
in for being assertively unassertive, if the phrase is intelligible, and
I do not think it unreasonable to suppose that this trick needs
rather elaborate treatment. " The good kind of sickly girl is refined " is a version of Type II ; whereas the equation in the bracket
is exactly like the militant lady's equation, and of Type I, so far
as it is present at all. There were also uses of the word, by the way,
with the purpose of euphemism ; the girl was on the face of it merely
sickly, but by expressing it with this word one put the matter
gracefully, and suggested that the reasons might be to her credit.
This is a still more pervasive suggestion in the word, which in some
speakers might be felt behind almost any use of it ; the logical form
is still " The good kind of sickly girl is refined ", but in so dim a use
this equation too might be put in a bracket.

It seems a plausible view, as one considers the ramifications of
this word, that any Marginal Meaning (capable of appearing alone
in some contexts) is automatically capable of appearing as a

Connotation when the word is used in its head meaning. There is no difficulty about the Type of the equation ; it would be Type II ; but the word would also give an equation of Type I with the terms in the opposite order. People, I think, do not drag a double meaning about in this way unless they are particularly attached to it ; and the peculiar clinging quality of the Victorian *delicate* was a rather specialised trick.

However this account of the word assumes that the people are talking, and putting in the Emotions by the tone of voice. My last example, to be sure, comes from a printed play, but we feel we know how the actress ought to say it. Yet, as soon as the thing is taken from print, the whole story about the Types is altered. In print this Emotion not required by the immediate verbal context has presumably to be supplied by a remoter context, perhaps a very remote one, such as your impression of the writer's style as a whole. The first use of *delicate*, the one about Amelia, has now become an equation of the aberrant Type V or port type. And yet a knowledge of the style can sometimes feel so like a knowledge of the spoken voice that we seem to pick up the intonation directly. One might say that at the second reading we often simply imagine the thing as spoken, but that we cannot really do it at the first reading. I think we sometimes can, but it is a fairly elaborate performance ; what we really pick up, and translate into the tone of a speaking voice, is the way the writer uses a series of pet words ; we shift the head meanings to suit him, and when we have done this the little equations fall into place as they would do if his voice were selecting the chief meanings. We would soon learn, for example, that a writer is using " refined " as the head meaning of his *delicate ;* and then " hence she is sickly " can be attached to it as an implication. The example is perhaps rather too violent ; a writer would not use the sentence about Amelia as it stands, in his own person, and a novelist who quoted the sentence need only add " she said proudly " to make you imagine the tone of voice straight away. The main moral to be drawn, I think, is that a writer can do a good deal to alter the relative status of the different meanings of a word within his own style ; he can impose a new head meaning or at least a new dominant one.

Incidentally, most writing on Shakespeare, if not positively aberrant, is a process of deciding what the equations in the words ought to be, and therefore how the actor ought to to say them, so that the audience can be given the structure of meaning in a more direct manner. When I assert that Shakespeare frequently uses *fool* with the chief sense " clown ", my evidence should be that this reading improves the sense of the whole passage on a variety of occasions ; but the theory seems pretty null unless an actor could say the word so as to convey the effect to an audience. I do not undertake to say how he should do it, but then the human resources in this field are very large, and I should fancy it would be quite possible ; perhaps by a certain gusto in the word, but more probably by his whole interpretation of the part.

In a simple case of Type I where the defining context is verbal there is no need for an Emotion to put in either meaning, though of course any equation is made more obvious if the word is said in a knowing or emphatic manner. In Type II it is the predicate that is likely to need assisting by an Emotion either in the context or the voice, as where *native* is said with a tone of scorn. In Type III the unexpected subject needs to be insisted on, and perhaps the general way to do it is to say the word with quotation marks, a thing we do mainly by an air of precision and a slight pause—" in my, or our, sense of the term ". In Type IV the two ideas tend to be viewed with a similar feeling, so that if any Emotion is expressed it will cover both ; thus in general Type IV is not affected by any puzzle about the degree of immediacy of the Emotion. In many cases of Type III there is no specific Emotion which would pick out the sense to be made the subject, but where there is one (as perhaps in *fool*) the effect of saying the sentence with the right intonation is to make the equation formally of Type I, though it still keeps the interpretation " A is typical of B ". But even this is a bad description, because the subject is being treated as the head sense, whereas for Type I the head sense should be a minor one. If the hearer accepts the subject as a head meaning the equation presumably becomes of Type II. Similarly, when Amelia is called *delicate*, the hearer may fail to understand the intonation which made it Type I, and then if he suspects an equation at all it must be of the aberrant Type V. There is thus a certain amount of shuffling possible among the types according to the way the thing is received, and this seems rather untidy, but I should say that it only recognises the facts of the case.

There may seem to be a confusion here about whether the Type is defined from the point of view of the speaker or the hearer, the writer or the reader. The subject of the equation is defined from the producer's point of view, as what he would say that the word really means here ; but the criterion about what can be deduced from the " immediate context " takes the point of view of the receiver. It might be better, one would think, to erect two series of types and consider these parties separately. But this I think would be an unreal opposition, creating more puzzles than it solved. Normally the receiver is trying to estimate what the producer means by a word, and the producer is not disregarding the need to be intelligible. Of course in cases of misunderstanding one needs to symbolise the two views separately, but even there each party is imagining the other to have gone through a process complementary to his own. (Various child-psychologists have emphasized that a child only talks to itself, but surely what it really does is to play at having a conversation between two people.) However I can give a definite answer to the accusation of confusion ; the types are regarded from the point of view of the receiver, and it is assumed that he is always trying to estimate what the producer took as the chief meaning of a word.

By the way, it might seem that Jespersen's grammatical distinction between a " junction " and a " nexus " needs to be brought into this account, as his nexus is supposed to deal with phrases or single words which carry assertions though they are not recognised to do so by ordinary grammar. I do not think that his scheme is any help here, whatever its merits in its own field. If we take a sentence like " the doctor's cleverness was great " (we need a rather clumsy one to bring out the alternatives) this may imply " the doctor was clever, indeed very clever ", and then, as I understand, " the doctor's cleverness " is a nexus and carries an assertion ; or it may imply " the abilities to be presumed in a doctor were in this case found in a high degree ", and then the phrase is only a junction. Or if we take an even flatter case, it seems clear that " Tom's nose was long " is not felt, as a matter of language, to carry a subsidiary assertion " Tom had a nose ", because this is taken for granted. But the things that are taken for granted by a given period or type of speaker often make more interesting covert assertions than the ones made clear by a " nexus " ; also they are more likely to be generalisations. The idea that all doctors are clever has much more flavour, or tells us more about the speaker, than the trick of saying that a particular one was clever twice over. I ought perhaps to bring the covert assertions made by phrases into my account, though it looks as if this one only adds an Implication to the word " doctor " (whereas a phrase like *birth-control* can simply be treated as one word) ; but in any case what I would have to consider would be junction-phrases and not nexus-phrases.

I want now to discuss a few examples of verbal equations so as to show the distinctions at work and try to convince the reader that they are useful. But perhaps the main piece of evidence in our time that rules of this sort are needed is a negative one. The trouble about the double meanings in *Finnegan's Wake*, it seems to me, is that since they are wholly artificial one cannot tell which way round they are meant to go. The effect is static, like imitation Gothic, and like that again because the essence of what it wants to imitate is an effect of movement.* To be sure, when Joyce is making a joke, usually a bawdy one, you get a movement all right, but this is rather misleading than otherwise about the intention as a whole. It would lead you to think, as E. M. Forster said about *Ulysses*, that Joyce wants to insult the universe ; whereas I take it that when a sexual incident is implied he wants this to be made dignified by comparison with the universe, not only to act as a comic illustration of it. In effect he wants all his puns to be of Type IV, but he cannot have that. I hope I am wrong, but it seems to me that all he produced by his method, in the last full application of it, was a titanic corpse.

I fancy indeed that Shakespeare sometimes makes the same mistake, though of course without this appalling persistence. The end of *Hamlet* is an example.

> FORTINBRAS :   *Let four captains*
> *Bear Hamlet, like a soldier, to the stage ;*
> *For he was likely, had he been put on,*
> *To have proved most royally : and, for his passage,*
> *The soldier's music, and the rites of war*
> *Speak loudly for him.*
> *Take up the bodies ; such a sight as this*
> *Becomes the field, but here shows much amiss.*
> *Go, bid the soldiers shoot.*

A Variorum edition reports a German critic as saying that this is a secret jeer by the myriad-minded author, intended to remind the wiser few that Hamlet was only fit to pretend to be a soldier on the stage. This view follows from the belief current among nineteenth century Germans that Hamlet *was* Germany, and displayed the lack of military willpower and of rough practicality which was the usual result of going to a German university. Few discoveries of a double meaning can seem more obvious nonsense. Most people, particularly actors, but I too, feel that the last words of the tragedy are enormously moving and wholehearted ; however surprising the praise of Hamlet may be, it is a paradox which Shakespeare was much concerned to drive home. Unless one believes, like Professor Stoll, that Hamlet is to be admired as a swashbuckler all through (whatever he says he has failed at) it seems obvious that

---

*In calling it a movement I may seem to be invoking something other than a simple equation. May I offer a cordial but belated acknowledgement to Mr. Kenneth Burke, who I find in *The Philosophy of Literary Form* (p. 75) uses the term " equation " and the equals sign for synecdoche etc. but an arrow sign for sequence and opposition. This seems a reasonable distinction, but he was not as I understand thinking of the analysis of single words, and there I don't think the contrast is much help. The movement I had in mind was simply that from subject to predicate, a narrow thing within one word.

the last scene is meant to sweep away any irritation that had been caused by " his weakness and his melancholy " ; Hamlet has suggested that he delayed out of cowardice, and we are now to be assured that he did not ; and the soldier he had most admired, though as the very opposite of himself, now gives him the praise he would most have wanted. Indeed Shakespeare too, as much as any actor, was continually representing heroes without having to test his own capacities as a soldier, and was to some extent personally involved in the claim that Hamlet would have made a good one. The feeling that Shakespeare is unlike Fortinbras comes out I think in " Such a sight as this Becomes the field ", as who should say " a becoming hat " ; corpses look nice on battlefields. The sentiment is an excessively " soldierly " one ; the author is straining his imagination. But in any case, whether Shakespeare is justifying himself or not, he cannot have intended to ruin his own play.

And yet there is a decisive case for the double meaning. The number of actual metaphors drawn from the theatre in the play is perhaps not remarkably large, though larger than usual (e.g. i.2.84 " these are actions which a man might play ", ii.3.31 " more audience than a mother . . . should o'erhear the speech ", iii.3.98 " a vice of kings ", iv.5.18 " each toy seems prologue to some great amiss ", v.1.291 " I'll rant as well as thou ", v.2.34 " that are but mutes or audience to this act ", v.2.396 " call the noblest to the audience " ; and I believe in the emendation of line 393 " let this *scene* be presently performed " because it fits the others). But in any case the play within the play, and the apparently irrelevant speech to the actors, and much else in the story, are more powerful than most verbal effects as means of putting this key metaphor forward. Hamlet is incessantly " acting a part ", and so for that matter are most of the other characters ; the main theme of the tragedy (echoed even by unlikely mouthpieces such as the King) is his self-consciousness or his failure to understand himself ; the parallels to the stage are central to the thought.* And this is a standard piece of Shakespearian technique ; it is the method of reiterative imagery, which a variety of critics (following Miss Spurgeon, I suppose) have proved to be important in the other main Shakespearian tragedies. One cannot suppose that Shakespeare did not notice this very prominent double meaning at the end, agreeing with the previous ones. On the contrary, he has gone

*Mr. Hugh Kingsmill has maintained (in *The Return of William Shakespeare*) that Hamlet is a grossly theatrical and therefore unreal figure, almost solely concerned with scoring off other people, which the dialogue lets him do much too easily, and only attractive to actors because " they have more humiliations than other men to avenge ". This view leaves out the merits of the play, but has enough truth to make the final pun pretty startling.

out of his way to " plant " the word twenty lines earlier, with

give order that these bodies
High on a stage be placed to the view

and no doubt felt that he had rounded off the " theatrical " theme
very neatly. But he was letting his machine run away with him ;
he had stopped thinking what the pun would " amount to " ; he
was content because he was weaving in another reference to the
theatre, exactly like Joyce weaving in the name of another river
or what not. Exactly like Joyce ; and the best thing the public
can do is to avoid noticing it.

No doubt one does not really want the word altered ; I suppose
it has a sort of pathetic charm, and probably some remote but
valuable meaning could be invented for it. Indeed this rather
trivial mood can be dissipated by trying to do so. " All the world's
a stage," is the obvious starting point ; particularly for the hero,
because he is dependent for his glory on the approval of the crowd.
Hamlet dies craving to be justified in popular opinion ; if only
someone goes on talking, he says, it will be all right ; and this
feeling, as Mr. Eliot pointed out, saves him from reflecting how many
unnecessary deaths his delay has caused. Cleopatra must fear to
have an actor " boy her greatness " if she yields to Augustus ; but
when Hamlet is staged his name is no longer wounded. All this I
think lets the word give a relevant idea, not one that Mr. Eliot
would think creditable but still not a ridiculous one. (Indeed
I daresay he was wrong to want the characters to be so unworldly.)
But for this line of thought, it seems clear, the theatrical stage needs
to be a secondary meaning ; it must come up as an Implication
about the various uses of a stage, a predicate of the equation.
Whereas if you make the word mean " carry him back to the
footlights, where he belongs " (" and mind he is *put on* in a star
part ") you are making the theatrical stage the chief meaning here
in spite of the demands of the context. In Elizabethan times the
theatrical meaning of the word, though common, seems still to have
been felt as a derived and therefore minor one, and the general idea
of any scaffolding or platform had a sort of natural claim to be the
head sense. The planting of this sense twenty lines earlier puts us in
much the same position as an Elizabethan, except that we are less
at home with it and therefore less ready to let it carry the theatrical
stage as a subsidiary idea. Thus the theatrical *stage* could only
act as subject here by an equation of the rejected Type V, and you
might say that I have no business to blame Shakespeare for leaving
open the possibility of it. But the technique of reiterative imagery
seems to me to complicate the thing ; it gives the theatrical stage a
claim to be the head sense of the term, so that the equation is of

Type III.   This again might be harmless, if you make it a matter
of " typifying " everything in terms of the theatre ; the point is
rather that once the theatrical stage is accepted as subject, or
" what the word really means here ", there is liable to be no equation and only a single farcical idea.   I cannot get away from feeling
that it would sound a neurotic piece of self-justification.   However,
after all this to-do, no doubt the proper moral to be drawn is that
Shakespeare assumed no one would give excessive attention to his
reiterative imagery, and that it could be trusted to work only in
the background of the mind.   This being granted, the example
still illustrates the point I was trying to make about Joyce.   The
same excuse could not be extended to him, because you cannot read
Finnegan's Wake at all if the reiterative imagery is left in the background of the mind.   And the example does at least show that it is
sometimes important to get the two ideas in the right order.

I am not sure how far I am labouring the obvious on this topic.
A writer can sometimes be found treating the kind of principle I
want to elaborate as already settled, but even then the rule does not
get formulated.   For example there is a passage in Aldous Huxley's
The Perennial Philosophy where he seems to argue not vaguely from
a double meaning but specifically from an equation of the first type,
and he treats the process as something obvious and well known.
What he says seems to me true, though perhaps it does not go as
far as he thinks ; but even so the conditions for a reliable deduction
of this sort need examining.

" The Sanscrit *dharma*—one of the key words in Indian formulations of the Perennial Philosophy—has two principal meanings.
The *dharma* of an individual is, first of all, his essential nature,
the intrinsic law of his being and development.   But *dharma* also
signifies the law of righteousness and piety.   The implications of
this double meaning are clear : a man's duty, how he ought to
live, what he ought to believe and what he ought to do about his
beliefs—these things are conditioned by his essential nature, his
constitution and temperament . . . Hence the almost total absence,
among Hindus and Buddhists, of bloody persecution, religious
wars and proselytizing imperialism."

On the face of it, one might think that a quite opposite moral could
be drawn from the same pair ; not " a man's nature defines his
duty " but " to obey the one law is the true nature of all mankind ".
The difficult thing to decide, in such a case, is which way round
the pair gets interpreted, and why one of the ways is chosen not
the other.   The answer given by Aldous Huxley seems to me
correct ; the equation that he wants can only arise when the immediate context demands the meaning " nature of an individual ",
and the meaning " the universal law of righteousness " has then got to

poke its way in and act as predicate. That is, it must be of Type I, and there is a reason for expecting the equation to be of this type, because the two uses of the word are very distinct, as in the *saddle* example ; in most cases the grammar, let alone the context, will be enought to show whether *dharma* is used about an individual or the cosmos. It does not seem plausible therefore to suppose that this equation is of Type II ; if the nature of the individual were the head sense, and you were talking about an individual, the idea of the moral nature of the universe would seem too remote to be added as an Implication. At any rate it could not appear (on the model of *native*) as another property of the same referent. What would be probable, if the nature of the individual were the head sense, would be the reverse case of an equation of Type I ; that is, when you were talking about the law of righteousness in general the idea of " someone's nature " would be liable to put itself forward, especially if the context had some definite class of persons in view. The equation would then become " the world *dharma* is (also) their *dharma* ", so that they would be expected to follow the universal law. The same effect would follow from an equation of Type III which made the world *dharma* " typical " of all individual *dharmas* ; and on the other hand it would be absurd to make each individual *dharma*, or whichever of them you had in view at the moment, typical of all the others and at the same time of the universal one. Finally we cannot suppose that *dharma* has a standard equation of Type IV, because there is a striking opposition of meaning between the two equations given by the two orders for the terms. I don't deny that a particular school of theology might get an equation of Type IV into the word, indeed Wordsworth may have got one into its approximate translation " Nature " ; but Aldous Huxley could not claim that all Sanscrit speakers would be likely to do this spontaneously, in the absence of some doctrine already held independently of the word. We must suppose then that the equation is of Type I, and that the connection between the equated meanings is felt to be fairly loose. It is only when we make the universal law of righteousness the head meaning of the word that we get the equation praised by Huxley which serves to weaken its claims. This is a mildly paradoxical result ; one would think that if the law of righteousness is the head or dominant meaning of the word it would tend to rule the others, not to be outfaced by them.

My ignorance of Sanscrit is no doubt making me argue in the dark here, but it seems to me that the English word " nature " has much the same structure of meaning. Here again the equation arises only when we talk about an individual ; " his character is disorderly " simply blames the man, as far as it goes, but " his nature is disorderly " tends to imply that if he follows his nature he will do better work in the end—because we all ought to " follow Nature ". I suppose we should call the abstract Mother Nature the head sense of the word ; certainly if we are given the word alone we tend to think of it first, but this may be merely because it requires no special grammar. It would seem natural here to follow Professor Richards' view in *Mencius on the Mind*, and say that the Emotion is what spreads over to the other Sense ; indeed the Mencian view of Nature was the chief thing he was discussing at the time. That is, we could say that Nature in general has a strong Emotion attached to it " Good ! Not forced ! Worthy to be followed ! " and that this seeps across into other uses. Its presence there will no doubt be supported by metaphysical arguments, but these will have been invented later, like a myth to explain a ritual, and their only real basis will be the emotive performance of the word. The point of difference with my account is perhaps not really very great. All I should claim is that a dim half-formed metaphysical argument arises at once when the emotive effect is first obtained, if indeed it does not have to be present before the new sense of the word, applying to the specific natures of individual men, can even establish itself. It seems to me therefore that the argument through the Emotion is only a roundabout way of doing what is done at once if you call Mother Nature the dominant sense of the word. But I agree that the dominant sense tends to have more emotive power than the others, and also that the sense which appears as predicate in an equation tends to be more emotive than the subject (this appears to be one of the obstacles against forming an equation of Type III, which tends to have an exciting meaning as subject). Incidentally, the double meaning of *dharma* is quite clearly not what prevented religious persecution among the users of Sanscrit, because there is a word in English and the other languages of Christendom which would yield practically the same covert assertion. The point that Aldous Huxley really wanted to make, as I understand him, was that the Sanscrit speakers based their religious and moral position on something like Nature rather than on a transcendent God who revealed universal laws.

This business of plodding round the alternatives may seem pedantic, and not as reliable as common sense even when complete. No doubt the plodding need not often be written down. But since arguments of this kind are often used we do seem to need a criterion which could make them valid. In particular, I think, you find sociologists and anthropologists going ahead rather too cheerfully with the idea that any double meaning found in the language of the speakers examined can be taken as evidence of an opinion held by their society. It seemed to me that I found examples of this, for instance, in *The Chrysanthemum and The Sword*, an excellent book by

Ruth Benedict about the Japanese. She gives an interesting examination of *giri*, a word for something like " personal honour ". There is a separate term *gimu* for the unlimited duties to the Emperor and one's parents, but *giri* covers (or covered) the limited duties to one's feudal superior, less close family relations, persons who have done one favours, etc., and then also the duty to clear one's reputation of insult (e.g. by vendetta) and to fulfil the proprieties (e.g. by giving respect where it is due). The reason why the Japanese welcomed the American occupying troops, she says on p. 173, is that " *Giri* had always meant equally the use of aggression or the observance of respect relations, and in defeat the Japanese turned from one to the other, apparently with no sense of psychic violence to themselves. The goal is still their good name ". Undeniably this is a neat point, but it is not clear how much weight Ruth Benedict meant it to carry. Did she prophesy, I wonder, when she was an official wartime advisor on such matters, that the Japanese would welcome the G.I.'s, and could she have made a confident forecast from this word in the Japanese dictionary alone? It seems to me that a good deal more information is needed before you can make such important deductions from the mere range of a word, and according to the method I am using here you would have to show that a definite argument was commonly based on an equation of two of its meanings at the period in question. I don't deny that a quite different line of deduction is conceivable, from the whole structure of moral ideas in the culture, and the book seems to contain an argument of that sort. But, if I understand how it goes, one would still have to ask what reason there is for supposing that *giri* reflects the actual structure. To do this, one would think, its various meanings would have to be highly integrated ; they would have to feel " really " connected. But it looks more like a rag-bag word, which has been extended piecemeal to cover a variety of minor duties ; so that (unless indeed a fashion for the equation had been established) a Japanese would feel it was only a trivial pun to argue that both these actions were *giri*. And on the face of it they were not done out of *giri* at all but out of *gimu*, obedience to direct orders from the Emperor.

We know that in English the suggestions of this sort in a moral word have altered every two generations or so, whereas the range of its meanings has been pretty stable. The reason is, of course, that not all the possible equations are used at any given time. In any case, it is often hard to be sure of these twists of feeling even in your own language, and it must be very easy to go wrong in a language which you have taken up to do a cultural survey. The range of distinct meanings is much easier to learn than how they are combined. Also the care with which the foreign meanings are teased out is not as a rule balanced by a similar treatment of the English meanings which are to interpret them. There is a tendency to imply " They, the objects of study, have very quaint ideas ; but we, the English-speakers or the scientific world, have sensible and transparent ones " ; whereas we may only be understanding the foreign ideas, if at all, through a similar complexity in our own. And this generally goes with an idea that the foreigners are sure to stay fixed in their peculiar thought-processes ; we must learn to be tolerant and understanding about them, and then we will realise that they have got to be kept just like they are. This would be prevented, and the method I think would become more reliable, if it were recognised that in any given period some of the possible equations in a word will be in common use and others used rarely if at all ; while some could not affect opinion anyway.

Indeed I think the main literary use of an adequate equation theory would be to clear up the feeling of a period style. At present our skill in feeling this is far in advance of our understanding. It is quite a usual examination question to give a list of quotations and say " spot the periods ", and this can be made very easy, but it is hard to explain to those who have failed why they ought to have known the answer. One of the forces that drove me to invent an equation theory was that I would get a feeling that a word took on a special sense in a certain period ; and then I would go and look in the great Dictionary ; and the sense I had in mind would turn out to be much older, and quite separate from the period feeling. Furthermore anything I could peg down as Emotions or what not would sometimes also be separable from the period feeling ; in fact it amounted to the assertion of some belief typical of the period. The equation theory of course settles this quite easily ; the stock assumptions of the period are being fitted out by the context with simple equations in its pet words. To be sure, it might be argued that when we get this period feeling what we really do is something much more abstruse ; literary taste is in play, and it makes in-numerable connections with all the uses of the word we have read dating from the period. I doubt whether we are as clever as all that, at any rate so regularly ; it struck me that my period feelings about words were much simpler objects.

On the other hand, the double meanings used occasionally by a rich stylist tend not to be equations at all, or only of a peculiar sort. I have written two books largely concerned with literary double meanings, and I looked through them for examples useful in testing an equation theory, but I hardly found any. In an ordinary literary use both the meanings are imposed by the immediate context, which has been twisted round to do it, and the suggestion is not " as everyone admits, so that language itself bears me out " but " as I by my magic can make appear ". You get many shades between one extreme and the other, and the idea of an " immediate context " is hard to make into a definite criterion here ; but I think we need to separate this kind of double meaning from the compacted doctrine, where the word itself seems to put the doctrine into our minds. Of course a single writer can put an equation into a word, but he needs to bring it out steadily as a way of recalling his doctrine, not only make a nonce-use of it for a special effect. And, going to the other extreme, no doubt there are permanent equations which are more important than the period ones ; but the period ones are easier to notice, and there is more need to notice them if you are to get the right reading ; and also they allow you to examine the machinery of change.

There is a case more or less halfway between the nonce-use of an ambiguity and the period flavour in a word, that is, the " key word " of a long poem, or complete play, in which the structure of meaning for the word is gradually built up. This is what I have chiefly tried to examine in the examples which follow, but I do not think that any sharp theoretical distinction can be drawn. There are all sorts of " key words ", from Pope's *wit* which is actually the topic of the *Essay on Criticism* to the much more casual use of *sense* in *Measure for Measure*, where two main types of pun on the word are made at different stages of the play and it seems natural to connect them. To pretend that every long poem has one key word which sums up all of it would of course be absurd. But one might expect to find more positive enriching of the key word as the long poem goes forward than usually occurs ; usually I think the author assumes the whole structure at the start and leaves the reader to pick it up as best he can. In any case, the peculiar structure which is to be picked up is usually one of the stock period flavours, made rather more definite ; the two things are not sharply distinct.

Perhaps it is as well to explain that I did most of the work on the large scale examples given in later chapters before I had arrived at the classification of Types given in this one. The remarks about which Type of equation is being illustrated were added at the end. Thus I am more sure of the general literary account that I am of the classifying fitted onto it. It is useful I think to have general rules suggesting how you should interpret an " A is B ", for example whether it goes " A is like B " or " A is typical of B ". But if two people agree on which sense is subject and which sense is predicate, I think, they commonly agree enough ; how the thing is to be interpreted is likely to be obvious, and which sense ought to be called the " head sense " is likely to reduce to a question of definition. However it is plain I think that there is a real field of activity for the critic which the term " head sense " ought to sum up and recall ; he needs to know the general flavour and proportions of any crucial word in the minds of the audience primarily intended, and he needs to know whether other uses of the word by the author in hand show that he does something special with it. The idea of a change in the head sense is I think often the best way to sum up one of these impalpable shifts of flavour in a word, even when the term is rather an over-simplification.

The problems of change of meaning have of course been studied very fully already, and most of the processes concerned do not involve equations of any kind. But I think there are cases where a word has to change its meaning, and yet there are several possible candidates for the position of the new head one. We left off examining *native*, earlier in this chapter, at the point where the slang use of the empire builders began to affect the talkers at home. The old head meaning could no longer apply, and one of the new Implications had to be promoted ; but more than one of them could have been chosen. Here I think the rules about choice of sentence-order can actually be found in play. They were that the subject tends to be more obvious to the hearer, less emotive, and narrower in range (or in some other way more " concrete ") than the predicate. No doubt the returning empire builders might keep the old Sense and merely limit the range of the Equation, using it only for colonial peoples and imposing it there through the Emotion of a tone of voice. Indeed this is more or less what happened, since the old head meaning has not been abandoned. Nor would they worry much about the Range ; on the whole, the type of speaker who would want to imply that the colonial peoples were " inherently subjected " would not want to imply that the English working classes were natural political leaders either. Thus one finds the word used about English labourers for the jovial reactionary facetiousness of Bulldog Drummond ; for example in *Challenge*, when the heroes disguise themselves as dockers, " two typical dockyard natives slouched out of No. 10 Heppel St." (p. 237). In this development the word practically means " working class ", though " uncivilised " is perhaps an equally prominent idea about the group in view. One can imagine it being used so in India ; no longer a rude thing to say in front of the rajah, but with a good deal of subtlety about which Indians were covered by it and which not, further down the scale. But, from the point of view of the people who had stayed at home, the natives the returned empire-builder was talking about were " non-European " ; this was the most definite fact that could be elicited about them, both as being obvious and as being clear-cut ; and also it was the least emotional or highly coloured, which was an advantage to those who were now to adopt the slang use because they could not express these feelings as if at first hand. Thus the three rules worked together, and " non-European " became the new head sense. The choice was if anything made from liberal rather than illiberal motives. It seemed rather more civil to take " non-European " as all the word really meant. It was actually as less emotive, for one thing, that ~~the massively emotive structure was formed.~~ But when the new head sense carried on with the old Implications it was found to say " all non-European persons are essentially inferior and fit for subjection " and so forth. The striking thing here, if I am right, is that this impressive assertion was not what anyone had tried to make the word mean ; it was an unexpected and rather embarrassing result of the working of a few simple laws of verbal structure.

Going back to the Emotions, it may seem that my accounts of *native* and *nature* (or *dharma*) fit together badly. In *native* the least emotive of the secondary meanings is supposed to be chosen as the new head sense, whereas in *nature* the emotive power of Mother Nature is supposed to give her a dominant position among the meanings of that word. But the dominant meaning of a word with several distinct uses (giving equations of Type I) is a different thing from the head meaning of a word which is integrated, in the sense that, though it includes various ideas, it applies them all to much the same group of referents (thus giving equations of Type II). And the effect of this contrast was to satisfy the only rule which I supposed to be at work ; the equations of both *nature* and *native* put the more emotive idea in the predicate. The rule does not always work, but it seems a strong influence in both these cases.

A similar change can be examined in *delicate*, where the original sense is apparently that of " giving pleasure ". One must not make it too simple ; the N.E.D. says " derivation doubtful ; connected with *deliciae* at some point ", and the Latin word itself has already a somewhat Puritan background. *Lacio* " to pull " has such other derivatives as " to attack, entice, deceive " and *de* in combination gives " to the uttermost, to exhaustion ". But in classical Latin it meant only " pleasurable " or " tender " ; there are uses meaning " spoilt " and " fastidious " in Plautus and then again in Quintilian, I am told, but the " pure Latin " sense would be the main influence on English. For the English word, the N.E.D. gives a first group of meanings now all obsolete, mostly extending from the sixteenth to the middle eighteenth century ; " delightful ", " voluptuous ", " self-indulgent ", " innocent ", " effeminate ", " fastidious ". Its other two main groups are " not coarse, not robust " etc., and " endowed with fineness of appreciation or execution " ; these are equally old but have survived. No doubt the human race has always been moral about delicacy, indeed my other word *refined*, as Dr. Johnson remarks somewhere, also carries a hint of weakness though not so much of it. But it seems fair to say that our two senses of *delicate*, " refined " and " sickly ", are implications from the idea of pleasure which were at some point promoted to Senses ; they proceed from the two equations " persons devoted to pleasure improve their taste but lose their health ". The Victorian matron whose brief remark about Amelia I have so often recalled would fiercely deny this connection with sensuality ; her equation of the surviving pair was meant to imply that the best people ignore the body and its pleasures, preferring chastity and the consequences of tight stays. The only ground for taking " sickly " as the head meaning, rather than " refined ", seems to be that it was used more frequently ; perhaps at first because it was so convenient as a euphemism. If a trifle baffling, the word was not more so than it was intended to be, and the arrangement had an air of great stability. But the worm was already at work ; a revival of the more commonsense Latin view can be observed in Swinburne and his following Decadents, where it conveys a shuddering and scandalous vision of the extremes of spirituality tottering into corruption. A simple formal cause can be given for this comic result. The notion of pleasure could be revived in the word because the Latin view is after all a very plausible one, because Swinburne could use learned classical contexts to force it home (by a general appeal to " paganism " rather than by philology), and because he need go no further afield than Shakespeare to recall the old meaning in English. There are " soft and delicate desires ", for instance, in *Much Ado About Nothing*, and Fortinbras, of all people, is described as " a delicate and tender prince ". But as a revival (therefore less obvious to the hearer, rule one) it must act as predicate; that is, the idea is added as an Implication by successive contexts and the equation is of Type II. The old pair now appear as one confused concept " A+B ", as if by an equation of Type IV. Thus the covert assertion in Swinburne becomes " Refined-sickly people are devoted to pleasure ", and this was an appalling insinuation for the drawing-rooms. I suppose he was also using a cynical version of the Victorian equation, though only dimly : " You can't get a woman to be refined unless you make her ill ", and the other words for refinement (*sensibility*, perhaps) ought to be considered at their stages of shift ; but the broad truth of this joke is I think clear through the complexity of the topic.

The question is now how useful Swinburne found *delicate*, and on looking through *Poems and Ballads*, the poetry of my schooldays, I was at first ashamed of having supposed it important to him ; his Baudelairean key notion is put across by a clear and splendid structure of metaphors, and only echoes and shudders into the meaning of particular words. Swinburne discovered *delicate* without much sense of triumph ; it did not discover him ; it is a simplicity for the imitator. But he did what I expected with it. The meaning " sinful pleasure " gets put in quite barely, for example, when Christ in the *Hymn To Proserpine* is said to have robbed us of " all delicate days and pleasant," or when the scandalous Aholibah kept as wall-paintings " horseman on horseman, girdled well, delicate and desirable ". However the main poetic technique, I said to myself, is a matter of very spaced-out and balanced metaphors, for example the ones in *Laus Veneris* about flowers and fire and then the fire of desire and the fire of hell and then the " inner flower of fire ". But then, I found, this whole group was handed on to the word :

> *And eyes insatiable of amorous hours,*
> *Fervent as fire and delicate as flowers,*

The eyes are insatiable *because* they are " delicate " ; the over-refinement of aristocratic overbreeding has collapsed into perverse cravings. There is one main theme in Swinburne's box of tricks where *delicate* isn't much help ; the praise of sadism :

> *Take thy limbs living, and new-mould with these*
> *A lyre of many faultless agonies ?*

No doubt you have to be very delicate for that, but the artistic perfection or the insane idealism of this vice was what needed emphasising, rather than the pleasure of it. However the word is at its best when given a firm connection with death and horror. *The Leper* leads off with it as a reliable dramatic irony :

> *Nothing is better, I well think,*
> *Than love ; the hidden well-water*
> *Is not so delicate to drink :*
> *This was well seen of me and her.*

The ideas of " pure " and " natural " in the well-water are clashed against a love so pure, so indifferent to the corruption of her body, that it comes near to necrophily. The word still describes a fastidious pleasure and is the more at home because it is of a ghastly kind. The idea that he positively liked to have her rotting away, because it added to the refinement of the thing, is a direct parody of what the drawing-rooms were already assuming ; and for that matter the latent sadism of the whole theme was already present in the tight-lacing. However all this is unfair to the poem, which I think a very fine one ; the sadism is adequately absorbed or dramatised into a story where both characters are humane, and indeed behave better than they think ; Swinburne nowhere else (that I have read him) succeeds in imagining two people. But the function of *delicate* in the first verse is clear enough. The word also holds a crucial position in the great scandal-piece *Dolores* :

> They shall pass and their places be taken,
>   The gods and the priests that are pure,
> They shall pass, and shalt thou not be shaken ?
>   They shall perish, and shalt thou endure ?
> Death laughs, breathing close and relentless
>   In the nostrils and eyelids of lust
> With a pinch in his fingers of scentless
>   And delicate dust.

One must quote the whole verse to do Lust justice, or he is too simple. Death has his laugh against both religions but seems only to use one method, whether the religion of Venus is finally dead or not, and the whole point of *delicate* was to insinuate the appalling lusts of the pure.

It seemed best, while introducing the idea of an equation, to use the rather " shocking " examples *native* and *delicate*, because in both of them the historical development is worth attention ; the reader I hope will feel that there was really something to be explained, and that the equation theory has at least tried to explain it. The ordinary user of the words had not intended them to grow as they did, to a point where the decadents or the jingoes could embarrass him with the result. But I shall not often deal with such cases ; as a rule, in a successful literary use, the equation does just what the writer and his audience wanted ; and this is even more true of the equations carrying the stock ideas of a period, where as a rule there is no tension between individuals or groups. Nor has the process of forming new equations much to do with that of forming new meanings in a word ; some of course arise from new Implications, but most of them I should think are between old meanings of the word. The process does often tend to raise an old but subordinate meaning of the word into a new prominence, but this kind of change does not get much attention even in the N.E.D. ; it is not likely to be regarded as a change of meaning. In any case I think it tends not to be permanent. The change in prominence occurs in connection with equations of Type I; the word comes to be frequently used in a subordinate meaning (though there is a more usual word for it available instead) merely so that the head meaning can rise in the background as predicate of the equation. This might tend to make the subordinate meaning into the new head one, so that the equation becomes of Type II. It might be argued that something like this happened with *sense* for good judgement ; in the same way, the effect of the equation in *dharma* was actually to weaken the claims of the head

79

sense, apart from any question of frequency. One might indeed expect a secular change from side to side, like the curving bed of a river. But, thinking of examples already given, it seems clear that *nature* and *law* have very permanent structures, whereas *native* and *delicate*, after a period while they are very tricky, simply go out of fashion till they have run clear again and the tricks are no longer obtrusive. It would be foolish to erect rules which were supposed to be automatic ; on the whole, talkers do what they think sensible ; and the real purpose of finding quasi-automatic rules in this matter is to break them, that is, to be able to point out cases where people are being unnecessarily misled.

I have been talking as though sense-changes always occurred through growth of implications, which is certainly not true, but that type of change produces the more interesting equations. It is impressive to see a new idea appearing in common words through an extension of their meaning before any theoretical writer " discovers " the idea and builds a system on it ; this I think really happens, but only through the growth of implications, as it were by case-law. Stern gives seven main types of sense-change, some of which are very unlike this, and I shall list them to show the variety of material which the equation process is likely to have to work upon. They are (1) Substitution, a change due to external non-linguistic causes, as when *ship* is used for the new object " steam-ship " (2) Analogy, between one word and another, as when the adverb *fast* changes (by method 6) from " immovably " to " quickly " and the adjective jumps after it (3) Shortening, as *private* for " private soldier " (4) Nomination, which includes invented names and metaphors. " Nominations are transfers in which a name is intentionally transferred from one referent to another ", and this intention is concerned with the form of the language, not as usual only with its import. Keats' Urn as " unravished bride ". (5) (Regular) Transfer, which is based on similarity and not intentional in the sense of (4), as when objects resembling a leaf in shape are called *leaves* (6) Permutation, which occurs when it is immaterial for the purpose whether a whole phrase is interpreted in one way or another, as with " telling his beads " ; this allowed *beads* to change from prayers to perforated balls (on a rosary) (7) Adequation, an adaptation of the meaning to the actual characteristic of the referents which the word is employed to denote, as when *horn* was taken to have a sense " type of musical instrument " distinct from its sense " object made of horn ".

On the face of it this list does not exclude the possibility of any change whatever, so it could never be tested to find whether it is complete ; but if you are sure that a change is not " intentional " the possibilities become reasonably narrow. The intentional group looks a rather helpless gesture, but I think it is logically necessary ; after all, if you made a rigid list without it, and some type of change were excluded (without which the list would be useless), it is conceivable that people might make one such change merely with the " intention " of proving you wrong. It is perhaps rather a farcical plan, but the mere possibility of it seems enough to prove that they do not *have* to follow quasi-automatic processes. Stern indeed remarks at one point (p. 173) :

> " I assume that the possibility of a change is made use of by the speaking community or group only when it serves some purposes connected with the functions of speech."

This would make them all rather intentional, and might imply that there is more use for equation-theory in considering the causes of sense-change than I have supposed. But the kind of choice that is made will often be very remote from that. Professor Bloomfield has made clear that many changes of meaning are simply a result of habitual choices between near-synonyms, a process that has to go through two stages ; and the reason why one word of a pair is favoured against another need not concern the word whose meaning is thereby changed. Thus " meat " originally meant food in general, but came to be used particularly often for edible animal flesh. However, this process might depend on a disfavour of the word *flesh*, not on any changed attitude to the word *meat*. Then food in general came to be frequently called, not meat, but " food " or " a dish " or " dinner " or what not, and this too might be because other words were fashionable not because *meat* had anything against it. In this way the sense-change could be pushed through without any consciousness of a double meaning at all—without anyone ever feeling that he was not using *meat* in the long-accepted way. Puns and double-meanings and suchlike are not represented at all in Prof. Bloomfield's index to his *Language*, and so far as I can find not in his text either ; indeed it is not clear how he could admit their existence. I consider this a weakness in his system, because after all they undoubtedly occur ; but his successful avoidance of them in his theory of sense-change does at least illustrate the truth that such changes need not involve anything worth calling an equation.

I am anxious to insist that the ordinary equation process has nothing to do with etymology, because otherwise I might find myself in rather bad company. For example the father of the great N.E.D., Archbishop Trench, may be found saying :

> " But there is a deeper feeling in the heart of man, bearing witness to something very different from this shallow explanation of the existence of pain in the present economy of the world—

namely, that it is the correlative of sin, that it is *punishment ;* and to this the word " pain ", which there can be no reasonable doubt is derived from " poena ", bears continual witness. Pain *is* punishment ; so does the word itself, no less than the conscience of everyone that is suffering it, continually declare."

If you came fresh from the factory conditions of the time and heard the good archbishop on this point you might perhaps have tried kicking that important figure. He might then have found himself claiming that though in pain he did not deserve to suffer. To be sure, the immorality of his argument does not prove that it is historically false. But an opposite argument is just as easy to invent ; if people made a term for " legal penalties " cover all suffering they must have thought their judge so bad that most of their suffering came from him, so that the word is a monument to the injustice of the ruling classes. Both of these vehement pictures are improbable ones, and I do not know what is the accepted theory. One might think that the Saxons misunderstood a word of the Normans, but the shift occurred in all the Romance languages. *Pine* as a noun was introduced before *pain* into England ; it is another derivative from *poena*, and was applied here originally to the pains of hell. The first use of it in the N.E.D. for mundane suffering happens to support the idea of the wicked judge—1154 " I cannot tell all the pines that did wreak men in his land ". The *peine fort et dure* was another rival form, and would be easily thought of as undeserved. The English *pain* is dated back to 1297 with the idea of penalty, but only just after (in 1300) it has already the idea of *taking pains*, " trouble as taken for the accomplishing of something ". This does not give a very theological impression, but the decisive changes had no doubt already occurred in French. It seems enough to think that the use of the word by the church for the pains of hell, which it considered to be deserved, gave the word a general impressiveness, and then lay speakers drew on this feeling to describe mundane pains as strong ones, whether deserved or not. The effect would be a mild sort of swearing rather than the trust in the justice of God, or the frank welcome to plague, which was what attracted the Archbishop. The machinery of change of meaning, an important and interesting subject, has I think rather little influence on the equations between the meanings once achieved.

Also (I hope it has been clear that I don't deny this) a word can have several independent senses without making any equations between them at all. To maintain that all possible equations arise would mean imputing an immense confusion to ordinary language. To be sure, it is perhaps rather surprising, if double meanings are as common as I am making out, that we avoid confusion as well as we do. When a word has a really " dominant " sense, and is used in a subordinate sense, one would think that the dominant sense is bound to put itself forward, by definition. But it can still be ignored if it is not felt to be relevant ; the only time when it can be forced on you against your intention is when it is felt to be relevant and satirical. And a word with a variety of meanings has often no dominant one. A speaker who wants to assert one of the possible equations has in general I think to show that this extra meaning is relevant, as well as emphasise the word to show that some extra meaning is to be expected. Also, to be received easily, the equation needs to be a stock one of the period ; two meanings may exist in a word for a long time, it seems to me, without anyone seeing any point in connecting them. The decision to take the connection seriously, to regard the equation as a general truth, is a fairly serious step on the part of a zeitgeist or an individual. Naturally it will have little to do with the word's past history.

It is clear then that the linguist has always to justify any claim he makes that an equation is being used ; he cannot merely presume it. To take one of our complex words in the N.E.D. and write down the equations between its senses is often to obtain, with that effect of ease which is the root of comedy, the series of stages of thought for which it has been used ; but this is only because you know the answers already. At the same time, granting that you must first know the spirit of the author or the period, I think that to write down the equations of the key words which carried it is really the quick and natural way to sum it up.

The most striking recent work on the kind of linguistics I am trying to consider here has been a very untechnical one ; it is in the dreadful book *1984* which George Orwell wrote while dying. What he calls " double-think ", a process of intentional but genuine self-deception, easy to reach but hard to hold permanently, really does seem a positive capacity of the human mind, so curious and so important in its effects that any theory in this field needs to reckon with it. In the nightmare of his book the emotional ground of the process is a secret but fully justified fear, and the case is so hideously special that it seems rather hard to generalise (indeed the book itself, I think, tends to frighten the reader into believing the possibility of what he does not really think possible). But no doubt this kind of process does occur, and is based on emotional grounds ; I am left uneasy whether my treatment here has a pureminded intellectualism which ignores the facts in view. I might protest that you can have a usable linguistic theory which doesn't apply to sheer madness, just as you can have a wave theory which doesn't apply to cases of turbulence ; but this is not much help unless you have some means of knowing where, and how often, turbulence is to be expected. Actually I think there is no such division ; the kind of analysis I am attempting here could be applied even to the ghastly paradoxes of the Orwell world such as " War is Peace ". Clearly this means that to be analysable doesn't make a bit of language good, but it was never supposed to. While considering the possible equation forms I gave a paragraph about " the paradoxes of the great religions " ; and all I can find to add, after trying to mull over the question again, is that I think it would apply to the very worst religions too. But then again, to take this way out of the theoretical dilemma does seem only another way to make my position a null one. It is rather hard to see beforehand what a line of argument is letting you in for ; but I suppose I really meant to argue all along that the human mind, that is, the public human mind as expressed in a language, is not irredeemably lunatic and cannot be made so.

Chapter 3

WIT IN THE ESSAY ON CRITICISM

I SHALL begin the examples with Pope's *wit* because, though
fairly elaborate in detail, it keeps to the simplest version Type
I as regards equation order. If one wants to examine how a
structure of meaning comes to be built up in a word it seems natural
to take the " key word " of a long poem, in which the process might
actually be seen at work ; and here the key word names the theme
of the poem. I approached the *Essay* rather coolly, as a handy
specimen likely to provide crude examples ; but I now think that
the analysis improves the poem a good deal, and indeed shows how
it was meant to be read. Critics may naturally object that the
Augustans did not deal in profound complexities, and tried to make
their words as clear-cut as possible. This is so, but it did not
stop them from using double meanings intended as clear-cut jokes.
The performance inside the word *wit*, I should maintain, was
intended to be quite obvious and in the sunlight, and was so for the
contemporary reader ; that was why he thought the poem so
brilliant ; but most modern readers (unless I wrong them) do not
notice it at all, and that is why they think the poem so dull.

The word appears on the average every sixteen lines of the Essay,
and by these frequent uses of it Pope was in effect building a system
on what was almost a slang word ; this is already a kind of assertion,
that one can think best in the fashionable language of the moment.
The implicit notions of the word seem to me to go neatly into
formulæ, but the effect is comic and somewhat unjust to Pope ;
the interesting thing is not that the Essay asserts the notions but that
by seeming to accept them it uses them to imply a hierarchy, and
thus puts them in their place. Pope continually plays off different
kinds of people so as to make himself look better than either, and in
the same way the smart flat little word *wit* seems meant to make
Pope himself look something more important. " And are, besides,
too moral for a wit " he makes an opponent say of him in the
Satires ; very possibly, we are to feel, but not too moral for a great
poet. The personal trick was a useful piece of machinery, but the
final effect is less trivial ; Pope and his rules are above the wits, but
smaller than such poets as can be conceived, even though all poets
are called wits. Thus my equations are not supposed to show
Pope's final opinions, only the basis of common assumption that he
accepted and played upon. The cleverness of the thing is that the
epigrams are irrefutable if you stretch the meanings of the words

far enough and give what the age demanded if you let them slip back. Yet to play this trick on such a scale comes at last to suggest more dignified notions ; that all a critic can do is to suggest a hierarchy with inadequate language ; that to do it so well with such very inadequate language is to offer a kind of diagram of how it must always be done.

What is now the most common and prominent meaning of the term, something like " power to make ingenious (and critical) jokes ", was I think already the most prominent one in the smart milieu which Pope was addressing. It was more than a century old (e.g., Falstaff says " I am not only witty myself but the cause that wit is in other men ") but the degree of prominence was a novelty. Also it is agreed that the special form " a wit " for a man possessing wit had taken on a new meaning at some time after the Restoration. I say " agreed " chiefly because it is in the N.E.D., which gives first an older use of the form : " 9 (trans. from 5) A person of great mental ability " (etc.), as in the Sonnets, " The wits of former days To subjects worse have given admiring praise ", and then this new use of the form : " 10 (trans. from 7) A person of lively fancy, who has the faculty of saying smart or brilliant things, now always so as to amuse ; a witty person ", for which the first example is dated 1692. This example and the following Augustan one under the same head both show wits as quarrelling with one another. " 5 " begins " Good or great mental capacity " and extends to " acumen " (apparently a critical power), whereas " 7 " begins " Quickness of intellect or liveliness of fancy " and includes the Falstaff example. Thus " a wit " for a person possessing Falstaff's sort of wit is given as a novelty for Pope, not yet invented when he was born. This seems rather improbable, but I think the great dictionary was right to assume an important change around that date. The sense " 10 " may well have become more frequent then, even if not first introduced ; but the reason for what one feels to be a novelty is that the form " a wit " then acquires a Mood. The N.E.D. " 10 " is really " 9£1 ", though the sense is also usually narrowed as a result. It is the obscure assertion " I have placed him ; I am an individual and he is a type ". This of course, if you were yourself a wit, could not logically be sustained, and anyway the type itself was not a very clear one. The Mood I think is needed to show why there was so much play of personal implication. It seems to have been put into many class-names of that rather schoolboyish period, for example into the queer word " parson ". The implication is that of the Comedy of Humours, in which one belittles a man merely by classifying him ; his Humour is supposed to be a " ruling passion ", so that all his actions are explained by it ; he is regarded as a mechanical toy.

Pope himself made much play with this claim in the Satires. It makes the speaker superior if only because it gives him a feeling of social power—he can manage people easily now that he has " placed " them. Thus the appearance of the Mood does not need explaining for this word in particular. But one could maintain, taking a historical view, that *wit* had been sinking in dignity, partly because of the gradual rise of *sense* to take over many of its functions, and that this might give a feeling of belittlement to the word even in the functions that it still had. Pope did not wholly accept this change ; as was said in effect by Warburton, he set out to combine the seventeenth and nineteenth century notions of wit, range of imaginative power with bright social criticism. The view of him as tied to a blind " classicism " is of course quite wrong ; he imagined he was striking a balance between Longinus's " The true sublime thrills and transports the reader " and Horace's " Fools admire but men of sense approve ". It is a mistake to suppose that his use of the word could not come near Coleridge's Imagination. Cowley's Ode *Of Wit* was in easy reach ; he if no other metaphysical was still read ; and what he makes the word mean, after labouring to cut out the idea of jokes, is almost exactly Coleridge's divine coadunative power.

> *In a true piece of wit all things must be,*
> *Yet all things there agree*
> *. . . . as the primitive forms of all*
> *(If we compare great things with small)*
> *Which without discord or confusion lie*
> *In that strange mirror of the Deity.*

This view indeed had become suspected in favour of the rationalism of Locke's theory of wit, but one could get a decent distance from Locke by insisting that the kind of wit now in hand was true.

A wit, then, or man who displays wit, may be a

1. bright social talker
2. critic of the arts or of society
3. poet or artist,

and in each class he may be divided into similar heads :

a. mocking,
b. acting as judge,
c. giving æsthetic pleasure or expressing new truths.

These divisions are perhaps only a matter of how he is applying his wit, and in all of them there is a doubt about what qualities of mind are so called. This is decided mainly by Emotions of admiration or satirical amusement, and the senses when translated back are I think best symbolised by plus and minus signs. No doubt in themselves Fancy and Imagination, or whatever the pair may be, are radically different and ought not to be symbolised in this way, but by doing it we imitate the pretence of Pope that they are similar. It is also convenient to introduce a sign " 4 " to cover the grammatical form " wit " as apart from " a wit " ; the plus and minus signs are originally attached to that, but they can be called in to qualify the persons possessing wit as well.

4+conceptual force, range of imaginative power

4—power to make neat jokes or ornament an accepted structure.

Because of the Mood, there is a rule that a wit must not have all these advantages at once.

We have now to decide how the equations go between these meanings, and no doubt it depends a good deal how you interpret the style. After I had written down my version I found an excellent school edition of the poem with notes by J. Churton Collins. His first note on the word *wit*, after saying that the various shades of meaning should be carefully distinguished, goes like this :

" Its derivation is from the A.-S. *witan*, ' to know ' so that its primary meaning is (a) the knowing power, pure intellect, mental capacity as in [line 17] and in lines 53, 61, 210 and elsewhere ; then (b) in a slightly wider sense, genius, as in line 657 ; then (c) as a synonym for ingenious or gifted writers, as in line 36 ; next (d) it comes to mean knowledge, learning, or ingenuity, as in 259, 447, 468, 494, 508, particularly ' polite learning ', 652. Next it is a synonym (e) for imagination or fancy, as in 292, 590, 717, 722. Then (f) it is employed for judgement, as in [the couplet 80-81], where it is employed in a double sense, imagination, and the control of imagination, i.e., judgement. Lastly, it is employed in the sense in which it was occasionally used in Pope's time and is generally used now ; namely, as ' a combination of heterogenous images, the discovery of occult resemblances between things apparently dissimilar ', as in line 28."

" Primary " at the beginning of this passage is a pun, carrying the equation " historically first, and therefore the chief meaning in Pope's time ". (" The first is the chief. ") The preface says that the edition is designed mainly for the use of students, both in England and in the Colonies. It seems to me that this otherwise excellent note is likely to give a foreign student an entirely wrong idea about the tone of the word, and indeed of the whole poem. Even when it gets to " lastly " the definition of a joke is so scarifying as to be quite unrecognisable, and at best this idea is at the bottom of the pile. I had been taking for granted, and I still do, that there is not a single use of the word in the whole poem in which the idea of a joke is quite out of sight. Indeed I think that the whole structure of thought in the poem depends on this. It was the deliberate policy of Pope to start from the slang meaning of the word, because it gave the tone of society :

> *Without good breeding truth is disapproved ;*
> *That only makes superior sense beloved.* (576)

and indeed because

> *The current folly proves the ready wit* (449)

Wit as joke could be relied upon as the " head meaning ", because the flippant reader could be trusted to think of it in any context ; the context in the poem often makes it very unsuitable, and the other meaning which is required then appears as the subject of the equation, the thing " meant by the word ", but the idea of the joke or the smart joker will still crop up as a predicate of it. To be sure, this could not be done unless the other meanings were in fairly easy reach ; if the use had too much feeling of strain, so as to give an effect of metaphor, the meaning " joke " would appear as subject because it would be felt as " what the word really means ". But the other meanings were still in regular use ; the point is merely that the term " a wit " made a false claim to simplicity. I take it then that " 1 " the bright social talker never appears as subject in an equation ; if the term is definitely used about such a man it appears flat. But when it is used about a poet or critic the word will compare either of these to the smart joker, and I think the critic is close enough to the idea of the coffeehouse wit to appear as predicate in some equations on his own. It seems to me that if you write down the more pointed equations, on this general principle, you get a fairly complete parody of the Augustan critical position.

$3=1$, $2=1$. Both poet and critic are social entertainers and must keep to the tone of polite society, since that is the final judge of the arts.

$3=2$. The poet is a critic ; he should judge his work coolly not rely on enthusiasm.

$3c=3a$. The normal mode of poetry, in itself merely a cultivated pleasure, is satire.

$a=b$. The satirist is a judge ; he tells the truth about life and upholds wisdom and virtue.

$4+=4-$. The field of imaginative writing is limited and simple; one can go ahead and give the correct rules.

$3b+=1a-.1\pounds1$. Even in authoritative writers one must expect a certain puppyishness.

I have written the equation about the nature of wit-in-the-abstract in terms of " 4 ", since it is more prominent there, but no doubt any use of the form " a wit " might be felt to raise the question of what *wit* can be ; a better symbol perhaps would be the generalised one " $x+=x-$ ". Incidentally, since the idea " $4-$ " is an attribute of the petty wit " 1 ", this equation still takes him as predicate and is therefore of Type I like the others. The Mood is now written " $1\pounds1$ " because it properly belongs to " 1 " the bright social talker. It is sometimes called in merely to give assurance— " we need not believe anyone who says this is all wrong, because he would belong to the class we are despising ". But it may also be used, speaking as one kind of wit, to imply that you need not attend to the adverse judgements of another kind, and this makes the structure less cramped than it appears. Such a twist of thought seems a fair case for the question-mark sign :

$$3c+? \ 2=1a-.1\pounds1.$$

As a true poet myself, I regard the critics as types ; they have an itching to deride and judge by fashion. Similarly for the learned critic about fashionable poets, or even for the gentleman about professional authors, which would for once return a special use of " 1 " (" $1b+$ ") to the position of subject for the equation. Sufficient play with the formulæ would no doubt impute a lot of things that aren't meant ; but these ones I think actually occur.

I had better begin the examples with one that shows " a wit " being treated with some contempt, as apparently there is a doubt whether this happens. The form comes in Mr. Churton Collins' list only as "(c) a synonym for ingenious or gifted writers ", with a reference to the following passage :

> Some have at first for Wits, then Poets passed,
> Turned Critics next, and proved plain fools at last.
> Some neither can for Wits nor Critics pass,
> As heavy mules are neither horse nor ass.
> These half-learned witlings, numerous in our isle
> As half-formed insects on the banks of Nile ;
> Unfinished things, one knows not what to call,
> Their generation's so equivocal :
> To tell 'em would a hundred tongues require,
> Or one vain wit's, that might a hundred tire.   (36-45)

Certainly Pope does not say, and could not say, that a wit as such is always contemptible ; but it is made clear that an inferior kind of wit (a witling) is very common, so that we expect him to be referred to when we hear more about wits ; and the final turn of contempt is a kick at some type of person who it seems is really a wit, though a vain one. You might even read *vain* as a sort of Homeric stock epithet, implying that all wits may be assumed to be vain ; and indeed these witlings are being satirised, however unfairly, for just that combination of functions which the term " a wit " seems designed to recommend. The whole passage is something like an attack on the idea of " a wit " in general. It comes early in the poem and helps to set the tone. But this of course is not a complete account of the thing. Pope is involved in the business of being " a wit " himself, and on the other hand there is no suggestion that all good writers are contemptible in the same way that " wits " are. He is kicking at his own vocabulary, and can hardly avoid kicking at himself ; and our chief impression after recognising this picture of the bad writers is that the good writers are something different and yet something to which it would not be sensible to give another name.

As a rule, indeed, the poem uses a limitation of one counter merely as the only way to exalt another one :

> *One science only will one genius fit ;*
> *So vast is art, so narrow human wit :*   (61)

or contrariwise

> *Great wits sometimes may gloriously offend,*
> *And rise to faults true Critics dare not mend.*   (159)

> *From vulgar bounds with brave disorder part,*
> *And snatch a grace beyond the reach of art.*   (153)

It is only by narrowing *wit* and *art* each in turn that he contrives to elevate the concepts they might be supposed to name. Incidentally wit in the abstract is given the negative role in this couple, and " wits " are given the positive one ; there is no animus against the form " a wit " as such. The only effect of the process, which does not feel at all like a contradiction, is to imply that there is a hierarchy which ordinary language cannot be expected to describe directly.

However even the " great wits " of this quatrain, if you took it alone, might still be rather lightweight writers ; cavalier love-poets writing with the ease of gentlemen, perhaps. Pope in this kind of use meant to include any poet, however impressive, among his wits, and I must now try to give convincing enough examples of the high use of the term ; most readers perhaps will have more easily believed in the low one, unlike Mr. Churton Collins. As he pointed out, the term is used for " the knowing power " taken in general :

> *Nature to all things fixed the limits fit*
> *And wisely curbed proud man's pretending wit.*   (53)

Of course there is still a joke in it ; the thinker is dwarfed when he pits himself against heaven, and can therefore be compared by implication to the coffeehouse atheist making blasphemous quips. But the meaning imposed on the term as the relevant one for the context is as high as any human mental power.

He, who supreme in judgement, as in wit,
Might boldly censure, as he boldly writ,
Yet judged with coolness, though he sung with fire ;
His Precepts teach but what his works inspire.　　(660)

There is no trace here of a desire to sneer at Horace by speaking
of his wit ; the antithesis seems to make it mean his imagination,
which was so strong that it needed strong judgement to control it.
But there is still room for the simpler idea ; when he came to
criticism, his " fire " might have expressed itself in making very
rude jokes about bad authors ; but instead of this boldness he
judged coolly and " talked us into sense ". A more definite, though
less warm, example is therefore given by the following antithesis :

Authors are partial to their wit, tis true,
But are not Critics to their judgement too ?　　(18)

Judgement being the main function of a critic, the wit of an
author can hardly be less than his creative power. This gives a
firm definition of the sense required by the context, even though
the secondary meaning is also particularly clear. What the author
likes best are the flashy parts, the jokes or the purple passages ;
he is always puppyish.

The passage about Aristotle is nearly an unambiguous use of the
high sense of *wit*.

Poets, a race long unconfined, and free,
Still fond and proud of savage liberty,
Received his laws ; and stood convinced twas fit,
Who conquered Nature, should preside o'er Wit.　　(652)

Mr. Churton Collins says that this means " polite learning ",
part of his group " d " which includes knowledge and ingenuity. I
found this a puzzling unit till I realised that he was claiming a
logical distinction between " products of wit " and " the capacity
to produce them ", and that this was meant to subdivide any
specific sense of *wit*. He had much better have said so ; his
Colonial students will have to be on their toes here if they are to
guess his meaning. But in any case I think Aristotle might preside
over both these logical entities. A more interesting question is
whether there is any joke about *wit* here. It is against the poets
rather than against Aristotle ; the shaggy barbarians, as they
droop before their conqueror, seem unlikely to have a very great
supply of the polished facetiousness of which they are so proud. Or
rather (as we should interpret this picture) the smart fellow who
thinks he can give a quick answer on questions of taste is really
more of a barbarian than he supposes, and ought to be thankful
that Aristotle took the trouble to make laws for him. This I think

is the suggestion intended ; but none the less the main statement intended is that Aristotle does preside over wit, and indeed is a wit, the chief one.

> *No longer now that golden age appears,*
> *When Patriarch-wits survived a thousand years :*
> *Now length of Fame (our second life) is lost,*
> *And bare three score is all even that can boast.*　　　(481)

I take it this is a much more definite joke ; Methuselah is absurd in himself, and the idea of his being witty for a thousand years is positively depressing. We are to feel that Homer (who has just been mentioned) cannot really be placed as a wit, because this points the contrast with the contemporary scene. The very name of a modern artist proves that he cannot stand up to immortality. But Homer is unflinchingly called a wit, and no doubt would prove to have the frailties of the species if Pope could meet him. There is an idea that he was a moralist, as Methuselah presumably was, and as Pope is, but it is not elaborated. Pope here is in effect satirising his own key term, but without any hint that some other would be better ; indeed no other would suggest so clearly that there is a hierarchy of literature which it would be ridiculous to peg down by terms.

> *Some to Conceit alone their taste confine,*
> *And glittering thoughts struck out at every line ;*
> *Pleased with a work where nothing's just or fit ;*
> *One glaring Chaos and wild heap of wit.*　　　(292)

No doubt this is a smack at Cowley and any other metaphysicals not yet forgotten, but the grandeur of the suggestions in the background prevents it from seeming an unfair one. There is perhaps an idea that great powers are seen most clearly in a tragically suicidal freedom ; they create their destruction. There is a doubt, as usual in the form " A and B of C ", whether " chaos " is qualified by " of wit " ; a heap of jokes is a trivial kind of chaos, but if we choose to read " a chaos of wit " there is a certain note of doom. The two readings are related, I think, by the idea behind *MacFlecknoe* and the *Dunciad*, that there is an ominous mystery in the way the lowest and most absurd things make an exact parallel with the highest. For this idea you invert the conventional equation and read " $4-=4+$ " ; Pope made fuller use of it later in life. If present here it is a case where the equation is Type II ; probably the only one in the poem. I have taken this example last of the " high " uses of *wit*, and will now go on to what might be called the social applications of the standing contrasts in the word.

We have already seen that *wit* in the abstract is alternately opposed to judgement and identified with it :

> *Some, to whom Heav'n in wit has been profuse,*
> *Want as much more, to turn it to its use ;*
> *For wit and judgement often are at strife,*
> *Though meant each other's aid, like man and wife.* (84)

Warburton makes an amusing attempt to clear this up ; but he had little right to be surprised, because the process of alternately identifying and separating a key pair of opposites is a fundamental one for the style.

> " Here the poet (in a sense he was not, at first, aware of) has given us an example of the truth of his observation, in the observation itself . . . In the first line, Wit is used, in the modern sense, for the effort of Fancy ; in the second it is used, in the ancient sense, for the result of Judgement. This trick, played on the reader, he endeavoured to keep out of sight . . . (by making a trivial change in the second line) . . . The truth is, the Poet had said a lively thing, and would, at all hazards, preserve the reputation of it, though the very topic he is on obliged him to detect the imposition ; in the very next lines, which show he meant two very different things, by the same term, in the two preceding."

Man and wife are allowed the same surname ; in the same way, Pope had every right to choose a term covering both his allied ideas and allowing a generalisation to be expressed about them together ; and it was graceful to choose an unassuming one. The writer unwilling to face the labours of correction is to be exhorted to do so, and the best exhortation is to tell him that this is only another part of the straightforward (the humanly vain) impulse to display his wit. This was the main use of identifying the poet and the critic, creation and polish, in the one key term ; and indeed Blake himself, with his hundreds of corrections in the poems dictated to him by the Holy Spirit, could hardly deny that inspiration and revision are part of the same process. Pope, I think, in making *wit* his general term, felt not only that it was persuasive to adopt the tone of polite society but that he was working against " the very thing that gives modern Criticism its character ; whose whole complexion is *abuse* and *censure* ". The good humour of the thing was meant to exhort the reader against pettiness. Here, I suppose, as so often, his method betrayed him, and the effect of the identity was rather the other way.

> *True Wit is Nature to advantage dressed,*
> *What oft was thought, but ne'er so well expressed ;*
> *Something, whose truth convinced at sight we find,*
> *That gives us back the image of our mind.* (300)

" True " is of course an invocation to the god in the machine of the term " wit ". It may be Imagination " + " or simply " wit that tells truth " " b ", perhaps only in personal satire " a ", which would reduce wit to jokes " —". *The image of our mind* is chiefly what we had already felt about the matter in hand, from our previous experience of it ; but it may also be something in the structure of the mind itself, not corresponding to anything in the outer world, a taste for myths for example (that is, " true " can mean truly beautiful, true to the facts of æsthetics), and this would let us approve of any degree of unreality in the wit. Pope clearly means to praise some kind of truth, but the usual drag towards the drawing-room has a powerful effect here. I think that the strongest resultant meaning is to impute a queer sort of democracy to the work of the gentleman poet ; the essential fact about a true, as apart from a vain, wit is that he is not a bore.

Dr. Johnson, from whom sympathy might have been expected, thought the definition both false and foolish ; novelty was not as unwelcome as all that ; such an account of wit " depresses it below its natural dignity, and reduces it from strength of thought to happiness of language ". This interpretation I think simply followed from having less respect for polite drawing-rooms. For a really solemn treatment of the couplet we must go to Warburton, whose note on it makes a bold attempt to keep Locke at bay and decides that it really means to recommend Optimism, or flattery towards Nature.

> " Mr. Locke had defined *Wit* to consist in ' the assemblage of ideas, and putting those together, with quickness and variety, wherein can be found any resemblance or congruity, whereby to make up pleasant pictures and agreeable visions in the fancy.' But the great Philosopher, in separating *Wit* from *Judgement*, as he does here, has given us (and he could therefore give us no other) only an account of Wit in general ; in which false Wit, though not every species of it, is included. A *striking Image* of Nature, is therefore, as Mr. Locke observes, certainly *Wit;* but this image may strike on several other accounts, as well as for its *truth* and *beauty ;* and the Philosopher has explained the manner how. But it never becomes that Wit which is the ornament of true Poesy, whose end is to represent Nature, but when it *dresses that Nature to advantage*, and presents us to her in the brightest and most amiable light."

This interpretation would not have occurred to me, but it is adopted by Mr. Churton Collins, and certainly helps to illustrate the rich confusion of these apparently simple couplets. However the main purpose of Warburton's note is to claim that the opposites have been reconciled : " whenever *Wit* corresponds with *Judgement*, we may be sure that it is *true*."

It seemed worth looking at this old puzzle because it serves to show what irrelevant problems arise if you do not interpret the poem in the light of its social tone, and this is largely a matter of getting the right play out of *wit*. I hope this view will not be taken to imply that all the uses of the word are facetious or contemptuous. Neither of these two last examples were so intended, and many uses are intended definitely the other way, to provide an escape from the harshness of the criteria that Pope was laying down.

> *As men of breeding, sometimes men of wit,*
> *To avoid great errors, must the less commit ;*
> *Neglect the rules each verbal Critic lays,*
> *For not to know some trifles, is a praise.* (262)

The tenderness of Pope towards a real poet has something touching about it; he feels that such a person is sure to need protection, and adopts rather the same tone towards him as towards young ladies. The real gentleman is expected to be a help in getting him treated decently ; it would I suppose be fussy to separate the wit of Sense " 1 ", the social talker, into two classes only one of which has " breeding ", but the distinction is fairly well marked. Incidentally it is clear here that the antitheses are not meant to be exclusive ; the first line opposes gentlemen to writers, but Pope certainly did not intend to say that a writer cannot be a gentleman ; the terms name functions of the complete man rather than types, and even the functions are called similar. The only way to make the head meaning " 1 " appear as predicate inside *wit*, in this example, is to distinguish the polite man from the joker, but even if you regard the man of breeding as one who makes jokes tactfully the head meaning " 1 " is still prominently in view.

What is perhaps the finest line about *wit* brings in " generous ", a crucial word for Pope though not a frequent one.

> *A perfect Judge will read each work of Wit*
> *With the same spirit that its author writ ;*
> *Survey the WHOLE, nor seek small faults to find*
> *Where Nature moves, and rapture warms the mind ;*
> *Nor lose, for that malignant dull delight,*
> *The generous pleasure to be charmed with Wit.* (238)

How are we to get away from Horace and " Fools admire, but men of sense approve " ? Can we sometimes forgive authors who do not copy Homer exactly? This background of stupid and frightened nagging, I think, gives the last couplet great power. It is generous, that is, indulgent and forgiving, of a superior critic to put up with mere " wit " ; what he likes is Homer. Also in a way it is noble (generous as well-born) to enjoy calmly what is available ; the best in this kind are but shadows, as a Duke said of Bottom. Only as a third alternative does the dangerous idea poke up ; that no one but the broad, unspecialised and in a way careless person (the well-born soul) can recognise a new development of the imagination even when it is thrust under his nose, and that even he only does it by rejoicing. The whole world of the Rules and the " slight faults " is dwarfed and trampled upon, and the bad rhyme is meant as a brave illustration of the virtues of carelessness which are being praised. *Generous* indeed still meant " brave " (a dictionary of 1623 actually defines it as " valiant, noble "); but the modern use of the word carries the point sufficiently strongly. There is again a certain tenderness towards the reader who is capable of doing this ; it is really very good of him, because he is sure to make a fool of himself quite often. What kind of wit he is admiring cannot be known beforehand, and the pathos of the inadequacy of man still hangs over the whole topic.

The feeling that there is something unpleasant about the whole business of being a poet was expressed by Pope with great dignity in his prefaces, and it is this touch of self-pity which gives the more human side of his incessant play on the word. There is a fine paragraph on the unpleasing fate of genius which seems to reach beyond the stock comparison to the joker and suggest rather the romantic view of the clown. (The passage about the patriarch-wits is a preparation for it).

> *Unhappy wit, like most mistaken things,*
> *Atones not for that envy which it brings.*
> *In youth alone its empty praise we boast,*
> *But soon the short-lived vanity is lost. . . .*
> *What is this Wit, which must our cares employ ?*
> *The owner's wife, that other men enjoy ;*
> *Then most our trouble still when most admired,*
> *And still the more we give, the more required ; . . .*
> *Tis what the vicious fear, the virtuous shun,*
> *By fools tis hated, and by knaves undone !* (494-507)

Wit appears essentially mistaken in this passage, even the good kind of wit which *the vicious fear,* and the reason must be that all worldly labours are mistaken by comparison to an assault on Heaven. This over-riding religious sentiment allows of a high view of wit (and Pope is using the first person) but even here a lower view is allowed to be a natural one ; why otherwise do the virtuous shun it ? The poet-outcast idea is no less strong in Pope than in Byron ; he must expect to be despised because of his merits, so if he is to use the language of the world he must at least pretend to despise himself. The idea that the young lyrical poet always arouses hatred seems to be made more plausible by dissolving it into the idea of the satirical " wit " who goads the mob ; but even this figure seems to enjoy his duty only so far as he remains childish, a Shakespearean fool perhaps. " Yet then did Gildon draw his venal quill " in the early days of Pope's *Pastorals* " when pure description took the place of sense " ; no doubt Pope would have denied that this opposition is a real one.

As the appeal goes on (it is the heart of the poem) the wit is urged to distinguish himself from the clown by behaving with good-nature ; as usual, the terms put into an antithesis are thereby made to overlap.

> *And while self-love each jealous writer rules,*
> *Contending wits become the sport of fools :* (517)

Their vanity is the chief reason why they deserve the slang term *wit ;* but if so, after all, it may well apply to many learned and profound thinkers. The next paragraph indeed recognises that Pope is urging the impossible, and the writer is asked at any rate to make his clownishness respectable by venting his spleen upon vice or blasphemy. In the Restoration period this was not done :

> *Jilts ruled the state, and statesmen farces writ ;*
> *Nay wits had pensions, and young Lords had wit :*
> *The Fair sat panting at a Courtier's play,*
> *And not a Mask went unimproved away.* (541)

We are back in the normal double attitude. It would seem a good thing that the dashing aristocrat under the Restoration set out to write verse and often did it well ; Pope can admit this without losing his tone of contempt, because the type of wit in view may be a merely social one, and besides, the lords of his own day are despised for not showing it. The government of his own day is despised for not giving pensions. The wit in need of a pension he could also despise for not being a lord ; so that the line gives him a full superiority all round.

> *Encouraged thus, Wit's Titans braved the skies,*
> *And the press groaned with licensed blasphemies.* (552)

It may be either *wits* or *Titans* who are ridiculously inadequate for this purpose ; *wit* may also have its gods, genuine good writers who are at home in the skies. There is again a touch of " $4 - = 4 +$ ", the ominous idea that the lowest is an exact parallel of the highest. Yet it is clear that the same machinery would allow him to despise any writer who deviated into infidelity ; already a wit, such a man would automatically become a comic kind of wit.

It is difficult to analyse this satirist without satirising him, but to say that his tricks were often used unfairly does not go very far. The contradictions of his self-contempt and self-justification are erected into a solid and intelligent humility before the triumphs and social usefulness possible to his art. And it is the same evasively contemptuous use of his formula which saves him from the abject reverence for rules and ancients of which he is commonly accused. The statements against the rules are, after all, very resounding :

> *We cannot blame indeed—but we may sleep* (242)

And in a later poem

> *Reason raise o'er instinct as you can*
> *In this tis God directs, in that tis man.*

He is always ready with his contempt for those who accept the rules he identifies himself with :

> *The rules a nation, born to serve, obeys ;*
> *And Boileau still in right of Horace sways.*
> *But we, brave Britons, foreign laws despised,*
> *And kept unconquered, and uncivilised ;* (716)

The " critic-learning " of the French does not seem to be called mistaken ; there is only a possibility that Boileau's claim to be heir of Horace might be wrong. But while Pope despises the English for breaking the rules he contrives still more firmly to despise the French for keeping them. The only final question about Pope, I think, since you cannot think him wrong after a full analysis of his meaning, is as to the quality of the contempt through whose action his meaning is imposed ; whether you find this a nasty little view of human affairs or a nobly stern one.

However I ought not to talk as if there was only one correct way of reading Pope, which required you to keep the author well in the foreground. It seems arguable that there are three ways of taking the text. In the first the words are merely English and not governed by any sense of what the style wants—you are feeling your way about to see what the point of it all is, and many of the effects won't come off. In the second the author (I think) has to seem prominent as poking his meaning at you, and you feel that various words have Moods in them. But no doubt there can be a third, in which the style to which you have become accustomed is viewed as a sort of dialect with its own rules and structure of meanings, and the author partly fades out. The Moods such as the one in *wit* can then be regarded as a couple of contrasted Emotions, a mixture of delight and contempt or what not ; and maybe this is the best way to read it. But I do not think that this refinement of the theory makes much difference, because in any case this couple of contrasted emotions needs to be put in by a Mood (so far as I can see). However much you ignore the Mood later, it is the main thing to get hold of in considering how the trick is made to work.

II.

We ought also to look at *sense* in the poem, for comparison. There are I think only 22 uses of it, and few of these make a direct opposition to *wit*; however some of course do :

> *In search of wit these lose their common sense* . . .　(28)
> *To teach vain Wits a science little known,*
> *T'admire superior sense, and doubt their own.*　(200)

On at least one occasion they are in effect treated as parallel :

> *Pride, where wit fails, steps in to our defence,*
> *And fills up all the mighty Void of sense.*　(210)

There seem to be no uses of the two together in which *sense* is belittled, but the possibility is envisaged :

> *Launch not beyond your depth, but be discreet*
> *And mark that point where sense and dullness meet.*　(51)

However in general *sense* is the more holy or deeply respected term of the two, though *wit* has grander claims.

Many of the uses of course merely refer to the " prose meaning " of the passage in question, e.g. :

> *The sound must seem an Echo to the sense*　(365)

But even these uses imply that *sense* is necessary to a good poem, and this is extended till the *sense* becomes in effect the imaginative material that a man had to work upon :

> [bad poets] *in a raging vein,*
> *Even to the dregs and squeezings of the brain,*
> *Strain out the last dull droppings of their sense,*
> *And rhyme with all the rage of Impotence.*　(609)

In a less negative context this would be not far from Wordsworth's *sense*. Pope also, I think, tried to get into the word the idea of the good humour of a reasonable man, which made it play an important part in the general outlook he thought he was recommending :

> *Nor in the Critic let the Man be lost.*
> *Good-nature and good-sense must ever join ;*
> *To err is human, to forgive, divine.*　(525)

No doubt this was opposed to the grim classical doctrine he inherited :

> *For fools admire, but men of sense approve :*　(391)

but then so were a good many of his other feelings.

I do not mean to make out that *sense* has a wide range here ; its importance is rather to provide a steady base note in contrast to the high gyrations of *wit*. That word treats genius with a certain playfulness out of deference to the democracy of the drawing-room ; but such a view could only be made plausible if the drawing-room were assumed to have a high standard. The whole strategy of Pope therefore makes large demands on the " common sense " which is to become adequate to the task of criticism.

Nature is another obvious candidate for analysis, but I think Nature here is simply everything, however diverse, that is outside wit, a source of wit as well as in various ways a contrast to it. No doubt latent philosophical ideas could be brought to light by examining both words, and I shall try to do it for *sense* later in this book ; but it seems clear that neither word is used in the poem, as *wit* is, for elaborate byplay.

Chapter 4

ALL IN PARADISE LOST

THE tricks in Pope are I think very clear-cut and perhaps suit my little machine rather too well ; they are liable to suggest a false generalisation. They had best be followed, if only for a brief interlude, by a case at the other extreme ; where, so far from being able to chart a structure of related meanings in a key word, you get an obviously important word for which an Emotive theory seems about all that you can hold.

The word *all* in *Paradise Lost* seems to me a striking example. My count gives 612 uses of the word in the poem, or about once every seventeen lines (almost the same as *wit* in the *Essay*). There are long patches, for example the Creation, where it is hardly used at all, and contrasting passages where it is repeated obtrusively (e.g., God's speech on Christ's sacrifice, iii.318-43 ; Adam's lamentation, x.817-850, where the sudden reappearance of the word marks the onset of repentance). At times it seems wilfully dragged in to give a passage weight (e.g., the repentant Eve " with tresses all disordered " x.11, and the departure from Paradise " They, looking back, all the eastern side beheld " xii.641) ; and in general, if I may merely assert what seems to me the main point, the word is a prominent feature of the style, with a set of tricks of its own—a Wagnerian *motif*—you could hardly parody Milton without bringing it in.

To be sure, its prominence in *Paradise Lost* is not surprising ; the poem is about all time, all space, all men, all angels, and the justification of the Almighty. But Milton was already using it in his typical way in *Comus*. It seems to be suited to his temperament because he is an absolutist, an all-or-none man. All else is unimportant beside one thing, he is continually deciding ; he delights in the harshness of a theme which makes all human history turn on an absolutely trivial action. The generosity of the proud man also requires the word ; when he gives he gives all. It is as suited to absolute love and self-sacrifice as to insane self-assertion. The self-centred man, in his turn, is not much interested in the variety of the world, and readily lumps it together as " all ". (Shakespeare has something like the Miltonic use only for proud and rigid characters like Coriolanus and Cordelia—" sure, I shall never marry like my sisters, to love my father all "). In a stylist, the word presumes economy of means ; it raises the thing in hand absolutely without needing to list all the others. The sound rolls the tongue from back low (the inner man) to front high (throwing him out and upward), and the vowel is the " organ " note for which Milton is praised, or the Virgilian moan at the sorrow inherent in the whole story. Thus the word has a good many connections with the whole theme of the poem, though its meaning remains very simple.

The argument here seems to me a difficult one to present, because a cumulative effect can only be suggested by examples, and yet to give even a representative selection of six hundred odd examples would become intolerably tedious. I think I can assume however that the cumulative effect is already known to anyone who has a feeling for the style ; one can almost say that Milton uses *all* whenever there is any serious emotional pressure. The puzzling question comes after admitting this : to what extent do the different uses enrich each other ; do they all, when you are at home in the style, get coloured by one key sentiment or covert assertion ? Now the main occasions for using the word can be classed under the following Emotions : Combativeness (claiming all, arguing all else away, etc.) pride (ruling all, disdaining all, etc.) love (offering all, disvaluing all but . . .) and self-sacrifice (standing as representative of all, giving up all for them). I think that equations may be drawn between any two of these, with the effect of defining a Miltonic type of character ; the kind of man who would feel in a wholehearted way that any one of these feelings entails any other is also the kind of man the style as a whole presents. But I think we can only connect the different uses in this vague and distant way ; certainly there is no variety of Senses in the word, which in itself is merely a logical connective.

That the word does not actually collect meanings is clear I think from the way the assonances work ; the emotion can be echoed into other words with the same sound. For example God's speech on Christ's sacrifice works up to a blaze of " all "s, but the best pair of lines in it (where a breath of Christianity seems to creep in for once) echo the sound only :

> *Therefore thy humiliation shall exalt*
> *With thee thy manhood also to this throne* (iii.314)

In the same way, I think, for one of the most echoing bits of pathos about the nuptial bed of Eden, Milton is drawing on the vowel for part of the resonance of a feeling he must not express more plainly :

> *In shadier bower*
> *More sacred and sequestered, though but feigned,*
> *Pan or Sylvanus never slept, nor Nymph*
> *Nor Faunus haunted.* (iv.708)

There is a strong *all* carrying the same moan in the next sentence.

Speculation along these lines is I suppose pretty useless, but I think an extra weight comes into the word because it is part of *Fall*; at one point indeed Milton spells out this delayed pun quite plainly.

> *Forsaken of all good, I see thy fall!*   (v.878)

On this hint I looked through the poem for cases where a stressed F comes one or two stresses before a stressed *all*, and found over 80 of them, though I rejected a number of possible claimants and of course did not count the V of the recurring *of all*. Maybe the frequency of F is high enough to make this a probable random distribution, but I should not have thought so, and many of the cases once noticed seem fairly pointed. Of course, a sound effect on this sort depends on the meaning, and reinforces it; but this kind of process seems very distinct from that of putting an equation into a key word.

On the other hand, one might reasonably claim that the suggestions of the recurring *all* do lead to poetic ambiguity*, and indeed are part of a profound ambiguity which gives the poem its whole dramatic strength. *All* is useful to Milton because of its very obscurity; it provides confusion only at the deep level where it is required. (One might suspect indeed that all " classical " styles work like this; they contrive to strip the words of apparent ambiguity by imposing instead some distant emotive contrast on them. But what Milton is really up to is so very *un*-classical that it is not likely to illuminate the normal case). I discussed the most plausible example of this effect in *Versions of Pastoral ;* Satan gloats over the harm he will do our parents, and then says :

> *Hell shall unfold,*
> *To entertain you two, her widest gates,*
> *And send forth all her kings ;*   (iv.383)

I said that Milton only uses *all* for " a wholesale and unquestioned emotion ", which is not true ; e.g., Satan when disguised as a good angel (iii.655) gets a cosy piety into his speech chiefly by packing it with *all*'s. But it is somehow very difficult to read *all her kings* here as anything but heroic generosity ; and of course how you read it makes a considerable difference to your view of Satan as a whole.

---

*By the way, the term Ambiguity, which I used in a book title and as a kind of slogan, implying that the reader is left in doubt between two readings, is more or less superseded by the idea of a double meaning which is intended to be fitted into a definite structure. You can still have a doubt as the whether one or other of two structures is meant but this is much less common and belongs rather to peculiar states of dramatic self-conflict. However the term still seems to me the natural one to use as long as a reader is uncertain, and the peculiar mixed feelings of Milton about his subject are I think certainly Ambiguous as the term is ordinarily used.

I take it that Milton, while certainly not condoning either Fall, in Heaven or earth, knew that he was piling up the case in favour of Satan and our parents as strongly as he could ; the fierceness of the thing, as he might have boasted, was that apparently justifiable sins were what produced these enormous consequences. That his feelings were crying out against his appalling theology in favour of freedom, happiness and the pursuit of truth was I think not obvious to him, and it is this part of the dramatic complex which is thrust upon us by the repeated *all*.

The question I want to raise is how far an exegesis of literary effects can go in terms of equations between connected meanings in single words, and how far we have to fall back on an Emotive linguistic theory instead. If this case is a fair sample, it looks as if one could say that the real contrast is between the different depths of unconsciousness which are being tapped. One could draw up equations for the effect of *all* in Milton, relating not so much senses of the word as whole contexts in which it has become habitual. But they would no longer be tracing a clear-cut, even if sub-conscious, mental operation, like those which let us talk straight ahead and get the grammar in order ; they would be concerned with something more like a Freudian symbol. Even so, I think the critic would still be dealing with verbal effects to which a " purely emotive " linguistic theory could not be applied. Of course I do not mean to deny that a reader can best absorb them by accepting and trusting his own emotions as he reads.

The next major example I want to consider is the Shakespearean use of *fool*, and here as in Milton's *all* there is no great need to fuss about puns. Apart from definite jokes the word excites no puzzles ; it carries with it wherever it goes its own aura of suggestion, which might well be called chiefly an Emotive one. But this does not prevent us, if we set out to understand the aura, from writing down a definite and I think illuminating set of equations between the senses of the word.

As to the recurrent controversy over the poem, my view is that the poem gets its great merit from presenting the real ambiguity of its theme with such dramatic and insinuating power. Critics keep on finding minor inconsistencies in the story and using them to belittle Milton, but I think very few of these are mere muddles ; they fit in with the major inconsistencies, which affect me as presenting a real and profound mystery. The attitude sketched by Blake in an epigram seems nowadays to be thought romantic and therefore bad, but the more you examine the poem, I think, the more you find it going to the heart of the matter (not only about Satan). Certainly it is hard to know what Milton thought he was doing, but I take it the man was so intensely self-assured that he hardly criticised his work—it had only to suit his feelings.

Chapter 5

THE PRAISE OF FOLLY

WITH Pope's *wit*, it seems to me, the performance of covert assertion is very definitely " in " the word ; a general background of ideas is implied by little tricks with the word, recognisable as such. I want now to consider the Elizabethan (and medieval) ideas about fools, and in the first place it must be clear that this very rich background, of philosophical as well as humorous thought, is much less dependent on a single word than were the social attitudes of Pope. Fool meant both " natural " and jester, but you could very well express the combination without it ; in fact it seems to have been more usual in the time of Henry VIII to talk about " Will Sommers, the king's natural jester " than about his " fool ". Even Shakespeare, who I think put a great weight of meaning onto the word even in some apparently casual uses, can call up the whole range of ideas without it :

> *for within the hollow crown*
> *That rounds the mortal temples of a king*
> *Keeps Death his court, and there the Antic sits*
> *Scoffing his state, and grinning at his pomp.*
>
> (Rich. II. iii.2.160)

In any case, the group of ideas in question is very ancient and widespread, and clearly did not depend on having a single word to express it. Furthermore, when we do try to express the ideas in terms of equations between senses of the word *fool*, it seems likely that two distinct sets of equations are required. *King Lear* and *The Changeling* start from the imbecile and the clown, and pile their dark and disturbing symbolism on those actual figures. But Erasmus' *Praise of Folly*, which can be taken as summing up the medieval view about fools, was still widely read in Elizabethan times and had an English translation on the market. (Incidentally it is a likely " source " for the idea that all the world's a stage.) This version does not start from a half-mad clown, or even make much use of such a figure, but from the ordinary simple man, who is held to be somehow right about life though more pretentious figures fail to see it.

Perhaps I had better try to summarise the doctrine of the book before looking for a formula. Erasmus argues that children are liked and admired, and what is it to be a child but to be a fool and an idiot ? Old men are mercifully made fools again, and folly preserves youth ; in women it makes beauty. There is no social peace without folly, for example flattery makes the right "understanding" between prince and people. Can any love another that first hates himself ? But without folly he would have to. Only flattery made men, who are naturally savage, unite into civil societies. Vainglory has caused the sciences. If wisdom, as must be confessed, is no more than a readiness of doing good and an expedite method of being serviceable in the world, to whom does this virtue more properly belong ? The wise man is modest and cowardly, the fool tries. Why should it be thought any scandal to be a fool, since the being one is part of our nature and essence ? Creatures living by instinct (owing to the providence of God) need nothing to complete their happiness. Fools are good company and can tell truth even to kings, which they need. Horace welcomes frenzy, and Plato ranks the madness of poets, of prophets and of lovers among those properties which conduce to a happy life. There are two madnesses, one leading to crime, the other when " by a harmless mistake in the nature of things the mind is freed from those cares which would otherwise greatly afflict it ". Madmen are happy laughing at one another, and fools make sport for the whole company. Flattery makes every man fond and indulgent of himself, which indeed is no small part of each man's happiness, and at the same time renders him obliging and complaisant in company, where it is pleasant to see how the asses rub and scratch one another. So among the saints, those are the most resorted to which are the most romantic and fabulous. Christ had the wisdom of the Father but partook of human folly, used ignorant apostles and told them to be like children or things devoid of reason. Monks esteem the first step to happiness a profound ignorance, and think carnal knowledge a great enemy to their spiritual welfare. Christ will receive those concerned about the details of righteousness only as scribes and pharisees. Ecclesiastes says that in much wisdom is much grief. St. Paul said " if any man speak as a fool, I more ". God has chosen the foolish things ; the lamb is foolish. The final happiness of Christians is an ecstasy, a sort of folly and madness.

The skit of course refuses to explain itself, claiming that :

" it would be equally hazardous to attempt the crowding together into narrow limits of a definition, whose nature is of so diffusive an extent, or to mangle and disjoin that, to the adoration of which all nations unitedly concur."

In effect it gives a series of paradoxes about a variety of types (simpletons, children, madmen of various sorts, saints) and leaves it to be guessed why the key word of the title should bring them together. But it is the relations between the Senses of the word referring to these types which ought to supply us with our equations. We could indeed say that the simpleton is innocent and natural ; this sums up most of the conception, and both words provide us with puns ; but the puns are merely repetitions of those in the key word. Also this summary leaves out an important part of its functions. Miss Welsford in her treatise on The Fool says :

"The first thing to be remembered is that the words ' fool ' and ' knave ' were constantly coupled together, but not always in quite the same way ; for sometimes they were treated as synonyms, sometimes emphasis was laid on the distinction between them."

Not always in *quite* the same way ; either as synonyms or as opposites. This curious truth is I think a general rule when two words are erected into a stock antithesis, because at least one of them will try to cover the whole field ; the same thing happens with wit v. judgement and the honest man v. the rogue. "Knave" here is the Biblical fool who says in his heart " There is no God ". The strength of the opposition, Miss Welsford goes on, was that it allowed of play between different conceptions of life :

"To religious moralists . . . a knave was simply a fool regarded ' sub specie eternitatis ', for he was neglecting his true, ultimate self-interest, and what could be more ridiculous than that ? The fool was therefore the actually worthless character that lurked beneath the veneer of wealth, learning and respectability. On the other hand the fool-societies were founded on the idea of the court-jester as the ' sage-fool ' who could see and speak the truth with impunity. From this point of view, the fool was the truth-teller whose real insight was thinly disguised as a form of insanity."

There is not merely a doubt about how far the term *fool* extended ; it had a commanding position at both ends of a scale. Furthermore it provided a means of escape from the conflict which the anti-thesis defined ; all men are fools in the eyes of God, but we are dependent on God and he will allow for it.

Thus the medieval picture took as its type of the fool Everyman in the presence of God ; his position was illuminated by comparisons to different kinds of folly, and assertions may be attached rather obscurely to the connections between them. All the elements of meaning appear again in Shakespeare, but the interest is now not in Everyman but in the dramatic figures of the clown and the lunatic. I cannot see, in particular, that Shakespeare makes any serious use of the idea that God will forgive us all because we are all fools, which was the crown of the structure of medieval fool-theory. Yet it seems clear that this line of feeling, as a whole, is recalled fairly often in the course of his play with the word.

In both versions it is a major activity of the Fool to make a fool of other people, so that this word gives a particularly strong case for

the surprising form " ? ", the return of the meaning of the word
upon the speaker. Everyman displays by contrast the folly of the
wise, and the clown jeers at his betters ; the contradictions that
appear in the doctrine were felt to be a gain, not an obstruction,
because they brought out this feeling of mutuality : " I call you a
fool of one sort speaking as myself a fool of another sort ". Indeed
on the theory of Socrates, that the fool is he who does not know that
he is a fool, any direct use of the word inherently recoils and it
can never help being mutual. Evidence for the complete obvious-
ness to the Elizabethans of this movement of thought is provided by
Jack of Dover's Quest of Inquiry, a collection of heavy jokes supposed
older than the surviving copy of 1604 ; here the mutual joke is
used in the first and last paragraphs as a sort of frame.

> " When merry Jack of Dover had made his privy search for the
> Fool of all fools, and making his inquiry in most of the principal
> places in England, at his return home was adjudged to be the fool
> himself ; but now, wearied with the motley coxcomb, he hath
> undertaken in some place or other to find out a verier fool than
> himself. But first of all . . . there came in a whole jury of penniless
> poets who being fellows of a merry disposition (but as necessary
> in a commonwealth as a candle in a straw bed) he accepted of
> their company ; and as from poets cometh all kinds of foolery, so
> he hoped by their directions to find out this Fool of Fools he was
> looking for."

Each story of the Fool of Somewhere then ends with the ritual form—

> " Well quoth Jack of Dover this in my mind was pretty foolery
> but yet the fool of all fools is not here found, that I look for."

Some fools are dupes some mockers some simpleminded, and there
is a castration of an amorous doctor after which the set form sounds
even more Biblical than usual. Somewhat rumblingly, but now
against the wits not the clown, the joke of the beginning is at last
smacked out at the end.

> " Well (quoth one of the jury) if we cannot find the fool we
> look for amongst these fools before named one of us will be the
> fool, for in my mind there cannot be a verier fool in the world
> than is a poet ; for poets have good wits but cannot use them,
> great store of money but cannot keep it, and many friends till
> they lose them, therefore we think fit to have a parliament of
> poets and to enact such laws and statutes as may prove beneficial
> to the commonwealth of Jack of Dover's motley coated fools."

There is a flavour about this, but no one would take it for a very
original piece of work, and it trots through the whole paradigm of
fool.

This kind of use for the word is by no means dead, but since
fool has now a much stronger suggestion of insult such a use of it is
kept for impressive occasions. The " youths " of Punch in my

first chapter would avoid saying *fool* in their mutual accusations of folly, so long as they were merely being facetious. But when M. Hackin discovered what are among the earliest surviving Buddhist statues in the caves of Bamiyan in Afghanistan, at the head of an officially recognised expedition organised like a small army, the occasion was an impressive one, and he found a couplet in English scrawled on one of the more inaccessible of their walls.

> *If any fool this high samootch explore*
> *Know that Charles Masson has been here before.*

This was a deserter from the British Army in India, early in the nineteenth century ; he gives the assumed name under which he wandered across Asia and eventually published an important travel book. There is a Kipling quality about the incident. The claim of the couplet is that he was a fool ; he does not want it forgotten ; the assonance of *fool* with *samootch* (cave temple) makes this a remote wild kind of fool to which the adjective *high* can be extended : " Great men do hard things, and the greatest know that it is foolish to do them. Only we, in the secrecy of this place, can rightly say that we are fools." No doubt he suspected he was a worse fool than that, and felt the horror of his isolation, but the grand echoes of *fool* were what made it satisfying. This gives the two main points about the hearty use of " fool " ; it is mutual, and it claims an escape into some broader way of judgement or larger air.

There is another Elizabethan figure who produces this effect of mutuality, though it is a much less verbal matter : the Revenger. His revenge will make more revengers, so that the blood-feud goes on ; the final holocaust which makes so many Elizabethan plays too absurd to revive was meant to show his power to drag everyone to his own way of feeling. It is this apparently far-fetched connection, I think, which puts so much weight onto the fooling of Hamlet, in itself an obscure threat of revenge. King Lear on the other hand threatens revenge noisily and pathetically but can only achieve folly. The supreme example of the connection is Iago, who must be treated separately. I do not mean that the mutual effect gives the chief thread of connection. Thinking in terms of stock theatrical types, the carping critic who supplies jokes against the other characters, as the clown does, can also be used in the plot as a revenger, because the key idea of the Malcontent who is somehow not part of human society includes both.

The derivation of *fool* is through a Latin word for " bellows ", late Latin " windbag ", and though this is not a Sense of the word the fool always talks ; " he was scant of news that told his father was hanged ". (" The fool also multiplieth words ". Ecc. x.12.) The stern contempt of the Biblical version of the word seems to grow on it with the rise of the Puritans ; the N.E.D. remarks :

> " The word has in modern English a much stronger sense than it had at any earlier period ; it has now an implication of insulting contempt which does not in the same degree belong to any of its earlier synonyms, or to the derivative *foolish*."

No doubt one reason for this is that the peculiar English form " ish " may imply " of moderate degree " (greenish) ; and perhaps the word was simply needed in its narrower form because there was a better supply of nouns than of adjectives to deal with the case of a moderate degree ; but I should fancy another reason is that a noun calls up an idea of metaphor more easily than an adjective, and that this was where the rudeness came from. *Folly*, the noun for the behaviour of a fool, gets an early implication " pleasure (probably sin) " ; the N.E.D. gives 1303 as its first date for the sense " Lewdness ", and Coverdale's version " because he hath committed folly in Israel " (Josh. vii.15) was retained in the Authorised text though with " wickedness " in the margin. However this allowed of an opposed feeling that the fool got more pleasure out of life than the virtuous, so was positively more sensible ; to commit follies was never to be the imbecile; and Dr. Johnson could nobly insist that " Thy love of folly, and thy scorn of fools " was high praise. The modern use of *fool* I think gets its power from a suggestion of nausea, which is a new stock reaction to the presence of a lunatic (not even an eighteenth century reaction). The first use of the word that feels like it comes perhaps in the *Tale of a Tub*, when Swift defined happiness as " a perpetual possession of being well deceived, the serene peaceful state of being a fool among knaves ". Yet the whole horror of his style was required to fix such an Emotion in the word here, because in itself the sentence could carry the amiable complex of Erasmus. Indeed I once gave this passage to a Chinese class to " spot the period ", and a student wrote that he had not supposed this good-humoured paradox to be European at all ; it was more likely to be a translation from some oriental philosopher. I feel sure therefore that one is asking a real question in asking how Swift managed to make the word act as it does here. And I should think that the fundamental answer, though it is a remote one from the point of view of analysing the style, is that he felt for personal reasons all our present day revulsion from lunacy. No doubt the modern world has in any case wholly rejected the Erasmus point of view,* but I think that the metaphor from the lunatic, though it has gone out of sight, is still working powerfully underground. This helps to give us the right

---

* Except for Dickens ; this I should think is why Dickens' line of sentiment often seems positively shocking nowadays.

impact from the language of *King Lear*, though in rather a different way from what was intended.

The main elements of meaning required to explain the performance of the word can I think be listed as follows :

1 person who is   *a.* stupid
                b. simpleminded
                c. lacking " common sense."

These belong together from the thirteenth century, but a clown may be felt to show common sense in his jokes though he is simpleminded, so we need to separate them.

1/1 mocked (early)
1/2 brash, ready to talk (derivation)
1/3 innocent, inexperienced
1/4 childish
1/5 duped (made a fool of) (1440)
1/6 loved and pitied as dependent (1503 ?)

2 clown, professional jester and mocker (with 1/1) (1370)
3 knave, obstinately and viciously stupid person (Biblical)
4 weakminded or idiotic person (1540).

The Erasmus group of feelings starts from the simpleminded person and sets out to praise him, perhaps chiefly because he is innocent but more generally because he has not been put wrong about life in the way that the sophisticated people have. This of course requires an elaborate play of paradox from the context, and the effect is that one Implication can be equated with another. I do not think that this process can make the head sense appear as predicate ; it is the " thing meant " to which the various Implications are attached ; what happens is that you are made to observe the surprising effect of attaching two of them at once. For the Erasmus group of feelings the Biblical fool " 3 " is merely one of these Implications (one of the sorts of person who follow their natural impulses in a simpleminded manner) ; I write it as a Sense because I think the definiteness of the uses in the translations of the Bible made it come to be felt as one later.

It may seem particularly absurd to play about with the English word to deal with the thought of Erasmus, who wrote in Latin (for that matter classical rather than medieval Latin) and probably never thought in English at all. If he could do it all in a " dead " language, where he was not allowed to shift the senses of the words, that may seem enough to prove that the shifts of the English word were not important. I could reply that I am only concerned to show the influence of his thought on the later uses of the English *fool ;* but the more important point is that the equations come to

very little. We can of course extract an idea such as " $1/4=1/3$ "
" the child is innocent ", and I think the two main paradoxes can
be written as doublets ;

$1/3=1/1$ The innocent are mocked (by the world).

$3=1/1$ Knaves are mocked (at Judgement Day).

$1b=1/2$ The simpleminded are ready to talk (they flatter).

$1/3=1/2$ The innocent are ready to talk (they blow the gaff).

As to the more general idea " the simple approach to life is the right
one in the end ", this seems to depend mainly on a repeated denial
of the stock Emotion of contempt " -1! ", expecially through the
mutual " 1? " " I too ". A complexity of feeling of this sort can
be put into classical Latin or any other language with a general
word for *fool*. A direct assertion of one of the equations would
require in effect another assertion of it in the context, but the word
would gradually collect a vague humorous memory that doctrines
of this sort were within call. I do not think that the clown, the
imbecile and the dependent pet need be brought into the main
structure. We do however need to leave room somewhere for the
mystical doctrine about the mercy of God and his indifference to
our worldly judgements, and I imagine this can be present as an
obscure fourth-type equation between " 3 " and " $1/3$ "—the knave
and the innocent may somehow be classed together in God's mind.

The Elizabethan equations, on the other hand, all take as subject
the imbecile or the clown.

$4=3$ One treats imbeciles harshly ; their condition is somehow their fault.

$4=1/6$ One treats them as tame pets.

$4=1$ Come, they are only foolish people

$4=1/1$ We laugh at imbeciles.

$4=2$ They laugh at us, and are critics.

$2=4$ Clowns are mad ; they speak from outside ordinary life.

$2=1/5$ Clowns get hard treatment.

$2=1/6$ The clown is privileged, a tame pet.

$2=1/1$ The clown imposes a situation of mutual mockery.

$2=1b$ He tells the plain truth, which no one else tells.

The difficulty about this list, I think, is that it seems too harsh for
most of Shakespeare, even though the contradictions allow a
moderate version to be chosen. It is the crude Elizabethan view
of a comic lunatic, an object for hearty laughter. But I am not
maintaining that the equations available in a word give the final
impression of a literary work that uses it. In any case, it is notable
that none of the Shakespearean tragic figures who go mad are
called " fool " except Lear, who requires separate treatment.
Hamlet can say with glee about himself " they fool me to the top

of my bent ", but that is a boast ; Emilia seems to call Othello a fool, but he is not primarily a madman. Though it is used so often, I think one could maintain that the word is often avoided when its large background is not required.

The reader may also object that Shakespeare's clowns are not meant to be mad at all ; this is likely enough, but they seem to assume that people will think them mad :

MALVOLIO : *Fool, there was never man so notoriously abused ; I am as well in my wits, fool, as thou art.*

CLOWN : *But as well ? Then you are mad indeed, if you be no better in your wits than a fool.*

Mad here is of course chiefly a strong term for folly or feeble-mindedness, but Malvolio is meditating revenge and the clown is even now taking it, so on that ground the more specific sense of the word would fit them. In general the fool (even the fool as idiot) is opposed to the madman ; they are Cibber's two brazen brothers, the silly and raging types of insanity. But the audience would not seriously deny that they were both insane.

The chief novelty of structure in these equations for *fool* is that we apparently have two head senses, and they are identified with one another both ways round. This is Type IV. It is true I think that a use of the word about a lunatic is always liable to suggest that he can say funny but searching things (like a clown), and that a use about a clown is always liable to suggest that he is half-imbecile. One might suppose that this double type of equation would excite a particularly firm belief in the false identity ; it seems like a necessary and sufficient condition in mathematics. But in fact the speakers are continually distinguishing between them, as in " my fool, that wants but little to be a reasonable man ". Or one might say that they excite the same Emotions, so that a thought of one of them suggests the other. This is obviously not true of the clowns and madmen on the stage. But it is true I think that the types both had a sort of magical aura ; both were outside ordinary society and there-fore in touch with wild forces, or anyway in a position to criticize society as aliens. The double equation structure, I should say, is only possible because this rather peculiar state of feeling treats them as two examples of a general truth, and in this way it can be classed as an effect of Mutual Metaphor. The concept arrived at by treating the whole complex as a sense of the word may be symbolized " 2+4 ", and I think that it never occurs as a predicate. I don't deny that you could use the word about a foolish man and reflect that he was like a clown, but the effect is then that you call him a clown metaphorically.

However it is hard to lay down any definite rule when there are two possible structures ; in the Erasmus structure a clown would be merely one of the examples of the innocent simpleton, and could be attached to him as predicate if the context suggested it. While a word is changing from one head sense to another the effect is rather like " turbulence " in a liquid, to which ordinary wave functions do not apply. The more important question is how the new head sense could get in, if it did. For the ordinary person, what happened was probably only that the new head sense could be established temporarily as part of the " style " of a play, once he had realised how it was going. The clown and the lunatic are then more obvious in the setting (rule one) and more concrete or definite (rule three). But we must also suppose that he had some kind of readiness to adopt this structure, even if only temporarily.

It seems clear that the Elizabethan state of language and feeling gave a writer peculiar opportunities to make full use of this group of ideas, and on the other hand that Shakespeare made much fuller use of them than anybody else. One must not suppose that the ideas were all obvious (because inherent in the words) ; indeed in most of his early comedies Shakespeare goes out of his way to tell the audience what to think of the clown. The most obvious case is in *As You Like It*, where the subject is made part of the play, but one comes to expect small positive statements like " This fellow's wise enough to play the fool, and to do that well requires a kind of wit " (*Twelfth Night* iii.1.67). The conception had to be built up gradually, both in his own mind and for his audience, before he got to the terrific uses of it in *Lear*. On the other hand the clown who bases his effects on " you are a fool too " was certainly not a romantic invention of Shakespeare's. Examples of clowns in difficulties include one of Henry VIII's (Will Summers came later and knew better) who asked for a patent to extract a tax of one egg from any man whose wife was unfaithful, and as soon as the paper was signed demanded one from Henry ; after Shakespeare's time Archie Armstrong could plead the privilege of his coat when arrested for giving the toast " Great honour to God and little Laud to the devil ". Both suffered for it, but then Elizabeth rebuked one of her clowns (appropriately named Clod) for not criticizing her sufficiently sharply. The reason why Shakespeare, to the convenience of later audiences, tended to explain his intentions about the clown may indeed have been that the clown tended to regard himself as a separate turn and criticize the play and the author (the actual part of Will Summers consists of little else in *Summers Last Will*). To make the characters theorize about the clown was to insist that he was part of the play. This may also explain why Shakespeare tends increasingly to say *fool* rather than *clown ;* the stage comedian was called a *clown* but the court clown was called a *fool*, and Shakespeare wanted to insist that he was representing a court fool not letting loose a clown on his stage.

I think we must also say that the state of the language was peculiarly suited for this purpose. According to the N.E.D., something important had happened to the word just before the Elizabethans took it over; the earliest affectionate use for a dependent is dated 1530 and the earliest use for a mere imbecile is 1540. Now the introduction of these two further meanings into the word was necessary to complete it as an instrument; given these extra two, the whole group of ideas could be imposed on the hearer by mere word play; to a far greater extent than at any other time, the very subtle thought of *Lear* was inherent in the language. To be sure, one had better not put too much weight on this kind of argument from the great dictionary, because it can never guarantee that earlier uses did not exist. Indeed it may well be that the collectors looked more carefully at periods in which they knew that something important had happened to the word; and what had happened might well have been the formation of Moods or Equations rather than simple new Senses. But even if this is true they are still recording something important; and whether or not the new meanings were introduced early in the sixteenth century it seems clear that an increased play between the meanings was being developed from then on.

Miss Welsford's treatment, I think, is a little confused in maintaining that the Fool was an essentially medieval conception which happened not to be fully developed till the Renaissance; if the Renaissance Magnificent Man chose to have clowns to remind him of his weakness before God it is no use classifying him as if he didn't. No doubt he felt that his new glory needed something to balance it. Whatever the cause, it is not till well after the destruction of the monasteries that the great families are recorded as keeping fools of their own like rival kings. One could hardly maintain that the development of the word produced the custom, because (for one thing) the custom was partly a matter of accepting a fashion from abroad; Velasquez gives striking evidence of it from Spain. But it is clear that the two developments are parallel.

The sense "imbecile" probably became prominent in the English word because of a new legal procedure under Henry VIII ("de idiota querenda") by which one could petition the court of wards for custody of an idiot (and control of his property) as being his feudal superior or as having interest in the case; "idiots and fools natural" was apparently the official English phrase and the phrase "begging for a fool" was a Shortening. "A natural fool" continued to be the more formal term, but the shortening gave *fool* the new sense alone. The N.E.D. group "Ic" "used as a term of endearment or pity" is harder to estimate or explain.

" How say you now by this, little young fool " (1530) is surely
pretence of jeering, such as people imagine puts a child at ease ;
nowadays people would be more likely to say " little silly " or what
not, because *fool* has got ruder, but it is in any case not a Sense
of the word. The Sidney sonnet, which is next quoted by the
N.E.D., seems to me in rather bad taste :

> *Love still a boy and oft a wanton is . . .*
> > *A sugared kiss*
> *In sport I sucked while she asleep did lie . . .*
> > *She makes her wrath appear*
> *In Beauty's throne ; see now who dares come near*
> *Those scarlet judges, threatening bloody pain ;*
> *O heavenly fool, thy most kissworthy face*
> *Anger invests with such a lovely grace*
> *That anger's self I needs must kiss again.*   (Astrophel, 1586.)

He really does treat her as a good deal of a fool, but maybe there
is meant to be a reminder of Erasmus-doctrine, as the word is
contrasted with superlatives. Some texts read " soul ", which
with the long " s " is easily mistaken for it. And the only other
use given by the N.E.D. under this head, from *The Winter's Tale*,
is by Hermione to her women after she has been accused of adultery ;
it is not playful at all.

> *Good my lords*
> *I am not prone to weeping, as our sex*
> *Commonly are : the want of which vain dew*
> *Perchance shall dry your pities ; but I have*
> *That honourable grief lodged here, which burns*
> *Worse than tears drown . . .*
> > *Beseech your highness*
> *My women may be with me* [in prison] *; for, you see*
> *My state requires it.   Do not weep, good fools,*
> *There is no cause ; when you shall see your mistress*
> *Has deserved prison, then abound in tears* (iii.2.159).

They are only fools from a very elevated point of view, but to
suppose that she merely uses the word as a " term of endearment "
is to underrate the strain and the paradoxical stoicism of the whole
passage. I should deny than that the N.E.D.'s " Ic " ever appears
alone, regarded as a sense of the word, but this is not to deny
that there were various rather complicated uses of the word in
which " Ic " is the main resultant feeling. The main thing one
learns from the existence of such a group of uses in a given period
is that people were using the word a good deal ; it lay near the
tongue, so to speak, even on occasions where it might seem irrelevant.

It would be tedious to give examples of how the equations about the lunatic clown were put into the word, as habitual ideas which might then appear without much help from the context. This of course was done by talking about such a figure and asserting the doctrines about him directly, and I suppose no one would deny that notions of this sort were actually expressed. The structure is built by equations of Type II, as the Erasmus one was, and the chief difference is that the lunatic clown is now assumed to be the head meaning of the word ; or at any rate to be such a distinct meaning that it can collect its own set of Implications. The cases of literary interest come when the word which has been thus enriched is applied to some other character, apparently just to call him foolish, but the head meaning " clown " imposes itself as " what the word really means here " and gives equations of Type III. But there is another confusing factor here. In Shakespeare, when the character in view is actually a clown, he is treated very much as an ordinary person; the portentous doctrine about him only hovers in the background, and though the equations are formally of Type II they may get a remoteness from the individual which makes them rather like those of Type III. This tends to appear as a problem about interpreting his character rather than about interpreting particular passages in the text.

A recent book by S. L. Bethell, *Shakespeare and the Popular Dramatic Tradition*, seems to me to put the point very clearly about Touchstone without any examination of the word "fool". His general theory is that the Elizabethans used what he calls " multiconsciousness ", a thing also found in cinema and musical-comedy audiences. It hardly deserves this grand name ; indeed he says to himself that it looks " suspiciously like dullness ; actually it is more like the acceptance of a mechanical contrivance without wanting to know how it works ". I think he is quite right in saying that this process occurred, and a certain narrowness in his interpretations makes the book more useful because it serves to isolate the precise point he is making. I should only want to add that Shakespeare often relied on this simple readiness in the audience and built something more interesting on top of it. As regards Touchstone, Mr. Bethell says that he has

" two irreconcilable characters, which are held in parallel throughout the play. The question of episodic intensification does not arise, since both ' characters ' may function in the same scene, or indeed at the same time. On his first entry and before he speaks, Celia refers to Touchstone as ' this natural ', and observes that ' always the dullness of the fool is the whetstone of the wits ' (i.2.57). When he does speak, however, we are surprised to find him, not a natural, but a mordantly satirical wit . . . shortly afterwards his good sense is displayed in (a) timely rebuke ... As the Duke says later ' He uses his folly like a stalking-horse and under cover of that shoots his wit ' (v.4.111). If, then, we take Celia's characterisation of him objectively and believe it, Touchstone must be accepted as both fool and wit." (p. 92.)

The play " is in fact no more naturalistic than *The Mikado* ", and the test of this view, Mr. Bethell considers, is given by the marriage of Touchstone to Audrey, which some critics have regarded as his " final cynicism ", " an acted comment on the romantical attachments of the others ". But his jokes are meant to be amusing, not cynical, Mr. Bethell goes on, and " a pathological cynic, such as would spite his own base desires with an ill-assorted marriage ", is not an Elizabethan type ; if Shakespeare had intended such a character he would have stated it very clearly.

" The true explanation of Touchstone's behaviour lies in the psychology, not of Touchstone himself, but of the audience. Professional jesters are witty, but they are also fools ; they are to be laughed *at* as well as with ... Shakespeare makes him witty because we do not tire of wit as we do of the ' natural ' ... The psychological difficulty is brushed aside, and we are given a character wise in speech and foolish in action—which seems to have been the character usually assumed by a court jester. The audience is thus required ... to enjoy the folly and the wit without any naturalistic sense of their incompatibility."

One might object that if this character was " usually assumed " by court clowns the picture of Touchstone is after all a " naturalistic " one. But no doubt Shakespeare carried the idea further than could often be managed in real life. The only thing I should want to add to this account is that these two ideas about Touchstone, which are supposed to be so hard to combine without a special prelogical mode of thought, are already combined in the very word by which he is classified. There is no need to say " both fool and wit " ; it is enough to say " fool ". For that matter the low sensuality which acts as a parody of the romantic lovers is part of the Biblical fool " 3 " ; it comes out for example in the whole-hearted accusation by Othello " She turned to folly and she was a whore ". Clowns of course are expected to be lustful as well as to make jokes about lust ; compare " Marry, here's grace and a codpiece ; that's a wise man and a fool "—the Fool in *Lear* describing himself and his master. Not indeed that Touchstone is supposed to be wicked for his folly ; one might say rather that the simple commonsense of his desire " 1b " is what blows the gaff on more pretentious people, and that this makes him inherently a satire without his having to make conscious jokes. But both halves are in play. I think it is no use denying (as Mr. Bethell seems to do) that some idea of parody is intended in our feelings about Touch-stone's marriage. Surely the whole thrill about his insolence when he says " I press in here, sir, amongst the rest of the country copulatives, to swear and to forswear " (dropped coolly into the middle of his account of his duelling experience) is that Rosalind and Celia his employers are among the pairs. It does not take a psychological theory to find a joke here. But this crashing sneer about the rapid arrangements of the lovers comes in as part of the conception of a " fool ", not as something to be explained about the particular one Touchstone.

Indeed the reactions of Jaques on discovering a court clown in the forest brings out much more clown-doctrine than Touchstone himself does. It is Jaques who has the self-contempt and delight in what he despises, which so much enlarge the concept of the mocker (of course Touchstone may be feeling this about Audrey— " praised be the gods for thy foulness ; sluttishness may come here-after "—but he does not have to insist upon it because it is anyway part of his role). The name Jaques means the lavatory and interest in filth ; he is like Apemantus, " who few things loves better than to abhor himself ", though he is in such a different play. The reason why he is charmed to find a clown in the savagery of exile is that such a creature is a silly toy of the very grandest people, of the utmost refinement and corruption ; no doubt, as the play goes on, a fool comes to stand for other aspects of civilisation, good humour and so on, but that is not the point for Jaques. (By the way, it was rather odd to say that a pathological cynic was not an Elizabethan type.) Critics have remarked that the Fool here, no less than in *King Lear*, is showing an extravagant fidelity and devotion which is accepted quite without comment. This situation seems to have been needed in a play if the clown's remarks were to carry much weight, but to give it direct attention would spoil the tone of the thing ; he is not wanted among the stage exiles as a high-minded character but as a real clown who has presumably joined them for a whim. The lords welcome him because they do not really enjoy Nature and adversity ; they only pretend to do so, with varying degrees of grace, as the best way of putting up with them. Immediately after Jaques' praise of the clown there is a more serious use of this double feeling, when the lords are discovered by Orlando. All comers to the forest are automatically converted, and the nobles are at their most civilised in its shade ; the paradox of the refinement of Nature is very firmly stated ; but Orlando's " He dies that touches any of this fruit " is the right way to deal with *people* in a state of nature, and his apology when he is treated with kindness and dignity, " I thought that all things had been savage here ", puts the weight wholly in favour of civilisation. The same paradox about Nature, indeed, is more grandly connected with clowns in *Lear*.

Jaques maintains that he is now ambitious for a motley coat, because his mockery of the world has been incomplete till now for lack of recognising the absurdity of the process itself. He goes on to claim that there is no other complete liberty ; the Duke accuses this of being the product of disappointed sensuality " 3 ", and uses the hideous metaphor of the man eager to pass on a venereal disease ; Jaques answers that to be free like a clown is to become universal. They go rather painstakingly, in fact, through the theory of the thing. In all this the pair who are contrasted in order to be identified are the clown and the satirist, who is only a fool as fooling others. But there is another pair who are more directly wanted for the paradoxes of the theme of pastoral. Touchstone, a natural who is informed of the refinements of the great world, is to be coupled with a representative of Nature ; he and Audrey are " two very strange beasts, in all tongues called fools ", and all their scenes are an elaboration of the simple pun on " 1 " and " 2 ". The plot is devised to throw a variety of types together on a background of raw nature, and these two are the rock-bottom specimens of court party and country party. The symbolism of their marriage is a joke about the clown as such, a social function, not about the psychology of poor Touchstone ; and the ideas treated here lightly but directly went on growing at the back of Shakespeare's mind.

I have tried here to deal with an actual Shakespearean Fool without treating the verbal structure as too crude, and want now to examine some of the applications of the word to other characters. As the structure was described, the sense " lunatic clown " " 2+4 " ought to poke itself forward as subject in many cases where the context does not directly require it. I am not sure how it is usual to read the grim decision of Macbeth ;

> *Why should I play the Roman fool, and die*
> *On my own sword ? Whiles I see lives, the gashes*
> *Do better upon them.*

Here in effect the context does require it ; probably the word *play* makes most readers accept *fool* as a direct metaphor from the clown. But I should want to take it rather further ; I think that *Roman* should get a stress in delivery (as should *why*, *play*, *fool* and *die* ; his bitterness gives a gnomic weight to the thing) so as to make him imply that he has got to play some kind of clown's part anyway. The only choice still open to him is whether he will be the bitter fool or the sweet one, to use the distinction made by the clown in *Lear*.

CLEOPATRA (to the asp) : *poor venomous fool,*
Be angry, and dispatch. O, couldst thou speak,
That I might hear thee call great Caesar ass
Unpolicied !
CHARMIAN : *O eastern star !*
CLEOPATRA : *Peace, peace,*
Dost thou not see my baby at my breast
That sucks the nurse asleep ?

The asp at first seems a fool merely because it does not understand what it is doing ; in itself the deadly creature is petty and rather pathetic. But then we find that if it spoke it would mock at Caesar, whose plan it is frustrating ; it would behave like a clown. Critics have suggested that Charmian in her cry of tragic praise for Cleopatra calls up an association with the Star in the East " which stood over the place where the young child lay "—a child that like the asp was not merely a natural one, and brought sorrow on his mother as well as greatness. We have just had a real clown labouring to make a mystery of the asp, wishing her joy of it, and explaining when asked if it will eat her that the devil himself will not eat a woman, or not unless he has dressed her himself. This is rather a strong joke against Cleopatra. I think she assumes that the asp's nature is to enjoy doing harm, so she pities it as a dupe because it is being used to do good ; she has a sympathy with such characters, and what she must do now is a necessity of her own partly venomous nature. However obscurely, the whole range of the clown-sentiment is called up ; the stupid malice and the mutual mockery, whether devilish or not, are felt to express some profound truth about the world.

> *But thought's the slave of life, and life time's fool ;*
> *And time, that takes survey of all the world,*
> *Must have a stop. O, I could prophesy,*
> *But that the earthy and cold hand of death*
> *Lies on my tongue.* (*1 Henry IV*. v.4.81)

Hotspur means chiefly that life is cheated by time, because our apparently great opportunities all end in death ; but this might be a comfort, since the same end would come even if he were not defeated. Life is made ridiculous by time ; we are clowns because our pretensions make such a contrast with our end. But if time keeps us as clowns we in our turn mock at time ; we criticise it, and know better. There was room here for a prophecy ; he dies still ready to gibe at the House of Lancaster.

Whether the reverse process can occur, that is, calling a clown a fool and meaning foolish people in general, I am not sure ; if it occurs it feels like a generalisation not like a metaphor.

OLI. : *What think you of this fool, Malvolio, doth he not mend?*

MAL. : *Yes, and shall do, till the pangs of death shake him. Infirmity, that decays the wise, doth ever make the better fool.*

CLO. : *God send you, sir, a speedy infirmity, for the better increasing your folly!*

The clown seems annoyed, and under cover of the habitual retort of folly is perhaps threatening revenge. (By the way, when a clown calls other people fools, as he continually does, I take it he is refusing on principle to distinguish between foolish people and clowns, so the symbol for this professional use of the term is "2+1".) But it seems possible that Malvolio is not so much despising clowns as rebuking the cruelty of the whole custom of maintaining them; their masters, he could imply, would laugh more heartily at greater suffering. On the other hand the obvious antithesis to *the wise* would be not clowns but "the foolish". Perhaps these foolish people are owners of clowns, as Olivia herself is. If we regard the answer as a surly rebuke to his mistress we have here for once an equation of Type I with the word; fool is used in sense "1" or "3" and adds "foolish (or stubbornly cruel) people are themselves clowns". But he is not in the least likely to insult Olivia, and seems really annoyed by the clown here; this more elaborate meaning might occur to Shakespeare but not to Malvolio. All the same, he does seem to mean a generalisation of some kind; here as usual he is an impressive though a harsh speaker. The black little piece of fun has two ways out to a larger air, the idea that tragic experience may lie behind wit and the idea that simplicity is learned through adversity. Or perhaps he really means nothing so agreeable. In any case, it is very rare for one of the characters to generalise about human nature with the clown as the illustration of it; you might think that was what a clown was for, but the clown seems to be the only person who does it.

There is a certain grimness about my equations which suits these examples, and indeed I think suits the whole Elizabethan attitude to the subject. But I must admit that there are uses of the word by Shakespeare which carry a different feeling; and indeed the reader may have felt that the equations are a bit too grim to describe Touchstone.

FORD : *Though Page be a secure fool, and stands so firmly on his wife's frailty, yet I cannot put off my opinion so easily; she was in his company at Page's house, and what they made there, I know not.*

(Merry Wives ii.1.241)

Such a use is intended to be grim, and yet there is a curious good-humour in the background. Page is said to be a fool because he imagines himself secure, and also he is *securely*, unalterably, a fool;

yet he is " safe " in the possession of folly, which will not allow him to discover what would disturb him. A certain cosiness in the phrase might make us feel that we can put up with being fools on such terms, or even that it is wise to accept a general necessity in the matter. No doubt he is called a fool because he will probably be " fooled ", but even so this group of ideas has rather little to do with the lunatic clown. The same idea is put more directly in Puck's " Lord, what fools these mortals be " ; no doubt he means in the first place that the lovers are ridiculous and comparable to clowns, but the background of the idea is something more cordial ; the mortals appear as running their heads simplemindedly into trouble (1/2, 1/3) and therefore as a kind of pet (1/6). We are moving among the ideas of Erasmus. And when we come to the proposal of Miranda to Ferdinand I have to admit that the clown is quite out of sight. The ideas are by no means simple, but they take the Erasmus structure only.

> FER. :   *I,*
> *Beyond all limit of what else i' the world,*
> *Do love, prize, honour you.*
> MIR. : *I am a fool*
> *To weep at what I am glad of.*
> PROS. : *Fair encounter*
> *Of two most rare affections !   Heavens rain grace*
> *On that which breeds between them.*

The peeping and lip-smacking of the old goat Prospero, like the bawdy goodwill of Pandarus, does perhaps make a bit of a clown of her ; but one must presume this was not intended.

> FER. : *Wherefore weep you ?*
> MIR. : *At my unworthiness, that dare not offer*
> *What I desire to give ; and much less take*
> *What I shall die to want.   But this is trifling,*
> *And all the more it seeks to hide itself*
> *The bigger bulk it shows.   Hence, bashful cunning !*
> *And prompt me, plain and holy innocence.*
> *I am your wife, if you will marry me ;*
> *If not, I'll die your maid.   To be your fellow*
> *You may deny me, but I'll be your servant*
> *Whether you will or no.*

> (*Temp.* iii.1.60)

I am assuming that " fool " never comes flatly into an important passage, and it is not hard to see why she is a fool here. She is the complete " innocent ", and that is why she is so valuable ; it lets her go to the heart of the matter. (1b=1/3.) The structure of the thought is sufficiently pegged by her saying

" innocence " a few lines later. Of course, she herself is not supposed to mean this ; she was already feeling conscious of her inexperience, and admits it as an apology when she starts to cry— or indeed the word is a kind of swearing at the nuisance of an obstruction of speech just when she has so much to say. But we are to feel it means a great deal more ; this is a pastoral or Robinson-Crusoe situation where one meets only the fundamentals of human life, and it takes a fool to meet them with so much splendour. And since it is fundamental (by the usual pastoral formula) it is felt to apply to everyone ; we must all be fools, if even she is one.

If then a Shakespearean use of *fool* is not a metaphor from the clown, I class it as a rather generalised memory of the Erasmus doctrine ; but if it is, as most of them are, I maintain that it brings in the darker and more tragic picture that he got from his madmen. The two structures need not conflict, though they seem normally to be independent ; and I think that *The Merchant of Venice*, which has a good deal of medieval feeling in its central allegory, gives a rather special case of a combination of the two. The negro prince represents pagan splendour and the lust of the eye ; he chooses the gold casket, and finds only death in it, but nobody calls him a fool. The admittedly undeserving suitor who gives and hazards all he has (and all his friend has too) is apparently to stand for the triumph of the humble Christian. Only the conventional man between them, who chooses reasonable silver and is too much of a gentleman to ask for more than he deserves, is met by a picture of an idiot and a schedule calling him a Fool. Erasmus would no doubt have liked the thing as a whole, but I doubt whether he would have rubbed the idiot in so firmly. And what the allegory meant to Shakespeare was probably something rather different from the Christian interpretation ; I think it was that you ought to accept the actualities of life courageously even if rather unscrupulously, and not try to gloss over its contradictions and the depths that lie under your feet. I do not know how to symbolise a direct fusion of the two structures.

Chapter 6

FOOL IN LEAR

THE preceding essay is meant to give a rough general background before I attempt a survey of *Lear*, which of course in the supreme exercise-ground of the word *fool*. I must ask the reader to be patient while some of the early uses of the word in the play are listed, also Nature and the gods have to be followed rather cumbrously. Going back to Bradley after drafting my piece, I was struck by how much I had unconsciously borrowed from him, how much broader and more adequate to the play his whole treatment seemed than mine, and what an enormous amount he gets said in his apparently brief and leisurely talks. It may be thought that there cannot be much more to say about *Lear*, so that the prospect of a new theory about it is merely depressing. I take heart from an article by George Orwell, in *Polemic* for March 1947, who said " The subject of *Lear* is renunciation, and it is only by being wilfully blind that one can fail to understand what Shakespeare is saying ". It is " Give away your lands if you want to, but don't expect to gain happiness by doing so. Probably you won't gain happiness. If you live for others, you must live for others, and not as a roundabout way of getting an advantage for yourself." I think this interpretation is right, but it had never occurred to me, and (whether through wilful blindness or not) it does not seem to have been said plainly before. That Lear wants a public show of love from his daughters, and reproaches them when they don't love him because he gave them so much, is of course on the surface of the play ; but this interpretation takes the idea much further. The critic who has most nearly anticipated Orwell seems to be Freud, who said that the meaning of the play was the tragic refusal of the old man to " renounce love, choose death and make friends with the necessity of dying ". But a refusal to do it is different from an attempt to do it which failed, and I think that Orwell is right in saying that Lear is described as making a confused attempt. The effect is that all through the play, even in the first scene which is usually taken as just romantically strange, the idea of renunciation is examined in the light of the complex idea of folly ; and this would imply that you are losing a good deal if you do not give its full weight to *fool*, a key term which is used (by the way) forty-seven times.

One might expect to get evidence about the Orwell view from the older versions of the story, or the way Shakespeare altered them,

or the contemporary historical parallels which it would suggest to
an audience (as in Miss Winstanley's treatment). There does not
seem much to be got. The older play of *Leur* makes him say :

> *The world of me, I of the world am weary*
> *And I would fain resign these earthly cares*
> *And think upon the welfare of my soul.*

which is quite specifically religious ; but you might say that
Shakespeare deliberately weakened this. It seems to be agreed
that he had read a number of different versions ; and the different
versions show a good deal of uncertainty as to how much Lear
gave away and why he did it. But the story was regarded as history,
and well-known, so that it was a bold step when Shakespeare gave
it a tragic ending which would be considered false. The main
point seems to be that he shortened the beginning drastically to
make room for his extra material, and thus removed what
indications of motive there had been. Nothing is left but the
speed and violence of one scene like a fairy-story, and the rest of the
play is the result. All the same, one expects a fairy-story to have a
moral, anyway on the stage ; otherwise it is liable to look silly.
As to Miss Winstanley, who maintains that the driving power of
the play comes from the civil war in France, the St. Bartholomew
massacre, and the murder of Coligny, also the cruelty of Mary
Queen of Scots to Darnley (two themes which would be felt as part
of one Catholic plot against Britain), I feel that she tells you a lot
about the mental background of the first night audience, but not
about the play. The recent events did not supply the moral ; if
anything the moral could be applied to the recent events. The
only relevant point, it seems to me, is that thoughts about the civil
war in France would as it were be part of the fear of civil war at
home ; the reason why it seemed sensible to give this bit of history
a tragic end was that it was about a division of Britain.

If the division is viewed as a religious renunciation on the part
of Lear, one might expect him to be one of the holy fools of
Erasmus. I doubt whether the holy fool was quite what
Shakespeare wanted, but the religious renunciation is suggested
clearly enough :

> LEAR : *Meantime we shall express our darker purpose.*
> *Give me the map there. Know, that we have divided*
> *In three our kingdom ; and tis our fast intent*
> *To shake all cares and business from our age,*
> *Conferring them on younger strengths, while we*
> *Unburdened crawl toward death.*

On the face of it he says that the plan is for his own ease and
convenience ; but *crawl toward death* is the language of mystical

piety in the mouth of so masterful a character, and the suggestion is that he will occupy himself with his prayers. The purpose of saying it in this rather misleading way is to announce a renunciation without any appearance of boasting about his highmindedness, which would be unsuited to the occasion. Of course we find him going hunting and so forth afterwards, but that is precisely George Orwell's point, that the renunciation was inadequate. We are directed to the idea of renunciation by his calling it a *darker* purpose ; in the eyes of the world it would be a gloomy one. I think that an Elizabethan audience would naturally interpret the speech in religious terms. (There is another reference to the idea later in the scene : " So be my grave my peace ".) They would also think the purpose *dark* because they would feel a very practical disapproval for any plan to divide England and thereby risk civil war ; Lear would therefore already seem a very wrongheaded man but one acting from other-worldly motives.*

Several critics have said that the play is deliberately worked out as a picture of a pre-Christian world, which is groping after the ideas of religion ; obscure Christian language is used about Cordelia, but the others are pagans even when they have religious thoughts. Shakespeare was of course aware that the period was pre-Christian, and it is assumed in the first scene that these people believe in the classical gods, or use those names for their gods. (Lear has also heard of Greek philosophers, and Mr. Edmund Blunden has ascribed to him a taste for classical reminiscences.) There is a curious passage :

> LEAR : *Now, by Apollo—*
> KENT : *Now, by Apollo, king,*
> *Thou swear'st thy gods in vain.*
> LEAR : *O vassal, miscreant!*

—where *miscreant* could accuse Kent of not believing in them. In any case there was an early Greek tradition (discussed by Mr. Robert Graves in *The White Goddess*) that the Hyperboreans worshipped Apollo and that his mother was born on their island ; the Elizabethans were rather keen on this sort of thing, and maybe Shakespeare would have claimed that Apollo was the one point he had bothered to get right about prehistoric Britain. But it is clear that the characters hold various religious opinions, and I think we get an impression as the play goes on, which would be historically quite reasonable, that these " gods " are not really the classical

---

* I don't think that to abdicate for religious reasons, like Charles V., would seriously be considered wicked as a breach of Hierarchy. However, abdication in favour of your children does get called unnatural in *Gorboduc*, as was pointed out by Dr. Tillyard ; no doubt Protestants would be more against it than Catholics. In any case, to divide the kingdom would be considered much worse.

ones. There are only three references to classical gods after the first scene, apart from a couple of oaths in iii.4, and they seem only stylistic conveniences (Kent " flickering Phœbus' front ", an intentionally affected phrase, Lear " do thy worst blind Cupid ", where the god is interpreted as a brothel sign, and " tell tales of thee to high-judging Jove ", which feels like monotheism ; indeed when Lear reaches the idea of " taking upon us the mystery of things " he simply mentions " God "). Mr. Wilson Knight treats this change as a mark of the religious development of Lear, though he also says that the last scene makes the idea of expiation or purification in Lear a " tinkling irrelevance ". This seems a typical case where one needs to think of the audience not the character ; I take it the classical gods in the first scene are meant to give the audience the right point of departure for the idea of the gods, and anyway need not prevent it from thinking of Lear as a naturally Christian soul.

Kent calls him mad and accuses him of folly as soon as Cordelia is cast off, and at the end of the scene Goneril and Regan accuse his bad judgement :

> REG. : *Tis the infirmity of his age : yet he hath ever but slenderly known himself.*

They are preparing to call him a fool as being in his " dotage ". Goneril has a curious remark which seems to imply previous renunciations :

> GON. : *Pray you, let us hit it together : if our father carry authority with such dispositions as he bears, this last surrender of his will but offend us.*

Of course he is an extremely headstrong man, and what is more he seems obsessed by his royalty ; it is already clear that he is unfit to carry out a renunciation when he curses Cordelia. (There is an inherent irony, on this view, apart from any madness, about " every inch a king ".) But there is room for an idea that, like so many overbearing extroverts, he has periodical fits of trying to counteract his faults by vehement acts in the opposite direction ; there is a saintly side of his character as well as the explosive one, and low characters might call him a fool for either. Miss Welsford pointed out that he seemed a fool to the bad for trustfulness and affection, but to the good for distrustfulness and unkindness. Shakespeare usually seems to expect his audience to think more highly than we do of his old men in high positions, and if you start with the idea that Lear abdicates for religious reasons you are ready for both sides of his nature.

In the next scene Edmund begins his plot, and tells his father that Edgar has often said

that, sons at perfect age, and fathers declined, the father should be as
ward to the son, and the son manage his revenue.

It is an objection to George Orwell's view that Gloucester, who cannot be supposed to have renounced anything, is so clearly parallel
to Lear. Indeed Orwell says that the play would be better without
him. But this passage carries on the theme ; the idea is that the
heirs of Lear would be tempted to invade his position anyway, so
that his plan is a madly rash one ; the effect of the partial renunciation is to let loose the evils which are always surging under
the surface of the normal civilised controls. Edmund then makes
cynical remarks about his father's belief in astrology, which serve
to press the idea home :

when we are sick in fortune (often the surfeit of our own behaviour) we
make guilty of our disasters the sun, the moon and the stars ; as if we
were villains on necessity ; fools by heavenly compulsion ; knaves . . .
and all that we are evil in, by a divine thrusting on ; an admirable
evasion of whore-master man, to lay his goatish disposition to the charge
of a star !

Apparently we have all these faults ; men in general are both fools
and evil. And it is commonly believed (we need not be impressed
by Edmund's denial) that we are made so by heaven ; this is a
preparation for the idea that the mysterious " gods " of natural
theology do us no good. The planets have the names of the
classical gods, and are " in heaven " in one sense of the word ;
but it was not considered irreligious to believe in astrology, indeed a
sceptic on such matters is rather expected (anyway on the stage)
to be a religious sceptic too. This helps to tie up " the gods " with
current opinion. The rationalist villain is easily connected with
Macchiavelli, but that author does not seem to me either necessary
for a source of this stage type or as prominent in the texts as some
critics have maintained. Anyway none of the wicked people of
the play, as Mr. Wilson Knight pointed out, have any doubts at all
about their wickedness ; they sin (as it were) naturally, and this
is a source of the doubts about Nature.

The next scene begins with the words :

GON. : *Did my father strike my gentleman for chiding of his fool ?*

so it is the Fool who causes the beginning of the storm against Lear,
rather than his shadowy train of deboshed knights. She calls Lear
a fool in her indignation : " old fools are babes again ". We then
see Lear calling for his Fool and his daughter simultaneously, and
being treated with insolence. The Fool has been pining away at
the loss of Cordelia ; his first entry comes when Lear has begun to
make himself ridiculous by encouraging a scuffle between the
rival servants ; he begins immediately to tease Lear for the folly of

his behaviour, and to claim that only he can tell Lear the full truth. Kent has the usual line intended to warn the audience that this clown is meant to be taken seriously :

This is not altogether fool, my lord.

The clown seizes the opportunity to say that " lords and great men . . . . will not let me have all fool to myself, they'll be snatching ". This folly that they insist on getting seems to be wickedness, the Biblical fool ; no doubt they are foolish too, but it is because they are wicked that Lear was foolish to give up his power over them. The clown is not yet a prominent symbol, and you could take the structure of the word as that of *The Praise of Folly*.

Lear greets him affectionately as " my pretty knave " and threatens him with the whip before he has spoken ten lines ; there are six references to the whip during this short period of their comparative happiness together, and at least two of them are threats. The position of Lear's Fool is clearly meant to be a miserable one ; we are to believe him when he says " I would rather be anything than a fool, and yet I would not be thee, nuncle ".

Goneril then comes in and announces that she will cut down the knights :

Not only, sir, this your all-licensed fool
But others of your insolent retinue
Do hourly carp and quarrel.

She still seems more annoyed by the fool than by the knights. Lear makes his first great speech about ingratitude and appeals to the " dear goddess " Nature to put unnatural and startling punishments on her. Bradley well points out that she has not yet deserved all this ; the speech recalls his curse on Cordelia ; indeed there seems room for a superstitious idea that his curses really affect Nature and bring bad luck all round. After the speech the shocked Cornwall says " Now, gods that we adore, wherefore comes this ? "—perhaps implying that Nature was not one of the regular gods and should not be prayed to. When Edmund said Nature was his goddess it implied he was the villain. Lear has just said that the most small fault of Cordelia, like an engine of torture, " wrenched his frame of *nature* from the fixed place " ; here for the first time he accuses himself of " folly ". It seems indeed to be a case of what I called impossible when considering *dharma ;* the nature of an individual is to decide the character of all Nature within the world of the play. No doubt you can say that Lear, unlike Edmund, assumes that Nature is good and will punish wickedness, so that there are two views of Nature in the play ; but one might also accuse Lear of believing that Nature is an amoral magical force which will obey his royal caprices.

Goneril then accuses him of dotage in explaining the situation to her husband. Lear returns to the stage after storming out, and the answer to his prayer is to learn that half his knights are already dismissed. He threatens to pluck out his eyes if they weep, because he wants to be angry and revengeful. When you know the story it gives him an obscure connection with Gloucester, but even so largely one of contrast ; I think the chief idea is that even now, he is deliberately blinding himself to the realities of the process of renunciation. He sets out to go to Regan, and it is Goneril who makes the clown go with him, by the words " You, sir, more knave than fool, after your master ". Outside the palace, Lear for the first time is seen to laugh at a joke by the clown ; it is a particularly obscure one, but still seems meant to call Lear a fool. Till the blow had fallen he was trying to resist this suspicion, and the clown was particularly unwelcome, but now he has admitted his folly and the clown seems on his side. The determination of Bradley to bring out the best in the good characters sometimes makes his judgements rather brutal, oddly enough ; I do not think we need say it was very magnanimous of Lear not to whip the clown. But no doubt he might have been expected to do it, so the clown has succeeded in making him appear tolerably human. Incidentally the clown says that Lear's asses have gone to get his horses ready, so that even the invisible knights are included in the universal accusation of folly. He then brings in the whip again:

FOOL : *If thou wert my fool, nuncle, I'd have thee beaten for being old before thy time.*

LEAR : *How's that ?*

FOOL : *Thou shouldst not have been old till thou hadst been wise.*

LEAR : *Oh, let me not be mad, not mad, sweet heavens ! Keep me in temper ; I would not be mad !*

There are two ways of looking at this. Bradley it appears would say that the teasing of the clown is intolerably irritating, and that Lear means " if this nagging goes on I shall go off my head ". But Lear makes his feelings much plainer than that, and on the other hand he often does not listen to people ; here he is giving the clown hardly any attention. During the jokes he has made two ejaculations about his own kindness and Goneril's ingratitude, and said " I will forget my nature " ; " let me not be mad " simply follows his own line of thought. All the same, I think the presence of the clown has suggested the idea. Lear considers the clown as mad, and the whip was used on actual madmen too ; I think this first outburst of the horror of madness was put into his mind by seeing a lunatic before him. (The two ways of acting it are of course very distinct.) The horses are ready, and the scene ends with an irrelevant bit of bawdy nonsense from the clown ; which Bradley wanted to throw out as spurious, and indeed on his view it is completely out of place ; but it is very much wanted if you are to treat the Fool as a real one.

The second act begins with the plots of the wicked, and then Kent attacks Oswald before Gloucester's castle. He complains that Oswald smiles at his speeches (which are very wild talk) as if he were a fool, and Cornwall asks if he is mad. Next Edgar in soliloquy explains that he will disguise himself as a mad beggar. Lear and the Fool then find Kent in the stocks, and realise that Regan will be no help ; Lear again expresses fear of rising madness, and the Fool calls Kent a fool (Kent admits that his actions lacked wit). It seems as well to point out these hints that Kent is in some peculiar sense another fool, because that completes the set of them for the mad scenes. The clown indeed insists that a wise man would abandon Lear, but adds some riddling lines ending " The knave turns fool that runs away, The fool no knave perdy ". Dr. Johnson tried to amend this into an Erasmus idea, that the knavish timeserver would be fooled at the final Judgement ; Bradley, I think successfully, argued that a knave who took the Fool's advice would thereby act as a fool, whereas the Fool himself won't take it because it is knavish. In any case anyone who comes near the charmed circle, whatever he does, is made a fool of some kind.

I am not clear how far we should suppose, as is commonly done, that the Fool is labouring to distract Lear from his anger and thus save him from going mad. He boasts of staying with Lear, but he has been sent with him, and would probably be afraid to go off alone. When we last see him he is again ordered to follow Lear, this time by Kent : " Come, help to bear thy master. Thou must not stay behind." This does not suggest that Kent took his faithfulness for granted. Of course it is pathetic if you suppose that the clown is already dying from his unrecognised exertions (and Kent is repaid when Lear at the end fails to appreciate him in his turn) ; but to believe this is to build a good deal on the mere silence of the text, especially as the silence is natural if you take a clown to be a low and unimportant person. The audience would not regard self-sacrifice as typical of clowns, and so far there has been nothing to suggest it. To be sure, the line just before his first entry : " Since my young lady's going into France, sir, the Fool hath much pined away " is meant to put him clearly on the side of the good characters. But he may *pine* because he is frightened and actually ill-used, not because he loves her so much ; what he expresses as soon as he appears is a keen sense of danger. I do not mean to deny that the Fool is affectionate towards Lear and Cordelia, his only protectors (why shouldn't he be ?), only that he is supposed to be a highminded and self-sacrificing character ; also I think that the malice which is part of his role comes out plainly enough in his jokes to Lear.

After Gloucester has made clear that Regan will be no help we do get an impression, for the first time, that the Fool is sympathising with the real anxiety of Lear, which is fear of madness :

LEAR : *Oh me, my heart, my rising heart ; but down !*

FOOL : *Cry to it, nuncle, as the cockney did to the eels, when she put 'em up i' the paste alive ; she knapped 'em o' the coxcombs with a stick, and cried " down wantons, down ! " 'Twas her brother that, in pure kindness to his horse, buttered his hay.*

Even here, I think the chief impression is not of any depth of sympathy but that the Fool understands about madness because he is mad himself. George Orwell's view of him is that he stands merely for the cynical side of Shakespeare, a man who had no intention of renouncing anything, or at any rate that he stands for worldly common sense. Both the simpletons mentioned are in effect cruel, and the brother may well be a knave, as greasing hay was more usually done by deceitful ostlers ; the worldly second anecdote makes one suspect a bawdy meaning in the first. Anyhow the Fool satirizes Lear's habit of giving orders all the time, even to his diseases, after he has renounced the power to get his orders obeyed. The text does not tell us the effect on Lear, because Regan enters at once ; no doubt the important effect is on the audience—it broadens the suffering of Lear into a whole world of coarse wickedness and folly, and at the end of the great scene with Regan that follows we first hear the rumbling of the universal storm.

Lear tells Regan that she is unlike Goneril and would not " oppose the bolt against my coming in ", which in fact Regan and not Goneril has just done ; this may be a pathetic appeal but sounds as if he is already confused. Apparently the old man has ridden all night after a day's hunting, and without the dinner he was calling for. Regan in effect accuses him of dotage, and Goneril when she appears again uses the word. Lear appeals to the heavens to help him :

If you do love old men, if your sweet sway
Allow obedience, if yourselves are old

and the immediate answer is that Regan takes Goneril by the hand. " O sides, you are too tough " implies that an explosion, even perhaps of madness, would be a relief, but as the insults sharpen he becomes wary and decides not to let them send him mad. They press him to say why he needs any knights as his followers, and this

brings the first cry of " I gave you all " ; but he is still able to
philosophize in a large-minded calm :

> *O reason not the need ; our basest beggars*
> *Are in the poorest thing superfluous*

—a lead-in to the theory that " there is no worst ", and perhaps to
his discovery that the beggars are worse off than he had supposed.
Again he appeals to the heavens, this time for patience, and now
their answer is his madness, because his patience cracks as he forms
a positive suspicion against them :

> *If it be you that stirs these daughters' hearts*
> *Against their father, fool me not so much*
> *To bear it tamely ; touch me with noble anger,*
> *And let not women's weapons, waterdrops,*
> *Stain my man's cheeks.*

His revenges will be the terrors of the earth—nothing will make
him weep—" Oh, fool ! I shall go mad ". The storm begins, and
Goneril remarks that he must " taste his folly ". The practical
question for Lear is only what kind of fool he will become, " sweet
or bitter " as the clown has defined it ; a simpering madness or the
violent madness of revenge. He feels the second would be better,
but in most of his insanity he is nearer to the first, which is more
like the ordinary conception of the Fool.

This speech to the heavens has an important position because it
touches off the storm ; at least there seems no doubt that it would
be taken so by the audience, who were accustomed to melodramas in
which thunder comes as an immediate reply. The storm in Nature
is no doubt partly the image of Lear's mind, but it is also an attack
upon him, whether from the stern justice of God or the active
malice of the beings he has prayed to. The use of the term *fool*
acts as a strong support for the theory of malice. The N.E.D.
quotes this example and makes it " 4 " to make foolish, infatuate "
as opposed to " 3 " " to make a fool of ; impose upon, dupe,
trifle with ", but the decision is very unsupported, because the
N.E.D. apparently considers both these senses of *fool* as verb to be
invented by Shakespeare. I think that the idea of stirring up his
daughters against him makes the word here an obvious case of
" 3 " ; in fact I think the compilers of the dictionary deliberately
invented their sense " 4 " to avoid a startling accusation against
the heavens in this one passage. It is commonly the business of a
clown to make fools of other people, and the heavens themselves, in
this break-up of the human order, are becoming fools like everyone
else, and malicious ones. Every time Lear prays to the gods, or
anyone else prays on his behalf, there are bad effects immediately.

You might object that this is impossible because Elizabethan stage thunder was a convention for the anger of God ; even supposing that Shakespeare would want it to mean the malice of Nature, nobody could understand him. But thunder could be ironical even in the crude revenge plays ; the revenger can take it as approving his plot though it really threatens him for his crimes. I don't deny that the faint suggestions of Christianity in the play held a very strong position against the repeated statements of a sort of Manichæan pantheism ; I only claim that both were in view, and if the heavens are supposed to resent what was said, this only makes more serious the blasphemy that Lear has put into our minds. The obvious effect, however it is interpreted, is that when he appeals to them not to fool him they fool him all the more. At this stage of the play, I think, the structure of the equations in the word has to move over from the Erasmus one, if you were taking it like that before ; it is becoming clear that the half-mad clown is the typical or central meaning of the word.

In the third act, as we approach the great mad scenes, a Gentleman tells Kent that Lear has with him in the storm

> *None but the fool, who labours to out-jest*
> *His heart-struck injuries.*

Here is the picture of the Fool struggling to save his master's sanity which the critics have admired, but the actual words only say that he is trying to make jokes adequate to so big an occasion. The phrase echoes another remark by the Gentleman immediately before ; Lear, he says,

> *Strives in his little world of man to out-scorn*
> *The to and fro conflicting wind and rain.*

The idea in " out— " is that of defeating an enemy by doing more of the same kind of thing ; if Lear can scorn Nature, or fool Nature, more than she does him, he will defeat her and be safe. The fool is busied in the same way ; if he can laugh at Lear's injuries more than they (being personified) laugh at Lear, he will have saved him. But I am not sure that we need regard this as a rational kindness towards Lear ; the ideas belong more to magic than to medical psychology. The main effect of the lines about the fool is to insist that what Lear is doing is like what a clown does.

We next see Lear exulting in the storm and the prospect of universal destruction ; he forgives the elements because he never gave them a kingdom.

> *then, let fall*
> *Your horrible pleasure ; here I stand, your slave,*
> *A poor, infirm, weak, and despised old man.*
> *But yet I call you servile ministers,*
> *That have with two pernicious daughters joined . . .*

Their pleasure in fooling him is a horrible one, and like most bullies they are slavish ; they take orders from the legitimate royalty which has got hold of the divine right. A pause after this outburst is filled by a bawdy rhyme from the fool and the arrival of Kent, who complains about the weather. In between Lear mumbles " No. I will be the pattern of all patience. I will say nothing ". To say nothing would be like Cordelia ; the irony emphasizes that he has no idea what he is really doing. But the remark seems to enlarge itself into a claim, that he really is in some mysterious manner the type of that patience which can experience reality ; much more so (we are told by the play, not by the character) than the incessantly patient but too passively despairing Gloucester, to whom everybody preaches the virtue that he seems to have already. After Kent has spoken Lear bursts out again, but this time in defence of the weather ; it comes from the " great gods ", he says : he will approve this pother if they punish the secret wickedness of mankind which he failed to recognize when he was king (if he had recognized it he would have known better than to risk his renunciation). Gloucester in describing the scene later says " poor old heart, he help the heavens to rain " ; it is a moving expression of sheer praise, but it means that he helped the disorder of Nature, which was in itself a hideous one. To be sure the whole accusation against Nature could be regarded as part of his madness, especially from the self-absorption in his own wrongs which is still present however he claims to universalize them ; but the madness itself is clearly regarded as a source of wisdom, and therefore somehow in accordance with Nature. In the same way the many comparisons of men to animals, as Mr. Wilson Knight pointed out, make them not merely in some harsh way " natural " but either wicked, because subhuman, or mad, therefore perhaps in touch with superhuman forces.

The practical remarks of Kent, offering the hovel, bring him to himself enough to say :

> *My wits begin to turn.*
> *Come on, my boy ; how dost, my boy ? Art cold ?*
> *I am cold myself . . .*
> *Poor fool and knave, I have one part in my heart*
> *That's sorry yet for thee.*

He is surprised at himself for it, and the claim of " yet " is I think false ; he would not have bothered whether the Fool was cold except for his new plan of universal magnanimity. It really is to his credit, and no doubt was felt to be a dramatic point, but I find it a bit unctuous of Bradley to say that this proves his character to be completely regenerated. The striking thing is rather the gulf between the two social positions. The Fool before entering the hovel speaks a vaguely bawdy prophecy, ending with the powerful line " This prophecy Merlin shall make, for I live before his time ". Bradley wanted to call this soliloquy of the clown spurious, like the previous one at the end of a scene, and it seems as well to have a definite answer. Mr. Bethell rightly pointed out that this joke makes the clown step out of the remote period as a contemporary, and that Edgar as poor Tom is also a contemporary figure belonging to the Elizabethan unemployment problem. The shock of the thing depended on its realism ; the lunatics which can actually be met are meant to rise in the mind as standing metaphors for cosmic affairs.

It seems to me that Lear's mood of magnanimity goes with an increased belief that he gave up the throne as an act of renunciation, or anyway with more attention to this belief ; the phrase " gave all " is repeated three times. It is a sinister phrase, because the self-pity of it marks the onset of insanity—" that way madness lies, let me shun that " ; and when he repeats it to Edgar—" did'st thou give all to thy two daughters ? "—it marks that madness has come. No doubt the appearance of the wild Edgar, just after Lear had prepared himself to sleep after praying, is the accident that made him unable to shun it any longer ; but the effect on the audience is to connect the claim that the renunciation was complete with the insanity. The Fool's remark that Edgar didn't give all but kept a blanket, " else we had all been shamed," acts I suppose as a satire against " giving all " from coarse common sense.

What Lear describes as his prayer before sleeping seems to be the words of his speech, but it is addressed first to " poor naked wretches " and then to " pomp ", people in authority. The only reference to a supernatural power comes in the final phrase, that if the rich give their superflux to the wretches it will " show the heavens more just ". This does not sound as if the gods are just of their own accord. " Take physic, pomp " seems to be a pun ; if the rich expose themselves to such physical conditions as the storm it will be medicine to them. There is a notion here that Nature does you good, but only when in its more appalling forms. He has " taken too little care " of the sufferings of the wretches ; all this, I take it, in contrast to " gave all ", is part of his obscure recognition that the renunciation he made was not an adequate one.

The horror of sex appears for the first time as soon as he is mad. Edgar's nature, he says, must have been subdued by his daughters :

> *Is it the fashion that discarded fathers*
> *Should have thus little mercy on their flesh ?*
> *Judicious punishment ! twas this flesh begot*
> *Those pelican daughters—*

so that even the legitimate act demands punishment, at any rate if the product is evil (" a disease that's in my blood "). The idea is echoed by obscure bawdy jokes from Edgar and the clown, and indeed serves to bring him nearer to their fooling—the clown has all along made jokes about sex which imply that the daughters will do harm. The change in Lear has been viewed as an irrelevant introduction of Shakespeare's own neuroses, and the horror certainly occurs in other plays of the great period, but it seems thoroughly in place here.

All the same, we must not let the " pattern " approach distract us from the " character " approach ; the horror of sex fits in well with the general rising horror, especially the metaphors about animals, but surely we are also to reflect that it is ridiculous and rather sordid when a very old man finds this topic so exciting. Lear wants disorder in sex, just as he wants disorder in any form, because he thinks it will help his revenge, which is from now on his major obsession on his wheel of fire. That is why, in spite of his weird holiness, it is reasonable to make him talk like the standard Malcontent, Jaques for example, who can be jeered at for choosing to be a " cynic " only because he is a " libertine ".

Lear then praises Edgar, dressed only in a blanket, because " Here's three on us are sophisticated ; thou art the thing itself . . . Off, off, you lendings. Come, unbutton here ". " Be contented, tis a naughty night to swim in ", says the Fool, treating this hunger of the mind as a kind of perverse pleasure, so that it is like the bawdy talk of a clown ; he goes on to talk of old lechers, a cue for the entry of Gloucester. I think the incident is connected with the later discovery of Edgar that " there is no worst " ; it is ironical for Lear to believe that this man is the rock-bottom—not only is he a pretence, but worse things are still to befall him. In any case, the whole scene is much more pointed if you take the original abdication as an attempt to renounce the world, but one which had too much calculation in it, so that he is now trying desperately to find what a real renunciation would be.

I am not sure how much weight we ought to put on the repetitions of *nothing*, mainly done by the Fool, which look back to " Nothing will come of nothing ; speak again ". Taken seriously they are all hints about renunciation, a process which regards the achievement of some aspect of nothingness as a positive gain. This was not too Buddhist an idea to occur to Shakespeare ; " Nothing brings me all things ", says Timon welcoming the prospect of death. But we would then I think have to go further and say that Shakespeare is criticizing the Negative Way of the mystics, because he also maintains very firmly that there is no rock-bottom above the water-table of lunacy. I rather doubt whether these echoes are worked out so intentionally ; the *nothing* of the play seems a clear enough dramatic irony which does not add up to anything more.

Gloucester (who produced the bastard Edmund) then comes to bring them help, and gives an echo of the prevalent sex-horror :

> *Our flesh and blood, my lord, is grown so vile*
> *That it doth hate what gets it.*

He means only that both he and Lear are hated by some of their children, but there is another idea for the audience : " We have become so depraved that we hate the sexual process by which we are produced ". Here again the sentiment is treated definitely as an evil one. Kent tells him that the king is going mad, and he says " I am almost mad myself " because of sorrow about Edgar ; " the grief hath crazed my wits ". (Nobody in the storm scenes is allowed to be wholly sane.) Lear then refuses to be separated from Edgar—" I still will keep with my philosopher ", " come, good Athenian ". That is, Edgar is taken to be an ascetic who has renounced the world deliberately (Diogenes perhaps) ; and the parallel again looks as if Lear thinks he set out to make a renunciation, but failed to take it far enough till he was forced to. (Edgar too of course did it involuntarily.) In their next scene, in the outhouse, Kent twice appeals to this idea when he says that Lear is mad because he failed to keep " patience ", which he " so oft had boasted to retain ". This is far from being a native virtue of Lear's, but it must have been what he intended if he originally proposed a renunciation. Just before Lear sleeps in this scene he gives his clearest expression of the feeling of mystery in the evil of the world—" Is there any cause in nature that makes these hard hearts ? " ; and there is a long pause before we see him again. The idea has been reached through the metaphors about the heavens fooling mankind, and Lear has searched for an understanding of them first in a clown (fool 2) and then in a lunatic (fool 4).

We then see Gloucester's eyes put out, and the fourth act opens with his meeting with Edgar. Edgar in soliloquy praises his own condition, as Lear had done ;

> *To be worst,*
> *The lowest and most dejected thing of fortune,*
> *Stands still in esperance, lives not in fear ;*
> *The lamentable change is from the best,*
> *The worst returns to laughter.*

The idea seems to be that since things can only get better there will be happy laughter at any future change ; but this is too absurd even as an argument to be rejected at once. The point I think is that if mad beggars like himself are the worst they are only a form of clown ; they can laugh as well as be laughed at. He " owes nothing " to the blasts of heaven ; he has no feudal duties towards Nature, who is an evil lord.

> *But who comes here ?*
> *My father, poorly led ? World, world, O world*
> *But that thy strange mutations make us hate thee,*
> *Life would not yield to age.*

Yield may be " turn into old age, which is hardly life " or " produce old age, as a result of living long " or simply " allow authority to old persons ", the normal process whose failure has made all this chaos. The confused rich phrase implies that a horror of the world, or at least a certain detachment from it, is somehow necessary, but its chief function is to mark the bafflement with which he sees his theory of the worst destroyed. Gloucester says

> *Ah, dear son Edgar,*
> *The food [fool ?] of thy abused father's wrath,*
> *Might I but live to see thee in my touch*
> *I'd say I had eyes again.*

Edgar ignores this aspect of the matter.

> EDG.: *Oh gods, who is't can say " I am at the worst " ?*
> *I am worse than e'er I was.*
>
> OLD MAN : *Tis poor mad Tom.*
>
> EDG.: *And worse I may be yet ; the worst is not*
> *So long as we can say " This is the worst ".*

This idea indeed is fundamental to the interest in madmen ; they cannot tell us directly what the worst is, but they allow us to peer into the abyss for knowledge about the bases of the world. Gloucester drives the point home when he is told that this is a " madman and beggar too."

> GLO.: *He has some reason else he could not beg.*
> *I' the last night's storm I such a fellow saw,*
> *Which made me think a man a worm ; my son*
> *Came then into my mind ; and yet my mind*
> *Was then scarce friends with him ; I have heard more since.*
> *As flies to wanton boys, are we to the gods—*
> *They kill us for their sport.*
>
> EDG.:   *How should this be ?*
> *Bad is the trade that must play fool to sorrow,*
> *Angering itself and others. (to Glo.) Bless thee, master.*

Christian commentators have insisted that this picture of the world is only a " passing phase of Gloucester's religious development " or " a temporary reaction of his superstitious nature ". I do not say that it is presented as a solid doctrine, but it joins very directly onto the fundamental imagery of the play. The gods are mischievous boys, so they are fooling us ; Gloucester does not say it in passing but as a summing-up of what Lear has repeatedly implied. In explaining Edgar's question, some critics think he asks how Gloucester became blind, others why he is himself forgiven—a fact which he hardly seems to realize, and indeed we must suppose he is now rather crazy because he doesn't. He may well wonder about things at large, but the thought is close to the previous words. He says " How can what father says be true ? " and goes on to talk about it. The gods are called fools both as lunatics (or malicious children) and as mockers ; this is the trade Edgar has adopted, and he feels it is too bad a trade for the gods. Miss Bradbrook has pointed out that, being disguised as a madman, he is vaguely thought of as possessed and unable to stop ; no doubt this crude assumption was a help, but I think we are really meant to doubt his sanity. He makes occasional claims that to go on pretending madness is a way to cure his father, but the shock becomes so much greater when the truth is at last told that it actually kills his father, which it clearly would not have done if told now. Apparently the shock is expected to kill Kent as well. Edgar in describing all this near the end has the grace to say it was a " fault " to keep on fooling his father, though at the time he claims to be healing his despair.

Perhaps he may have felt that to go on pretending madness was a sort of penance to bring good luck, but one may suspect darker feelings to be at work. After all, his function towards Gloucester is a direct parallel to that of the Fool towards Lear, and the Fool does not neglect his trade of mocking. After Edgar has imposed a false death on the father who has wronged him he describes himself as he was till then as a sort of grotesque devil. (The reason why the interpretation can be so complex is that the stage effect is so crude and as it were mythical.) At any rate his words here seem to blame him for the part he is playing ; he is a *fool* both to his own sorrow and to other people's, and the word means that he is both dupe and mocker to both kinds of sorrow.* It is a fearful trade,

---

*Edgar's soliloquy in bad couplets at the end of the hovel scene seems meant to remind us that he has only been pretending madness, and anyway breaks the rule that he always acts madly when dressed in a blanket. Critics have suggested that it is an interpolation. But there is a relevant irony in making him say that it is a comfort to have others in misfortune, just before the blinding of his father ; the comforts he invents are all weak. The speech is needed to give time to change the furniture on the inner stage, and the reason why it is clumsy may well be that Shakespeare added it later for this purpose, rather in cold blood. But perhaps the clumsiness can be made positively good if the words are acted as a strained effort to hold on to sanity.

then, if the gods lead it, but this at least helps to define the gods. The clash of these two great sentences makes us see them as creatures cruel and senseless through their own suffering, the contempt of whose irony unites them to what they mock. This idea of a suffering demi-urge has of course been recognized by critics, but not in the straightforward way that seems to me required ; Bradley for instance uses the idea as the rhetorical climax of a lecture when he says the play gives us " a consciousness of greatness in pain and of solemnity in the mysteries we cannot fathom ". No doubt a Christian can regard these gods as merely Nature and therefore subordinate to God. But they are not subordinate in the play. If we regard it as the root idea of tragedy that the sacrifice of the hero re-unites his tribe with Nature or with supernatural forces, then it is in these passages that we find the idea fully at work.

Gloucester, to be sure, does not seem in any mood of revolt ; he accepts Edgar as guide because " Tis the time's plague, when madmen lead the blind " ; his troubles are fitting when such things have happened to royalty ; and he asks the heavens to continue the good work, supposing as Lear did that it will help the poor.

> *Let the superfluous and lust-dieted man*
> *That slaves your ordinance, that will not see*
> *Because he doth not feel, feel your power quickly :*
> *So distribution should undo excess,*
> *And each man have enough.*

This kind of " patience " only leads to the request to be led to Dover Cliff for suicide. Indeed, I am not quite certain that Shakespeare approved of the idea of distribution to undo excess ; Lear's own attempt at it led to disastrous enough excesses. The irony, if it is there, at any rate makes the difficulty of a successful distribution seem a sharp one ; the horrors of poverty and the fear of social disorder are stressed about equally.

We next see Goneril indignant with Albany for sympathy with Lear, and she calls him a fool four times ; one of them is just before his entry, and clearly means " clown "—" my fool usurps my body". The effect on the play I think is to make her more important by fitting her into its major imagery ; the internecine lust of the two sisters has begun to illustrate the themes of sex-horror and the self-destructiveness of evil. Also the word marks the entire certainty of Goneril that her view of the world is the right one. We then have news of Cordelia's feelings about her father, and it is obvious that Goneril would call Cordelia a fool too :

> *You have seen*
> *Sunshine and rain at once ; her sighs and tears*
> *Were like a better way*

The puzzling text is right, I suppose, because nature and man are still deeply connected ; she is like a better way for everything to happen, including the weather ; as a rule Nature happens in Goneril's way (or simply Lear's). Miss Spurgeon pointed out, on the other hand, that the play's general imagery of violence is imported even into this picture of love and reflection. Kent remarks that only astrology could explain why she is so different from her sisters, and this keeps us in the world where Nature makes things evil as well as good.

> COR.: *Alack, tis he ; why, he was met even now*
> *As mad as the vexed sea ; singing aloud ;*
> *Crowned with rank fumiter and furrow-weeds,*
> *With charlocks, hemlock, nettles, cuckoo-flowers,*
> *Darnel, and all the idle weeds that grow*
> *In our sustaining corn.*

The corn appears to sustain also the idle weeds, so that they are rogues, battening upon the commonwealth, and Lear is at least an outlaw, if nothing worse ; that is why he is profound like the sea (it is singing with pleasure even when angry). Mere nature is still not harmless, though wonderful, even in the sanctified thoughts of Cordelia ; it is healthy only when human affairs are in order. But she believes it still has herbs which are " unpublished virtues " and can heal him again.

After a bout of plotting between Regan and Oswald we return to Gloucester, who at the moment before his intended suicide does something to clear up the gods :

> *Here, friend, 's another purse ; in it, a jewel*
> *Well worth a poor man's taking : fairies and gods*
> *Prosper it with thee ! Go thou further off.*

Here they seem as petty as the fairies, so that there is less blasphemy in calling them wicked. He then, to be sure, apologizes to the " mighty gods " and says that he would not kill himself

> *If I could bear it longer, and not fall*
> *To quarrel with your great opposeless wills*

so that he took his blasphemy about " wanton boys " seriously enough to feel that the necessity of repeating it must be avoided at all costs. And yet there seems to be an idea that he can get away from " the gods " by getting out of Nature.

Indeed, the " extreme verge " on which he is said to stand may be meant to recall Regan's remark to Lear " Nature in you stands on the very verge of her confine " ; Lear is ripe to get outside the world of ordinary experience, in one way or another, and the fearful aspects of Nature are always compared to him. Even the pebbles on which Gloucester is to fall are " idle " like Lear's weeds. " This great world " Gloucester is soon to say at the spectacle of Lear in madness, " shall so wear out to nought." Edgar, as soon as Gloucester has survived his imaginary fall, tells him that " the clearest gods " have preserved him ; it is one of the lies intended to heal his despair. But Edgar (and for that matter Albany) is definitely made to hold orthodox opinions, however much irony may be contrived against his expressions of them. The characters, as Bradley pointed out, nearly all express views about nature and providence, and hold extremely various ones ; no religious opinion in the audience need feel attacked ; but it does not appear that any of the views are made to seem adequate to the mystery of the world as it is presented.

Edgar tells Gloucester to " bear free and patient thoughts " ; free, I suppose, from a fixation on his wrongs and on the horror of the world such as drove Lear mad. The words form an ironical cue for the entry of that hero, " every inch a king " (and therefore still unable to renounce his royalty), but now full of infantile fancies which make him more than ever like a fool ; " look, look, a mouse ; peace, peace, this piece of toasted cheese will do it." Gloucester's reminder that he is a king sets him off on his supreme expression of sex-horror ; also he calls Gloucester mad if he cannot see how the world goes without eyes, and runs off into a denunciation of worldly convention and injustice. He does, of course, absolutely no justice to Gloucester, who has been blinded in trying to save him from the consequences of his folly ; indeed, he seems to jeer at Gloucester for being blind, in a thoroughly clownish manner. But he comes back to advise Gloucester, with one of those triumphant recaptures of the obvious that make Lear such a wonderfully convincing dotard :

> *I know thee well enough, thy name is Gloucester.*
> *Thou must be patient ; we came crying hither.*
> *Thou knowest, the first time that we smell the air*
> *We waul, and cry. I will preach to thee, mark ;*

GLO.: *Alack ! Alack the day !*

LEAR.: *When we are born, we cry that we are come*
> *To this great stage of fools,*

—but then his mind is drowned again under a scheme to kill his sons-in-law, with *kill* six times repeated. Nobody, I suppose, doubts that clowns are meant here, with the word *stage* to insist upon it, but after all, the babies cannot be supposed to know all this about human affairs ; " smelling the air " of the world, their first contact with Nature in any form, is what makes them denounce her as essentially unsuited to the human spirit. Nature is still the most prominent of the many clowns in view. It is a comic impudence for the entirely impatient Lear to preach patience to Gloucester, but the idea is that his impatience and his clowning are what have taught him to understand the nature of the world.

I went too fast over the denunciation of injustice, which leaves him feeling at home with the universe and relaxed, so that he pulls off his boots. It is at the climax of this rage that he makes his most distinct expression of the scapegoat idea :

> *None does offend, none ; I say none. I'll able 'em.*
> *Take that of me, my friend, who have the power*
> *To seal the accuser's lips.*

This is what sets him free to recognise Gloucester and take his boots off. The royal prerogative has become the power of the outcast to deal directly on behalf of mankind with the Devil or other extra-human forces ; the people he is going to save apparently include the wicked in power, whom he has just been denouncing, as well as the poor whose sins are viewed as natural ; so he can escape for the moment from the craving for revenge. The "wheel of fire", of course, goes on turning, and the craving soon comes round again.

During his repeated cries of *kill*, a gentleman comes to capture him :

> *No rescue ? What, a prisoner ? I am even*
> *The natural fool of fortune. Use me well ;*
> *You shall have ransom.*

Natural in the sense " imbecile " is insisted on by *fool*, the other half of the stock term (they define each other, like " look-see "), and yet the main sense of " natural " carries so crucial a conflict for the play that it still rises here. It surely means something good, at any rate in Lear's intention ; the wicked are unnatural, but Lear has found his way back to unsophisticated nature, like the *fool*. Yet taking the phrase as a whole, it says that fortune keeps making a fool of him ; that is, he keeps having bad luck because nature has a spite against him. " Loyal and natural boy " Gloucester calls Edmund in the hour of deception, and the irony carries behind it a doubt of Nature herself ; what is called natural is disordered, and one is most likely to be betrayed by one's natural children. Nature is Edmund's goddess. But then again, Timon of Athens, who is close to Lear in spirit and date of writing, uses " fools of fortune " (iii.6.106) to mean " trencher-friends ", false pets, who are determined to keep in with fortune ; the phrase I think may go either way. Since Lear now feels that death would be welcome he feels he is a toy of fortune because he can no longer be hurt (" I will die bravely, like a smug bridegroom "). To be sure, he will die bravely *because* he is a King (" my masters ") ; but also because he is genuinely a Fool now and has a right to the title. The gentleman, after expressing pity, remarks :

> *thou hast one daughter*
> *Who redeems nature from the general curse*
> *Which twain have brought her to.*

and in spite of its pious form this reports a common agreement at
the time with Lear's denunciation of Nature. The effect of the
scene on Gloucester, and perhaps the effect of hearing that the
enemy army is approaching Cordelia and she is inadequately
protected, is to make him say :

> *You ever-gentle gods, take my breath from me ;*
> *Let not my worser spirit tempt me again*
> *To die before you please.*

He is so symbolically patient that he can praise even the gods. But
the idea that the spectacle of Lear's madness gave him strength to
have still more patience does not explain what wisdom it has
conveyed.

The change in Gloucester may be parallel to that in the protean
Edgar, who now adopts a standard rustic accent to quarrel with
Oswald and kill him with a stick. The good people are in contact
with Nature, and therefore can appear as pastoral rustics ; it is like
Lear's use of the idle weeds. No doubt in a way, as critics have
asserted, these details give a feeling of greater trust in Nature, but
the idea is not so much that she is found to be gentle as that the good
characters are now more at home with her wildness and roughness.
While Edgar is handling the decisive letter of Goneril and preparing
his plot, the voice of Gloucester speaks up wishing that he was mad.
" How stiff is my vile *sense* " is a particularly rich use of that word ;
chiefly for " sanity ", *vile* because it seems disloyal to outlast the
king's ; but *vile sense* is commonly used for the senses as a source of
pleasure, so that he might be regretting the past " sensualities "
which have coarsened his " sensibility." He is still patient, but he
recognises that it would be an achievement if he could get to the
condition of Lear.

The great scene of the meeting of Lear and Cordelia rises far
above the problems about madness and what it teaches ; they are
happy through their tears because they love entirely and ask for
nothing. One cannot speak of trust, because if she has poison for
him, Lear will drink it ; there is no need for trust. But all the same,
we are to be in no doubt that this divine goodness and gentleness in
Lear has been learned through madness ; not merely through
suffering, but through having been a clown. And the reason why
the real renunciation, now at last achieved, is so pathetic is that it is
so close to imbecility. I do not deny that the scene stands out in
memory as a chief one of the play, even as the " meaning " of the
play, which would then be one of regeneration. But surely it is also

true that this mood of greatness arises in him as a sort of wild flower, almost unconnected with anything else. The play does not allow him to keep it, and indeed gives us an immediate warning. The scene is followed by a brief dull conversation on the apronstage, while the inner set is altered (no doubt coats of arms were the important objects, to show which camp one is in) ; and Kent tells a Gentleman "Tis time to look about; the powers of the kingdom approach apace ". The kingdoms of Heaven and Hell are perhaps not what give weight to this phrase ; the wicked who have got hold of the divine right are simply the kingdom of this world. But anyway, it is not Lear who is going to " look about " ; we think of him as hardly conscious.

The fifth act begins with the plots of the wicked and the battle in which the French are defeated, a thing the audience would approve in itself, though its effect is the capture of Lear and Cordelia. Gloucester is comforted in the famous words of Edgar :

> *Give me thy hand, come on.*
> GLO. : *No further, sir. A man may rot even here.*
> EDG. : *What, in ill-thoughts again ? Men must endure*
> *Their going hence, even as their coming hither ;*
> *Ripeness is all. Come on.*
> GLO. : *And that's true, too.*

It looks back to the preaching of Lear, that the new-born child howls immediately at coming to this stage of fools, when it has so far merely smelled the air of the world. If birth sets the standard for dying, we do not need much patience to live up to it ; the great thing is to get it over and leave the world. To be sure, I agree with the many critics who have praised the passage that it contrives to suggest a great deal more than this, but I think that they have wilfully ignored its background, which is the malcontent view of Nature as the supreme clown. It may work by contrast as well as parallel ; *ripeness* implies that the natural process is somehow good, however much the echo from Lear's preaching says it is bad. But I think we clearly need both halves ; that is why this apparently simple remark has so much power.

The scene of Lear and Cordelia as prisoners begins at once, and Cordelia says that if suffering alone she could " outfrown false Fortune's frown ", a phrase that looks back to Lear and the Fool " outscorning " the tempest.

> COR. : *Shall we not see these daughters and these sisters ?*
> LEAR. : *No, no, no, no ! Come, let's away to prison :*
> *We two alone will sing like birds i' the cage.*
> *When thou dost ask me blessing, I'll kneel down*
> *And ask of thee forgiveness ; so we'll live,*

> *And pray, and sing, and tell old tales, and laugh*
> *At gilded butterflies, and hear poor rogues*
> *Talk of court news ; and we'll talk with them too,*
> *Who loses and who wins, who's in, who's out,*
> *And take upon's the mystery of things*
> *As if we were God's spies ; and we'll wear out*
> *In a walled prison, packs and sects of great ones*
> *That ebb and flow by the moon.*

" *Gilded butterflies :* here, gay courtiers " says the Arden text plumply; " *the mystery of things :* the mysterious course of worldly events." However, some doubt is admitted about *God's spies :* " Johnson renders, ' angels commissioned to survey and report the lives of men'. Warburton explains, " Spies placed on God Almighty to watch his motions ". But the motions of God are also shown by real butterflies, creatures who are symbols of thoughtless folly, and the charm of the metaphor is that it comes as an accident. Lear only thinks of the courtiers after he has said what he will do to the butterflies ; if any gilded rogues come in he will treat them the same way. This gets the politicians so much under control that they still seem brief mayflies at the end of the speech. But they are certainly not the chief mystery he is going to plumb ; and indeed to take the mystery of things *upon yourself* is an undertaking that only the mysteriously wise imbecile is entitled to. The few activities that he does suggest are so mixed that though wise they still seem to have the incoherence of folly ; the idea is guarded from clear statement, but we are to think of him as sane and yet leave him all the halo that he acquired in his madness and all the inconsequence that he learned from the clowns. She makes no answer, and no doubt she is certain that her sisters mean to kill them both.

> EDM.:   *Take them away.*
> LEAR.: *Upon such sacrifices, my Cordelia,*
>   *The gods themselves throw incense. Have I caught thee ?*
>   *He that parts us shall bring a brand from heaven*
>   *And fire us hence like foxes. Wipe thine eyes ;*
>   *The good-years shall devour them, flesh and fell,*
>   *Ere they shall make us weep ; we'll see them starve first.*

He did not think of it as a *sacrifice* in the previous speech, but now when she weeps he tries to present it as a renunciation, and therefore valuable. He asks if he has caught her because he fears he has not. It appears that they *were* parted, however briefly, when she was hanged. Maybe the reference to *heaven* makes " the gods " responsible again. The last words, so far from being regenerated, recall with a most painful irony his blustering speech to Goneril, about the terrors he would discover for her instead of weeping, and how his heart would break into fragments before he would weep—"Oh, fool, I shall go mad." Bradley admits this, and indeed at one point (p. 274) though not at another (p. 290) says that the sacrifice which involves taking upon oneself the mystery of things is "scornfully rejected."

We are not much concerned with the fate of the wicked, except to recognise that Albany can call it firmly "the judgement of the heavens". I want also to put in a word against a fine phrase by Mr. Wilson Knight, about the decision of Edmund to try to save Lear and Cordelia; "again", he says, "the Lear universe travails and brings forth its miracle". I think this idea would only occur to a critic who assumes that bad characters on the stage are meant to be devils. Edmund has not been shown as a bloodthirsty man, but simply as a ruthlessly ambitious one; he has no longer any reason for wanting to kill these people. (If he hoped to survive, his only chance would be to save them at once.) Nor, for that matter, is it surprising that he should accept the challenge of the disguised Edgar to trial by duel without inquiring whether he is a gentleman. An Elizabethan who got hold of a title by dubious means often did make a romantic display of courage, usually with references to the chivalric past; it was the best way to get people to accept him. Naturally Edgar is prepared to defend his honour in a dashing manner; he really is dashing, and he has had his father killed simply to get himself honoured. The line between good and bad characters is drawn very sharply in this play, but the first-night audience was, I should think, more ready than we are to see the merits of Edmund. So I do not think this good action surprising, but I agree that the movement of thought which leads to it is a very striking one. "Yet Edmund was beloved" implies that this is the only thing he can look back on with any sense of peace, with any assurance that his life was not worthless; both sisters have died of their lust for him, so after all he was somebody. It is perhaps a little fatuous of Bradley to say his father would have loved him if he had been better ("he has been out nine years, and away he shall again"; even when staying at his father's castle he evidently does not live in the main building). But after all the sex-horror of the play, which has been piled so nauseatingly onto these villains, it is a really magnificent twist to say that love was the only good thing about them.

Edgar is now properly dressed and therefore sane, indeed rather verbose. People are recovering their proper social positions, and the service Kent did for Lear now seems to Edgar "improper for a slave". It is perhaps worth noting, as part of the puzzle about his and Gloucester's religious opinions, that he now speaks in favour of suicide :

> *O, our lives' sweetness,*
> *That we the pain of death would hourly die*
> *Rather than die at once—*

This does not look as if the decision of Gloucester not to kill himself meant that he had attained a deeper trust in Nature. However, perhaps Edgar shows this deeper trust when he talks to his dying brother :

> *The gods are just, and of our pleasant vices*
> *Make instruments to plague us.*
> *The dark and vicious place where thee he got*
> *Cost him his eyes.*

It is an echo of Lear's reflection on the sufferings of Edgar— " judicious punishment "—where the punishment seems to be for an entirely legitimate sexual act. In any case, even the resentful Edgar and the sex-resenting Shakespeare cannot have believed all through the play that Gloucester deserved to have his eyes put out ; the sort of justice imputed to the gods is what is called "poetic", happening through agencies which have obviously no real sense of justice. And the way the gods do it is by " plaguing " us, and by inventing " instruments ", that is, instruments of torture ; they are also facetious and full of mean jeering tricks. I think that this pious acceptance of the gods does a great deal to recall the old picture of them as criminal lunatics.

The longwindedness of Edgar, and even the deaths of Goneril and Regan, are used to prolong our anxiety about Lear and Cordelia. Edmund repeatedly says he will do good and exasperatingly doesn't do it. At last things are in train to fetch them, and the prayer of Albany is answered by the famous irony of the stage direction :

ALB.: *The gods defend her. Bear him hence awhile.*

(Enter Lear with Cordelia dead in his arms.)

Nobody, I think, has denied that this crack at the gods is intentional, whatever it is taken to mean. Also, the death of Cordelia, and the death of Lear in consequence of it, are different from those of any other Shakespearean tragedy in that they seem wilful ; a point well made by Johnson and elaborated by Bradley. Nothing but death is possible for Macbeth and Othello, and at any rate nothing else is expected for Hamlet ; Timon goes roaring up to a death so desired and obvious that no cause for it need be assigned ; but with Lear and Cordelia the whole movement of " necessity " is finished and we last saw him planning a life of mystical gaiety. The death is like a last trip-up as the clown leaves the stage ; its shock and senselessness (of course I do not deny that it is essential to the effect) are as far as Chehov from normal tragedy.

There is a sort of terror about the pathos of Lear, and it arises chiefly because he is always on the edge of absurdity. The power of the last speech comes from the repeated delusions, the boasting, the pretence that Cordelia is still alive, and the unjust indifference to Kent. " Is this the promised end ? " asks Kent, who might mean the death in religious peace which Lear had aimed at by renouncing the kingdom, and had therefore deserved, so that in a way it had been promised. As a rule Kent means something practical, and it seems likely that Edgar misunderstood him. In any case his question in reply, " or image of that horror ? ", makes a final comparison of Lear to the cosmos and envisages, like several previous comments in the play, the ending of a world which it describes as insane. " Fall, and cease " continues the pious Albany, and I do not know that any critic has tried to call this a reconciliation with Nature.

It is rather hard to know just how much weight to put on these repeated hints about the end of the world. Many Elizabethans (though we now think of their period as such an expansive one) expected the end of the world quite soon, for various bad reasons deduced from the new astronomy ; the idea was that Nature had been proved to be in decay (the heavens were not perfect, as Aristotle had supposed) and would now decay fast. Perhaps one should not put too much weight on the chance that Shakespeare was echoing these learned theories, indeed, it seems likely (as far as one can see anything through the confusion of the subject), that he was rather opposed to them, though willing to make play with any topical idea. But one can be sure, I think, that some of the first-night audience did regard these hints about the end of the world as a further count against Nature, who was being blamed already. The religiousness of the Elizabethans did not stop them from entertaining the idea that there might be a quite unhealable Breach in Nature, and it was never heretical to expect the end of the world soon.

The chief problem of interpretation here is :

> *And my poor fool is hanged ! No, no, no life !*
> *Why should a dog, a horse, a rat have life,*
> *And thou no breath at all ?*

Fool has been taken as a kindly reference to the otherwise unrecorded fate of the clown, and this has a renewed attraction for our modern hard-boiled school, who regard it as a bit of tidying-up pushed in as a belated afterthought. The line breaks out as a wail after a tedious ten lines by Albany about rewards and punishments for the nobles, and even before that Lear was only dropping brief irrelevancies to Kent. His mind might have wandered to the clown ; he believes that "Caius" is dead too. However, this interpretation of the word would make the sentence contradict the movement of thought that it introduces, and must therefore be wrong ; the passage is in verse, whereas random wanderings are always in prose. The argument is that other creatures are alive but not Cordelia, and the whole impulse of the speech is concentrated on her. On the other hand the N.E.D. theory that *fool* was used as a term of affection should not be carried to the point of thinking that this use excluded the normal meaning of the word. It seems extraordinarily out of place to describe Cordelia. In fact, the word seems likely to puzzle the audience whichever way round you take it. One must suppose, as Bradley did, that his mind has wandered so far that he no longer distinguishes the two ; but this should not be softened into " a very old man failing to distinguish two of his children ". The Fool has not been required after the storm scenes, because the mad king has taken over his functions completely. But Lear is now thrown back into something like the storm phase of his madness, the effect of immediate shock, and the Fool seems to him part of it. The only affectionate dependent he had recently has been hanged, and the only one he had then was the Fool ; the point is not that they are alike—it is shocking because they are so unlike—but that he must be utterly crazy to call one by the name of the other. Presumably the audience was meant to accept it as mere raving and thereby get the right poetical effect ; it is meant to recall the whole background of clownery which is what he has discovered about the world. (And no doubt, if you deduce that the Fool was hanged too, that is consistent with the tone of the play ; but Lear was not likely to have inquired.) I do not pretend to know how to fix an equation onto such a use. But I think there is another touch of the same process (in the mind of Shakespeare, if not of Lear) when he says :

> *Never, never, never, never, never !*
> *Pray you, undo this button. Thank you, sir.*

The last time he talked about unbuttoning was when he tore off his clothes to be like the naked beggar, in search of the rockbottom which is the worst. There is no worst ; the only rockbottom he can find is the grave, and it is a release. In the next two lines he dies of a passion of joy at the false belief that Cordelia has recovered.

We should now be in a position to reconsider the George Orwell theory, the view that Lear's abdication is meant as a renunciation of the world, and that the moral of the play is " If you renounce power you must not also try to wield it indirectly by making people love and admire you." Bradley, who was a great assembly-point for critical theories, had evidently never heard of this idea. He describes Lear's plan as rather selfish, though not fatally rash till he changed it to spite Cordelia. This might mean that Bradley took for granted that there was a renunciation and that it was inadequate, but at the end of his treatment he gives a full discussion of whether the play recommends renunciation, and uses that word, and it never even occurs to him that Lear's plan might be an example of one. Indeed, he says that Gloucester (who made no renunciation —except in his attempt at suicide, to be sure, where he uses the word) provides the only sub-plot in Shakespeare which merely repeats the main story.

I must try to give a summary of Bradley's position about the gods, as it has the great merit of exploring the alternatives. He recognises that Lear and other characters describe Nature and the gods as wicked, but considers that this, if it were more than a cry of pain, would develop into the orthodox view that one had best renounce the world in favour of Heaven. Lear is thus learning to make a renunciation at the end, not learning that the one he made at the start was no good. On the other hand, Bradley feels that Shakespeare is too humanist to hold this position for long, or except in moments of indignation. After all, the world which produced the bad characters is convulsed by them and kills them all off a few weeks after they start to sin, whereas the good characters are made steadily better by their experiences in the world. The play might be called " The Regeneration of Lear ", and this is enough to refute any theory that the world as such is evil. But then again, the death of Cordelia (and in consequence of Lear) is presented as an un-necessary accident ; Bradley discusses how this can be satisfying, and decides that it can hardly satisfy at all except by a vague assumption of Christian belief. " The more unmotived, unmerited, senseless, monstrous, her fate, the more we feel that it does not concern her." Nothing matters except to build up a good character, and once that is done the sooner you die the better. Bradley does not put it so brutally, and appears to describe an unwanted death as a renunciation in order to put it gently, but it is what his argument requires. " I might almost say ", such is his phrase, that the " moral " of the play is given by *the gods defend her*, followed by the entry of her corpse, because prosperity " breeds " all kinds of vices. The remark about vices is not directly applied to Cordelia, but I do not see what else he can mean except that Cordelia would have become corrupted after a happy ending, so that the gods defended her in the only possible way. We can call this pessimism if we like, he remarks ; it is in the play, but cannot be prominent in it, or the play would no longer be tragic.

The main thing about this argument, no doubt, is that it succeeds in turning the blasphemies against the gods into the orthodox view held by Mrs. Gamp, that the world is a Wale. I do not know how seriously he took his last little twist of piety, the view that Cordelia was sure to become corrupt. It is curious how often the puritan high-mindedness can be found interlocked with an almost farcical cynicism. But even if involuntary it seems to me a *reductio ad absurdum* of his line of argument. (The way to make it tolerable, I suppose, would be to say that death-wishes in the audience are being satisfied, but it is always hard to join ideas about the deep unconscious onto the structure of conscious judgements with which you follow a play.) And it seems no better to say, as other critics have done, that the accident of her death is meant to express the same feelings as Thomas Hardy's nasty fancy, in *The Dynasts*, of the Spirit Ironical. To believe in a spirit who only jeers at you is superstitious without having any of the advantages of superstition ; besides, it has a sort of petty wilfulness, it comes of trying to think of something nasty to say. If this is the atheist view of the tragedy it is as disagreeable as the Christian one. Whatever one says about this huge play feels very inadequate, but the Orwell theory seems to me to fill a gap, and to be consistent, and to suit the actual development of the imagery. Perhaps, as he expresses it, it belongs to our age rather than Shakespeare's, but I do not know why it should be a remote one then ; indeed one might say that a Jacobean audience, being trained in theology and fine points of conscience, would pick it up more easily than later audiences.

This is not to deny, of course, that pious members of an audience might adopt Bradley's point of view at any date ; indeed, George Orwell, as I understand him, means that such an other-worldly point of view is actually presented for consideration, though he calls it a deadly one and believes that Shakespeare did not hold it. But the reason why Cordelia gets killed is no longer a problem; that the execution was carried through after the change of government is just the kind of thing that happens in the confusion of a "liberation", and indeed is almost typical of the forces that Lear had set loose. The point of interest is the doctrine that " if you want a renunciation, you must be prepared to go the whole hog ". Orwell would deny that Lear is " regenerated " ; his picture of the thing shows the old man " still cursing, still not understanding anything " at the end. Indeed, I think that if Lear really seemed regenerated to the point of accepting his calamities (including the death of Cordelia) the play would become sickly. And on the other hand Bradley's remarks about renunciation, which in his text is a mere euphemism for unwanted death, become much more relevant if the audience thought that the play began with one. But on the Orwell view I do not see that we can regard the blasphemies against the gods as pious ejaculations in favour of Christianity. Not indeed that they are specific attacks on it ; they are not more shocking than the Book of Job. The point surely is that the world is a place in which good intentions get painfully and farcically twisted by one's own character and by unexpected events. Lear has failed to understand the nature of what he has undertaken, and is falling between two stools ; the very nature of things is tripping him up. The standard process of comparison in the double plot is not therefore nullified by becoming a repetition; Gloucester is deliberately deceived by Edmund, but Goneril and Regan do not deceive Lear more than he forces them to ; if then Lear is " like " Gloucester in being deceived it is because Lear has deceived himself. Well may Gloucester achieve patience and Lear plunge with increasing violence into the mysteries of folly. A record-breaking display of evil is let loose by the process, and this forces us to hold in balance the ascetic and humanist views of the world ; but the balance is held even, and the gods remain a teasing riddle.

They are in any case peculiar objects, because they are offered neither as the mythology of a definite historical period nor as a belief of the playwright. The view that they represent merely Nature, behind whom is the good God, does not seem to me a very obvious one for the audience. " God " and " the gods " were almost alternatives in the theatre ; a listener might well take these gods as a term for God adopted to evade the blasphemy laws. But this need not make him think the play intentionally blasphemous ; as in reading the classics, one would feel in a certain sense irresponsible when following the thought of pagans in such matters. What we gather directly about the gods is that they are confused ; apparently they can suffer as well as cause suffering, but in any case they can fool and cause fooling. What is so disgusting about Hardy's Spirit Ironical is that nobody has a chance to call it Fool ; these gods are more intimately involved with mankind. The foolish Lear can compare the storm and the heavens to himself, and the stock metaphor from the clown and the lunatic can be extended to include the cosmos. Such is the impression from a literal reading, I think, and critics have either evaded it or hailed it as being anti-Christian. But, if you take it as simply a result of working out the key metaphor as far as it would go, you need not expect it to have a clear-cut theological conclusion ; the problem for the dramatist was rather to keep such a thing at bay. The effect of the false renunciation is that Lear has made a fool of himself on the most cosmic and appalling scale possible ; he has got on the wrong side of the next world as well as on the wrong side of this one. I do not think one need extract any more theology from the gods.

A rather interesting distinction, I think, needs to be drawn here. If you assume that a key word, or better no doubt a whole pattern of related key words, is the proper thing to follow in considering a poetic drama, you get a noticeably different result in this play from the result of the Victorian assumption that the characters ought to be followed separately. Maybe both are different from the result of a simple visit to the play, but the play could be produced to suit either assumption. What the key-word or " pattern " approach brings you to, I submit, is a fundamental horror, an idea that the gods are such silly and malicious jokers that they will soon destroy the world. The question whether Shakespeare meant this or not is still quite a live controversy, and usually thought to be independent of any question of critical technique. It is most often raised about the words of Gloucester, " As flies to wanton boys are we to the gods ; they kill us for their sport ", and I have noticed critics on both sides showing impatience with those who are so blind as to disagree with them. As part of the description of a character the words are not very important, because Gloucester soon gets out of this mood of despair, though only into another one ; but as part of the pattern of clown-imagery in the play they make a big moment, easily recognized as one in the theatre. I think that the moralizing critic could not usefully attempt to deny this. But he could still reasonably claim that the parts of a play which the author left obscure or atmospheric, so that a verbal analysis is needed to dig them out, are not *therefore* the decisively important ones—why are we not to suppose that Shakespeare threw in a gloomy "atmosphere" rather recklessly, and that the attempts of later critics to make a tidy doctrine about it can only mislead them ? We might, indeed, have reason to think that Shakespeare was putting into the atmosphere notions which he dared not express more frankly, and then we would have reason to give them serious weight. But in *Lear* I am not sure that the hints had the importance of being unsafe. It is thoroughly Christian to say that Nature is inadequte to the human spirit, and that the world will come to an end. As for the attacks on " the gods "—the Olympian troupe, if that is in question, does behave fairly clownishly in the myths ; one could argue from the text that a bad kind of paganism is considered and rejected, and certainly a Christian audience need not be shocked to hear a pagan discover for himself that his gods are bad ones. I can't see that Shakespeare had anything to worry about from the ecclesiastical courts. On the other hand, of course, I do think that the suggestions of a fundamental horror in the play were meant to be prominent, whether you interpret them as some profound intuition about life or prefer to say, more simply, that the theme released a lot of real bad temper in him. In any case, from the point of view of his immediate actors and audience, I submit, it was reasonable and not theologically suspicious to have this background of cosmic horror, because the play was about the huge evils which could follow from a false renunciation.

Where there does seem room for a religious view is through a memory of the Erasmus fool, that is, by being such a complete fool Lear may become in some mystical way superlatively wise and holy. It seems hard to deny that this idea is knocking about, and yet I think it belongs to the play rather than the character. The idea is already present, in its flattest form, if you think " it is very sad, but after all I am not really sorry it happened, because it teaches us so much". And the scapegoat who has collected all this wisdom for us is viewed at the end with a sort of hushed envy, not I think really because he has become wise but because the general human desire for experience has been so glutted in him ; he has been through everything.

> *We that are young*
> *Shall never see so much, nor live so long.*

Chapter 7

THE ENGLISH DOG

FROM the sixteenth to the eighteenth centuries a number of English words, *arch, rogue, fool, honest, dog* and so forth, went through a cycle of curious slang or "emotive" uses that invoke patronage, irony and sympathy, and though we still give them slang uses we keep on the whole to the last stage of the cycle. It seems to me important, as a matter of history, to understand how the cycle went, because a man tends finally to make up his mind, in a practical question of human relations, much more in terms of these vague rich intimate words than in the clear words of his official language. Also they are interesting words for linguistic theory or plain dictionary-making, because some of their uses get a strong "period" feeling, a thing it is often essential to understand if you are to get the point of a piece of writing, and yet a thing it is difficult to list even for a dictionary on the grandest scale. One is in doubt how far the period feeling was genuinely put into the word, as its meaning in this special use, how far we imagine it there by association whereas during the period the feeling was simply everywhere—it comes out for us in this word only through a rival use that makes it evident. So that once you let yourself "read things into" these words they seem to mean a great deal ; indeed absurdly too much, except that this gives you a handy way of summing up part of the thought of the period, and an insight into the way that this part came to seem obviously true because always suggested by language. Also I think that this family of words carried an interesting and controversial part. It is a commonplace that the formulae of a religion like Christianity or Buddhism may be interpreted in many ways, some exalted, some merely civilizing, some definitely harmful, and that when actively at work in a society they form a kind of shrubbery of smaller ideas, which may be the most important part of their influence, yet which also may be a half-conscious protest against the formulae, a means of keeping them at bay. There is a main puzzle for the linguist about how much is "in" a word and how much in the general purpose of those who use it, but it is this shrubbery, a social and not very conscious matter, sometimes in conflict with organized opinion, that one would expect to find only able to survive because somehow inherent in their words. This may be an important matter for a society, because its accepted official beliefs may be things that would be fatal unless in some degree kept at bay. Chat about rogues and other Rabelaisian figures tends to be cosy from a safe distance, and I am not trying to say that the exponents of the hearty uses of these words were nice people ; they may have been of great value to our society but very nasty. The web of European civilization seems to have been slung between the ideas of Christianity and those of a half-secret rival, centring perhaps (if you made it a system) round honour ; one that stresses pride rather than humility, self-realization rather than self-denial, caste rather than either the communion of saints or the individual soul ; while the words I want to look at here, whether in their hearty or their patronizing versions, come somewhat between the two, for they were used both to soften the assertion of class and to build a defence against Puritanism.

Rogue and *arch* have I suppose had no literary triumphs, and can be used quickly to show the background from which this family of slang arose. *Arch* has degenerated into facetiousness more completely, but appeared in the sixteenth century with the same aura of romantic villainy, and the same mystery about its birth, as the less temporary *rogue*. Skeat suggested and then denied that it was connected with a Saxon root " arch- " for " low and thieving " and got its character from the clash between this and the Greek " arch " for " old and ruling " ; there is at any rate an irony in its first conception, from the contrast between the accepted versions of *arch-*, e.g. archbishop, and the arch rogue ; indeed, only the weight acquired by the ironical contrast explains why " arch " as *chief* was not used more generally. I suspect that many uses also draw on the Latin *arch* and the curved bow of the archer, suggesting arched eyes of pretended inquiry, the back arched in mock dignity, curled separated fingers, or muscles stiffened in a moment of social tension. Thus the word goes with an unwilling admiration both for the rogue's ability and for a certain comic force in him which makes moral condemnation seem irrelevant ; there is already a suggestion of the clown. This softened very little while changing its milieu at the Restoration :—

> " Last night I supped at Lord R.'s with a select party ; on such occasions he is not ambitious of shining : he is rather pleasant than arch : he is comparatively reserved . . . "

Rochester when " arch ", one would suppose, had not the coyness suggested by the modern use ; the word means more nearly " outrageous ", mainly in the way he " rallied " people. Playful uses may be found earlier but as a special treatment of a word in itself insulting. With the Augustans the word becomes somewhat fatuous because always playful, and the " arch rogue " descends to asking the innocently piercing question which in the nineteenth century would be asked by a child.

Rogue is a word of darker origin which appeared suddenly in the sixteenth century and rose almost at once from slang to the statute book. It was needed because of a great and dangerous increase of vagabondage, due to the failure of monastery charity, the supplanting of small farmers by great newly-rich landowners, the change from plough to sheep, and so forth ; thus it stood for a class regarded with fear as well as horror and yet with a sort of sympathy because their condition was not their fault. The sympathy gets very little rational expression, and is mixed up with the sneaking sympathy of mankind for the successful criminal, also with the Noble Savage feeling, but it gives a clear historical reason for the mixed nature of the word. Of the many suggested derivations, which I cannot criticize, a few are worth quoting for their inherent interest. Ben Jonson fancied it was derived from " erro ". Two derivations from *rogo*, through the ideas " begging " and " arrogant ", make a neat clash ; an obscure English *rug* " pull or catch ", hence later a cheap woollen cloth, hence Shakespeare's " water-rugs ", a shaggy breed of dog, takes us to the dog idea ; the verb *rag* " to tear " maintained a long life in dialect as " scold " before its nineteenth-century emergence into upper-class slang ; and there was a word *roger* for " a wandering beggar who pretended to be from a university ", which has probably some real connection. The sound effect is likely to have been important in getting the word accepted (whatever the source it must have been unknown to most accepters) ; it clashes " roam " with the final " g " of " dog ", a sound at the back of the throat which suggests either outcasting and contempt or a pointing at one's inner man. It is more definite to look at an early account of them : Harman's *Caveat for Common Cursitors* (1566). They come only fourth in the hierarchy of vagabonds, so it was never the extreme word for a desperate character.

> " A rogue is neither so stout nor so hardy as the upright man. Many of them will go faintly and piteously when they see, either meet any person . . . halting though they need not, requiring alms of such as they meet . . . but you may easily perceive by their colour that they carry both health and hypocrisy about them."

The story illustrating their habits makes them rob a person of four marks and extract a promise that he shall drink " twelve pence for our sakes to-morrow at the alehouse ". The good wife says " they be merry knaves. I warrant they mean to buy no land with your money ". A subdivision of the class is viewed more gravely.

> " A wild Rogue is he that is born a rogue. He is more subtle and more given by nature to all kind of knavery than the other, as beastly begotten in barn or bushes, and from his infancy traded up in treachery . . . when they meet in a barn at night, every one

getteth a mate to lie withal . . . Then, when the day doth appear, he rouses him up, *and shakes his ears*, and away wandering where he may get aught to the hurt of others."

It is the latent comparison with dogs which is so powerful here ; one is forced to suspend the horror so fully expressed in the rest of the paragraph ; to be delighted that such independent creatures can be so gay and strong. The genuineness of the effect depends on its being incidental ; you must feel in real danger from robbers and anxious to get them cleaned up. " Few venture to go alone in the country," said an Italian visiting England, " excepting in the middle of the day, and fewer still in the towns at night, and least of all in London." In 1589, just after the Armada and Tamburlane, " a band of about five hundred " disbanded soldiers, back from Drake's expedition to Portugal, " threatened to loot Bartholomew Fair. Martial Law was proclaimed. Two thousand City militiamen turned out . . . to scatter a horde which was menacing the capital . . . It was at least six months before the panic abated " (*Elizabethan Underworld*, Edited by A. V. Judges, 1930. Introduction, p. xv). One needs to remember this sort of thing before treating as mere gaiety the hearty tone about rogues, or about Dogberry's incompetence at catching them ; it is trench humour, like the jokes on venereal disease.

I should like to put here a verse from Luke Hutton's *Black Dog of Newgate* (1596) to show the solidity of feeling which might appear behind the rogue business, and that it was not only written up by literary fanciers (Hutton seems to be accepted as genuine). While starving in Newgate and waiting execution this highwayman hears the voice of the prisoner chained to the outside wall, who begged food there not only for himself but for all his fellows.

> *Woe's me, thought I, for thee so bound in chains.*
> *Woe's me for them thou begs for to sustain.*
> *Woe's me for all whose want all woes contains.*
> *Woe's me for me that in thy woes complain.*
> *Woe's me, woe's you ; and woe is to us all.*
> *Woe to that dog made me to woe a thrall.*

The beggar who speaks for the others takes on the functions of Christ, and seems to include the others in himself. A queer suggestion of mutuality, not merely that we are in the same boat but that you could say about me what I say about you, clings to the words I want to examine, and finds a direct and splendid expression here.

To find what became of this sentiment in the eighteenth century one had best avoid finished and artificial works like the *Beggars' Opera*, but I think so sensible a man as Fielding would have sympathized with Horace Walpole's affectations on the subject. It made life " very Gothick " to have the highwaymen still so powerful ; " so that one cannot travel, even at noon, without arming oneself as if for a battle. To such a perfection have all the arts been brought." Walpole plays this game with all the cards in his hand ; he is an aristocrat because he is a hereditary Whig and revolter against tyranny : at one end of the thing, he knows that Shakespeare was a rogue and vagabond in law ; at another, so was Sir Robert Walpole in the *Beggars' Opera*. It is rather like Queen Victoria's claim to be a Jacobite, but also a little like what Jefferson meant when he said he hoped a truly democratic America " would never go ten years without some sort of revolution ". The main point, of course, is that by Walpole's time one was much safer ; the thing has become playful ; even the realistic and seriously humane attitude of Fielding does not suggest that the rogues are many and dangerous enough to excite trench humour.

With this goes the emergence of " you (gay, young) dog " beside " you rogue ", and both terms may now be applied to respectable characters. The humour of mutuality in the word shifts from the good citizen's feeling about the vagabond to a man's feeling about those in his own set. But I have missed out a stage in which this shift was forced through. The Restoration aristocrat, or rather the kind who affected language through fashionable slang (and in a less degree the genteel wit of the other Charles' days, shadowed by the same threat from the forces of Puritanism), combined pride in a display of rakishness with a queer sort of political scepticism, quite compatible with being a Tory. It was easy for him to use "rogue" in the old sense about a friend. This would imply that the friend was out-and-out, fit for power, and yet that he had a reckless courage felt to be " generous " (a key notion for the words) more because it meant throwing his life away than because he or anyone was helped by it ; that he had accepted a sort of social outlawry by becoming an end in himself. When Steele and Addison set out to make respectability fashionable they did not attack (or directly admit) this feeling in the words—it was part of the accepted social tone that they meant to build upon—but perpetually clashed against it the older feeling that such a man can be patronized ; and they had considerable success in fixing the mixture. It is easy to write absurdly, and hard to know one's way, about this " gay dog " business. The flippant Etherege, who started the Restoration comic tradition, thought drunkenness an unforgivable fault in a young man, and approved rather solemnly of liaisons in high society because that was the only way to make it go in for intelligent conversation ; in his indignation with the society that was so shocked by him when he was ambassador at

Ratisbon he writes more like Matthew Arnold than a " rogue ". Whereas Rochester, who really had the touch of suicide that the gay tone pretends, who was perhaps tricked into the effect of suicide by a belief that it was fashionable, hardly ever uses such words, and in his best work, which is his most desperate, rises outside their tone altogether. The hearty use of " good fellow " dates back at least to Chaucer (where it describes the kind of man to whom the Sumnour would lend his concubine), and there were plenty of people under Victoria inventing slang phrases of this sort, but there was not a general political revolt against Puritanism to make it catch on. The point for the linguist is not that the Restoration gentry were unusually roguish, but that during the Restoration a fairly permanent way of feeling had enough influence to affect certain words.

" Dog " is an important one. The word plays an unusual trick in first getting its hearty feeling in one or two special phrases, which seem already to depend upon a feeling about dogs denied in other uses of the word. Before the Restoration the dog of metaphor, by and large, is snarling, a sycophant, an underdog, loose in sex and attracted by filth, cruel if it dare ; " love me, love my dog " means " love the meanest thing about me ". There is the Biblical dog, a pariah, living on crumbs and Jezebel as they drop (" a dog's chance "—he is dependent on human society and yet friendless in it) ; also the dog-faced Thersites of Homer, a mean and envious mocker (staying in the manger, barking at the moon). Shylock is eminently a dog of this sort and often called so ; a man so placed can hardly be expected not to pervert justice, though this is a warning for you, not an excuse for him. It is not clear how far this feeling would apply to actual dogs ; they do not get the full weight of it, but the change in a stock proverb seems to show that the earlier feeling was that they deserve pity as being normally (yet therefor rightly) ill-treated. "As good a deed as to help a dog over a stile," 1546, an act of supererogatory and unconventional mercy ; whereas the version of 1638, " help a lame dog over a stile ", puts in the adjective to make an otherwise natural action pathetic, and is a direct metaphor for helping a man. It is clear anyway that very mixed feelings are there to be drawn upon.

The derivation of the word is not known, but something can be said about the effect of the sound, which makes it particularly ready to carry a duality of feeling. (In discussing sound like this, one is concerned with what *can* be felt in the sound in special uses, not with a thing that forces itself on your attention all the time.) Compare the opposite sound *God*, which begins at the back of your throat, a profound sound, with which you are intimately connected (" ich "), and then stretches right across to a point above the teeth, from back to front, from low to high, with a maximum of extension and exultation. " D " does not stop the movement as " b " would by closing your lips, so that the idea can shoot upwards straight out of you. The suggestion of retching in the " g " (" gob ") is absorbed by this, and an effect of disgust appears only in swearing, for which the word is well suited. In " dog " you do not simply do this backwards ; both consonants have to be pronounced forwards though the vowel goes back, and the effect can hint at a change of mind. The " do " sound is all in the front, connected with an external object ; it moves the tongue out and down with an effect of giving (as in the Aryan root) or of ejecting something from the front of the mouth. Then (with a sudden movement of affection, or a discovery of the truth, or a final anathema) the word reaches across to something deep, personal to you, and despised.

Orion makes a fine discourse on dogs in *Summer's Last Will and Testament*, which it seems he has taken from Sextus Empiricus' *Pyrrhoniae Hypotyposes* ; it shows the kind of thing you could feel about actual dogs, as apart from metaphorical ones, without coming very close to them. Being a hunter, he is concerned with the dog's natural wisdom, faithfulness, and so forth ; one might connect Shakespeare's view of dogs with his not coming from a hunting class and his evident sympathy, in *Lucrece*, for the hare.

The more obvious Elizabethan view, the idea of the dog as a cynic (which Nash throws in to his set of claims), seems to be in part a learned innovation. Few people nowadays observe their dogs to grin, and those who do take it as a charming smile, but the grin of dogs seems then to have been part of their reputation for satire. I take it that the medical use (1615), " Convulsions we call Cynic or dog-spasms because by the contraction of these, men are constrained to writhe and grinne like dogs ", is a foreign or ancient association of ideas that still needed to be explained. The Biblical " grin like a dog and run about the city " would insist on this aspect, whatever the original meant, and Ben Jonson seems to connect this with the idea of a man " grinning in the rage of his lust ". It is curious to compare Pope's version of the reminiscence from this Biblical phrase :

> *Nor like a puppy dangle through the town*
> *To fetch and carry sing-song up and down.*

This important puppy is quite a different dog. No dog grins in Chaucer. I suspect the Elizabethan dog's grin needs a more learned treatment than I can give it. However, there was a more obvious element in dog behaviour that fitted the cynic ; the habit of making water often and on conspicuous objects, actually (I believe) as a signal to the next comer, but mistaken by men for a symbol of contempt. The *Return from Parnassus* (1601) makes the point clear about Marston as cynic or malcontent : " What, Monsieur Kinsayder, lifting up your leg and pissing against the world ? Put up, man ! Put up, for shame." This notion of the dog as cynic could of course be used with warmer approval, as in the claim made for himself by the Fool in *Lear* : " Truth's a dog must to kennel, when Lady the brach may stand by the fire and stink." The connection seems to have been settled and proverbial ; thus Joseph Hall's *Characters* end the section on the Malcontent with " Finally, he is a querulous curre . . . in the deep silence of night the very mooneshine openeth his clamorous mouth ".

This connection with cynicism is puzzling to modern sentiment, which tends rather to stress the unreasoning fidelity of the creatures ; and certainly there were contrasting ideas. Various combined words show a feeling of low but sturdy and permanent usefulness about them—e.g. *fire-dogs*, and *dogs of iron* to support a steeple (1458). Also a charming mixture of ideas seems to be at work in the word *fawn*. The N.E.D. gives this as a development of " fain " in the sense " rejoice at pleasure ", and gives it a special origin through a phrase about dogs " faining " or " faining with " their tails (from 1225). The word might also make them *desire* or *welcome* what they wag their tails at, or indeed " congratulate their own tails ", and the pun with " feign " would help the shift toward servility ; in welcoming a master with uneasy attempts to make peace they are " lying with their tails ". Shakespeare, as has often been pointed out, had a sort of fixation of disgust between the words " spaniel " and " candy " ; the dogs always appear slobbering and melting their sweets, and the cynic imagined as *dog* always at bottom wants to get on in the world he despises. The word *hypocrite* itself, indeed, seems to have something of the double meaning of " fain " and " feign ". The N.E.D. rightly refuses to separate into two senses the uses for conscious and unconscious hypocrites, and ends its list with a nineteenth-century statement that the two are inseparable. Seeing that the examples can hardly ever be separated it is interesting to find More giving an ambiguous explanation after his early use of the word—" Ipocrites that *fain* to have virtues that they lack ". The word being needed for purposes of insult has steadily refused to make a distinction which many of its users must have known would be charitable.

Lear brings in dogs fifteen times, or more if you count synonyms ; partly because it stresses animals in general, to call up the mysteries of nature. They chiefly appear as snobs, cruel to the unfortunate, also either as flatterers or as habitually flattered (" They flattered me like a dog " iv.4.158). The Fool has a phrase " dog in madness " which apparently appeals to hydrophobia, in a determined effort to make metaphorical dogs join the variety of lunatics already represented in the play. This is no part of the ordinary symbolism, which makes dogs typically, even if offensively, sane. Shakespeare had thus reached the height of his anti-dog sentiment just before the mysterious pro-dog gestures which are part of the cynicism of *Timon*.

The merits of a dog in ordinary Elizabethan metaphors about men come out only through the two phrases " shaking its ears " and being " a dog at all things ". The Variorum edition of *Twelfth Night* gives seven contemporary references for " go shake thine ears " under a use of it by Maria (ii.3.126), and decides that it is an expression of contempt used always for helpless asses. Actually only two of the references name an animal at all ; one of these, *Julius Caesar* iv.1.26, names an ass as metaphor for a laborious fool, but Shakespeare is very capable of re-applying a stock phrase, and the more obvious one names a dog. " Thou must get thee packing, thou damned dog, and go shake thine eares, for in me thou hast nought " (Stubbes, *Christall Glasse*). Of course, one could put the phrase on to any such animal, and I only need to show that it went easily on to dogs. No one could say that the ass rather than the dog was at work in my quotation from Harman, about the rogue who shook his ears and went off looking where he might do aught to the hurt of others. The phrase there has a strangely eighteenth-century feeling ; it is made delightful that the rogues should be independent, and somehow encouraging that they should be like dogs. The idea behind the phrase is that the dog (for instance, in shaking the water out of its ears after being thrown into the pond) shows a cheerful stoicism based on independence and indifference to dignity. The paradox of the independence of a specially dependent creature is as clear here as in Fool.

The dog can easily be made to seem important as blowing the gaff on human nature,* but only the phrase " a dog at all things " allows it a more general admiration. Nash had used " he is old dog at expounding " some years previously in a context of contempt, and this, perhaps, is the root form. Lodge uses " he is dog at recognisances and statutes" (*Wits Miserie*, rather later) in the sense of " a clever scamp ". I suppose there is an additional joke when Sir Andrew Aguecheek says he is " dog at a catch ", as it suggests the dog howling in sympathy while his betters sing ; and there is a terrible point in the phrase when De Flores in *The Changeling* says he is "dog at a house on fire" ; the lust of the underdog is witty at

---

* I have kept on using " blow the gaff " for something like " give the low-down ", with the extra idea of puncturing something inflated. It is too meaningless to be a good phrase, and apparently it is used by criminals merely for " betray a plot to the police ". But I have failed to think of any better one.

contriving ruin. The phrase in cases like this, though it can be hearty in a degree, starts from patronizing the " *old* dog " who leads the pack ; it stands for the absurd but specialized powers of the country wiseacre, knowing not rationally but by the instinct of long experience. This stress on instinct could however shift over to the idea that the young aristocrat has natural good manners, so that the word was ready for the chance it took at the Restoration.

The brief sixteenth-century fashion of swearing by Dog's wounds instead of God's might also be mentioned ; the dog is God's opposite in sound so you can swear by him as the scapegoat—blame everything on the dog. Cf. " By no devils, I will not go " ; " I swear by no God I will repay on Thursday." These are more desperate but still feel that they evade responsibility. Similarly the American " doggone ", supposed to have developed in the latter half of the nineteenth century. So far as the dog is connected with God by sound it is easy to make him a devil, as in the black dog of care and the black dog of Newgate, and this makes him important. The idea of sexual looseness also carried weight in this direction ; the high-class rogue sentiment of the Restoration could use this for " cuckold-maker ; outside or above the safe tidy world of marriage " (cf. " bitch ", which remained firmly rude because women could not make a joke of not being chaste). At what date Arbuthnot's John Bull acquired his Bull-dog, whose original function was to bait the Bull, I have been unable to discover. This breed of dog is pre-eminently " dogged " in the later sense of that word, which Dr. Johnson did not put in his dictionary ; but he said that the Duke of Devonshire had a " dogged veracity ", which meant high praise, and that a man could always write verse if he would set himself doggedly to it. The old sense was " cursed, malicious ", then " fixedly malicious ", " obstinate " (as the harsh view of Fool made a man obstinate), and from this it took its eighteenth-century twist into " having rugged strength of character ". Various elements which had given the dog strength as a symbol of evil could still give it strength as a term of praise.

This is far from " gay young dog " as a rib-digging term of affection, a phrase for a careless creature sniffing his way from one pleasure to the next. No doubt " dogged " itself was felt to be connected with the verb, and the verb took this direction because " dogging a trail " was one of the more important activities of a dog and happened to need naming. Besides, the other actions wanted of dogs are dogged processes like going on barking till someone comes. But the " sea-dog " is rugged and independent, unyielding, a pioneer, dogged in short, though he has no such connection with the verb. It gave the eighteenth-century use a considerable range of praise. Though become respectable, the human dog keeps something of the independence of the outcast; he is at least un-doubtedly sure of what he wants, and the suggestion of slyness adds to his competence and keeps his animalism from stupidity. There is also enough " blow-the-gaff " feeling about calling a man a dog to give him a fundamental sincerity (as if by reflection from the speaker); he does not hide the truth about himself and thereby shows the truth about us all.

It might seem that the playfulness of the eighteenth-century use, the shift from the outsider to the clubman, would destroy all that deserved respect in the words; for what deserved respect in the earlier use was the power to combine breadth of sympathy with a sense of danger. But the new uses found for them were no less serious. I shall take Dog here and assume that Rogue, Arch, Honest, etc., did the same, because in a way this was the most important one. Dog, it is absurd but half-true to say, became to the eighteenth-century sceptic what God had been to his ancestors, the last security behind human values. " Men are no more than animals. No man by any effort can escape the charmed circle of self-interest." " Materialist " ideas of this sort were in the air, not so often believed as feared to be possible. " Yet if the worst is the dog, humanity is still tolerable." I know of no parallel development on the Continent to the English dog, though *honnête* did a good deal of the work*; it gives one a sense of Voltaire's real qualifications to discover England when one finds him, in old age, with wary but genial admiration, shaking his head over Dr. Johnson to Boswell and calling him (" in the English phrase ") " a super-stitious dog ". The stress, of course, is on *superstitious;* with the stress on *dog* it would have seemed as rude then as it does now. *Dog* is unstressed because the phrase assumes that everybody is *some* kind of dog, so that that is not the distinctive feature of Johnson. It is the pastoral idea, that there is a complete copy of the human world among dogs, as among swains or clowns. I think there are two elements in the thought behind this word, which can be distinguished roughly as rationalist and humanist.

The eighteenth-century rationalist limited very sharply the impulses or shades of feeling he was prepared to foster—not merely Enthusiasm was cut out but the kind of richness of language that

---

* Montaigne covers this whole range of ideas, and does not regard them as new : " among the most moderate opinions, I meet with some discourses that go about and labour to show the near resemblance between us and beasts, and what share they have in our greatest privileges, and with how much likelihood they are com-pared unto us " (II.xi). Dogs are prominent in his emphasis on the point, and he has a baffling remark " Do we not daily see monkeys ragingly in love with women, and furiously to pursue them ? " (*Raymond Sebond*). All I am claiming for the English as against the French is that the French do not seem to have gone in for the joke phrases.

Gray lamented over in a passage from Shakespeare—and yet could pursue Reason with gusto and breadth, without emotional skimpiness ; there is a savour in his work which a man such as Herbert Spencer has lost. The feeling that the dog blows the gaff on human nature somehow attached itself to the ambition of the thinker to do the same, and this helped to make him cheerful and goodhumoured. His view of our nature started from a solid rock-bottom, a dog-nature, which his analysis would certainly not break in digging down to it ; this made him feel that the game was safe, and the field small enough to be knowable. Whereas Shakespeare felt that " there is no worst ", and the corresponding depths to him were fearful degrees of lunacy ; " fool " was his earth-touching word, not " dog ".

If one considers the richness of the intuitive poetry, of the emotional life the language took for granted, in the seventeenth century, it is surprising that the eighteenth could make so much of its more narrow material, could base so much poetry on a doggish mock-heroic. It was the simplicity of this feeling, on the other hand, which let them prune down so far towards rationalizing their emotional life without killing the tree. But there was a danger of killing it. A surprising number of the great writers went mad, and most of them feared to ; indeed, the more you respect reason the more you must fear the irrational. Thus another use was found for the Dog in the way it stood for the Unconscious ; for the source of the impulses that keep us sane, and may mysteriously fail as in drought. Its process of thought is a mystery, but the results are homely and intelligible ; it makes what we do not know about the roots of our own minds seem cheerful and not alarming. Swift, for example, kept himself sane for as long as he did on secret doses of this feeling (and on the collection of beggars to whom he gave the money gained by cheese-paring) ; its goodhumour and humility are somehow at the back of and make endurable the most regal solvents of his irony. Yet he would shy very decidedly from the humanist application, and his ideal animal is the pointless " calculating horse " (the horse as generous has a point all right, but not the horse as Cold Reason).

The humanist application corresponds to the hearty use of these words, as the rationalist one does to the patronizing use. Of course humanism was a complicated affair, and the term has not always been used to mean what I mean here ; I am using it for something vaguely anti-Christian. The reason the early humanist put so much weight on learning correct Latin and reading classical literature in bulk was—not exactly to put the anti-Christian idea across under cover, but to put it across in a way that would allow the pupil to digest it within Christianity ; as something that applied to life in a different way, rather than conflicted. The fundamental novelty was an idea that " Man is no longer an abortive deity, born in sin, necessarily incomplete in the world, but the most triumphant of the animals ". To call him a dog playfully is thus to insist on his rights ; he is better than a dog, but has the same reasons for being cheerful. It brings in a sort of pastoral feeling to do this ; that there is a sweetness or richness in the simple thing, that to cut yourself off from it would be folly, that it holds *in posse* all later values ; also the fact that you need to remind yourself of it may show how encouragingly far it has been left behind. The essential here is that you can start building yourself into a man, and not hate yourself, on the basis of being that kind of animal ; the trouble about Evolution was that one could not feel the same about monkeys.

There was, indeed, a widespread feeling towards evolution before Darwinism, such as both uses of dog-sentiment would suggest. Bentley claimed rather absurdly to find an example of it in Milton, and said " he remembered this senseless notion spread about " ; Coleridge speaks of " that absurd notion of Pope's ' Essay on Man ', of man's having progressed from an orang-outang state ".

> *Still as one brood, and as another rose,*
> *These natural love maintain'd, habitual those ;*
> *The last, scarce ripen'd into perfect man,*
> *Saw helpless him from whom their life began.*

Sure enough, these laboriously obscure lines can hardly mean anything but the development of men from unreasoning creatures— what is a natural sentiment to us, for instance, was not so to the first brood. There is a more dangerous hint a few lines later, that the idea of good was developed only because it " preserved the kind ". The striking thing, however, is that critics were so ready to pick up a hint of this line of thought. The fact that monkeys were so like men was " sadly humbling " to Boswell ; Monboddo only dared to say what many had suspected, and Johnson agreed he was not a fool. Swift might fall back on the Houyhnhnm in accepting this about the Yahoo, but that was a refusal of humanity ; the only real animal to use was the dog. And, indeed, it is comforting to reflect that this apparent evasion was to a great extent the truth. Whatever the spiritual quality we dislike in monkeys may be, there is no positive evidence that our common ancestors shared it ; and even if they did, for a much greater period of time they were straightforward mammals like a dog or a squirrel. Even our ancestral reptile, in the pictures, is made to stand up on its legs and look about it like a puppy. There is a curious agreement, at any rate, that if we are animals this is the kind of animal we would like to be.

What the human state of nature may have been is no clearer in

Warburton's notes on Pope than in the text, but the bishop has a surprising remark about a monkey.

> *Superior beings, when of late they saw*
> *A mortal Man unfold all Nature's law,*
> *Admir'd such wisdom in an earthly shape,*
> *And show'd a Newton as we show an Ape.*

". . . it was not Mr. Pope's intention to bring any of the Ape's *qualities*, but its *sagacity*, into the comparison. But why the *Ape's* it may be said, rather than some more decent animal, particularly the *half-reasoning elephant*, as the Poet calls it ; which, as well on account of this excellence, as for its having no ridiculous side, like the Ape, on which it could be viewed, seems better to have deserved this honour ? I reply : Because as a shape resembling human (which only the Ape has) must be joined with great sagacity, to raise a suspicion that the animal, thus endowed, is related to man ; so the spirituality, which Newton had in common with Angels, joined to a penetration superior to Man, made those Beings suspect he might be one of their order."

Few men but Warburton would have decided that the elephant had no ridiculous side on which it could be viewed. But the feeling that a monkey is indecent is normal enough, and went deep into the troubles of Darwinism. The idea that the dog pisses against the world, on the other hand, has done hardly anything to make us think dogs indecent. Warburton goes on to call this couplet a new species of the sublime, peculiar to Pope, in which he has the Art to combine Wit and Sublimity ; " this seems to be the last effort of the imagination to poetical perfection ". If the thing required such unique powers of imagination, one is tempted to feel, it may perhaps mean more than Warburton's official explanation of it. Indeed one might think that the discovery of the great apes was one of the decisive forces in the shift towards seeing the Renaissance Magnificent Man as the most triumphant of the animals. It is difficult to find out exactly who had seen apes and when ; the creatures need to be big, I fancy, if they are to impose any searching reflections. Monkeys are absent from the modern heraldry of the Boy Scouts, but in 1303 the Fitzgeralds had some kind of monkey big enough to carry a child out of a burning house, if you believe the story about their coat of arms. Live apes arrive in Europe later than you expect ; hardly at all till the nineteenth century, and probably Pope was thinking of a monkey (the division between the terms is late). But the Prince of Orange had a chimpanzee, the only ape that kisses, in 1641, and a travel-book in 1670 believed that apes walking erect were used as general slaves in Abyssinia, and the English had a fair account of Pongo the gorilla from an escaped captive called Martell in 1698, who was copied by Buffon. Monboddo saw a stuffed Orang at Versailles, where it had died of drink. But Monboddo's theoretical writing, though certainly inspired by the problems of the ape, is very insistent that the interesting cases are some entirely human creatures who merely happen not to have discovered speech ; these people (about whom he has elaborate and quite false information) set an interesting problem to the linguist and the philosopher, but it is very unfair to them when people mistake them for apes.

I doubt whether there is a case for saying that the actual sight of apes was what startled Europe into a change of thought. The time would have to be earlier than Descartes, whose assertion that animals are machines but men are not was important mainly because it gave great publicity to the question, together with an evidently wrong answer. Christianity requires a sharp distinction between the creatures with eternity before them and those without, and given the mechanist scientific idea a rigid mechanist view of animals was the only one that fitted comfortably. This would be enough to raise a new puzzle about the relations of men and animals, seeing that it is difficult to take a crudely mechanist view of a dog you go hunting with ; so that if we are to consider the apes a crucial factor we must show that they put ideas into the mind of Descartes ; and there were reasons to make him think that way even if he had never heard of them.

However, even if the ape affected the philosophers, and he probably did not very much, the importance of the dog is of a different kind ; you get a great deal of him in casual speech as a way to fix a line of sentiment. Thus Boswell and Johnson both speak of the Laird of Col as the best example of the natural man, which only showed the more clearly that they were something higher. He was Johnson's social superior if not Boswell's and had been educated in England, but they insist on the romance of idealizing him as a savage. Of course it was a joke, but the joke brought in feelings that were important to them.

"Young Col told us that he could run down a greyhound ; ' for (said he) the dog runs himself out of breath, and then I catch up with him '. I accounted for his advantage over the dog, by remembering that Col had the gift of reason, and knew how to moderate his pace, which the dog had not sense enough to do."

It is very winning to see Boswell patting him on the head, as the better dog of the two.

"Dr. Johnson said, ' He is the noble animal. He is as complete an example of an islander as the mind can figure. He is a farmer, a sailor, a hunter, a fisher ; he will run you down a dog ; if any man has a *tail*, it is Col.' "

The phrase seems to have grown out of his reflections on Monboddo, whom he had recently met, but it is no longer concerned with controversy against Monboddo. It is tremendous praise, and while it is ringing in our ears we can understand the generosity latent in more satirical uses of the word. The important point about the noble animal is that he is a deeply reassuring object to contemplate. The fact that he can be patronized as no more than fundamental makes you think better of the race of man.

This is the sea rather than the gay dog, but it is interesting that Johnson accepted the Noble Animal, the humanist feeling about such an animal, so frankly in jokes and casual talk. *Tom Jones*, he thought, was wicked because it was an attempt to make the hearty dog-sentiment into a system of morality ; whereas in serious talk you must keep to the rationalist one, as a sane recognition of the Old Adam. So far, indeed, as this meant praising the masculine virtues of the man who wastes all his family's money (and the feeling easily tumbles across into that) Fielding retracted it in the more feminist *Amelia*, which Johnson admired. But there seems to be a more fundamental issue. *Tom Jones*, Johnson said,

" resolves virtue into good affections, in contradistinction to moral obligation and a sense of duty."

Fielding was

" the inventor of the cant phrase, goodness of heart, which is every day used as a substitute for probity, and means little more than the virtue of a horse or dog."

Johnson here has to use a synonym for *honesty* and put *horse* beside *dog* to keep the slang senses from rising at him.

It seems to be true that there is an ethical theory latent in the jokes on *dog*, that Fielding took it seriously, and that it is not Christian because it does not start from the Fall of Man. But the theory, as such, cannot well have been what made Johnson complain, because it is still there in *Amelia*, which he approved of.

" The behaviour of this man alone is sufficient proof of the truth of my doctrine, that all men act entirely from their passions ; for Bob James can never be supposed to act from any motives of virtue or religion, since he constantly laughs at both : and yet his conduct towards me demonstrates a degree of goodness which, perhaps, few of the votaries of either virtue or religion can equal."

(III.v.)

Religion is not necessary because man is naturally good ; but this appears only in revolt against another doctrine which a Christian might consider false, that only those actions are morally good which are done on principle and against the grain. The feeling was too universal to be formalized as a sect ; if someone tries to, the joke language about dogs is dropped and we receive lectures from the

Noble Savage. By calling a man " you young dog " one certainly
need not mean that he had no, or a new kind of, moral sense, still
less that he was a free-thinker, and if it meant sexual freedom it
generally meant disillusionment about that as well. The feeling is
strong when Gray's Divinity encourages Jemmy Twitcher with

> *He's a Christian enough that repents and that itches*

or when Pope's Duchess is

> *A very heathen in the carnal part*
> *But still a sad good Christian at her heart.*

Indeed the phrase " a sad dog " brings out the feeling particularly
sharply. It is chiefly like " a sad muddle ", which makes other
people sad who have to deal with it ; also it is sad that he should
be so much of a dog—being a bit of a dog would be all right. But
I think there is an obscure humour from the idea of the dog being
sad too ; he seems gay, but no, he is always in a great mess. At
bottom he feels the sadness of the thing, just as we do. Perhaps
there is a feeling that this dog has the right Old Adam to build a
New Man upon, and that he is discovering virtue for himself by
independent experiment. Such a joke manages to absorb the
humanist version into a Christian view and also to back it with a
rationalist version ; a very complicated piece of play. It is surely a
striking reflection that a great deal of the thought of a man like Dr.
Johnson, and probably the parts of his thought which are by this
time most seriously and rightly admired, were not carried on his
official verbal machinery but on colloquial phrases like the one about
dogs ; phrases that he would have refused to analyse on grounds of
dignity, even if he had been able to. No doubt you need to know a
great many other things before you can understand the working of a
society ; but there is a claim to be made for the branch of study I am
touching on here. You need to know, as well as the serious opinions
of a man in the society, how much weight he would allow, when
making a practical decision, to some odd little class of joke phrases,
such as excite, he would feel, sentiments obvious to any agreeable
person, and yet such as carry doctrines more really complex than the
whole structure of his official view of the world.

Chapter 8

TIMON'S DOG

THE study of metaphor in Shakespeare would obviously be valuable if one knew how to set about it, but there is a large question as to which metaphors should be taken seriously. The very laborious work of Miss Spurgeon, in which all the metaphors are counted and classified, left one doubting whether there is any significance in figures that lump together a descriptive metaphor and a normative one (let alone the problem of what an " image " may be). This is certainly not a reason for dismissing her results, because no doubt all metaphors are in part both, but the interpretation of them is bound to be tricky. The extreme case of normative metaphor is clear enough in principle. The thing becomes a " symbol " and involves a high degree of what would be called "pregnancy" if free from metaphor—e.g., *man* in "He was a man; take him for all in all, I shall not look upon his like again ". That is, various adjectives are taken as typical of the noun, and there is an obscure assertion that it ought to possess them ; in the case of metaphor, this gives further obscure assertions about what is typical or proper for the thing described. One might say that the only metaphors to pick out and examine are those used like this ; Miss Spurgeon, I take it, would have claimed that even the most careless or conventional metaphors have a kind of statistical total effect, and no doubt both processes occur though they need to be distinguished. But the most interesting case, or anyway the difficult one to handle, lies between the two. A way of making the metaphor a " symbol " is in view, but though the thought centres round the metaphor, and it is continually used, the author will not accept its symbolism.

The use of *dog* in *Timon* is a handy and interesting case, and I want here simply to discuss that without plunging into a general view of metaphor. Miss Spurgeon had a small triumph over some critic who said that the metaphor of gold was fundamental to the play ; her actual count found one doubtful metaphor from gold and a continual protean metaphor from dogs. He could still claim that gold as an implied metaphor is more important than most of the actual ones of her counting ; Timon still handling gold in misery is a symbol stronger than most verbal effects, and indeed, the metaphor of a golden nature as a noble and magnanimous one raises the whole puzzle of the play—how far Timon's nobility is essentially that of a rich man, even when it becomes sacrificial and suicidal.

But the dog too cannot be dealt with by addition. I am indebted to Mr. Wilson Knight for pointing out the extreme subtlety of thought in this uninviting play, but feel sure that he over-simplifies by making Apemantus a mere symbol of Nasty Cynicism and Hate. There is an unusually strong case for his viewpoint here because Shakespeare himself was over-simplifying, but Shakespeare does not cheat Apemantus either of his jokes or of the arguments for his side. I shall try to show that Shakespeare is both presenting and refusing a set of feelings about *dog* as metaphor, making it in effect a term of praise, which were already in view and became a stock sentiment after the Restoration. It is a popular but tactfully suppressed grievance that Shakespeare did not love dogs as he should, and I think the topic is really a large one ; when you call a man a dog with obscure praise, or treat a dog as half-human, you do not much believe in the Fall of Man, you assume a rationalist view of man as the most triumphant of the animals.

It seems necessary to define special terms for dealing with cases like this. The first sort of " symbol " is a normative metaphor, making a strongly pregnant use of the word ; it tells you what to think about the class it appears to name, or tells you which are the " typical " specimens of it. The new sort has in view two alternative ways of doing this, so as to imply a conflict of judgements. I shall call that a " double symbol ". And thirdly, such a word may come to imply a way of reconciling the contradiction, though no doubt this will only be " in the word " in a peculiar sense ; perhaps that the doctrine of the author is felt to be absorbed into his whole style, and particularly present in the style when he uses this key word. I call such a word a " master symbol ". It is a specially elaborate kind of fourth-type equation, whereas the double symbol seems to be a pair of rival third-type equations, and is anyway a pair of rival pregnancies. " Dog " in *Timon* is then a double symbol but not a master symbol.

One can see that it *could* have been a master symbol ; indeed, this I think is why it is important to define terms, so as to make clear that it is not. Apemantus is continually called " dog " (in a play clearly meant to be taken as symbolic) with the sense " snarling and envious critic ", also as " ill-conditioned "—he will " famish, a dog's death ". But this kind of critic is a person of recognized value in Shakespeare ; there is much of him in Jaques and Hamlet as well as Iago. At one end, as the character who though somehow low will tell the truth, he joins on to the respected figure of the Fool ; at another, he is the disappointed idealist. Contrariwise, Apemantus continually calls the courtiers of Timon " dogs " with the sense " flatterers ", and puzzles are contrived to include Timon in this as well. But the flattery given by a dog is a type of how you can be foolish and mercenary and yet sincere ; the creature shows love to get still more food but is really affectionate. This was an obvious point in Erasmus' *Praise of Folly* (and therefore certainly known to Shakespeare). Erasmus was maintaining that flattery was not mere lying but belonged to the valuable kind of fool, and said " What is more fawning than a spaniel ? Yet what more faithful to his master ? " Thus both the opposed types of dog could be praised. But this would not impress Shakespeare, who found spaniels particularly disgusting because of the way they melted their sweets. (Actually the Latin of Erasmus only says dogs, but spaniels come into the first English translation, which Shakespeare is more likely to have read.)

We may recall what Miss Welsford says of Erasmus' *fool*, which really is a master symbol. It could be applied either to the respectable people (scribes and Pharisees) who would be fooled at the Judgement Day, as would the proud rogues, or to the unpretending people, failures in the eye of the world, who give sound criticism under the guise of folly ; thus it held the crucial positions at the two ends of the scale in hand. Furthermore, it implied an escape from the conflict of these criteria—all men are fools in the eye of God ; we are dependent on God ; it is our nature and he will allow for it. Now the metaphorical dog came to give a different escape, one that suited a rationalist individualism ; its humour implied that you could start from the rock-bottom low man because he was a decent kind of animal. Shakespeare believed that " there is no worst ", and would have no truck with the rock-bottom sentiment. Yet the dog in *Timon* holds the key-positions at both ends of a scale ; furthermore it gives a hint of escape from the conflict that made the scale important, because there is a hint of liking for dogs in general. Certainly the great majority of the metaphors imply hatred of dogs, and the fact that the dogs *might* have been used to praise both ends of the scale is not relevant. But Shakespeare, elsewhere, normally made the metaphor from dogs rude. The curious thing is that this play also praises dogs, and apart from the fooling of Launce (who was like a dog himself as a kind of " natural ") they are praised nowhere else in Shakespeare.

I shall try to list a paragraph of dog-praises ; perhaps only the last is clear, but it affects the interpretation of the others. One may doubt over the first words of Apemantus to Timon :

TIM. : *Good morrow to thee, gentle Apemantus.*

APE. : *Till I be gentle, stay for thy good morrow ;*
When thou art Timon's dog, and these knaves honest.

The main point of this is to make Apemantus mention dogs at once and whenever possible, but, however little it means, *dog* is somehow parallel to *honest*. One can read it as dramatic irony—when Timon becomes a cynic (what people call Apemantus a dog for) and the knaves become honest in the sense of showing their villainy, then Apemantus will try to be gentle to Timon before the cave. But the only relevant point is that Apemantus regards becoming a dog as some kind of forward step. Timon himself catches the trick of talking about dogs when he exposes the courtiers at the pretended banquet—" uncover, dogs, and lap "—the " flatterer " sense, but from then on he too can mention actual dogs with an obscure cordiality. Having found one honest man in his old steward (not in Timon or Apemantus) he gives him money on condition he gives none to mankind :

> *But let the famished flesh slide from the bone*
> *Ere thou relieve the beggar ; give to dogs*
> *What thou deniest to men.*

Not hearty praise of dogs, but there is something more like it in the crucial scene with Apemantus :

APE. : *What man didst thou ever know unthrift, that was beloved after his means ?*

TIM. : *Who, without those means thou talkest of, didst thou ever know beloved ?*

APE. : *Myself.*

TIM. : *I understand thee, thou hadst some means to keep a dog.*

One might think the dog was prepared to love him for such means as he had, therefore was a flatterer, but the paradox admits that in a way he had no means, and that one would expect a dog to be faithful even so.

APE. : *I was directed hither ; men report*
Thou dost affect my manners, and dost use them.

TIM. : *'Tis then, because thou dost not keep a dog*
Whom I would imitate. Consumption catch thee.

This retort seems baffling rather than effective. Timon wants, or at any rate proceeds, to deny that he has imitated Apemantus ; but if Apemantus is like a dog, and Timon would imitate his dog if he had one, probably he has imitated Apemantus as the nearest thing. Nor is there any clear insult in telling him so. And if Apemantus' dog would be a flatterer (kept dog) he would be quite a different animal from Apemantus, a cynic (pariah dog) with no one to keep him. Certainly, Timon goes on to the paradox of calling the cynic a flatterer, but this seems to be derived from the confusion, and the bewilderment of the two critics on their central issue is already visible in their first words. Finally, in a surprising remark of

Timon to Alcibiades, it is hard to deny that dogs receive obscure but real praise :

> *For thy part, I do wish thou wert a dog,*
> *That I might love thee something.*

The merits ascribed to dogs would I suppose be " affectionate ", " faithful ", and in view of the money-hatred in the play " indifferent to money ". But there is little interest in their merits, and the first impulse seems to have been a fellow-feeling for men who are called dogs, gained because contempt for man had extended to self-contempt. Men treat Timon and Apemantus as dogs ; Timon and Apemantus notice at last that they cannot escape being men, so that there is some logical puzzle for them in railing against mankind ; let them then praise dogs, among whom they are metaphorically included as cynics, and in rebuking man they may half-praise themselves. But the dog from this angle is disgusting rather than cynical, chiefly because he enjoys smells that we agree to call disgusting. Timon and Apemantus take pleasure in recognizing the worst ; they are pleased therefore by dogs' pleasures and view dogs as their allies.

The idea of pleasure in self-contempt goes deep into the Elizabethan theme of the Malcontent, and I do not know where else it has been put so clearly. We are told it about Apemantus in the first scene, before he has appeared. The Poet has described the existing situation in his play :

> *yea, from the glassfaced flatterer*
> *To Apemantus, that few things loves better*
> *Than to abhor himself : even he drops down*
> *The knee before him, and returns in peace*
> *Most rich in Timon's nod.*

This need not be unfair to Apemantus. To look to a higher world because of the faults of this world is always to accuse oneself of its faults, so that all other worldly pleasures in men might be classed as perverse pleasure in self-contempt ; not to see them so would be hubris. Timon himself as a cynic is too little aware of this logical puzzle (thus remaining Renaissance rather than medieval) :

> Tim. :   *all is oblique :*
> *There's nothing level in our cursed natures*
> *But direct villainy.   Therefore, be abhorr'd*
> *All feasts, societies, and throngs of men.*
> *His semblable, yea himself, Timon disdains.*
> *Destruction fang mankind.   Earth, yield me roots.*

In digging for roots, however far from mankind he may now be, he is trying to keep one man from destruction. We are told clearly that he " disdains himself ", but he does not follow this up when railing at other people. Actual pleasure in disdaining himself he avoids recognizing.

The idea that there is nothing direct but villainy is a generalization of the ascetic outlook seen best when it works the paradoxes of *The Fable of the Bees*. What is direct is the satisfaction of a simple appetite (digging for roots) ; if you take so exalted or insane a view as to call all satisfaction of appetite villainy, on the grounds that it is worldly and self-centred, you are safe in agreeing with Timon. All the less simple satisfactions (meditation on God or pleasure in self-contempt) may at least be paralleled by perversions of appetite and treated as identical with them. The only trouble is that Timon is still wicked to dig for roots, but he could claim that as a minimum. Yet on a similar ground one could claim the pleasure of self-contempt as a spiritual minimum (without it there is hubris). Thus, when Timon and Apemantus meet before the cave, each has strong grounds for priding himself on his own version of self-contempt and despising the other's. Nobody pretends that *Timon* is a very good play, but given the Malcontent theme this is the cleverest treatment of it ever written.

A main source of their puzzle is that they seem only to have exchanged the senses in which they are dogs ; Apemantus has become a flatterer and Timon a cynic. The only effect from their teasing this problem is to suggest that each may always have been both. Yet they are meant, of course, to be quite opposite characters ; the play insists on this by very unfair means, as when Timon finds gold in the desert and can thus go on throwing it away, still more when he turns out to be an important general, the only man who can defend Athens against Alcibiades. In the last words of the play, after the victorious Alcibiades has read out the epitaph of un-remitting hatred which Timon erected over himself when he buried himself (it does not appear that he also killed himself ; he simply chose to die), we gather that the good influence of Timon will make all the Athenians forgive one another in a Christian manner ; it is he, in effect, who is to

> *make each*
> *Prescribe to other, as each other's leech.*

This is hard to treat as anything but a daydream of self-justification, but the whole point of it is that Timon was somehow right, owing to his golden nature, whereas Apemantus was wrong.

In the first scene, with a delicate irony on the part of Shakespeare, the Poet describes how he has written what amounts to the play of *Timon* as a means of flattering Timon and getting money out of him. It is in his list of flatterers that Apemantus (interested in a similar exposure) is described as chiefly enjoying self-contempt. Some such puzzle is necessary to the position of Apemantus in the play, for he has to be brought to the feasts as if he is to comment on them. He himself claims to have come partly to glut his eyes with the falsity of the world (pleasure in contempt) and partly to do Timon good ; the Poet would claim that this was itself flattery of Timon, showing that Timon's money could collect even incorruptible philosophers to advise him.

TIM. : *Now Apemantus, if thou wert not sullen, I'd be good to thee.*

APE. : *No, I'll nothing ; for if I should be bribed too, there would be none left to rail upon thee ; and then thou wouldst sin the faster.*

This claim to goodwill becomes plausible when he follows Timon to the cave, but by an ingenious twist the accusation of flattery is made more plausible as well.

TIM. : *Depart.*

APE. : *I love thee better now than e'er I did.*

TIM. : *I hate thee worse.*

(Till now they have hidden both love and hatred.)

APE. : *Why ?*

TIM. : *Thou flatterest misery.*

Poor Apemantus backs out and claims to have come out of ill-nature, and this again is made to prove him a knave. He flatters Timon's misery as well as his own by the offer of friendship ; they are to enjoy railing and self-contempt and thereby feel superior to mankind. Also this has a real likeness to flattery, because Apemantus is a cynic only from the accident of his birth :

TIM. : *If thou hadst not been born the worst of men*
Thou hadst been a knave and flatterer.

This is easily retorted ; Timon has become a cynic only through " change of fortune ". The claim that Timon was always a flatterer is less simple, but Apemantus starts on it as soon as he is rebuffed. At any rate Timon had better become one now :

APE. : *Shame not these woods*
By putting on the cunning of a carper ;
Be thou a flatterer now, and seek to thrive
By that which has undone thee . . .
What, thinkst that the bleak air, thy boisterous chamberlain,
Will put thy shirt on warm ?

Under cover of the irony or self-protection of this false advice the poetry offers Timon the mood of the exiles in Arden rejoicing in Nature because she does not flatter. Timon is in no mood to admire anything, certainly not Nature ; her use is to provide symbols of the faults of men, and the attraction of " preparing

himself " a grave by the sea is that it stands for eternal bitterness
and infertility. On this view Apemantus is the better dog of the
two, and his rudeness has offered the romanticism as tactfully as
possible. When this is exposed as " flattering misery " he makes
the more searching point :

> APE. : *If thou didst put this sourcold habit on*
> *To castigate thy pride, twere well : but thou*
> *Dost it enforcedly ; thou'dst courtier be again*
> *Wert thou not beggar. Willing misery*
> *Outlives uncertain pomp . . .*

Again ; he was a courtier when he was holding a court. The harlot
Timandra has the same kind of accusation against him ; " Is this
the Athenian minion, whom the world voiced so regardfully ? "
This is a refinement of money hatred that Marx failed to pick out of
the play ; Timon's generosity was a way of begging for affection,
and it makes him the same kind of dog as the spaniels he could hire.
Timon might answer to the main point that he has in fact found gold,
and stays in misery from disillusionment about friends or hurt pride ;
but that would not answer the claim that he was a spaniel.

The answer of the play is no doubt that he has a noble nature, and
Apemantus a mean one ; but people agree that Timon gets his
apotheosis too easily, and it is not only a fidget of logic to complain
that the dog theme is unresolved. The most convincing claim for
Timon appears when he urges the thieves, in Apemantus' manner,
to go on thieving, and gives such profound reasons that one of them
decides to stop. No one would pay so much attention to Apemantus;
Timon keeps a certain grandeur and generosity which works for
good however much he wants to do harm. But the paradox amounts
to denying Timon's ascetic position, with which Shakespeare seems
to identify himself so wholeheartedly, and the final arguments
against Apemantus are little better than snobbish.

> TIM. : *I, to bear this,*
> *That never knew but better, is some burden.*
> *Thy nature did commence in sufferance, time*
> *Hath made thee hard in't. Why should'st thou hate men?*
> *They never flattered thee ; what hast thou given ?*

The unreason of the question has the pathos of Lear thinking
Edgar had been sent mad by daughters, but he goes on, less like
Lear, to exult over Apemantus for low birth. After a bout of that,
we have :

> APE. : *Art thou proud yet ?*
> TIM. : *Ay, that I am not thee.*
> APE. :   *I, that I was*
> *No prodigal.*

Tim. :   *I, that I am one now.*
Were all the wealth I have, shut up in thee,
I'd give thee leave to hang it. Get thee gone.

Apemantus is clearly right in saying Timon cannot claim to be otherworldly ; he is proud of good birth or of being born into money, and apparently proud of having just found some. But Timon's apparently simple insults amount to a claim for aristocracy ; the accident of birth has saved him from meanness of nature, and the otherworldly life can be reached only through a sort of success in the world. It is a splendid answer, but not only to Apemantus ; it throws a crucial paradox into the whole cult of asceticism, known to Shakespeare chiefly as Christian. One would think a Christian audience would be bound to reflect that Apemantus is more like a saint than Timon is. And even here the dog rides the conflict ; on the one hand a low creature which distributes contempt, on the other it is good-humoured because self-satisfied about its direct pleasures (what else has Timon felt in generosity and glory ?). Yet in the play the only effect of the idea is that Timon can go off unanswered into neurotic insanity, and Apemantus is forced for contrast into a reasonable view of life in which he can cut no figure. They are left with only abuse to entertain themselves :

Tim. : *Choler does kill me that thou art alive.*
I swoon to see thee.

Ape. :   *Would thou wouldst burst.*

It seems likely that Shakespeare wrote the scene both in bitterness of spirit and as a hurried working-over of a play whose somewhat thin plot was already drawn up. To do that, he had to bring out some of his root ideas in a crude form, a process he would find irritating, but this has the convenience of letting us see them clearly. The striking thing, I think, is that the dog symbolism could be worked out so far and yet remain somehow useless. One would not expect it to solve the puzzles any more than *fool* does elsewhere, but it should make us feel better about them. Actually, after all the argument, its parts remain quite separate—the dog does not manage to become a " symbol " that includes cynic and flatterer, flattery and affection, so as to imply a view of their proper relations. It remains a bridge over which they exchange puzzles, and the generalization of it amounts mainly to letting you feel the same kind of distaste for a variety of different people. Yet the range required for the jovial Augustan dog-sentiment, and even the feeling about dogs, are all present ; the thing is offered and refused. There is no palliation fit for Timon, and he can find no rock-bottom above the grave—it would be stupid to say that mere full use of the metaphor would have made the play better. But this kind of analysis seems to me to show that the metaphor had a large use, that the refusal was tested, that in an obscure but continuous fashion there was a palliation held in view.   And anyone who wants to clear up the very baffling topic of metaphor (perhaps too fundamental to be cleared up) needs I think to hold in mind cases like this, the most radically complex type, and the fact that machinery like this may be at work even in a metaphor of settled convention and apparently simple form.

Chapter 9

HONEST MAN

THE Highlanders raised cries of " honest man ", in Boswell's *Tour to the Western Isle,* after a farmer's wife had sat on Dr. Johnson's knee. "But what", as Boswell very sensibly asks, " could he have done ? " There would have been another puzzle for the lexicographer if he had tried to explain the word. The cry is both patronising and cordial, even both mocking and respectful ; the farmers meant that he had seemed frankly pleased, therefore a good fellow, but also virtuous, therefore both worthy and absurd. At least, that is what I should have thought it meant, but Boswell insists very firmly that this was a " Scottish phrase " and merely " an expression of kindness and regard". He ought to have known, but then he was also concerned to pass things off adequately smoothly. No doubt it is a plausible view that the Scotch had stuck to the older use of the word. One feels it would have been clear enough on the spot ; but the text leaves it very doubtful.

Uses of this kind, very complicated but somehow obvious within their own group of speakers, seem interesting in themselves and likely to bear on questions of linguistic theory. I cannot attempt to explore all paths which lead from this point, for example, to explain what is considered honest in big business, or why it is only in English that this romance word has come to mean telling truth. It has been a rich and shifting but always somehow real and intelligible term of praise, so that it would illustrate, if you could get the performance clear, what people in a given group were prepared to praise, why they were prepared to praise it (that is, what twist of moral feeling made them choose to praise it by this word), and again, perhaps chiefly when different groups meet each other, how far people were able to suggest or impose their moral outlook simply by the way they used the moral word. Clearly the first thing to get clear is the historical development, which is very completely recorded (under a bad system of classification, I think) in the N.E.D.

In Chaucer's time it meant " deserving and receiving social honour ", and any humour or irony put on top does not affect this basic feeling. The poignant and in time cloying simplicity of most of the characters in the *Canterbury Tales* comes out in a steady vague use of it—" I am speaking seriously and keeping moral judgment in play." Owing to this frequency it can come down to mean hardly more than " conventional ", as when the Pardoner

is asked for a tale without " ribaldry " and says he can't think of
that unless he has a drink :

> *I moot thynke*
> *Upon som honeste thyng, while that I drynke*

(The sense " chaste " is already strong.)   The nearest I could find
to the later rich uses comes about a man hiding himself abroad :

> *And eek men broghte hym out of his contree,*
> *From yeer to yeer, ful pryvely, his rente,*
> *And honestely and slyly he it spente*
> *That no man wondered how that he it hadde . . .*   (A 1440)

" Sly " only meant clever, it seems, but that makes little difference.
The sense of "honestely" seems to be "not in the riotous pleasures
that attract attention ", so " in a respectable way ", also "steadily
and carefully, like a good tradesman." But it carries a kind of
interest in this process, which the story tells us no more about.   He
must have been a very worthy capable man.   And then there is the
monk who always brings " some manere honest thing " as a present
to help the process of seduction (B 1240) ; something worthy of this
generous giver.   The sustained and always double irony of Chaucer
can be felt in the word here but does not darken its simplicity.

About the middle of the sixteenth century a vague slang use of
honest for general praise among friends, on a good fellow basis,
became strong enough to cut itself off from the feeling of moral
approval.   This is quite different from even habitual mild readiness
for irony, because it makes a serious use liable to be misunderstood ;
it therefore necessitates a change in the head sense.   My only basis
for giving this date is the way the word gets cut out of successive
translations of the Bible.

> " And those members of the body, which we think to be less
> honest, on these we put more honesty."—(I Cor. xii.23).

Tyndale's version, 1526.   This gets changed to " honourable, . . .
more abundant honour"; the N.E.D. classes the sense as "looking
respectable."

> " And Solomon said, If he will show himself an honest man,
> there shall not a hair of his head fall to the ground ; but if wicked-
> ness shall be found in him, he shall die."—(I Kings i.52).

Coverdale's version, 1535.   The Authorized text (1612) makes him
" a worthy man ".   Some cases of the older use of " honest " were
kept in, but they can be regarded easily as an extension from
the new root sense " not lying, not cheating, not stealing ".   Cases
like these two had to come out because they might be laughed at
from the slang point of view.   Thomas Wilson's *Logic* (1551) gives
a good picture of the slang use, which he does not regard as new.

" The fault of a logical deduction . . . is in the matter, when words are doubtful and may diversely be taken.

> *I had good cheer in such a man's house.*
> *Ergo, he is an honest man.*

Here the fault is in the definition, for if I would go about to define an honest man, everybody would laugh me to scorn, if I would thus define him. Whatsoever he is that doth as he would be done unto, and wrongeth nobody, but liveth still uprightly, godly, and continently, the same is an honest man, or else not. Notwithstanding in talking of honest men, evermore the wealthiest are considered, and therefore this and such like talk is commonly used. An honest man, saith another, for he will eat his meat I warrant you, he is none of those scrupulous consciences, he hath the Bible in the house you may be sure."

There seems to be an intentionally amusing puzzle between the unscrupulous conscience and the Bible in the house, but it goes to show that this early hearty use had no animus against Puritans. This man is not a Chestertonian Catholic ; maybe he keeps the Bible because he is cheery on the reformation side, and takes a practical view of Salvation by Faith. (Sir Thomas More seems to have thought that a common attitude.) The last of Wilson's examples is the use for a friend taken alone :

" Thou art to blame, quoth he, to deprave such a man's estimation, for by God's mother he is a very honest man, for he is my special friend, I would thou shouldst know it, and therefore cease thy railing."

There is nothing raffish about these uses, except in the idea " not over-scrupulous ", but they gave the word a new and rival feeling, so that the old use had to fall back on things that could not be misunderstood, that undoubtedly deserved solid praise. Hence we get the three elements that would now be given as the head sense, " not lying, not stealing, keeping promises ", though the older general sense went on living in the background.

But in the new sense the word at once developed irony. As something normally demanded, not something admired when pointed out, it could be used for patronage, especially by contrast with the hearty use among friends. A man you praised for mere honesty was in a position where it was hard to be honest, or could not be praised for anything else. The clash of this with the permanent claims of the word then gave convenient twists to express both pastoral sentiment and rogue sentiment ; you could retain a touch of the patronage in warm praise for simple people, and also praise rogues with it as not being hypocrites, where one sense of the word is used directly though the effect is ironical. The hearty use among friends could then throw in both pretended patronage and a hint that the friend was a rogue ; hence you could imply that you preferred your friend to be a fundamental rock-bottom man, and that this figure is independent of the laws of society. Also, the truth-telling aspect then acquired the prominence which it still holds ; this tended to imply that the rogue or friend was an amusing critic, a man ready to blow the gaff. However, the development of the hearty use goes on mainly among low or raffish people until the Restoration, when it comes to power in a slightly new form.

The following example from George Herbert gets its play from pastoral sentiment and patronage :

> *Shepherds are honest people ; let them sing ;*
> *Riddle who list, for me, and pull for prime ;*
> *I envy no man's nightingale or spring ;*
> *Nor need they punish me with loss of rhyme,*
> *Who plainly say, My God, my king.*

The claim is that he can write good poetry though he is plain and direct (does not write a conceited ostentatious style) and though he uses genuine religious beliefs (does not use pagan mythology or the myth of chivalry that the mistress is perfect). The force of the trick is that *shepherds* may be all parties concerned. Either (A) the personages or authors of pastoral poetry, which uses the conventions that he attacks—if they are genuinely pagan and really have feelings about the spring (which they generally don't), even if they are only *pulling for prime*, for that matter, acting on a vanity as trivial and touching as a country game, still let them write in their vain style and leave Herbert to his. A touch of rogue-sentiment here but mainly patronage. Or (B) they may be people with genuine good taste who like simplicity, such as Herbert claims for this piece of writing itself (with absurd untruth), or simple poor people who need edifying poetry—let them have something from Herbert that they can understand. This is the double claim of pastoral. Or (C) they may be parsons like Herbert, looking after flocks, rather low people socially, as he felt, and he gave up a career to become one. These people are not likely to write poetry well, but after all they are worthy ; let them write as they please. It is clear I hope that *honest* can follow *shepherd* through the whole set of tricks. The elaboration of the style is a kind of parody that makes the directness of the last line more moving.

As to the many rich uses in Shakespeare, I think the chief point is that he avoids the simple hearty use between equals, perhaps disliking the raffish twist of it which was to become powerful after the Restoration ; and I think these feelings are at work about " honest Iago ". But there is only room for two small points. The apology of Lucullus for not lending money to Timon in distress, Timon who has made his fortune ; " Every man has his fault, and honesty is his ; I ha' told him on't, but I could ne'er get him from 't." This sums up the charge that he " keeps too fine a house ". Of course the main purpose is to satirize the bad excuse. There might be some satire on men like Lucullus who misuse *honest* to mean " riotously sociable ". The main sense is " generous to friends ", claiming to soften the idea " too much so ", with a suggestion of patronage " simple, easily deceived ". (" Honest Tom at the fair " in a Victorian novel forewarns you that Tom is going to be cheated.) But I suspect that Lucullus in his embarrassment is making an affected archaic use, " seeming worthy of social honor ", hence, " making a show ". This would let him at bottom make a fair point against Timon, who is not drawn as ignorant of human deceitfulness before his disillusion, indeed, as making it an excuse for further hysterical or grand folly. The extraordinary breadth of the word then, with its habit of satire, makes this a possible hint. And the clown in *All's Well* (I, iii) is worth quoting for the animus of the hearty uses against Puritans. (Not the early one, but these later low-class ones.) He has been saying that it will be convenient to have his proposed wife unfaithful, for reasons, as Mr. Bonamy Dobrée well pointed out, that would have suited lords in Restoration comedy.

COUNTESS : *You'll be gone, sirrah, and do as I command you.*

CLOWN : *That man should be at woman's command, and yet no hurt done ! Though honesty be no Puritan, yet it will do no hurt ; it will wear the surplice of humility over the black gown of a big heart. I am going, forsooth.*

Some puritans, though the surplice was a rag of iniquity, were ready to humble themselves before the law and wear it over the black gown of Calvinism ; a big heart is a proud one, but I suppose might also be tender or generous, as nowadays. Behind all this complicated and growling irrelevance he is saying the two opposed things he wants to—" Honesty (telling the truth) does no harm, though the truth is never refined " and " All right, I can stop ; an honest man (a hearty chap) can hold his tongue like other people."

For the simple hearty use among friends, without irony or patronage, one must go outside the works of Shakespeare to comparatively low characters like Bellafront in *The Honest Whore* (First Part, 1604). The title chiefly means that she is transformed by love and made an honest woman by marriage ; indeed it is a fairly simple-minded work (as the savage Second Part, written later, implies). But there are also paradoxes on the word in the first scenes, when her customers praise her as she is already :

By God, when you know her, as we do, you'll swear she is the prettiest
kindest sweetest most bewitching honest ape under the pole.

When she falls in love with Hippolito, who is in love with the
heroine, falsely reported dead, she offers to become an honest whore
in being true to him only. This of course gives it another twist.
But there is more interest in her uses of the word about men while
still unreclaimed. On her first view of Hippolito he is brought to
her house by a trick, to win a bet that he would go to a brothel
soon after the report of the heroine's death. He soon stalks out
again, and Matheo explains his rudeness to the lady as not due to
any offensive morality but to unhappy love :

MATH. : *All this is for a woman.*
BELL. : *A woman? Some whore. What sweet jewel is't ?*
MATH. : *Would she heard you . . .*
BELL. : *Prithee, a buss, and tell me ; I warrant he's an honest fellow,*
if he take on so about a wench. Good rogue, who ?

There does not seem to be any patronage—indeed, the seeds of the
refining love for him have just been sown ; but nor is there any kind
of moral praise ; this is simply the kind of man she likes. The
point is perhaps clearer when she is disliking somebody :

BELL. : *I cannot abide that he should touch me.*
CAS : *Why wench, is he scabbed ?*
BELL. : *Hang him, he'll not live to be so honest nor to the credit to have*
scabs about him. His betters have them.

The objection is that he won't pay. One need not appeal to this
as direct naturalistic evidence ; no doubt the joke is carefully
constructed to discredit her with the audience. The idea that
she takes syphilis for granted is an attack on her mode of life, or so
one would suppose, though it can be ignored as soon as she reforms.
All the same, it had to be a plausible enough way for her to talk.
In a way there is still a plain connection with honour ; the word
means " having the qualities honoured in our set ". " Unhypocritical and courageous " could be dug out of it as relevant ideas,
but she does not seem to mean anything as definite as that. The
language is not at all strained, and the point of the joke is that this
sort of use is common. By the way, we are also given a patronising
use ; the wife of the patient Candido says that not even being
cuckolded would make him angry, and the swaggering Fustigo
replies " the honester citizen he ".

Shakespeare, of course, recognised the existence of this line of
talk ; Mrs. Quickly is very near it when she says to Falstaff, " Well,
fare thee well ; I have known thee these twenty-nine years, come
peascod time, but an honester and truer-hearted man—well, fare
thee well." But I think that he was bored or irritated by the flat

use and always arranged to give the word more point ; here " true-hearted " lets *honest* mean a good deal, whether as " faithful to friends " or in some more obscure way as " with the right kind of feelings ", ready to share his pleasures perhaps. The muddle of her ideas is made actively pathetic. I take it that there had been a serious change in this use of the word since Wilson described it in 1550, though the meaning or rather lack of meaning seems just the same. In its bare form it is now found only among people whom the respectable would look down on, people who are accustomed *not* to be honest in one of the rock-bottom moral senses of the word ; because these senses have now become more prominent in it, so that only the raffish would ignore them.

However, in *The Roaring Girl* (1611)—another play by Dekker in collaboration—the same tavern milieu can make a more curious and touching play with the word.

SEBASTIAN : *I would be nearer to thee, and in that fashion*
That makes the best part of all creatures honest.

He is pretending to propose marriage to Moll the Roaring Girl ; he could not be supposed to do more than pretend. She was a real tavern figure of the time, and the belief that she was a Lesbian would be clear to the audience though it is kept out of the play. Honest sex, let alone marriage, would make her a bit better, as it does all animal creatures. But she is not called unnatural ; the effect is that Sebastian expresses a pathetic humility about the conditions of life and offers honest marriage. He does this as part of a plot to catch a richer and more suitable woman, and later in the play Moll is able to throw the word back at him, with the same clinging but reflective pathos ; she will help the plot.

MOLL : *Any honest pity*
I'm willing to bestow upon poor ringdoves.

An *honest* pity—she is not helping sin ; but an honest *pity*—she is not one to fuss about marriage ; any creatures who have these necessities, as she has not, she will help as she can, and she is more generous to Sebastian than he deserves. Moll is a particularly odd specimen of the Noble Savage, in fact ; she can look at ordinary life from outside it, so that her dignified uses of *honest* can bring in the bawdy ones (" flat and natural ", " not hypo-critical ", etc.). The muddle of the word that she accepts is to her only a touching symbol of the muddle among the ringdoves that she observes. You notice that the appeal to animals comes in each time.

With the Restoration cult of independence, it seems to me, the word reached a clear new sense, derived from truth-telling but not implied in it, that of " frank to himself about his own desires ".

There is now a covert assertion that a man who accepts his nature as it comes, who does not live by principle, will be fit for such warm uses of *honest* as imply " generous " and " faithful to friends ", and to believe this is to disbelieve the Fall of Man. The praise in the word is still strong, and praises you for not being a Puritan. For example the scene where Valentine's dun is kept at bay by being treated as an equal and a friend.

VALENTINE : *I was much obliged to you for your Supply : it did me signal service in my necessity. But you delight in doing good.—Scandal, drink to me, my friend Trapland's health. An honester man lives not, nor one readier to serve his friend in distress : Tho' I say it to his face. Come fill each man his glass.*

SCANDAL : *What, I know Trapland has been a Whoremaster, and loves a wench still. You never knew a Whoremaster, that was not an honest fellow.*

Valentine's use (with *man*) is hearty but holds the patronizing use in reserve if he refuses to drink. Scandal, giving his reasons, is clear that the hearty use (made clear by *fellow*) can be employed outright. This is very like Bellafront's performance with the word but more militant and tricky, and said by more word-conscious people. The two prominent ideas are " generous, faithful to friends " and " pleasant company, one of our set ", and these are if anything opposed to the Independent version—" sturdily true to himself ; lives his own life with no nonsense about it." Such a man might simply make use of his friends. Yet it is from this idea (" getting solid pleasure, not caring what people say ") that Scandal argues to the others. This line of joke seems a very clear case of covert assertion within the word. He might indeed imply " we raffish fellows prey on the dull ones ", which would get out of the contradiction, but that is not in sight here. There is an obscure paradox that the selfish man *is* the generous one, because he is not repressed, has " good nature ", and so on. Also, he tends to have " natural ease ", which was then specially prominent as a test virtue of the gentleman. Courage, a more real test in a duelling society, can safely be presumed in him. It is quite a body of doctrine.

But the type of man who might have formulated the doctrine tends to revolt against it. There was a certain gangster grimness about the Restoration that made the cheery use of *honest* too much of a cheat. You find Wycherley and Rochester getting away from it in the two possible directions, one by analysis into bleak independence, the other by a kind of tact or innocence that swept it aside.

The Plain Dealer is a play about the word *honest*, like *Othello*, or probably more. I mean that Wycherley took a play by Molière

about telling truth in social life and translated this as being
" honest ", and what he thought about that turned into a very
different play. But he did not translate it as the hearty version ;
Manly is remarkably far from any good-humoured use of the word.
When he is called " honest Manly " it might have the patronizing
sense " easily deceived " (because so friendly and natural) ; but
Wycherley does not mean that either. The play does not want us
to think, what seems obvious, that Manly is too much of a fool to
choose his friends. It criticizes him mainly through Freeman,
who says, (" if I am to tell truth ") " I should tell you that the
world thinks you are a mad man, a brutal, and have you cut my
throat, or worse, hate me. What other good success of all my
plain-dealing could I have, but what I've mentioned ? "

The honest man here is the independent man, the Noble Savage,
with an unusually frank stress on that hero's brutality. (Manly is a
sailor and has come from wild parts of the world.) Many savages of
course really are noble, but the phrase meant to praise them for
something else. They were the free mind, not spoiled by convention, looking up at the stars and discovering natural morality,
etc. The trouble is that real savages have particularly rigid conventions. But Manly can do it ; he is brave and " generous ",
so he can admit his own nature to his own mind. There is no
friendship, he says, " therefore, I had rather choose to go where
honest downright barbarity is professed, and where men devour each
other like generous hungry lions and tigers, not like crocodiles . . ."
Generous still meant mainly " of good stock ", so that the paradox
would look less stark. Well-bred horses were generous, just as all
lions were magnanimous. Pope gave him the word as a stock
epithet :

> At half mankind when generous Manly raves,
> All know 'tis virtue, for he thinks them knaves :

and the effect is still doubtful. Yet " generous " in something
near the sense " free with money " was a main element of the hearty
use of honest by Scandal. Wycherley's honest here is clearly more
than " not lying ", something like " accepting its own nature, therefore as good as it has the power to be ". Yet all normal meanings
that would give praise are denied. In trying to imagine what he
means one keeps shifting to the memory of accounts of actual
savages—how did he suppose that this tribe kept itself going ? The
main effect is a blind Samson's attempt to ruin honest and generous,
those vaguely complacent terms of praise, the two pillars of the
temple. Floundering among their mixed virtues his only rock-
bottom is Independence, and the only cheerful side of this cult
belongs not to him but to the casual Freeman, who wants to marry

the rich widow Blackacre. Oldfox is proposing marriage to this character, the most repulsive of the play (and Wycherley knew it when he drew her son) :

WIDOW : *Thou withered, hobbling, distorted cripple ; nay, thou art a cripple all over : wouldst thou make me the staff of thy age, the crutch of thy decrepitness ? me . . . a relict and executrix of known plentiful assets and parts, who understand myself and the law ?*

FREEMAN : *Well said, widow ! Faith, thou wouldst make a man love thee now, without dissembling.*

Here is a real sentiment based on the love of freedom, but it is not clear that honest Manly would be capable of it. Freeman could apply to the widow the raffish good-humoured version of *honest*, but not Manly.

Rochester is a very odd case for our topic. He actually lived as the genteel rake was pretending to do, and died of it at about thirty ; partly through an awful unresolved force, but partly from a mistaken idea that his habits were fashionable. Still it was too large a mind for the evasive fashionable use of *honest*. The word never appears in his poetry, and in his few surviving letters, where we find it often, the effect has an honest warmth not far from Victorian sentiment :

" O ! That second bottle (Harry !) is the Sincerest, Wisest, and most impartial Downright Friend we have ; tells us truth of our selves, and forces us to speak Truth of others ; banishes Flattery from our tongues . . . And (before God) I believe, *the errantest Villain breathing, is honest as long as that Bottle lives*, and few of that tribe dare venture upon him, at least, among the *Courtiers* and *Statesmen*."

The trick would be too obvious for such a man ; if he wants the word at all he means it. The only exception (just for completeness) comes in the Advertisement he wrote for himself when he fooled everybody disguised as an astrologer. " Alexander Bembo " has studied in " Palmestry, Mathematics, Alchemy, and even in Government itself, but the rest . . . I find more safe, I think equally honest, and therefore more Profitable." There is nothing hearty about *honest* here ; it is the cold irony of Swift.

We must now look at *Honest* in the *Pilgrim's Progress*, a person our last characters would not have expected to find at all among ignorant fanatics, and it is true that he has a refreshing effect upon the allegory. He cannot be summed up ; the analysis of the idea is in the story. He is old, brave and rugged, is called " a Cock of the right kind ", at first too modest to tell his name, at last says " not Honesty in the abstract, but Honest is my name " (perhaps " not the root idea but the mixed virtues that are so called "), comes from the town of Stupidity, which lies four degrees beyond the City of Destruction, for stupefied ones are worse than those merely carnal (we have seen the accuracy of this ; it was Rochester who lived in the City of Destruction), though brave had much to do with Fearing, a man, he says, that had the root of the matter in him (Rochester never learned this about his friends), and has been acquainted with Self-Will. This man believed that one could be a good pilgrim though cheating and keeping many wives like the pious Jacob and Solomon, and that " to do this by way of opinion, seems abundance more honest, than to do it, and yet hold contrary to it in opinion ", which Honest quotes as a " pleasant " warning against hypocrisy. (Self-Will is the cult of Independence in a lower and more theological walk of life.) Honest is a great observer (so was Manly), asks a riddle whose answer is generosity (an idea that haunts the rich uses of the word), in convinced only by deeds (blows the gaff), cuts down the giantess Diffidence at one blow but has to leave Giant Despair to Great-heart (this needed faith, not truthfulness or goodnature or common-sense or courage), and at the end, very pleasingly, refuses to agree with the other characters about the advantages of death. Indeed when Christiana is dying with holy satisfaction he makes an alarm-ingly satirical remark : " I wish you a fair day when you set out for Mount Sion, and shall be glad to see you go over the River dry shod." When dying himself he finds the river too deep and can only be carried over by Good-Conscience.

Bunyan has played me off the field here, so that he is hard to analyse. In most examples one can avoid pedantry because the situation shows both what idea of honesty the speakers had and to what actions they thought the idea would apply. But if we come to Bunyan to find how far the raffish high-class use of *honest* was actually echoed among tinkers we find him too broad and too intelligent for what we need. He let Honest go as far as possible while yet remaining a successful pilgrim, but just how *honest* impinged on the intended reader it would take heavy work to say. The only clear point is that the puritans could give the word a performance of their own.

The next step in the development is a return irony that tends to join these uses obscurely separated between classes. It is amusing to set against Wilson (1551) the claim of Steele (*Tatler* 71) to have taught the Augustan polite world to make a hearty use of *honest*. This particular paper is supposed to be a letter from Oxford thanking him for social information : " He that drinks till he stares is no longer called towrow but honest. . . . Their language is very mightily refined." It seems just what Wilson was describing, but the trick that Steele means to boast of by his irony was something more complicated. Given the Restoration hearty use, a high-class anti-Puritan raffishness, he has pushed this over onto the older patronizing use ; the moral man of the world can thus accept the language of the great, but use it for a tactful suggestion that on this issue they are low. With this successful trick goes a fall in the stock of " natural ease ", in the Restoration an inherent possession of any gentleman who was an honest fellow. Excessive natural ease, in a world more ruled by polite drawing-rooms, could now be called " honest " in the patronizing sense till then reserved for the lower classes. The only point where Steele and Addison failed was in trying to fix a sense of *honest* meaning " chaste " when applied to men. I know of no other moral revolution which had so early-Chinese a linguistic basis.

Pope sums up the triumph with a Roman gravity which must often seem smaller than what he intended ;

> *A wit's a feather, and a chief's a rod ;*
> *An honest man's the noblest work of God.*

His nineteenth-century editor, with that excellent rationalism of Johnson which at worst clears the ground for further understanding, said that this is " unfair to man and derogatory to God". But, in Pope's time, if you could be an honest man in all senses, you were going a long way. *Wit* and *chief* light the word from two angles ; it is clearly the function of *honest* to exclude the faults of either. Yet since they are alternatives this is impossible in ordinary practice ; the honest man in achieving normality reconciles a contradiction and becomes a half-divine figure of pastoral. It requires a certain humility, or readiness to be outfaced, to deserve the term that can be used for patronage ; yet the man who can be both unlike the wit, vain, easily hurt and blown from his course (even the highest sort of " wit "), and unlike the chief, narrow, harsh, fond of power—the man who can recognize and fulfil both his own nature and his duties to society is the Type of man, the measure of all things. Pope indeed retains a certain patronage towards the most ideal men he can conceive, perhaps even compared to the chiefs and wits in Pope's own set ; but it is from this that he gets the dignity of his assertion ; only God could afford to take such a tone, so a sentence that takes it to point out God's noblest work is sure to be well-informed. The whole word is involved in this apparently straightforward couplet ; all the faults suggested in *wit* and *chief* are opposed to virtues that *honest* could be used to praise.

So flat a use cannot forever bank upon double ironies, and I suppose the right judgement for a modern critic is that the line is not as impressive as Pope meant it to be. The point of quoting

it here is not to praise it but to suggest that Addison's tricks with
the word were in the air, easily remembered without a special
context. (One might give the hearty and patronizing uses to the
wit, the rock-bottom one to the chief.) Now Addison's trick
requires a kind of militant comic primness; the speaker pretends
to be simple and humble but is in fact comparing or combining
different ideals. What the decent bourgeoisie, who were rising
in the world and buying country houses, would call honest, is
played off against what some at least of the court aristocracy
would call honest. But to say this is to describe an actual play;
it is the whole conception of the *Beggars' Opera*. Macheath
(highwayman) is a satire on aristocratic, Peachum (fence) on
puritan-tradesman, ideals, so that each has his own sense of *honest* ;
Macheath has the hearty raffish use and Peachum the smug prim
use " respectable "—one that starts from the rock-bottom virtues,
touches them with the older general meaning, and comes to imply
" having a steady eye on the main chance". A " reliable " man,
though only in the sense that he is sure to have money. Poor
Addison must be counted among his originals. The simple use of
the word by Macheath can be dealt with quickly ; the robbers are
deciding whom to attack :

MAT : *The fellow with the brown coat with a narrow gold
binding, I am told, is never without money.*

MACHEATH : *What do you mean, Mat ? Sure, you will not think of
meddling with him ! He's a good honest kind of fellow,
and one of us.*

" In our set," in the business of thieving. The main joke at the
time would be that he described some politician. But there seems
to be no cliquishness or conscious irony about the thing ; this is
just one of the satisfactory kind of men. Honour among thieves
indeed is an obvious virtue to the romantic Macheath but not at
all to the Machiavellian Peachum.

PEACHUM : *Slippery Sam—he goes off the next sessions, for the
villain hath the impudence to have views of following his
trade as a tailor, which he calls an honest employment.*

This is of course direct irony, and does not show how he would
use it for praise. It was a stock joke that tailors were dishonest,
so that there is a joke here from impudent plausibility. But also
that they were cowardly ; now "brave" is clearly part of Macheath's
idea of *honest*—it includes all the virtues of the duelling rakes.
Peachum expects the men who rob for him to have the aristocratic
virtues, though he himself need not be brave—he is an honest
tradesman. The word shifts its ideals with the type of man it
describes, and the principle of the habitual sneer of Peachum is

to accept all the conventions. Here he echoes the sneer of the lord at the bourgeois and still adds " none of us good bourgeois think much of tailors". The reader may feel here that too much meaning is being piled onto a small joke, but the song by Peachum that begins the play offers the word as a kind of blank check which the subsequent ironies are to fill in ; and the development is done by Peachum and Lockit. They take the spirited use of it by Macheath and his robbers as a kind of lever, with which to work the word away from the rock-bottom " not lying, not stealing". One essential for this trick was that the word was partly, but not wholly, specialized onto the virtues required for different walks of life. Hence the force of the always implied comparison to lying politicians and spendthrift lords—these people cannot finally claim a different morality from that which condemns the low characters of the play. Here is the song :

PEACHUM : *The priest calls the lawyer a cheat,*
The lawyer be-knaves the divine ;
And the statesman, because he's so great,
Thinks his trade as honest as mine.

This baffling version was supplied by Pope ; Gay's version was " And there's many arrive to be great, By a trade not more honest than Mine," which would not raise the puzzle of the word firmly enough. The new one clearly smashes poor Walpole, who outfaced it by applauding the play (and suppressed the sequel) ; the question is how Peachum can be proud, what sense of *honest* can he plume himself upon, as he sits there betraying the honest highwaymen ? He has nothing left, I submit, but Independence. He is a steady tradesman who knows his job and can make a decent living out of it ; this is what people, very properly, call an honest tradesman ; and of course he does " Social Service " and all the rest of it, because it is only through him that the highwaymen ever get captured—he makes up his quarrel with Lockit the prisonkeeper " for the benefit of the world". And the greater danger of his valuable job makes the dignity of the politician (who also betrays his allies) ridiculous ; Peachum is more " honest " as " deserving Honour". Gay hated him far more than Macheath, but the whole point of the irony is that he had a real claim to the word as then used. Indeed the least sympathetic side of him, his smugness, was again included in possible uses of the word ; it is prominent in the suggestions of "an honest tradesman " and even in " honest Tom at the fair". The social satire is pretty fairly balanced.

Under the pressure of satire the two notions of *honest*, or the two classes, begin to approach, and Lockit, who is rather less hated by his author than Peachum, is given a crucial use of the word not far from Macheath's. (Peachum is fetching drink, at their meeting.)

LOCKIT (alone) :   *Thus gamesters united in friendship are found,*
Though they know that their industry all is a
cheat . . .

Like pikes, lank with hunger, who miss of their ends,
They bite their companions, and prey on their
friends.

Now, Peachum, you and I, like honest tradesmen, are to have
a fair trial which of us two can over-reach the other.

Whatever the ironies the main feeling is pleasure. " It is amusing to think that the honest tradesman would have the hypocrisy to disapprove of us." " This is a quiet cosy sort of cheating, between friends, like the tradesman's, because we dare not hang each other." And yet again " This is a real trial of strength ; I would be proud to over-reach Peachum. Let us enter into it heartily and be as savage as the very business men themselves ". But even in this version he feels above the business men or the honest tradesmen, because it is a " fair trial ", because he would enjoy cheating Peachum even if he lost money by it in the end—he feels he has a little of the dignity of the gambling lord. Regarded as an attack on the tradesman spirit, in fact, the play would over-reach itself— both parties can claim the same raffish type of regard from courage and pleasure.

The moral outlook of Fielding can be felt in his use of the word, though it is partly a matter of codifying a notion that had long been present in it. Good actions, he says at some length, come from good impulses, not from good principles ; Tom Jones is the ideal normal man because he has so much " honest warmth", and indeed though very tough he is always bursting into tears. Dr. Johnson thought this wicked because un-Christian, but the reaction of most readers was less philosophical. They agreed that Tom was a good fellow but objected that he was not really a gentleman ; the life of impulse made him too much " honest Tom " in a patronizing sense. It is remarkable surely that the word itself, in its power of directly calling up an intimately known mood or feeling, could carry both the new theory and the two objections to it—Johnson had only to appeal to " real honesty " to bring up ideas of paying on the day agreed, whatever your immediate feelings, etc. The notion of Independence is still strong in Fielding's version, but only justifies acting on your immediate feelings and being rather casual about sex, whereas in the Restoration period it justified more positive selfishness and indeed high-grade crime (say in a political career). The later but not the earlier version allowed of being erected into a reputable system (though rather vaguely), as in fact occurred. But I should not say that Fielding invented a new sense of the word ; he is only trying to codify the feelings which were accepted in it. The point was rather that the more grimly raffish uses, under the strain of the double ironies, have been cleared away.

This notion of a kind of wholeness of nature, of not having any conflicting impulse at the back of the mind, of not needing to be cautious at the moment in question, goes on clinging to the word and gives I think an obscure pathos to a very direct use of it by Jane Austen :

> He then shut the door, and coming up to her, claimed the good wishes and affection of a sister. Elizabeth honestly and heartily expressed her delight in the prospect of their relationship. They shook hands with great cordiality ; and then till her sister came down, she had to listen to all he could say of his own happiness, and of Jane's perfections ; and in spite of his being a lover, Elizabeth really believed his expectations of felicity to be rationally founded . . . .

(Giving her reasons.) It might of course mean only that the congratulations which would have to be given anyway were in fact given with a sense of their truth. One does not see Miss Austen talking heartily about an " honest fellow ". A bucketful of little wriggling ironies has to be thrown over the moment, to keep hold of good sense. But still, just for that moment, with the door safely shut, there was Elizabeth flushing through her primness and speaking " honestly ".

Even here there is a certain reconciling of disparate groups ; the word marks the point where Elizabeth is less different than usual from Tom Jones. One of the more permanent functions of the word, when the double ironies had died down, was to soften the assertion of class, or contrariwise to maintain the assertion in a softened form. In an evasive way, yet both from its fundamental rigidity and its readiness to make allowances for established types, it worked for the unity of society. A Victorian gentleman, while Gladstone was being discussed, could remark (in his pompous manner) " honest Jones, our butcher, thinks the man a windbag ", and this could chiefly mean that he was himself in doubt. Gladstone might be above Jones's head, or Jones might have sturdy commonsense : in any case what you needed here was a certain breadth. A slow and rather dumb readiness to collect the evidence, a quality that Jones probably has, is in view, however much Jones may be a fool. " That's an honest fellow " (so we'll ask him to dinner) came to imply not merely that he was a gentleman but that gentlemen

don't need to think about being gentlemen—what they like are
plain nice people—who of course *are* gentlemen (or you wouldn't
bother about whether they were nice). And "that's an honest
lad, that Sir Charles" (so I'll vote for him) meant that the lower
classes understood him and did not resent his claims to superiority.
An obscure echo of the double ironies about class seems to ring on
in these more genial or more cautious phrases.

An early Victorian song by Maturin brings out the strength of
the word as it still is, without any fuss about a peculiar context.

> *'Tis good to be merry and wise, my love,*
> *'Tis good to be honest and true,*
> *'Tis good to be off with the old love,*
> *Before you are on with the new.*

For each word " 'tis good " may imply approval of my love because
he is so or advice because he isn't ; both if the adjective has two
senses ; and for that matter the two senses may go either way
round. *Wise* might mean " clever, knowing with women " ; then
the first and second lines are contrasted and must be reconciled by
the person advised. But the first line insists on its own contrast.
Merry (have many loves), *wise* (have one true love) ; *merry* (enjoy
love, which is perhaps best from one only), *wise* (obtain none,
from fear or virtue). These it is good to combine ; it may be wise
to be merry (have two loves, change love lightly) or possible to
be merry though wise (having none, having one, having two but
in good order). Like or opposite, their complex of advice mirrors
itself in the blanker couple parallel to them, which can therefore
entrench itself more deeply behind ironical simplicity. *Honest* looks
simple here ; but if it is hard to be both merry and wise it must be
hard to be both honest and true. This forces the hearty sense of
honest to contrast itself with the promise-keeping one ; and immediately the patronizing use with its implication of folly arises
behind them darkening the whole air. The poor fish has been
trying to be dashing. "I am sorry for you, fool that you are,
when I see you forced, as all humanity is forced, to reconcile in
yourself these shifting and contradictory virtues. But by the same
token you cannot cheat me." The breadth of the humour comes
from the conscious flatness with which the adjectives are set down
and let loose ; " I did not invent the profound meanings in these
common words and cannot save you from having to make what
you can of them."

Chapter 10

HONEST NUMBERS

I PROPOSE now to try to analyse these uses of *honest* and list them as if for a dictionary. It seems clumsy, to be sure, to put the evidence and the conclusions first in a separate chapter, and then the machinery all by itself with nothing to grip on. But there is a real difficulty of "style" here, because if you jam the literary criticism and the linguistics together, detail by detail, you interfere with the normal processes of judgment. The thing becomes disagreeable to read and also likely to excite suspicion, quite rightly I think, because the only way to decide about the examples is by "taste" (granting that taste needs a good supply of examples and an adequate assurance that contrary ones have not been suppressed), and if you are being badgered by theory at the same time it is hard to keep taste in focus. It seemed best therefore, in this rather large-scale case, to try to make the results convincing in ordinary prose before trying to arrive at formulae.

As a source of historical information, the N.E.D. is particularly good on the word *honest*, and I need to explain why it is not supposed to have done enough. It does little about the interaction of senses with "feelings", which for a word like this is the chief difficulty, and since it has to give a historical survey it does not attempt to show the structure of the word at a given date. The main point in showing "structure" would be to say which sense acted as the head one, because the interaction of senses with feelings turns largely on that. I do not say that the work could ever be done completely ; no doubt different groups would be giving the word different structures even at one date, and to give all the structures of all words would only mean writing the history of opinion in the most prolix possible manner. My own chart is meant to run from the late sixteenth century to the present day, with the Restoration use added when it arrives and many of the others gradually dropping out ; the only stage when there is a practical need to form a new chart, I think, is the middle sixteenth century, when " not lying, not stealing, keeping promises " becomes the head sense instead of " deserving and receiving social honour ". In the N.E.D. version the ideas " not lying, etc." (which I call " 1 abc ") have not even a subsection to themselves ; the N.E.D. " 3c ", which includes them, begins " dealing fairly and uprightly in speech and act ". This is much too warm for the idea of honesty as " an elementary requirement such as one ought to be able to take for granted ".

My " 2 " is the memory or influence of the archaic sense, which appears enormously predominant in the N.E.D. version and heads two main sections. But it seems to me that the sense has changed even when the archaism is invoked, because it has turned into the inner virtue of " keeping one's own honour " ; there is an echo of the process by which the knight-errant became a symbol of the highminded gentleman. "Not cheating " and so on made definite enough suggestions about what the public part of honourable behaviour ought to be, so a use that recalled the connection of *honest* with " honour " was felt to deal with the inward part. I write my " 2 " in brackets to show that it is normally only " at the back of the mind"; it could be treated simply as an Implication (and therefore written with "/") but it acts differently from the other Implications since it has a different origin. My " 3 " and " 4 ", both written as Moods, are the patronizing and hearty uses of the word. The N.E.D. lumps together these very distinct objects as its " 1c " " vague praise, esp. patronizing ", and then they crop up again for example in its "3d" "ingenuous, not concealing character good or bad." The reason why the N.E.D. has to separate these two subsections is that its main heads are merely logical ; " 1c " comes under " I " " held in honour " and " 3d " under " III " " having honourable principles ". In general to make logical distinctions of this sort during talk would require an elaborate personal hint, such as " Few but I would honour him here ", which I should write as a Mood. In the case of *honest*, the peculiar shift of the idea of " honour " to inward virtues might have allowed the N.E.D. logical technique to be useful for once, if it had been used rightly. (The first main head " I ", however, I suppose, had better have been used to give the early structure as a whole and no more.) Finally, it seems to me that there are patronizing uses in which the sense becomes " foolish ", for example ; at least this idea becomes so prominent an Implication that there is no obvious Sense if it is not counted as one ; and the N.E.D. does not in general bother with Implications of this sort unless they succeed in becoming promoted into Senses at a later date.

There is a major objection to my chart, because the hearty use which is classed as " 4 " and supposed to emerge after the Restoration is also what started the whole development of this structure of the word, in the middle sixteenth century. However I claim that the Restoration use brings in a new Sense "4" "not deceiving himself " as a result of a militant performance with the Mood " £4 ". The Mood in itself might appear earlier. And the original sixteenth-century feeling of social acceptance for the person called *honest* can best be written as an Emotion ; it was derived from the old Sense " deserving and receiving honour " when viewed somewhat casually, but it can be attached either to the new head sense " 1 " " not lying, etc. " or the eventual sense " 4 ". Indeed the Emotions which produce the four main uses can all appear with the head Sense " not lying, etc.", and without implying any change of meaning ; the Emotions differ according to the degree of importance which " not lying, etc." has for the occasion. There has to be a stabilising of these feelings into conventions before the sense-changes can emerge. I do not think there is any need to introduce further emotions for the other heads ; thus there is no " 3 ! ", and " 1 ! 3 " is the Emotion suited to 3 but separable from it.

The other symbols are meant to recall their meanings under 1 when used for other numbers. I use symbols " + " and " — " for a pregnancy-process according as the idea of honesty in view is made a more or less thorough and searching one (whether the spirit or the letter is in view) ; this is distinct from the speaker's Emotion about the person who exemplifies whatever idea it may be. There are three major Implications, " reliable ", " respected ", and " brave " ; each of them keeps the same number after the dash " / " all through, however the ideas are re-interpreted. The "a, b, c" for the three elements of the head sense are used again for any parallel ideas in 2, 3 and 4. This should make the chart easier to interpret ; it involves a certain amount of overlapping, but that I think only shows how the same idea may be reached in different ways.

My scheme for *honest* then runs as follows :

1. a. Not lying. b. Not stealing. c. Keeping promises.
   1 ! 1. approval. 1 ! 2. respect. 1 ! 3. " presumably ". 1 ! 4. social acceptance.
(The four Emotions are parallel to the four main heads.)
   1/1 steady, reliable 1/2 respected 1/3 brave 1/4 chaste (chiefly used of women).
   1— technically honest. 1a— telling verbal truth. 1b— keeping within the law in money matters. 1c— keeping the letter of a promise.
   1+ keeping the spirit not only the letter. 1a+ frank, going out of one's way to tell truth. 1b+ generous about money. 1c+ faithful to friends, employers, etc.

(2) Keeping one's own honour, not merely receiving and deserving honour from others as in the archaic use.

2a telling truth without regard to popular prejudice. 2b indifferent to money, taking it for granted. 2c fixed in purpose.
   2/1 independent. 2/2 highclass. 2/3 brave.
   (No " 2 — ", as honour has no minor degrees.)
   £3 The patronizing Mood.

£3+ He deserves praise for these minor virtues.

£3 — I am on a higher level than he is.

3 — simple, naive, stupid.

3+ solidly true to the facts of our nature.

3/1 — smug 3/1 independent 3/2 — lowclass 3/2 worthy.

3a having something to be hypocritical about, but not hypocritical 3a— because shameless, etc.

3a+ having manly vigour, bluff.

£4 The hearty Mood. "He is a man in my set, one I am easy with."

4 Not deceiving himself, or those to whom he is intelligible by sympathy, about his own desires or emotions.

4/+ a reliable member of our set (as 1/1).

4/— likely to act for himself (as 2/1).

4/2 — not insisting on his social dignity (as 3/2).

4/2+ always recognisable as a gentleman (as 2/2).

5 Of women : chaste.

The equations between these senses had better be given at once, to save trouble in looking backward and forward. No doubt there are plenty of minor ones such as " 1a = 1b " " not lying entails not stealing " ; you would call this out if the argument in view was " we know that he didn't lie, on an occasion when a bad man would have lied, so we can presume he won't steal ". These various virtues are only given the same name because they are presumed to belong together in the character of the worthy citizen. But the more interesting equations arise from the hearty and patronizing uses, and take as subject the characters to whom those uses are normally applied ; if you write them down with that equation-order you get a fairly complete account of pastoral sentiment and rogue sentiment. Also the obscure process of using tact about the assertion of class is I think dragged into a rather unfair daylight.

Pastoral 3—.3/2 — = 1bc " Simple and unpolished people do their duty "

= 2/1 " . . are independent because unsophisticated "

= 2/2 " . . are Nature's aristocrats "

= 1a+ "and tell the essential truths about life".

3 — = 3+ " Simple people are true to the facts of our nature ".

Rogue   3+ = 1bc " The man who is true to the facts of our nature does no more than he need in fulfilling the demands of society ".

3a = 2/2 " The man who will not be a hypocrite is Nature's aristocrat "

$3a = -1a$ " . . and knows when to tell lies ".

$3a+ = 4/1+$ " A frank rogue is a good fellow, fit for our set ".

$4/ = 4/1+$ " The independent man is the reliable one ".

$4 = 1b+.1c+$ " The man who accepts his own desires is generous and faithful to friends."

Class $\quad 4/2+ = 4/2-$ " The really gentlemanly thing is never to insist that you are a gentleman."

When a word is so elaborately developed as an instrument for covert assertion I do not think there is much necessity to fit the results into the four Types. The function of the Types is to show how equations get into a word without being expected ; but when people start playing games on this scale with a fundamental word it becomes a sort of echoing-chamber, and the equations *are* expected. However some come more easily than others. The subject of the equation is presumed to be clear from the context, as the type of person you are talking about, and to add as predicate " 1 " or " 1+ " with any " abc " is easy, as a return to the head sense. This is Type I ; the uses get so far from the head sense that the type normal for a not highly integrated word can naturally come into play. On the other hand when rather remote Implications appear as predicate (such as " 2/2 ") the equation is Type II ; the ideas are knocking about in the word and ready to be called out on a remote hint from the context. There are no examples of Types III and IV. What I write as equations of the form " X+=X- " perhaps do not really have any order ; they are recognitions of a paradox in the two possible views of the case, a different kind of process from an ordinary equation, and to read them backwards does not seem to make much difference. However, the subject is the one that applies more obviously to the person in view.

There is a more serious formal problem, I think, than that of defining the Type of the equations. As the panorama of the word unfolds itself there is increasing difficulty in telling the Equations apart from the Senses. The performance for example in the Sense " 3a+ ", where contempt for the man described is combined with a high valuation of the virtue he exemplifies, that is, where the Mood is patronising but there is a positive pregnancy, seems to be already elaborate enough to amount to a covert assertion. I don't deny that there may be a sort of doctrine in asserting the reality of such a concept ; this process could be written " Ǝ3a+ " ; but I think that when a man wants to appeal to such a notion in his argument he generally does it by packing hints into the context which in effect buttress the main notion with other ones allied to it ; and so the technique is that of asserting an equation, even when the equation amounts to a tautology and the existence assertion is what he is really aiming at. Perhaps in any case the Senses and Implications in this chart need more defence than the Equations derived from them, and I shall try to provide it.

The Implication $1/1$ " reliable, steady " will not be much doubted, and might be counted as a Sense ; the main point of the word is to impute a general reliability. It is allied to " $1c$ " " keeping promises ", as both involve passage of time. I have treated " $1/1$ " as a main source of the idea " independent ", which is important because of the paradoxes attached to it. The Independent Man may no doubt be found very unreliable, because he acts for himself and not for you ; but this is not in sight when the man praised is steadily keeping his own honour ($2/1$) or practising sturdy lower-class industry and thrift ($3/1$). These are what give the idea its foothold in the word, and it can then stand up and produce paradoxes under 4. I don't maintain that the process was an automatic one ; a general interest in the problems of independence had to be on foot, echoing into a variety of other words ; but given this interest in the idea of independence the word *honest* was well adapted to produce surprises about it. $1/2$ " respected " seems hardly to need listing, but I have used it to bring out the ideas of social class in the other main types ; the archaic $2/2$ implies a gentleman ; the patronising $3/2-$ implies low class (lower than the speaker's) and in fact might be treated as negating the stock Implication " $/2$ ", but the process is not as direct as that ; and the jovial $4/2$ creates a minor paradox by ostentatiously waving the issue aside. One might argue that implications about social class are really a matter of Range ; that one had better write " Of tradesmen : smug " as well as " Of women : chaste". They are not different in principle, but no Implication of the word was really limited to tradesmen, and if you classed " smug " like this you would have to explain away half the uses of it as metaphorical. Certainly, when we get to $1/3$ " brave " the reader may become impatient, and say that this is so obviously not a meaning of " honest " that I might as well call " female " a meaning of the word, which happened always to be combined with the meaning " chaste". But the ideas arise in quite different ways. Not to be exposed to scandal about sex, if that is in view, was a natural condition for the archaic " receiving and deserving honour " ; the use settles down gradually to apply only to women, since chastity was more essential to their honour than to men's, and the word was crystallizing round a few essential virtues. The Implication $1/4$ "chaste", therefore, has to reappear on my chart as an eventual Sense 5 " Of women ".

But courage in the same way was essential to men, and a wide variety of uses of *honest* could make you reflect that the virtue now praised by the word was (like so many others) a test of courage. Dr. Johnson remarked that courage was the fundamental virtue because no other could be sustained without it, and in a duelling society a doubt about your courage meant disgrace. The archaic sense "receiving and deserving honour" would certainly treat courage as one of the necessary conditions for *honesty*. The reason why I think the idea needs insisting on is that it gives an important backing for the praise of the rogue and for the rather obscure virtues of Independence. "/3" "brave" is unaltered in the main heads "2" and "4" but makes a paradox in the patronising head "3"; the low man has no class duty of courage but may be praised for showing courage in peculiar ways.

The machinery is now already rather elaborate under the main head "1"; the suggestion in "1+" of keeping the spirit not the letter might be supposed to give the shift from conduct to character found in "2" and "4", and the narrowness of "1—" might produce the contempt of "3", especially as there are emotions "1!3" to support them. But the word was not so easily tampered with, and a further change in the sense required positive ironies. The main mood under this head seems to be "1+£" "I am understating his merits but this is enough for the purpose."

My chief use for "(2)" the archaistic use is that "2/1" brings in the idea of Independence. It is allied to "1+" "doing more than the rules demand", since both have an idea of being more than conventionally honest. Of course, it might be argued that any broadening "1+" of the ideas, since they were only just becoming clear-cut, would merely return them to the old vague one "(2)". But the feeling of putting a mild pregnancy into a use is habitual for a great number of words, and in most of them entirely different from the feeling of calling up an archaism; so that the two processes would still feel different here. There is no negative pregnancy for "2" because personal honour has no minor degrees; the mixture "1—.(2)" is a joke if conscious, and when taken as settled turns into the Moods of 3 or 4; indeed, this clash is what makes the word so rich. The mixture "1+(2)", the normal use for "(2)", may imply that almost any moral concept is part of "true honesty"; this is one of the main means of holding the word together. I think that an obscure background use of "(2)" remained fairly common; the word was accustomed to power in homely situations, and such a character does not easily give up one of its old claims. The class idea in "(2)" tended to return to the speaker, since the archaism implies that he understands the feelings of men of honour: "2/2?" "I am high-class too." I am not sure whether this could spread over into the patronising use, where it would help to make him of higher class than the person described ; in any case, it is not an important source of the idea of patronage.

The patronising Mood " £3 " arises because if you praise a man for a virtue commonly taken for granted you imply that it cannot be taken for granted about *him*. The process is essentially double, because though you praise for an obvious virtue you still praise ; thus the Mood has two parts. No burst of emotion is needed to impose this ; it appears through an otherwise unnecessary use of the word. It might be argued that the early patronage must have involved the vague sixteenth-century hearty use, because that was what started the whole development. But this hearty use was not universal ; Thomas Wilson himself, for example, would have used it ironically if at all. All that is required for the patronising use is a feeling that the word now only describes elementary virtues. If you accept a hearty feeling in the word as well, you are engaged in something more complex which approaches rogue-sentiment, and I think the main use " 3 " had to become settled first.

The two parts of the Mood are " I approve of his having these obvious virtues " and " I am on a higher level than he is " on the scale in hand ; they can be symbolised separately as " £3+ " and " £3— " to deal with cases where one of them is emphasised more than another, but the normal " £3 " includes both. I write the sign in that order instead of " 3£ " to point out that there is no simple sense " 3". The Mood, indeed, presumes the Sense " 1— " and might be written " 1—£1 ", but this would only be confusing ; and once a trick of patronage becomes habitual it can be applied to a variety of senses of the word. However, this broadness gives a certain instability, because a sense of the word which makes honesty an unusual virtue, such as "(2)" or even " 1+ ", has only to appear in the background to disturb the patronage. It might seem that the Mood based on the presumption of an obvious virtue must simply disappear, but there may be two criteria at work, e.g. " I am higher socially but lower morally ", so that there is now a feeling of paradox. This case might be written " £3+.—£3—.2/2?". Also " £3 " is much used for ironical humility, whose trick is to imply a higher criterion than the one it pretends to use. (On the other hand " £4 ", the hearty, use tends to be aware of a criterion among the senses of the word commonly thought higher than the one it uses, and to deny that it is so.) But the apparent good humour of ironical humility in " £3 " can be used for further contempt ; " I take the lowest ground so as to be fair to him, and my word he still looks low." Such an irony tends to emphasise, what is always inherent in " 3 ", the idea that the person described would accept what is said as serious praise ; *honest* gets a sort of quotation mark as " what the person described calls honest". This makes him " smug ", which can appear as quite a strong Implication in the word (it is probably what Iago means by " whip me such honest knaves"). I should class this as a parallel idea to " reliable " and " independent " ; it is reached through the Mood but tends to buttress itself on those ideas, so I write " smug " as " $3/1-$ ". The Mood tends to imply that the person is stupid, whereas " $1-$ " " doing the minimum to be called honest " tends to make him sly. The contradiction is reconciled by calling him smug ; being unimaginative he can act badly without realising it. But all the ironies in the patronising use are liable to ricochet ; the speaker who implies " smug " does it through a word of praise, and cannot help appearing to admit that he regards this quality as a virtue ; he may, therefore, possess it himself. Many of the uses of the Mood were intended to be harsh, but an obscure geniality is what makes them so rich ; even Iago has to pretend to be amused in his contempt rather than merely indignant (which might make him look jealous).

However, the more usual sense resulting from this Mood is I think " foolish ", which may be made " $3-$ ". The man unnecessarily called honest is in a low position, and the industrious poor are expected to be dull ; also the speaker claims to be doing something clever with the word, and this makes him call the other man stupid by contrast. The implied quotation of the other man's use of the word can also make him look simple-minded. There are less disagreeable ways of getting at the same result ; " honest Tom at the fair " is going to be cheated, so he is viewed with pity and given any praise we can find. The intention in calling him honest may be a charming one, but it still helps to make *honest* mean " stupid ". Owing to its generality this should I think be called the Sense resulting from the Mood, whereas other defects in the man which might justify the use of the Mood are Implications in that they require support from the context. For example the mere presence of *knaves* in "honest knaves" is a context which makes the defect some kind of moral one rather than stupidity. The positive versions can arise easily enough, as they do about " Honest Tom ", but they involve a second twist of the word, in that they contradict the irony by adding to it the normal feeling of praise, and the resulting Sense is likely to be vague. I make " $3+$ " " solidly true to the facts of our nature ", and the idea that this can be said of a " $3-$ " person (" simple, stupid, naive ") is already an equation carrying the ideas of pastoral ; it may seem unnecessary to add any other pastoral equations. But I think there is a difference in the way they come to be used. You put in " $3+$ " because you want to, because feelings of that sort are in your mind and therefore echo into your uses of a variety of words ; but the fact that in this word the feeling can be supported by so many stock contexts (dutifulness, truthtelling, the class paradox, etc.) gives it a much stronger and more permanent position there. The word is useful for arguing about the idea and tends to remind you of it ; it develops a structure which tends to impose a doctrine.

We now come to Rogue as apart from Pastoral sentiment, and the fundamental difference is that the notion of truthtelling " a " is transferred from the predicate to the subject of the equation. The swain may tell simple truths or illustrate profound ones ; but the rogue can only get a foothold in the word *honest* by being " not a hypocrite " " 3a ", and this irony on the word has to define the character before other ideas are attached to him. In the simplest case he is a thief, and the joke is that " 1a " fits but " 1b " doesn't. In " 3a− " you reduce the merit of not being a hypocrite by adding Implications to explain it away ; the most general one is " shameless ", but " stupid " " 3− " and " low-class (coarse)" are in easy reach. For positive rogue-sentiment you require " 3a+ ", and in finding grounds to praise the man you draw, in the first place, on the idea of courage. The sense " having manly vigour, bluff " draws upon " 1/3 " " brave " and might be written " 3/3a ", but it seems to fill the position " 3a+ " without requiring specific hints at the idea of courage. Indeed, a low man may show lack of hypocrisy by confessing his fears, so that he breaks any class rule of courage " 2/3 ", and this can still be treated as rather " bluff and vigorous " behaviour. It has at any rate the merit of showing Independence, the other key idea about the rogue, because it shows he does not care whether other people think him brave or not ; this is already suggested by the idea of " not being a hypocrite " (and I suppose by the definition word " bluff"). The form " 3a/1 " could be used to emphasize it ; I am not sure whether the use really drew support from its archaic parallel " 2/1 ". In the equations for rogue-sentiment I have avoided taking " 3a+ " as subject except in the one which tries to connect the patronising with the hearty use ; the more clear-cut " 3a " is all that is required, and one might argue that " 3a+ " is itself the concept of the Rogue and therefore should not be used in the equations which define it. In the same way I do not use " 3+ " " solidly true to the facts of our nature " as subject in the equations for the swain ; it appears as predicate in " 3−=3+ ", but that is hardly a full-blown equation, only a way of expressing the inherent paradox of a cordial use of patronage. On the other hand I think " 3+ " does appear as subject in the rogue equations, and there draws on the obscure idea of truth in its definition, the idea not of blowing the gaff but of corresponding to the facts of life. It comes in, I think, as a sort of generalisation of the stock lack of hypocrisy in the rogue. For the shift of " 3+ " from predicate to subject to be plausible we have to suppose that the pastoral sentiment was well settled in the word before the more elaborate rogue sentiment was piled onto it.

We have still to consider how far a hearty feeling "in my set, one of my intimates " was used in building up either of these groups of sentiment. In both it would be literally false, because the irony cuts the speaker off from either rogue or swain, and in neither is it, so to speak, logically necessary, to explain how the uses got into the word. The " + " forms draw on the inherent moral praise in the word not on any hearty uses; indeed, these tended rather to weaken its moral claims. But I think a certain paradoxical use of the hearty feeling, an idea that this kind of talk was a way of treating the man as an intimate even though he so definitely wasn't, gave an added momentum to the two groups of sentiment in the word once they had got started. The appeal to common humanity which is their justification, after all, implied that we are all in one " set " fundamentally. The man whom I call *honest* " 3+ ", in particular, somehow reminds me of the facts of human nature and therefore forces me to feel that I am like him. The Moods that result from this will depend on the view of human nature that he suggests, and there are two possible extremes ; we might write them " 3+.I£+ " " I find it comforting that I am like him at bottom" and " 3+.I£ — ". " It is a grim and humbling truth that I am like him at bottom." The first perhaps was in the minds of the Highlanders who said " honest man " after the farmer's wife had sat on Dr. Johnson's knee. The second appears when Manly in *The Plain Dealer* says that it is better to tear your friends in pieces honestly, like generous lions and tigers. But I do not think that these special uses need listing in a chart.

In the hearty use " £4 " itself, " He is a satisfactory member of my set ", there is no reason to deny complete continuity from the middle sixteenth century to the Restoration ; the only questions are who used it and how far they recognised the contradiction about Independence. What I give as the Sense " 4 ", " not deceiving himself", derives of course from " a " " truthtelling ", as did the defining virtues of the Rogue ; it seems derived from patronising uses *about* the Rogue. On the other hand, the Mood " 4 " " in my set ", without any clear supporting Sense, had largely become peculiar to the talk of rogues about one another. This combination is easily explained if we suppose that the Restoration aristocracy adopted the tone towards one another of thieves but continued to think about it like lords. However, it is no use dating these things too sharply, and we must suppose that individuals could play this trick before the political changes had made it a fashion. The Sense without the Mood is in any case not hard to put into the word if your interests lie in that direction ; the idea of truth-telling was increasingly prominent in *honest*, and " 4 " is merely a special form of it.   There is an emphasis on the inner world of character rather than on action, but these are already implied in the word by "(2)" and " 1+ ".   The obstacle is that if you impute an entirely individualistic meaning to a word consecrated to everyday social relationships you run at once into moral paradoxes, and a certain readiness for them was necessary before the meaning could emerge. The effectiveness of the double appeal to rogues in " 4 " and " £4 " was that it could suggest to the listener some way of resolving the paradoxes ; not merely " we are all rogues " but " a man of the world, with a sense of humour, can pick his way without soiling himself through these philosophical morasses ".   Given the Sense, there is a logical route towards the Mood ; if you know that your listener is a case of " 4 " you must be one of those to whom he is intelligible through sympathy.   But the more probable way of making the Mood rise in the social scale was the affectionate pretence of insult ; you pretend that your friend is a rogue, and this is not really insulting because you must be supposed to pretend that you are one too.   Rogue sentiment is then in play, with the idea " we can afford to talk like this, in our closed circle, among ourselves ".   This does not involve the Sense " 4 " directly, though it gives a powerful support for it ; on the other hand, the trick was not likely to occur until the rogue-sentiment had reached a point where the Sense would be found plausible.   On the face of it there is now a firm denial of the connection with honour "(2)" ; but with the return of the word to a high-class use, as between equals in good society, the idea that the man of honour keeps up his standards for his own sake can make a paradoxical re-appearance.   The ideas of " stupid " " 3— " and " smug " " 3/1— " are, however, really denied ; we assume that the man in our set will not be offended at our use of the word, therefore that he can see the obscure humour of its contradictions.

The chief contradiction, as I put it in my chart, is a very unescapable or inherent one because the equation is between " 4/1+ " and "4/1—", and these should not need inserting separately by the context.   The man who is Independent (because he steadily follows his own desires) is also supposed to be trustworthy (steady as one of our set).   However, I do not claim that this pervading assumption was often clearly recognised ; it gets attention chiefly on the painful occasions when it is found to be false.   What could more easily be " put across ", as a covert assertion which might convince the hearer, was an equation such as " 4=1c+ " " the man who accepts his own desires is faithful to his friends ".   Here the two elements are remote from one another, therefore more easily put in separately by the context, and the simple-minded hearer can accept the predicate as a normal moral use of the word. A very similar paradox could of course be got by using not " 4 " but " 3a/1+ " " unhypocritical and independent—leads his own life with no nonsense about it " ; but this is still part of the patronising use, and the idea that there is honour among thieves does not affect you so deeply as the presumption that there is honour among your own raffish friends. The puzzles the rogues themselves may have met with in their hearty use do not seem to have been adequately recorded ; very likely they did not put enough weight on the word to find it actively misleading. Macheath, of course, is a highly sophisticated object, since he is a satire both on the highwayman who aped the lord and the lord who imitated the language (among other things) of the highwayman.

The polite use of the word for implications of class has still to be considered, and the difficulty here is that the whole joviality of the thing lay in a determined vagueness. There does not seem to be a tendency to call up Implications from the context, so as to assert an Equation of a clear-cut sort ; and I think the only Equation that need be listed is the inherently obscure one between the two halves into which the hearty use splits the implication of class. " 4/2+ " = " 4/2— " " the really gentlemanly thing is never to insist that you are a gentleman, indeed not to think about the matter ". Except, of course, that you can think about it in terms of the irony of these evasive words, and think as harshly as you choose. The two parts arise because the man the aristocrat treats as an intimate does not seem to him particularly aristocratic, and yet is presumed to be, or he would not be so treated.

The development of the English word is so complete that a kind of freewill problem presents itself ; one might be tempted to think the process inevitable and indeed automatic. The word was in unstable equilibrium, because so near " honourable " that any difference was likely to be picked up and exaggerated to make the word more useful. A disturbing irony was applied. The centre of gravity (the central meaning) fell with increasing momentum into a new position of stable equilibrium. There was a pendulum movement of irony about this point, but after about two centuries the oscillation was damped down. I should agree with this analogy so far as to think that no particular historical event (such as the Restoration) really had very much effect on the development ; if the history had been different there would probably only have been different emphases within the same range. The development of the word is part of a whole development of thought expressed in language, and indeed you might say that whatever caused the word-changes also caused the public events. But if it is suggested that this development of *honest* was inevitable there is a decisive retort ; the same romance word exists in many European languages, and the English development is unique. None of the others have made telling truth their central meaning. The French *honnête* played the patronising tricks but not (I understand) the roguish and jovial ones ; in Italy and Spain nothing has been done to tamper with the honour of the word. I suppose one could connect the English development with an early reaction against feudal ideas of honour, with the Protestant stress on bare truth and the money-making virtues, and perhaps with a certain distaste, whether modest or snobbish, for allowing a word always to exact solemn praise for commonplace virtues.

I ought, perhaps, in all this, to have given more attention to the control experiment of considering why *honest* was not used in cases where the analysis looks as if it might have been. A word which carries light irony easily is no use where there is a real intention to make the irony deceive the audience ; for example Mark Antony could not have said " They are all honest men " over the body of Caesar, because his intention would have been understood too quickly. He needed to take a word not susceptible of irony, and then gradually irritate the audience to the point where they would deny its meaning of their own accord. More generally, it was because " honourable " was in reach when required that the word for the more social and less solemn aspects of honour was free to develop on its own ; on the other hand, the connection of the two words, the possible antithesis between them, would tend to keep alive in *honest* a sort of shrubbery of ideas about honour. So long as these appeared as subsidiary to an unbreakable main sense like " not cheating " they could not be driven out by irony from an opponent.

On the other hand, for many casual but not ironical uses of *honest* it might seem that what is meant is simply " good ". No doubt *honest* was often used as an " intensifier " to add emotional weight or interest to a mere vague feeling of " good ", and by what is called the process of Fading this would tend to give *honest* a sense " good " no longer with emotional weight. The process may well be a source of the original sixteenth-century hearty use, but the ideas which *honest* was wanted to express were too important for the process to be complete ; a strong reaction was called up which in effect gave the word new claims. Even the casual and humorous uses of *good* and *honest* therefore remain very different. For example, there is a passage in *Prancing Nigger* about a Scotch choreographer who had come to Cuna Cuna (in the Tropics) late in life, I think as a governess, and then found her true bent :

" Self-expression had come with a rush, and her ' arrange-ments' sometimes embarrassed even the good Cunans themselves." What is *good* doing here, and why would *honest* be wrong for the purpose ? The Cunans are clearly " true to the facts of our nature " " 3+ " ; a certain dullness " 3— " is imputed to them, since they do not want Modern Art to go too far, or on another possible view of the case they are worthy " 1+ " ; and on the other hand they are not hypocritical " 3a ", so that if they are embarrassed it is a measure of the startling character of the work. " On paper ", as people say, this makes *honest* fit the case very perfectly ; but if you try substituting it for *good* the sentence feels rather clumsy. I think that this case is like " So are they all, all honourable men ", though for the opposite reason. There the whole purpose was to make the irony a serious one. Here the whole charm is to make you feel that you are seeing the position for yourself, so that it needs only to be touched in with the most evasive lightness ; *honest* would be out of place here, because it is too masterful, too accustomed to make assertions out of its little ironies. Such at any rate is the picture of it that I have been trying to draw.

Perhaps I have treated the paradoxes of the word too much as delusions to be exposed ; one ought also to consider what means there were for making them reasonable. The idea that the self-centred and sensual character will be generous, reliable, and faith-ful to friends can on the one side be treated as a piece of Restoration brutality ; the idea is that we are allies because we both cheat husbands and tradesmen, and the paradox about independence can be evaded by an idea that " anyway we don't need a great deal of helping in our set "—the insolence of wealth replacing that of crime. But on the other hand it was supported by the philosophical ideas of the Enlightenment, which are not yet given up, nor should I want to give them up myself ; the man who satisfies his own nature " 3+ " and is honest to himself " 4 " is expected to have generous feelings " 1b+ " from his own unobstructed nature, not from the rules of " 1— " or the effort of principle in " (2) ". Before the Restoration you do not find the careless good breeding and natural ease of the gentleman singled out for much praise, and it is the security of this idea that made it plausible to keep a hearty use of the word for the clique and a patronising use for outsiders running concurrently. The gentleman plumed himself on his truth to nature, in a roundabout way, and could afford to play with an Equation " 4/2=3+ ", the good fellow is the swain. This part of the idea could do a good deal to keep it from mere scoundrelism. And indeed, I do not think that the idea in its full form need be treated as an absurd flattery of our nature. The Freudian view of the primitive gift, if you drop its infantilism to take a wider view of

the naivety of our selfishness, becomes " to show that you are willing
to take your pleasure in that person's company " ; there is some
element of generosity in all social pleasures. This merely generalises
the idea that " the man able to lead a life of pleasure is carelessly
generous ", which is one of the presumptions of the hearty use of
the word. And to connect this with praise for recognising the truth
about yourself, which the development of the word imposed as a
mysterious suggestion, amounts to a doctrine with which the
psycho-analyst could hardly disagree. At the same time the humour
inherent in the irony of the word, and insisted upon so far as it made
a covert defence against Christianity, admits or might protest that
the doctrines involved are only partial truths. The best uses of
such a word are very good ones. But the average ones were fairly
coarse, and there were grim possibilities in the way of cheating.
After this attempt at idealising the full use of *honest* we had best
turn to Iago.

Chapter 11

HONEST IN OTHELLO

THE fifty-two uses of *honest* and *honesty* in *Othello* are a very queer business ; there is no other play in which Shakespeare worries a word like that. *King Lear* uses *fool* nearly as often but does not treat it as a puzzle, only as a source of profound metaphors. In *Othello* divergent uses of the key word are found for all the main characters ; even the attenuated clown plays on it ; the unchaste Bianca, for instance, snatches a moment to claim that she is more honest than Emilia the thief of the handkerchief ; and with all the variety of use the ironies on the word mount up steadily to the end. Such is the general power of the writing that this is not obtrusive, but if all but the phrases involving *honest* were in the style of Ibsen the effect would be a symbolical charade. Everybody calls Iago honest once or twice, but with Othello it becomes an obsession ; at the crucial moment just before Emilia exposes Iago he keeps howling the word out. The general effect has been fully recognised by critics, but it looks as if there is something to be found about the word itself.

What Shakespeare hated in the word, I believe, was a peculiar use, at once hearty and individualist, which was then common among raffish low people but did not become upper-class till the Restoration ; here as in Iago's heroic couplets the play has a curious effect of prophecy. But to put it like this is no doubt to over-simplify ; the Restoration use, easy to feel though hard to define, seems really different from its earlier parallels, and in any case does not apply well to Iago. I want here to approach the play without taking for granted the previous analysis. But I hope it has become obvious that the word was in the middle of a rather complicated process of change, and that what emerged from it was a sort of jovial cult of independence. At some stage of the development (whether by the date of *Othello* or not) the word came to have in it a covert assertion that the man who accepts the natural desires, who does not live by principle, will be fit for such warm uses of *honest* as imply " generous " and " faithful to friends ", and to believe this is to disbelieve the Fall of Man. Thus the word, apart from being complicated, also came to raise large issues, and it is not I think a wild fancy to suppose that Shakespeare could feel the way it was going.

Four columns of *honest* in the Shakespeare Concordance show that he never once allows the word a simple hearty use between equals.

Some low characters get near it, but they are made to throw in contempt. 'An honest fellow enough, and one that loves quails' is said by Thersites in contempt for Ajax ; 'honest good fellows' is said by the Nurse in Romeo, but of minstrels that she is turning away ; 'as honest a true fellow as any in Bohemia' is from Prince Cloten and to a shepherd ; 'I am with thee here and the goats, as the most capricious poet, honest Ovid, was mong the Goths' gets its joke from making the clown patronise Ovid. The nearest case is from Desdemona :

> EMIL. : *I warrant it grieves my husband*
> *As if the case were his.*
>
> DES. : *Oh, that's an honest fellow.*

But Emilia is butting into the talk with Cassio, and Desdemona, in this careless reply to silence her, has a feeling that Iago though reliable and faithful is her social inferior. This indeed is a sufficient reason why Iago talks with irony about the admitted fact that he is " honest " ; the patronising use carried an obscure social insult as well as a hint of stupidity. Critics have discussed what the social status of Iago and Emilia would actually be, and have succeeded in making clear that the posts of ancient and gentlewoman-in-waiting might be held by people of very varying status ; the audience must use its own judgement. The hints seem to place Iago and his wife definitely enough well below Desdemona but well above Ancient Pistol, say. Now at the same date as the refusal by Shakespeare to employ a flat hearty use of the word, there are uses by Dekker (for example) which only differ from the Restoration ones by coming from people of lower rank or bad reputation. One need not say that Shakespeare always had a conscious policy about the word (more likely the flat hearty use bored him ; it was a blank space where one might have had a bit of word play) but his uses of it in *Othello*, when his imagination began to work on the loathsome possibilities of this familiar bit of nonsense, are consistent with his normal practice.

Most people would agree with what Bradley, for example, implied, that the way everybody calls Iago honest amounts to a criticism of the word itself ; that is, Shakespeare means " a bluff forthright manner, and amusing talk, which get a man called honest, may go with extreme dishonesty ". Or indeed that this is treated as normal, and the satire is on our nature not on language. But they would probably maintain that Iago is not honest and does not think himself so, and only calls himself so as a lie or an irony. It seems to me, if you leave the matter there, that there is much to be said for what the despised Rymer decided, when the implications of the hearty use of *honest* had become simpler and more clear-cut. He said that the play is ridiculous, because that sort of villain (silly-clever, full of secret schemes, miscalculating about people) does not get mistaken for that sort of honest man. This if true is of course a plain fault, whatever you think about "character-analysis". It is no use taking short cuts in these things, and I should fancy that what Rymer said had a large truth when he said it, and also that Iago was a plausible enough figure in his own time. The only main road into this baffling subject is to find how the characters actually use the term and thereby think about themselves.

I must not gloss over the fact that Iago once uses the word to say that he proposes to tell Othello lies :

> *The Moor is of a free and open nature,*
> *And thinks men honest that but seem to be so.*

This is at the end of the first act. And indeed, the first use of the word in the play seems also to mean that Iago does not think himself honest. In his introductory scene with Roderigo, he says of the subservient type of men " whip me such honest knaves " ; they are opposed to the independent men like himself— " these fellows have some soul ". Later there is a trivial use of the word by Brabantio, but the next important ones do not come till near the end of the act. Then Othello twice calls Iago honest ; Iago immediately (to insist on the irony) has a second meeting for plots with Roderigo, and then in soliloquy tells the audience he will cheat Roderigo too. Next he brings out the two lines just quoted ; he is enumerating the conditions of his problem, and the dramatic purpose, one may say, is to make certain that nobody in the audience has missed the broad point. The act then closes with " I have it " and the triumphant claim that he has invented the plot. Even here, I think, there is room for an ironical tone in Iago's use of *honest* ; he can imply that Othello's notion of honesty is crude as well as his judgements about which people exemplify it. For that matter, Iago may simply be speaking about Cassio, not about himself. He has just said that Cassio is framed to make women false, and he certainly regards the virtues of Cassio as part of his superficial and over-rewarded charm of manner. But I think that, even so, Iago has himself somewhere in view ; to claim that he did not would be overstraining my argument. The introductory phrase " honest knaves " is of course a direct irony (made clear by contradiction) ; it can only mean that Iago has a different idea of honesty from the one that these knaves have. To be sure, you may be meant to think that he is lying by implication, but even so, this is the lie that he must be supposed to tell. However, I do not see that the uses at either end of the act put forward definite alternative meanings for the word ; they lay the foundations by making it prominent. It is then, so to speak, "in play" and is used with increasing frequency. The first act has five uses; the second eleven; the third twenty-three; and the last two only six and seven. One might argue that the character of Iago is established in the first act before the verbal ironies are applied to it, since "honest knaves" is only a sort of blank cheque; but even so we learn a good deal more about him later.

Both Iago and Othello oppose honesty to mere truth-telling:

> OTH. : *I know, Iago,*
> *Thy honesty and love doth mince this matter,*
> *Making it light to Cassio. . . .*

> IAGO : *It were not for your quiet, nor your good,*
> *Nor for my manhood, honesty, or wisdom*
> *To let you know my thoughts.*

No doubt the noun tends to be more old-fashioned than the adjective, but anyway the old "honourable" sense is as broad and vague as the new slang one; it was easy enough to be puzzled by the word. Iago means partly 'faithful to friends', which would go with the Restoration use, but partly I think 'chaste', the version normally used of women; what he has to say is improper. Certainly one cannot simply treat his version of *honest* as the Restoration one—indeed, the part of the snarling critic involves a rather puritanical view, at any rate towards other people. It is the two notions of being ready to blow the gaff on other people and frank to yourself about your own desires that seem to me crucial about Iago; they grow on their own, independently of the hearty feeling that would normally humanize them; though he can be a good companion as well.

One need not look for a clear sense when he toys with the word about Cassio; the question is how it came to be so mystifying. But I think a queer kind of honesty is maintained in Iago through all the puzzles he contrives; his emotions are always expressed directly, and it is only because they are clearly genuine ("These stops of thine", Othello tells him, "are close delations, working from the heart") that he can mislead Othello as to their cause.

> OTH. : *Is he not honest?* (Faithful, etc.)

> IAGO : *Honest, my lord?* (Not stealing, etc. Shocked)

> OTH. : *Ay, honest,* ("Why repeat? The word is clear enough.")

> IAGO : *My lord, for aught I know. . . .* ("In some sense.")

> IAGO : *For Michael Cassio*
> *I dare be sworn I think that he is honest.*

OTH. : *I think so too.*

IAGO : *Men should be what they seem,*
Or, those that be not, would they might seem none.

OTH. : *Certain, men should be what they seem.*

IAGO : *Why then, I think that Cassio's an honest man.*

Othello has just said that Cassio " went between them very oft ",
so Iago now learns that Cassio lied to him in front of Brabantio's
house when he pretended to know nothing about the marriage.
Iago feels he has been snubbed,* as too coarse to be trusted in such a
matter, and he takes immediate advantage of his discomposure.
The point of his riddles is to get " not hypocritical "—" frank about
his own nature " accepted as the relevant sense ; Iago will readily
call him honest on that basis, and Othello cannot be reassured.
' Chaste ' (the sense normally used of women) Cassio is not, but he
is ' not a hypocrite ' about Bianca. Iago indeed, despises him for
letting her make a fool of him in public ; for that and for other
reasons (Cassio is young and without experience) Iago can put a
contemptuous tone into the word ; the feeling is genuine, but not the
sense it may imply. This gives room for a hint that Cassio has been
' frank ' to Iago in private about more things than may honestly
be told. I fancy too, that the idea of ' not being men ' gives an
extra twist. Iago does not think Cassio manly nor that it is specially
manly to be chaste ; this allows him to agree that Cassio may be
honest in the female sense about Desdemona and still keep a tone
which seems to deny it—if he is, after so much encouragement, he
must be ' effeminate ' (there is a strong idea of ' manly ' in *honest*,
and an irony on that gives its opposite). Anyway, Iago can hide
what reservations he makes but show that he makes reservations ;
this suggests an embarrassed defence—" Taking a broad view, with
the world as it is, and Cassio my friend, I can decently call him
honest." This forces home the Restoration idea—" an honest dog
of a fellow, straightforward about women ", and completes the
suspicion. It is a bad piece of writing unless you are keyed up for
the shifts of the word.

The play with the feminine version is doubtful here, but he
certainly does it the other way round about Desdemona, where it
had more point ; in the best case it is for his own amusement when
alone.

* Cassio does not call Iago *honest* till he can use the word warmly (ii.3.108) ;
till then he calls him " good Iago " (ii.1.97, ii.3.34)—apparently a less
obtrusive form of the same trick of patronage. Possibly as they have been
rivals for his present job he feels it more civil to keep his distance. However the
social contempt which he holds in check is hinted jovially to Desdemona (ii.1.165)
and comes out plainly when he is drunk ; Iago returns the " good " to him and is
firmly snubbed for it as not a " man of quality " (ii.3.108).

And what's he then that says I play the villain?
When this advice is free I give and honest,
Probal to thinking, and indeed the course
To win the Moor again?   For 'tis most easy
The inclining Desdemona to subdue
In any honest suit.   She's framed as fruitful
As the free elements.

Easy, inclining, fruitful, free all push the word the same way, from 'chaste' to 'flat, frank, and natural'; all turn the ironical admission of her virtue into a positive insult against her.   The delight in juggling with the word here is close to the Machiavellian interest in plots for their own sake, which Iago could not resist and allowed to destroy him.   But a good deal of the 'motive-hunting' of the soliloquies must, I think, be seen as part of Iago's 'honesty'; he is quite open to his own motives or preferences and interested to find out what they are.

The clear cases where Iago thinks himself honest are at a good distance from the Restoration use; they bring him into line with the series of sharp unromantic critics like Jacques and Hamlet:

For I am nothing if not critical

he tells Desdemona to amuse her; his faults, he tells Othello, are due to an excess of this truthful virtue—

I confess, it is my nature's plague
To spy into abuses, and oft my jealousy
Shapes faults that are not.

There seems no doubt that he believes this and thinks it creditable, whatever policy made him say it here; indeed we know it is true from the soliloquies.   Now this kind of man is really very unlike the Restoration 'honest fellow', and for myself I find it hard to combine them in one feeling about the word.   But in a great deal of Iago's talk to Roderigo—'drown thyself! drown cats and blind puppies . . . why, thou silly gentleman, I will never love thee after '—he is a wise uncle, obviously honest in the cheerful sense, and for some time this is our main impression of him.*   It is still strong during the business of making Cassio drunk; there is no reason why he should praise the English for their powers of drinking except to make sure that the groundlings are still on his side.

Perhaps the main connection between the two sorts of honest men is not being indulgent towards romantic love:

OTH. :   *I cannot speak enough of this content,*
It stops me here; it is too much of joy.
And this, and this, the greatest discords be
That e'er our hearts shall make.   (Kissing her).

* It is a very bold and strange irony to make Othello repeat the phrase " love thee after " just before he kills Desdemona.

IAGO : *Oh you are well tun'd now ;*
But I'll set down the peggs that make this Musick,
As honest as I am.

The grammar may read ' because I am so honest ' as well as
' though I am so honest ' and the irony may deny any resultant
sense. He is ironical about the suggestions in the patronizing use,
which he thinks are applied to him—' low-class, and stupid, but
good-natured '. But he feels himself really ' honest ' as the kind of
man who can see through nonsense ; Othello's affair is a passing
lust which has become a nuisance, and Iago can get it out of the
way.

It may well be objected that this is far too mild a picture of
Iago's plot, and indeed he himself is clearly impressed by its
wickedness ; at the end of the first act he calls it a " monstrous
birth " and invokes Hell to assist it. But after this handsome
theatrical effect the second act begins placidly, in a long scene
which includes the " As honest as I am " passage, and at the end of
this scene we find that Iago still imagines he will only

> *Make the Moor thank me, love me, and reward me*
> *For making him egregiously an ass*

—to be sure, the next lines say he will practise on Othello " even
to madness ", but even this can be fitted into the picture of the
clown who makes " fools " of other people ; it certainly does not
envisage the holocaust of the end of the play. Thinking in terms
of character, it is clear that Iago has not yet decided how far he
will go.

The suggestion of " stupid " in a patronizing use of *honest* (still
clear in ' honest Thompson, my gardener ', a Victorian if not a
present-day use) brings it near to *fool ;* there is a chance for these
two rich words to overlap. There is an aspect of Iago in which
he is the Restoration " honest fellow ", who is good company
because he blows the gaff ; but much the clearest example of it
is in the beginning of the second act, when he is making sport for
his betters. While Desdemona is waiting for Othello's ship, which
may have been lost in the tempest, he puts on an elaborate piece
of clowning to distract her ; and she takes his real opinion of love
and women for a piece of hearty and good-natured fun. Iago's
kind of honesty, he feels, is not valued as it should be ; there is
much in Iago of the Clown in Revolt, and the inevitable clown
is almost washed out in this play to give him a free field. It is
not, I think, dangerously far-fetched to take almost all Shakespeare's uses of *fool* as metaphors from the clown, whose symbolism
certainly rode his imagination and was explained to the audience
in most of his early plays. Now Iago's defence when Othello at

last turns on him, among the rich ironies of its claim to honesty, brings in both *Fool* and the Vice used in *Hamlet* as an old name for the clown.

IAGO :   *O wretched fool,*
           That lov'st to make thine Honesty, a Vice !*
           Oh monstrous world !   Take note, take note (O World)
           To be direct and honest is not safe.
           I thank you for this profit, and from hence
           I'll love no Friend, sith Love breeds such offence.
OTH. :   *Nay stay ; thou should'st be honest.*
IAGO :   *I should be wise ; for Honesty's a Fool,*
           And loses that it works for.
OTH. :   *By the world,*
           I think my wife be honest, and think she is not.

What comes out here is Iago's unwillingness to be the Fool he thinks he is taken for ; but it is dramatic irony as well, and that comes back to his notion of *honest ;* he is fooled by the way his plans run away with him ; he fails in knowledge of others and perhaps even of his own desires.

Othello swears *by the world* because what Iago has said about being honest in the world, suggesting what worldly people think, is what has made him doubtful ; yet the senses of *honest* are quite different—chastity and truth-telling. Desdemona is called a supersubtle Venetian, and he may suspect she would agree with what Iago treats as worldly wisdom ; whereas it was her simplicity that made her helpless ; though again, the fatal step was her lie about the handkerchief. *Lov'st* in the second line (Folios) seems to me better than *liv'st* (Quarto), as making the frightened Iago bring in his main claim at once ; the comma after *Honesty* perhaps makes the sense ' loves with the effect of making ' rather than ' delights in making ' ; in any case *love* appears a few lines down. *Breeds* could suggest sexual love, as if Iago's contempt for that has spread to his notions of friendship ; Othello's marriage is what has spoilt their relations (Cassio ' came a-wooing with ' Othello, as a social figure, and then got the lieutenantship). In the same way Othello's two uses of *honest* here jump from ' loving towards friends, which breeds honour ' to (of women) ' chaste '. It is important I think that the feminine sense, which a later time felt to be quite distinct, is so deeply confused here with the other ones.

It is not safe to be *direct* either way, to be *honest* in Othello's sense or Iago's. The sanctimonious metaphor *profit* might carry satire from Iago on Puritans or show Iago to be like them. Iago is still telling a good deal of truth ; the reasons he gives have always

---

* And make thyself a motley to the view. Sonnet CX.

made him despise those who are faithful to their masters, if not to their friends. It is not clear that he would think himself a bad friend to his real friends. He believes there is a gaff to blow about the ideal love affair, though his evidence has had to be forced. Of course he is using *honest* less in his own way than to impose on Othello, yet there is a real element of self-pity in his complaint. It is no white-washing of Iago—you may hate him the more for it— but he feels he is now in danger because he has gone the ' direct ' way to work, exposed false pretensions, and tried to be ' frank ' to himself about the whole situation. I do not think this is an oversubtle treatment of his words ; behind his fear he is gloating over his cleverness, and seems to delight in the audience provided by the stage.

In the nightmare scene where Othello clings to the word to justify himself he comes near accepting Iago's use of it.

EMIL. :   *My husband !*
OTH. :   *Ay, twas he that told me first :*
          An honest man he is, and hates the slime
          That sticks on filthy deeds . . .
EMIL. :   *My husband say that she was false ?*
OTH. :   *He, woman ;*
          I say thy husband : dost understand the word ?
          My friend, thy husband, honest, honest Iago.

From the sound of the last line it seems as bitter and concentrated as the previous question ; to the audience it is. Yet Othello means no irony against Iago, and it is hard to invent a reason for his repetition of *honest*. He may feel it painful that the coarse Iago, not Desdemona or Cassio, should be the only honest creature, or Iago's honesty may suggest the truth he told ; or indeed you may call it a trick on the audience, to wind up the irony to its highest before Iago is exposed. Yet Iago would agree that one reason why he was honest was that he hated the slime. The same slime would be produced, by Desdemona as well as by Othello one would hope, if the act of love were of the most rigidly faithful character ; the disgust in the metaphor is disgust at all sexuality. Iago playing " honest " as prude is the rat who stands up for the ideal ; as soon as Othello agrees he is finely cheated ; Iago is left with his pleasures and Othello's happiness is destroyed. Iago has always despised his pleasures, always treated sex without fuss, like the lavatory ; it is by this that he manages to combine the " honest dog " tone with honesty as Puritanism. The twist of the irony here is that Othello now feels humbled before such clarity. It is a purity he has failed to attain, and he accepts it as a form of honour. The hearty use and the horror of it are united in this appalling line.

Soon after there is a final use of *fool*, by Emilia, which sums up the clown aspect of Iago, but I ought to recognise that it may refer to Othello as well :

EMIL. : *He begged of me to steal it.*

IAGO : *Villainous whore !*

EMIL. : *She give it Cassio ! no, alas ; I found it,*
And I did give't my husband.

IAGO : *Filth, thou liest !*

EMIL. : *By heaven, I do not, I do not, gentlemen.*
O murderous coxcomb, what should such a fool
Do with so good a wife ?

(*Iago stabs Emilia and escapes*).

On the face of it she praises herself to rebut his insults, which are given because she is not a " good wife " in the sense of loyal to his interests. But her previous speech takes for granted that " she " means Desdemona, and we go straight on to Emilia's death-scene, which is entirely selfless and praises Desdemona only. I think she is meant to turn and upbraid Othello, so that she praises Desdemona in this sentence : it would be a convenience in acting, as it explains why she does not notice Iago's sword. *Coxcomb* in any case insists on the full meaning of " fool ", which would make a startling insult for Othello ; the idea becomes not that he was stupid to be deceived (a reasonable complaint) but that he was vain of his clownish authority, that is, self-important about his position as a husband and his suspicions, murderous merely because he wanted to show what he could do, like a child. She is the mouthpiece of all the feelings in us which are simply angry with Othello, but this judgement of him is not meant to keep its prominence for long. Indeed as her death-scene goes on the interpretation which the producer should reject is I think meant to come back into our minds ; the real murderous coxcomb, the clown who did kill merely out of vanity, was Iago. The cynic had always hated to be treated as a harmless joker, and what finally roused him into stabbing her was perhaps that he thought she had called him a clown. The Lion and the Fox are thus united in the word, but as so many things happen in the play by a misunderstanding. It is perhaps an unnecessarily elaborate interpretation (the reference to Iago is much the more important one) but I think it is needed for our feelings about Emilia that she should not deliberately give herself the praise which we none the less come to feel she deserves.

Some other words which combine the ideas of truth-telling and generosity are affected by the same process as *honest*, though without becoming so important. Desdemona while giggling at the jokes of Iago in the second Act says, " Is he not a most profane and liberal counsellor ? ", and Othello echoes this *liberal* when he catches from Iago the trick of sneering at the generosity of Desdemona.

OTH.   . . . *here's a young and sweating devil here*
            That commonly rebels. Tis a good hand,
            A frank *one.*
DES. :   *You may indeed say so,*
            For twas that hand that gave away my heart.
OTH. : *A* liberal *hand* . . . .
EMILIA : *No, I will speak as* liberal *as the air*
            Let heaven and men, and devils, let them all
            All, all, cry shame against me, yet I'll speak . . .
            So, speaking as I think, I die, I die.

Indeed the whole power of Emilia's death-scene is that she ties up a variety of sacrificial virtues into a bundle labelled " mere coarse frankness ". *Honest* itself seems to have rather minor connections with truth-telling, but the play as a whole is far from indifferent to that virtue, and Emilia has to steal the limelight from Iago in the eyes of those who preferred a character who could blow the gaff.

The only later use of *honest* comes when Othello's sword is taken from him by the State officer ; a mark of disgrace, a symbol of cuckoldry ; two possible negations of honour and honesty.

OTH. :   *I am not valiant neither,*
            But every puny whipster gets my sword.
            But why should honour outlive honesty ?
            Let it go all.

The straightforward meaning, I take it (though commentators have disagreed a good deal), is something like " I have lost my civilian reputation, because the killing of my wife has turned out unjust ; why then should I care about my military reputation, which depends on keeping my sword ? " But the poetic or dramatic effect clearly means a great deal more. The question indeed so sums up the play that it involves nearly all of both words ; it seems finally to shatter the concept of honesty whose connecting links the play has patiently removed. There are thirteen other uses of *honour* (and *honourable*) ; four of them by Othello about himself and five by others about Othello.* The effect has been to make Othello the

* The remaining four can all I think be connected with Othello. His wife's honour concerns him directly—the comparison of it to the handkerchief even implies that he has given it to her (iv.1.14) ; Cassio, we hear, is to have an honourable position—because he is to take Othello's place (iv.3.240) ; the state

personification of honour ; if honour does not survive some test of
the idea nor could Othello. And to him *honest* is ' honourable ',
from which it was derived ; a test of one is a test of the other.
Outlive Desdemona's chastity, which he now admits, outlive
Desdemona herself, the personification of chastity (lying again, as
he insisted, with her last breath), outlive decent behaviour in,
public respect for, self-respect in, Othello—all these are honour,
not honesty ; there is no question whether Othello outlives them.
But they are not tests of an idea ; what has been tested is a special
sense of *honest*. Iago has been the personification of honesty, not
merely to Othello but to his world ; why should honour, the father
of the word, live on and talk about itself ; honesty, that obscure
bundle of assumptions, the play has destroyed. I can see no other
way to explain the force of the question here.

There is very little for anybody to add to A. C. Bradley's
magnificent analysis, but one can maintain that Shakespeare, and
the audience he had, and the audience he wanted, saw the thing
in rather different proportions. Many of the audience were old
soldiers disbanded without pension ; they would dislike Cassio as
the new type of officer, the boy who can displace men of experience
merely because he knows enough mathematics to work the new
guns. The tragedy plays into their hands by making Cassio a
young fool who can't keep his mistress from causing scandals and
can't drink. I don't know why Shakespeare wanted to tell us
that Iago was exactly twenty-eight, but anyway he is experienced
and Cassio seems about six years younger. Iago gets a long start
at the beginning of the play, where he is enchantingly amusing
and may be in the right. I am not trying to deny that by the
end of the first Act he is obviously the villain, and that by the end
of the play we are meant to feel the mystery of his life as Othello
did :

> *Will you, I pray, demand that semi-devil*
> *Why he hath thus ensnared my soul and body ?*

Shakespeare can now speak his mind about Iago through the

---

officer is " your honour " because he represents the source of that position. The
only difficult case is

> *Three lads of Cyprus—noble swelling spirits*
> *That hold their honours in a wary distance* . . .
> *Have I this night flustered with flowing cups.* (ii.3.53.)

It will be hard for Cassio not to get drunk with them because they are " tough " ;
their boastful virility is likely to make them dangerous customers unless they are
handled on their own footing. I think they act as a faint parody of Othello's
Honour, which is a much idealised version of the same kind of thing. And on
the other hand Iago does not use the word at all when he is making contradictory
speeches in favour of " good name " and against " reputation ", because that
would make it less specific.

convention of the final speech by the highest in rank :

> *O Spartan dog,*
> *More fell than anguish, hunger, or the sea!*

Verbal analysis is not going to weaken the main shape of the thing. But even in this last resounding condemnation the dog is not simple. Dogs come in six times. Roderigo when dying also calls his murderer Iago a dog, and Othello does it conditionally, if Iago prove false. Roderigo says that he himself " is not like a hound that hunts but one that fills up the cry "—Iago is the dog that hunts, we are to reflect.* Iago says that Cassio when drunk will be " as full of quarrel and offence as my young mistress's dog " ; now Iago himself clearly knows what it feels like to be ready to take offence, and one might think that this phrase helps to define the sort of dog he is, the spoiled favourite of his betters. He has also a trivial reference to dogs when encouraging Cassio and saying that Othello only pretends to be angry with him " as one would beat his offenceless dog, to affright an imperious lion ". It seems rather dragged in, as if Iago was to mention dogs as much as possible. The typical Shakespearean dog-men are Apemantus and Thersites (called " dog " by Homer), malign underdogs, snarling critics, who yet are satisfactory as clowns and carry something of the claim of the disappointed idealist ; on the other hand, if there is an obscure prophecy in the treatment of *honest*, surely the " honest *dog* " of the Restoration may cast something of his shadow before. Wyndham Lewis' interesting treatment of Iago as " fox " (in *The Lion and the Fox*) leaves out both these dogs, though the dog is more relevant than the fox on his analogy of tragedy to bull-baiting ; indeed the clash of the two dogs goes to the root of Iago. But the dog symbolism is a mere incident, like that of *fool ;* the thought is carried on *honest*, and I throw in the others only not to over-simplify the thing. Nor are they used to keep Iago from being a straightforward villain ; the point is that more force was needed to make Shakespeare's audience hate Iago than to make them accept the obviously intolerable Macbeth as a tragic hero.

There seems a linguistic difference between what Shakespeare meant by Iago and what the nineteenth-century critics saw in him. They took him as an abstract term ' Evil ' ; he is a critique on an unconscious pun. This is seen more clearly in their own person-ifications of their abstract word ; e.g. *The Turn of the Screw* and *Dr. Jekyll and Mr. Hyde*. Henry James got a great triumph over some critic who said that his villains were sexual perverts (if the story meant anything they could hardly be anything else). He said :

---

* Mr. Granville-Barker indeed said that Iago was " like a hound on the trail, sensitive and alert, nose to the ground, searching and sampling, appetite and instinct combining to guide him past error to his quarry ."

' Ah, you have been letting yourself have fancies about Evil ; I kept it right out of my mind.' That indeed is what the story is about. Stevenson rightly made clear that *Dr. Jekyll* is about hypocrisy. You can only consider Evil as all things that destroy the good life ; this has no unity ; for instance, Hyde could not be both the miser and the spendthrift and whichever he was would destroy Jekyll without further accident. Evil here is merely the daydream of a respectable man, and only left vague so that respectable readers may equate it unshocked to their own daydreams. Iago may not be a ' personality ', but he is better than these ; he is the product of a more actual interest in a word.

II

It struck me on reading this over that it is not likely to convince a supporter of Bradley, since it bows to the master as if taking his results for granted and then appears to include him among the nineteenth-century critics who are denounced; also, what is more important, it does not answer the central question that Bradley put—" Why does Iago plot at all ? " I shall try now to summarize Bradley's position and explain the points at which I disagree from it.

We are shown, says Bradley, that Iago is clear-sighted, and he appears to have been prudent till the play begins ; he must have realized that his plot was extremely dangerous to himself (in the event it was fatal) ; and yet we feel that he is not actuated by any passion of hatred or ambition—in fact, so far as he pretends that he is, he seems to be wondering what his motives for action can be, almost as Hamlet (in the immediately previous play by Shakespeare) wonders what his motives can be for inaction.* Some recent critics have objected to this sort of analysis, but I think it is clearly wrong to talk as if coherence of character is not needed in poetic drama, only coherence of metaphor and so on. The fair point to make against Bradley's approach (as is now generally agreed) is that the character of Iago must have been intended to seem coherent to the first-night audience ; therefore the solution cannot be reached by learned deductions from hints in the text about his previous biography, for instance ; if the character is puzzling nowadays, the answer must be a matter of recalling the assumptions of the audience and the way the character was put across. Of course it is also possible that Shakespeare was cheating, and that the audience would not care as long as they got their melodrama. Indeed there are lines in Iago's soliloquies which seem

---

* One might indeed claim that Iago is a satire on the holy thought of Polonius—
" To thine own self be true . . . thou canst not then be false to any man."

to be using the older convention, by which the villain merely announced his villainy in terms such as the good people would have used about him. But I should maintain that the character was an eminently interesting one to the first-night audience (they did not take the villain for granted) and that even the crudities could be absorbed into a realistic view of him. Such at any rate is the question at issue.

Bradley's answer is in brief that Iago is tempted by vanity and love of plotting. Iago says he likes " to plume up his will/In double knavery ", to heighten his sense of power by plots, and Bradley rightly points out that this reassurance to the sense of power is a common reason for apparently meaningless petty cruelties. Iago particularly wants to do it at this time, because he has been slighted by Cassio's appointment and is in irritating difficulties with Roderigo, so that " his thwarted sense of superiority demands satisfaction ". But he knows at the back of his mind that his plot is dangerous to the point of folly, and that is why he keeps inventing excuses for himself. Bradley opposes what seems to have been a common Victorian view that Iago had " a general disinterested love of evil ", and says that if he had a " motiveless malignity " (Coleridge) it was only in the more narrow but more psychologically plausible way that Bradley has defined.

All this I think is true, and satisfies the condition about the first-night audience. The thwarted sense of superiority in Iago is thrust on them in the first scene, and they are expected to feel a good deal of sympathy for it ; at the end of the first Act they are to appreciate the triumph with which he conceives the plot. However the question " why does he do it ? " would hardly present itself as a problem ; obviously the play required a villain ; the only question likely to arise is " why does everybody take the villain for a good man ? " Bradley of course recognises this question but he deals with it in terms of an ethical theory supposed to be held only by Iago, whereas you clearly need to consider how it was understood by the audience ; and the effect of this twist is to take Bradley some way back towards the idea that Iago embodies Pure Evil.

He says that Iago has " a spite against goodness in men as a thing not only stupid but, both in its nature and by its success, contrary to Iago's nature and irritating to his pride ". Not only that, but " His creed—for he is no sceptic, he has a definite creed— is that absolute egoism is the only rational and proper attitude, and that conscience or honour or any kind of regard for others is an absurdity." Bradley therefore finds it contradictory and somewhat pathetic when Iago shouts " villainous whore " at his wife, or implies that since Cassio would like to be an adulterer it is not so bad to say he is one (iii.1.311). This, he says, shows that Iago has a " secret subjection to morality ", an " inability to live up to his creed " ; also the soliloquies betray a desire to convince himself, so that his natural egoism is not perfect. Perfection is attained, however, in the way he hides his ethical theory from other people ; when we consider his past life, says Bradley, " the inference, which is accompanied by a thrill of admiration, (is) that Iago's power of dissimulation and of self-control must have been prodigious ". Since a thrill about his past life is not properly part of the play, this amounts to an admission that the stage character is not consistent. In effect, Bradley is agreeing with Rymer here.

It seems clear that Iago was not meant as a secret theoretician of this sort, and that the audience would not be misled into thinking him one. His opinions, so far as he has got them clear, are shared by many people around him, and he boasts about them freely. To be sure, he could not afford to do this if they were not very confused, but even the confusion is shared by his neighbours. When Iago expounds his egotism to Roderigo, in the first scene of the play, he is not so much admitting a weak criminal to his secrets as making his usual claim to Sturdy Independence in a rather coarser form. He is not subservient to the interests of the men in power who employ him, he says ; he can stand up for himself, as they do. No doubt an Elizabethan employer, no less than Professor Bradley, would think this a shocking sentiment ; but it does not involve Pure Egotism, and I do not even see that it involves Machiavelli. It has the air of a spontaneous line of sentiment among the lower classes, whereas Machiavelli was interested in the deceptions necessary for a ruler. Certainly it does not imply that the Independent man will betray his friends (as apart from his employer), because if it did he would not boast about it to them. This of course is the answer to the critics who have said that Roderigo could not have gone on handing all his money to a self-confessed knave. And, in the same way, when it turns out that Iago does mean to betray Roderigo, he has only to tell the audience that this fool is not one of his real friends ; indeed he goes on to claim that it would be *wrong* to treat him as one. I do not mean to deny there is a paradox about the whole cult of the Independent Man (it is somehow felt that his selfishness makes him more valuable as a friend) ; but the paradox was already floating in the minds of the audience. No doubt Shakespeare thought that the conception was a false one, and gave a resounding demonstration of it, but one need not suppose that he did this by inventing a unique psychology for Iago, or even by making Iago unusually conscious of the problem at issue.

Indeed, when Iago is a conscious hypocrite, I should have thought that he was laughably unconvincing :

> *Though in the trade of war I have slain men,*
> *Yet I do hold it very stuff of the conscience*
> *To do no contrived murder : I lack iniquity*
> *Sometimes to do me service ; nine or ten times*
> *I thought to have yerked him here under the ribs.*

" Tis better as it is ", answers Othello rather shortly ; they are his first words in the play. Iago's attempt to show fine feelings has only made him sound like a ruffian in Marlowe. But this is not at all likely to shake Othello's faith in him ; the idea is that, if you are in the way of needing a reliable bodyguard, you must put up with something rough. It is true that the soliloquies make him seem a more intellectual type ; and when he says, as a reason for murdering Cassio, " He has a daily beauty in his life, Which makes me ugly ", one can hardly deny that Shakespeare is making a crude use of the soliloquy convention. But even this line, though false, is only so in a marginal way. We feel that Iago would not have used those words, but Shakespeare is already committed to the convention of making him talk poetry. The trouble is that the phrase seems to refer to the *moral* beauty of Cassio, on which Bradley expresses some delicate thoughts, and indeed this line is probably what made Bradley believe that Iago has both a clear recognition of goodness and a positive spite against it.* But it is plausible enough (as a " second level " interpretation of the crude convention) to say that Iago only means that Cassio has smarter clothes and more upper-class manners, which give him an unfair advantage over Iago (for one thing, that is why Iago fears Cassio with his nightcap). The resentment of the lower classes towards the graces of the upper really has been known to take ugly forms, and Shakespeare with his new coat of arms was ready to go out of his way to reprove it. The phrase comes late in the play (early in the fifth Act) where Iago can in any case be treated simply as the villain ; it is assumed that the feeling of the audience has been swung firmly against him. Mr. Granville-Barker said that it is a " strange involuntary phrase " which Iago " quickly obliterates under more matter-of-fact language " ; and marks the point where " even his nerve is strained ", so that he is beginning to bungle a

---

* Mr. Wilson Knight, in *The Othello Music*, also regards the " daily beauty " speech as the essence of the matter ; in the same way, he says, Iago hates the romance of Othello and the purity of Desdemona, and " this is his ' motive ' throughout ; other suggestions are surface deep only ". No doubt he is drawn as a cynic, but I do not think the audience would take cynicism as such to be something purely devilish and consciously devoted to destroying goodness or beauty in any form ; because the cynic had a claim to be a puritan.

situation which has got more complicated than he meant (he has obviously got to kill Cassio anyhow). This seems to me an excellent tip for a modern actor but not necessarily part of the first idea.

As to the puzzle about why he is not suspected, he boasts of that too, in a prominent place, at the end of a soliloquy and a scene (Act ii.1).

> *Knavery's plain face is never seen, till us'd.*

Shakespeare here outfaces the difficulty by a challenge to the audience : " You would have been fooled too, though you may think you wouldn't." And the reason seems clear enough from the preceding soliloquy, though it is not what Iago meant to say. His accumulating resentments at his inferior position have become explosive, so that he imagines slights from every direction ; but people cannot expect this because it seems to them natural that his position should be inferior. And yet (says the line) his knavery has always had a " plain face "—his jeering wit and his sturdy independence had always been his stock-in-trade.

I have gone into the matter at perhaps tedious length without using the word " honest " at all, because there seems a suggestion of trickery or triviality about saying that the character is only made plausible by puns on one word. Perhaps this is a risky manœuvre, because the more I succeeded in it the harder it would become to claim that the puns on " honest " were essential to the play. But it is clear I think that all the elements of the character are represented in the range of meanings of " honest ", and (what is more important) that the confusion of moral theory in the audience, which would make them begin by approving of Iago (though perhaps only in the mixed form of the " ironical cheer ") was symbolised or echoed in a high degree by the confusion of the word. When opinion had become more settled or conventionalised, and the word had itself followed this movement by becoming simpler, there were of course two grounds for finding a puzzle in the character ; but, of the two, I should say that failure to appreciate the complexity of the word was the more important ground, because after all the complexity of moral judgement had not become so difficult—what people had lost was the verbal pointer directing them to it. I think indeed that the Victorians were not ready enough to approve the good qualities of being " ready to blow the gaff " and " frank to yourself about your own desires " ; and it is not likely that any analysis of one word would have altered their opinions. And I must admit (as a final effort to get the verbalist approach into its right proportion) that my opinions about the play date from seeing an actual performance of it, with a particularly good Iago, and that I did not at the time think about the word " honest " at all. The verbal analysis came when I looked at the text to see what support it gave to these impressions. But I do not feel this to be any reason for doubting that the puns on " honest " really do support them.

III

Since Bradley there has been a drive to clear the text of subtleties of character at all cost and recover the point of view of the Elizabethan audience ; I ought to try out my theory against some representatives of that. The view of Miss Winstanley, that Shakespeare is drawing on ephemeral political allegories all the time, seems to me very probable ; they were a major interest of the period and dramatic in themselves. But it seems to me that, if he used this material, he digested it so completely that it throws almost no light on what the details mean in the final play. Her account of *Othello* is that Othello is Philip II and Iago his great enemy Antonio Perez, who had recently visited England to plot against Spain with Essex. Spaniards were called by their enemies both Moors and Jews, so that the relations of Othello to Iago (who is so nearly a stage Jew that he talks about his " tribe " iii.3.160) stand for the fatally divided Spanish nature. Desdemona is Venice ; if she accepted Spanish rule the results would be fatal, and the issue was in doubt at the time of writing. Also James I was negotiating an unpopular treaty with Spain, and Shakespeare as a patriotic Protestant gave him a warning against that country. A lot of details (for example the handkerchief) fit the Spanish legend very impressively. Perhaps the chief advantage of making Desdemona Venice is that it gives more force to the final speech of Othello ; the turbaned Turk who traduced Venice to him, he says, was stabbed at once ; Iago was not, but at least on a previous occasion . . .

That some of the audience would interpret the thing like that seems hard to deny ; it was how their minds habitually worked, and the play yields with surprising readiness to that kind of working. But it must also have been part of the regular business of a playwright to say with outraged innocence that he had never thought of such a thing ; Shakespeare succeeded in avoiding trouble about political allegory in his plays, which others didn't. And if Othello is Philip II, that character gets remarkably high praise ; it would seem easier to deduce that Shakespeare was a secret Catholic (a view often maintained) rather than a' patriotic Protestant. If the deductions are so muddling it seems possible that they were intentionally muddled. Miss Winstanley has a powerful piece of writing, both of her own and from quotation, about how

Philip II stifled everybody connected with him, either morally by suppression and suspicion or quite literally; therefore he was Othello, who suffocated his wife. But the very strength of her picture of the contemporary idea of Philip seems to me to kill the identification; Othello carries a feeling of fresh air and wild open country; it would be laughable to make Perez say that Philip had a free and open nature. You may think that Othello was " really " a jealous character, but it has to be in a different way; there has to be some point in such a resounding line as

> *I think the sun where he was born*
> *Drew all such humours from him.*

What does seem to me illuminating is the idea that the good side of the terrible Spanish character belonged to something that could be despised, their half-Moorish and therefore half-negro ancestry; admittedly they had an extravagant amount of Honour, but it was the Noble Savage cropping up—" so now I will isolate that aspect of them ". This was the starting point; the reason why an Othello was interesting. But the Othello we are asked to believe in is no longer even like a Spaniard; in fact one could connect him with Spaniards the other way round, as one of the Noble Savages they were ill-treating. It seems to have been a regular claim of people like Drake that the West Indians or what not would welcome them and supply their ships on the basis of both hating the Spaniards. To be sure, one feels there is more to be known; whether Shakespeare had ever seen a negro seems a relevant question which might be answered.* One would like to know why the idea of marrying a European princess to a negro comes into *The Tempest* and *The Merchant of Venice* as well as here. (The negro prince chooses the gold casket and the Spanish prince the silver one for the hand of the Venetian lady, and a Jew supplied the money to choose the lead one, so that the whole racial complex is there too.) Anyway " when your eyes roll so " does seem an observed detail. Miss Winstanley asserts as obvious that the audience would despise and hate a Moor, as in *Titus Andronicus;* this needs a good deal more documenting. A certain amount of racial prejudice would help to give Iago a long start with the audience, and this I think would add to the dramatic effect; but if they had as much as she supposes they would surely refuse to accept the play.

* Mr. G. B. Harrison has produced some amusing evidence that there was a negress prostitute in Shakespeare's London, who may have been the Dark Lady. But he does not seem to me to realise the linguistic difficulties of interpreting his evidence—what degree of dark skin got you called a negress, and was there a period joke about misapplying this term, whatever it meant, to a dark English-woman?

As to Iago, who has a Spanish name (though "our country disposition" seems to imply he is an Italian), I think that less light is thrown upon him by the political allegory. Miss Winstanley says we are to believe that the lascivious Moor obviously *has* seduced Emilia, because Philip II (at any rate in the contemporary myth) had seduced the Princess of Eboli and thereby made the formidable Perez his enemy. Hence there was no problem at all about the motives of Iago. Now, it is easy to believe that Perez was felt as unfathomably wicked, especially because he was plotting against his own country, and that this feeling of awe was transferred to Iago. No doubt other impressive villains would be remembered too (the objection "nobody could be so wicked" would not occur), but it seems better to take Iago as a traitorous Spaniard rather than an Italian Machiavel—the Borgias were Spaniards, anyway ; and the idea that he is the Jewish side of the tainted Spanish nature seems to me good though unimportant. But, as to the main point at issue, the more you pile up this mysterious political background to his wickedness, the less need you have to give him a simple motive. If the wickedness of Perez was unfathomable it was not "explained" by Philip's seduction of the Princess of Eboli ; and I think any tricks in the production of the play to make it obvious that Othello had seduced Emilia would only confuse the main shape of the thing. It is clear that Shakespeare drops the historical parallel whenever it is inconvenient ; indeed if the characters are to symbolise both individuals and countries the parallels can only fit here and there. I think therefore that the only relevant part of the historical parallel for Iago is that his wickedness is felt to be a startling alien thing, needing somehow to be made intelligible, though it undoubtedly exists ; and Shakespeare then sets out to make it intelligible in very homely terms, such as English villains would use. So far as you treat the character as a coherent one the whole symbolical background becomes unimportant, and the puns on *honest* take the stage.

IV

In the simpler process of disintegrating the characters the chief names are Professor Stoll and Professor Schucking, who have expressed a great deal of sympathy for the position of Rymer. The first point here seems to be the view (mainly of Professor Schucking) that what a character in an Elizabethan play says about himself ought to be accepted flatly, without wondering why he says it, because that is a "convention". Iago calls his own behaviour knavery, and a real person who did that would be a cynic, but Iago is not a cynic, only a conventional villain. It seems to me enough to say that Iago thinks a sturdy chap should use knavery when necessary ; he is prepared to accept the word for some of his actions not so much out of cynicism as out of " blow-the-gaff " spirit. He also gets excited by the idea of doing a remarkably wicked thing, and when in this mood can be interpreted as a simple villain, but he is seldom in it. The force of the argument however depends on getting a large number of cases, all of which are most simply interpreted in terms of this standard convention. Now I do not think Professor Schucking cites a single case from Shakespeare where one cannot get out of his theory somehow ; Cordelia *is* meant to be abrupt in her first reply (when stating her virtues)— she is consistently laconic, whatever else is true about her character ; Julius Caesar *is* meant to be self-absorbed, because there must be a case for the conspirators, to make them intelligible, and on the other hand Brutus *is* meant to be rather self-righteous ; Henry the Fifth *is* meant to have a command of forthright self-praise, even though Shakespeare is in the business of hiding his doubts about the character to make a straightforward patriotic play ; Lady Macbeth showed by her subsequent career, not only in her early soliloquies, that she knew the action she wanted was a criminal one. (The question of course is not merely about soliloquies but any case where the puppets make announcements about their own characters or actions.) It is wilful to put up a struggle to make the author stupider than he appears ; and one might naturally ask why this secret convention was kept up, when the contrast with the surrounding naturalism would make it an obvious butt.

However, I think that such a line of approach is valuable so long as it is not interpreted stupidly. Precisely because the final judgements were left so open, Shakespeare needed a first-level judgement, what the groundlings were working on, or how an old-fashioned play would have handled it ; and here the character's account of himself really could be accepted simply. This gave you a solid basis on which to build something more interesting ; it prevented the whole structure of judgement from becoming confused. But there had also to be a second level justification, if only to prevent the smarter parts of the audience from laughing. And I do not see why one should deny that, with a fortunate self-indulgence, but like other hurried writers, he sometimes left bits of his own opinion of a character lying about even when they were more a criticism of the play than a development of it.

Granting that the convention existed, even if only partly accepted by Shakespeare, one still needs to ask what the point of it was ; why it could be retained. I think that the answer was given by Mr. Eliot in his lecture on the influence of Seneca, in which he said that Othello's last speech was a repulsive attempt to cheer himself up and ignore the realities of what he had done. Stoicism had been a refuge for the individual (usually a slave) from a hostile world, and it was attractive to Elizabethans as a means of holding oneself together in a period of intellectual confusion. The elementary case is Parolles' " Simply the thing I am Shall make me live ", and this feeling that the individual is self-sufficient is echoed by a series of tragic heroes. Thus, apart from its dramatic convenience, the trick of self-portrayal was wanted ; it was connected with the growing cult of Individualism. It seems to me that this both accounts for the " convention " (so far as it stands out in a work whose technique is otherwise less crude) and allows us to judge how much of it is really being used.

Professor Stoll maintains that the character of Othello is a fundamental contradiction, being both very jealous and not jealous at all, or that we are tricked into believing that he has a character which is at variance with his actions, and that the whole dramatic effect depends on this. It is hard to be sure how much this theory is meant to say. That there is usually a tension between a Shakespearean character (as judged by his speech-rhythms and so on) and his actions no one need be anxious to deny ; the dramatic effects are heightened to the verge of paradox ; but that the audience is not meant even to *try* to resolve the contradiction, however inadequately, seems to be more than Professor Stoll always wants to maintain. It is agreed anyway that the so-called technique of long and short time is used with great extravagance in this play, so that the incidents run on consecutively but the characters talk as if weeks have passed ; they seem to use poetry as real people use lapse of time. Iago's plot once started has to be carried through fast or it would be discovered ; there is no reason why it should not be fast, but if it starts on the wedding-night even an audience can observe that Desdemona has had no time to be unfaithful. When one sets out to maintain that the characters are consistent in such a play it is not very clear what story one is calling credible. I do not have to maintain that the thing has an unbeatable amount of reality, only that the puns on *honest* make it better if they are observed. The failure to observe them, I can claim, has led to Professor Stoll's view that Iago is a ridiculously obvious villain with a " convention " attached to him that he is impenetrable, and Othello (as well as both jealous and not jealous) a fool with a " convention " attached to him that he is a man of strong judgement. Minor improbabilities, on this view, are deliberately thrust in to carry off the major ones ; for instance, Desdemona does not travel to Cyprus in Cassio's ship because the jealousy has to begin out of an absolutely clear sky (Shakespeare

" will no more give Othello evidence or justification for suspicion
than the predisposition itself ") ; and Emilia is brought into scenes
where one feels she cannot help guessing the truth, because it is
important to insist on the convention that *no one* could see through
Iago—otherwise Othello would seem a fool. As to the repetition
of *honest*, the effect is so crude that frank spectators no longer find
it tolerable :

> " It is true that nowadays—and possibly it was the case in
> Shakespeare's time as well—Othello's endless repetition of ' honest '
> at moments when he is being ' led as tenderly by the nose as
> asses are ' has been known to make the pit titter or laugh outright.
> Bulthaupt says he has observed this, and I have done myself. But
> this can only be considered a miscalculation of effects, not un-
> heard of among dramatists today".

" In real life ", he says later, " so importunate a reputation for
simple truth-telling would be worse than no reputation at all.
It is another case of Shakespeare's overdoing the matter ".

Of course my answer is that simple truth-telling was not what
was meant. But I am anxious to consider the merely verbal point
in terms of the real problems of the play. The first question, it
seems to me, is how Professor Stoll, reading the play like this, can
still claim to admire it ; and the answer leads us back to the protean
question of Emotive language. To be sure, he writes with an
appearance of hearty distaste for the play, but he also claims that
it is saved by Shakespeare's tact, style, and " feeling for what
belongs together " ; he " shows the sweep of his vision, or rather
the sweep of his own emotions ", and he can distinguish one
character from another by delicate but superficial observations.
Professor Stoll also sketches an argument that the emotions expressed
are natural ones, unlike those in a melodrama, although the
characters behave out of character ; but if this is so I can't see
what makes the emotions natural. The idea seems to be (it comes
out very clearly in the comparisons of the play to music) that the
audience is given a contrasting series of emotional exercises, as one
has contrasts in a well-planned dinner. " Sudden conversions and
lapses are only the most implausible part of a system common in
Elizabethan plays, . . . whereby the chief characters, before all is
said and done, run the whole gamut of emotions." But surely a
play might have this kind of merit and still make the characters feel
real ; most people would say that Shakespeare was better than
Beaumont and Fletcher precisely by doing so. If you have that
in mind already, the learned argument reduces to a mere assertion.
The idea that tragedy is a series of thrills crops up again as an
idea that the words are " purely emotive " in their operation :

" Iago explains his method—to put the Moor into a jealousy so strong that judgement cannot cure. And this he does as if the Moor were a hypnotic subject or a brainless beast, by repeating the words *good name, jealousy*, and *cuckold* almost as if he were crying ' sick 'im ' to a dog."

Professor Stoll seems irritated by it here, and takes it to prove that the characters are unreal ; but he quotes Professor Richards to support the view that it does not matter if statements in poetry are frankly false ; thus you can appreciate a tragedy while thinking the plot all nonsense, just as you can appreciate poetry while thinking that its Emotions have nothing to do with its Sense. I don't deny that there are cases which push you fairly near this position ; you ought to be able to appreciate in literature beliefs you don't agree with, and realise the general merits of a bit of poetry before you have grasped it. But when these rather subtle points are broadened into a confident dogma they lead I think to bad criticism. If what Professor Stoll says is true, *Othello* is a bad play, and he would have done better to admit it.

However I do not deny that there are myths which carry out the Stoll theory, in having a permanent appeal because incompatibles are joined. The idea of Fate is commonly important to them, as a sort of name for the assumption of the story, that the incompatibles were joined when at their height ; and the *truth* of such a myth is that it frequently seems somehow apposite to human affairs—it sums up a lot of human experience because things may appear to happen nearly like that, or because you ought to be warned against allowing them to. The story of an entirely unjealous man who was made fatally jealous by an obvious villain (who could only deceive him because of Fate) would I suppose be one of the most elementary possible myths of this sort. But, even granting that this is the fundamental material of *Othello*, it seems clear that the play needs to be, maybe not more plausible, but anyway more interesting than this. Indeed a myth in this flat form, the sentence after a name in a mythological dictionary, has never been more than material requiring elaborate treatment, whether by poets or priests. The idea that the myth is somehow enough, because it excites Emotions, leads I think to a radical doubt whether Professor Stoll is explaining something or " explaining it away ". After all, if we have these titters from the pit, which he finds good evidence for his theory, surely it is not enough to say that the play is like a myth, and that is *why* it is so successful.

I should claim then that the puns on *honest* and the ideas behind them provide something that is needed ; they at least allow Iago a reasonable basis for his legerdemain. The word imposes a confusion between the man of worldly good humour and the man with a subtle puritanical conscience, and so far as one can imagine such a character it does I think cover many of Professor Stoll's objections.

> " An honest man who undertakes to tell you such a thing does not twist and turn, tease and tantalize, furtively cast forth the slime of slander and ostentatiously lick it up again. Nor when you ask him what he is driving at does he purse his lips and pat you on the shoulder, and say : ' It were not for your quiet nor your good. Never mind me ; I am an uncleanly prying devil, etc.' "

Professor Stoll, it is clear, has a very definite picture of an " honest man ", just as Rymer had. But the puritan conscience has always gone in for discovering enormous sins in the very act of being particularly righteous ; so far as Iago is a puritan, nothing could be more " in character " than his fuss about scruples and his doubt of his own defiled judgement. And, so far as he is a worldly good fellow, nothing but a great occasion would make him call this machinery into play. What Professor Stoll is really saying is that he finds the Jacobeans nasty and confused people, and I do not say that he is wrong ; but it does not follow that Shakespeare described them inconsistently.

> " Through all his jealousy . . . (Othello) never conceives the possibility of Cassio's surpassing him in personal charm or wit, but takes her only for a ' cunning ' or ' delicate ' courtesan, without a heart, without the right to love and choose."

This is a chivalrous objection, and one which I think Shakespeare himself could have appreciated ; but as regards the play in hand it is surely a comic anachronism. Othello " did all in honour " ; it was not a question of whether Cassio was " charming " but of the rigid duties of a fantastic code. The jealous thoughts he falls into are befouling ones, but even so it is his duty to wade through them ; he must pursue this theme until his Honour is cleared. And since he also connects Honesty with Honour he regards the rough Iago as the best person to tell him how to do it. Indeed both of them are versions of the Independent Man (and are old comrades in arms, as Iago insists at the beginning ; a point which Professor Stoll repeatedly denies). Othello takes an early opportunity to explain to Iago

> But that I love the gentle Desdemona,
> I would not my unhoused free condition
> Put into circumscription and confine
> For the sea's worth.

and he echoes it again later, e.g. " Why did I marry ? This honest creature doubtless . . ." (iii.3.240). Of course his happiness in the marriage is shown as almost unearthly; but he feels almost from the beginning that this makes it precarious. To put the matter somewhat coarsely, the marriage is only satisfactory to him if it is admittedly perfect and a feather in his cap ; once it is causing trouble among his officers it is already disagreeable, and he is prepared to accept the moral view of Iago that all sex is disgusting as such. Mr. Wilson Knight, with an unusual flash of realism, said that Iago rightly calls Othello fantastical, since there is something sentimental about his language ; it is over-decorative. " A proper understanding of Othello's style reveals Iago's ' motive ', so often questioned." This is much more to the point than saying that Iago hates beauty and virtue in any form, and it does not make Othello unreal ; an Elizabethan who took Honour seriously (Essex or Herbert of Cherbury, for instance) really did think in rather this way. Perhaps I am a bad judge of inconsistency, because it seems to me that few writers have dared to make people as eccentric as they really are ; but I should say that such a character would regard suspicions as impossible till they were suggested to him by an " expert ", and then would let them fill his mind very easily.

After calling him credible in his period one still has to consider what his period would think of him, both author and audience. The references in the *Shakespeare Allusion Book*, though very indefinite, seem to take for granted that he was both jealous and an object of pity. " The greeved Moor " (elegy on Burbage), " Honest Iago and the jealous Moore " (Digges on Shakespeare), " Jago for a rogue and Othello for a jealous husband, two parts well penned " (notebook of Wright) ; there are no surprises to be got from this sort of thing. As to what Shakespeare thought about it himself, another way of making Othello unreal is to say, like Mr. Hugh Kingsmill, that he is simply an outburst of Shakespeare's personal feelings of jealousy, and " very slenderly attached to his character as a general ". Indeed it would fit the Stoll formula neatly to say that Shakespeare is expressing a compulsive jealousy of his own in a self-righteous manner, and therefore attaches it to a man entirely unjealous by nature. His feelings are " externalised " merely in the sense that he tries to make other people feel as he does without giving them the chance to criticise him. But after all he set out to kill this idealised person, and kept enough balance to scarify the self-righteousness by some piercing criticisms against him. Professor Stoll, to be sure, argues that the tragic hero of the Elizabethan popular audience had no Aristotelian " flaw " but was viewed wholly with admiration (including Hamlet when he scolds himself) ; it makes a neat contrast to the view of Miss Winstanley, that they would regard a Moor with positive loathing. I do not see how he can get round a line like " she was too fond of her most filthy bargain ". Othello indeed remarks " who can control his fate ? " (though it reads almost as a throwaway line) and on this view we are merely to feel pity for the gallant barbarian with whom Shakespeare is identified ; but I think the Shakespeare reaction to the word *fate* is very steady ; there is always a side of him like Edmund in *Lear* which sees through Fate and recognises it as an excuse. No doubt there were the passing delusions of grandeur in the old actor, which Mr. Kingsmill has described so convincingly, but on the whole I should have thought he felt himself extremely unlike Othello.

The crucial question for Professor Stoll seems to be whether Othello was naturally jealous or not. I know that a critic ought at least to put up a claim to understand human nature, but I cannot show any *expertise* here ; because it seems to me that Othello's principles about the matter were all wrong, let alone the way he applied them. The advent of contraceptives has taken a lot of strain off the topic, but I am not sure that the attitude of the Elizabethans was as simple as they pretended. I understand that murder of one's wife out of jealousy was not at all usual among Elizabethans, let alone usually condoned as *crime passionel*. Indeed the rancour of their incessant jeering at cuckolds is not easy to understand if these figures were simply considered ill-used ; it has much more the air of a propaganda drive against a body which had excited popular resentment. They were too comfortable, if nothing worse ; they must be made to do their duty ; let them consider Othello, for instance ; there's a really highminded man for you. A savage, or a Spaniard, or something ; that's the type you ought to imitate. The fact that Shakespeare could appeal to these feelings does not tell us on which side of the fence he would be found. He had certainly experienced jealousy, but I fancy Mr. Kingsmill's insistence on it is connected with a desire to minimise the importance of Mr. W. H. The Sonnets, after all, are the main source for his picture of Shakespeare's private life (in *The Return of William Shakespeare*) and yet I cannot see that " Take all my loves, my love, yea take them all " is at all close to the attitude of Othello. For that matter, I cannot imagine Othello leaving his wife his second-best bed. I think in fact that the play has a certain wilful heightening of the conduct to be expected of a man of honour, in a manner which we recognise more easily in a Victorian melodrama. Robert Bridges found the play " more exasperating than anything else ", and one does not get this kind of irritation from an outpouring of personal agony (which *Timon* probably is), only from a glossy " smash hit ". But this effect of wilfulness, of concocting something as unpleasant as possible, disappears I think if you take the play as an attempt to isolate a racial or national type of the Man of Honour —an idea which most recent critics have laughed at as absurdly un-Shakespearean.

Indeed, I think the interesting question is not whether Othello was " naturally jealous " but whether Iago was. There is usually in a Shakespeare tragedy a certain doubling of the main theme—if a play is about jealousy we expect to have two jealous men, of different sorts. This becomes clearer if we realise that there was a very different way of looking at the subject. Iago, we gather, normally lives in a state of passive suspicion about his wife (or " peevish " jealousy, as she calls it), willing for her to further his interests but not sure how far she has gone in doing it. An attractive wife was an asset, and it would be impolitic to pry into her technique. If Cassio had such a wife he would be damned for the way he would use her. (At least, I cannot see any other relevant meaning for " almost damned in a fair wife ". But on any theory the line is obscure and something of a loose end ; maybe at the beginning Shakespeare expected to make more use of this aspect of cuckoldry than the final play does.) The play thrusts this theme on us chiefly when Cassio kisses the two women on arriving in Cyprus, and Iago expresses suspicions about Desdemona which it is obviously more his business to apply to Emilia ; he admits this at the end of the scene. It is clear that he knows a lot about jealousy ; indeed, the broad effect is that he is dragging Othello into his own state of mind.* The first thing he does about the marriage is to try to make the father jealous ; he is always emphasising that no women can be trusted ; he speaks very feelingly about the pains of the condition (" Good Heaven, the souls of all my tribe defend " from it—" Not poppy, nor mandragora ", and so on). But all this is a habit of feeling which he dare not ordinarily act upon ; and even here he only gets relief by pushing it off onto somebody else. It is " thought abroad ", he says, that Othello has enjoyed his wife, and the point I am trying to make is that the complacent husband who had got a job by it was a fairly common object (especially at court) ; the only dangerous thing about it was that one might get jeered at so extremely savagely. For example, the poems in Campion's *Observations on English Poetry* (1602) seem to be merely stock themes treated in the metres recommended, and one of them is the happy cuckold who prays daily that his state may continue, because the lover takes all the trouble and expense so that the husband is practically the adulterer. " Mock him not with horns, the case is altered ", says the poem, but of course this is a comically low man

* Iago's phrase

> Oft my jealousy
> Shapes faults that are not

claims I think to use only the Biblical meaning of the word, but helps to spread the idea. For that matter the pathetic but ridiculous jealousy of Bianca over the handkerchief, as Mr. Granville-Barker pointed out, adds to the coarseness of the kind of jealousy we are to impute to Othello as he peeps at her.

and even he has to deny it " stiffly ". The ever-useful N.E.D. quotes under *cuckold* a report that the honourable Spaniards of the sixteenth century used to punish " unrepining cuckolds " by parading them mounted on asses ; the idea here is that a man might naturally not repine, and would naturally be attacked for not repining. (The word seems to have gone out in the middle of the eighteenth century ; the point of the insulting metaphor is of course that the husband is feeding the other man's child.)   I take it then that Iago's grizzling on the subject is rooted in an idea that he can't afford the heroics of Othello about his own domestic Honour, and yet this is another reason why he may become unjustly treated as a butt ; his general explosive mood of repressed resentment breaks out in this form too.   Indeed, he actually tells Othello that there is nothing to worry about ; plenty of people have to put up with it ; in fact Othello's Honour might be better served by winking at it.   This line of talk is useful to him because it drives Othello to the opposite extreme.   But it also to some extent drags Othello into Iago's own view of the matter, particularly when Othello is made to spy on a Cassio who is apparently jeering at him in the conventional style. This is his period of deepest degradation (" I see that nose of yours, but not the dog I shall throw it to ") ; and there seems to be a suggestion here that he kills Desdemona merely to avoid the standard cuckold-mockery.   Shakespeare goes out of his way to make Emilia say " Who would not make her husband a cuckold to make him a monarch? Tis a huge price for a small vice." The scene is one of great pathos because it underlines the innocence of the already doomed Desdemona, and Emilia seems to be only making a joking answer to a child ; but the remark at least fits in with the nagging worries of her husband on the matter.   And it is not at all clear that he would have disagreed with her ; it is only clear that if he agreed he would be agonizingly suspicious that people were dropping hints.   There is a puzzling incident (iv.2.148) when he calls his wife a fool because she rallies him for his suspicions of her ; he seems to feel that the rules of this form of competition are painfully complex, more so than she recognises.   From his own point of view, the only really wicked part of his plot (the only cruelty which could not be regarded as revenge) is its effect on Desdemona ; and towards her, as Bradley pointed out, he seems to show a certain embarrassment. (The clamouring Roderigo twice makes a pat appearance as if to suggest that that is what forces Iago to hurt her further.)   But I suppose Iago greatly resented the high-class affectation of purity in the presumable adulteress ; and perhaps resented it even more when he suspected that she did *not* go to bed with Cassio ; these people, he feels, can get advantages from their " charm " (very obscenely) without doing anything you can lay your hands on.   The coarseness and the puritanism are inextricably mixed, and the main result is an obscure but very bitter feeling that women put men into a false position about their " good name ". (Of course, I assume his feelings are very sincere when he talks to Othello with horror about the loss of " good name ", just as much as when he jeers at " reputation " to comfort or humiliate Cassio. One of the chief ways to lose good name was to be exposed to jokes about horns.) No doubt all this acts as a defence of the murderous high-mindedness of Othello, because the only alternative point of view about adultery which is shown to us is such a low one ; but still it is not pretended that no other view except Othello's can be conceived.

I have tried to make all reasonable concessions to the adverse critics, and I think I can now turn round and claim that the thinking behind the " melodrama " is not at all crude, at any rate if you give Iago his due. It is only because a rather unreal standard has been set up that the blow-the-gaff man can take on this extra-ordinary power. It is not merely out of their latent " cynicism " that the listeners are meant to feel a certain sting of truth in Iago's claim to honesty, even in the broadest sense of being somehow truer than Othello to the facts of life ; and they are still meant to feel it even if it makes them hate Iago all the more, as indeed the play intends it to do.

In this kind of way, finally, it seems natural to come back to the idea that Iago is meant to be a devil and to represent Pure Evil, as the Victorians thought, but by a different route. For that matter, my remarks about Professor Stoll deal with his earlier treatments of the play ; in *Shakespeare and Other Masters* (1940) he writes of it with much more appearance of liking and treats Iago as a simple devil. Certainly the text leaves room for this idea ; Othello undoubtedly, at the end, wonders whether Iago is a devil. " This of Iago's is the supreme melodramatic villainy ", the final flower of a long development of the Vice and the Machiavel and what not, says Professor Stoll contentedly. And the justification " for Iago's humour and vulgarity is structural.... He cannot be permitted to keep to the high pitch of tensity in his soliloquies and his final defiance . . . or he would be unendurable and fail of effect. And for him to unbend there is no other good and plausible way." Villainy and humour were known to go together in a moderate degree, and this was enough basis for combining them in an in-credible degree. As for the motive, his obvious hatred for Othello is quite enough—" To be successful, a slanderer and intriguer must obviously be above the suspicion of a grievance." I find this too frank a preference for melodrama, and the idea that such a thing obviously couldn't happen *really* (the story must have been con-cocted) strikes me as a rather innocent bit of optimism. In the same way, the ridicule which Professor Stoll likes to heap on subtle commentators in their studies, as compared with the broad simplicity of the stage, does not sound to me as if he had done much acting or producing ; surely the fact is that there are many ways of putting on an Iago, some better than others, and a love of broad simplicity does not get you very far. He is actually misleading, I think, when he says that the devil Iago simply enjoys his Evil and is " not tormented by it " ; when Iago says " I hate him as I do hell-pains " it does not sound like enjoyment, and the mere suspicion that he has been cuckolded " gnaws his entrails ". An actor who allows him both suffering and humour is already committed to some attempt at " interpreting " him as a credible character. But, after all these complaints, I have to admit that something very like a devil is what is wanted ; a performance should not soften the character but manage to make us accept it, when it is played all out, as both wicked and coarsely funny.

The real question thus becomes what a devil is wanted to be, and the answer I think is Miss Maud Bodkin's, in *Archetypal Patterns* :

> " Iago seems to Othello so honest, so wise, beyond himself in human dealings, possessed of a terrible power of seeing and speaking truth, because into what he speaks are projected the half-truths that Othello's romantic vision ignored, but of which his mind held secret knowledge."

In an appendix, defending this kind of language against Professor Stoll, she points out that what is really in view is the spectator or reader, " experiencing the romantic values represented in the hero, and recognising, in a manner secretly, the complementary truths projected into the figure of Iago ". On her account this is always the way people use their idea of a devil, and it is enough to justify calling Iago one. I have really only tried to supplement it, by considering the word *honest* and its ramifications, so as to elucidate what kinds of truth he must be supposed to contain.

Chapter 12

SENSE AND SENSIBILITY

THERE was a good article on *sensibility* in *Psyche* for 1935 by Caroline Thompson, from which I want to start ; partly to criticise it, but feeling grateful to her for giving the work such a firm basis. This family of words is obviously very difficult ; the mere number of them is distracting (*sensuousness, sensuality, sensitivity, sensationality*), and the N.E.D. counts thirty meanings of *sense* alone. Indeed, the head of the family seems to me to need the most attention ; it has most tendency to make up people's minds for them. Caroline Thompson gives a rather gruff treatment to the aesthetic member of the family, using on it the language of the psychologist, and it struck me that this gave one an opportunity to generalise about the linguistic machinery in play.

The thing she sets out to explain about the word is that, though it is rightly used to describe and praise discriminating reactions, it can be twisted round to describe and praise excessive reactions. The field of sensibility is then analysed into four parts, reception of, and reaction to, stimulus and context ; and she claims, I think, to explain the suggestions of the word as due to simple confusion between these elements. A covert metaphor is also made important, one that compares the human creature to a weighing-machine or pointing-needle, and it is not clear how this comes in ; but I understand her to mean that while we make this comparison naturally and rightly about any receptions (esp. receptions of stimuli), yet in the case of this one word, owing to its confusion of meaning, we extend the comparison wrongly to reactions (esp. reactions to context). Thus the reason why praise of excess comes into sensibility is that a balance which can register small differences is easily disturbed; as soon as the confusion of meaning has put the balance analogy into the wrong place, the word implies that a sensitive person is easily disturbed in his reactions. This belief, she tells us, is untrue ; and it leads to a more serious error, because the word now encourages you to show violent reactions as a proof that you have delicate discriminations. Most people would agree that this second deduction was a mistake, but it is less clear that you can call this mistake inherent in the word. *Sensibility* also tends to specialise on tender or pitiful emotions, and I understand her to explain this as choosing reactions particularly like those of the delicate balance, since they show that you are easily hurt. The article avoids any basic distinction between emotions as such and judgements or decisions.

SENSE AND SENSIBILITY

The author seems to class emotions partly as receptions-of-stimuli or first-reactions-to-stimuli (because even if we have strong feelings we ought to have good judgement), but also partly as reactions-to-context (because they ought to be proportioned to the context, not to the stimulus). I agree that " emotion " is a slippery term here, and had better not be made fundamental with regard to *sensibility* ; but she may be getting too much help from the blanket term " reaction ". Anyway it is an interesting account, particularly in giving a plausible explanation by covert metaphor when the metaphor is one that most users were probably unaware of.

Of course, one has to limit an article somewhere, but it is dangerous to take only one word of a stock pair. It looks as if the trouble with her account of *sensibility* is that she leaves out *sense* or takes it for granted. To begin with, *sense* has the same four elements in its field as *sensibility*. It is therefore certain that you cannot explain the suggestions of *sensibility* as due to mere confusion between the four elements, as she apparently claims to do, because the suggestions of *sense* go exactly the other way. And I suspect her of an unconscious tendentious use of this suppression. There has been a war between *sense* and *sensibility*, a war in which the English *sensible*, though not the French, was taken captive by the enemy ; and there is still fire in the embers. While reasonably good-humoured on the point, Caroline Thompson has a distaste for sensibility, and treats the suggestions of the word as mere fallacies—from the point of view of good sense. I should agree heartily that the war between sense and sensibility leads to nonsense on both sides when carried to extremes, and she would agree that the best people have the merits of both of them ; but it is no olive-branch on her part to apply the wisdom of peace only to the slogan of the enemy. In effect she is getting a delusively clear view of the fallacies of *sensibility* by treating those of *sense* as basic truths. We hear a great deal about the fallacious hint in *sensibility* that it is a good thing to have strong feelings, but nothing about the opposing hint in *sense* that it is better not to have feelings at all. In the same way we are flatly exhorted not to be like weighing-machines, but the human creature is at least in some degree really built like a weighing-machine—those made for delicate accuracy have had to sacrifice strength, range, or speed. By and large, people really do divide into those good at sense and those good at sensibility, and you must be thankful if they are good at either. So far as Caroline Thompson sets out to rebuke romanticism she is in danger of the typical romantic mistake, that of ignoring human limitations. Poor Marianne in Jane Austen is then treated as a mere social climber who made use of a fashion for sensibility. But the book is called *Sense and Sensibility*, and we are told in the first pages that Marianne after all had good sense too ; therefore, after a full exposure of the errors of sensibility, the book is able to end happily, when Marianne has learned through suffering how these virtues are best combined.* The striking thing here is not that people were helpless when they used the word *sensibility* but that they balanced its fallacies by using a cognate word open to fallacies in the opposite direction ; this after all is a curious source of wisdom, and one that the linguist might well examine.

However, I make these complaints more from fearing this kind of mistake in my own treatment than from finding it in Caroline Thompson's. She set out to describe the possible fallacious uses of *sensibility* and explain how they arise ; obviously a useful thing to do, and I suspected her of doing more only because it was done so fully. But surely the interesting question is not why we make mistakes with such a word but how in the world we ever come to use it rightly. It is because this seems to me the crucial question that I have kept back, in this essay, what historical remarks I can make till near the end. I want to build up the structure of opposition between *sense* and *sensibility* with extremely little appeal to the past, because I think that that is what most of us succeed in doing. Perhaps in putting this weight on the ordinary speaker, I am in some danger of a bogus free-will problem, which should first be pushed away ; a problem that takes that form, though it is really a question of the level of intelligence brought to bear on the case by the speakers in question. You cannot have a science without regular rules, and it looks as if you cannot have rules in linguistics unless people are sufficiently stupid. They are so often careless about language that you can make plausible rules on this basis, but after all it is stupid to have a theory that everybody is stupid. The issue arises here because I am assuming that we build such words by a primitive, or anyway not specifically logical, process of thought, and I must be careful to avoid saying that this makes the thought expressed by them necessarily fallacious. Except perhaps as a first approximation, you do not even want a theory saying that *most* people are stupid ; you want to give the fundamental process at work, that can

---

* It is perhaps fair to point out, what is rather in favour of Caroline Thompson's view, that *Sense and Sensibility* (the earliest Jane Austen novel apart from the suppressed first version of *Pride and Prejudice*) is a pretty full-blown piece of romanticism, more unlike her later books than critics generally allow. Marianne can " scream with agony " and be convincing about it ; the sensible Elinor can pass a whole morning in meditation which " goes like a flash ". Critics are fond of saying that Jane Austen never shows men apart from women, but here (reported, to be sure, in a harangue) we have Willoughby seeing all the way in front of him, as he drives all night through storm to the supposed death-bed of Marianne, the face of deathly agony with which she had received his insults and rejection. It is a detail that you might get in Dostoevsky. But still, though she knew what she was talking about when she dealt with romantics, she was trying to hold the balance between sense and sensibility.

be followed almost without thinking, and then show how the more integrative or intelligent processes are built on this foundation. The cheerful comparison is, after all, the discovery of grammar. People were talking grammar before grammarians existed ; and this not because they were stupid nor yet because they were mysteriously wise ; the rules merely held the language together. It seems to me very likely that there is an inner grammar of complex words like the overt grammar of sentences, and if so the mysteries of human folly are not our immediate problem. You can deny this comparison, certainly, if you say that the suggestions in a word like *sensibility* were collected by historical accident and are now learned, each one separately, by every speaker, but I think this makes us both cleverer and more slavish than we are. Of course, there is some truth in it ; for that matter there is a good deal of historical caprice in grammar, but one can also find general rules. It seems clear that the complex structure of opposition in *sense* and *sensibility* is in part re-invented by anyone who sets out to use the words seriously, and the first question is how he does it.

But before trying to answer that, it seems as well to offer a more fundamental defence of these words, to try to show how a confusion between reception and reaction, stimulus and context, can ever be useful. Otherwise the speakers are liable to seem too stupid altogether. Coming at the matter from a psychological angle, it may seem merely imbecile to mix up sense data with either emotions or judgements, so that the words look too odd to have any coherence at all. Even before it occurs to you that "sense" means the opposite of "sensibility", or Jane Austen's "sensible of" the opposite of her "sensible", or "a sense of something far more deeply interfused" the opposite of common "sense", you may be looking for the historical accidents through which this muddle arose. But in fact, we cannot help thinking as these words expect us to do. Indeed, I should say the English could claim that their present extreme muddle with this family came from having faced first the realist and then the romantic issues with more of the permanent human balance than their neighbours. Yet there was no reference to verbal history when Mr. T. S. Eliot, for instance, said that in the Elizabethan period " the intellect was at the tips of the senses " ; he was going through an independent process of thought with the original machine that formed the words. Actually the only thing he gained by this remark, which was so intriguing that some people took it for a definition of metaphysical poetry, was to imply "sensibility" without suggesting anything Caroline Thompson would disapprove: for example, a self-indulgent tenderness. But the phrase does something to show that the combination of meanings in the word cannot be escaped. " What the creator of character needs is not so much knowledge of motives as keen sensibility ; the dramatist need not understand people ; but he must be exceptionally aware of them." True enough, but all that Mr. Eliot is doing here, in the same essay, is to expound the paradox of the word. On the face of it one cannot be " exceptionally aware " of people without understanding them, unless indeed this phrase only means being prying and touchy—" intense " about the obvious kinds of information. The issue raised by the word is as to how the understanding is done— what parts you have to be conscious of, whether it comes to you in flashes or exists as a structure which you could expound. A great part of our understanding has to be " intuitive ", done by an integration of parts too complex to be spread out, and this will inevitably seem a direct " part of the sensation ", because we are not conscious of anything between the stimulus and the final result. Such cases are clearly the field or justification of both *sense* and *sensibility* ; they are the reason why this theoretically odd connection of meanings is a normal one for the human mind.

Evidently the same reason holds for the confusion of stimulus and context, but this needs saying more loudly, because it amounts to a confusion in the behaviourist use of " context ". The behaviourist may know the context of a rat in a maze, but he would not have known the context, supposing he had been present, when Newton saw the apple ; let him not pretend then to know Rousseau's context. A mathematician will often take an absurdly small context—' me seeing a stick '—and argue from what is inherent in that to a theory of continuity ; a philosopher commonly takes ' me seeing my table ' and finds inherent in it his theory of knowledge. You do not know his real context till you know what he has to say. It is the distinguishing mark of the expert of sensibility that he does the same ; from the small specimen he leaps to the universal truth, commonly with references to infinity, and when he is wrong you do not want to introduce a larger context but a middle-sized one such as the human creature really knows about. It is of course quite true that *sensibility* tends to assume a narrow context. " She had enough sense to know he disliked her "—she is judging from what she knew before. " She had enough sensibility to know he disliked her "—though he is pretending to like her she can plumb, by her immediate sensations, into his secret reactions of dislike. But take a roaring specimen of sensibility, take Laurence Sterne crying over the dead donkey. It would be no use for an advocate of *sense* to come up and tell him to consider a wider context. His context is the temporal universe and the suffering of all mortal creatures, and he knows it very well. What he claims about his immediate sensations is that they include a reaction to an enormous context, and are therefore indulged ; the suggestion that he is right to fuss about small things is carried not merely on the idea that he is like a recording needle but on the claim that he can see large things ' in ' them. Often he would claim to see them logically, just as the properties of all triangles are inherent in ' the triangle '. Indeed, I fancy there is a hint of this when we say " the horse is a noble animal ", thus dignifying the horse, but " pigs are dirty ". It is inherent in the nature of a horse to be noble (an analytic proposition —take any horse) but all pigs just happen to be dirty (a synthetic one). The notion of inherence goes as deep into our language as our thought, and you cannot pick on *sense* and *sensibility* to carry all the blame for using it.

Granting then that we are not simply shocked by the words, the starting-point of our problem is that though they both combine the ideas of reception-of-sensations and reaction-to-contexts they make opposite covert assertions. I set out to explain this type of covert assertion within a word by the equation form " A is B ", where A and B are the two meanings of the word brought into play in a given use. In reasonable language the notion of identity can shift to that of a relation between the elements, as in the English sentence, and the covert assertion becomes for instance " A is included in the larger class B ", " A entails B ", or " A is like B in possessing a character prominent in B ". I think that imputing the false identity is a primitive process, and that making it logical is a secondary one, which the mind will only take so far as seems to be required by the particular occasion. If so, there is no way of getting a direct opposition between *sense* and *sensibility* except through the order of the terms equated.

We can see how an order is put in by considering the forms of the two words. *Sensibility* looks like " ability for sensing ", or anyway is concerned with some quality of the power of sensing ; whereas *sense* (when used as a term opposed to it) must have some chief meaning which is quite distinct from the senses, because otherwise there is no reason why it should not mean the senses only. We get a similar result from considering the standard context for an elementary use of the two words ; when you are asked to show *sense* there is commonly no immediate occasion for using the senses, but when you are asked to show *sensibility* what is wanted is commonly a direct though aesthetic reaction to them. Two other points are needed to decide on the form. A reception and a reaction do not easily fall into one class, so we had best begin interpreting the equations by the idea of " likeness ". Also, the appeal of an equation is to a sort of normative process : " language itself agrees with me that this is what you would expect ; that is why I can leave the idea to show itself without elaborating on the word." In an equation which tells you how to interpret your sensations, this idea easily becomes " what I am assuming here is normal ; it ought to be true even if it isn't ". Actually " normal " goes better with *sense* and " ought " with *sensibility*, but we can put " good " into both accounts.

The covert assertion of *sense* is now " a good reaction is like a reception " (in being direct, obvious, unexcited, certainly true as far as it goes). *Sensibility* retorts " a good reception is like a reaction " (in being complex, likely to need training or special powers). Also context evidently goes with reaction and stimulus with reception, so where *sense* implies " a good reception to the whole context is like the reception of a stimulus " (because a practical man can pick out the one right conclusion) *sensibility* will retort " a good reception of the stimulus is like a reaction to a whole context " (a man of feeling can see the universe in the meanest flower that blows). No doubt I am putting a good deal into the brackets, but the ideas follow from the presumption that *sensibility* names a kind of special power of sensing, and that *sense* is radically opposed to it. The idea of normality belongs to A, because that is the thing-talked-about, which you are concerned to get right ; the function of B is to supply qualifications to the thing which make it normal. Of course, the whole assertion is also taken as a " normal " truth, but the two appeals to normality go together. We could leave out the word " good " and still make sense of the equations, but the direction of the thought is clearer when it is put in. The assertion of likeness does not bring out all the properties of B, only those relevant to the assertion. For example *sense* does not imply that a good reaction is often painful and commonly outside your control, though this is true enough about reception of stimuli ; the word considers sensations as means of knowledge not of suffering. This kind of limitation is usual with metaphors; for example, " O rose of all the world " is not intended to make you think of thorns. Indeed, you might argue that B is the one that goes through a normative process ; because it is idealised, only parts of it are to be chosen. But they are chosen in view of what is wanted for A, as in the ordinary process of metaphor.

We ought now to try " entails " instead of likeness, to see if that works better. But " a good reaction entails a reception " seems to be a mere truism; it only says that you cannot react to a stimulus without having the stimulus first. " A good reception entails a reaction " (for *sensibility*) has indeed an air of being profound ; the aesthetic judgement of the critic is felt to be inherent in his power of seeing all that is in the picture. There is no need to deny that *sensibility* often puts this idea forward ; but when the word is used in opposition to *sense* the two are felt to be somehow parallel, and I think both use the idea " likeness ".

Also, I think that both equations are of Type II, but in the case of *sense*, at any rate, we have first to consider an earlier stage. The use of the word for good judgement seems to have been borrowed from French and Latin, but the original process of extension (whether in English or not) is easily imagined. It is given by such a remark as "Use your sense, man, which *looks* the right one?" said of two plans of campaign already outlined. *Looks* here is a simple metaphor, and it is clear that *sense* is a close parallel. There is nothing to look at, and what is wanted of you is some elaborate act of judgement; the metaphor is brought in to say "the act of judgement here is as easy as using your senses". Now if the only settled meaning of the word is "the faculty of receiving sensations" I am not sure that the metaphorical use of it need be called an equation at all; at any rate, the equation is not a regular part of the word. But as soon as this becomes a stock metaphor, so that the word is regularly used in contexts where it could be replaced by "judgement", that idea becomes one of its secondary meanings. The equation is now of Type I; it only arises when the context requires the secondary meaning, and takes the head meaning as predicate. But in modern English we have accepted this shift of meaning very completely for the grammatical form *sense* used alone; we take it only to mean "good judgement", except so far as we insert a secondary idea, that this is arrived at through the senses. In fact, I think, it has become a separate word whose head meaning is "good judgement", and if we class it like that the equation becomes of Type II. The memory of the original meaning acts as an Implication, and need not be regarded as a separate meaning of the modern word at all. With *sensibility*, I think we take a special capacity for sensing (of some kind) as the head meaning of the word, and the idea that reactions are involved comes in as an extra. The typical use of it, parallel to that of *sense* for a plan of campaign, would be about something like window-curtains. "Use your sensibility, man, which *looks* the right one?" would imply that the judgement is somehow inherent in the sensations. Thus the head meaning again acts as the subject and is required by the context, so that this equation is also of Type II. No doubt it may be said that *sensibility* "really" means a special power of reacting to the senses, and I agree that some such idea comes in as predicate, but "a special power of sensing" (without further analysis) is what it appears to mean. Both words have their pairs of meaning well integrated together, so that Type II rather than Type I is where we should expect to find them. Indeed, the reader may object that they are not ambiguous at all, when they are used as an opposed pair (since this is enough context to remove the quite irrelevant meanings); it is a delusion, he might say, to think that there are alternative "senses" within either of them to be equated. But I can answer that the predicates in these equations are not independent Senses, merely Implications. Indeed, the point is not that the words are ambiguous, still less that the users think them to be, but that the field with which they both deal is itself complex, as the users are vaguely but quite reasonably aware.

So far we have hardly found any trace of the fallacies which Caroline Thompson believed to be lurking in *sensibility*, and which I retorted were also lurking in *sense*. The equations appear as general doctrines, to be sure, but as very innocuous ones. We must now examine where the fallacy comes in. I am not clear whether she meant to say that the metaphor of the recording needle was really in the minds of most users, or whether she took it as a device of exposition ; but her accusation, at any rate, was that *sensibility* says that a reaction is like a reception, like it in a whole group of ways which you can sum up by saying that it is like the behaviour of a recording needle. If you have good taste you will be easily disturbed ; you can no more help having a brainstorm or a flood of tears when disturbed than you can help seeing what is before your eyes ; and you are particularly praised by the word if you take a somewhat passive attitude to life, open to impressions, for example if you easily feel pity and tenderness. In short, " a reaction is profoundly like a reception ". It no longer fits the case to say a *good* reaction, except as one speaks of " a good cry " ; there is no idea of normality ; but one could make it " a reaction *ought to* be profoundly like a reception ", because this extremity of feeling is praised. I should say that *sense* retorts " a hardheaded man will ignore any feelings arising out of particular cases while he is carrying out his plan ; he will stick to the main chance ; he will use his senses only as tools or spies to help him in the great purpose of getting rich ". Here the idea is " a reception ought to be part of a reaction, wholly subordinate to it ". Or the hardheaded man may believe only the evidence of his senses, and stand no imaginative nonsense ; here the idea is " a reception is inherently a reaction ", because his senses themselves give him his philosophy (they are a means of knowledge, not of feeling). To be sure, these ideas seem rather far-fetched when regarded as deductions from the two ideas within *sense*, but so I think would the other ones from *sensibility* if they did not follow neatly from the metaphor of the recording needle. Each set of ideas has undoubtedly been held by people who would use one of the words assertively. And all of them, when you write down their equations like this, go the opposite way round to the ones considered so far.

It might be comforting for the theorist to say that they go the wrong way round because they are fallacies. But I think there is a fair amount of truth in what *sensibility* tells us about the recording needle, and there are plenty of other doctrines lurking within *sense* beside these crude ones. The word has been used to claim that the senses give us an unconscious wisdom like that of the animals, or that what seem mere sensations are already partly interpreted when first received. A wide variety of people, from Hobbes to Wordsworth, have made play with it, and the root idea common to these philosophical uses appears to be " a reception is profoundly like a reaction ". We cannot assert that all these ideas are fallacies, and they go the same way round as the crude ones.

On the whole, in these more doctrinal or generalising uses of the words, the speaker tends to give a context that emphasises the less obvious part of their total field of meaning so as to bring the whole word into play. The context of *sense* will now actually direct your attention to the senses, and that of *sensibility* will seem to take you away from them to some psychological process which is being praised. (Whereas in a simple use of *sense* for good judgement there is no immediate occasion for using the senses, and a simple use of *sensibility* asks for a direct though aesthetic reaction to them.) It may be thought that this is enough to explain the new order of terms ; what is suggested by the context becomes the " chief meaning " and therefore the subject of the equations. But to make the reader think *about* the senses in connection with a word for good judgement feels very different from making sensation the chief meaning of the word. We do not feel that the meaning of the word is changed round when it is used like this, only that its doctrine is being taken more seriously.

It is therefore, I think, important to notice that, in spite of what looks like a change in the order of terms, we still keep the same term as the fundamental one, or as the first thing to consider. *Sensibility* in its new equations treats a reception, in various ways, as a sort of key idea for explaining what a reaction ought to be, and *sense* holds on to a reaction of some kind as a means of interpreting or finding profundity in the mere use of the senses. It might of course be argued that these are still the head meanings, and now appear as predicates after the occasional chief meanings put in by the context ; the equations have thus been moved from Type II to Type I. But the word when taken more seriously seems to become *more* integrated, not less as you would suppose from its entering Type I, the horse-saddle type. Both *sense* and *sensibility* now use their different main ideas as a sort of quarry ; in each case you are to dig into the main idea and find aspects in which the other elements of the field are " like " it. But to do this you must take the elements as more seriously related than by mere likeness ; you treat the false identity with more conviction. The effect, I think, is not " B is like A (in all properties of A)" but " A is the typical specimen of B ". That is, the Type II equation has become a Type III equation ; and this does not require any change in the order of terms (because the head meaning is still subject) but does suit a new context, one which appears to demand the secondary meaning. That is, the machinery for getting deep or extravagant deductions out of *sensibility* is to think " a reception is the typical specimen of the whole complex field of receptions and reactions ", and to get them out of *sense* you make the subject of this sentence "a reaction". It is true that the innocent listener, who does not at the moment take this attitude, can get the main point by imputing " likeness " and connecting the terms the other way round ; I should think this has some importance for the spread of the trick, by making it less obtrusive and therefore less likely to be challenged. We had a rather similar alternation of the order of terms in the word *delicate*, where the doctrine " Being a refined girl entails being sickly " could be insinuated in the less outrageous form " this is a good type of sickly girl, and therefore refined ". But here the lines of interpretation with the two orders are much more sharply distinct ; in the simple use of *sense* the judgement and the sensation are admitted to be quite different, though they are compared ; in the doctrinal use they are seriously included in one vast kingdom, and good judgement is made king of it. I am not sure whether the two orders can really act as alternatives here.

It may be objected, however, that this scheme of opposition in the words posits a distinction which people never thought of, and ignores a simple one which they did think of. On the face of it (to repeat the point about the difference of the forms) *sense* is the simple and general word for all degrees of a capacity, whereas *sensibility* brings in, through " ability " or what not, the idea of a high degree ; it tends to imply some theoretical view of the matter, and perhaps by being a " long " word can suggest a high-falutin tone. Actually both words involve degrees of power and both can carry theories, but one shows it more than the other. Now a pregnant use like " He was a *man* " has two aspects which may be stressed in different degrees : " This is the ideal, what such a thing ought to be, what really deserves the name ", and " this is the normal or average, and therefore, as the name admits, good enough ". " Well, that *is* a lobster "—that lobster is unusually large and fine ; but " I don't care if his books are all nonsense ; I only want people to be *human* " —actually, you are asking for special qualities, good humour and so on, but the use of the pregnancy is to claim that you aren't asking much, and that a man lacking in these qualities is almost a freak. Cases of the second, as here, are usually the first in disguise, and indeed, I suppose would not otherwise deserve to be called pregnancies, but the disguise makes a difference. A common but rich word (*human* and *sense*) will tend to the second, while a special and apparently definite word (*lobster* and *sensibility*) will tend to the first.

Sensibility will, therefore, tend to mean " a high degree of power for sensing, and I have a special notion of what sensing is ", whereas *sense* will keep to " the qualities that ought to accompany a normal act of sensing " even if an extended notion of sensing appears. They will, therefore, tend to pick out, from the same complex field, different elements to put first in their equations. For *sense* directs you to what ought to accompany the sensation, whereas *sensibility* is concerned to extend the notion of sensing itself. Also, *sensibility* will come to praise a special type of person, whereas *sense* will carry a sturdy agreement with the common man ; this is the main basis of the emotion-judgement distinction. In the more doctrinal uses, the individualist idea in *sense* will also tend to cut out emotion, because our expressions of emotion are largely carried on other-regarding formulae. You can, of course, feel strongly while feeling selfishly, but you tend not to say so ; most expressions of emotion are punctured if treated as individualist, and this curious asceticism has given a certain stoic dignity to the cult of " sense ", which rather depends on such paradoxes for its claims.

I do not have to deny that these contrasts are at work ; I need only say that they are why we come to take the difference of equation order as somehow obvious. The two processes reinforce each other. Thus it is equally possible to derive the emotion-judgement opposition directly from the contrasting orders of the equations. If *sense* takes the reaction as the ' main thing ' it is not to be swamped by the feelings of the moment. As soon as *sensibility* takes the reception or reaction-to-stimulus as the ' main thing ' it is bound to attach importance to emotions, because they seem called out by sensations more directly than judgements are. This is even more the case in the more ambitious use of the word, when a narrow context is the first thing to consider but the final context is indefinitely large. You must have a definite final context to decide on action (make a judgement), but you are often not sure what your feelings are about, and an emotion turns cosmic (" the context is everything ") without much difficulty. But all this merely adds to the weight of the slogan *sensibility* ; it does not imply that the divorce from *sense* is complete, and that a partisan of *sensibility* has to admit that this virtue does not involve judgement. The partition was never finally made ; it was merely used to build up the difference of equation-order which was never recognised.

But another kind of objection, which I should think more searching, might also be made. I said that both words must be expected to use the notion of inherence ; it could be answered that *sensibility* is the only one to take this notion seriously. *Sense* is treated as a kind of metaphor, but in *sensibility* people tend to feel that the judgement really is inherent in the sensations. In my set of terms, the difference would be that *sensibility* interprets the equation either by " entails " or by " typical ", whereas *sense* holds on to " is like " whether it is taken to carry a doctrine or not. And the reason is, as before, that *sensibility* is the kind of word that is expected to carry some special doctrine, whereas *sense* is unassuming and flat, even if it is used in a militant way.

At this point, I think, the historical approach can profitably be used. It is not true that *sense* could only get from " sensations " to " good judgement " by a metaphor under specific conditions. It could get there by a variety of routes so great as to be quite baffling. Our present structure of the word was invented around the time of the Restoration ; the speakers then took to regarding the " good judgement " use as a simple metaphor, in the course of a general drive towards simplification. And the two types of equation, " A is like B " and " A is typical of B ", came into play together; the rise of *sense* for " good judgement " goes hand in hand with the rise of sensationist or plain-man philosophies. The process is practically complete before *sensibility* is taken up as an opposing term. The general feeling about *sense* in the Restoration and Augustan periods is I suppose too obvious to need examples; what is needed is to analyse this period flavour. The suasive power of the word seems to come from treating all reactions or good judgements as of one sort, though, in fact, they presumably range from the highest peaks of imaginative insight, or the greatest heart-searchings of " enthusiasm ", to fundamental but humble processes like recognising a patch of colour as a table. *Sense* tells you to concentrate on the middle of the range, the man-size parts where we feel most at home ; and it can do this because the simple use of the trope (which is now taken as a pattern) is an appeal to you to show a normal amount of good judgement, " like everybody else ". A full-blown use of the word will appear to treat it as meaning *only* " good judgement ", and indeed, good judgement of a rather narrow sort ; but the idea of sensation is not forgotten, indeed, it is having an important effect by recalling the wide range of the field which the word claims to cover. For that matter the common uses of the word for an " inner sense " or a " sense of " honour or agony or what not could meanwhile extend the range in the other direction. Good judgement appears as the king of this large and confused region, the thing you should think of first, the right handle to take hold of the bundle. It seems to me, in short, that the Restoration speakers tried to do what my opponent has suggested, that is, to reduce this meaning of the word to a simple metaphor working by " likeness ", and the effect was the contradictory one of giving it a particularly strong inherence doctrine.

The evidence for these assertions seems pretty clear in the N.E.D.

Under SENSE " 11 " it gives " Natural understanding, intelligence, esp. as bearing on action or behaviour ; practical soundness of judgement " as first used in 1684 ; by Roscommon, in the line " Pride . . . proceeds from want of sense or want of thought " which was in effect borrowed by Pope. In the same way under " common sense " it gives only " a minimum without which a man is foolish or insane " as sixteenth century, and reserves for the eighteenth century a new idea " b " " good sound practical sense, combined tact and readiness in dealing with the everyday affairs of life " ("nothing is more uncommon " 1726). The first use of *good sense* for " native soundness of judgement " is given as 1688 : " natural good sense hath a mixture of surly in't." But, in spite of these repeated claims that there was *some* important change in the word after the Restoration, it seems clear that there was only a different feeling in the word ; what was new was not the idea of judgement itself but the structure into which it was fitted.

To begin with, the main meanings of the word already existed in Latin, and were therefore well known before the Restoration. The use of *sensus* for " good judgement " is classical ; that for " meaning " comes in Augustan poets but not in prose till later; however, it is frequent in Quintilian, who seems a likely influence. The N.E.D. " 2 " " an instinctive or acquired faculty of perception or accurate estimation " is very near to good judgement : " there is, saith Tully, in the dog a marvelous perceiverance and sharp sense to know who doth him good " (1567). The N.E.D. " 8 " is " capacity for mental feeling ; sensibility " and quotes Marston[*] and the *Yorkshire Tragedy* ; it appears as connected with an older " 7 ", the idea of inner senses of the mind contrasted to the bodily senses. The N.E.D. " 18 " is " an opinion, view of judgement held or formed by an individual ", as in Othello's " in my sense tis

---

[*] A lengthier quotation from Marston had better be given here. His point of view, I think, is that a tragic extremity of sensibility is the only " sensible " thing to feel, so that the usual oppositions in the word collapse. Caroline Thompson could certainly complain that he admires people for having the strongest possible feelings of a certain kind.

> *Therefore, we proclaim*
> *If any spirit breathes within this round . . .*
> *Who winks and shuts his apprehension up*
> *From common sense of what men were and are,*
> *Who would not know what men must be, let such*
> *Hurry amain from our black-visaged shows.*
> *We shall affright their eyes. But if a breast*
> *Nailed to the earth with grief ; if any heart*
> *Pierced through with anguish, pant within this ring :*
> *If there be any blood whose heat is choked*
> *And stifled with true sense of misery ;*
> *If ought of these strains fill this consort up*
> *They arrive most welcome.* (*Antonio and Mellida* II Prologue.)

happiest to die ". This heading ends a series of the form " sense of " ... " pain " or what not, all sixteenth-century. The N.E.D. " 23 " is " the meaning of a speaker or writer ; the substance, purport or intention of what he says ". This dates back to 1400, and seems to be earlier than the allied use for " sense of a word, or sentence " ; but there are contemporary uses by Wyclif for the anagogical and other senses in Scripture, which probably helped to bring the word into wider use. The " meaning " series might seem irrelevant here, but it goes on to "27" "discourse that has a satisfactory and intelligible meaning " as in the *Merry Wives*, " Believe it, he speaks sense ", also " 28 " " what is wise or reasonable ", generally in the negative form " there is no sense in it ", dating from 1600.

The comparison that comes to mind, I think, is the musculature of the human cheek. You can name and isolate lines of specially strong and frequently used muscle, in rather different places for different people, but the main fact about the cheek is that it is a single network or sheet of muscle. The dictionary here distinguishes four ways in which the word was extended from sensations to judgements, but it is not to be supposed that the ordinary speaker distinguished which of them was in play. The idea that the shift could only happen by a flat metaphor in a peculiar context, " which *looks* the right one ? ", is, therefore, absurdly false. But I think it is relevant here ; it is a kind of rationalisation of the structure which suited the Restoration, and still feels plausible to us now. The idea of metaphor gives a certain positiveness and underlining to the word, and draws your attention to the contrast of meaning as none of the earlier uses did. But which use has most of the inherence doctrine at the back of it would, I think, be impossible to say.

The rapid rise of *sense* both in frequency and range of meaning during the fifteenth and sixteenth centuries requires an explanation of its own. In Chaucer's time *wit* covered the whole range of the modern *sense*, apart from a learned borrowing of the Latin word in philosophy, and I think the rise of *sense* involved most of the ideas of the Renaissance. In its obscure background both then and in the present-day mind are such ideas as that a sensible man will be a bit of a sensualist, well rooted in the earth, and that his judgements will be based on an evidence of the senses supposed to be free from " theory ". The accident of translation by which the first N.E.D. example of *sense* for " good judgement " happens to be about a dog suggests how philosophical puzzles about animals (and sensitive plants) were behind the development of the English word. It seemed at first abstract and non-committal, rather like our " reaction " ; it went back to the fundamental situation of any experiencing creature, and did not force you to say that the dog had " wit ". (Not that this was too shocking ; the N.E.D. gives examples of it.) It was a fundamental question for the Renaissance whether man was the most triumphant of the animals or a spirit miserably born in sin, and I think the word had an important part to play, though an unassertive one.

Thus there is a connection between the Renaissance development and the Restoration one, and a certain hardening of the word towards a rationalist philosophical position may have been already in the air in Shakespeare's time. I am ignorant about the French use from which the Restoration English one may well have been borrowed ; the first use of *bon sens* in Littré is from Descartes, but he seems not to try to go earlier. The Restoration speakers might easily imagine that they were borrowing a more civilised use of the word from the French, but even if they did they would still be affected by its English tradition. After looking at the background of the Renaissance development, it seems to me, one can get a rather fuller picture of the Restoration development. What happens is that there is a more positive vote for the dog of Tully ; the background of associations becomes rather cruder and more like a specific doctrine. Some such hardening occurred to a variety of Restoration words, as part of a general desire to escape the effects of enthusiasm and theology ; it is not a matter of a verbal opposition to *sensibility*, whose major uses had not yet appeared on the scene. As to the more doctrinal uses, the man of sense (judging from the direct evidence of his senses) is a good deal of an individualist—" hath a mixture of surly." But this is far from making him isolated ; for one thing because he agrees with the common man, but also from a more subtle idea that he can handle a complex human situation. There is a suggestion, much more extrovert than anti-emotive, one that rises almost to song in Stubbs' *History of the Royal Society*, that the only way to get at the truth (such as the senses ought ideally to give) is to know how to sit on a committee.

Indeed, so far from being dry and anti-emotional at this period the word has a temporary development of more clear-cut uses for the emotions as well. This may be a reaction by the puritans against the philosophical uses of the word, but I do not think they were felt as sharply distinct. The N.E.D. " 16b " gives " I fulfilled with great sense ; I preached what I felt, and I smartingly did feel " 1666, and a more normal example from the early eighteenth century " a bad life, of which he spoke with some sense "—that is, with a good deal of the strong emotion proper to the occasion. And meanwhile the placid uses of *sensibility* by Addison, for example, do not suggest emotion but only " power of making delicate aesthetic judgements ". Furthermore, a development of " a sense of " (e.g. impending doom) goes on during the eighteenth century, so as to make the form imply a dim and intuitive emotion not clearly attached to any of the senses.

The N.E.D. is confusing about this development, distinguishing its
" 13 " and " 14 " merely by whether an " object " or a " state of
things " is being sensed, and including in both of them examples of
earlier date which do not imply "more or less vague". "A
doubtful sense of things Not so much seen as felt " (1596) has to use
another word to show that the effect was doubtful ; and Othello's
" What sense had I of her stolen hours of lust ? " does not imply
that Othello's feelings would have been vague if he had had any.
When he talks about Iago's " noble sense of a friend's wrong " he
implies very strong and definite feelings. But the suggestion for
example about Gray's Etonians, who had " no sense of things to
come ", is that you might expect them to have a kind of intuition
of things to come ; the form was getting ready for the great use
made of it by Wordsworth. This shift towards a vague or emotional
intuition is clearly not worked from any idea that *sense* is good
judgement ; it comes in as the sort of knowledge that an animal gets.
When Wordsworth has a sense of something far more deeply
interfused the dog of Tully is still snuffing along the trail. Even
in its later stages, then, the suggestion of *sense* is very far from that
of the simple metaphor arrived at by the type sentence " which
looks the right one ? " This came to be regarded as its backbone,
but it had rich associations, and its chief element was a certain
claim to direct your attention the right way in the field that it
covered. And when it came to be opposed to *sensibility* there was
not felt to be a simple opposition between emotion and judgement
but between two general attitudes to life. It seems to me that to
read equations into the words is the natural way to handle these
broad but vague covert assertions, and if you take the whole
development of *sense* you can hardly say that it has less inherence
doctrine than *sensibility*.

I am perhaps over-simplifying the picture by aiming only at the
use of *sense* for " good judgement " ; there may be a reverse action
when the word is taken to mean " sensation ". However this only
seems to occur among the specialised uses of philosophers, and
probably did not affect the main development. Monboddo
provides an example of it ; he was not using the standard equation
" good judgement is the type of all mental powers ", and indeed
thought he was reacting against it ; but that makes him show all
the more clearly how hard it was to get away from. He set out
to distinguish the powers of animals from those of men, and to decide
what new powers were brought in by language. The Idea was
brought in by language, and it is described in very absolutist
terms : " the perfect idea must contain nothing but the very
essence " and so on—it is very far removed from sensations. He
reasonably objects to Locke's use of *idea* to cover both sensation and

thought or concept, and claims that the rest of Locke's philosophy merely follows from this trope; a particularly bold trick, he remarks, because the word was stolen from Plato. To be sure, it is not certain that the invention of language (an unnatural thing) itself introduced concepts ; they may be native to Man ; but anyway they mark his crucial difference from animals. However Monboddo then goes on to point out that a great deal of what amounts to thought goes on below this level ; a dog can't form Ideas, but he can compare his immediate complex of sensation with his memory of previous ones, and the effect is that he can make a good choice between two paths, and indeed he can know that while all men are men, his master is an individual man. But all this is merely a matter of Sense. " The union of the senses in a general perception is entirely a matter of sense not of mind." It seems clear from the context that Monboddo does not think of this as the version of *sense* for good judgement, but he is drawing on that for his effect. The curious thing is that he is doing just what he complained of Locke for doing, but with the opposite intention ; he generalises the notion of direct perception to include a special class of mental operations, which he wants to take as typified by sensing, and then he talks as if they are " nothing but " sensation. Here then we get a private equation for the word *sense* being built up, with the opposite order: " sensations are typical of the mental operations possible to dogs." But this of course is not a rival to the stock equation of *sense*, because the whole trick of the style depended on not letting the reader suspect that *sense* as " good judgement " was even the word he was using. All the same, the end of the argument was not out of line with the historical development of *sense* ; that was what made Dr. Johnson so suspicious; it ended with a claim that some creatures believed to be apes were really men, and even in general (or about dogs) it pushed the intellectual claims of animals higher than before.

Another form of the objection based on inherence theory might be stated as follows : " So far as the idea of an equation in a word is definite, it only provides an intellectual doctrine when there is a notion of inherence to support the false identity. Now here the inherence obviously takes the same direction in both words, because both start from the reception of sensations and imply that certain mental qualities are inherent in that." I have in effect admitted this by arguing that the words used different types of " pregnancy " both starting from the idea of sensation. Taking the emotion-judgement opposition for granted, the equations are now " good judgement is inherent in a normal use of the senses " and " delicacy of feeling is inherent in a high power of using the senses ". I agree that these notions would arise naturally from the words, and for that matter the sentences are fairly true. But there is surely a difference in the readiness with which the words can be felt to assert these things. The second remark can be felt in a fairly casual use of *sensibility*, but you have to brood over *sense* to extract the first remark. This fits my account of the order of the equations. *Sensibility* will give this notion at its first degree, through " a good reception is like a reaction", but *sense* only at its second degree through " a reception is profoundly like a reaction ", which I chose to rephrase as " a normal reaction is the typical specimen of the whole reaction-reception complex ".

But such a reply would not satisfy a man who took the inherence theory with enough seriousness. If we say that all important covert assertions are based on inherence doctrines, and if this process is always felt to be different from the pretence identities used in ordinary metaphors, then both sets of equations go the wrong way. For *sensibility* ought to have an inherence doctrine in its first version, which I treat as only based on " likeness ", and ought only to intensify this when taken more seriously, whereas I think it does something quite different ; and *sense* ought not to be able to extract an inherence doctrine from an ordinary metaphor. I should claim then that, if my account is right, it gives something like an *experimentum crucis* to decide between two theories. It is not found to be true, I maintain, that a covert assertion has to invoke the feeling of inherence before it can carry a general doctrine felt to be important. The importance of the doctrine is a matter for the opinion of the speakers, not a matter of how completely they are deluded by the false identity ; they may recognise the trope as a simple metaphor and still think the meaning profound ; and on the other hand they may feel that " something is inherent in something else " on quite trivial occasions. We need not therefore plunge deeply into an inherence theory in order to get a theory of the equations in complex words. But we do need to understand the idea of pregnancy, which I think is best dealt with in the less dignified form of " the right handle to take hold of the bundle ".

It should now be possible to decide about Caroline Thompson's account of the fallacies inherent in *sensibility*. They are made to depend on her recording needle, and one would like evidence, particularly from the French who gave us the word, about how this metaphor came in. The scientists used *sensibility* for their purpose (not a separate word *sensitivity*) till well into the nineteenth century, and the N.E.D. has an obscure poet using her metaphor just after the Restoration ; but in ordinary uses of the word this metaphor or technical analogy seems to have been out of sight. Indeed I expect one could find evidence of a primitive tribe with a word like *sensibility* and no knowledge of balances. The fallacies she described were of course made, but as a dismal result of war. If you say " people have either sense or sensibility, and the only good ones are those who have sensibility ", then you will try to prove you have sensibility by proving you have no sense. Or if you back sense you will become the ' reserved ' frustrated sentimentalist, games-cult lout, permanently alarmed money snob, or heaven knows what else among the more dismal figures of our island story. But I do not think one need treat the fallacies as part of the semantic structure of the opposition, because while you are willing to accept both words you can escape either fallacy.

Finally, I ought to make clear that I do not offer these two pairs of equations in the words as the only ones that can appear in them, or have appeared in the past. The bits quoted from the N.E.D. about the actual history of *sense* will indeed have made my contribution to the topic look rather paltry ; I shall try to fill it out with two large-scale examples from Shakespeare and Wordsworth, both of which use a different structure in the word. What I was aiming at here was something more elementary, though in looking for it I had to wander over the field. An ordinary hearer or reader, when the words crop up as an opposed pair, is expected to see directly how they are being used ; and what he does cannot be very elaborate. It is because the historical background is so rich and still so much alive, I maintain, that one can fairly do what seems absurdly unhistorical, make a set of equations from first principles. When you have so unmanageable a history behind a stock opposition the words get worked down till they are a kind of bare stage for any future performance. It is no longer the first question about the words to ask when and how, in history, the various elements were introduced which the full form makes possible. What the user needs, and feels that he has, is an agreed foundation on which to build his own version ; a simple basic difference between the words from which the whole opposition can be extracted. One is forced to ask what it can be ; I suggest that it is a difference in the order in which the similar elements in the words are equated, and that any subsequent difference is put in by developing the type of equation as required.

Chapter 13

SENSE IN MEASURE FOR MEASURE

THERE are only about ten uses of the word in the play, but I think almost all of them carry forward a puzzle which is essential to its thought. It is not denied that the word then covered (1) " sensuality " and (2) " sensibility ", and I maintain that it also covered (3) " sensibleness ", though in a less direct way, through the ideas of " a truth-giving feeling " and " a reasonable meaning ". Clearly the equations between these three could carry very relevant ironies, though the effect is not so much a covert assertion as something best translated into questions. Are Puritans hard ? (Is not-one not-two ?) Are they liable to have crazy outbreaks ? (Is not-one not-three ?) Is mere justice enough ? (Is three two ?) To be sure, these questions look very unlike the flat false identity of one idea with another, but I think the state of the word then made them easier to impose. It seems to have been neither analysed nor taken as simple ; it points directly into the situation where it is used, implying a background of ideas which can be applied to the situation, but somehow as if the word itself did not name them ; it is a shorthand term, rather than a solid word in which two of the meanings can be equated. And yet, as the play works itself out, there is a sort of examination of the word as a whole, of all that it covers in the cases where it can be used rightly ; or rather an examination of sanity itself, which is seen crumbling and dissolving in the soliloquies of Angelo.

No doubt, in any case, the play is not fully satisfactory, and it has been argued that the suggestions of extra meaning are merely the result of Shakespeare doing the best he can with a bad plot. Mr. R. W. Chambers, in *Man's Unconquerable Mind*, seemed to feel that the Bard had been unfairly insulted by modernistic persons, and urged truly enough that he made the plot less disagreeable than he found it. But no one, I take it, maintains that Shakespeare set out to write an attack on virginity (or for that matter on James I, if he is the Duke). The rebuttal does not come close enough to the idea in question ; nor, I think, does Mr. Dover Wilson's gallant and romantic defence of Prince Hal, or Dr. Tillyard's patient and illuminating collection of evidence that the scheme of the Shakespeare History plays was drawn from a pompous contemporary myth made up to flatter the Tudors (a thing which he seems to admire more than it deserves). Nobody has denied that the Histories build up the Tudors, or that Prince Hal was meant to be

270

a popular success. What has occasionally crossed the minds of critics, for quite a long time now, is to wonder what Shakespeare thought about it, and whether he cannot sometimes be found grumbling to himself about the plots that he was using, in a way that the audience was not expected to notice. No doubt this puts the contrast rather too strongly. I think a certain double attitude to Prince Hal is meant to be made public ; indeed the idea that he could not be both a reliable friend and a popular hero is a very straightforward " moral ", even if not a prominent one. But in any case the question how many of the audience noticed the two levels of meaning does not seem to me crucial. As the evidence about the Elizabethan mind piles up, we are tacitly asked to believe that Shakespeare could not possibly have disagreed with it, or have dared to show that he disagreed. I think he was a more self-indulgent kind of man than that, as well as not such a stupid one. Of course the plot had to be something that would go down, but when he came to write the thing (pretty fast) the characters had to say what he could imagine for them. *Measure for Measure* is I think one of the most striking cases where the feelings in his words jib at a wholehearted acceptance of the story, without being planned as a secret meaning for the wiser few or even marking a clear-cut opinion in the author. Perhaps I am making too much fuss about adopting this common-place point of view, but the idea seems to have been much blown upon lately by historical-minded critics, and yet I cannot see that they have brought any evidence against it.

However, the recent drift of various British critics towards royalism is mild compared to that of various American ones towards behaviourism, which happens to go in the same direction. At least I imagine that that cult, so powerful in linguistics, is the ultimate reason why so many American critics of Shakespeare claim that their work is " objective ". If we give *objective* its full claims, to " wonder what Shakespeare thought about it " becomes a disgraceful self-indulgence ; a critic should limit himself to rigid proofs, like the scientist that he is. That is, in effect, he should talk about the author as one of a type, not as an individual acquaintance ; to a certain extent this really gets done, and it seems clear to me that the method produces superficial criticism. No doubt the timidity of the thing saves a critic from the more flamboyant errors of the last century ; and you may reasonably say that we cannot make Shakespeare into a personal acquaintance. But it is enough to refute the behaviourist, on this issue, if he admits that we can make *anybody* into a personal acquaintance ; that we can ever get any " insight " into another person's feelings. One of the things a critic has normally claimed to do is to show this sort of insight about authors ; there is nothing that I can see in the theory of behaviourism, only in its " atmosphere ", to get this forbidden ; and if a critic insists that he has no such insight, it seems to me, he is only saying in an unnecessarily pompous manner (and sometimes quite falsely) that he is unfit to do his work.

I shall assume then, in the old-fashioned way, that the first thing to consider about *Measure for Measure* is why Shakespeare was interested in the story ; because this interest is what will cause any drag there may be against the obvious theatrical values of the characters. We are to imagine him coming across it in the Italian, perhaps translated offhand, of Cinthio's collection of 1565, which he was already using for the plot of *Othello*, and then looking up Whetstone's dramatisation of it (1578) for some extra tips. It was a clumsy plot, needing a good deal of tinkering, but it would carry a part of what was on his mind. This was very complex. There was a strand of loathing for sexuality in any form, partly no doubt as an intellectual agreement with the Puritans, but one that he recognises as a diseased frame of mind ; and contrasting with this a loathing for the cruelty which this line of feeling produced in Puritans, above all for the claim that to indulge the cruelty satisfies justice. The contrast was one with many ramifications, and my own guess is that he saw the wicked deputy as one of the Cold People of Sonnet 94, the lilies that fester and smell worse than weeds ; he christened him Angel ; after that he found the plot interesting. He was not in the mood to write comedies, and the old real situation of the Sonnets, however irrelevant, was a source of energy. The first speech describing Angelo is a series of reminiscences from the Sonnets, and after that he develops on his own. I think that a use of *sense* in Sonnet 35 helps to show why the word became a crux of the play.

> *No more be griev'd at that which thou hast done,*
> *Roses have thorns, and silver fountains mud,*
> *Clouds and eclipses stain both Moon and Sun,*
> *And loathsome canker lives in sweetest bud.*
> *All men make faults, and I even in this,*
> *Authorising thy trespass with compare,*
> *Myself corrupting salving thy amiss,*
> *Excusing their sins more than their sins are :*
> *For to thy sensual fault I bring in sense,*
> *Thy adverse party is thy Advocate,*
> *And gainst myself a lawful plea commence,*
> *Such civil war is in my love and hate,*
> > *That I an accessary needs must be,*
> > *To that sweet thief which sourly robs from me.*

" I bring in reason, arguments to justify it " or " I bring in feelings about it, feel it more important than it really was (and therefore excuse it more than it needs) " or " I bring extra sensuality to it ; I enjoy thinking about it and making arguments to defend it, so that my sensuality sympathises with yours". Sensuality is the predicate, I think. In any case the subtle confusion of the word is used for a mood of fretted and exhausting casuistry ; the corruption of the best makes it the worst ; charity is good, but has strange and shameful roots ; the idea of a lawsuit about such matters is itself shameful, and indeed more corrupt than the natural evil. If he associated the word with this passage it would carry most of the atmosphere of *Measure for Measure*.

The first use of the word in the play is by the gay Lucio, when he goes to Isabella at her nunnery to tell her about the pregnancy and ask her to beg for her brother's life. (To avoid obscurity I shall summarise the plot here and there in brackets. Angelo, left in command of the dukedom, has revived an old law imposing death for sex outside marriage, and this falls on Claudio though he is already betrothed and prepared to marry.) It is hard to get clear about Elizabethan politeness, but I take it Lucio is a bit muddled though still casual. He wants to respect her highminded-ness, but he has to treat the scandal as trivial to induce her to help, so he falls into a verbose style which the bitter woman thinks is mocking her virtue.

> *A man whose blood*
> *Is very snow-broth : one who never feels*
> *The wanton stings and motions of the sense ;*
> *But doth rebate, and blunt his natural edge*
> *With profits of the mind ; Study, and fast . . .*
> *. . . hath pick'd out an act,*
> *Under whose heavy sense your brother's life*
> *Falls into forfeit : he arrests him on it . . .*   (i.4.57)

" Profits of the mind " with its Puritan commercialism makes an effort to get the nun's point of view, but " blunt your natural edge " is a phrase he would more naturally use (say) of making yourself stupid by heavy drinking. He clearly feels, though he cannot say outright, that Angelo's habits have cost him his " common sense ". However we must guard against taking this as part of his intended meaning for *sense*; the meaning " sensuality " is very unequivocal. Indeed one might say that this clear-cut use of the word is put first in the play to thrust the meaning " sensuality " on our attention and make us treat it as the dominant one. Yet the word acts as a sort of euphemism, and this suggestion is supported by the jaunti-ness of Lucio's whole tone. The form implies that sensuality is only one of the normal functions of the senses, and the rest of the speech implies that to neglect them is to become *blunted, heavy* (cruel) and so forth. Lucio does not want to annoy Isabella by saying this plainly, even by the relative plainness of a covert assertion ; but it can hang about in his mind, and there is evidence that it does so when *sense* crops up again as the " meaning " or " intention " of the heavy Act. This sort of thing needs to be distinguished from asserting an equation, and indeed is prior to it. If you say that I am ascribing magical powers to Shakespeare in making him put all this into the speech of Lucio, the answer is that the word was hanging about in Shakespeare's mind in the same way.

The next use is an aside of Angelo when first fascinated by Isabella (he will bargain to give her her brother's life in exchange for her body).

> *She speaks and 'tis*
> *Such sense, that my sense breeds with it.   Fare you well.*   (ii.2.143)

Pope emended *breeds* to " bleeds ", making him express pity only, which is quite off the point. It shows I think how obscure the Shakespearean structure of meaning in the word had become to the Augustans ; because the meaning " sensuality " is obviously wanted here, if you can feel that it is linguistically possible. Angelo's first use of the word is " wise or reasonable meaning ", and then the meaning " sensuality ", which Lucio has made dominant for this stage of the play, pokes itself forward and is gratified by the second use of the word as a pun. Even in the second use I am not sure that " sensuality " can be called the chief meaning of the word ; the suggestion of *breeds* is rather that both the " meanings in his mind " and his " sense-data " have sensuality growing inside them—added to them, so to speak, as an Implication. So I think one could class both uses as equations of Type I, with sensuality acting as a dominant ; however it is quite enough to feel that the word is given two simple meanings one after another. Presumably the capital letter when the word is repeated merely means that the actor should emphasize it to bring out the pun.

In real life it seems rather unlikely that this pun would occur to Angelo. It occurred to Shakespeare, and was wanted ; to Lucio it could occur spontaneously, with a cheerful feeling that sensuality goes with sensibleness ; but to Angelo the combination of meanings in the word can only appear as a hideous accident. The only touching side of Angelo is that he is genuinely astonished by his desires. (It is taken for granted that he could not make love to her in the ordinary way, though there is nothing to prevent him.) Yet the real irony, apart from the verbal accident, is that her coldness, even her rationality, is what has excited him ; the two things are patently connected as in the word, though not in his system of ideas. Possibly with his usual injustice he feels that what she has just said (" if *you* remember a natural guiltiness ") is already a loose way of talking. It is curious in any case to remember the decision of the N.E.D. that the meaning " good judgement " for *sense* does not appear till the later half of the century ; this passage is not using it alone, but gets all the effect of it.

In the next use, after the interview is over, Angelo is not thinking of the word as a pun, and indeed the possible connections have become so elaborate that the meanings are hard to tie down.

> What's this ? What's this ? is this her fault or mine ?
> The Tempter or the Tempted, who sins most ?
> Not she : nor doth she tempt : but it is I
> That, lying by the violet in the Sun,
> Do as the Carrion does, not as the flower,
> Corrupt with virtuous season. Can it be,
> That Modesty may more betray our sense
> Than woman's lightness ? . . .

(ii.2.163)

The Arden edition's note says, very properly, that *sense* here means " sensuality, desire " ; that of course is the most prominent idea in Angelo's mind. But the recent punning may easily be recalled, and the immediately preceding metaphor is not obvious. In any case, why is our sensuality betrayed by being excited and released ? We may be betrayed, but why it ? To be sure, the modest woman may make the sensuality show itself, betray its presence ; but if you adopt this rather strained meaning for the phrase the word need not mean " sensuality " uniquely. What is betrayed is perhaps our general tendency, our " gist or drift ". Or again she may trick our sensuality into wrong actions, but this implies that our sensuality is normally present and usually good ; it is nearer to Lucio's attitude than to Angelo's. Nor does this attitude feel the meanings of the word to be sharply opposed. Indeed I am begging a question when I translate one of the meanings as " sensuality ", because that tends to imply that the sexual desire in question is of an evil kind, whereas *sense* in itself does not have to add this Emotion. In the play it seems to be added insistently, not only by Angelo but by the presence of Isabella at the first use of the word ; but perhaps Angelo is trying to exorcise this Emotion by the picture of the violet. There is a parallel confusion to that of *sense*, I think, in *season* ; indeed part of the strength of a ready-made puzzle like that of *sense* is that it can impose itself as pattern on neighbouring words. The Arden note gives " benign influence of summer " for *virtuous season*—the warmth rots the carrion but makes the flower sweet. This idea is certainly present and gives a tidy metaphor. But it would make Isabella the sun, whereas she is clearly the modest violet, which he is lying by. If the sun is the natural strength which causes sexual desire, that itself can be good, the metaphor will imply. But if the violet is giving the *season*, the idea seems to be the smell of it, like " *seasoning* " in food, pepper for instance. Unlike the public and clear sunlight, this brings in ideas of privacy and of exciting the senses. He is no longer sure what the natural process can be, to which he contrasts himself, and has gone far towards accepting the confusion of meanings as a single and " profound " one, as in Type IV. I hope I have also shown that " sensuality " can still be regarded as a dominant, appearing only in the predicate as for Type I ; and of course the passage is fully intelligible if you take " sensuality " as the only meaning of the word. In general I have not worried about the possible use of a deliberate ambiguity of equation structure, but when a character is actually puzzling about a word it is not surprising that the author should leave one open.

The next use of the word is in his second interview with Isabella.

> ANG. :   *Nay, but hear me,*
> *Your sense pursues not mine ; either you are ignorant,*
> *Or seem so craftily ; and that's not good.*   (ii.4.73)

The pathetic or disgusting assumption of superior morality, in this rebuke to her for not understanding the bargain, finds an echo in the stock pun. Her meaning does not follow his, and also her desires do not start running when his do—that's not good ; a girl ought to be docile. The Folio punctuation implies that ignorance would be bad as well as craft. " Now I give my sensual race the rein " he says soon after (ii.4.160) ; he is the only person in the play to use the adjective, and it is felt to go with a split in the meanings of *sense*, which should be harmoniously combined. In " your sense pursues not mine " the immediate context very definitely imposes " interpretation " (" the sense you put on my words ") as the chief meaning, indeed to suppose it means " sensuality " is a satire on Angelo ; but by this time it is so strong a dominant meaning that it arises easily.

There is a long pause before the next use of the word ; Angelo has now settled down into crime, and can combine the meanings harmoniously enough in a way of his own.

> *He should have lived*
> *Save that his riotous youth with dangerous sense*
> *Might in the times to come have ta'en revenge*
> *By so receiving a dishonour'd life*
> *With ransome of such shame.*   (iv.4.8)

It is still with superior morality that he looks back on the most repulsive of his supposed actions. (Claudio begged Isabella to pay the price of his life, and she wished him dead for it. The Duke arranged that Angelo had Mariana instead, but no man in an Elizabethan play can tell one woman from another in the dark, and Angelo believes that he has killed Claudio after taking the price for saving him.) The *danger* of keeping the bargain and letting Claudio live would be that he would feel too deeply about it ; *sense* covers " sensibility " here. But the reason why he is sure to have a keen sense of honour is that he is *riotous*, he is " sensual ", for that either shows that you have strong feelings or develops them. In either case Angelo despises him for it ; he is himself one of the cold people. The idea " meaning, purpose " is still possible in the word, but it is unimportant beside this startling irony.

There is no need to make these interpretations rigid, especially in so fluid a word. The simple view of the uses by Angelo is that he always means "sensuality" when in soliloquy and always pretends to mean something else when talking to other people. But this corresponds to the view of him as a hypocrite and villain all through ; if you take the character as capable of struggle and development you need to suppose that his language carries the marks of it. At first he felt it as abnormal that the dominant meaning should emerge at all. In this example one does not need to invoke the idea of a " dominant meaning ", because Angelo is explicit enough to make the immediate context impose both the meanings required ; *riotous* gives " sensuality " and *dangerous* (to Angelo) gives " sensibility ". *Riotous* is said first ; to be sure, it is further away than *dangerous*, but it would be rather absurd to call this a less immediate context. I think " sensuality " is the idea that comes first in his mind, and acts as chief meaning of the word ; if you had to choose only one meaning, what the logic of the passage requires is " sensibility ", but it is regarded as a consequence. This is the order of the terms in the equation ; the idea is " sensuality entails sensibility ". He seems indeed to have moved the idea " sensuality " from being an intrusive dominant to being what he considers the head meaning of the word. He has no more to say with it, and does not use it again ; the main force of its irony now turns against Isabella, and " sensuality ", till now so prominent, becomes only a solemn paradox making a darkness in the background.

> DUKE :   *Away with her ; poor soul*
> *She speaks this in th'infirmity of sense.*   (v.1.47)

(Isabella is appealing against Angelo to the Duke at the gates of the city.) The use is simple enough, but the Duke is teasing

Angelo, and a double meaning would be in order. He could hint at such ideas as " in the disorder of strong feeling—she has much to make her excited " or " in the weakness of mere reason and truth, which are inherently feeble beside the public monsters of hypocrisy and law ". I think it is possible that the voice of Shakespeare behind him is preparing an irony of another kind. The Duke is still toying with the word a few lines later :

> *By mine honesty,*
> *If she be mad, as I believe no other,*
> *Her madness hath the oddest frame of sense,*
> *Such a dependency of thing on thing,*
> *As ere I heard in madness.* (v.1.59)

If she has reason it is of a queer kind, not common sense but the obscure wisdom that Shakespeare expected in clowns and the half-mad. It is true that she would put an odd construction on *sense* (give it an odd *frame*) ; she is too other-worldly to use it in the common way. There is no pressure behind the passage, but I think it adds to the cumulative effect. Then Mariana has a use, important because free from irony ; and her rhetoric (it is like that of Troilus) gives the word a fine chance to spread the peacock tail of its meanings. She has the shame of begging in public to be married to Angelo, who deserted her because she lost her money.

> *Noble Prince,*
> *As there comes light from heaven, and words from breath,*
> *As there is sense in truth, and truth in virtue,*
> *I am affianced this man's wife, as strongly*
> *As words could make up vows : And my good Lord,*
> *But Tuesday night last gone, in's garden house,*
> *He knew me as a wife.* (v.1.223)

There is meaning in a true statement ; there is purpose in making one ; it is wise to tell the truth frankly. But the series goes from *sense* to *virtue*, and this tends to call out another part of the word's range. The kind of truth that is in virtue seems rather to be constancy or correspondence to natural law. Desire or passion, sensuality or sensibility, may make her constant ; and she can decently assert them both in public ; to be constant is to have the common sense of our normal feelings. The meanings are not merely compatible but undivided here ; this is what the whole word is meant to do.

The next and final use raises a question about what Shakespeare himself thought of the play. Isabella still believes that Angelo has murdered her brother, and Mariana begs her for his life.

> MARI. : *Sweet Isabell, take my part :*
> *Lend me your knees, and all my life to come,*
> *I'll lend you all my life to do you service.*

SENSE IN MEASURE FOR MEASURE

DUKE : *Against all sense you do importune her :*
Should she kneel down, in mercy of this fact,
Her Brother's ghost, his paved bed would break,
And take her hence in horror. (v.1.433)

In the Duke's earlier plotting with Isabella, the chief impulse he appeals to in her is the desire to be revenged on Angelo, not to save her brother ; indeed in her first revulsion when he begs for his life she says " 'tis best that thou diest quickly ". Almost at the end of the play, the Duke tells her that he could have saved her brother but acted with " slower foot ", apparently because he wanted some more fun with his plot ; but after all Claudio is better dead : " That life is better life, past fearing death, Than one that lives to fear. Make it your comfort, So happy is your brother." " I do, my lord ", is the brisk and hearty answer. Here, by the way, we find Bradley's principle, that the characters are better dead, in full command of the stage ; Angelo in his turn " craves death more willingly than mercy ". But Isabella does not apply it to Angelo. We are given a further test of the quality of her feeling, in the appeal of Mariana for his life. She does react with the mercy enjoined by her religion, and this is certainly meant to be to her credit, but she attains this height by an impulse of personal vanity so repulsive as to surprise even Dr. Johnson.

I partly think,
A due sincerity govern'd his deeds
Till he did look on me. (v.1.448)

She knows the history of Mariana, who is appealing for Angelo's life beside her ; in fact the Duke has told her that when Mariana lost most of her marriage portion Angelo " swallowed his vows whole, pretending in her discoveries of dishonour ". Afterwards, when Isabella's brother is presented to her still alive, she does not speak to him at all ; no doubt the plot gave no room for a long speech, but the Bard is not as tongue-tied as all that if he can think of anything for a character to say. The apologists have objected that flippant modern critics merely do not understand the old reverence for virginity if they dwell on such points. But it is impossible to suppose all these details are accidental ; they are not even clumsy ; they are pointed. It seems to me the only working theory to suppose that Shakespeare could not quite stomach the old reverence either.

And on this view the final use of *sense* can carry a good deal of meaning, though if you suppose the Duke meant all of it he is not likely to have married her afterwards. " Against all reason "— " all normal decent feeling "—" all depth or delicacy of feeling " ; whatever kind of *sense* is meant here, she lacks it. For a moment, in the elaborate and teasing balance of the play, Shakespeare turns even against mercy, or at least against the abstract rule of mercy from which she acts. She is too otherworldly to feel the thing like a sane person ; she is not sensual enough, the word might argue, to have tolerable human feelings.

This is certainly not what the Duke thinks ; here as always, however savagely he tests her, he finds her ideally right. If he means any irony in the word, apart from the general triumph in knowing better than his audience which he is enjoying in all these uses of *sense*, it is that she is altogether above " sense ", above the whole view of life which even a good use of the suggestions of the word would imply. Miss M. C. Bradbrook, in an essay on the play (*Review of English Studies* XVII.385), has maintained that the Duke did not expect Isabel to forgive Angelo, but accepts her superior wisdom when " her justice recognises the one grain of good in him ". I am not sure how much a verbal analysis can prove, and I would think this view wrong without one, but surely those who support it must find it less plausible when they notice that this use of the word is the last of a series of uses by the Duke in this scene, and that the previous ones (whatever else they mean) have all carried secret boasts of superior knowledge. It does not seem to me that there was any subtle unconsciousness about the matter ; I think Shakespeare felt he was " polishing off " the series of puns on *sense* by this very dramatic final use of it. But if he meant to kick away his key word at the end, it seems to me, he could not manage to do it. This is not to say that he took the same cheery view of the affair as Lucio ; the play repeatedly tells us that Lucio took venereal disease for granted, and I think this practical argument gave the basic emotional drive in favour of purity. Claudio ends the old story with a brave and generous action, giving himself up in the expectation of death to save the life of Angelo, now married to his sister ; Shakespeare would not allow him so much dignity, and altered the plot. This seems good evidence that he found the behaviour of Claudio disgusting. But he could not convince himself, it seems to me, even that the Duke was agreeable, let alone that Isabella was. The pomposity of the man he probably found natural, but the touchiness, the confidence in error, the self-indulgence of his incessant lying, must I think always have been absurd.

Various critics during this century have tried to show that Shakespeare in his heart disliked his pompous old men, Prospero for example, and merely assumed that the audience would put up with them sufficiently to make the mechanics of the play tolerable. On the other hand Mr. Wilson Knight, who is highminded and warmhearted in a rather Victorian manner, tends to make these old men into practically undiluted symbols of heavenly virtue. The Duke raises this problem particularly sharply, and I should not agree that the problem is for some logical reason inherently unreal (" if we dig into the picture we only go through the canvas ") ; surely any producer has to make up his mind about it. Mr. Wilson Knight considers that :

> " The Duke's ethic is born of his knowledge of good and evil potential in himself. And his remembrance of his own evil, which is crucial to his ethic, is kept alive by Lucio's chattering of his supposed vices at his side. Lucio causes the Duke to distrust the ideal of purity in Isabella by continually suggesting that such an ideal is a form of insincerity. Iago causes Othello to distrust his ideal of purity by suggesting its impurity ; the two triangles may thus be shown to bear a close resemblance to each other."

I think this parallel is a searching one, but I do not see that the text gives us any encouragement (apart from one very obscure piece of doggerel closing the third act, in which the unreal style lets the Duke act as a sort of chorus) for ascribing to the Duke an idea about ethics which is simply the playwright's. Mr. Wilson Knight seems to regard as important evidence the Duke's remarks about not liking to stage himself before the people's eyes (the idea comes in twice, but he stages himself very elaborately at the end of the play). The same feelings had been expressed by James I, to the annoyance of the public, and the audience might well notice the resemblance ; this is an argument against supposing that the Duke was frankly ridiculed in performance, because it might be dangerous, but Shakespeare could not assume that everybody would interpret the foibles of James as a proof of a high and selfless view of ethics. In any case, the higher you pitch the ethics of the Duke, the more surprising you must find his behaviour.

It seems hard not to regard him as a comic character. Indeed the play gives us a sufficiently memorable phrase to sum him up ; he is " the old fantastical Duke of Dark Corners ". In the fourth scene the Friar points out that, if the Duke defends the revival of the old law by Angelo, he should have revived it himself ; that would have been more impressive. The Duke replies :

> *I do fear, too dreadful :*
> *Sith 'twas my fault to give the people scope*
> *'Twould be my tyranny to strike and gall them*
> *For what I bid them do . . . Therefore indeed, my father,*
> *I have on Angelo imposed the office*
> *Who may, in the ambush of my name, strike home*
> *And yet my nature never in the sight*
> *To do it slander.*

To be sure, he seems to be lying as usual ; we heard him specifically tell Angelo " Your scope is as mine own, So to enforce or qualify the laws As to your soul seems good " ; and he goes on to tell the Friar that he is testing Angelo. But surely on the stage this excuse is too prominent to be forgotten, and the combination of vanity and cowardice cannot be intended for praise. It does have a note of puritanical self-examination, as Mr. Knight would claim, but I would not call that enough to give it a high spiritual ethic. No doubt it could be carried off by grandeur of manner ; but when the Duke buzzes from Claudio to Isabella, all agog, and busily telling lies to both, I do not see how the author can be banking on the simple-minded respect of the audience for great persons. The subtlety of his justice has been praised, and indeed there is a curious passage where he claims that all his prisoners are either executed or released. But he is asking why Barnadine had been kept in jail seven years ; the excuse of the provost is that " his friends still wrought reprieves for him " while there was no proof adequate to kill him on. What the Duke urges Mariana to do (" He is your husband on a pre-contract ; To bring you thus together is no sin ") can only be distinguished, if at all, by a technicality from what Claudio is to be killed for doing (" she is fast my wife Save that we do the denunciation lack Of outward order ; this we came not to, Only for propagation of a dower ") ; and the Duke apparently approves of the law which would kill Claudio, at least he tells the Friar that he does, at considerable length. Incidentally this law would also have killed Shakespeare, whose first child was born soon after marriage ; his distaste for lust at the time of writing did not (I take it) carry him so far as to make him agree with the Duke here.

But perhaps all this is picking holes. What makes the Duke ridiculous on the stage is the fuss he makes about the backbiting of Lucio, that is, precisely what makes Mr. Knight think him so high and pure. The Duke of course is in disguise when Lucio tells him these things, and he answers by boasting about himself, in a phrase which seems an obvious dramatic irony, " let him but be testimonied in his own bringing forth, and he shall appear to the envious a scholar, a statesman and a soldier ". He anxiously questions Escalus in the hope of hearing something better, and continues to drag the subject up when we are thinking about the plot. The soliloquy " Oh place and greatness " (iv.1.60), while Isabella is trying to induce Mariana to play her part, is so much out of key that at first we think he is talking about Angelo. In the final scene, the mutual petty accusations of Lucio and the Duke, working up to " yet here's one in place I cannot pardon ", are good farce and nothing else. No doubt there was a casualness and good-humour about the Elizabethan stage, so that the great man could be laughed at for a bit and resume greatness when required ; but this is only to say that there was room for Shakespeare to put in mixed feelings of his own.

But it is true, I think, that there is an agreeable side of the Duke ; it becomes dramatically prominent on the occasions when he is proved absurdly wrong. He is certain (iv.111) that Angelo will be sending a pardon for Claudio to the prison (thinking he has enjoyed Isabella) ; and he keeps boasting to the provost of his superior knowledge. When the letter is opened it orders an earlier execution under cover of night. The Duke immediately starts plotting again, apparently unperturbed, but the fact that he could not imagine the depth of evil that he is playing with does, I think, operate on us as somehow to his credit. From then on his tricks seem less offensive ; the claim to divine foreknowledge has been broken. Also by this time it has become clear that nothing less than the fantastic behaviour of the Duke could have kept the play from being a tragedy. The whole force of the case against Angelo is that, in the ordinary way, he would have been completely safe ; he is a symbol of justice itself, as Escalus points out (iii.11,end); he can only be imagined as vulnerable if he is handled by very strange means. In the same way the Duke's final test of Isabella, that she must forgive Angelo still believing he killed her brother treacherously, is a result of his general expectation of mercy ; the fact that she agrees to it for bad reasons is not one that he is likely to realise. One might even find it pathetic that the intended nun should say " I partly think A due sincerity governed his deeds Till he did look on me ". Her new sensual vanity seems meant to imply a partial awakening of her senses after the battering she has gone through ; and her decision to marry the Duke is perhaps not so grossly out of character as critics have supposed.

What is really offensive about the Duke is the other side of this quality which can be found agreeable ; it is offensive, I mean, that he should treat his subjects as puppets for the fun of making them twitch. But here, I suppose, the Character is saved by the Plot. It seems a peculiarly brutal flippancy that he should not only trick Isabella about Claudio unnecessarily but take pains to thrust the imagined death of Claudio upon her mind. His moral claims about it—

> *But I will keep her ignorant of her good*
> *To make her heavenly comforts of despair*

—do not seem to me tolerable even on Bradley's principle ; he is playing at being God. But there is a question here of the mechanics of working on an audience ; we forgive him for it because Isabella turns out not to care a rap about Claudio, and we wanted to know whether she would. The reasons why it seems all right, if you followed them up, would lead to quite a different view of the story.

And yet I think the play is a whole in spite of this chasm in one's view of the two good characters ; even if Shakespeare was only grumbling to himself about them, an audience could share his feelings without ruining the performance. The Duke's flippancy about justice corresponds to a deeper and more desperate feeling in the author, elaborated throughout the action and insisted upon in the title, that the whole business of public justice is fatuous and hideous, whether compared to the mercy of Christ or the humanity of private life. There is an echo of the same idea when Pompey shifts over comfortably from a bawd to a hangman. Mr. Wilson Knight was quite right to feel that there is a subtle ethic in the play somewhere, and that it is mixed up with Christianity. But I think there is a balancing idea to this, one that accounts for the unpleasantness of the two good characters. It is perhaps simply the idea that one must not act on these absolutes prematurely. Even granting that the conditions of life are inherently repulsive, a man makes himself actually more repulsive by acting on this truth ; you cannot get outside the world and above justice, and a ruler who sets out to do this (except under very peculiar circumstances, by luck) is merely bad at his job. And the same ambivalence clings to the divine Isabella. In a way, indeed, I think this is a complete and successful work of the master, but the way is a very odd one, because it amounts to pretending to write a romantic comedy and in fact keeping the audience's teeth slightly but increasingly on edge. And on this view, I should claim, the performance with the word *sense* is made to echo the thought of the play very fully up to the end.

In all this I have taken the text for granted, but the case for revision made out by the New Cambridge editors is I think stronger here than for any other play, and I need to consider whether that alters the case. The theory is that the play was cut down for a court performance before James I on Dec. 24th, 1604, when the two passages flattering his distaste for crowds, and a passage referring to a court masque, were added ; that the original text was lost ; that the court play was collected from the actor's parts and padded by another hand to the public stage length soon after Nov., 1606. The padding was done by adding jokes for Lucio, also sententious rhymed couplets, and by turning some of Shakespeare's verse into longwinded prose. I doubt whether this makes much difference. All the references to *sense* are unaffected. Certainly the changes tend to make the Duke more ridiculous ; the farce of his relations with Lucio is now largely due to the reviser, and the irrelevant self-regard of the " Oh place and greatness " speech (iv.1.59) is explained because the reviser took it out of the speech at iii.2.178, where it is relevant, and used it to hide a join in the text. The phrase by Lucio about " the old fantastical duke of dark corners " is added by the reviser. But if the Duke had originally been the half-divine figure described by Mr. Wilson Knight it seems unlikely that this despised hack would have presumed to alter him so far ; it is one thing to add to the jokes which had been found popular, and quite another to reverse the intention of a playwright who was still a leading member of the company. For that matter, the reviser is supposed to have added the doggerel lines at the end of III.2, spoken by the Duke, which are the strongest evidence for Mr. Wilson Knight's theory of his high and subtle ethic. If we are to believe in this hack, it looks as if he was trying to keep the balance of the original conception, and not so very coarsely either. Indeed I think one might push the argument the other way ; a special version was needed for the court performance in front of James, making the Duke much less funny, and afterwards some new jokes against the Duke could be written in on the lines of the original intention.

The editors also produce a reason for the silence of Isabella when reunited to her brother ; she was originally reconciled to him by his mistress Juliet, and then the part of Juliet was doubled with Mariana, so all this had to be cut. I should have thought that some of Isabella's reply could easily be salvaged, and the play only wants three handsome women (anybody could take Mistress Overdone)—the same as *King Lear*. In any case, it seems hard to guess what she could have said that would greatly alter our impression of her, and the same doubt might perhaps occur to the author. But, even if we accept the whole theory of revision, I do not think it much affects the interpretation of the " key word ".

We should now be able to look back and deal with the attitude of R. W. Chambers, which is by no means his alone. A variety of recent critics (young rather than old) have emphasized the strength of the Christian symbolism in the play, and treated it as a Morality Play about the dialectic of Justice and Mercy, ending in an atonement won through love. On this view the Duke is implicitly compared to God, who goes among his people and judges each case on its individual merits ; he is the king of love wooing the human heart, and the symbolism is worked out in detail. I think this is in the text all right ; and for that matter it would be foolish to suppose that a pro-Christian play on this theme would have to be " reactionary " ; any attempt to apply the anarchic mercy of Christ to the actual processes of government must be a pretty revolutionary affair. But I think the play simply did not work out like that ; Shakespeare undertook to use this traditional theme, and found he did not like his saints when he had got them. It is thus an interesting example, by the way, of how wrong an " analytical " critic can be when he industriously digs out a " symbolism ", even one that is really there.

However, it might be objected that this theory is untenable unless it is taken very far, further than I should want to go. The ostensible Christianity in the play is very strong (the whole speech about " Be absolute for death " is powerfully in the Duke's favour ; Claudio himself does not question the justice of his punishment for " too much liberty "). Therefore, it may be said, any irony against it in the play must also have been strong, if it were to be effectually present at all. We must, therefore, suppose a situation in the playhouse like Verrall's interpretation of Euripides ; people must have quarrelled on the way out. Now, of course, we are extremely ignorant about Shakespeare's audience, but I do not believe that this happened either ; for one thing, it was just what the censorship system was designed to prevent. Nor, by the way, do I think that the word " justice " needs a thorough-going treatment here, analysing it into different conceptions of justice which are to conflict in the minds of the audience and form ironical equations in the word. I think that the audience would consider a death penalty for the fault of Claudio quite patently *un*-just, so that no subtlety about different sorts of justice need become prominent. On this question of public opinion, and on Shakespeare's probable opinion, Mr. Hotson's *I, William Shakespeare* gives a useful light ; the very reputable man who became overseer of Shakespeare's will made an arrangement similar to Claudio's for the same reason, and finally regularized his marriage, when the families agreed about the money affairs, just before *Measure for Measure* was probably written. No doubt, within the circle, there would be a touch of sardonic fun about this retrospect, but nobody, it seems obvious, was seriously entertaining the idea that he ought to have been killed for it. Claudio himself accepts guilt, and the sex-horror of the play requires him to ; but he is drawn as a weak character ; the manly thing to say would have been all men are sinners but that not all sins deserve death from the law. The religious politics of the thing are after all very clear ; they are intentionally confused by the presence of nuns and friars, but Geneva was the only place where a law like this was conceivable. The more we make Shakespeare sympathetic to the old religion and the sanctity of virginity, the less likely we make him to have approved the Duke's law. And, on the other side of the *via media*, the audience would not be at all shocked by a suggestion that nunneries make for a narrowness of human feeling. It seems to me, therefore, that the ironies against the good characters would only strike the audience (or rather the kind of spectator who might have made trouble) as a balanced Anglican position, not put forward more obtrusively than the theatre was allowed to do. I don't mean that this is what Shakespeare felt about it ; I am only concerned to show that my interpretation of the play is not wildly far from what a contemporary audience could be expected to recognise or endure.

As to the view that the gallants joking about syphilis are intolerably flat and crude, and therefore must have been put in by a hack reviser, I think the point needs to be made that they were exactly what Shakespeare wanted, whether he bothered to write them himself or not. The jokes are trench humour, not made out of insensitivity to a common mortal danger but to keep up strength, and jokes of this sort usually seem bad to an outsider. Indeed, the whole development of Puritanism can be viewed as a consequence of the introduction of syphilis (usually dated around the beginning of the sixteenth century). The point I think is important for the play because it gives a certain practical basis for the conflict between justice and mercy, which otherwise appears as a mere flat contradiction. One can interpret the Duke as saying " There's too much syphilis in this town ", and trying to find a way to reduce it without getting personally unpopular ; on this view Claudio is obviously innocent because unlikely to spread disease. I must agree that this practical view of the case seems to be very remote from everyone's mind. But then the question whether the Duke proposes to continue enforcing his law is simply dropped ; on any view, the questions that the play raises are not answered. It moves over, as the key-word does, from a consideration of " sensuality " to a consideration of " sanity ", and then the action is forced round to a happy ending.

The idea of such a word as a " compacted doctrine " hardly applies here ; the equations can be made to give a variety of minor doctrines, but it is not clear how well they fit together. Indeed, whether they can be fitted together is treated as a problem, part of the play as a whole, and yet the word itself is used easily and with conviction. It seems to me another case of the incomplete double symbol, like the dog in *Timon of Athens*. And the word which can be treated like this, as one would expect, is in an unstable condition, because it is getting too hard to use. Metaphors about dogs can be complicated without getting in anyone's way, but a word like *sense* needs to be tolerably handy ; and before the century was over it had settled down into a simpler form.

But though the change seems natural it may be more mixed up with politics, and therefore less inevitable, than this account would imply. Indeed, to call the later structure of *sense* the " Restoration " one, already suggests that it was part of the reaction against Puritanism. Even this play which turns on the word, in spite of its apparent fantasy, is full of a brooding sense of what would happen if the Puritans came to power, as they did in the next generation. One might argue, in fact, that these Jacobean uses of the word are already a weapon against the Puritans, which the Civil War only hardened and sharpened. And yet there seems no doubt that this would be going too far. The poor little word was too busy to be so much of a partisan; neither side had a monopoly of it. Indeed, if one can trust the earliest references in the N.E.D., what I am calling the Restoration use of it did not appear till around the death of Charles II; it was eventually produced by the Restoration settlement, but was definitely not produced by the Civil War. I wish I had more decisive evidence, particularly about the Commonwealth uses. But the broad point seems clear; the word was made to echo contro-versial questions that were both subtle and pressing, and Shakespeare had a keen nose for this kind of quality in a word; but it was not made to come down on one side of the fence till considerably after his time.

Chapter 14

SENSE IN THE PRELUDE

ONE does not think of the poetry of Wordsworth, even the parts which expound his philosophy, as depending on a concentrated richness of single words. There are of course " key " words like Nature and Imagination, and these may in reality be very puzzling, but he seems to be making a sturdy effort to expound them in discursive language. The apparently flat little word *sense* has I think a more curious part to play. It comes into practically all the great passages of *Tintern Abbey* and *The Prelude* on the mind's relation to Nature. And so far from being expounded it might seem a kind of expletive that he associates with this line of thought, or a convenience of grammar for expressing it. Yet in fact, of course, whether or not Wordsworth is drawing on Hartley or Coleridge, his whole position depends on some rather undeveloped theory about how the mind interprets what it gets from the senses. Nor does the word drop from him casually ; in the great majority of uses he makes it prominent by putting it at the end of the line, and this tends to hold it slightly apart from the stock phrase it comes in, so that some wider meaning for it can be suggested.

Taking Mr. de Selincourt's edition for the 1805 manuscript, I found 35 uses of *sense* at the end of a line and 12 elsewhere ; the (posthumous) 1850 text has 31 uses at the end of a line and 11 elsewhere. There are changes moving the word in both directions, but both texts put just under three-quarters of the uses of *sense* at the end of a line, and these I think include all the important uses. The figures are minima, because no doubt I missed some. I did not count any of the derivative words, even *senseless*. *Tintern Abbey* only uses the word three times, and makes " feeling " do much of the work ; but the crucial stylistic inventions for Wordsworth's *sense* come in those three.

The most frequent version of it, as one might expect, is the form " a sense of . . . " which the N.E.D. explains as " not by direct perception but more or less vaguely or instinctively ". This was not a hundred years old, perhaps a good deal less. I shall quote a series of examples with *sense* at the end of the line to show how the effect adds up. The most famous example, from *Tintern Abbey*, has not yet got used to the position for *sense* but gets the corresponding *of* at the start of the next line.

> *A sense sublime*
> *Of something far more deeply interfused . . .* (T.A. 95)

> *While here I stand, not only with the sense*
> *Of present pleasure, but with pleasing thoughts*
> *That in this moment there is life and food*
> *For future years.*   (T.A. 62)

For the surface meaning, *sense* is dragged in here very unnecessarily.

> *my brain*
> *Worked with a dim and undetermined sense*
> *Of unknown modes of being.*   (Prelude i.392)

There is a suggestion here from the pause at the end of the line that he had not merely " a feeling of " these unknown modes but something like a new " sense " which was partly able to apprehend them —a new *kind* of sensing had appeared in his mind.

> [the soul]   *retains an obscure sense*
> *Of possible sublimity . . . .*   (ii.317)

> *Place also by the side of this dark sense*
> *Of noble feeling, that those spiritual men*
> *Even the great Newton's own ethereal self,*
> *Seemed humbled in these precincts thence to be*
> *The more endeared.*   (iii.268)

He is trying to do his best for Cambridge and give it *sense* at the end of a line ; but the language is thin, indeed to put his *sense* and *feeling* together always acts as a dilution.   But presumably it means " Wordsworth's sense that *they* had noble feelings ", so that it would again imply a peculiar mode of knowledge.   Most of the later examples of the form are comparatively trivial.

> *And though an aching and a barren sense*
> *Of gay confusion still be uppermost . . .*   (iii.627)

> *How arch his notices, how nice his sense*
> *Of the ridiculous . . . .*   (v.310)

> *This only let me add*
> *From heart-experience, and in humblest sense*
> *Of modesty . . .*   (v.585)

> [from astronomy]   *I drew*
> *A pleasure quiet and profound, a sense*
> *Of permanent and universal sway . . .*   (vi.130)

> *a sense*
> *Of what in the Great City had been done . . .*   (viii.625)

> *When every day brought with it some new sense*
> *Of exquisite regard for common things.*   (xiv.262)

And, to end with something more worth attention,

> *a voice*
> *Labouring, a brain confounded, and a sense,*
> *Death-like, of treacherous desertion, felt*
> *In that last place of refuge, my own soul.*   (x.413)

I only noticed five cases where " a sense of " is used without *sense* being at the end of a line. They come fairly late in the poem and carry none of this weight (e.g. " sense of beauty " viii.74, " of right " ix.388).

The word, of course, can also be used merely for one of the senses :

> *As we grow up, such thraldom of that sense*
> *Seems hard to shun.* (xii.150)

Here it is the sense of sight, or rather the pleasure in scenery, which tends to have too much power. The word is simple enough, but even here he is not merely thinking of reception of sensedata.

Also, examples of *sense* meaning only " good judgement " or " common sense " undoubtedly occur :

> *that were to lack*
> *All sense . . .* (iii.368)
>
> *To tell us what is passion, what is truth,*
> *What reason, what simplicity and sense.* (vi.113)
>
> *Words follow words, sense seems to follow sense.* (vii.507)

In one place we even have a bad kind of *sense* :

> *The tendency, too potent in itself,*
> *Of use and custom to bow down the soul*
> *Under a growing weight of vulgar sense. . .* (xiv.159)

" Oppress it by the laws of vulgar sense " is the 1805 version. The idea I suppose is " what vulgar people call good sense, knowing the price of things, etc." It comes very late in the poem. In any case, all these are in a way negative uses ; in the positive ones he makes " good sense " something larger than the ordinary idea of it. Even

> *real feeling and just sense* (xiii.172)

has a peculiar emphasis. In spite of his disadvantages, he reflects, he might have had a good effect on the French Revolution if he had tried, because any man might

> *That with desires heroic and firm sense* (x.166)

had made a bold stand. In the 1850 version, this has become " strong in hope, and trained to noble aspirations " ; Wordsworth perhaps felt that the reader could not be expected to know how much he had felt *sense* to imply. Even the phrase " common sense " makes an appearance in the 1805 version, but certainly looks bigger than usual. It is about the unfortunate child who has been educated from books :

> *Forth bring him to the light of common sense*
> *And, fresh and shewy as he is, the Corpse*
> *Slips from us into powder.* (1805 v.354)

While cutting this out of the 1850 version, Wordsworth put back

" common sense " a little higher up, in a flat appeal to the reader which feels rather out of the style. In any case, though the idea " common sense " occurs, an adjective will often be added to this version of *sense* to make it carry higher claims :

> *one whom circumstance*
> *Hath called upon to embody his deep sense*
> *In action, give it outwardly a shape,*
> *And that of benediction, to the world.* (ix.401)

Good judgement here becomes practically the Creative Imagination applied to politics.

> *He deemed that my pursuits and labours lay*
> *Apart from all that leads to wealth, or even*
> *A necessary maintenance insures,*
> *Without some hazard to the finer sense.* (xiv.368)

This rather pompous stuff is almost exactly the prosaic use of " sensibility " ; it is viewed as a special degree of " good judgement " but hints vaguely at something more artistic. The passage is the same in the 1805 version.

I think it is important that Wordsworth refuses to say " sensibility " in these poems at all, except once about babies (ii.270) and once about the growing child who still has some of the claims of the baby (ii.360). Babies are entitled to a " tender, delicate, easily hurt " kind of sensibility, what " The Man of Feeling " had been proud of, but not (in Wordsworth's view) adults. Excessive sensibility was, I suppose, connected in his mind with the modish affectations of the people who used Poetic Diction, and he would not have liked his contemporary Marianne Dashwood, but to make a direct attack on the word might have been confusing. Cutting it out had an unexpected but rather helpful consequence ; it put a lot of extra work on *sense* and thereby made the word more fluid.

There are points, indeed, where the language tells us plainly that a new kind of *sense* is in question. To begin with a slighter case, he suggests that poets

> *Have each for his peculiar dower, a sense*
> *By which he is enabled to perceive*
> *Something unseen before* (1805 xiii.304)

and perhaps this will show Wordsworth what used to happen at Stonehenge. The 1850 edition reduces the suggestion of vanity in this fancy by removing *sense* from the end of the line. Again we have :

> *Nor less do I remember to have felt*
> *Distinctly manifested at this time*
> *A dawning, even as of another sense,*
> *A human-heartedness about my love*
> *For objects hitherto the absolute wealth*
> *Of my own private being and no more.* (1805 iv.232)

This seems to throw light on a use of the word twenty lines earlier :

> *Yes, I had something of another eye*
> *And looking round was often moved to smiles*
> *Such as a delicate work of humour breeds.*
> *I read, without design, the opinions, thoughts*
> *Of these plainliving people, in a sense*
> *Of love and knowledge.*   (iv.213)

Such is the 1805 version ; I give the line reference to the 1850 one for convenience. There it is altered to " now observed with clearer knowledge ". Wordsworth, no doubt, felt that this use of *sense* would hardly be intelligible, and indeed it must mean that he read them with a new faculty of sensing. Unfortunately, he chose to get his pet word back into the text somehow, and it comes in the first line of the paragraph, very intelligibly, but with a disagreeable complacence :

> *Yes, I had something of a subtler sense.*

The passage about the Chartreuse, which was entirely rewritten, gives a more striking example of how he came to alter his idea of the word :

> *be the house redeemed*
> *With its unworldly votaries, for the sake*
> *Of conquest over sense, hourly achieved*
> *Through faith and meditative reason.*   (vi.458)

The 1805 version has no example of *sense* meaning sensuality, and this I should think was deliberate. Even for the 1850 one, Wordsworth did not allow it to come at the end of a line. His own " conquest over sense " is something of an unwanted irony here.

More general examples of the same process are given by " The incumbent mystery of sense and soul " (1850 xiv.286) and " By sense conducting to ideal form " (xiv.77), where he is introducing at least the hint of a dichotomy in the course of re-writing ; *sense* appears to be the opposite of soul, and the " mystery " is that they can be connected at all. However, I do not want to make out that the re-writing shows an important change of opinion. In any case, there are signs that his use of the word had changed in the six years between ending Book VI and starting Book VII ; all the impressive examples come before that. What is really in question, I think, is not any theory in Wordsworth's mind about the word but a manipulative feeling, of what he could make it do ; a thing more familiar perhaps to poets than critics, and one which a poet easily forgets ; the period during which Wordsworth could feel how to use this word was, I think, very brief. In general, I agree with a recent defender of the older man (M. E. Burton *One Wordsworth*) who says that he did not try to hide his early political and religious opinions any further when he re-wrote, indeed, he sometimes enlarged upon a vaguely unorthodox idea such as the world-soul ; he was merely " improving the style ". But this improvement, which was mainly a process of packing the lines more fully, meant invoking Milton and his sense of the unrelaxing Will ; whereas the whole point and delicacy of the first version was to represent a wavering and untram- melled natural growth. The improvement was, therefore, about the most destructive thing he could have done, far worse than changing the supposed opinions. Incidentally, I think there was also a good influence of Milton, already strong in the first version, which came from a very different side of that author's feeling about the world ; it is remarkable surely that the first paragraph of *The Prelude*, describing how Wordsworth is now free to wander where he chooses and write as much as he likes, makes two distinct quotations from the throwing out from Paradise of Adam and Eve (" The earth is all before me " (i.14.), " Whither shall I turn ? " (i.26)). Indeed the repeated claims that it was somehow a good thing to have lost his first inspiration are a rather close parallel to Milton's baffling but very strong feelings about Paradise.

I have tried to review the general background of the uses, and must now approach the important ones.

> *in such strength*
> *Of usurpation, when the light of sense*
> *Goes out, but with a flash that has revealed*
> *The invisible world, doth greatness make abode.* (vi.600)

Maybe this tidier version of the great passage is an improvement, but the 1805 one certainly demands attention :

> *in such strength*
> *Of usurpation, in such visitings*
> *Of awful promise, when the light of sense*
> *Goes out in flashes that have shown to us*
> *The invisible world, doth greatness make abode.*

It is not long after the Chartreuse passage, and perhaps Wordsworth in making his changes remembered the ascetic view of *sense* he had put in for the monks. The removal of the sensuous world, in the new version, is the point of vision. But this idea was already present in the old one ; the *invisible world* clearly means to suggest something like it. I am rather reluctant to insist on the ambiguity of the passage, because in general the style does not want any con- centrated piece of trickery ; Wordsworth is trying to state his position, even if he fails. But the trick he has stumbled upon here is as glorious as such a thing could be. *The light . . . goes out* can mean " light proceeds from the source " as well as " the source fails ". By combining the two, Wordsworth induces his baffling *sense* to become a lighthouse occasionally flashing not on any spiritual world but on the dangerous and actual sea, which at other times is invisible merely because the captain is in darkness. I am not certain, to be sure, whether lighthouses already flashed in Wordsworth's time, and the essential image is the last bright flash of the guttering candle ; this in itself allows mere sensation to carry mysterious and rarely seen powers. The ecstasy both destroys normal *sense* and fulfils it, and the world thus shown is both the same as and wholly different from the common one. The verbal ambiguity in the first version only drives home the paradox which he retained in the later one.

The most fundamental statement of this theory of the senses is made about the famous baby at the breast :

> *For him, in one dear Presence, there exists*
> *A virtue which irradiates and exalts*
> *Objects through widest intercourse of sense.*
> *No outcast he, bewildered and depressed . . .*
> *For, feeling has to him imparted power*
> *That through the growing faculties of sense*
> *Doth like an agent of the one great Mind*
> *Create, creator and receiver both,*
> *Working but in alliance with the works*
> *Which it beholds.* (ii.238—60)

The 1805 version brings in *sensations* and *sentiment* but does not have *sense* twice :

> *In one beloved presence, nay and more*
> *In that most apprehensive habitude*
> *And those sensations which have been derived*
> *From this beloved Presence, there exists*

" a virtue " and so on, and

> *For feeling has to him imparted strength*
> *And powerful in all sentiments of grief*
> *Of exultation, fear, and joy, his mind*
> *Even as an agent of the one great mind,*

" creates " and so on. The earlier version is thus rather more pantheist, emphasises emotion more, and is perhaps less dependent on key words ; the notion that feeling " returns as power " had come to seem a settled epigram to Wordsworth when he shortened the second part of this quotation, and in the same way it seemed an adequate theoretical coverage to say " faculties of sense " rather than list the child's emotions, which might suggest that he admired it (as the Chinese sage Laotze did) because it yelled so loudly. In the first part of the quotation the change makes the idea prettier and cruder ; the original point was that the " sensation " of affection, and I suppose of resistance as well, towards the mother are what teach the " senses " of the child to grasp the world, a thing which must be done by an interchange like that between persons. *Sensations* here are not sensedata, and thereby free from the ambiguity of *sense*, but a more highly developed compound of emotion and knowledge even than *sense*, and therefore convenient for forcing us to understand it. Indeed, the 1805 version has no unambiguous term for sensedata, and I suppose would have denied the reality of the concept ; in the 1850 version Wordsworth sometimes inserts " bodily " before *sense* to make a passage clearer (e.g. xiv.88) but the earlier version hardly ever descends to this (once in 1805 xi.272).

Obviously the meaning " good judgement " is given a very back seat when the word is used for such a theory. It need not be ignored or denied, but it is only a middling part of the range which has now to be covered by the word, and we are more interested in the two ends of the range. Using the word for the baby makes the process more complete. No doubt the baby does have to use good judgement, but its powers of mind are applied to such extraordinary things from our point of view, the building up of the idea of space for example, that we do not think of them as needing " good sense ". The whole poetical and philosophical effect comes from a violent junction of sensedata to the divine imagination given by love, and the middle term is cut out.

The uses of the word so far, however striking, can be said to keep within its previous range. It appears that Wordsworth also invented a new form, " the sense " used absolutely, and the new form must be supposed to imply some new meaning. There are, to be sure, precedents for the form, but only with a context that makes the meaning an obvious one. The N.E.D. has " 5 " " pierced to the sense " (to the quick), " 11b " " if they had had the sense to do it they could have . . . ", and " 1e " " the process of ink-making is noisome to the sense ". Perhaps this last heading, defined as " that one of the senses indicated by the context ", would cover Lucio's " wanton stings and motions of the sense ", which otherwise seems to be ignored. Pope has a use which feels more like those of Wordsworth, " darkness strikes the sense no less than light", but I take it he meant quite narrowly " the sense of sight ". None of these would prevent the bare and blank use by Wordsworth from appearing a novelty. He has already got it in *Tintern Abbey*, and it is already tearing upon the tripod :

> *well pleased to recognize*
> *In Nature and the language of the sense,*
> *The anchor of my purest thoughts, the nurse,*
> *The guide, the guardian of my heart, and soul*
> *Of all my moral being.* (T.A. 108)

" The " does not refer back to any *sense* previously defined, but this very sentence is expressing his theory ; it goes

> *Therefore am I still*
> *A lover of the meadows and the woods . . .*
> > *of all the mighty world*
> *Of eye and ear—both what they half create,*
> *And what perceive; well pleased to recognize . . .*

Thus one feels that " the sense " is a combination of " that sense " (the kind of *sense* just adumbrated) and " the senses " in general. The new grammar was really needed by the poetry ; even Wordsworth could not have got away with saying that the language of *the senses* was the soul of all his moral being. " *Language* " does much of the work—the senses can no doubt " show " us profound things (like Professor Wittgenstein) through the means by which they " tell " us every-day things ; but the traditional idea of the weakness and corruptibility of the senses would have been bound to poke up its head. With the new grammar " the sense " can take over some of the defining work from " the language " ; we may even take " the sense " as a peculiar power of imagination and its " language " as the mere sensedata from which we learn it. Either term could serve to ward off misunderstanding.

After this invention of the form he used it without any help from the context.

> *Nor, sedulous as I have been to trace*
> *How Nature by extrinsic passion first*
> *Peopled the mind with forms sublime or fair,*
> *And made me love them, may I here omit*
> *How other pleasures have been mine, and joys*
> *Of subtler origin; how I have felt,*
> *Not seldom even in that tempestuous time,*
> *Those hallowed and pure motions of the sense*
> *Which seem, in their simplicity, to own*
> *An intellectual charm; that calm delight*
> *Which, if I err not, surely must belong*
> *To those first-born affinities that fit*
> *Our new existence to existing things,*
> *And, in our dawn of being, constitute*
> *The bond of union between life and joy.*
>
> *Yes, I remember when the changeful earth*
> *And twice five summers on my mind had stamped*
> *The faces of the moving year, even then*
> *I held unconscious intercourse with beauty*
> *Old as creation, drinking in a pure*
> *Organic pleasure from the silver wreaths*
> *Of curling mist, or from the level plain*
> *Of waters coloured by impending clouds.*   (i.544—66)

The 1805 version is noticeably better in the last five lines, but there is no important difference elsewhere :

> *A Child, I held unconscious intercourse*
> *With the eternal Beauty, drinking in*
> *A pure organic pleasure from the lines*
> *Of curling mist, or from the level plain*
> *Of waters coloured by the steady clouds.*

The next paragraph says he would stand looking at the water

> *bringing with me no peculiar sense*
> *Of quietness or peace*

but " gathering . . . New pleasure, like a bee among the flowers ".

Wordsworth, I think, realised that he had to use hidden devices so that he might talk as if he had never heard of the meaning " sensuality " ; the chief function of *pure* here is to keep it out of view. But apart from this hidden denial of a meaning (a common and important process), which adds obscurity to the uses of the word, there is a curious blankness even about the meanings allowed. I have quoted at length here to show how the context before and after leads us in the two opposite directions. The second sentence, or paragraph, begins by saying that he remembers taking a pure organic pleasure in the scenery at this period (when he was ten). But the beginning of the first long sentence makes a careful distinction between his love for the scenery and the " joys of subtler origin " ; and these are what he is claiming to remember. I am not saying that there is a real contradiction in this obscurity, only that it imposes a double meaning on " the sense ". If the child were enjoying the scenery we would expect the term to mean or anyway to include " the senses ", but our attention is first directed away from them so that it means some " inner sense ", and *the* in the singular makes it look like the supreme sense of Imagination. But then the next sentence pushes it back to the sensations from the scenery again. I take it that the child felt a gush of well-being from far within, apparently without cause, but marking some profound adjustment to life ; and Wordsworth goes on to say that he remembers attaching this feeling to the scenery. The effect is that, though Sensation and Imagination appear as the two extreme ends of the scale in view, so that one might expect them to be opposites, the word is so placed that it might equally well apply to either. And the middle of the scale, the idea of ordinary common sense, is cut out from these uses no less firmly than the idea of sensuality. That is, instead of falling into the usual fallacies about good sense, you are forced to keep the whole range of the word in view, and there is a claim that the whole range of the word has been included in one concept. At least, I do not see what else the claim can be.; and I suppose most people would agree that the word is made to echo Wordsworth's doctrine somehow.

A conceivable meaning for *the sense* is the archaic " common sense ", that which correlates the messages of the different external senses. It is " the senses regarded as unified ", and that is already a kind of rudimentary power of interpreting them. It was not then so remote as to be quite familiar to Wordsworth. On the other hand, the passage as a whole obviously means " My Imagination was already stirring ", but which of the words means his imagination, if *the sense* does not ? This may be an unreasonable process of thought, but it seems to describe the way we are driven to give the term an obscure but splendid claim. It must be remembered that, here as so often in the poem, the language is in any case extremely loose ; the theoretical turns of phrase in the first paragraph lead us to expect the " bond of union " to be between the child and the external world—an epistemology is being given—but the peroration sweeps this aside to contemplate only " life and joy ". No doubt the reason why this seems fine is that one accepts *life* as the child and *joy* as inherent in Mother Nature, but such extreme optimism is made plausible only by being left vague. In the same way *the sense* feels inherently vague ; but this is no reason why we should not try to account for its behaviour.

In the " Statements in Words " chapter I gave as an example of the fourth type the use of *law* for " both human and divine law " ; the law you are talking about will commonly appear to be one or the other, but you may imply that such laws as this one satisfy the conditions for both. In such a case, though the order of terms for the equation is indifferent, it will be fixed on any particular occasion. The Wordsworthian use of *sense*, if I am right, is a much more thorough example of the process, not merely because the unifying concept required is much more obscure, but because in any one use of the equation you are not certain which term is meant to come first. However, I should claim that these two sorts of equation can be classed together for the purpose in hand, which is to consider what the different forms of interpretation can be.

Granting that the Wordsworth one is an equation of some sort, it is still not obvious how this equation could be translated into a sentence. " Sensation is Imagination " is a possible slogan, but both this and its inverse seem very open to misunderstanding without making the real point. " Sensation and Imagination are included in a larger class " is merely dull ; besides, the important thing may well be that they overlap to form a narrower class. " Sensation and Imagination interlock " seems the best way to put it. But I think it is fair to say that Wordsworth had not got any translation ready ;

he was much better at adumbrating his doctrine through rhetorical devices than at writing it out in full.

To be sure, I do not mean to claim that the form always carries so much weight ; for example it is used in the 1805 version to build a graceful piece of deliberate tedium, later omitted.

> On I went
> *Tranquil, receiving in my own despite*
> *Amusement, as I slowly passed along,*
> *From such near objects as from time to time*
> *Perforce, intruded on the listless sense,*
> *Quiescent, and disposed for sympathy.* (1805 iv.379)

Even here it can be read as something like " imagination " ; indeed, you might say that Wordsworth, rather pompously, is thinking of his imagination as a pet dog which never left his side. The example shows that the form was still connected in his mind with the actual process of receiving sensations. But, in contrast to that, another of these fairly trivial uses shows him treating it as a sort of technical term. During the French Revolution, he is saying, many young idealists and theorists felt that they must learn to deal with practical affairs :

> *The playfellows of fancy, who had made*
> *All powers of swiftness, subtlety, and strength*
> *Their ministers, who in lordly wise had stirred*
> *Among the grandest objects of the sense,*
> *And dealt with whatsoever they found there*
> *As if they had within some lurking right*
> *To wield it . . .*
> *Were called upon to exercise their skill* (xi.129)

—in the real world. This is particularly baffling because *the sense* appears to be the despised Fancy. In ordinary English, that is, you would expect it to refer to a sense *of* a kind already mentioned, and a sense of fancy is the only plausible candidate. But it is considered ironical that these people thought they had a right to deal with whatever they *found there*, that is, in *the sense* or among its *grandest objects*. Of course, it may be said that fancy often deals with grand objects, only not practically enough. The irony of Wordsworth is always cumbrous, and he does not mean to express contempt for these people by it (the passage is hardly altered from 1805) ; nor therefore, you might argue, for their kind of fancy. I do not see how to disprove such an argument, but I believe that at this stage of the poem he regarded *the sense* as practically equivalent to " Imagination ", so that it comes in as a natural opposite to Fancy (the irony against these people is due because they supposed that fancy would work where imagination is required). I think, indeed, that he would have been startled to find anyone identifying the two opposites for reasons of grammar. The interest of the example, supposing that this account is true, is that he was taking his new form as something well established.

I ought now to give some account of *feeling*. One might think that it was the opposite word to *sense*, rather as *wit* is in Pope ; but Wordsworth does not oppose the two words, and the effect when he puts them together is one of verbosity rather than anything else. Both of them (and *sensation* too) are concerned with both knowledge and emotion ; a feeling of impending doom is very like a sense of one. The choice between using one or the other is I think often made on rather obscure grounds of tact. " A sense of " impending doom claims that there is really something there to feel, though your interpretation of it may be wrong, whereas "a feeling of it" admits that you may be wholly mistaken. However, this contrast may be used in a rather contradictory way. If you want to say that you have come to a decision, though you realise the subject is complicated, you say you " feel ", and whatever the other man says you can still have your feeling. To say you have a *sense* that your plan is the best would really be milder, though it makes a larger claim, because it is not wholly closed to argument. " When people begin to ' feel ' ", Samuel Butler noticed, " they are always taking what seems to them the more worldly course ". It is because the subject is so complicated (not a thing you could claim to know about) that they are prepared to act in a way which might seem against their principles. This rather odd social development makes it hard to nail down a difference between the words in general. I should fancy that Wordsworth made more use of *feeling* in *Tintern Abbey* because he was writing with more direct conviction, though no doubt it is also true that he had not yet fixed his technical terms. But in any case it does not seem possible to exchange the words in his later work :

> *So feeling comes in aid*
> *Of feeling, and diversity of strength*
> *Attends us, if but once we have been strong.* (xii.270)

The whole passage is a very fine one. But why could not Wordsworth use his technical terms here ?

> *A single operation of the sense*
> *Gives power, and diversity of strength . . .*

Why, I wonder, does my invention look so ridiculous ? No doubt it fails to meet the point about " diversity " ; it seems a narrow piece of theorising. But also I think it feels out of the style because it makes *the sense* too definite ; only some high idea of " the sense of imagination " will fit the requirements of the assertion, whereas

Wordsworth always (even in " the grandest objects of the sense ")
left room for the alternative reading by which it meant the
processes of sensing in general. Indeed, this double meaning was
required by the theory which he used it to expound.

The reader may also have felt my little attempt ridiculous because
he remembered the context, which is a particularly strange one.
" I am lost " Wordsworth is just going to say ; he uses *feeling* for a
reason not really unlike that of Samuel Butler's people ; and in any
case he is actually talking about feelings rather than some act of
imagination which would transcend them. He first describes the
fear of the child losing its guide on the grim moor, and the
" visionary dreariness " of the place, and then says that this place,
when he came back " in the blessed hours Of early love, the loved
one at my side ", gave him ideas of " pleasure and youth's golden
gleam ".

> *And think ye not with radiance more sublime*
> *For these remembrances, and for the power*
> *They had left behind ? So feeling comes in aid . . .*

It is not even clear that the child used *the sense;* the only strength
he showed was to face and recognise the horror of the thing.
And what kind of strength does Wordsworth now require, out
walking with the bride rather coldly planned for ? Apparently even
a time of agony in his childhood was better than—more than that,
it gave him strength to endure—the chief pleasure he could arrange
for his middle age. Of course, he would have denied that he had
meant this, but he is reporting experiences, without much distortion
for the sake of theory, and it would be no use to try to simplify his
opinions.

Mr. James Smith has pointed out a similar jump in the famous
passage on crossing the Alps, and it has the advantage for my
purpose of falling into an " A is B " form. Critics have insinuated
that the experience was a good deal " written up ", judging by
Wordsworth's travel diary; but if you examine the language of the
poem it is sufficiently frank. On being told that he had crossed the
Alps, he says, " Imagination "—

> *That awful Power rose from the mind's abyss*
> *Like an unfathered vapour that enwraps,*
> *At once, some lonely traveller. I was lost;*
> *Halted without an effort to break through;*
> *But to my conscious soul I now can say*
> *" I recognise thy glory "; in such strength*
> *Of usurpation . . .* (vi.600)

—and " the light of sense goes out ". The 1850 version says rather
more clearly than the 1805 one (" and now recovering, to my soul

I say ") that he only recognised the Imagination afterwards ; but they both say it. The next paragraph, indeed, calmly begins by saying that what this news caused at the time was " a melancholy slackening ". But they hurry on down the gorge and see

> The immeasurable height
> Of woods decaying, never to be decayed . . .
> Winds thwarting winds, bewildered and forlorn . . .
> The rocks that muttered close upon our ears,
> Black drizzling crags that spake by the way-side
> As if a voice were in them; the sick sight
> And giddy prospect of the raving stream . . .

Nature is a ghastly threat in this fine description ; he might well, as in his childhood, have clasped a tree to see if it was real. But what all this is *like*, when the long sentence arrives at its peroration, is " workings of one mind " (presumably God's or Nature's, so it is not merely *like*),

> Characters of the great Apocalypse,
> The types and symbols of Eternity,
> Of first, and last, and midst, and without end.

The actual horror and the eventual exultation are quite blankly identified by this form of grammar. Now, of course, the historical process of learning to enjoy mountains really was a matter of taking this jump. I do not want to appear more prosy than Jane Austen on the subject. Her chief discussion of it comes in *Sense and Sensibility*, chapter xviii, and we find she is perfectly at home with horror ; the man who says he likes scenery to be cheerful is suspected of trying to be singular, but on the whole, it is felt, he is only rebuking excess or sympathising with farmers—at bottom he likes horror all right, like any other person of taste. One need not say, as I understand Mr. James Smith to do, that owing to a narrow theory about Nature Wordsworth is forcing an obviously wrong interpretation onto his feelings here. The point of identifying these two very different states of feeling, as a matter of style, is to insist that they are profoundly connected ; one of them grows out of the other, or something like that. No doubt some kind of pantheism is implied, because Wordsworth feels that Eternity is turbulent like the Alps and not calm like the Christian God. But the last line of the passage contradicts this idea by putting the calm back, and in any case the metaphysics would be a deduction only ; what he sets out to do is to describe the whole development of his feelings about crossing the Alps, and he asserts it as a unity.

I have been wandering away here from the verbal approach and the word *sense*, and I needed to do so, because if my account of *sense* is to be convincing I need to show that a similar process is at work generally in the poem. The word, I maintain, means both the process of sensing and the supreme act of imagination, and unites them by a jump ; the same kind of jump as that in the sentence about crossing the Alps, which identifies the horror caused by the immediate sensations with the exultation that developed from them. And in both cases, one might complain, what is jumped over is " good sense " ; when Wordsworth has got his singing robes on he will not allow any mediating process to have occurred.

A sturdy Wordsworthian, I suppose, would answer that there really is a consistent theory expounded, and that my linguistic approach merely ignores it. But then the Hartley theory, which Mr. Herbert Read describes as " practically what would now be called Behaviourism ", left much the same gap to be jumped. Perhaps I should quote some of his exposition of it (in his *Wordsworth*):

> " According to Hartley's psychology, our passions or affections are no more than aggregates of simple ideas united by associa-tion, and simple ideas are ideas surviving sensations after the objects which caused them have been removed. First, sensations, which arise from the impressions made by external objects upon the different parts of our bodies ; then simple ideas of sensation ; finally, under the power of association, all the various faculties of the human mind, such as memory, imagination, understanding, affection, and will."

Indeed, there is at least one passage, in the rejected manuscript Y given in Mr. de Selincourt's edition, where Wordsworth positively asserts the connection of ideas which I claim to find buried in his use of *the sense*. After the child has grasped simple ideas, he says :

> *And the world's native produce, as it meets*
> *The sense with less habitual strength of mind,*
> *Is pondered as a miracle,*

he grows up wanting to believe myths and legends ; but the wiser man after maturity will abandon them and return to the Nature which the child experienced,

> *as it were*
> *Resolving into one great faculty*
> *Of being bodily eye and spiritual need*

and there is a very fine long passage about the strength which his thought can then attain. There is no unwillingness to expound the idea in this rejected and rather bold document ; we are plainly told that the new faculty combines sensation and imagination. Perhaps I am taking a narrow and stupid view, but the idea seems to me to remain pretty unintelligible, however plainly and lengthily it is expressed ; and at any rate most readers of the poetry, who have not read Hartley, must pick up the idea in the form which I have tried to describe. Besides, Wordsworth seems to have followed Coleridge in going to the opposite philosophical extreme, from Associationism to Idealism, without feeling that the change needed to be made obvious in these poetical expressions of his theory. It does not seem unfair to say that he induced people to believe he had expounded a consistent philosophy through the firmness and assurance with which he used equations of Type IV ; equations whose claim was false, because they did not really erect a third concept as they pretended to ; and in saying this I do not mean to deny that the result makes very good poetry, and probably suggests important truths.

Chapter 15

SENSIBLE AND CANDID

JANE AUSTEN'S uses of *sense* and *sensibility* seem to be very clear-cut, and not in need of detailed examination. But I am not so sure about her use of *sensible*. The adjective was likely to be a no-man's-land between the two factions, but the eighteenth century seems to have made a firm decision that " sensible of " went one way and plain " sensible " the other. (There are already examples in Shakespeare of this modern use, though perhaps mainly as a joke.) Mr. T. F. Powys, particularly in the title " Mr. Weston's Good Wine ", a quotation from *Emma* (the wine made Mr. Elton propose to her), and elsewhere in his stories, has suggested that Jane Austen puts not merely a profound but positively a macabre irony into the primness of her language and her themes. This goes too far, but it is more plausible, I think, about her use of *sensible* than any other word. When Mr. Wickham says that Lady Catherine has the reputation of being very sensible and clever, for example, one does not quite know what to make of it. Or Lady Bertram when her husband returns from Antigua :

> " She had been *almost* fluttered for a few minutes, and still remained so sensibly animated as to put away her work, move pug from her side, and give all her attention and the rest of her sofa to her husband."

Probably it means " visibly " animated ; showing it to other people's senses ; but there may be a hint that as a rule she has not enough sensibility even to have good sense ; she has risen for once to the level of being " in her senses ". Jane Austen would easily feel that good sense requires the proper amount of emotion for a given occasion. When Elizabeth accepts Mr. Darcy we are told :

> " The happiness which this reply produced was such as he had probably never felt before ; and he expressed himself on the occasion as sensibly and as warmly as a man violently in love can be supposed to do."

You must " suppose " it for yourself ; the maiden lady is not going to do it for you ; and the phrase seems to me exactly balanced between the ideas that he showed as much good sense as could be expected (not much) and that he was as warmly sensible of the greatness of the occasion as anyone can imagine. But I am not sure whether she meant this to carry some real irony or whether she was just embarrassed, concerned to get through the love scene adequately without becoming fulsome. The word is too close to each of the opposed pair of cognate words to develop its own structure.

There is a franker piece of embarrassment over this family of words, in the same novel, when Elizabeth explains why she is prepared to believe (though it seems a shocking thing to have to say) that Lydia has really run away with Mr. Wickham :

> " She has been doing everything in her power, by thinking and talking on the subject, to give greater—what shall I call it ?—susceptibility to her feelings, which are naturally lively enough."

So in the earlier novel did Marianne, and it was called sensibility, but Lydia is not given so much licence. Sensuality is what Elizabeth would call it if she were not a lady, but she can make the point well enough, with decency and charity, by using a scientific word and perhaps the idea of the recording needle.

Candid ought to be considered as a parallel and contrast to *honest;* they were both driven down to truth-telling from more complex ideas. I am putting it here partly because it goes well with Jane Austen and partly because the structure seems like that of *sensibility*. It is, perhaps, the most beautiful of the words obscurely connected with truth, and the date of the destroying irony is pretty clear. The ingenious lady in *The School for Scandal* (1777) had not Candour but an Affectation of it ; however, this was coming to be regarded as a common danger ; and the song " Save Oh save me from the candid friend " (1798) amounts to an attack on the word. That is what this metaphor, I suppose, always means, an attack on the people who made a wrong and intriguing use of it, but an attack under conditions that prevent the old structure of the word from being recovered. However, the process was a slow one and is hardly yet complete. One would suppose that the Victorian fear of outspokenness was the strongest enemy of the grace of the word, and it is hard to invent a reason why the song should appear as early as 1798. Perhaps it is part of the feeling that the Augustan settlement had become artificial ; the word presumes a code of manners which had become vulgarised, and the attack on it is a sort of minor parallel to the attack on Poetic Diction. Jane Austen (whether you date *Pride and Prejudice* at 1796 or 1813) feels that the old word names a real virtue, but that it is rather wonderful to meet a contemporary example of it.

> " I would wish not to be hasty in censuring any one ; but I always speak as I think."
>
> " I know you do ; and it is *that* which makes the wonder. With *your* good sense, to be so honestly blind to the follies and nonsense of others ! Affectation of candour is common enough—one meets it everywhere. But to be candid without affectation or design—to take the good of everyone's character and make it still better, and say nothing of the bad—belongs to you alone. And so you

like this man's sisters, too, do you ?   Their manners are not equal to his."

The meaning here looks extremely single ; the word means " not desirous to find fault ", and so far from being a way of arriving at truth it involves being " honestly blind " to people's faults.   But even when this meaning is isolated you still have to " take the good " which is really there, however much you exaggerate it.   Indeed, the difficulty of bringing off the trick of *candour*, which was a greatly admired one, is that you have somehow to convince yourself that what you say is true.   (*Honestly* I think only means " without lying " here, Jane Austen has no tendency to make it elaborate.)   It is thus essential to the idea that what you say should be "favourable" but also, as a secondary meaning, " sincere ".   There seems also to be an idea that a candid person makes people better by encouraging their good qualities, but this is a rather remote Implication and not a necessary part of the standard use.   The noun can still take the eighteenth-century meaning when used with sufficient pomp, at least I think it appeared in a *Times* editorial during 1937:

" It is a time when no one may safely say quite all that is in his mind.   Candour must discipline itself to the attainment of the one supreme object, namely, peace not of might but of reason and humanity in Western Europe."

One might think candour must simply " shut up ", but that is not how the muffled sentences work.   The appeal of the word is that you will show real candour (the disciplined kind) if you refrain from exposing some low but important compromise.   Since the word works both ways, there is an added suggestion that this silence will be a way of telling the real truth.   But only the noun, not the adjective, would have done what *The Times* wanted here ; being *candid* has become " blowing the gaff, rather naively ".

The word, of course, comes from Latin, but through seventeenth-century French ; it was not borrowed by the English till after 1630. Apparently the meanings were all present in late Latin and were borrowed piecemeal.   As is not uncommon for a word of this sort, the romance languages seem partly to re-invent it and partly to grow up to it.   The first uses in English merely leave the word open for a variety of metaphorical praise :   " White, splendid ; fortunate, innocent."   Then (in the N.E.D.) :

3 free from bias ; fair, impartial, just (1635).
4 free from malice ; ' not desirous to find fault ', ' gentle, courteous ' ; favourably disposed, favourable, kindly (1633).
5 frank, open, ingenuous, straight-forward ; sincere in what one says (1675).

One must admire the great work in " 4 " for making the definitions grow slowly from the idea of the just judge to that of the judge prejudiced in your own favour. But " 5 " I think confuses ideas which are more seriously opposed ; telling truth against yourself (the early one) and exposing other people to their faces (the late one). All the defining words cover both, and this hides a thing you want to know—the process that took the word from one to the other ; I imagine it was a clear-cut jump due to irony. What does emerge is that the ideas of the just and the favourable judge belong to Charles I, and the idea of some form of truth-telling to Charles II. It is tempting to connect this shift with the Royal Society and the interest in the " laws " of Nature, rather than with any other feature of the Restoration. The word offers a remarkably different ideal truth-teller from the *fool* as clown or the *honest* man or the *wit* or the man of *sense*. One has only to move back to France and say " Candide " to see how firm the connection remained with the innocent simpleton who can judge life as it is ; that was what amazed Elizabeth about her candid sister who yet had sense. But the word had no ground for darkening this idea with ideas about low class or scandal or abstinence or assertive talk ; the root idea of whiteness is never lost, and the splendour of its purity comes partly from knowing what to ignore.

Jane Austen's use of the word here, though in a way so central, is very far from the unquestioning use which could assert an equation in the word as normal. It examines rather sceptically just what kind of truth-telling is involved, and the result is a definition not a covert assertion. A candid person picks out the good points in a person's character and ignores the bad ones, without affectation or design. The judgements are favourable but also unbiased and sincere; one could write this as " 4 (3.5) " ; but the formula still would not express the logical complexity of the thing. There are three aspects of " 5 " truth-telling in view ; what you say may be true, and you may think you are not suppressing anything (" sincere "), but your over-all judgement of the person's character may be quite false. Indeed, in a way you are *not* " unbiased " (" -3 "). A simple equation, as the notion of truthfulness gradually became an important implication in the word, would be " the kind umpire is truthful "; he does not suppress your good points out of malice, so he is a trustworthy source of information. But in the full use, I think, and even in Jane Austen's, however much she may seem to deny it, the notion of a peculiar kind of truthfulness has become the head sense of the word. " The truthful umpire is kind " does not look seriously different from its opposite, partly I think because we take both to mean " the ideal umpire is both kind and truthful ". But a perfectly accurate judgement is not in view ; in fact the word asks you to feel (as Pope did about the " generous " critic) that the candid person is touchingly good because his method is so likely to deceive him. The thought is something like "The innocent and unsophisticated mind, expecting others to be as open as itself, is the really just judge, because the rest of us are blinded by malice and self-interest". The paradox of saying that the over-favourable judgements are "really" the correct ones can lead to further reflections, as that such treatment makes the other people better, or at any rate that such behaviour will receive some kind of heavenly or magical reward ; but I suppose they are not part of the meaning of the word. In such a case, as in the doctrinal uses of *sense* and *sensibility*, the analyst has to appeal to the idea of pregnancy. The kind of truth-telling which has no self-interest is made the right handle to take hold of the bundle ; the reader will agree, I think, that the various meanings of the word actually do make it present a rather confusing bundle when it is called in to handle a practical situation. And this kind of truth-telling is then felt to be *inherent* in the other two ideas, of being a favourable judge and of being an unbiased one ; that is why I find myself putting "really" into the sentence expounding the equation. It is thus another example of Type III, but in the end a rather pathetic one. As soon as people feel that this rather strained doctrine is being used to cheat them they can kick the whole card-castle over ; all they have to do is to use the word in its head sense when the other ideas are ironically out of place.

Chapter 16

MESOPOTAMIA

I OUGHT now to give an example of the unnoticed equations of Type III which I said often occur in controversy, and the simplest way to do it is to take an example already worked out in full by Professor Richards. Whether I really disagree with his account I am not sure, but if I do it is only in a marginal way; however, I need to make the most of the possible disagreement to show what is needed if his account is to fit my formula. The question one might disagree over, as I understand it, is whether the decisive processes of a controversy are carried in the structure of single key words or (so far from that) as whole " proofs ", patches of argufying, which are remembered without paying much attention to their parts. Obviously this is important for my equation theory, and there seems room for experiment on the question if one could get it stated sufficiently clearly.

No doubt there are possibilities between these extremes. An equation in the word " it " may be imposed by leaving open two things which *it* can refer back to, and yet the word itself would carry hardly any stress in ordinary use ; the natural way to phrase the effect is that the equation is imposed by the whole sentence. I am not sure how far one could learn the trick of doing this for a particular argument without realising that it was a trick, but I should think one could. In the same way putting two words in apposition tends to impose an equation between them, and this trick seems an easy one to pick up. However, in both these cases it can be said that a single equation is what the argument is to turn on, or is what has to be remembered, whatever grammar is used to impose it ; so I think that cases like this could be counted on my side of the controversy.

Interpretation in Teaching actually describes such an experiment. Professor Richards handed two passages round a class and asked for criticisms on the arguments in them. One was a sentimental speech about love from *Elmer Gantry*, with an indignant critic's remarks appended, and the other was a discussion by the Regency grammarian Campbell on the nature of grammar. Both these very different passages turned on statements that something *is* something else ; the first could be summed up as " love is music—no it isn't " and the second as " Grammar is merely a codification of usage, and therefore must not attempt anything else ". In the first the identity assertions seem obviously meant as metaphors, whether good or

bad, while the identity in the second is offered as a definition of
" grammar ". The Cambridge students seem to have been pretty
clear about this. They come in for a good deal of scolding in the
book, because some of them accepted the metaphors and echoed
them in their discussion, and some accepted the definition without
examining its truth. But they were sufficiently forewarned about
the forms of logic not to write down blank false identities, however
they may have been thinking. I tried the same passages on a class of
Chinese students, who did not regard a dress of logic as a necessary
decency. The papers were not at all stupid, and in an unconnected
way made a lot of good points. But they commonly agreed with the
identities and then went on to say something that denied them.
"Of course, love is music, but jealousy isn't. I remember a man
who . . ." or " I think grammar is a statement of usage. A great
scholar need not keep the rules of grammar, but ordinary people
must." One did not know whether they had missed the logical
point or not thought it worth mentioning, and if regarded as a
psychological experiment they would, I think, give rather different
evidence from the Cambridge ones ; not that either are at all
decisive.

Professor Richards' analysis, of course, deals with cases like this,
cases that might be called pre-logical thinking. But his account
makes the pre-logical (or usual) thinking a matter of whole sentences
or paragraphs ; if I understand him, it is only in logical thinking,
which recognises that the definition of a term is different from statements about an already defined term, that the analyst can usefully
attend to the meanings of single words. He compares this change of
approach to the change from the fluid to the crystalline state. In
the fluid state the words " cannot be said to have any meaning " ;
no doubt the single words have functions, but such a word is hardly
more than an aggregate of potentialities, like what you feel for a
syllable used in many words. In connected speech the mind is able
to perform an extraordinarily complicated process of balancing and
eliminating the possible resultant meanings from the interaction of
these loose aggregates, and the point or purpose of the whole speech,
a thing gradually discovered, is not attached to individual words.
No doubt this process actually occurs. But in general, and more
clearly than usual in these bits of schoolwork, the language performance is about a topic which can be given in a single word. After
writing one sentence about grammar, or love, the student would sit
back and wonder what other ideas he had about grammar, or love.
And, precisely because of the fluidity of words in general, the word
recognised as the topic is able to grow a more inclusive structure in
the process. The previous remarks adhere to it. I should agree,
of course, that it is misleading to treat such words as having single

meanings, because I claim that they have equations. But I should disagree on a point which is in a way prior to that. It seems to me that the key words, the " topic " words, are far more in command of this kind of discourse than they are of a logical argument. Precisely because they have not got single meanings, they can be made to sum up the process of thought. Professor Richards introduces a kind of joke technical term, the " Mesopotamian " use of a word, to mark the peculiar degree of emptiness he describes ; but this I think loses all its value from being applied to both of two opposite extremes. It seems to cover both the word used as a blank cheque (" I will now introduce the term ' phlogiston ' ") and the word used as a compacted doctrine (" Phlogiston for ever ! "). There was an old woman who got great comfort from that blessed word Mesopotamia, and the derivation of it is " between two rivers ", between two meanings. The point of the joke, as I understand it, is to say that the effects of the word on her were " merely Emotive " because the senses of it were wholly confused. I should suspect that the old woman was giving the word some wrong meaning, or simply telling lies. But I don't deny that the supposed process might occur in a softened brain ; all I claim is that it does not account for the Regency argument about grammar.

Professor Richards falls with gusto on that piece of sophistry because he believes that the Usage doctrine has kept grammarians from being any use, and also believes that classes in grammar ought to be used to teach students to think more clearly. Before summarizing the arguments, I had better try to make the issue real by giving an example. Let us take the treatment in Fowler's *Modern English Usage* of ' fused participle ' (" Women having the vote is bad "). Fowler says that the use of this grammatical form is growing rapidly and ought to be stopped. Then he gives two arguments. An absurd one from the classics, that we ought to make English like Latin and say " Women having the vote *are* bad ", but that we had better not do this either, because it is often not what we mean. Then an effective proof by examples that the thing becomes confusing in long sentences. A sensible reader, I think, will get some profit from the point about long sentences and go on using the construction for short ones. Now it does not matter whether you say that Fowler is writing " grammar " here or not. He is not merely codifying current usage. Nor for that matter is he issuing " laws " ; he is trying to persuade you, and where his arguments come (say) from undue reverence for Latin you can reject them. But in the strict Usage doctrine there is no room for this natural process. A grammarian must merely codify usage, because otherwise he would be issuing laws.

The question is now how the Regency grammarian made the

Usage doctrine plausible.   This is the essential part of his argument:

> " It is not the business of grammar, as some critics seem pre-
> posterously to imagine, to give law to the fashions that regulate
> our speech. . . . For, what is the grammar of any language ?   It is
> no other than a collection of general observations methodically
> digested ; . . . modes and fashions . . . no sooner obtain and become
> general, than they are laws of the language, and the grammarian's
> only business is to note, correct, and methodise them."

Professor Richards points out that when *grammar* is used in the first
sentence of this quotation it must be supposed to mean something
which some people think might give laws, and they could not think
this about a collection.   Campbell must, therefore, be changing the
meaning of the word and, indeed, " giving laws " about it, when
he says it is " no other than " a collection.   The crux of the process of
suasion is that you do not easily think of this retort, because you do
not take the definition so seriously ;   you accept it as a description
before you see what it implies.   You feel (this seems what is meant
by taking it as only a description) that grammar is other things as
well, really, but that the description covers the field and shows you
how to direct your attention ;   the apparently rigid logic of " no
other than " might only imply that all the aspects of grammar could
be viewed under this head.   As the argument proceeds, there is an
idea that usage means good usage, or that the " standard " is the
usage of the " best " speakers, and this acts as a vague source of
plausibility.   Great play is made with " law ", so that the grammarian (unless he keeps to the definition) is a tyrant ;   what right
has this pedant to issue laws ?   These contrasting ideas are merely
stirred into the brew to feed the growth of the original false identity ;
if you took them seriously they would imply that some other body
is expected to issue laws.   Then we are told " language is a living
thing ", as if it were some kind of dragon, and the business of the
grammarian is to count the paws.   But of course he is *part* of the
living thing, and the real argument can only be that he is less
important than some other part, the Gentry perhaps, or contrariwise the Folk.   The " business " of the grammarian is another term
used for suasion ;   he must stick to his job, and merely count the
paws.   The business of a doctor is to heal people, but it is also
considered his duty (among other things) to help the police in murder cases.   Similarly, it might be the duty of a grammarian not to
limit himself to his business.   This, I think, shows that the mere
definition of grammar is harmless, because it need not stop a
grammarian from doing anything useful.   The stirring and suasive
part of the argument is in the false deductions from it.

I have repeated part of Professor Richards' analysis of the deception, and think it clearly correct.   But, as I understand him, he tries

to take each successive use of the term " grammar " as having a single meaning and to maintain that the trick is to move from one to another. We first, he would say, read " grammar " in a Mesopotamian sense, then accept the definition of it as a codification of usage, then in subsequent uses of the word we slip back to some normal wider meaning (e.g. " criticism of language forms ") and yet feel that the deductions from the definition still apply. This is how we are deceived. Now, even here, you must somehow have both meanings of the word within reach, or you would forget the old deductions. However, I don't deny that deceptions of this sort do occur ; perhaps you remember a phrasemeaning rather than the wordmeaning, which you fail to examine. But suppose a man tried to repeat the argument after it had convinced him ; suppose he " walked round the garden again ". The effect due to surprise would have to take another form. If he only remembered the definition, he would forget the sophistry. That is, he has somehow to take for granted the other idea of grammar, the one his opponent has ; because it is used in the argument. Nor is this hard to do ; everybody in childhood has been told to speak " correctly " because " that is how people talk ", and later he comes to assume that the way he talks is the correct one. About anything established there settles this curious double sentiment, that it is both right because it is customary and customary because it is right ; and the idea of what is normal, since both are contrasted to the confusion of actual occurrences, allies itself to the ideal of what is best. The pure Usage doctrine is a product of revolt against one part of this sentiment while appealing to another part. The immediate revolt is against the false analogy of Latin, but this becomes a revolt against such obscure magical ideas as that language ought to obey an ancestral lawgiver or correspond to some truth in the heavens. Such a revolt does not escape from its own psychological background, and there is a feeling that what we actually do has these magical virtues, so it ought not to be tampered with. I submit that doctrines of this sort, carrying a primitive aura, are very suitable for expression in the equation form. Everybody knows the two definitions or rather feelings about the matter, and for the two doctrines he has only to equate these feelings in the two possible orders. A " revolution " in his view of grammar will occur when he puts " B is A " instead of " A is B ".

We must now try to write the equations down. If we take the two phrases, which I said were anybody's idea of the distinction, and pair them off, we get " how people actually talk is how they ought to talk " and " how people ought to talk is how they actually talk ". But these are both the Usage doctrine, and the same thing happens if we put " usage is correct ", " correctness is usage ". This is not a surprising result, because it is the nature of " correctness " which is in question ; does it depend or not on rules drawn from outside the language ? To bring this in we need an idea of the normal or the ideal, which as before can be got by putting " good " before the subject of the equation. " Good usage is correct " gives us the traditional doctrine all right, and the Usage doctrine is concerned with denying this idealism—" correctness is merely usage". The alternative form " correctness ought to be usage " gives the idea clearly enough, and we can now invert the sentence as it stands to get the traditional doctrine " usage ought to be correct ". But it is a weakness of these equations that the idea which is taken more seriously is in each case made the predicate. *Grammar* is certainly an " integrated " word without any obvious double meaning, so that we do not expect its equations to be of Type I (like the mountain-saddle) ; the subject of an equation here ought to be the head meaning of the word for a speaker who believes the doctrine it asserts. The case looks very similar to the second batch of equations in *sense* and *sensibility*, when those words were made to express general doctrines : we can again swap the word-orders by changing from Type II to Type III. In Type III, the new head meaning is regarded as the fundamental or even the only one, and this is very suitable here because the Regency grammarian actually claims that his meaning of the word is the only one. Also, we need a vague idea of magic or power, which is applied by one doctrine to the old rules and by the other to the actual customs, and this process supplies it by emphasising " inherency ". Another advantage of Type III is that it does not presume that you conceive both elements of meaning distinctly at the same time ; the double meaning of *grammar* is likely to remain pretty obscure. In such an equation, you realise that the referent is somehow mixed and then merely pick out one part of it as the right handle to take hold of the bundle ; this part is made the subject, and the predicate is the bundle as a whole. We can indeed arrange phrases in which the old Authoritarian and the new Usage doctrine appear as the same equation in the two opposite orders : for the Authoritarian doctrine " a locution that keeps a rule is the typical specimen of a usage ", and for the Usage doctrine " a locution in common use is the typical specimen of a rule ". But these are rather artificial, because the strength of this type of equation is that the predicate does not have to be definite ; it is merely all the other meanings of the word. This makes the equation much easier to remember and keep in play ; the Authoritarian doctrine is " How people ought to talk is the typical specimen of what grammar is about ", and the Usage doctrine is " How people actually talk . . .". The convert has only to deny whenever convenient that it is " about " anything else.

The reader may object that it would be more sensible, when analysing an argument which makes play with logical terms, to use the idea of definition. " What is defined as what sums up usage is also what teaches the rules " should be the Usage doctrine, and " What is defined as teaching the rules is also what sums up usage " should be the traditional one. This puts the pairs in the same order as the equations with " typical specimen ", and it may seem that I have been boggling very unnecessarily before arriving at the obvious. But it is not at all clear, I think, until you try out the alternatives, that this coherent and sensible piece of thinking is actually what the mind does. Indeed, I think it only does so when it works very carefully. When the casual reader comes across " grammar is no other than a codification ", etc., he feels that he is to select from his confused experience of the meaning of grammar the part that makes this assertion a tautology. But he does not abandon his past experience ; in spite of the logical form of the sentence, this part merely appears to him as the most important fact about grammar, or rather the most important one for the passage now in hand. The order for *his* equation, as he reads on, will be that of " correctness is merely usage ". But such a man is only being tricked by the argument, and is not likely to be good at repeating it. On the other hand, the convert will really make the new definition the head sense of the word, but he will retain contact with his past experience of the meanings of the word by regarding it as a mixed class of which the new head sense is the " type ". The casual man adds an Implication onto the word, and treats the equation as in Type II. The convert accepts the re-definition and will in future make equations of Type III.

This, I think, he must do, because if the defining property is not also treated as the " typical " property, or anyway as much the most important property, we are likely to get a paradoxical effect. " Grammar in itself is merely a codification of usage ; but the important thing about it is that it tells you how to use language." This looks like a way of expressing the Usage doctrine, but it is not what Campbell wants at all. It suggests the parallel with the doctor ; a grammarian may have other duties beside his " business ". Of course, it still leaves doubtful whether grammar issues laws or gives advice, but it gives you an escape from the sophistry of the argument. Such a movement of thought is too genuinely logical to explain how the passage works ; so it proves that the form " what is defined as . . ." is not what we are looking for.

It is perhaps rather surprising that the definition should be so unimportant, but the reason, I think, is that the Range of " grammar " is still the same however you define it. It is " what grammarians do ", and this gives the referent a sort of solid quality, as in the case of

" cats ". To accept a new definition of it is not to give up what you know about it already ; you can feel " That covers it, but there's more than that *in* grammar ", or " *to* a cat ". It is this vague feeling which we draw upon for the predicate of the equation ; but the feeling is not merely primitive or illogical, indeed, it keeps us in contact with reality ; a sound argument has to draw upon it no less than a sophistry.

We should now be able to return to Professor Richards. " What can be the meaning of the term *grammar* ", he asks, " when Campbell first uses it in this passage ? " He points out that the assertion " grammar is nothing more than a codification " cannot be merely a definition of a term previously blank, or it would have no suasive power, and it cannot be a statement *about* grammar in which grammar is taken to have some meaning other than codification, or it would be at once rejected. He therefore says it could only have a " Mesopotamian " use. But if this joke term is meant to describe a word with a sort of magical quality, such as the old woman found helpful, surely the magic is being put in the wrong place. The first use comes before the spellbinder has got to work. It is merely our ordinary mixed idea of grammar, which includes both codifying how people *do* talk and telling (perhaps other) people how they *ought* to talk. If an idea like this is pre-logical, we are all pre-logical, and had better remain so. No doubt the reader's idea of the word is already meant to be altered when he gets to the end of the sentence ; from then on he is supposed to have put the new equation into it, whether by regarding " codification " as the most important property or as the head sense. He has established an asymmetrical relation between the parts of the word's meaning. But I cannot see that this need be viewed as a merely unintelligible use of language, like that of the old woman. It occurs in many correct logical arguments, and anyway it is not magical in the sense of yielding to Emotion rather than reason. Finally, the grammarian himself no doubt meant something rather different by the word, because he knew the answer already ; perhaps he meant only the Range of the word, the class usually named by it, and went on to give the defining property of this class. But he might simply use the term in inverted commas : " what *you* think of as grammar is a wrong idea ; here is the right one." I do not think that this need be called a Mesopotamian use either.

After pursuing the matter in detail, Professor Richards remarks that :

> " Whether we say we have two ' views ' of grammar taken in one and the same sense, or that we have two *senses* of the term is optional. It depends on how we elect to use the word *sense*."
>
> (P. 252.)

And to support the one-meaning view, he goes on, we could define grammar as " the only worthy proper right and useful way of studying language ". Both parties would agree that this was what they were talking about, and their difference would lie in the way they went on to describe it. This, which amounts to giving the word an Emotive definition, does seem to settle the matter without further fuss. But the effect is to put the opinions into the predicates of the two equations, thus making the two rival uses of the word into qualifying pregnancies only. I should maintain that these have an actual difference from typifying pregnancies, and that a convinced disputant is using a typifying one. Of course, our choice of terms is optional, and we need not bother about this rather subtle difference all the time; but what is optional is not necessarily indifferent; and it is better to formulate the thing in such a way that we can make this distinction if we want to. I hope my formulation does not seem too elaborate ; the elaboration belongs only to the process of defending it. What struck me about Professor Richards' account was that he said all that could be said about the complexity and deceptiveness of the play with language on which the passage relies, but that after expounding and indeed solving the problem he failed to show the simplicity of the answer.

There seemed also to be a more general doctrine in question, which I have not yet considered ; the idea that a passage as a whole may have a meaning, while its component words are practically meaningless. Certainly when a man is talking straight ahead he cannot be supposed to give individual words a great deal of attention, and in arguing that one of them has a particular structure the theorist must be supposing he gives it that structure in his subconscious mind. But this is not as wild as it appears, because the subconscious mind is patently doing a good deal of work anyhow ; for one thing it is getting the grammar in order. There is another objection of this kind which seems to me more important. In verbose (rather than illogical) discourse, it is sometimes possible to distribute the meanings among the words in a variety of ways, and the verbal analyst might think he was getting a very complex ambiguity by working this out, whereas, in fact, it would add nothing to the total effect. The purpose might well be only to nail a meaning home by repeating it, and a number of near-synonyms may be connected for this purpose by a perfunctory but quite elaborate grammar. However, I think it is still possible, in such a case, to write down the possible alternative structures of meaning in the words ; the fact that it is not worth doing does not make it theoretically wrong. It would be wrong if it did not correspond to anything in the speaker's mind, but he cannot be supposed to string his sentences together without any mental operations at all. And, indeed, we should beware of despising verbosity ; he may well have some extra purpose in his repetitions, such as to discourage possible misunderstandings. I think Wordsworth's " language of the sense " (to take a mercifully brief example) is an example of the more worthy process ; you can parcel out the meaning either as " the important truths we are told by the senses " or as " the bodily processes by which the Sense of Imagination tells us truths ". The chief effect of this double structure in the phrase is to make sure that *the sense* does not imply sensuality ; (a reader may protest that sensuality does teach us truths, but that is a question for Wordsworth not for his exegetist). It also serves to keep in play the two meanings of *the sense* so as to impose a fourth-type equation between them. That is, the existence of two pairs of alternative meanings in the two words, which converge to define the phrase-meaning, also makes one of the pairs more prominent as a "double meaning", and this echoes a permanent doctrine which Wordworth wants to suggest repeatedly. Up to a point, in fact, verbosity is rather a powerful weapon for making the words spread themselves, and I do not think there is any reason for supposing that it gives them no individual structures which could be examined.*

* Re-reading R. G. Collingwood's *Philosophical Method*, which imputes a vastly (perhaps infinitely) higher degree of complexity than I do to any word when used philosophically, it struck me that mine would appear to a philosopher an absurdly brash and summary treatment. And yet, in spite of my admiration for the book, I cannot see what else he can be describing except a very complex repeated use of the little bits of machinery I am trying to get clear. The idea of an *essence* which is different at every stage of a discussion is particularly hard to treat otherwise. In fact, though intended so differently, it looks to me like a grand exposure of philosophy from the inside.

Chapter 17

PREGNANCY

IN writing about *sense* and *sensibility*, I sometimes appealed to our experience of a " pregnant " use of a word for comparison. It is the most familiar example of the typifying process, but needs to be examined on its own. Till recently the term was used vaguely, as a metaphor, for any word with a hidden meaning which could ripen. It has now been given a more specialised sense, and had better be kept to that, but even that, I think, has two sorts. For lack of terms, I used " pregnancy " in the first chapter to describe what was to be symbolised by plus and minus signs after the number, that is, a shift that makes the meaning of the word warmer and fuller, or contrariwise less so. This symbol only marks one meaning of the word, imposed by some play of feeling ; but we also talk about " pregnancy " when what we really have in view is an equation between this sense and the usual one. I think the terms " a pregnant *use* of a word " and " pregnancy " in general should be kept for the equation, but the extra sense of the word is most naturally described as " the pregnant sense " even if it appears alone.

The stock example of a pregnant use in its full form is given by Hamlet when speaking about his father :

HOR. :   *I saw him once ; he was a goodly king.*
HAM. :   *He was a man, take him for all in all,*
        I shall not look upon his like again.
HOR. :   *My lord, I think I saw him yesternight.*

Only the most general term may be used for King Hamlet, and the reason is that he is unique. No doubt it could be denied that there is any equation here ; all that the passage requires is a peculiar but single meaning for the word *man*. I agree that the argument does not proceed through the equation, as it did when the matron called Amelia *delicate*. · But it seems clear that Hamlet cannot get his " peculiar but single " meaning for the word without appealing to some general background of ideas about what men ought to be ; these are both taken for granted and taken as the underlying reasons for his judgement in the present case. So I doubt whether the distinction here, between an equation used to carry an argument and an equation carrying an assumption, is really important ; one might feel later that the assumptions of the period are what need attention, and contrariwise if you had pointed out to Hamlet what he was assuming, he would only have felt that strengthened his case.

Stern's description of pregnancy in *Meaning and Change of Meaning* is as follows :

> " It implies concentration on characteristics of the referent that are, or are considered to be, essential and typical, mostly from a moral or intellectual point of view, and it often involves a valuation of the referent."

This seems true enough, but *mostly* and *often* cannot give a definition, and it is at least a tricky business to stop the first part of this account from applying to any case of his ' adequation '. His stock example of an adequation is the horn used as a musical instrument. This came to be thought of as " essentially " a musical instrument, so when other such instruments not made of horn appeared they were called horns too. Now if the referent is the individual horn spoken of (phrase-referent) you certainly " concentrate on its essential characteristic ", so that adequation is pregnancy. But though it might be said that King Hamlet alone is the referent of *man* here, still the process clearly involves some reference to men in general. If the referent of *horn* is the whole class of horn objects (word-referent) then the adequation changes the referent to the class of horns used in music. But in the pregnant use of *man* you presumably narrow the class of men to those truly manly, in this case to King Hamlet alone, and the two processes are still not distinct. The difference, of course, is that you forget the central meaning of *horn*, whereas you are somehow " arguing from " the central meaning of *man*. Indeed, it is this double element of meaning, I submit, which makes it reasonable to suppose that an equation is at work. But it is difficult to call the virtues of King Hamlet essential to being a man, or typical of men in general, when only one man has been found to possess them. The terms ' essential ' and ' typical ', in fact, simply repeat the puzzle Stern has to consider—an excellent way, of course, to describe it, which is what he was doing. " He was so typically Mongolian that he could hardly walk ", said a recent travel-writer, giving a lively case of the kind of ' typical ' in question. It means that this Mongol came fairly near the traveller's idea of a caricature of a Mongol, a thing that most Mongols were very unlike, and to meet one fairly like it was remarkable enough to be reported. The reason there is a puzzle here about *referent* is, I think, that this term was invented to avoid certain fallacies about concepts, and when the speakers themselves make a hearty use of such a fallacy the term does not suit them. The characteristics picked out by pregnancy are ' typical of ' *the concept*, though, indeed, this term may well be misleading, for the concept has become a kind of totem or flag, with a life quite independent of the class it is supposed to represent. Thus the business of a pregnant use is to assert an equation between two referents, for example, the class of men and something that had best be called the ideal man, since the whole method of the trick is to shift from an idea to an ideal. These two may exist in your mind quite separately, as they clearly do in Hamlet's. The normal use is to assert the equation " the specimens of the class are the ideal " ; for instance, a reference to Englishmen in a patriotic speech will firmly imply that they are all ideal Englishmen. In a case like Hamlet's, where you admit that most of the specimens are not ideal, the equation will easily shift to exhortation, " let them be the ideal ", or to praise for any that are, or again to an obscure magical feeling, which seems strong in the example from *Hamlet*, that if you find one such specimen it is a kind of god, because it is Man and not merely a man. But the same trick can be used for depreciative pregnancy—" a very woman " is the example given by Stern—where the suasive part only tells you that this is how you had best regard a woman, even if the woman in view has not yet shown herself ' typical '. Of course, a number of these entities can be extracted from one class-name ; for instance the main business of political propaganda is to put across your ' type ' of the worker or the business man, the specimen you want people to think of when they think of workers or business men.

In this case, however, it might seem that there is no limitation on what virtues the ideal man is supposed to have, so that the effect is mere praise. In a serious case of typifying, as when the propagandist establishes his Type of the business man or the worker, a good deal of effort is put into describing this type ; but the pregnant use of *man*, it may be said, is purely Emotive. It is true that Hamlet takes his meaning for granted, whatever it may be, but surely the whole force of the trick is to imply that he has some meaning in view, some virtue which most men do not have but ought to have. His claim may be false, but the important point for linguistics is that he makes a claim. To decide what these virtues can be, one can only try to think of past contexts in which they might be suggested. No doubt there could be an occasion when a woman or boy was suggested to do some important bit of work, and the reply was " No, it needs a man ". The virtues required on that occasion might now come forward to fill the gap. But it seems clear that a listener could follow this use of *man* without remembering any such occasion even in his subconscious mind. A good deal of sociology would be needed to fill out this gap which seems so obvious to everyone. I imagine it really depends on the custom of telling a boy to be a little man (indeed, to be like father, which would fit the Hamlet situation very closely) ; this is at once part of every man's background and so remote from any context he is likely to recall that the disposition to understand the pregnant use seems to exist on its own. Such a case seems the ideal one for an Emotive use ; and, of course, I agree that the thing is communicated almost entirely in terms of feeling ; but I still think that it can only be analysed by taking it to impute specific virtues.

I have tried, so far, to describe the process and recall the reader's experience of it ; I need now to classify it and say which way round the equations go. The answer, however, seems to be the rather unsatisfactory one that they can go either way round, and perhaps the best approach to it is a confession. I regarded this example from *Hamlet* for a long time (it is given by Stern) as a handy working model of a " pregnant use " ; because the sentence can only make nonsense, I thought, unless you take *man* to mean the ideally complete man, with King Hamlet as the unique case in which this ideal has been realised, at any rate in the experience and expectation of Hamlet. But there is a chatty note in the Arden edition which shows that this view of Hamlet's remark has been considered unusual. " Edwin Booth ", it says, " in delivering this speech, paused after ' man ', giving it as if something higher than ' king ' "* (Booth was an American actor, and no doubt emphasis on this point went down well with his audiences.) Other actors, clearly, used to run the sentence straight on so as to imply a bit of grammar left out : " He was (such) a man (that), considering all the different ways in which he was excellent, I shall never see another to equal him." The Second, Third and Fourth Quartos have no stops in the line ; the First (which may have been punctuated from the voice of Burbage) has commas after *man* and the second *all* ; the Folios give the comma after *man* again and a colon after the second *all*, but even so this may be only to mark emphasis on the following line. Most modern editions follow the First Quarto in the matter. The majority of readers, I am forced to suppose, have not taken *man* here as a pregnant use at all, or at any rate not one which is decidedly and necessarily pregnant ; that would require a strong stop after *man*, not after the second *all*, the only place where it is ever inserted. And yet it is hard to believe that the discovery of Edwin Booth was altogether new ; the antithesis of *man* to *king* is as sharp as such a thing could be. It is not necessary to suppose, of course, that the " idealistic " Hamlet (because he had progressed beyond " feudal "

---

* Mr. Granville-Barker, claiming to take the actor's point of view, made a valuable analysis of the spoken rhythms intended in this passage—Hamlet repeatedly echoes the verse rhythm set by Horatio ; but then Mr. Granville-Barker says " the echoed cadence, as a test, condemns the reading, once beloved by actors, ' He was a man. Take him for all in all . . .' by which Hamlet is oddly made to imply that kings as kings were not of much account." But no, the echoed cadence is a semicolon ; not a comma, nor indeed a full stop. The argument from rhythm deserves full weight but only acts as a reinforcement of the dramatic ambiguity.

ideas of revenge no doubt) was taking a democratic or anti-monarchical point of view, and assuming that the human virtues are best illustrated by the lower classes. There might, indeed, be a feeling which a modern reader is tempted to confuse with this, but even so the line of thought would be what I call Pastoral rather than Proletarian. The claim is simply that King Hamlet carried the fundamental virtues to a remarkable extreme ; it is not, therefore, an unlikely idea to occur to Hamlet. But it seems clear that the emphasis of the actor can vary so as to make it occur to Hamlet in a greater or lesser degree ; this partial process is what is hard to symbolise, but there seems no doubt that it is the normal one. Indeed, as we listen to a sentence, we often cannot fix the required shade of meaning on the words near the beginning till we have heard the end ; we are regularly exercised in the partial process, therefore, even when the final meaning appears single and definite, and this is why the alternative meanings are often less fully cut out at the end than we think.

The Hamlet case is fairly straightforward if we suppose the Booth delivery, a pause after *man*, throwing it into opposition with *goodly king* as giving higher praise. " What the word really means here " has to be the pregnant sense, the ideal man, even though the normal meaning of the word is sure to arise as predicate ; and then the following clauses (saying that such a man is unique) serve to heighten the paradox. The actual sentence " He was a man " means " He was brave, decisive, reliable, not passion's slave " and so forth, and then the equation adds " *such a man* is the ideal to which *all men* should strive, by which they should be tested ". In the second version, for which the delivery must suggest the grammar " He was a man who —well, all I can say is . . ." the chief meaning of the word is " men in general ", but unless the word is slurred over almost completely there will be *some* effect from Hamlet's demand that we should think in universal terms of value, and not merely praise the man as a king. The ideal man will, therefore, come in as predicate, but can come in varying degrees ; whereas in the first version, where he is subject, he has to be there completely. In the second version the sentence says " I think of him as a man rather than as a king ", but may imply this only vaguely, since it is incomplete ; then the equation adds " and a good specimen of a man has manly virtues ". Here the merits expected of a man arise as a Connotation, and the equation is Type II. In the first version the equation must I think be put into Type I ; the criterion is that the contrast with *king*, and the tone of voice in which *man* is uttered, and the clauses which follow, all form an " immediate context " imposing a special sense of the word, and then the usual sense appears as predicate.

This at least seems the only reasonable way to take it, but you might say that the speakers are not being reasonable. There is a sort of pretence in such a use, you might say, that the " real " or only genuine meaning of *man* is the ideal man, so that this meaning " A+ " is taken as the head one, and the equation " A+=A " is of Type III. No doubt this arrangement is the ideal towards which a pregnancy strives, but it can seldom be achieved ; if it were completely accepted, we would need a new word to cover the work of naming " men in general ". The position is therefore different from that of *sense*, where we have come to accept the meaning " good judgement " as the head one ; at most we only pretend to take the ideal man as the head meaning of *man*. And even then Hamlet's use would not qualify for Type III ; because the subject of this equation, whether regarded as the head meaning of the word or not, has to be imposed very firmly by the immediate context. I suggested that all equations with the interpretation " A is typical of B " might be fitted into Type III ; Hamlet's use of *man* clearly breaks this rule, and I think most of the typifying pregnancies do. Perhaps one could describe them as a sort of playing at Type III.

To be sure, we might get a case where " A+ " acts as subject though the immediate context does not demand it ; then we must either regard " A+ " as the head meaning of the word, so that the equation is genuinely one of Type III, or as a minor meaning which has imposed itself as the subject, so that the equation is of the aberrant Type V. But at any rate these cases are rare. If you take a rosy generalisation like " man is a spirit ", or the phrase H. G. Wells was so fond of, " Man will reach out to the stars ", there is an opportunity for the thing. The immediate context can be satisfied by the meaning " men in general ", and you might think that the ideal man is made subject of the equation all the same. The feeling of the whole passage, it might be argued, makes the ideal man the " only strict and proper " meaning of the word. But I suspect that the function of the pregnancy is merely to make you forget that men may be evil spirits or may do harm in the stars when they arrive. In that case, it is only a qualifying pregnancy, with the equation " men in general are the ideal man (or if they aren't they ought to be, and we will assume they are) ". The imperative with " as " perhaps gives a better way of putting it ; " take men here as the ideal man ". If you make it a Typifying Pregnancy you must be more definitely prepared to exclude someone ; only nice men will be given a passport to the stars, and rough men don't count as spirits. To be sure, whichever way round you put the terms, there is only a contradiction which may be interpreted in various ways ; but if you feel that the ideal man is " what the word really means " in your sentence (it seems to me) you are implying some doctrine which you take seriously. The Connotation process works at a lower level of tension. Perhaps one reason why the tension is usually low in this word, even when the feeling is warm, is that the doctrine remains vague ; if we had two groups of speakers, one saying that the ideal man was virile and the other that he was humane, our use of the equations would have to become more clear-cut. It is true that in general *manly* and the pregnant *man* are " virile ", whereas the pregnant *humanity* and *human*, not having their sex to consider, are " humane " ; but it is not clear that any virtues are excluded from the man who reaches out to the stars. Indeed, women are probably meant too, though the word concentrates on the male (often by a Type III equation) so as to leave them very much in the background.

Contrariwise we need to consider what Swift may have meant, or how his meaning should be formulated, when he said he detested man but loved Tom, Dick and Harry. Or rather, to be definite, he said in a letter to Pope (of 29th Sept. 1725, explaining the design of *Gulliver's Travels*) :

> " I have ever hated all Nations, Professions, and Communities, and all my love is towards individuals ; for instance, I hate the tribe of lawyers, but I love Counsellor such a one, and Judge such a one ; Tis so with Physicians (I will not speak of my own trade) Soldiers, English, Scotch, French, and the rest. But principally I hate and detest that animal called Man, though I heartily love John, Peter, Thomas and the rest."

Mr. R. G. Collingwood, in *The New Leviathan*, says that this was meant to show that the Yahoo was an abstraction only, man conceived as lacking in the voluntary co-operation which makes the good society possible. This seems rather too good-natured if intended as a summary of the feelings of Swift. One might argue, indeed, that the feelings were not rational at all ; Swift gave the word *man* a tied Emotion which did not fit its referents when he encountered them. This process very probably occurred, but it seems clear that something else was going on in his mind too. Thus he may have put a depreciative pregnancy into the word, so that he regarded the Typical Man as vermin but realised (like Hamlet) that most actual men were not examples of the type he had in view. I think he meant a bit more than that again ; the difficulty is to know how far the phrase was a humorous confession (that he was unreasonable) and how far he thought the attitude a coherent one. It is quite coherent to say that you expect men to be bad, and so when a man behaves not too badly you get positively fond of him ; whereas people who expect their neighbours to be angels are always claiming they have been disillusioned. But if you can say this of " Peter " in general you must be admitting that your expectations are generally pitched too low. The phrase " Tom, Dick and

Harry " has a suggestion that these are low-class people, and the random names given by Swift seem to have the same kind of effect in removing dignity from the people in view. But it is clear from the previous sentence that he is not thinking chiefly of the beggars he befriended (in whom the universal rascality of man had a tolerable excuse), and anyway Swift regarded lords as Tom, Dick and Harry too. Certainly you might make him mean, as Mr. Collingwood might seem to do, that the systems which men have produced are what are hateful, whereas with any particular man you can feel that he would be all right under a better system. Probably Pope did not put as much faith as this in systems ; and the suggestion of the previous sentence is that even professions and communities founded on good principles are sure to become corrupt. The simplest explanation would be that even in these communities he can find a few good men, but this seems to be knocked on the head, at any rate as a unique meaning for the passage, by " Peter, Thomas, *and the rest* ". Or he might imply inverted commas and mean " What pompous writers about the Dignity of Man call man ", " what a eulogist of the law would call a lawyer ", and so on ; because what he could not bear was pride. I think there is enough feeling of resistance to common opinion in the passage to put this idea in, but even so it is not prominent (he was chiefly defending himself for the Yahoos). Or, finally, he might mean that the faults of any man are detestable when you regard him as a stranger, but when you know him as a familiar companion (and this could be the suggestion of the Christian names) you get fond of him in spite of his faults ; it need not be regarded as an inconsistency but as an instinct without which we could not carry on. This, I think, was the main idea, but one cannot say that it stands out very prominently. In any case, " I detest man " does not require you to put the detestation inside *man* before it will make sense, whereas the utterance of Hamlet (if it is to have its full dramatic force) actually requires an idealising pregnancy. On the whole, I do not think one need say that *man* is given a pregnancy here at all, though the idea " men in general, regarded as strangers ; man regarded as an abstraction " does seem to be required and could be called a Specialisation. Taken as a joke the thing pretends to expose an unreasonable pregnant use, but it was not only a joke ; and, when you take it seriously, the problem is not how to interpret " man " but how to interpret the Christian names and the phrases like " such a one ".

There is another possible line of distinction here, which perhaps made me unfair to the man who reaches out to the stars. It came up in the chapter on Sense and Sensibility as the difference between " that *is* a lobster " (that lobster is unusually large and fine) and " I only want people to be *human* " (have good-humour and so on).

That is, the pregnant sense of the word may give either the normal or the ideal specimen, and there may also be some confusion between the two. It is still true, I think, that both sorts can give equations both ways round ; you can feel " men *ought* to be normal men " just as easily as " they ought to be ideal men ", and " normal men are typical of men in general " is less absurd than " ideal men are ".

The two orders for the equation in a pregnant use, I maintain, are distinguishable in theory even though sometimes hard to distinguish in practice, and they need different names ; I call them the typifying and the qualifying pregnancy. Both may be either normalising or idealising, but only normalising ones can be depreciative (written " A— "). It might, indeed, be argued that a qualifying pregnancy is not really a pregnancy at all, but I think there is no doubt that the word is actually used to cover some such cases. The force of the objection is rather that the qualifying pregnancy needs to be prevented from including too much. In thinking of men " as having " ordinary virtues you hardly do more than when in saying " there are twenty bricks " you think of bricks *as* countable objects, or when in saying " that's a nice old brick wall " you think of bricks *as* coloured and mellowing with age. Nobody would want to call this a pregnant use of the word *brick* ; if anything it is a Specialisation. The criterion for a qualifying pregnancy, I take it, is that the added quality is felt as in some way required or demanded; it is halfway to a typifying pregnancy ; and the equation has to be either " an ideal A is B " or " a normal A is B ".

Looking back at *native*, the Implication " non-European " came to be felt as a normal attribute of natives, or rather of the word when used with its colonial complex of feeling ; at this stage " non-European " was attached to the word by a (depreciative) Qualifying Pregnancy ; and the switch over to a Typifying Pregnancy, with " non-European " as subject of the equation, would almost coincide with the process of making that idea an independent meaning of the word. It is thus quite a serious step, and not an especially difficult one to recognise.

All this may seem to have little to do with *sense* and *sensibility*, which need not be described as pregnancies at all. But the mode of action of both, when they are treated as a source of doctrines, is I think the same as that of pregnancy. While dealing with the same complex field each picks out one element of it as " typical or essential ", as the thing you bear in mind when dealing with the rest, and it is from this process that the two words get their suasive power. Also, the curious double action of the equations is a normal result of this mode of thought. You have no intention of changing the ideal, and the class of specimens is commonly fixed, but you will argue almost in the same breath both from the ideal to the specimens and from the specimens to the ideal. You are thus ready to alternate between " a good, or normal, or ideal A is B " and " B is the typical form of A ". The difference, of course, is that with *sense* and *sensibility* the " B " is not a vague warm use " A+ " but the accepted head sense of the term, so that the alternation is made less likely than it is in the pregnancies ; I do not think it need be recognised as part of the formula for their equations. But the formula seems to demand a cast-iron accuracy from the listener if he is to get the right effect at all ; and the idea that he can pick it up gradually, because the alternating progress does not send him entirely wrong, seems to me to make the whole picture more plausible.

Chapter 18

METAPHOR

MY business with metaphors here is to discuss their relation to the equation process—whether that is a sort of metaphor, or a metaphor a sort of equation, or if not what connections they have.

There is some danger of going too far afield here. Language is full of sleeping metaphors, and the words for mental processes are all derived from older words for physical processes. What appears to be an existence assertion can therefore often be regarded as a more complex figure of speech. However, the speakers often do not so regard it, and to say that their language is " really " metaphorical does not take us much further. A memory of the derivation of a word (though the present sense may have been formed from it by metaphor) is likely to appear if at all as an Implication; it is often used to fix and clarify the present meaning of the word, not to make it more complicated. However, it has been maintained, with particular eloquence recently by Professor Richards, that all language is " radically metaphoric ". All language is sorting, he says; even in wordless thinking, a thing can only be thought of by classifying it as *of* a sort. The mind " takes no hold if there is nothing for it to draw from, for its thinking is the haul, the attraction of likes ". " Our thought in all cases is being guided by its causal context, and this is only another way of putting the matter." I do not deny the importance and truth of this general account, but to say that you can only call a cat a cat by a metaphor seems to me unduly startling. Certainly, we compare a new experience of a cat with our previous experience of cats, but it is difficult to join this fully extended idea of metaphor onto the ordinary uses of the word. " In metaphor, more narrowly defined ", says Professor Richards, " we cross sorts to make occasional new sorts, but the sorting process is fundamental." On this basis he appears to make a frontal attack (in *The Philosophy of Rhetoric*) on the belief that metaphors proceed by imputing likeness between tenor and vehicle. These, by the way, are his terms for the thing-meant and the thing-said respectively, which badly needed naming, and I shall assume the terms are in current use. But when you examine his language carefully, it seems to me, he is merely saying that the point of likeness need only play a minor part in the total effect. One can agree with this fully and still believe that the hatpeg is functionally important even when hidden by the hat ; for that matter, his radically general sense of " metaphor " itself proceeds by likeness, if I understand him—the haul is the

331

attraction of likes. It seems no more than reasonable that tropes not proceeding by likeness should be given another name. (By the way, Stern also gives a list of metaphors not working by similarity, in fact it seems a traditional view, but his examples seem to me either reducible to likeness or cases of some other trope such as Part for Whole.) Professor Richards seems to take, as a typical example of his Disparity Action, Hamlet's phrase " what do such fellows as I crawling between earth and heaven ", and says :

" When Hamlet uses the word *crawling* its force comes not from whatever resemblances to vermin it brings in but at least equally from the differences that resist and control the influences of these resemblances. The implication there is that man should not so crawl."

Certainly this is the point of the metaphor, but the idea of unlikeness would not be roused unless the likeness had first been imputed. Having thus generalised the idea of metaphor in two different ways, Professor Richards goes on to use phrases which would imply that any of my equations ought to be called a metaphor ; thus metaphor is said to cover (*Rhetoric*, p. 116)

" all cases where a word gives us two ideas for one, where we compound different ideas of the word into one, and speak of one thing as though it were another."

This seems to me an inconvenient generalisation, because some cases of double meaning (compounding two ideas of the word into one) feel entirely different from what is ordinarily called metaphor (speaking of one thing as though it were another), and I think they do actually work in a different way even from Professor Richards' most general sense of the term.

Indeed, it seems a reasonable view that a metaphor is the opposite of an equation. A metaphor goes outside the ordinary range of a word, and an equation " argues from " the ordinary range, treating it as a source of traditional wisdom. The only reason why this distinction is not clear-cut is that many metaphors are themselves traditional, and have therefore gone part of the way towards extending the word's range of meaning. Nevertheless, two meanings definitely within this range can get connected not at all because an old metaphor is revived but to impute some new relation, sometimes not involving likeness at all, and anyway not involving the likeness which was the old ground of the shift, nor yet treating any new likeness as the peg which makes the new combination possible ; it is possible merely because it is already supplied by the word. Such a process, I submit, needs to be called by a different name from metaphor.

None the less, it might be argued that every metaphor carries a covert assertion, even if a trivial one. One might say then that metaphors are one of the sorts of equation, instead of the other way round. I do not think this is so either, unless you limit metaphors to " true " metaphors by a special definition. In the first place, a newly invented metaphor does not put its covert assertion " into the word " ; the word simply means one thing and is used for another, and the assertion that these things have a point of likeness is made by the whole phrase or sentence rather than the word. Of course, this phrase " in the word " is itself metaphorical, and may seem a shaky ground for distinction ; but until the metaphor is habitual the implied assertion cannot impose itself as a piece of common knowledge. It may be convenient sometimes to extend the idea of an equation to nonce-uses. But if we try to include in a theory about double meanings everything that might be required for the exegesis of a piece of writing I feel sure that we will fail ; what is wanted is something more modest, an account of the tools which a writer finds already prepared for him. In the second place, many metaphors seem too obvious to carry equations ; they do not feel like covert assertion but like direct description. Here again, an appeal to feelings does not have much logical cogency, but I have to define my term " equation " as seems best, and I have only feelings to go by in trying to hit on a good definition. The term had better correspond to what the speakers themselves feel to be a rich or suggestive or persuasive use of a word, rather than include uses like the *leg* of a table. Now a number of writers on metaphor have distinguished between two types of it, the " transfer " like the leg of the table and the Metaphor proper, which Stern puts under Nomination. The ground of the distinction has varied a good deal, but it seems clear that the distinction is a real one ; and I propose now to give it yet another ground. Metaphors, I suggest, are not transfers, and also do carry equations, if and only if they imply a pregnant use of the term for the vehicle. Thus " true " metaphors are the only ones with equations. This cuts out the very trivial examples, though it still leaves us with a lot of minor ones ; and it clears up the point about " in the word ", because pregnant uses are in the word in any case.

I ought now to try and sketch the alternative grounds which have been put forward for the distinction between metaphor and transfer. Stern in *Meaning and Change of Meaning* distinguishes true metaphor as intentional, emotive, dependent on context, and accompanied by " psychic resistance " ; he also quotes from Stahlin, without fully accepting, the conditions that true metaphor " does not involve an essential identity of the two referents " and that " the designation is taken from another sphere of experience from that to which the actual referent belongs ". The last has an air of picking out something important, but Stern objects that when you call a grasping moneylender a Jew :

" there is no *essential* identity involved, since the moneylender is not literally a Jew ; the designation is figurative. But it seems to be doubtful whether we should say that the designation is taken from an alien sphere."

Without wishing to join in this piece of continental fun, I should claim that " Jew " in such a case is given a pregnant use (implying among other things " moneylender "), as it would still be if the moneylender were literally a Jew, and that this is why the thing seems evidently not a " transfer " like the leg of the table. One possible meaning for the German phrase about Involving an Essential Identity is that a transfer is easily absorbed as a literal meaning of the word, perhaps with a rather narrow definition of it ; Professor Richards has pointed out that the leg of a table is both literal and metaphorical at once, according to which of two equally plausible ideas of a strict " leg " may come into your mind. This seems clearly a sufficient condition for calling such a case merely a transfer, though perhaps not a necessary one. Going back to the criteria of Stern, it seems to me that his " intentional, emotive, and dependent on context ", so far as they are justified, all follow from his " psychic resistance ". The thing is felt as a sort of break in the flow, requiring interpretation, exciting attention and perhaps other feelings. The only trouble about this as a defining property is that we hear nothing about other cases where there is psychic resistance ; we have no control experiment. Surely a man reading a bill often feels a strong psychic resistance to absorbing the meaning of the figures, and yet without any tendency to treat them as metaphorical. Why should it be assumed that there is never any such resistance to a simple transfer ? Indeed, the ladies in *Cranford*, who put the legs of their tables into trousers, probably did feel a psychic resistance to saying " the leg of a table ", and this not because they found the analogy remote (a case of " true metaphor ") but because they took them for real legs. The kind of psychic resistance in view, therefore, needs defining more narrowly. I submit that it is the feeling of resistance to a false identity, which we have already found fundamental in the equation form. The reason why resistance is called for is that you have to pick out the right elements from the vehicle, the parts of it which are treated as " typical and essential " for the case in hand ; if you merely accept the false identity you may fall into nonsense. And when the vehicle is typified it becomes pregnant by definition. Whereas in the case of transfer, though a logician might produce possible alternative grounds for the shift, the hearer feels that there is no difficulty and nothing to be typified. Perhaps I am trying to make too many different criteria collapse into one line of distinction, but the distinction itself seems a genuine one. The rose of metaphor is an ideal rose, which involves a variety of vague suggestions and probably does not involve thorns, but the leaf of transfer is merely leafish.

There are sure to be doubtful cases on the borderline. My first example of Type I was the mountain-saddle equation, and maybe this would be regarded as a clear case of transfer. How the thing works is presumably not in doubt ; the question is whether it is worth calling a true metaphor (now become a stock one) and an equation (even when stock). No doubt many uses of *saddle* for mountain-saddle do not make any double reference at all. But I think you often get cases where there is Psychic Resistance over a question of identity, because the shape is not obvious—you are being told the lie of the ground, which you cannot see from where you stand; the minor confusions of the contouring have to be ignored before the essential fact can emerge. When the word is used " predicatively " like this, so that the fact that the thing is a saddle is what is in question, I think you get a sort of equation even if you accept " mountain-saddle " as a separate meaning of the word, and the idea of the original metaphor is practically forgotten. Of course, if the comparison is treated poetically it is undoubtedly metaphorical, but I should have thought it was already a metaphor if used as a source of information. For you are classifying the bit of mountain as of a certain type, and thereby thinking of it as a simpler shape than it really is ; this typifying is already a faint pregnancy ; and if you remember the horse-saddle as the standard shape, as it is natural to do, the pregnancy becomes a metaphor.

We ought to make some attempt at connecting the idea of metaphor to the idea of Range, that is, a class named by the word as apart from its defining property, or a class for which a particular defining property is given to the word, as in the use of *honest* for " Of women : Chaste ". The mind does not in general use words without attaching to them both a class and its defining property, however vaguely, but owing to the creative looseness of the mind it can sometimes use defining properties which, apart from the aggregate of experience which can be tapped by one word, remain obscure. Cases where a word seems to leave its usual Range successfully often occur when the conscious mind has its eye on a few important elements in the situation and the classifying sub-conscious is called on for a suggestive word. This is how people invent metaphors, but you can get the same effect of surprise from an unexpected word which seems to fit very well, even when there is no need to call it a metaphor. The process may be like a " construction " in Euclidean geometry ; you draw a couple of lines joining points which are already in the diagram, and then the proof seems obvious, though till then the right " aspect " of the thing was nowhere in sight. It seems clear that when a man is hitting on the *mot juste* he does not have to notice whether it is a metaphor or not. So I am very willing to agree with Professor Richards that the notion of metaphor ought to admit of an extremely wide generalization, something that would apply to any case where you feel that the word " fits ". But I feel that this more general notion needs to be something present in metaphor and yet capable of appearing without it, and the notion of a " pregnant " use which picks out the right handle to take hold of the bundle seems to be what is required. Any pregnancy can be regarded as a confusion about Range, or a failure to make the defining property fit the class, though I do not think that that formulation is a convenient one when you try to follow the process in detail.

One might think that the real difference between metaphor and transfer, the criterion which people have fumbled after without catching it, is that a true metaphor yields more than one ground of likeness whereas a transfer does not. This simple answer is I think certainly wrong. It would make the *saddle* a transfer, since the likeness there is only one of shape, but that might be reasonable. On the other hand it could hardly avoid making a metaphor out of the *leaf* of a book, which is so often used as a standard example of a transfer. The ideas " thin " and " flat on the surface " might be said to make up one idea about the shape ; but both leaves are also " not heavy " and " normally attached to a more solid object by one outside part ". The ground of likeness is thus rather complicated, but we still do not feel that it has the richness of a true metaphor. The effect of the pregnancy, if I am to sustain my definition, has to be of a different kind.

Here I need to recognise that a more elaborate account of our dealings with metaphor has been given by Father S. J. Brown, in *The World of Imagery*. As I understand him, he maintains that whenever the tenor and vehicle are drawn from different " orders " (and this was one of the suggested criteria for a true metaphor which I listed before) the assertion made by the metaphor has the form of a proportion scheme. For example the metaphor in " You should try to root out your faults one by one " requires (p. 48) :

(1) a main idea *faults* (" a "), the real subject of the discourse, (2) a concrete image *weeds* (" x "), unexpressed but implied, (3) a perceived resemblance or analogy between " a " and " x ", involving in this case the further metaphor that the *soul* " b " is like a *garden* " y ", (4) a momentary and tacit identification of " a " with " x ", in such a way that language properly applicable to " x " may be used of " a."

The resultant meaning of the metaphor is then given by the proportion scheme " a:b=x:y ", " faults are to the soul as weeds to the garden ". The term *identification* here seems to be only a way of describing the belief in this statement of proportion. The ground of the comparison, the point of likeness, is still not expressed by the proportion scheme ; which merely controls the interpretation of the metaphor (or of the " identity ", perhaps) by giving the fields from which the two ideas are drawn ; and the fields are in some sense part of the range of the words themselves, so there is no great difficulty about finding them. But as the book goes on, Father Brown is not content with this proportion scheme, at any rate in doctrinal cases ; a more complex arrangement is required before such a metaphor can be said to make a wholly true statement. " Ye are the light of the world " is made to involve an eight-fold proportion " the relation of the relation of apostles to the enlightenment they give to that of spiritual cause to spiritual effect is identical to the relation of the relation of a source of light to the light it gives to that of physical cause to physical effect ". Cause and effect, according to Aquinas, though not univocal terms are also not merely equivocal ones, but analogous, so that there is really something in common between the two sorts of them. When Christ made this metaphor he may, therefore, have meant something exactly and permanently true, though perhaps only the Logos could know just what it was. It is tempting to reply that a linguist is concerned with the more common trope employed by the race of man. But the leap here to the ideal case is only like that made in elementary geometry, for example, where we argue about perfect straight lines although we know that we cannot draw them. It would be an important step to decide what a metaphor must do if it is to tell an exact truth, even if we never in practice make it do that completely.

I think, indeed, that a still more rationalistic view might well be taken. Before dealing with " You should root out your faults one by one " Father Brown expresses a doubt, perhaps of a theological kind, in a subordinate clause ; " leaving to those competent to judge it the feasibility of this piece of advice ", he will examine the imagery it contains. But this question is more relevant than it appears ; we do not know what the metaphor means till we know what advice it is giving. Father Brown says, " the point of resemblance may be called the point or scope of the comparison involved in the metaphor ", and in this case it is simply that vices and weeds are both found where they are not wanted and ought not to be. There is a term going begging here, because the same thing is called the point and the scope ; I have usually called it the " ground ", and perhaps the " scope " had better be kept for all the likenesses one might consider, rather than the one operative one, as it sounds broad. But in any case the real function of the metaphor here, or in ordinary English the *point* of it, is to suggest a technique for getting rid of faults. You are to take them out, even the roots, one at a time ; for example, make sure you are not cheating at all before you proceed to give up envy. No doubt one could force the parallel to give different advice. The only metaphorical word here is *root*, and others could be chosen, e.g., " Rid your soul of its weeds ". There is a theory that if you scythe a bed of nettles for three successive years the roots are exhausted, so that you can " rid yourself " without " rooting one by one " ; on the other hand, you might say that the original advice is too superficial rather than too meticulous, and that you ought to dig two spades deep over the whole garden, even where there are no weeds. But whichever way you take it the parallel must be supposed to recommend some process. To say that its function is Emotive seems to me merely a way of saying that it is a frigid piece of decoration ; the vices themselves are better equipped to excite emotion than the weeds. No doubt there is an encouraging suggestion that the activity required is a merely practical one, but even this seems to involve a vague idea of a technique. Now the two processes which are said to be alike will in general depend on the verbs ; " rid " the soul, "root out " or " dig under " or what not the weeds. These would make a third term in each half of the proportion scheme, and indeed there seems no reason why the structure should not have more terms still. It is in any case a paradox that in Father Brown's account *root*, the only word which shows that there is a metaphor, does not come into the final sentence at all. A scheme which put it in would include the " point ", and one would think it had better also include his " scope ". But this is merely the idea that weeds and vices are unwanted, so perhaps it reduces to one of the Emotions involved. It seems to me that a suggestion of further argument, of possible deductions from the parallel, is a very regular part of the effects of a metaphor ; whereas Father Brown only considers whether arguments can be based on metaphors later in the book, and there he is chiefly concerned to say that they are treacherous.

I take it that his rather intellectualist approach was forced upon him to avoid belittling the words of Christ, and then he felt he should balance this by recognising that most metaphors are essentially emotive. Thus the creation of new metaphors, he says, is " the outcome of an emotional mood reacting . . . on the imagination " and so on. Metaphor, he goes on to say, does not necessarily obscure thought, indeed, it may be " quite clear and illuminating, but only on two conditions ; it must be easily resolvable into the underlying simile or comparison, and that simile or comparison must be obvious ". This seems to me a wrong result due to confusion about what the Emotions may be, or perhaps to suspicion of them. Professor Richards has put the opposite point of view very resoundingly :

METAPHOR

> "It is a fundamental truth that we can sort things rightly without knowing how we sort them. If we could not do this we could never know anything. . . . Between merely recognising things and being able, in reflection, to discern the respect of likeness there is an immense gap in development. Chimpanzees perhaps cross it here and there ; the lower animals probably never do."

Obviously a metaphor may be a matter of " insight " ; it may be used to survey a whole complicated matter as if from a height ; it is a device for letting you handle the proportions of the matter intuitively, instead of fiddling about with first one part and then another. Mr. Herbert Read was getting at the same point in *English Prose Style* when he said :

> "Metaphor is the synthesis of several units of observation into one commanding image ; it is the expression of a complex idea, not by analysis, nor by direct statement, but by a sudden perception of an objective relation."

It is clear that we may do this before we can explain it ; in fact, the " underlying simile " may be much more obvious to the subconscious than to the conscious mind. It is ordinary experience that we can often " see our way through " a complicated situation, when it is presented in a handy and practical form, though to tease out all the elements and put them into a theoretical argument may be slow and hard. Original pieces of thinking have, I suppose, nearly always been started on metaphor, and so far from being peculiarly " emotive " and indulgent of folly a metaphor is often a loophole for common sense ; when a man is dutifully deceiving himself he will often admit the truth in his metaphors. Indeed, there is evidence from the psychologists that the thought behind a metaphor may be wider than it looks at first sight ; Spearman made some experiments which were claimed to show that the mind can " educe correlates " when the ideas are extremely faint, so long as they are " definite ". In any case, there is no advantage for a theory of metaphor in confusing this kind of process with one that drowns the intellect in a storm of passion.

Professor Richards has described some metaphors as " irreducible ", in that an adequte translation of their sense cannot be made by finding a ground of likeness and asserting it in a proportion scheme. He seems to imply that such metaphors are always used not for their Sense but because they suit the Emotion, Tone or Intention of the speaker or writer, and I am not sure that this follows. Of course, I do not deny that they are chosen because they suit the man's feelings, but he cannot tell whether his feelings are merely Emotions or some subtle kind of Intuition, and I do not see that we can decide offhand either. More exactly, they are chosen because what the speaker feels about the tenor is like what he feels about the vehicle, and in a phrase like " she's a duck " there would be no point in denying that the likeness is entirely concerned with his sentiments or attitudes ; both objects are viewed with affection, amusement, patronage, and a sense that they are reliably limited and complete. At least, that seems the usual way of taking the thing, though even here there is a suggestion of a technique in dealing with the creatures ; a tendency to specific actions would appear to be in view, not merely an Emotion. But it seems to me that other phrases apparently just like this one, such as the ones I was looking at in the " Dog " chapter, bring in such a very complicated background that they are best viewed as a meeting-ground of two rival theologies. There is no objection to calling them Emotive—indeed, it is not clear what else they could be called—but this term ought not to be erected into an excuse for dullness when we are trying to understand them.

A distinction could be drawn (as I said about Hamlet's use of *man*) according as an argument goes through the metaphor or not. " Being across the stream I felt safe from the tiger, judging that like all cats it would dislike wetting its fur." Sense " 1 " " domestic cat " has an Implication " hating wetness ", and this is transferred to Sense " 2 " " any member of the cat family ". The process, I think, is felt to be a metaphor, but the man takes the classification seriously enough to make deductions from it, even if he implies humorously " this was the best I could at the time ". The equation, of course, is " tigers are like cats ". But consider " Mrs. Thompson's sure to like cream in her tea because she's a cat ". Sense " 3 " " malicious woman " may be felt to carry a profoundly suitable metaphor, so that the ground of the shift though obscure is felt to be real. And as a joke the argument pretends to go through the metaphor, that is, to make a deduction from the classification of such women among (animal) cats. But it seems clear that the real argument would not, supposing there is one, even when the metaphor is taken as a source of wisdom. The argument is something like " polite but malicious people, who reserve their force and don't ask for sympathy (qualities which are enough to get them compared to cats) are always fond of petty but concentrated luxuries (also like cats, and the reasons are the same as whatever they are in the case of cats) ". That is, you are claiming to understand these people already ; the use of the metaphor is to say the thing vividly, not to give reasons for it. Indeed, the reasons are just about as obscure, though not beyond conjecture, when you think about the cats as when you think about the people. This gives the application of the metaphor a sort of remoteness, and one might describe the effect by calling the metaphor Emotive, but there may still be a good deal of thought knocking about behind it. Here, as in the case of pregnancy, the distinction about where the argument goes does not seem to me a fundamental one.

A hearty pursuit of these lines of thought tends to bring back an unpleasant complexity into the distinctions which I have been trying to treat as simple. If it is merely two relations, perhaps rather remote ones somewhere in the field, which are being identified or compared, let alone two "feelings", the idea of likeness between tenor and vehicle may become very strained. The distinction between likeness and identity must indeed be supposed to collapse, because there must be some degree of elaboration of the proportion scheme after which you could say that there is an identical relation in both the two things compared. Putting it another way, once an equation between tenor " A " and vehicle " B " has been established on the pretence of likeness, so that it is presumed to have the form " A is like B ", we might easily shift the interpretation of this equation to some much more complicated form. The reason why Professor Richards was so keen to make all language metaphorical, I suspect, was partly that he felt one can never be sure what is a verbal fiction and what is not. In any word, then, we may be having to make some elaborate play with proportion schemes before we can use it sensibly at all. This view has been put very dramatically by Scott Buchanan in a charming little book, *Symbolic Distance*, which uses the analogy of projective geometry all the way through. *Every* point (or simple meaning) can be regarded as origin of an indefinite number of line-pencils, each of which would lay out on any line sideways to it a cross-ratio (or one of Father Brown's proportion schemes) ; and *every* line (or direction of thought) through this one point makes it carry an infinite number of invisible cross-ratios (or proportion schemes) reduced to noughts divided by noughts. The book itself seemed to me rather like this, because it was so suggestive that it no longer suggested anything ; and I think at this point we must become irritated with the claims of the sub-conscious mind no less than with those of the Logos. We had better stick to what the fool of a conscious mind is doing, if we can be sure that it is so distinct from our unconscious wisdom. It seems to me that what we start from, in a metaphor as distinct from a transfer, is a recognition that " false identity " is being used, a feeling of " resistance " to it, rather like going into higher gear, because the machinery of interpretation must be brought into play, and then a feeling of richness about the possible interpretations of the word, which has now become a source of advice on how to think about the matter, so that we regard it as " pregnant ". It does not seem much use trying to symbolize how we go on with the thinking, for one reason because it may be so different in different people. As a rule, I think, the proportion scheme can be shown without further symbolism as the way in which the equation gets interpreted. But in trying to simplify the thing like this, it seems hard to deny, I am making the idea of pregnancy carry a heavy load.

If it is agreed that all (true) metaphors carry pregnancies, I have still to decide whether they are typifying or qualifying ones, and the answer, I think, is that they may be either. (The decision that qualifying ones can count as pregnancies thus turns out to be convenient in dealing with metaphor.) In a standard metaphor such as " Richard I was a lion " it seems clear that the pregnancy is a typifying one ; the equation says " courage is the typical property of lions ", and then the actual sentence, when we take the subject of the equation as the chief meaning of the word, will say " Richard I was brave ". The lion is so definitely treated as a symbol that this seems a natural account. But it is clear that we might also read the copula in the sentence as meaning " is like ", and then the equation must take the qualities of the lion as predicate ; " Richard I was like a lion ", " and lions are brave ". Furthermore, even granting that the ground of the metaphor is treated as typical, there can be other ideas which appear merely as qualifiers. Even in this simple example the feeling may go either of two ways ; we may think " bravery is typical of lions, and they are magnanimous ", or we may think " and they are cruel ". And this is the part that may need attention or lead to surprising results ; the reason why metaphors can be so rich is that they easily carry both sorts of pregnancy at once.

Stern's account of this metaphor is that we fail to think of a good word for " brave " so we take a word that includes " brave " among other things and presume we can lop off the rest of its meaning. All the other elements in the complex *lion* are simply disregarded ; we do not think of the lion's tail, he says. This seems to be the old question of thought by images ; it is a matter of taste. On such an account I doubt if the use would be worth calling a metaphor, and in the case of a symbolic beast I think it is clearly wrong. But in less striking cases, no doubt, we sometimes do tumble on an apparently adequate word without realising how little it fits, so that in effect we are using metaphor unconsciously. Whether the metaphor can be made to carry important implications later is then a matter of luck, and the first use of it should, I think, simply be called a Transfer invented for the occasion.

" Richard was a lion " happens to use a copula which we can translate as " is like ", and such a form might be used while the metaphor was being introduced so that it could be swallowed easily. But in a normal full metaphor (" Seven times the lion of England renewed the charge " or what not) there is no let-out of this kind. Normally, in the terms of Professor Richards, you have a " tenor " which is " what is really meant " and a " vehicle " which has a fixed meaning quite different to that. On my definitions the tenor has to act as subject and the vehicle as predicate, so the equation is of Type I. However, this is not sufficient, because Richard himself seems to be what is " really meant ", and the equation merely becomes " Richard is a lion ". The process of interpretation has not yet started. Also the term " typical ", when we proceed with interpreting by that, is itself a very slippery one ; you can say " courage is typical of lions ", but it might well be more relevant here to say " lions are typical of courage ". Indeed, though I am unwilling to make the thing elaborate, there seems no doubt that two processes of typification are going on. The vehicle is made typical of the tenor, and the ground of the likeness is made typical of the vehicle. The lion typifies the virtues of Richard (because it is brave) ; but to do this the lion needs to have courage as its typical virtue. In the ordinary pregnant use of a word the difference between typifying and qualifying is fairly recognisable, and may have practical effects ; but in a metaphor the pregnancy gets put into a whole situation of typifying, and the difference becomes unimportant.

However, I think it can be observed, if we compare " Richard was a lion " to " You should root out your faults one by one ". In the second sentence the only metaphorical word is *root*, and I do not see that any quality is taken as typical of rooting. We could, perhaps, say that " take " is the tenor here, since that would make the sentence unmetaphorical if it took the place of the vehicle. Then we get the other kind of typifying all right ; " rooting out is the typical process to consider when you wonder how to take out your faults ". But it seems clear that *root out*, in itself, does not yield anything till the considering has got started ; " and a normal process of rooting out ", you might go on, " involves feeling down to the bottom to make sure none of the root is left, before you go on to the next weed ". This is the order of ideas required for a qualifying pregnancy ; you do not know at once what is typical of rooting, and certainly do not give the word an unusual chief meaning. Of course, the contrast depends on how far the ideas are already fixed ; if your ideas are very settled on this topic you may feel " Getting the whole of the thing out is what is essential in all forms of rooting out ", and put that equation into *root* as soon as the word appears, just as courage is the stock typical property of lions. I am only concerned to argue that the metaphor might be taken either way, and that whichever way it is taken the metaphorical word is treated as a pregnant one. And no doubt the full understanding of the metaphor may require a more elaborate process of thought, involving proportion schemes and so on ; but I think that the double structure of the pregnancy gives us a good start.

It is agreed that metaphors easily excite images ; indeed, some writers simply call them images. One reason for this, I think, is that they typify ; the rose of metaphor is not all the various sorts of rose but the ideal rose, and this is easily felt as specific so that you can picture it according to taste. A " type " is already a sort of picture, indeed that seems to be the origin of the word. Owing to this process, it is likely to have accidental properties added to it merely to make it definite. This is rather confusing for the purpose in hand, because we want to have one property picked out by the pregnancy, not a heap of them, some of which aren't relevant ; but I think the extras can simply be treated as the effects of a " qualifying pregnancy " added after the " typifying " one. It is clear that the same process can go on without any use of metaphor at all. The pictures of the Aryan Man in the popular textbooks, which Hilaire Belloc laughed at to good purpose (" be as like him as you can "), did not merely give this figure his racial features in a specially complete form but made him a modest and high-minded product of one of the more expensive English public schools. He was not only idealised but particularised. Of course, the ordinary pregnant use of a word cannot carry this process so far, and if it did the speaker and hearer would be sure to have different pictures, but it has a tendency in that direction. In the same way, we expect the vehicle of a metaphor to be " concrete " whereas the tenor is " abstract " ; it is concrete, if for no other reason, because there is a pretence that it is specific. The same feeling comes out in the curious grammatical form " the spur *of* fame ", " shall I now drop the needle of insinuation and pick up the club of statement ? " The N.E.D. treats this use of the genitive as analogous to " a cake of soap ", " a house of brick ", " a piece of paper " ; the vehicle is a particular thing " made out of " the general mass of the tenor. One might also feel, I think, that insinuation *has* a needle, just as Jove has a thunderbolt, because that is his mode of operation. But taken flatly as a piece of grammar the " of " feels very like " which is ", indeed, one could actually say " the needle which is insinuation ". And the order of terms here, if I may complete the circle of ideas, is that of " A is typical of B ".

Writers on metaphor often speak of an identification or fusion of the two ideas presented, and I should applaud this as recognising that the same process of false identity is at work there as in the equation form. They might simply mean that the possible interactions, the different equations one might impute, are so various and hard to tease out, though they do not interfere with one another in practice, that the two meanings seem to have become organically connected. But certainly it is not always clear what this " identification " means ; even the modest use of the term by Father Brown seemed to be thrown in as an extra, an imaginative gratification by the way. I think there is a way of taking it in which would mean something quite different. Both these stock terms are treated with some irritation by Professor Richards (*Interpretation in Teaching*, p. 121), who says :

> "A taste for the fusion metaphor in discussing metaphor, and the implication that fusions are superior, is perhaps connected with the feelings behind the term *creative*. Tenor and vehicle are like two men acting together. We do not understand them better by supposing that they somehow fuse to become a third man who is neither. Moreover equal prominence and fusion (if we take fusion strictly) are not the same, and it is obviously best to make as few assumptions here as possible."

Of course, I agree that these terms are worth very little unless one takes them seriously and interprets them. The case where the two men produce a third man, according to my theory, only occurs in an equation of Type IV, and I do not think that a recognisable metaphor is likely to do it. Such a case does require " equal prominence ", but it does not appear that most writers who describe the effect of metaphors as a fusion would say that fusion only occurred when tenor and vehicle had equal prominence. What these writers are trying to describe by their metaphor, I think, and what I am trying to describe too, is a fundamental (and therefore primitive) process of thought which is at once re-interpreted by the healthy mind. What Professor Richards dislikes, on the other hand, is a suggestion that readers of poetry had better remain content with what he calls " somnial magic ", or rather that they should deliberately cultivate a barbaric habit of thinking by false identity. I approve his moral but suspect him of distorting the facts to preach it. The stimulus to interpret the false identity ought to come at once from the " psychic resistance " to it, and the combination of these two processes, I am maintaining, is the only equipment we have for absorbing and starting to digest an unexpected metaphor or equation.

Equal prominence for tenor and vehicle, I think, is of the nature of allegory, though it is not usually given that name unless it goes on for some time.

> *O could I flow like thee, and make thy stream*
> *My great example, as it is my theme !*
> *Though deep, yet clear, although gentle yet not dull,*
> *Strong without rage, without o'er flowing full.*

Professor Richards pointed out that some of the adjectives apply more directly to the river, some to the poem, and that your attention is kept moving from one to the other. It is certainly a fine case of Mutual Comparison ; both parties are elevated by it ; both are made interesting and real. I should only say that it is different from the ordinary process of metaphor; the effect of sustaining the comparison is to call out feelings of sympathetic magic. It is an invocation; the river is asked to make a good poem, and in any case, the river is what the poetry is about, so that it is not even obvious which is tenor and which is vehicle. Part of the function of an allegory is to make you feel that two levels of being correspond to one another in detail, and indeed that there is some underlying reality, something in the nature of things, which makes this happen. Either level may illuminate the other, and the words which apply to both are therefore (if taken seriously enough) given equations of my fourth type. But an ordinary metaphor does not carry fourth-type equations; it may involve all the other three, but there is no question of the order of terms becoming indifferent. Of course, it would seem fussy to deny that the adjectives here are metaphors, but the reason why they have " equal prominence " is that they are allegorical and therefore take a special type of equation.

No doubt this feels like a high degree of identification or fusion between tenor and vehicle. But I think there is no need to limit those terms to such a case; and indeed, I suspect that a quite different process is often what is in view when people have this feeling. Long ago there was a controversy in the *Times Literary Supplement* about Father Brown's book on metaphor; he had placidly offered an example, without giving the answer, as a difficult but rewarding test of his proportion scheme, and it appeared that the scheme could not be made to fit. The problem was the word *time* in a passage from Shakespeare:

> What custom willed in all things should we do it
> The dust on antique time would lie unswept
> And mountainous error lie so highly heaped
> The truth could not o'erpeer.

Much ingenuity was exercised, and I thought without success, on trying to get a proportion scheme for *time* here; but surely the main point is that it is the abstract idea common to all the processes which are compared. You may no doubt object that Old Father Time contrives to appear as an Antic, another case of the ubiquitous clown, but that is only tied onto the passage as a decoration and will not fit the argument simply. Or you might say that *time* to Shakespeare meant " occasion, period, opportunity ", so that it is not fully abstract but one of the elements of the proportion schemes. But, though a " past period of history with all its special conditions " is somehow in view, the question is whether we are to keep the custom now, after this lapse of time. As so often in Shakespeare, you could get a tidier metaphor by an emendation (putting " laws " instead of *time*) but you would lose the effect not merely of richness but of breadth, or even of simplicity. What has happened, it seems clear, is that, instead of "educing a correlate" for a proportion-scheme, his mind has "educed" what was to have been the hidden ground of the comparison ; and it is only by thinking of specialised meanings of the word that we can partly justify its claim to be a term in a proportion.

Thus the two ideas compared here do not merely illuminate one another, as in an allegory ; they produce a third more general idea which reduces them to the status of examples or illustrations. The metaphor as such is destroyed, not because the examples are not worth having or not alike but because we are no longer interested in which is the vehicle and which is the tenor ; they are on the same footing. This process too, I submit, corresponds to my fourth type of equation within a single word. In a clear-cut case like this, where there is no doubt about the third idea, I suppose the process should simply be called Generalisation ; but in a case where we have a feeling that it has occurred but the third idea remains vague we need a special term, and I am inclined to call it Mutual Metaphor. The objection to the name is that it seems to describe a kind of metaphor, whereas it marks a virtual abandonment of the metaphor previously used ; but I think people still feel that the process is somehow metaphorical, so that the name is not out of place ; indeed, the people who wrote letters to the *Times Literary Supplement* all seem to have accepted *time* as a metaphor in this passage from Shakespeare. If we call it a Mutual Metaphor we are left with Mutual Comparison to describe a case like " without o'erflowing full ", and this seems a clumsy arrangement because the cases that are real metaphors have to give up that term to the cases that aren't. But the effect of allegory is to keep the two levels of being very distinct in your mind, though they interpenetrate one another in so many details, and this feels like Comparison, whereas what I am calling Mutual Metaphor gives much more effect of making the two cases collapse into one. Here then is Professor Richards' " third man " resulting from the process of " fusion ", and he is not such a witch-doctor as he was suspected of being ; but he does not appear at all frequently.

Incidentally, when you do get cases of Professor Richards' Disparity Action in a pure form, I think they can be classed as Mutual Metaphor and not as Metaphor. The most promising candidates are the refrains of ballads :

> She leaned her back against a thorn
> (*Fine flowers in the valley*)
> And there she has her young child born
> (*And the green leaves they grow rarely*).

The effect of the contrast is not simple ; perhaps it says " Life went on, and in a way this seems a cruel indifference to her suffering, but it lets us put the tragedy in its place, as we do when we sing about it for pleasure." And you might say that the birth of the child and the growth of the plants are treated as both natural, so that in a remote way they are compared. But the flowers in the valley and the girl on the hill are both meant to be really there ; she will illuminate them as soon as they her. The likeness, I think, comes in if at all as a faint Mutual Metaphor, so that there is no need to call the thing a Metaphor as such even when further meanings are extracted from it.

Finally, though Metaphor and Mutual Metaphor are distinct in principle, I do not deny that they can be combined. Mr. Middleton Murry, in discussing metaphor, made some interesting comments on one of the great phrases of Cleopatra ; and according to his interpretation, at any rate, the passage gives us an example :

> *My desolation does begin to make*
> *A better life. 'Tis paltry to be Caesar.*
> *Not being Fortune, he's but Fortune's knave,*
> *A minister of her will ; and it is great*
> *To do that thing that ends all other deeds,*
> *Which shackles accidents, and bolts up change,*
> *Which sleeps, and never palates more the dug,*
> *The beggar's nurse, and Caesar's.*

" It is not the dug but Death which is the beggar's nurse and Caesar's. Death which in the previous line was the child sleeping against the heart becomes the bosom that receives mankind. We may say it is the mere verbal suggestion which links the metaphors . . . but the one metaphor grows immediately out of the other. The vague ' thing ' from which the images take their rise, swiftly groped after, shapes before our mind's eye, and finally achieves a full realization—the beggar's nurse and Caesar's."

That is, *nurse* appears at first to be in apposition to *dug*, but shifts so that it is in apposition to *that thing*. On the first view, the person after death " takes no more food and pleasure from Nature who sustains us all ", on the second he " returns to Nature the universal spirit on losing individuality ; and she gives him the same comfort whether he is Caesar or beggar ". As the reflections on Death continue, the idea of it is extended to become also the source of life ; there is a generalization of the darkness to which we go, so that it includes the darkness from which we come ; and a vague pantheism arises to justify the word as one new concept. There is a reason for this, as Mr. Murry points out, in that Cleopatra being an incarnation of Love conceives Death as a consummation of love ; the earlier phrases in the list treat it as a sort of vow of constancy, then the final phrase treats it as the source from which life comes, and it is a sort of act of sex. (I agree with him in preferring *dug* to *dung*, but the idea of flowers growing out of decomposing manure has the same pantheism and gives the same ambiguity of syntax.) The process of thought seems intelligible, though of course very rich, and I do not see why it led Mr. Murry to say that we cannot avoid transcendentalism. I bring it in here to discuss whether it is Mutual Metaphor, and cannot pretend that the difference of that trope from Metaphor is very obvious here. The two ideas attached to death are " love " and " peace ". The peculiar absorption of consciousness during the orgasm (the collapse of one's everyday mental connections) seems to be the basis of the first stock metaphor ; the second is obvious, but she heightens it by making the person at peace a baby, abandoned to sleep more deeply than grown-ups. (" Dost thou not see my baby at my breast ", said of the asp, may be cited as evidence that this idea is really present.) Having now got the baby into the picture she can connect these rival ideas of death, as sleep and as the source of new life, and the compound is a new idea (however vaguely adumbrated) of the universal spirit into which she will be dissolved. My definition of Mutual Metaphor said that tenor and vehicle are treated as examples of some wider concept which transcends them, and upsets the ordinary scheme of interpretation ; here two vehicles have to combine with each other as well as with the tenor, and an ambiguity of syntax is needed to tie them all up ; but the result seems to deserve the same name. I am not sure that any technical term is much help here, but this name does seem to me to sum up what Mr. Murry was describing, without dragging in any metaphysics except the bits of it which we can reasonably suppose were in the mind of the author. And I think this trope is present in the metaphors here in proportion as you take them to yield equations of the fourth type.

Chapter 19

A is B

SINCE I am assuming that the covert assertion in a word is normally to be translated " A is B ", I need to examine that grammatical form by itself ; not indeed with any aim at completeness, but to decide whether, on the one side, the actual behaviour of an intra-verbal equation can be covered by " A is B " reasonably well, and on the other whether " A is B " can be interpreted in other ways not found in intra-verbal equations. The aim is to find whether this way of interpreting an equation is likely to leave an important meaning out or put in one which isn't there.

We are concerned mainly with what may be called gnomic uses of " A is B ", in which both terms are used generally and somewhat vaguely. I said when introducing the idea of an equation that we are not concerned with cases where " B " is a simple adjective attached to the noun " A ", nor yet with cases where " is " serves to introduce a complex relation so that the predicate has several terms (e.g. " A is the broker in the sale of B by C to D "). But the chapter on metaphor may well seem to throw doubt on this simple view. " Fame is the spur which the clear spirit doth raise . . . to scorn delights " ; here " is " introduces a complex relation, but *spur* is a straightforward metaphor, and the function of the following clause is to give the other terms of the proportion scheme (not very definitely, perhaps, but *raise* makes the horse jump). However, the fact that the parallel can be pursued does not prevent the main point of it from being obvious at the start ; the flat way to take it is " Fame is like a spur, because . . ." whatever proportions come in later. There is a greater difficulty about " owls are wise ", which may not be a metaphor, of an obscure sort, according as you suppose or deny that wisdom in owls is " not the same as " wisdom in men. Even in men the idea is capable of being analysed into more complex terms, perhaps " accustomed to certain mental processes which produce certain good effects ", where both the *certains* are blank cheques. If we take it as a metaphor, it must carry a rather elaborate proportion scheme, probably with many terms. And if we say " owls have the wisdom of Nature " we only sharpen the doubt, I think, because " the wisdom of Nature " may define one of the sorts of wisdom or may appear as the regular grammatical form which announces a metaphor, like " the spur of fame ". Maybe the reason why " owls are wise " gives a rather blank impression is that the fancy is rather a silly one ; but " horses are generous ", though also obscure, does not, I think, feel blank in this way ; indeed, it may well have had a historical importance in the cult of chivalry. I think the idea is either that the horses in view are " well-bred " (hence " brave ", etc.) or that they are " willing to give all their strength ", so that the idea of metaphor is not needed ; but even so they seem to be compared to a type of man. It is thus possible to be in doubt whether an " A is B " statement is metaphorical or not. However, I think that this kind of doubt does not apply to the gnomic sentences of the form " A is B " which I want to examine here. Indeed, it is rather a striking fact about them, I submit, that they do not feel metaphorical at all, and if treated as metaphorical lose most of their claims.

I had better begin with a group of examples. Beauty is truth, truth beauty ; perfection is finality ; communication is civilisation ; hoc est corpus ; That art Thou (Hinduism) ; crime is disease (disease is crime) ; vouloir c'est pouvoir ; le style c'est l'homme ; l'état c'est moi ; might is right (right is might) ; God is Love ; time is money ; matter is mind (mind is matter) ; work is prayer ; knowledge is power ; the woman *is* beauty, of course, that's admitted (Mrs. Bloom in *Ulysses*). None of these feels metaphorical, and people who believe " hoc est corpus " or " That art Thou " would strongly deny that they are metaphors. Father Brown, indeed, argues at some length that the institution of the Mass should not be regarded as a case of metaphor. We can turn any of these phrases into metaphors by adding a genitive clause, as in " communication is the civilisation of fools " or " time is the money of philosophers ", and the whole line of interpretation becomes quite different. I think this can be said with some assurance, and for that matter there is not much doubt about what the original sentences mean ; we interpret them fairly easily, however odd the process may be. Surely the term " metaphor " would lose most of its usefulness if it could not be used to mark the distinction Father Brown had in mind.

The importance of the order of terms varies a great deal in these sentences. *Might is Right* and *Matter is Mind* yield directly opposed doctrines when inverted ; but *prayer is work* only gives a rather different doctrine, *power is knowledge* leaves me doubtful whether the inversion is only a weaker way of putting the same idea, and *civilisation is communication* and *beauty is woman* are practically unchanged after being inverted. When we say " A is A " for pregnancy, as in " an explosive is an explosive ; it must be surrounded with constant precautions ", the order seems necessarily indifferent : but this is a delusion, because the pregnant use always comes second. " The thing has the properties which ought to be obvious to you from its definition ", so that second use of the word has this definition as chief sense, whereas the first assumes that you have some loose notion covering the Range. Mrs. Eddy (I learn from *Our New Religion* by H. A. L. Fisher) summed up her doctrine as

> *God is all in all. God is good, good is mind.*
> *Good spirit being all in all, nothing is matter.*

She pointed out that these sentences give the same message when read backwards, which proves mathematically that they are true. What it proves, I suppose, is that she pairs off either two of the good words or two of the bad words, and they are all simple names either of the good or the bad Thing. However, there is none of this semantic collapse about " civilisation is communication ", so there are real cases where the order is indifferent.

The form makes clear that the machinery of false identity is in play, and therefore any such assertion is likely to feel profound. But this is not to say that we are tempted, even at a primitive level of thought, simply to accept the identity, because at a primitive level we also assume that different names stand for different things. This makes the sentence act differently from the equation within one word. The copula, as I have said so often, can be interpreted as " entails " or " is part of " or " is like " or " is typical of ", but this does not take us very far ; most of the slogans feel much the same if you put " entails " or " means " in the place of " is ", but they are still gnomic, they still have to be explained. (The sense " means " for " is " does not merely re-define " A ", as is clear from the form " What is that to me ? ") In any case we prefer to accept the feeling of false identity as far as we can, and rather than abandon it we are prepared to shift the senses of the terms identified. The main distinction as to how they shift, I think, is that the predicate feels rather more adjectival than the subject. This has been connected with an idea that " the subject of a proposition is always used in extension, and the predicate in intension ", but I think that makes the point too rigidly. The point is rather that you can take a wide sense for " B ", and colour all this field with the feelings due to a normal sense of it (I do not mean that this is a case of " x.y! ", because the normal sense is also in play), and meanwhile you take a narrow sense for " A ", the " essential " one, so as to include only such cases as the epigram wants to deal with. Thus a philosopher who said " matter is mind ", though no doubt leaving his position very obscure, would at least imply that he was an idealist. We let the word *mind* include all sorts of ideas about mind, and at the same time are ready to give him a good deal of choice about its defining property ; whereas we expect that *matter*, being the subject, will keep to its ordinary Range even if not its ordinary definition. Here the effect of holding matter captive is that mind can surround it and absorb it, as when one amoeba eats another. On the other hand, if we suppose him to mean " matter is typical of mind ", or the norm in terms of which mind must be interpreted, we have made him a materialist ; clearly this is not what would be expected from the sentence, but in speaking we would expect a stress on *mind*. To say it with a stress on *matter* would be more baffling, perhaps because that makes the " typical " idea more possible, but even so it would not be clearly in play.

> ". . . Eckhart was to some extent the victim of his own literary talents. *Le style c'est l'homme*. No doubt. But the converse is also partly true. *L'homme c'est le style*. Because we have a gift for writing in a certain way, we find ourselves, in some sort, becoming our way of writing. We mould ourselves in the likeness of our particular brand of eloquence." (*The Perennial Philosophy*.)

" The style is the man " is I take it " the style is a sign of the man " ; everything important in the character is mirrored in the technique. The interpretation " part of " is not wanted ; the style is in one way all of him and in another way outside him. " It is typical of him " is all right if you can regard it as part of him, but so far as you can't some different idea is needed. " Is like " would be the obvious translation, but that would make the aphorism too much of a metaphor ; there is an inherence doctrine at work, and the idea " entails " seems to be wanted as well. Perhaps " part of " and " entails " together make " typical ", whereas " entails " and " like " together make " sign or symbol ". As to the inversion, it seems rather a strained joke by Huxley, and by his own account the interpretation is " A becomes B ". This would be a new type, but it is not a common one ; " the egg is the hen " feels to me merely odd. One might regard it as a combination of " identical with " and " entails " ; the effect of the egg is in a way still the same thing as the egg. This version is worth noticing as a possible one, but I think it is only made tolerable here by the joke, which pretends to take it as an exact parallel to its inverse. Here we must consider the written style as something unplumbable and rich and inherently various, whereas the poor little personality of the writer is a thin and sketchy imitation of it ; a sentiment congenial both to Huxley's flippancy and his Buddhism. In both versions of the aphorism the most obvious point is that the predicate feels large whereas the subject feels definite and fixed.

I spoke of taking a wide sense for " B " as if this could be done at random, but a kind of typifying process is at work there too. The way you form the generalised idea is by using only some of the defining properties of the old class, the ones that at present seem " essential " to it, so the new definition will often apply to more things. But this choice of the essential elements can be made in a fairly *ad hoc* manner, probably in the direction suggested by " A ". Thus in " work is prayer " we generalise the idea of *prayer* until it will even cover work—the idea becomes something like " real service to God ", at least so I suppose, and yet still keeps the stock Emotion " holy " which belongs to the ordinary idea of prayer ; whereas if anyone asks about the patient labours of forgers or cat burglars the epigram is ready to reply " that isn't *proper* work ", the essential kind of work which is in view, so that this must be a narrower kind of work than usual. It would not be sufficient to argue (as I did in the simple case " A is A ") that the predicate takes the pregnancy ; both terms are made pregnant, because we shift from the ordinary meaning to an " essential " version of it ; but the subject is narrowed and the predicate broadened. Hence we can generally interpret the copula as " part of ". It does not sound so good to re-phrase this example " work is a kind of prayer ", because to do so weakens the strain which for the purposes of rhetoric ought to be inside the words themselves ; but I think it gives the same meaning, and only makes work feel rather less holy. I do not think " work is typical of prayer" is the normal interpretation, though it is a possible strained one. And to read it " work means prayer " or " entails prayer " only seems to take us back to the idea that work is a kind of prayer. In the same way, in " God is Love ", *God* keeps its old referent—he appears as the same person we were calling God before, even if the new property which is imputed to him is a decisively important one ; but *love* is both ideal (the best kind of love) and extremely general (all the love in the world). The reason why " Love is God " feels puzzling is that we are not sure which definite idea to take about love, how much sex to put into it for instance, nor yet how we are to generalise or diffuse the idea of God ; the slogan is likely to mean some kind of pantheism, but we cannot tell what till we hear more.

If now we take " work is prayer ", analysed like this, as the standard type of " A is B " assertion, we have a rather teasing puzzle on our hands. In one way or another, both terms are said to be pregnant. But a pregnant use itself carries an assertion of the form " A is B ", and all we have done by our trustful effort to explain one " A is B " is to land ourselves with three of them. There is a strong smell of unreality about treating the thing like this, but it would be merely inconsistent to say that the equations don't count if the words are arranged as " A is B ". We must suppose, I think, that the sentence relates the two meanings which are " what the words really mean here ", and these are the subjects of their equations. The sentence has got to say that proper work is general-but-real prayer. The equation inside *work*, to give it the right subject, must, therefore, be of the form " Honest work is the norm of all kinds of work ", whereas the equation inside *prayer* must be of the form " the most

general kind of prayer deserves the same feelings as the narrow
kind " ; or, putting in more interpretation, " Everything that serves
God ought to be respected, like direct worship of him ". The actual
sentence will now say "honest work serves God". This I think
seems a reasonable account, but *prayer* is not getting a straightforward kind of pregnancy ; we cannot suppose that, as the slogan
is ordinarily interpreted, usefulness to the public is taken to be what
is " typical and essential " in the idea of prayer. So far from that,
it seems to me, prayer is made typical of public service, and our idea
of prayer itself stays much where it was. But even this feels very
strained. Perhaps my idea of the meaning comes down unnecessarily heavily on the side of Works as opposed to Faith. The generalization of prayer need only make it cover " any process by which you
try to make God look on you with favour and therefore allow what
you want to happen ". This does not look an unreasonable account
of prayer ; and if you limit *proper* work to work which is done
humbly, leaving the issue in the hands of God, but with so much
effort as to prove to him that your wishes are serious ones—then it is
plausible to call this work a form of prayer. In effect, I should
think the epigram is bound to recommend Works (that is, doing good
to other people), if only as a proof that you have faith, but you can
extract a meaning from the word *prayer* without bringing that in.
However, in any case, this general meaning of *prayer* is given together
with a typical or central example of itself, that is, ordinary praying.
And this element regarded as the Type has to come as predicate in
the *prayer* equation, whereas the Type was subject in the *work*
equation. In the terms which I have defined earlier, *work* takes a
typifying pregnancy and *prayer* becomes a qualifying pregnancy after
first being generalized ; this is why their meanings get stretched in
such different ways. Of course, I do not mean to deny that the
stock Emotions of both words are intensified in the process ; no
doubt we are to feel something like " How hard good people work ! "
in *work* and " How holy is prayer ! " in *prayer* ; but I do not see that
this gives much help in deciding on the logical structure.

This kind of structure, I think, is the standard one for an " A is
B " slogan, but we must guard against supposing that people can
only take the thing in one way. It would be easy to be merely
deluded by *work*, and forget that the slogan would yield an immoral
moral if applied to cat burglars ; then *work* has no pregnancy.
And if cat burglars were suggested afterwards this man would be
likely to dismiss them impatiently, with an idea " of course work
ought to be proper work ", so that he gives the equation the order
of terms due to a qualifying pregnancy. But I think he is missing
one of the points of the slogan, which is that even his own work
ought to be examined to make sure that it is real good work, before

it can count as prayer. And then again, the slogan might be used for a very different purpose, as when a man is excusing himself from going to church because he wants to dig in the garden. The idea which will now be altered, if you agree with his use of the slogan, is not that of work but that of prayer. He is trying in fact to make *prayer* carry a typifying pregnancy, something like " Practical service is the essential, the only real kind of prayer ". This is a strained use of the word, indeed an attack on it, but the new meaning of the word is still acting as the subject ; the difference is that it is now taken as " typical " of the ordinary one in the predicate. The meaning of the sentence, as apart from the equations in it, seems now to reduce to an identity along the line " Honest work is practical service ". But we do not feel the sentence to be empty because there is an alternative formulation " Honest work is typical of prayer " ; the idea of " typical " cannot go in both places at once, but can be put into either with much the same effect. It is clear, I hope, that this man's way of interpreting the thing is really different from the standard one, because it would yield quite different opinions and, indeed, different practical results.

A reader may have been objecting all along that this discussion of the pregnancy in *prayer* is otiose, because the slogan obviously treats it as a metaphor. Now, I have to admit that *prayer* here behaves in the same way as a metaphor ; the word is stretched to carry an unusual meaning, and this is taken to be " like " its ordinary meaning. My criterion for saying that it is not a metaphor is simply that I do not think people feel it as one. But I also think that a good reason can be given for the feeling ; what the slogan aims at is a sort of permanent classification, for example, the inclusion of both work and prayer in the more general idea " service " ; and this feels quite different from asserting an analogy. A Buddhist monk, I should fancy, might turn the slogan into a metaphor by saying " work is the prayer of laymen ", that is, the two things have similar functions in the two different walks of life ; obviously this would be quite different. The point is perhaps clearer in " matter is mind ". One could not suppose this to be intended as a metaphor ; not because it would make nonsense, but because the business of the philosopher who is presumed to speak would be to build a classification in which matter would be included in a hierarchy of mindlike objects. Here again the crucial word " like " is involved, but so it is in all classification ; a cat is like other cats, but we need not deduce that to call it a cat is metaphorical. To be sure, I suppose people might take " work is prayer " as metaphorical, but the effect would be that they refused to take the slogan seriously. Indeed, the man who uses it to belittle prayer is even further from metaphor than the man who uses it to dignify work.

In effect, no doubt, we can put the important change of meaning into A, not into B ; we do this for example in the scientific utterance " light is a vibration in the ether ". Here " light " has to be taken to mean the invisible cause of light, not the sensations ordinarily given that name ; and on the other hand we tend to assume that this vibration is like any other. The shift of meaning in " light " is very definite, and of a kind often called metaphorical ; it is putting the cause for the effect. But the suggestion here is that this is the essential meaning of " light ", what a scientist ought to mean by the word (instead of babbling about his feelings). One could still say, therefore, that A takes not an extended use but a typifying pregnancy; and on the other hand B is at any rate prepared to be given a more general meaning than usual, if we reflect that this vibration must be of a peculiar kind. When you take the assertion seriously it requires the full form. But then again, it can be interpreted without shifting the wordmeaning as a case of " A is caused by B ", the vibration causes the sensation. This is not a prominent version of " A is B " and indeed will only suit an immediate effect (not a chain of causes), because it can only come from " entails " by the idea " if you have the sensation the vibration must be here too ". But I think it occurs ; for instance we could say " Hunger is lack of food " without too much strain. What is remarkable, I think, is that we feel no need to choose between these two interpretations of " light is a vibration " ; they simply reinforce each other, whereas in overt grammar we have been taught to choose either one such form or the other. Furthermore, there is a certain magical quality about the sentence, giving the scientist a touch of the necromancer (" light isn't what you think at all ") ; and this too can be put in alternative places ; either as an equation within the word *light* " the sensation *is* its cause " or in the whole sentence " the sensation *is* a vibration ".

We do not get the same tug from the familiar meaning when *light* appears as the predicate in a scientific utterance, because there we are more ready to have it generalized. One can say " radiant heat is light " with no more strain than " tigers are cats ", in a case where the comparatively unfamiliar thing already presented (the subject) is being classified with a familiar one as predicate. The copula then becomes quite firmly " is part of " and the predicate " all vibrations in the ether " or " all the cat family ". But here again there is an alternative view of the whole affair, one which would make the order of terms unimportant. We are bound to start, it may be said, from the ordinary idea of *light* or *cats*, and then jump away from them to something which will yield an identity to the " A is B " sentence. We therefore extract the elements which " A " and " B " have in common, or in which they are alike (a process which Spearman would include in his second fundamental power of the mind) and then the sentence merely says that these elements are alike or the same—if we have selected the right ones. In effect, therefore, it merely asserts the existence of these common elements, or the existence of a general idea which includes both " A " and " B ". For this purpose the order of terms is inherently unimportant, and the effect is like a fourth-type equation. But it is clear that this process cannot easily stand alone ; otherwise we could make sense of " Red is Blue ". This could be regarded as " red is in red's part of the spectrum what blue is in blue's part of the spectrum " (a proportion scheme, with *blue* a metaphor) or " both are colours " (a Mutual Metaphor). The idea that the same " thing " may have different names in different parts of its range is very familiar, and regularly used in all kinds of " A is B " assertions. But it will not carry us as far as " red is blue ", and the reason I think is that we require an alternative grammar which would generalize the idea of *blue*, a thing we are not prepared for.

It should now be possible to explain why some cases of " A is B " mean the same either way round. " The woman *is* beauty ", as I understand it, says that in painting landscapes, building cathedrals, designing patterns for your tribal pots and blankets, and all that, you have to use spatial proportions of some sort, and you had best learn them from the proportions of the female form. It is important to see that the slogan is not mere verbal nonsense ; Mrs. Bloom, who uses the phrase in *Ulysses* during her reflections in bed, no doubt did not mean very much, but she felt that there was a theory about the thing. Indeed, the historical background is large ; I take it the original idea was a Greek one, that the human body (especially male) is the norm of all proportions, and then the Victorians had felt that the male nude was rather indecent but the female one was idealistic. Thus while chiefly expressing a lazy resentment against men Mrs. Bloom is able to invoke an idea that woman are the standard or test of beauty. The obvious form of translation for the sentence is " a (normally beautiful) woman is the Type of beauty in general ". One could, no doubt, also treat the copula as meaning identity, after making considerable shifts of meaning in the separate words ; " something which is normally found in women is identical with the defining property of all beautiful things (and therefore deserves to be regarded with love and wonder) ". The effect would be to put the assertion " A is typical of B " inside the word *beauty*, as its equation, but I think this version is too strained to be at all prominent. If now we take " beauty is woman ", and this way of putting the idea does seem to me a conceivable one, we have presumably to narrow or make concrete the idea of *beauty* and generalize or idealize the idea of *woman*. Taking the essence of beauty can I suppose be felt as making the idea narrower, and taking Woman as a sort of goddess can be felt as an expansion. Mrs. Bloom's version feels as if it applied more directly to actual women, such as herself, because we only tend to " normalize " the subject, whereas the new version tends to suggest that the slogan is only true of an ideal female type, perhaps one which is seldom obtained ; this is the line of difference we would expect, because the predicate is idealized.

In " beauty is woman ", to be sure, the predicate *woman* takes a typifying pregnancy, instead of shifting to a more general idea and then giving it a qualifying pregnancy, like *prayer* in " work is prayer "; indeed, the same is true in Mrs. Bloom's version if we regard the predicate *beauty* as pregnant. The rule that the predicate takes a peculiar sort of pregnancy only applies when the new meaning given to " B ", in view of the requirements of " A ", is a rather remote one from the point of view of " B ". Here for some reason the requirements of the two words can work together, and this I think is the main reason why the slogan can be inverted ; also this makes it like the fourth-type equation, in which the order is indifferent because the two meanings serve to adumbrate a third one. But the slogan will not invert completely ; it is clear, I think, that only Mrs. Bloom's version allows the sentence to be interpreted as " A is typical of B ". The other version puts more strain on the individual words, and has to be interpreted " the distinctive property of all beautiful things is identical with the ideal woman ". Perhaps it is important that the copula is emphasized (in speaking) ; the emphasis is on the identity of some two things whatever they may be. This may help to make the order of terms unimportant, as may the mere difficulty of inventing any other meaning for the connection, however it is phrased.

" Communication is civilization " can only be supposed to mean that these entities are found together in a fixed proportion, so that having more of one entails having more of the other. Here, of course, there is no puzzle ; if a slogan is interpreted like this the order of terms is inherently indifferent. Actually I found it in a book about the development of the primary town civilizations from neolithic village ones, a context in which it is made fairly plausible. No doubt the slogan may also change your ideas about what civilization is, or about how far a given state should be called civilized ; but it will only do this in a secondary way, when you try to classify things after being convinced that the general rule holds. Some kind of argument in favour of the rule has to be supplied or invented before it is believed, but this will presumably not claim that moving from place to place is the " essence " or " type " of being civilized. So I think that this slogan, however untrue, is a fairly pure case of a mutual " entails " relation. All the same, so far as it goes on to change your ideas about the terms equated, it is liable to erect a new concept; and I think one could take both these epigrams as having a sort of likeness to equations of the fourth type.

We have now to consider why " Might is Right " is the opposite of " Right is Might ", in contrast to these last two examples. I gave a short discussion of this case in my previous book *Pastoral*, and a reviewer said that I was offensively rubbing in the obvious. It is a melancholy thing if I must now be offensive at greater length, but the case seems to me so far from obvious that I am still not sure I understand it. The resultant meanings, of course, were obvious to everybody in the First World War, but the processes of interpretation that everyone went through to arrive at them seem to me very subtle. No doubt there is a rough general rule in approaching such a sentence, by which the first term in the identity is given the right-of-way in any conflict between them. This was the explanation I gave in the book ; the German phrase " Macht geht vor Recht " encouraged such a theory. But " God is love " does not mean that God has the right of way over love, and " matter is mind " does the opposite and gives mind the right of way over matter. It seems clear that " Might is Right " (in English, anyway) has to use a confusion of several modes of interpretation. Our standard form is " the proper sort of might entails the general sort of right ", and the same for the opposite slogan inverted. But surely the strength of " might is right " was to claim that even an apparently improper kind of might was enough to give you right ; and in the opposing slogan an obvious kind of right had to be sufficient to give might, not some special kind, or the argument might go off in some unwanted direction. If we abandon specialised meanings for the two words we are thrown back on " might entails right ", " right entails might ". But the man who maintains that might entails right would certainly add that if you have no might you have no right ; otherwise the slogan does not do what he wants, because there may be a conflict of rights even though only one side has might. But in that case, if you are sure you have right, you can argue backwards and infer that you have might. This lands us in the slogan of the opponent. (It is parallel in fact to " communication is civilisation "). Thus it is clear that there must be some other interpretation in view which keeps this one at bay. We might think of it as re-definition ; you are told to use the term A in future where previously you had used the term B. Cf. " A triangle is a plane figure bounded by three straight lines ": in future you are to say " triangle " instead of the description. The suggestion is therefore "Efface discussion of right and bear in mind our might " and for the opposite slogan " Never calculate chances ; to be in the right is the only thing to be considered ". This is certainly not the only interpretation, because the terms forming the predicate are still present in the mind and are not negated ; indeed, *right* in the first slogan is some kind of justification and *might* in the second some kind of hope or claim. But when combined with the " entails " version it is enough to bar out the *reductio ad absurdum*.

However, in putting it like this, I am perhaps only going a long way round to say that the slogan itself is like an equation of Type III —" Might is the typical and essential part of the might-right complex ", the right handle to take hold of the bundle, indeed, the " only real " part of it, except that the rest of it is still somehow there. The opposing slogan is of precisely the same form, and it is now obviously a contradiction of the first. I do not think there is any need here to look for equations inside the words, because the primitive mode of thought has come out into the open and belongs to the whole sentence that connects them. All the same, I think there can be variations in the way the slogan is used, and these would take us back to our normal form : " The typical or ideal kind of might entails a general kind of right, and deserves the feelings attached to right in the strict sense of the term." If the speakers assume that their own kind of might is an ideal kind they can of course put a typifying pregnancy into their use of the word, and this will prevent them from feeling that the slogan is frankly immoral. Even the form " Efface discussion of right " could be taken to mean " We know that our might is of the ideal kind ; do not admit any derogatory suggestion that it is not ". The opponent, on the other hand, in holding the slogan up to detestation, takes it to mean that might is the " only real " kind of right in the sense that right will no longer be considered at all ; this is pure re-definition, in the peculiar sense I am giving to that term, and would mean that there is no longer any such thing as a " might-right complex ". But even the opponent really knows that there is some kind of moral problem involved, or he would not be satisfied by his own opposing slogan " right is might ". It seems to me that both sides have to agree that there is some such confused field in view, and that is why, although one may need other translations to mark minor shifts or emphasis, I think that the main one has to be the clumsy form which I have given.

Incidentally, this idea gives us a point of likeness between " might is right " and " matter is mind ", two slogans which seemed entirely unlike except that each yields its opposite when inverted. The people who disagree over " matter is mind " and " mind is matter " are agreeing over a more fundamental question, since they both assume that the contrasted entities can be included in a large unity. This would be readily admitted about mind and matter. It is not so easy to fix on the point of agreement between " might is right " and " right is might ", but it seems fair to say that both parties assume the State to be a demi-god. Neither slogan is used about individuals, at any rate about individual men. There is, indeed, a similar problem about God, who is said to be both all-powerful and all-good, and according to Aquinas these attributes of God are distinguishable by us but not distinct as they exist in him. A state which receives worship, or a people with a " destiny ", are in the same position as God because they are expected partly to create the standard of rightness by which they are to be judged. This idea, I think, was clearly present in " Might is Right ", and though " Right is Might " is a less reckless piece of self-justification there does seem to be an assumption in it that virtue gets plenty of reward. I think that both pairs of slogans have a suggestion of Mutual Metaphor, though not of Metaphor, because they erect however vaguely a third idea behind the two which they consider. Going back to the equations inside a word, it might be argued that all equations of the third type have a rudiment in them of the process which makes an equation of the fourth ; because they raise in the background a new notion " the A+B complex " however strongly they make " A " posture in the foreground.

The practice of making deep philosophical assertions in the form " A is B ", obviously prominent among the Germans, seems to have come in with the first translations of the Hindu sacred texts. The " That art Thou " of Hindu mysticism (" with the accent on the thou ") may well have a historical connection with " Might is Right ", though nationalism is about the last idea it was originally intended to convey. The idea that everything is One seems to have been particularly welcome, not merely where the intellectuals were moving away from Christianity, but where a lack of national unity made them feel insecure. Boston was taking a special interest in transcendentalism during the thirty years or so up to the American Civil War ; and perhaps one could claim the line from Vico to Croce as showing the same movement in Italy, the third striking case of a country trying to become One. The relations of Marxism to Hegel are a more baffling topic, but the One might be taken to imply either that the whole world should become communist or that no activity can be independent of the class struggle. I do not think that much weight can be put on this historical approach ; plenty of people have said " A is B " without having studied pantheism. Indeed, the French seem particularly fond of the form for epigrams without being prone to the metaphysics. But, if someone objects that my treatment of the " A is B " slogan tends to drag in too much undigested philosophy, I can answer that slogans of this type have really been used to hint at those philosophical ideas.

II

The account given so far seems to me a fairly complete picture of the " A is B " sentence so far as it is parallel to an equation inside a word ; but the sentence can also be inverted for emphasis, a process which seems to have no parallel in the equation, and I need to deal with that because otherwise cases could easily be found which do not fit my account. By the way, an inversion which leaves the grammar in doubt cannot be done in all languages with a form for the accusative ; indeed, it seems to be an eccentricity in Greek and Latin that they refuse the accusative after the copula. Russian, for example, which says merely " the house white " for " the house is white " (as against " the white house " for the phrase), gives the adjective an accusative form if it has one, even in this verbless sentence, just as the English language is determined to say " It's me " if the sentence is short.

Inversion for emphasis can of course be done with any sentence, as by the transcendental ladies in *Martin Chuzzlewit*, who said something like " Howls the profound, and sweeps the deep ". A stress on the first noun of an " A is B " will easily imply that the order has been inverted, because in an ordinary sentence the subject is assumed to be already known ; the interesting part, which will get the stress, is what is being said about it, the predicate. A gnomic " A is B ", where this is no longer true, will normally have an equal stress on both. I doubt whether any of my examples can be inverted by stressing the subject, except possibly " *matter* is mind ", which might conceivably give matter sufficient over-riding importance to imply a materialist philosophy. The distinction is perhaps clearest when the relation is that of symbol to thing symbolised ; thus Moses in interpreting the dream of Pharaoh says " the seven lean kine are the seven lean years ", a straightforward statement ; " *the seven lean years* are the seven lean kine " would have been more dramatic without altering the thought. (The symbol is the natural subject because it is what you are given to start with, the thing which the predicate is to explain.) The standard form of definition often begins with the new term to be defined, and it then takes a stress because it is supposed to be new : " A triangle . . . is a plane figure ", etc. There is a suggestion in Euclid that he knows all the answers already, and is not going to tell you how he found them out ; this traditional order for a defining sentence is slightly unnatural and gives the same feeling. I think it should be regarded as an inversion, and in any case a more openhearted style will be found to put the sentence the other way round. The result is that, if we suppose " A is B " to be a definition (or re-definition) of one of the terms falsely called identical, it is not obvious which of them is to be changed. The N.E.D. extracts two meanings for the copula from these alternatives :

10. " To exist as the thing known by a certain name ; to be identical with. ' Myself am king of Naples.' "
11. " To be the same in purport as, to amount to, to mean. ' The seven lean kine are the seven lean years.' "

These seem to correspond to " A plane figure bounded by three straight lines is (called) a triangle " and " a triangle is (or means) a plane figure . . ." The great work adds the idea of identity to the first because otherwise the mere naming appears to say so little. An " A is B " slogan tends to alter the meaning of both its terms, and the fact that we use both ways round for a sentence intended as a definition is perhaps a help in keeping all the possibilities open.

Indeed, we seem to have various forms for inverting the order when we feel we would like it to go the other way. " It is a sickly girl who is refined " can be used as a way of inverting " refined girls are sickly ". On the face of it a stress on the copula " A is B ", as in " woman *is* beauty ", merely claims extra belief in the false identity, and thus tends to encourage typifying or inherence doctrines ; " that *is* a lobster " says that it is an ideal lobster. But I find myself haunted by the idea that it can sometimes change the order too. I think it does so only in special cases where it suggests a definition formula. However, there is a straightforward inversion if we say " A is identical with B ", because that gives a much more direct appeal to the order of the definition formula ; it might also be analogous to the pair " the trigger fired the gun "—" the gun was fired with the trigger ". The way to re-phrase " God is Love " would be " Love is identical with God ", not the other way round, although here the suggestion of definition is easily ignored. To take a more actual example, Coleridge attached great importance to a belief which he defined by saying " that the former " (the existence of things without us) " is unconsciously involved in the latter " (the existence of our own being) :

" that it is not only coherent but self-identical, and one and the same thing, with our immediate self-consciousness."

It seems clear that if Coleridge had used a less German style and left out " identity " his phrase would have been " To say ' I am ' *is* to say ' there are things ' ", (or what not), rather than the other way about. " I entail things ", that is, my consciousness presumes some other things beside me, but I come first. Professor Richards in *Coleridge On Imagination* remarked that to change the order would imply another philosophy ; Coleridge " identified the existence of things with the existence of the self " whereas a materialist " reverses the step, and finds the explanation of the self in the behaviour of certain sorts of things ". The materialist would either say (something like) " the chemical actions of my brain cells are my consciousness " or " my consciousness is identical with the chemical actions of my brain cells ", reversing his order for the new grammar. (By the way, Professor Richards' use of the equals sign in this passage is the opposite way round from that of my "A is B" equation, no doubt because he was following Coleridge's order.) In an " A is B " the " A " is what we start arguing from, whereas in " A is identical with B " we are proving something about A and shifting the idea of A onto the idea of B ; B is therefore the more fixed.

A similar though less definite inversion seems to follow from inserting *really*, as in the following passage from Eddington :

"Whilst the physicist would generally say that the matter of this familiar table is *really* a curvature of space, and its colour is *really* electro-magnetic length, I do not think he would say that the familiar moving on of time is *really* an entropy-gradient. I am quoting a rather loose way of speaking, but it reveals that there is a distinct difference in our attitude towards the last parallelism. Having convinced ourselves that the two things are connected, we must conclude that there is something as yet ungrasped behind the notion of entropy—some mystic interpretation, if you like—which is not apparent in the definition by which we introduced it into physics. In short, we strive to see that entropy may *really* be the familiar moving on of time." Here again B seems the more fixed. As I understand it, Eddington accepts the usual order for these summary assertions but throws in *really* to see if it makes them feel different, and argues that the one about time won't stand up to it but the one about colour will. (We are prepared to believe that colour isn't what we think, but time has got to be more or less what we think, because it is fundamental even to the process of gaining knowledge ; the scientist would be sawing off the branch he sits on if he denied that.) I think the effect of *really* is to make the predicate into the right handle to take hold of the bundle, the thing you are to dig into for further wisdom ; in the case of time, this has to be the familiar experience, so the sentence with *really* needs inverting. That is, the predicate of " A is *really* B " acts like the subject of a third-type equation. I should like to add that I have a very great respect for the way Eddington could carry on a profound discussion in this apparently popularizing language ; any good scientist, I strongly suspect, conducts his formative thinking in this kind of way, but few of them have enough nerve to say so afterwards.

The reason why we sometimes want to juggle with the order is, I think, that there are some fundamental rules or rather feelings about the matter, and these may conflict with the logical require-ments which are what I have tried to consider so far. In general, the subject is the stimulus, the immediate situation which neither of the talkers will deny, and the predicate is the speaker's reaction to it. Thus in general (as I said before) we want the subject to be the more obvious to the hearer, or more clearly relevant to the context, also the more concrete or narrower in range (the more " like a noun ") ; whereas the predicate is " what is being said about it ", therefore the more emotive or more likely to cause action. The emotive rule, I think, was what made it rhetorically more effective for Coleridge to use the form " is identical with " and thus put self-consciousness at the end. The reason why it sounds pompous (or magically clever) when the mathematician first introduces a new term as the subject of a definition is that we expect the subject to be the more obvious to the listener, but here it is something previously unknown. Forms like " It's a poor heart that never rejoices " and " It's a long lane that has no turning " merely put in the " it's " because they want to invert the order that is convenient for grammar so as to get the " entails " relation the right way round (" if we never rejoiced that would prove we had poor heart "). But the recent spread of this form, until half the sentences in a *Times* leader may begin with " it ", seems to come from a rhetorical desire to get in the predicate first and thus treat it as fixed or agreed upon before the nebulous subject to which it is attached is allowed to drift into the mind. (" It is indubitably the path of wisdom to assume that, whatever . . .") Be this as it may, I should claim that my rules for interpreting an " A is B " assertion follow naturally from these more fundamental ones. The subject is the more likely to receive a typifying pregnancy because its meaning is to be taken more narrowly, whereas the predicate is free to be interpreted more broadly, and to have more emotive effect, because it carries the speaker's " reaction ".

For completeness, I ought to add the copula which feels like the style of Gibbon, and is merely a façade ; it has no interpretation.

"But Bombay, with its eighty textile mills increasingly in Indian hands retaining the profits in the country, is the great money power. The harbour which could shelter the navies of the world is the nearest great port to Europe."

We already see in the first sentence that this journalist likes to put the real information into a subordinate clause, and the second sentence merely attaches two more predicates to *Bombay*. Of course, you could suppose he intended some mysterious strategic hint, but the trick has a merit apart from this pretentiousness ; the departure from colloquial English saves him from chattering, and he uses a merely formal grammar to let him string information together briefly. I do not think a gnomic sentence or slogan ever lets the copula become null like this.

" Is " can also be replaced by " as ", but I do not think that this

brings in any complications. Several common English verbs
have analogues among prepositions ; *have* goes with *of* in the same
way. There is a real likeness here because both deal with possession, whether or not this is why people tend to write " I meant
to of gone ". In the same way one can always change " A is B "
into " Regard A *as* B ". Regard God as Love, Might as Right,
woman as beauty, time as money, work as prayer, the sanctified
bread as the body of Christ. The last is not theologically adequate
because the assertion of identity is now weak, but the order is the
same in the new sentences and an inversion would change the effect
in the same degree as before. The new form obviously suits a
metaphor (" regard fame as a spur ") and might seems to suggest
that all of them are metaphorical. But I can still regard the subject
as in a class to which it really belongs, regard a cat as a mammal, or
regard it in the light of what it entails, regard so much time as so much
money. The range of the two forms seems to be exactly the same.

One might now try to generalise further, and say that two terms
merely connected by " and " also form a unit of this sort, so that
the choice of order makes a difference to the implications. I do
not think this is so. When Gibbon at the end of his history says
that he has described " the triumph of religion and barbarism "
he is putting in a lot of implications, but it seems to me that the
order of the terms is merely a question of rhythm. One can think
of connections either way round : " the triumph of religion
weakened Rome and thus let in the barbarians ; religion had already
destroyed the elegance of civilisation and made it barbaric " or
" barbarians came in, and naturally they were at home with religious
enthusiasm ; the collapse of civilisation indeed had already made
the citizens of the empire barbaric, therefore they felt religious ". To
put the two words on the same level is a powerful trick, and I should
claim that the process can be counted as a small variety of Mutual
Metaphor ; but it does not seem to be a trick which depends on the
order of terms.

I ought, also, to consider which way round the equation goes
when two words are in apposition. So far as they are presented as
two shots at the same idea the second is presumably less obvious
but more what the speaker wants to say, also there is an alternative
grammar dimly in view which could put " which is " between them ;
on both counts the first will tend to be the subject and the second the
predicate. But you do not know that the pair is being presented
till you have got to the second, so in a striking case of this trope you
might feel that the second (now the subject) is equated to the first :

> the stunted unlucky heir
> *Of twisted bones, reciting a father's gnarled disease,*
> *His lesson from his book.*

(Spender's *Elementary School Classroom*). The idea is something like " That his disease cuts him off from ordinary experience is the only lesson he can be expected to learn " ; so the apposition is enough in itself to carry the question raised by the whole poem. In effect, *lesson* is a metaphor, and indeed has already been introduced as one by *reciting*. The simple equation in a metaphor goes " the tenor is the vehicle ", so that the words are again equated in the order of appearance—" his disease is his lesson ". However, a striking case which is not felt as metaphorical might change the order. On the whole I think such a case tends merely to be a vague fourth-type equation ; at least I cannot see how to decide on any order for Wordsworth's string of phrases in apposition to " a sense sublime of something far more deeply interfused ". The phrase " A or rather B " seems to be regularly used to imply, " The thing is commonly called A but I think it should be called B ", which yields the same equation order as an ordinary apposition (with a Mood to interpret it). The journalistic trick of putting a comma between two words when what is meant is " and " gives a disagreeable effect chiefly because the confusion between apposition and addition is bad in itself ; there may be a lot of difference between meaning two things and meaning two shots at one thing. But it tends also to suggest an unwanted equation between the two, and thus make the order of the terms important, whereas with " and " the order would not have signified.

I have now said what I can find to say about the matter, but have not yet broached the somewhat hag-ridden phrase " Beauty is Truth, Truth Beauty ", though it was on my list of " A is B " forms. I propose now to round off this chapter with an examination of how it works in the *Ode to a Grecian Urn*.

III

There is perhaps rather too much controversy in this book, due to a lack of intellectual grasp in the author ; I find it hard to choose between theories at all in this field except by coming across examples in which one theory works better than another. At any rate, after blaming the Stern and Richards views of the beginning and end of the *Grecian Urn* for making the language too Emotive, I found myself blaming Mr. Cleanth Brooks for not making the poem as emotional as it ought to be. He treats it (in *The Well-Wrought Urn*) as an entirely coherent philosophical position expressed by irony and paradox, and certainly this seems a less ungenerous approach than the view of Robert Bridges, that it was " uneducated " of Keats to let philosophy leak into a poem. But it seems to me to make rather bad philosophy, and rather a dull poem, which the thing need not be. Mr. Brooks dislikes " biography " as a means of explaining verse, since a poem ought to be complete in itself, and he is not very patient with personal expressions of feeling from a writer who is engaged in building one of these complicated structures. It is hard to feel anything very directly about the poem, now that it has been made so much of an " example ", but I think it needs to be viewed as a strong if not tragic expression of feeling, and when so viewed is still good.

Mr. Brooks feels that the whole third stanza of the Ode is a falling-off ; " there is a tendency to linger over the scene sentimentally ". This is the stanza that begins " Ah happy, happy boughs " and ends by saying that human passion leaves " a burning forehead and a parching tongue ". If we are to try to defend it, says Mr. Brooks, " we shall come nearest success by emphasising the paradoxical implications of the repeated items ... Though the poet has developed and extended his metaphors furthest in this third stanza, the ironic counterpoise is developed furthest too." It seems to me more like dropping an irony ; this stanza is concerned to tell us directly about the feelings of Keats. He is extremely *un*-happy, we find, especially about his love affair, but also from the tedium of the pursuit of beauty or pleasure and from the expectation of death. I do not get this from " biography " but from taking the opposites of the three things the stanza calls " happy ". Also there is a very dramatic effect, ignored by Mr. Brooks, from the juxtaposition of this stanza with the next :

> ... *A burning forehead, and a parching tongue.*
>
> *Who are these coming to the sacrifice ?* ...

It is a cry of awe from the parching tongue, as the poet sees new victims approach, and the stanza goes on to say that none of them will ever go home again, so that their town will be mysteriously desolate. Mr. Brooks has more than a page trying to rationalize this idea, and save it from being thought " an indulgence ... which is gratuitous and finally silly ". The town cannot really be left desolate merely because these people are carved on a pot. " The poet ", says Mr. Brooks, " by pretending to take the town as empty ... has suggested in the strongest possible way its reality for him—and for us. It is a case of the doctor taking his own medicine ; the poet is prepared to stand by the illusion of his own making." If this were all, I think it would still be pretty gratuitous. But the poet has just told us he is desolate too (if the critic will condescend to notice anything so sentimental) ; there is a comparison. The idea that the pursuit of beauty eats up the pursuer, who therefore sacrifices himself to it, is really not a remote one for a romantic poet ; though I have to admit that I did not realise how directly it was brought in till I tried to think what was wrong with the account of Mr. Brooks. These people's homes will be left desolate because they have gone to make a piece of art-work, and so will Keats' home because he is spending his life on his art. Beauty is both a cause of and an escape from suffering, and in either way suffering is deeply involved in its production. Here is the crisis of the poem ; in the sudden exertion of muscle by which Keats skids round the corner from self-pity to an imaginative view of the world. None of these people can get anything out of the world except beauty, and at once we turn back to the pot with a painful ecstasy in the final stanza ; there is nothing else left. This is the force behind the cry " Beauty is Truth " (obviously, I think), however the terms of it are to be interpreted.

The chief puzzle about it is that one feels the poem has raised no question about truth before ; it is " gratuitous " again ; the reconciliation may be all right in itself, but has got hold of the wrong couple. This, I take it, was why Mr. Middleton Murry defended the philosophy of the last three lines but doubted their value in the poem (thus taking a position precisely opposite to Professor Richards'). Such an objection would not occur to Mr. Brooks, who takes it as doctrine that a lyrical poet is concerned with philosophical truth. Already in the first verse, he points out, the pot is called a historian, so it is expected to tell truth, but its history has " no footnotes " and is merely an imaginative insight ; " if we have followed the development of the metaphors . . . we shall be prepared for the enigmatic final paradox ", in which the urn " speaks as a character in the drama and makes a commentary on its own nature ". This is sufficient for an answer to Mr. Murry, I think. But we cannot suppose that the aphorism is merely dramatic, in the sense of being a suitable remark for a silent pot (suitable only because of its complacence, perhaps). If we were sure that Keats did not agree with the pot the climax would become trivial. However little we are to use biography, it seems fair to quell this doubt by remembering that Keats had wrestled with the idea in prose. " The excellence of every art is in its intensity, capable of making all disagreeables evaporate from their being in close relation to Beauty and Truth. . . . What the imagination seizes as Beauty must be Truth ", and so on. That is, I take it, his mind was working on the ideas of Coleridge. But there is remarkably little agony in Coleridge's theory of Imagination (remarkably, I mean, for so unhappy a man) ; whereas Keats was trying to work the disagreeables into the theory. It seemed to him, therefore, that the aphorism was *somehow* relevant to the parching tongue, the desolate streets, and the other woes of the generations not yet wasted. He, like his readers, I think, was puzzled by the remarks of the pot, and yet felt that they were very *nearly* intelligible and relevant. It struck me that the philosophical approach of Mr. Brooks gave a slightly wrong twist to :

> *Thou, silent form, doth tease us out of thought*
> *As doth eternity. Cold pastoral !*

" It is enigmatic as eternity is, for like eternity its history is outside time, beyond time, and for this very reason bewilders our time-ridden minds. It teases us." It teases us *out of thought* ; it stops us thinking ; the idea is more suited to a mystical ecstasy than a metaphysical puzzle. And we have reached this condition through a " sacrifice " ; for that matter, the usual function of an Urn is to hold the ashes of the dead. What it tells us is a revelation, and revelations are expected to be puzzling. In short, if we recognise the stress of feeling in the rest of the poem, I do not think a reasonable man should withhold his sympathy from the end of it.

This may seem hardly worth distinguishing from Professor Richards' remark that the overlap of the ranges of Beauty and Truth at three points " gives to the equivalence, either as a gesture or as having some indefensible sense, a peculiarly strong suasive force ", which accounts for its power to convey a feeling of deep acceptance of the aesthetic experience. " The poem is perhaps unusual in having an aesthetic experience for subject as well as aim." And yet I feel there is some difference here so real that it decides whether the experience of reading the poem is a good or a bad one. There should not be a complacent acceptance either of " some indefensible sense " or of a mere emotive stimulus ; the thought of the reader needs somehow to be in movement. The fresh reader who is wondering what the pot can have meant is no doubt in the best position, but we cannot say that that is the only good way to read it ; at least, that may be true, but it amounts to saying that the poem is only good till it is found out. It seems clear that we have to imagine what went on in the mind of Keats, as he wondered what the pot can have meant—we, it is understood, being those who have lost our innocence in the matter by reading the contradictory babble of the critics. Nor need this be done with tacit contempt, as for a man puzzling over questions which are soluble ; and here I think the comparison to a drama really is relevant ; if Keats' life were an imaginary one in a play, and these phrases were put into his mouth, nobody would complain about the aphorism or find it anything but an impressive tragic detail.

But though the final meaning is left open in this way the structural meaning in the poem is tolerably fixed and firm. The essential dramatic process is that by feeling the beauty of the pot Keats is led to make reflections on human life ; in the same way the metaphors which are Emotive when merely applied to the pot, in the first lines of the poem, become Cognitive when applied to the real theme. The beauty of the pot presumably tells truth so far as it is a sound guide to the pot, and what it tells him is how to digest his sufferings and turn them into beauty. Thus there is a movement of thought in the reader (going through a Mutual Metaphor to get the right topic) which corresponds to what happened in the mind of the poet ; the poem has gone through the process which the identity is meant to sum up, so that Keats felt he had the right to assert it at the end. (" The feelings about the pot are, or have been shown to contain, important truths.") And indeed, so far as the thing is an aesthetic theory, he was surely right in feeling that something about it was important and general. Emotions well handled in art are somehow absorbed into the structure ; their expression is made also to express where and why they are valid. This would not be enough to carry off the claims of the final assertion ; Keats wanted us to feel, I think, that the wise pot meant a good deal more by its aphorism. But as far as he, the poet, was concerned (not knowing more than he needed to know), there was at least enough meaning to make the poem coherent.

We should now be able to consider the mechanics of the thing. The assertion goes both ways round. " Beauty is truth, truth beauty " ; and on such principles as I have been able to find, this must make it like an equation of Type IV ; either each entails the other, or both are examples of some third notion in which they are included. This extreme form of the assertion however is a sort of afterthought ; " Beauty is Truth " comes first, as the immediate idea arising from the context, and this is given further claims by throwing after it " Truth beauty ". But the first alone need not be a wild piece of romanticism ; it was Aristotle, after all, who first tied all the arts to making a correct Imitation, and his view was prominent in the eighteenth century. Dr. Johnson is found praising Bonhours, " who had shown all beauty to depend on truth ", and was himself fond of such remarks as that " the legitimate end of fiction is the conveyance of truth ". Mr. J. W. Krutch, in his recent study of Johnson, remarked that he would differ from Keats by not adding " truth beauty ", and I take Mr. Krutch to mean that this order of the terms is the only one that makes the beauty of an idea the criterion of its truth. But if we read the identities as " A entails B ", surely " Truth is beauty " is the right way round for Johnson's view. Yet it certainly feels like asserting that there are no ugly truths ; indeed, this would also follow from the interpretation " A is part of B " ; all truths are to be included in some kind of beauty. A third-type interpretation would suit Johnson's view ; " Truth is the right handle to take hold of the bundle ; the first

thing to consider in explaining or criticising an example of beauty."
But this could not also work on " Beauty is Truth " without coming
back to the idea that there are no ugly truths. It is that, of course,
which so many people have found offensive in Keats's ejaculation ;
there is a flavour of Christian Science ; they fear to wake up in
Fairyland, and probably the county of Uplift. But I think this
threat is removed if one takes the poem as essentially about the
unpleasantness of the life of the artist, which is not in itself a too rosy
theme. In any case, it is not clear to me why Johnson's view should
be considered secure against working the identity backwards ; if
beauty can only be obtained from truth, and we know that a given
story is beautiful, why are we not to assume that it is also true ?

The point where romanticism comes in, I think, is not in adding
" truth beauty " but in the assumption that " what the Imagination
seizes as Beauty " will be a vision grasped as the result of a life of
pain and effort, by a brief ecstasy from which the artist sinks back
exhausted. A supernatural state is attained, at great cost, and the
identity stated both ways round can then mean " all the eternal
values are united in the divine "—also in the poet, but only while
the mind " is like a fading coal ". This is what the mystery is about,
and indeed Mr. Aldous Huxley has rebuked the poet (in *The Perennial
Philosophy*, p. 158) for not taking the doctrine seriously enough and
fancying that his petty little verse forms had anything to do with
the matter. Here the identity becomes I think a full case of Mutual
Metaphor, or a full parallel to an equation of Type IV, because the
third notion which is supposed to be brought forward has not much
likeness to either of the two things identified.

But it seems clear that there are various subsidiary ideas at work,
to give the thing body, besides the simple one that the beauty of the
pot is what has led Keats to this line of reflection. Apart from any
ecstasy, the capacity to feel the value of an instant in life as satisfying
in itself, and as in a way summing up the rest of life, is claimed as
crucial to the artist ; indeed, he escapes death by it. The capacity
to seize on the typical in a complex situation is a common requirement for both truth and beauty, and this again could emerge from
taking the identity both ways round. The idea that " we recognise
truth through the sense of beauty or fitness ", an idea that Keats
certainly held, though it is getting near to the forbidden one that
there are no ugly truths, can be balanced by the idea " receptivity
to the outer life (truth) is what gives fullness to the inner life and
control over it (beauty)"—that is, the poet needs to experience his
burning forehead and his parching tongue. These are " entails "
relations going the two possible ways round, so that giving both orders
tends to balance them. And one of the overlaps that Professor
Richards suggested in the range of the two words, " expressing an

intuition or a personality is being sincere ", does, I think, hover somewhere in the background. Keats in a famous letter expounds a view of the world as a Vale of Soul-making, in which we are to learn to approach the divine by developing our personalities ; it is clear then that he would not agree with the sharp distinction drawn by Mr. Aldous Huxley, and would consider that the final mystery was really approached by these personal interpretations of the equivalence. This version will go with either order of the terms, which would help to link it with the final one. Other versions could be listed, for example the forbidden idea that all truths are pleasant can be absorbed into the idea " the delight in beauty gives us the strength to recognise truth "—" delight in the terribleness of Nature gives one strength to control it " ; but I am not sure that this is not remote from the poem, whereas the others, I think, are part of its immediate background of ideas.

However, to say that all this was present for Keats, as a feeling that the pot had summed up a far-reaching mystery, does not say that the lines are good ones, and that the reader ought to feel it too. If often happens that a poet has built his machine, putting all the parts into it and so on very genuinely, and the machine does not go. I think that " Oh Attic shape ! Fair attitude ! with brede " is a very bad line ; the half pun suggesting a false Greek derivation and jammed against an arty bit of Old English seems to me affected and ugly ; it is the sort of thing that the snobbish critics of his own time called him a Cockney for. One might feel, as Robert Bridges clearly did, that the last lines with their brash attempt to end with a smart bit of philosophy have not got enough knowledge behind them, and are flashy in the same way. I do not feel this myself, only that the effort of seeing the thing as Keats did is too great to be undertaken with pleasure. There is perhaps a puzzle about how far we ought to make this kind of effort, and at what point the size of the effort required simply proves the poem to be bad. But in any case, I do not think the lines need be regarded either as purely Emotive or as a fully detached bit of philosophising.

Chapter 20

THE PRIMITIVE MIND

I HAVE been taking for granted that the use of false identity is in some sense " primitive ", and ought now to give some evidence for it. The idea is perhaps rather out-of-date. Anthropologists have become more doubtful than they were about their inherent mental superiority to tribesmen, and even about where the primitive is to be found. One must go back to M. Levy-Bruhl for a thorough-going argument that the reason why the primitive mind is inferior to our own is that it works by " identities ". But the doctrine need not be contemptuous, and we have also to consider the Noble Savage. Mr. Owen Barfield has maintained that the so-called civilised mind is merely living upon its capital ; that whatever wisdom we still have is drawn from magnificent rich words which were devised before the dawn of history, and that our prying rationalism is gradually but fatally destroying them. These opposed views deserve at any rate to be recalled. In the main, I think Mr. Barfield's view simply needs to be cleared away, but he is right in recognising that the primitive process is something which we still use and need.

I am not sure how far he means to carry his theory in that excellent book " Poetic Diction ". Sometimes he maintains that a language has a period of flower, when its words are as full and handy as they can be got ; a melancholy but very arguable view. What I think needs clearing away is his alternative theory, that human thought had most wisdom when language first started. Surely this is grotesque, and it haunts the book too thoroughly to be a joke. His pages on the word *ruin* show the English language building up a " total meaning " of his sort quite in the primitive manner, and this did not start till the sixteenth-century ; I have tried to show how a fine rich meaning was built up in *candid*, and this seems to have been done by the wicked eighteenth-century rationalists themselves, who are the high priests of murder for dissection. No doubt a language tends to get stuck, and an idea abandoned long ago may turn out valuable if there is a word which lets it be revived. There is a case for saying that this was happened in *ruin* and *candid*, because they developed extra meanings which were already in Latin. But this would not support the theory that a language is doomed to die after a limited period like an individual man, and it would actually refute any theory that such words can only grow in a language so long as the thought of its speakers is " prelogical ".

Pneuma is one of Mr. Barfield's key examples. The mixture " breath, wind, soul ", we are told, is not a root sense with two metaphors but one rich profound ancient total meaning. It seems clear that this kind of meaning need not be so much " in " a word as in a general readiness to use the metaphors and take them seriously. " The wind bloweth where it listeth " (John iii.8) may mean the Holy Spirit or what we would call " life ", the breath of vitality ; we seem to get the literary effect all right in English without the profound Greek word. As to the word itself, I do not pretend to more learning than I can find in the dictionary, but that seems fairly conclusive. Homer does not use it, only a cognate word and that only for " strong wind ", and when *pneuma* first appears in Greek it is only used for " wind ". One must agree, no doubt, that a tendency to make the metaphorical connection " wind, breath, soul " must go back at least to the primitive Aryans ; there is that queer stuff in the Vedas about the different breaths. Still, for the Greek word, and among the recorded Greeks, we find metaphorical uses being added as secondary meanings to a root meaning, and not a Total Meaning which gets progressively cut down. No doubt Mr. Barfield would say that the Greeks' apprehension of metaphor was quite different from ours, but I do not see how there would be a radical enough difference to suit his purpose.

Mr. Barfield connects the invention of such words with the invention of myths, very rightly no doubt, but he cannot simply identify them. He never gives the one myth embodied in *pneuma* or the one word that embodies the myth of Persephone. His dislike for science makes him unreasonable here ; he seems to regard " I have no stomach for the business " as embodying a myth, though it is exactly like " I haven't the brains for it ", and that isn't allowed to be a myth because a doctor would agree with its assumption. It seems clear that there was a widespread view that the life was in the breath (as we would say the mind is in the brain), and this belief, no doubt, affected the word *pneuma*, but there is no need to suppose it was a myth in the sense of a story about the gods. No doubt such a myth could easily arise, which would give the word the other meaning " wind ". But the more seriously you took the myth, or felt the myth in the word, the more reason you would have to distinguish the meanings. Your breath may be the same sort of thing as the wind, but it is definitely not the same as " the breath of the wind-god " or " the exhalations of evil spirits ". By the time a word has got as much " total meaning " as this, there is a tug between its different parts or uses ; it will make what I call " equations ", and I do not think it gives what Mr. Barfield means by a " primitive undivided " total meaning. Nor does it seem likely that this was the first stage in the development of the word ;

the thing is too complicated. Contrariwise some group of speakers may have believed very completely that the life is in the breath, and expressed this so fully in language that they had one word " breath+soul ", which they put to both uses without feeling that there were two senses. There is no tension from theology about the thing ; they believe the theory as we believe the mind is in the brain; and they combine the senses as we use " light " for the waves and the sensations and the lamp that gives them. My only point is that this need not be " primitive ". It is easy to suppose a theology that was slowly democratised, as in Egypt ; in the First Empire only the Pharaoh's breath would be a soul (whatever that was), and every-body's breath might start to be a soul some time in the Middle Kingdom, so that everybody had to pay the priests. This talk about " primitive " language seems only to turn to the start of the history book ; language has been going on a long time. What we want from " primitive " language, if that is to explain the development of complex words, is a process that may work at any time, and therefore among ourselves, though perhaps feebly.

Now Piaget's account of a " wind-breath " theory at the beginning of *The Child's Conception of Causality* gives us plenty of it. The children of five or six that he examined had a queer idea of " participation " between wind inside and outside the body, and tended to say that wind is produced by man, God, breath, or machines. There can be little doubt that these tendencies of thought, hanging about in the sub-conscious mind, make the metaphor of the word a natural one. But the children are quite clear about the *difference* between wind and breath ; they merely give the two things odd relations of cause ; and the historical Greeks can hardly be supposed to be more childish. And then again, if a word means "air in motion" or "a current of air", it combines breath-sent-out and wind automatically and without metaphor, just as a black and a white cat are both cats. But this is not at all what Mr. Barfield means by his " total meaning " which does not involve metaphor ; at least it would destroy his argument. It seems clear at any rate that the primitive Aryans and the children were not using this general notion ; and as for the historical Greeks, I see no reason to doubt that they used plain metaphor, as in " Bill, punch him in the wind ". And if there is any primitive process at work in building the metaphor it must surely be the one we have evidence for ; the quasi-identifying of wind and breath from a vague magical belief that they have connections of cause.

An ingenious mythmaker, however, could again deny the distinc-tion recognised by the equations. We have supposed a word that picked up senses " breath, soul, wind ", by participation, theories of cause, and simple metaphor ; there is a feeling of tension between these different ideas, and contrariwise they can be given equations that connect them, for example, when talking about Boreas or Will-of-the-Wisp. The theologian can now put in a tearing equation between all three, and produce the central notion of the thought of India : " the soul of each man *is* at bottom the soul of the world ". The enormous respect of Mr. Barfield for primitive total meanings is based on an idea that they involved in a dim but powerful manner such assertions as this ; they are supposed to proceed from a view of man's relation to Nature which implies profound and urgent truths such as mere reason cannot attain. Certainly in attempting to refute this view one is in danger from deep waters. It seems only good sense to say that a rabbit knows that space is continuous, and you might say that the five conditions for continuity laid down by Dedekind and Cantor are inherent in its mind " unconsciously " ; you might then dwell on the truth that creatures with ideas like rabbits' were a necessary stage in the production of Dedekind and Cantor. The only trouble with this is that it doesn't tell you much about a rabbit. Just as Piaget's children connect breath with the wind, so they connect any shadow with the most striking shadow they know of ; the striking case " participates ", in the sense that it comes into their mind when they think " why ? ", and is then said to be the cause ; the shadow of a book on the table has come in from outside under the trees. The performances on *shadow* and *breath* seem clearly alike, but the idea of participation only comes into shadows at the start by making them rather mysterious. Ghosts are called " shades ", the devil has no shadow, and Plato's shadows in the cave are no doubt an important piece of philosophical mythology ; but I do not see that there was any general doctrine to be extracted from the word. The fact that there was one to be extracted from " breath-wind-soul " seems to me a mere piece of luck, such as is sure to occur if the process is used often. I am not denying that the children may have a dim perception of the highest truths, only that these truths are in any plausible sense the " total meaning " of their words. Certainly the equations of " breath-wind-soul " may become an important source of such truths when men are already struggling to express them ; it is a great help, it may be the only method, to pick out those few of the muddled words of the language which can be twisted so that they sum the new doctrine up. But to say that what was sometimes possible was always " totally " inherent is merely to put your reverence in an odd place, and the reader may be excused if he shifts his attention to your private reasons for doing so.

A detail in the book which concerns numbers seems to round this point off. Mr. Barfield says " in *couple* and *brace* the idea of ' twoness ' has evidently first been abstracted and then re-clothed in imagery ". I suspect that is only because he does not want his mysterious wise process to arrive at so flat or mental an idea as " two ". There may be as much unconsciousness here as anywhere else. Primitive people no less than the practical gamekeeper possess the idea of " two ", but they need not trouble to invoke it before bracing two birds' legs together for ease in carrying. When you slit the leg and push through the claw you certainly do not feel you are " re-clothing twoness in imagery ", nor yet when you count the bag as so many of these carriable objects. I do not know whether the idea of twoness was discovered later than human speech, by extracting a general idea from all the words like *brace* and *couple*, or whether a set of words was developed independently (more than one tribe uses the names of the fingers) for the " abstract " process of counting. But throughout historical times you get words like " couple ", in which there is an important idea wrapped in a total meaning, and yet the idea has an independent life in the common word for " two ".

A similar position to the Barfield one was taken up by Professor Coomaraswamy, e.g. in *Figures of Speech or Figures of Thought* (1946), though in a more balanced way and with more stress on pictures and statues than on language. Most of what he says seems to me true and important, but he too is haunted by the idea that the first user of any traditional symbol must have been an explicit and subtle metaphysician. This may be all right as a claim for the arts of India, where civilisation is undoubtedly old, but when he goes on to champion the South Sea Islanders he makes greater demands on faith. It is an absurd piece of western materialism, we are told, to believe that the Trobriand Islanders are " ignorant of the causal connection between sexual intercourse and procreation " ; because " it is clear " that " their position is essentially identical " with that of the universal tradition, found in Aquinas as well as the Upanishads, by which the spirit has to give life if the bodily act is to be fertile. But the evidence about the Trobriand Islanders, without which anybody would have guessed that they were telling some holy or prudish lie, was that they habitually castrated all their male pigs to make them fatter, and the race of pigs was only kept up by wild boars who paid their visits secretly at night. Now, of course, Professor Coomaraswamy, if he had been forced to attend to the actual argument, could have answered that this was a corruption of the ancient profound philosophy ; and there may be other arguments for such a view ; but the Trobrianders themselves cannot be called an impressive argument for it. Indeed I think they rather suggest that, if there was any profound religious thought at the foundation of their matriarchy, it was expressed in some form fairly easy to misunderstand.

Both writers, no doubt, were influenced by distrust of scientific language and its covert claim to be the only true sort, and one must heartily agree that a great deal of bogus scientific diction contrives to be at once a corpse and a cheat. Hence, says Mr. Barfield, we must start out towards meaning from the meaningless, that is, from the rich disorder of primitive words, not from the special set of meanings developed by scientific language, especially as this set has certain harmful implications such as the cutting-off of subjective from objective. This becomes an attack on the Ogden and Richards *Meaning of Meaning*. Of course he has every right to choose a historical approach, if that is all. He can hardly claim to be writing himself entirely in rich primitive total words ; he writes clearly and well. One could make a dilemma, I think, about the wicked scientific words ; either they are simple though dead, and then at least they are safe tools, or else they are full of delusive suggestions, and then they are what he likes, they are primitive total meanings. It is more important to see that the development of science in the seventeenth century really did make a conscious return to the primitive in language, without needing pre-history or remote tribes. One must use the practical English of the artisan and avoid words carrying hints of scholastic philosophy ; no doubt the chief idea was that these words were safe and simple, but in fact they also made active suggestions. The trouble with bogus causes like " a dormitive virtue " was not that they made false suggestions but that they stopped thought ; to have a name for the cause of this one effect was to feel you needn't generalise. The common words were not only clear but widely applicable, that is, easily extended, in fact they had a looseness of their own, which was of a useful kind. Professor J. B. S. Haldane gave a striking example (though not a seventeenth-century one) in an article on " The Origin of Life ". In practical work you speak of " seeding " crystals ; a saturated solution which might produce several forms of crystal is given a small seed crystal of the form required. This was a kind of metaphor—an easily remembered name for the process, which also described it ; but it came to suggest ideas about the structure of the primitive cell and make a partial bridge between living and dead matter. The change of meaning falls entirely within the scientific field, but surely it yields just the type of profundity that Mr. Barfield expects only from primitive words.

With the theory of M. Levy-Bruhl I am not competent to enter into controversy ; he comes in here as a witness to the importance of the false identity process, and so far as I criticize his text it is merely to push him further than he went. It seems that later anthropologists have swung away from his type of approach, calling it armchair mosaic work based on missionaries' false reports, and claiming that the primitive mind is in no way different from our own. There is not much help from an anthropologist like Dr. Malinowski, highly conscious of the difficulties of translating primitive thought, who would claim that you must understand the whole culture of a tribe before you understand any of its thought-processes, that language must be dealt with by " context ", and that the context is always very complex. The danger of this view, in spite of its fundamental truth, is that it tends to stop you from saying anything on the matter. To get any scientific theory one must generalise, and the process does not seem especially dangerous here ; it seems reasonable to expect a simple trick, easy to fall into, at the basis of the kind of thought we call primitive. For a radical and general attempt to find its rules of action one must go to M. Levy-Bruhl, and it seems clear that there is some large truth behind the formulations that he can support with such ample evidence. Perhaps in any case a theory that the senses of a rich word interact is too obvious to need the pomp of support from anthropology. But it is tempting for a verbal critic to stray onto these writers about the roots of the mind, psychologists as well as anthropologists, because they continually say " A is B ". This gives me a kind of double ruff ; if they deny that the process is fundamental their own language needs interpreting. It may seem little use for the verbal analyst to play wren on the eagle back of the scientist, but the parasite has his strength ; at worst he can use his probe on the eagle.

A foreword to the English version of *The ' Soul ' of the Primitive*, added perhaps because M. Levy-Bruhl felt that somehow the point was still not very clear, says that he set out to examine " the notions they possess of their life-principles, their soul, and their personality " but that now " an examination of the facts available has led me to recognise that, properly speaking, they have not got any notions of them. I find myself face to face with pre-notions." This is admirable, but to set out to describe pre-notions in terms of notions is to face a linguistic problem, one that needs to be solved as such. Instead, he hovers between expounding mysticism and treating an equation-form as a plain statement. " My picture, my shadow, my reflection, my echo, etc. are literally myself " and so on, even though " the most undeveloped of savages really knows that his shadow is one thing and himself another " ; and so far as this is explained at all the explanation is that " in his representations, that which is generally predominant is not the objective but the mystic elements ". This method does curiously little harm, but only because at bottom his readers already know what an equation is ; as they get hold of the psychology they automatically get hold of the linguistics, even though both are couched in what is in fact a mass of meaningless sentences. The principle M. Levy-Bruhl assumes is that an anthropologist must not add to primitive thought his own sophisticated notions. But if he merely babbles like the savage he leaves to the reader the original difficulty of the field-worker, and while doing this, I think, he tends to slip in a sophisticated mysticism. He claims, to be sure (*How Natives Think* p. 38), that his term *mystic* does not refer to " the religious mysticism of our own communities, which is something entirely different ", but is used " in the strictly defined sense in which 'mystic' implies belief in forces and influences and actions which though imperceptible to sense are nevertheless real ". But everybody believes in things like that, and in trying to make sense of his treatment of it as peculiar to savages one is driven back on the ordinary meaning of the word.

He tends also to hunt for European words that will play something like the primitive trick, but the tricks might not be the same at an important point, and anyway there is no advantage in putting the main idea in so queer a place. Thus the terms " image " and " double " are supposed to be nearer the primitive mind than " spirit " ; but while some savages in his examples use a rather casual idea of the soul as an image or a double some do not. The only advantage in using these terms for all cases is in their effect on *us*—they give us a vague idea of two things distinct yet identical, so encourage thought by equations. It is perhaps less misleading when he uses " individuality ", which has nothing in it but the fog required ;

> " The contradiction which the author finds perplexing arises from the fact that he does not see that the dead man's individuality comprises both the dead body in the grave and what he calls the ' spirit ' which is at a distance."

This learned word *individuality* is wonderfully well suited to express primitive thought, but it really cannot claim to explain anything ; the fundamental thing is the contradiction, an equation between " ghost " and " corpse " which makes them distinct but the same. And the main field for explanation is what the ghost was before it was equated.

Previous writers, M. Levy-Bruhl remarks, have suggested about the custom of destroying a man's property at his death that " it is meant to provide the dead man with all that he requires, so that he may not be unhappy in his new state, and, if it is an important personage, to furnish him with the means of maintaining his rank— to rid the living of objects which death has rendered unclean and therefore unusable—to avoid any risk that the dead man, exercising jealous supervision over the survivors, may be tempted to return and seek his possessions ". Evidence is then brought to show that this is only done when there is a " participation " between the dead man and his property ; for instance old men will sometimes avoid wearing their new clothes, as it seems a pity to have them destroyed at the approaching funeral—not simple ownership but being sweated onto and such like is what makes it necessary. " We may admit "

" that the motives we have indicated are those which natives attribute to themselves and yet ask ourselves whether, as a matter of fact, their customs ought not to be referred to other collective representations which are peculiar to mystic pre-logical mentality."

And " the motives are to be accounted for by the bond, not the bond by them ". Yet at the end of this long passage all heading in one direction he decides that the valuables destroyed are *useless* " apart from the mystic bond that unites them to the individual who has made and used and possessed them ". Now the belief that the spear will miss if another man throws it is no doubt an actual motive, and M. Levy-Bruhl is right to point it out, but it is on the same level as the others. And no doubt there is one motive force directing all the interpretations, but it is simple fear of death. The trouble with M. Levy-Bruhl here is that he thinks like one of his primitives ; he interprets the equation anew and claims his version as the real motive. We may note, however, that civilisation is at work in him too, and he has to throw in " mystic " as a rival interpretation. But he has made it quite clear that the " bond " is a simple equation. —" Tom's *are* Tom ". What Tom has made his own, in ways decided on other principles, holds the relation of contradictory-identity with himself. I am not saying more than M. Levy-Bruhl said ; indeed, the way he shifts off the main issue at the end may be only a slip in writing. But the linguistic reason for the shifts is that French, like English, makes the " A is B " form seem only a loose descriptive substitute for something else, so that you are tempted to use it without taking it seriously.

Certainly, in any one successful case, the equation will be interpreted as something so like a clear notion that it yields a clear plan of action, but the puzzle of relating this to the other notions produced in other cases is not faced by M. Levy-Bruhl's style. Thus if you get hold of a man's nailparings you can kill him, and we are told that this is because " he *is* his toe-nails " ; but a child that cuts its upper teeth first ought to be drowned, and the only way to avoid this is to collect all cast hair and nails and teeth till the first set of teeth has gone, and then drown the collection ; this too is because " he *is* his toe-nails ", though it saves his life. M. Levy-Bruhl merely states the equation, but if you only knew this much about a particular savage you could not prophesy his behaviour. The equation itself does not mean anything, either to the savage or to M. Levy-Bruhl ; it is simply a thing that their minds will do. But from it you can get notions or plans of procedure, and you choose the one you want at the time. This, of course, is where the emotions come in, which he makes so crucial ; but one need not suppose that reason has been drowned in a storm of passion ; there has only to be a definite enough preference to interpret the equation.

While attracted by " mystic " M. Levy-Bruhl was against " spirit ", partly through irritation with the hopeful reports of missionaries; and I rather sympathize with this clash of prejudices. But his attack on the claim that savages believe in " spirit " presumes an Aristotelian dichotomy, with mere matter fundamentally distinct from soul (equated to form) ; he cannot much disturb the missionaries by proving that the primitives have not decided on all that. On this kind of point one must agree with Professor Coomaraswamy's objections (and I suppose with James Joyce's, for an attack on M. Levy-Bruhl seems to loom through one section of *Finnegan's Wake*). Actually, the concept held by Lucretius, that spirit is a " subtle matter " with special powers, one that it was still respectable for Donne to expound in sermons, would seem on his evidence to be rather widespread among primitive minds. When he calls this a " preconcept " he throws all our notions under suspicion ; not only definite, it has satisfied some of the best minds of Europe. You may, of course, say that the savages have not really got this concept, but the distinction is a baffling one ; at times they will talk and act as if they had got it ; the natural way to phrase the effect is that they reach such ideas but fail to hold them. Thus there is a missionary (*Spirit*, English version, p. 276) who contrived to crawl home after being wounded and was regarded with awe. Apparently he crawled fifty miles, so it is not specially savage to feel awe here. " There sits the *soul* of Y.", as they pointed him out on the verandah, is a good case of the equation so fully asserted by M. Levy-Bruhl's method— " ghost-man-corpse ". But another man in the same tribe met him suddenly and said " yes, I know it *was* Y., but who are you now ? ", and this can only be the idea of possession. Another tribesman gives a clear logical statement of the theory that if you tie the legs of the corpse the ghost cannot walk, and if properly reported must have given these entities two words. M. Levy-Bruhl says that this " amounts to saying, though not quite openly, that the two are identical "—so far from " not being open " he makes the same analysis of primitive thought as M. Levy-Bruhl. Surely the striking thing is this apparent clarity; the normal process of thought seems independent of the primitive one, and may extract from it various notions of *spirit* without feeling the need to hold on to any of them. Evidently the primitive process is something you can fall back on, and I do not see that the term " preconcept " gives any help. The reason why the concepts can vary is that the permanent thing is the equation in some key symbol from which they are derived ; and this is what the theorist should isolate, whether he calls it a preconcept or not.

The term " mystic " hangs about a good deal, though from time to time M. Levy-Bruhl attacks it and removes all its meaning. Taken with " collective representation " and " common consciousness ", borrowed from Durkheim, it comes to very little ; all objects of religious thought are symbols of the forces immanent in the tribe, moral forces for example, a view which you could hold while believing that moral forces are also transcendent ; and the enthusiasm of an orator is " mystic " if he feels his audience is with him. No doubt primitive people often use a distinction of this kind, so that much of their thought is sensible by our ideas and only the holy or magical parts are " primitive ". The question is what you gain by using the term " mystic". It seems enough to say that in such thought they think by equations, usually those inherent in their traditional symbols ; they feel, therefore, that they are sinking into the accepted symbols, bringing out the wisdom buried in the symbols, a thing that belongs to the tribe not to one speaker ; whereas in ordinary life you take one end (meaning, context) of the symbol and put it to an independent practical use. This may in turn lead to a feeling that when they use such equations they are mysteriously one with some greater being, or what not, a feeling that would ordinarily be called mysticism. I have no wish to deny that a good deal of genuine mysticism may go on in primitive tribes ; but it is only confusing to extend the term to the earlier stage, in which the person to hold in view is less Plotinus than (say) Lloyd George.

Thus the use of " mystic " goes back to the terms " representation collective " and " conscience commune ". The puzzle here becomes at one point obvious in English because we separate " conscience " from "consciousness", though Shakespeare could make play with not having done so. One of Durkheim's English translators rather pathetically claimed that the collective consciousness is generally the collective unconsciousness, so that he was right in using the English " conscience ", but in many of his sentences the word is obviously feeling the strain. These terms assume that the basis of the thought they describe is in "concepts" which " represent " or at least display " consciousness " of some referent, but then we have to learn that the collective representations are "not always, strictly speaking, representations", and then, on a distant page, that they are not always " collective "—a man may expect the ghost near the fresh corpse of his own accord. By this time there seems nothing else that a preconcept can be except an emotion, which gets mixed up with the concept by some unknown process usually connected with groups. Whenever the authors admit that they are not really dealing with concepts they see no other possible basis for the thought except " collective mental states of extreme emotional intensity ", and this is also described as "mysticism ". But when they are actually explaining something they use an equational form of grammar, and this seems much more to the point than any explosion of passion. No doubt orgiastic ceremonies sometimes give one a renewed power to accept tribal beliefs, but this tells you little about what the beliefs are.

M. Levy-Bruhl gives what seems to me a rather unfair piece of evidence to prove the intensity of emotion required for primitive modes of thought. He quotes a speech of an Eskimo shaman, apparently untouched by missionaries, sympathetic to the scientific approach, glad to tell the truth clearly, who has decided that the religion he administers is a low product based upon fear. "Nous ne croyons pas, nous avons peur " begins this fine piece of rhetoric, admirably suited to the French language, and he proceeds to illustrate the epigram in detail and drive it home with every phrase. But there is a good deal of fear in most religions, and he was comparing his society not to ours but to his own ideals or to the strong character of one explorer. All that he tells you about the snow huts, and it is good to know it, is that they are the scene of free speech and rousing speeches. It is ridiculous to accept such talk as proof of a debased and morbid mentality ; the tribe has produced Aua, and he has the very accent of the Noble Savage. It is not fair to produce him in the opening pages of " Le Surnaturel et le Nature dans la Mentalité Primitive " so as to tinge the whole topic with a lurid purple.

However, I do not mean to deny that emotions are often at work ; identities are generally called into play when a subject is puzzling and exciting. Nor do I want to maintain that the savage identities are always developed as equations inside a single word. This would take us back to Mr. Barfield, or rather to Max Muller, who seems to have revived the classical attempt to explain mythology by linguistic error. It appears that most savages are willing to change their language, able to maintain distinctions not clear in it, and more liable to be impressed by non-linguistic symbols. *Both Sides of Buka Passage* gave an interesting case of a group of tribes all quite sure of the distinction between two sorts of ghost though only some tribes gave them two words. No doubt it is we who tend to push the primitive modes of thought into the interior of single words, because we have made some attempts to tidy the overt logic of our grammar. But this distinction need not be made sharp ; everybody's grammar has to be used for practical affairs, and a magical idea is generally given in a single word which carries a good deal of Emotion. The main difference seems to be that the tribes make a franker magical use than we do of sentences in the " A is B " form.

The most obvious use of false identity arises in totemism ; indeed, on this issue the primitives simply lectured the scientific observers until they had drummed the idea into their heads. When the Bororo of Brazil insisted that they *were* parrots, with no double meaning about it at all, and thus annoyed the anthropologist (" as if a caterpillar should claim to be already a butterfly ", he rudely objected), they knew with the clarity of a theologian that what they wanted to assert was precisely the identity of two ideas already distinct. If these people are " primitive " they are evidence that the human mind is inherently metaphysical. It is melancholy to read that the anthropologists got them down in the end, and they now parrot off phrases such as that they are only of the same substance as parrots. But in such a case the false identity had been conventionalized into a dogma ; the more interesting question is how it was arrived at. Indeed, this question has been connected with the profounder one of how a "concept" is ever arrived at ; Durkheim denied any use of concepts to animals and suggested that they were discovered through the invention of totemism. They may not have received attention till they were impressively misused, but that is another thing. It is hard to believe that a dog has no apprehension at all of the truth that while all men are men, his master is a particular man ; a power to behave *as if* you were thinking in concepts seems to appear rather early in the scale of life. The stage when the fallacies arise (as in telling the dead bear to come and be killed easily next time because you have put butter in his mouth) is when this skill has been partly translated into a set of public symbols, and it seems obvious that the cause is a standard type of misuse of them. The fallacy " This bear is The Bear " is an example of a regular equation " the specimen is the class ", and we appeal to the same trick when we say " the horse is a noble animal ", thus dignifying the horse, whereas " pigs are dirty ". A development of this was the main device of metaphysical poetry ; the individual who is a class is now usually compared to the Logos who was an individual man. It was the same equation which made the Nightingale in Keats immortal. So permanent a device need not be tied to the origins of anything ; you certainly do not have to be ignorant of the idea of a concept before you can make the trick work.

All the same, it is agreeable to speculate about the origins of language, and there is a reason for expecting some form of totemism to appear very early. Most of our words are now dead symbols, that is, only interesting in view of their referents, though it is part of the business of a writer to give them a life of their own. But when people were first coming to agree on public symbols they would only agree on symbols interesting enough to receive attention in themselves. The first public symbols are therefore likely to be double symbols, and in fact a totem will stand both for the tribe and the mysterious forces of outer nature. It is therefore used both ways. " The Emu is all the Emu men " asserts tribal unity, but " All the Emu men are the Emu " gives them dignity and security against the outer world. The equation belongs to Type IV, the most advanced one. But in arguing like this one must beware of imagining that existing totemic tribes are any nearer the origins of language than we are ; for that matter, the spectacle in Jane Austen's England of rival camps distinguished by *sense* and *sensibility* gives a rather neat parallel to a tribe divided into two totem-classes.

Totemism in fact is rather too much of a gift for the equation theory. In other matters, it might be argued, the equation process cannot say anything important about primitive thought, because the real question is how the concepts arose which are afterwards equated; for example, it may explain why people expect the ghost near the fresh corpse, but cannot explain why they believe in ghosts to start with. However, we have included the assertion of an Implication as a predicate in Type II, and there the equation arises before the new Sense does. An implication can easily have a casual relation to the head meaning, so that the equation is interpreted by " entails ". This fits in very well with one of the more plausible theories of the origin of ghosts. Savages and children are said to explain hearing, if they try to, by supposing a little man in your ear who hears (" there must be something in the ear which hears ; the only known things that hear are complete creatures ; therefore what hears in the human ear must be a small man)". In the same way if they explain living they suppose another living creature inside you, and when you die it has merely gone away. The process here is that of forming a dim notion of an abstract cause and then using it as subject of an equation " the cause is the result ". I do not say that this has to occur inside a single word ; it may not be a verbal process at all till it is expressed overtly as " A is B ". (Incidentally, it would be worth making a world survey of the derivations of words for ghosts.) But in civilised speech the same process regularly occurs within single words, as in " light is a vibration of the ether ". Our sensations of light are certainly not a vibration, whatever may be their cause ; but the plain man had already been saying " I left the light on all night ", assuming that the cause of the sensations deserved the same name as the sensations. The shift of meaning in a word from the thing to its cause will be often made for mere convenience, and the equation of the two meanings may then be made to yield an argument not at all in view when the extra meaning was acquired.

The example of *light* comes from Durkheim, who used it for an excellent point against Levy-Bruhl's theory of " participation ". It is not true, he said, that savages have " a general and systematic indifference to contradiction " or " a single and inclusive inclination for indistinction " ; when they do use this process, it is for a special mode of thought still essential for the modern scientist.

" Today as formerly, to explain is to show how one thing participates in one or several others. . . Is not the statement that man is a kangaroo or the sun a bird equal to identifying the two with each other ? But our manner of thought is not different when we say of heat that it is a movement, or of light that it is a vibration of the ether, etc. Every time that we unite heterogenous terms by an internal bond we forcibly identify contraries."

This seems rather at variance with his remarks a few pages before, that we nowhere really see beings mixing and metamorphosing themselves into one another, therefore some powerful force must be at work to make the savage suppose it ; a force which Durkheim identifies with religion, and is then tempted to treat mystically. In view of eggs and caterpillars, let alone such fundamental issues as the relations of mind and matter, the idea that things do not really mix and metamorphose seems rather optimistic. But he has already identified religion with his " conscience commune ", which I think makes the problem unnecessarily complex.

The point which I wanted to demonstrate is merely that the use of false identity is common among primitives, as well as among ourselves, and perhaps there was no need to do it at such length. How far the thought of this kind expressed by primitive! is due to equations within single words I do not pretend to decide ; much of it is clearly in the overt grammatical form " A is B ".

Re-reading Bertrand Russell's *Analysis of Mind*, after this was finished, I was struck by how much better his treatment of vague ideas had been than mine. However I do not see that his treatment uncovers actual fallacies in mine.

Analysing memory, in the simple form where an image of an event is accompanied by the belief " this occurred ", he points out (p. 180)

if the word " this " meant the image to the exclusion of everything else, the judgement " this occurred " would be false. But identity is a precise conception, and no word, in ordinary speech, stands for anything precise. Ordinary speech does not distinguish between identity and close similarity. A word always applies, not only to one particular, but to a group of associated particulars, which are not recognised as multiple in common thought or speech. Thus primitive memory, when it judges that " this occurred ", is vague but not false. . . . A word is general when it is understood to be applicable to a number of different objects in virtue of some common property. A word is vague when it is in fact applicable to a number of different objects because, in virtue oι some common property, they have not appeared, to the person using the word, to be distinct. I emphatically do not mean that he has judged them to be identical, but merely that he has made the same response to them all and has not judged them to be different.

I fully agree that this kind of vagueness is different from my equation process, in which there *is* assertion of false identity. All I have to claim is that the second easily grows out of the first, as soon as the possible deductions from the confusion are themselves vaguely realised ; Russell would not deny this, and indeed claims in the same passage that the process explains Bergson and Hegel.

With any sceptical comment of this sort, for that matter, my little machine is quite at home ; it merely puts in tabular form a frequent accusation. But Russell himself in the same book can be found saying with serious conviction (p. 142):

the sensation that we have when we see a patch of colour simply *is* that patch of colour, an actual constituent of the physical world, and part of what physics is concerned with.

How then do I analyse this sentence if it is true ; that is, suppose A really is identical with B, can we still not say so without using " false identity "? The answer must be, I think, that the rhetorical form is still used for a sort of pretence of false identity, in that the sentence is framed so that we realise how different A and B would appear to the opponent ; one might regard this intellectually and call it the device prior to irony which keeps alive both sides of the debate, or one might merely say in a literary manner that it invokes the old magic to give the proper effect of shock. In a case like this the italicised copula ought certainly not to be explained away as meaning anything different from identity, such as " is like " or " is typical of ", and I hope I am not thought to be saying that no assertion of this kind can be true, which would imply that no reduction of otiose terminology is ever possible. The point is that a good sentence of this kind presents its drama ; it says " you were wrong to attach these distinguishable properties to distinct objects "; just as the end of a detective story can say " the embarrassed curate *is* the murderer of the bishop ". Russell's assertion of an identity here seems to me possibly true but not certainly true, and this book needs to include at least one case where the analyst does not pretend to know the answer.

Chapter 21

DICTIONARIES

MUCH of the work of this book has been an attempt to do on a large scale, for individual cases, the sort of work that a dictionary has to do summarily ; and I ought now to consider how far a dictionary could use the results. One might no doubt make a dictionary of reasonable size which only listed words that carry important equations ; but it is not clear beforehand which they should be, and I suspect that people would be rather unwilling to use a dictionary which exposed them to a continual risk of disappointment. A certain claim to a workmanlike completeness is necessary if a dictionary is to seem more than a toy. Short dictionaries could, I think, be improved, and I will try in this chapter to say how, but most of the symbols used in this book would be out of place. In a dictionary claiming completeness I hope that all my symbols, or something corresponding to them, would be useful ; but the undertaking would of course be an enormous one, and the N.E.D. collection of material is not likely to need improving except in minor detail. The idea of a still bigger dictionary than the N.E.D. is obviously impracticable if not ludicrous. But a revised edition of it is presumably envisaged for the eventual future, and it ought not to seem presumptuous for any member of the public to discuss how it should be recast. My general proposal is that the interactions of the senses of a word should be included, and if this is to seem reasonable I need to show that such a plan could be carried out without making the dictionary much longer. The obvious way to do this is to show that in its present form it is unnecessarily long, and I shall make here a few complaints about it to illustrate that point ; but I ought first to say clearly, what I hope is already obvious, that such work on individual words as I have been able to do has been almost entirely dependent on using the majestic object as it stands.

In any case most of the length comes from the examples, and as a rule they already illustrate the process of interaction, so that you would not need any more of them. The symbols I have put forward are in themselves of course very brief ; what would need a certain amount of space would be marking the turn to a new head sense at a given period, and the resulting change in equation structure. However, as a rule the dictionary claims that a new sense of the word appeared when the new structure did, so that one would only need a few lines of re-interpretation. There seems no doubt that HONEST would have to be a bit longer, but I think that SENSE and WIT might actually be shorter.

You could gain a good deal of space, and at the same time a good deal of clarity, by cutting out the thesaurus work of the definitions, by using numbers in brackets after a defining word on occasion to refer back to its own definition headings, and by arranging that you do not repeat the major part of a previous definition under a new head when you only want to define a slight change in it. The business of referring back is already sometimes used in the N.E.D., and I do not mean that it should be carried so far that the text cannot be read straightforwardly ; the purpose should be to guard against specific misunderstandings that might come from making the definitions short. All this no doubt would give the page a rather mechanised appearance, but people are more used to that nowadays than they were when the dictionary was started. I want now to recommend this point of view with a few complaints about the entries on SENSE and WIT.

The N.E.D. numbers for SENSE, not counting sub-heads, run up to thirty, and if this is necessary it seems reasonable to inquire how we ever pick out the right one. A few are stock phrases, and the function of the dictionary is to show how the word is applied when in such a phrase. A few, at the other extreme, are not " in " the word at all, but are uses, requiring no explanation, to which it was often put. For example " 21 " says that the word was often used in combinations such as " anagogical sense " for interpreting Scripture, but it is not claimed that *sense* alone came to mean the whole phrase. The group is historically important because it gives examples from Wycliff in 1400, more than a century before the other sources for the whole group " 19—23 ", also no doubt because it gives a reason why the word came into frequent use. But this " 21 " belongs under " 20 " " one of the meanings of a passage ", and it would be clearer to put it there because then the earliest examples could be shown first. This is an extreme example, but serves to point out that the meanings fall into large groups ; there are many meanings treated as distinct which obviously go together. I do not mean that they can't be distinguished ; the dating of the historical rise of the whole range requires elaborate treatment, and it would be ridiculous to complain at having the work done so magnificently. But since the conclusion is that the range " 2—7 ", for instance, all appear in the second half of the sixteenth century, I do not see that it is useful to treat the parts as distinct senses ; the fact that the speakers evidently took them as " going together " deserves also to be shown, and the suggestion that one developed out of another is misleading. Combining the definitions and treating the examples (still in the same groups) as illustrating parts of it marked by letters would do more to interpret the same evidence, and would be shorter. No doubt this is a rather marginal matter, but to say there are thirty meanings is anyway rather absurd. The only definitely bad entries are " 13 " and " 14 " (already mentioned) ; " a more or less vague perception or impression *of* (an outward object, as present or imagined) " and " a more or less indefinite consciousness or impression *of* (a fact, state of things, etc.) as present or impending ". The logical distinctions between an object and a state of things, a perception and a consciousness, vague and indefinite, imagined and impending, all seem to me confusing and trivial ; and both sets of examples begin with apparent early uses which obscure the fact that this feeling did not get into the word till the eighteenth century. Even here, though the two ought to be combined, I do not mean that the logical distinction ought to be ignored ; but it is enough to put " (an outward object, a fact, state of things, etc.)".

WIT has a rather more mature treatment which shows the principles more clearly. There are only fourteen heads, and it is admitted that one sense can " connote " another. The over-riding distinction " I " " denoting a faculty " and " II " " denoting a quality " is retained, but after " 2 " we are told " for the corresponding pregnant uses see " 5 " and " 6 " (these have to be put into " II " because to have a faculty in a high degree is to have a quality). We have :

1. the seat of consciousness or thought, the mind ; sometimes connoting one of its functions, as memory or attention.   1100

2. the faculty of thinking or reasoning in general ; mental capacity, understanding, intellect, reason (arch.).   1297

5. good or great mental capacity ; intellectual ability ; genius talent, cleverness ; mental quickness or sharpness ; acumen. (The earliest quotations may belong to other senses, e.g. 6 or 11).   1297

6. wisdom, good judgement, discretion, prudence.   1200

I thought at first that the use of the distinction between " 1 " and " 2 ", a thing which in itself would be hard to rephrase briefly, was meant to appear in the corresponding " pregnant " versions ; but this is not plausible when you try to work it out, and the note under " 2 " must refer to that sense only.   The contrasting " 5 " and " 6 " correspond to the different parts of " 2 " separated by the semicolon ; it took me a long time to invent this theory, but I now offer it with some confidence.   At any rate " 5 " and " 6 ", cleverness and good judgement, are distinct ; in fact they have often been treated as opposites.   And Pope could use *wit* to cover both while recognising the distinction ; but this was because his *wit* was heavily weighed towards " 5 " and could only just be stretched to include " 6 " as well.   If the word could simply mean both, in the early sixteenth century, say, it had no way of getting a grip on the distinction.   Here then we have a definite example of the problem suggested by the thirty meanings of *sense*. Surely, in any period, a case where the hearer could be certain that *wit* " 6 " was meant and not " 5 " must have been extremely rare. To be sure, there is a certain play in the joints of " 6 ", because its four units (separated only by commas) begin with " wisdom " and are graded down to " prudence ". Some of the examples definitely mean " wisdom ", for example, the first one 1200 " God's son is God's word and God's wit ". But one might regard this as a combination of knowledge (" 11 ") and reasoning faculty (" 2 "). It does not mean God's prudence, and I do not see that any one of the examples can be limited to the group " good judgement, discretion, prudence ". Certainly there is the sub-head " a wit " (getting is a chance and keeping a wit) but this demands sharpness as well as prudence ; it could be classed under " 5 " as an example of " acumen ". We are told quite plumply that " Brevity is the soul of wit " is an example of " 6 ", commonly misunderstood as the modern " 8 " ; Dr. Johnson said so too ; but what argument could be given to prove it ? The Victorian Samuel Butler remarked very truly that brevity was the soul of a lot of other things. I should have thought that Polonius meant to straddle " 2 " or " 5 " and the modern " 8 ", which was already in use ; but even granting that he didn't, how could the contemporary audience find out ? Surely the important point is that they couldn't ; that until the development of *sense* for " good judgement " this idea was actually hard to isolate, because, if you tried to make *wit* mean only that, you had no way to cut out its implications of cleverness and knowledge. The later uses of *wit* for " good judgement ", on the other hand (Swift—" they had the wit to recall Aristides "), are an obscure irony (" they weren't clever, but at this point they were cleverer than usual "). I should maintain then that to treat the group " 6 " as a *separable* sense of the word is not merely unnecessary but actively misleading, both at the earlier and later dates.

The struggle of the N.E.D. to show the complete historical development of a word tends, I think, to land it in two opposed types of confusion. A number " x " will appear with its examples, not because the sense was felt to be distinct at the dates given, but because the context which the examples illustrate led eventually to a different sense " y ". On the other hand, examples will be listed under " y " which date from a period before the separate meaning " y " existed, and do not belong to it at all, but are supposed to show that the growth toward " y " could be a gradual one. Both practices are confusing, and I think that what is required is a symbol meaning " forerunners " under which both sets of examples could be listed without prejudice ; the obvious way is to start the group with these cases, inside a square bracket, And indeed the N.E.D. sometimes does it ; the most obvious ground for revision of the great work is that it developed gradually and has no unified technique.

We then get a puzzle which has defeated me altogether :

7. Quickness of intellect or liveliness of fancy, with capacity of apt expression ; talent for saying brilliant or sparkling things, esp. in an amusing way (cf. Sense 8).

8. That quality of speech or writing which consists in the apt association of thought and expression, calculated to surprise and delight by its unexpectedness ; later always with reference to the utterance of brilliant or sparkling things in an amusing way.

From the middle sixteenth century onwards, uses of the word are confidently put down for " 7 " and not for " 8 ", for " 8 " and not for " 7 ". I cannot see that any distinction can be meant except the logical one between the capacity to produce the quality and the quality which the capacity produces. Practically all the examples quite certainly envisage both. In an ecstasy of subtlety, the dictionary quotes under " 7 " a definition of wit by Boyle about both " conceiving and expressing ", and under " 8 " a definition of wit by Locke about both " assemblage of ideas and putting those together with quickness and variety". Both of them, it seems to me, were positively claiming to include both. It therefore seems very likely that what the dictionary meant was some other distinction, but I do not know what. If the logical distinction was meant, it is extraordinarily confusing to re-write the whole definition, which ought to have been equally suited to both the capacity and its product, so as to throw in innumerable other possible distinctions. Why is " 7 " especially amusing and " 8 " only amusing later ? Why is " 8 " surprising and not " 7 "? Why does " 7 " not deserve the evidently careful phrase " apt association of thought and expression " ? It seems to me that a cast-iron rule is needed to make this kind of confusion impossible. You should never re-phrase a whole definition in order to recall one of the logical elements of the total meaning. And whenever this rule would make you repeat a long phrase several times you should give the phrase once to define a symbol and repeat the symbol instead.

I hope that this makes out a case for saying that important additional information could be put into the N.E.D. without adding to the number of volumes. However, I do not pretend to feel sure what it should be. I think that some equations need to be listed, but a dictionary need not distinguish my four types as such. If you list an equation " $2=5$ ", say, of which " 5 " is the major sense, the equation is presumably of Type I, with the immediate context requiring "2"; otherwise it is of the rejected fifth type which need not be listed. If " 2 " is the major sense the equation will be of Type II or III according to which sense the immediate context requires. But this is not the distinction which requires listing, I think ; the important question is whether (being a serious case of Type III) the equation can be interpreted " 2 is the typical part of the 2+5 complex ", and this could be shown briefly by putting " 2=2+5 ", followed by a sentence showing how the possibility was used. To show an equation of Type IV a dictionary need only put " 2+5 ", since it can assume that nonce-uses of confusion are not what it is listing.

This amount of symbolism, however indecorous it might appear, really does seem to be needed, because it is important to make the reader notice that the senses can combine and interact. I do not think a separate symbol for Emotions is needed ; it would be enough to use the exclamation mark where it is required in the word defining a given use, a thing which is at present avoided rather absurdly; that is, one need not also offend the eye by writing " 2! " and so on. Probably it would not in any case be needed often. Moods certainly need listing in some cases, and are already shown to be moods by the sentence defining them, which uses quotation marks and the personal pronoun. Perhaps " Md. " as a symbol introducing them would be less offensive than my " £ ". The symbol " / " for Implications does not seem offensive, and would clear up many cases where examples of a sense appear to be listed from a date before the sense had established itself.

However, I cannot write down these proposals without feeling how unlikely they are to be acted on, and perhaps it is not really very important to improve the N.E.D. The great work is not what a man wants unless he knows the language intimately already, and then he ought to be able to struggle through the mistaken definitions and concentrate on the historical evidence in the examples. What is much more urgent is that short dictionaries should be improved, because they are intended for people who actually need help. The rest of this chapter will be concerned with the problems of short dictionaries, and I think that also has the convenience of letting one see what is required by any dictionary in a sort of diagrammatic form.

I ought not to be petulant about the failures of dictionaries to put in the sort of thing that interests me, if the reason is merely that they have no room. But I find myself saying indignantly, like Alice in Wonderland, " there's plenty of room " ; it seems clear to me that dictionaries might be made much more useful without taking up more space. And the matter is of considerable importance. To an Englishman who has had an expensive education the English-to-English dictionary no doubt does not seem very crucial ; partly because he knows a fair lot of classical derivations, and partly because the mistakes he made in first learning his own language have been weeded out of him by teachers correcting his " essays ". But the self-educated Englishman is very dependent on luck in whether the dictionary happens to be intelligible, on a point where he has got confused. And English-to-English dictionaries are widely used by foreigners with a very vague knowledge of English. In the Far East, at any rate, the confusion of translation equivalents is so great that many students have been warned against the interlingual dictionary. What they need is an English-to-English dictionary which is guaranteed against circularity, does on the other hand give working rules to distinguish near-synonyms, and also gives warnings of the unexpected tricks that a word might play, especially by an unlooked-for sense poking up. I know that this is a large order, but that is all the more reason for giving some attention to it.

How you are supposed to interpret what is put in a dictionary has been left extraordinarily obscure. It seems clear that different parts of the account given for one word may have been put there for different purposes, and that to use a dictionary with success, let alone to make one, you ought to know what they are. It may be only ignorance which keeps me from knowing where this subject has been worked out, but the ignorance seems to be pretty widespread. Webster's Dictionary is the only I know which even makes a brief comment on the distinction between comma and semicolon, a thing that obviously plays some vital part in the performance. I inquired about this from the secretary of the N.E.D. a long while ago and got the official answer that " there had been no intention of compiling a thesaurus " ; this seems to imply that no two even of the words separated only by commas (" actually, really, truly, positively ") are offered as equivalents for the purposes in hand. But, once a dictionary has adopted the practice of circular definition, it is in a sense committed to compiling a thesaurus in a cumbrous manner—because the reader does not know what other use the practice can be, and why once started it should not be completed. This gives him another puzzle in a field already complex. Under one word we have a series of groups of defining words and phrases. Any one such word or phrase, separated from the rest by commas or semicolons, may have been put in for the following reasons (1) to mark a new grammatical construction, which does not involve a separate change of meaning (2) to draw attention to a logical distinction between parts of the meaning, which is commonly ignored because the word means both ; the same distinction can usually be drawn within several of the word's meanings, so that if this plan were consistent all the permutations would have to be counted separately; (3) to suggest a feeling or tone which the word sometimes carries as well as one or more of its meanings, though the word cannot be used to give this feeling and nothing else ; (4) to qualify an adjacent word or phrase in the dictionary entry, so that they are meant to make one definition together, and finally (5), what most people expect, to peg down a separate sense, a part of the range of meaning which can be used alone. Even under (5) there are often several possible lines of opposition by which a word or phrase may be trying to distinguish itself from the adjacent ones. And on top of all this (6) the reader is never sure that the word or phrase has not been put in merely out of thesaurus-interest as another possible synonym. He has to keep in mind the question " what sort of reader is this meant for? Am I thinking of something too obvious or too subtle ? " It is often a highly-skilled piece of work to decide why the author put in a given word or phrase, and it is a curiously irrelevant one from the point of view of a man looking up a word in a dictionary.

It seems to me that something like the technique obviously in play in an English-to-Basic dictionary is what every English-to-English dictionary requires, and I hope that a large-scale English-to-Basic dictionary will be prepared. There is, of course, no need to do all the defining in the Basic words ; you can allow two stages of referring back without making the use of the thing too burdensome. The great interest of such a plan is that it makes all the problems of dictionary-making far more clear-cut. I want here not so much to recommend one method as to consider what is required, and is very often not provided even by a good dictionary. In taking a series of examples from the Concise Oxford, I am going to one which is admittedly very good, and also unusually articulate about its intentions.

One might think that the great advantage of using Basic is simply that you avoid circularity, as in BROAD " wide ", WIDE " broad ". But this method though often irritating has a use, because many people use a dictionary as a thesaurus. You know you want a word something like A but rather different—there *is* a word that fits, you feel sure, but you can only think of A. Then if you have a nice muddled dictionary and look up A, and then look up the more promising words under A, jumping up and down all kinds of scales of specialisation and generalization, you will as like as not hit on X. The person who does this is assumed to know the language already ; he wants to be reminded not informed. And what he would find convenient would simply be a page-number after the word A referring him to a group of synonyms. This, of course, would add to the length, but after treating this function separately the author could leave out many of the alternative forms which most dictionaries feel obliged to put in.

Furthermore, much of what is put after single words in a dictionary can only conveniently be done for a group of synonyms. When a word is taken alone, the reader does not see what the distinction is *for*. Each word of a group is in effect defined by a vague process of hinting at the others from which it has to be distinguished. So in many cases to accept the thesaurus approach would make the thing shorter as well as clearer, because the distinctions are only made once. They could be collected under the most general and least tricky of the group. The introduction to the C.O.D., to be sure, makes some excellent points about the system of cross-reference which should be used, and undertakes to give them (1) from the word treated to another word for the purposes of contrast, distinction, correlation, or the like, and (2) from any member of a group to the word under which the group is collected or further explained ; also (3) and (4) for proverbs and compounds. The method (1) is used between SLANDER, LIBEL and SCANDAL, for instance, to bring out the legal distinctions which are the point of the separate definitions, and (2) is used for technical points which can be handled very quickly, such as the different kinds of printers' type. This is excellent in principle, but there was quite as much need to use (2), for instance, on the group of scolding words.

However, other claims have been made for the circular thesaurus technique. The C.O.D. speaks with pride of its :

" unprecedented abundance of illustrative quotation ; define and your reader gets a silhouette ; illustrate, and he has it in the round ! That at least was our belief, and we hailed as a confirmation of it one or two letters from persons unknown congratulating us on having ' produced a live dictionary ', or ' treating English at last as a living language '."

One of their aims was " to give a vivid picture of the English that was being spoken and written at the time ". No doubt, the more illustrations a dictionary has room for the better, but I should connect the ideas behind these phrases with the extraordinary lengths to which thesaurus work was carried, rather confusing the illustrations than otherwise. Here for example is most of the entry on ROUGH, which does not so much give " quotations " as a panorama of rough things with a jungle of other adjectives that might be applied to them. It seems as well to give RUDE for comparison.

ROUGH : Of uneven or irregular surface, not smooth or level or polished, diversified or broken by prominences, hairy, shaggy, coarse in texture, rugged, (*r. skin, hands, paper, back, road, cloth, duty ; book with r. edges. . . r. leaf. . .; r. rice. . .*) ; not mild or quiet or gentle, unrestrained, violent, stormy, boisterous, disorderly, riotous, inconsiderate, harsh, unfeeling, drastic, severe, grating, astringent, (*r. manners, soldier, play ; r. water, sea, weather, road ; r. words ; r. elements of the population, quarter of the town ; r. usage, handling ; r. remedies ; r. baritone voice ; r. claret ; r. tongue,* habit of rudeness ; *r. passage ; rough work ; r. paces. . . r. luck ; r.* MUSIC) ; deficient in finish or elaboration or delicacy, incomplete, rudimentary, entirely or partly unwrought, merely passable, inexact, approximate, preliminary, (*r. nursing, style, welcome, kindness, plenty, accommodation, sketch, drawing ; r. work* and see above ; *r. state, attempt, makeshift, circle ; r. stone,* not dressed ; *r. DIAMOND ; r. justice ; r. translation, estimate ; r. copy* of picture etc., reproducing only essentials ; *r. draft ; r. COPY ; r. coat ; r. coating ; r. and ready,* not elaborate, just good enough, not over-particular, roughly efficient or effective).

RUDE : Primitive, simple, unsophisticated, in natural state, rugged, unimproved, uncivilised, uneducated, roughly made or contrived or executed, coarse, artless, wanting subtlety or accuracy, (*r. times, men, simplicity, ignorance, chaos ; r. produce, ore ; r. scenery ; r. plough ; r. beginnings, methods ; r. path, verses, drawing ; r. fare, plenty ; r. winter, style ; r. observer, version, classification*) ; violent, not gentle, unrestrained, startling, sudden, abrupt, (*r. passions, blast, shock, awakening, remainder*) ; vigorous, hearty (*r. health*) ; insolent, impertinent, offensive, (*r. remarks, say r. things ; be r. to,* insult).

I quite see that this ambition to make your dictionary " living " may be valuable and important. Fowler is teaching English to the English, and he is appealing to them to maintain their language and feel it as they can feel it and not let it decay. This is the only sane ground on which to write about " Modern English *Usage* " and at the same time say how it ought to be improved—you are appealing to a language-sense which you can call into play in your reader. In a case like the entry under ROUGH, the reader is being reminded of the range of feelings in the different uses of the word ; a lively stimulus to his writing. That is the idea. I cannot imagine anyone deliberately looking up ROUGH in a dictionary with this purpose in view, but he might. All you can object is that the use of the thing must be very narrowly to remind and not to inform. And after all most people use dictionaries in order to be informed. Even inside England probably the majority of users do it, and the dictionaries are used widely by foreigners with little knowledge of English. For that matter the same principle is used far too much in interlingual dictionaries ; I remember opening the standard pocket Japanese-English one and finding against some characters only

An inch of steel, the merest of a weapon.

This blank verse line is as " living " as it could be, and in most cases would lead into absurdity any unfortunate man who copied it out. What he needs is as nearly as possible the opposite ; something that would warn him of possible absurdities when writing English, and of the unexpected tricks that may be being played by an English author in his reading.

It may be objected that this is unfair as a complaint about the entry on ROUGH, because there the difficulty is from the idiomatic uses, and these have to be treated separately with nouns to illustrate them. But with most of the nouns the word simply takes the only metaphorical extension that it could. The heap of examples only frightens the reader and puts him off, if all he is meant to gather from it is that the word is often used metaphorically. And when there really is a puzzle the machine breaks down. What is he to make of " a rough claret ", is it *drastic* or *riotous*? You may say he must wait till he tastes it, but " a rough soldier " might lead to serious misunderstanding. This character may be *inconsiderate* and *unfeeling* but he is not (as the phrase is used) inherently *disorderly* nor yet *harsh*, and I am taking adjectives from the section where he is listed. You would be more likely to guess the right meaning for yourself by going through an independent process of metaphor than to pick it out of this list. And suppose you were actually trying to decide whether to describe some action in writing as RUDE or ROUGH, and looked up both words to compare them ; how much wiser would you be after pushing your way through these two jungles? The only obvious difference is that the same two main groups of meaning are put in opposite orders ; this is an important clue, because the primary ideas start from opposite ends and then stretch across the same field, though the dominant meanings are no longer at the opposite ends. But we are told in the introduction to the C.O.D. that there is no fixed principle governing the order, so we can deduce nothing from it. In any case, this vast supply of synonyms for ROUGH (startling, hairy, entirely unwrought) is obviously a thesaurus out of place. By all means list it under ROUGH but do not offer it as a definition.

One would think that " which sense is listed first " ought to be an important point of dictionary technique, but it had probably better not be made one. If you say that the dominant meaning always comes first you imply that every word has got one, which a word like POST apparently hasn't ; and in a case like RUDE I think it is more intelligible to put the primary meaning first, as the C.O.D. does, because that shows what sort of difference the word has from ROUGH even when it hasn't much. I suggest then that even in a short dictionary the distinct senses ought to be numbered and " D " and " P " ought to be written after the numbers for the dominant and primary sense respectively if they exist ; this would not take much space. " H " for the head sense might also be kept ready for cases where this is separate from the dominant one. It is then also possible to write another number in brackets to mark the cases when a double meaning is likely to intrude. Take for example " rude health ", which rightly has a clause between semi-colons to itself in the C.O.D. The foreigner reading a novel is a bit startled by this phrase, and the dictionary gives him an official reassurance that RUDE here only means " vigorous, hearty ". This starts him in the right place maybe, but it is not true and lays a trap for him when he is using the language himself. In modern uses there is nearly always a twist of humour from the Primary meaning " primitive (implying coarse)", and a stronger one will rise when the context allows it from the dominant meaning " offensive ". The feeling that the phrase is archaic tends to keep back the dominant meaning here but easily lets in the primary one, and even the dominant one can arise as an unwanted joke. (I call the sense " offensive " dominant because when someone is simply called *rude* there is no suggestion that he is " primitive "). In the same way a *rough copy* may as the C.O.D. claims mean " reproducing only essentials ", but there is likely to be also a suggestion that it is " inexact " or " not smooth " ; of course, only a fool would believe the dictionary here and use the phrase for an official precis, but a dictionary ought not to be actively misleading. In any case, the main heads, which the C.O.D. separates by semi-colons, have to be numbered, because it is ridiculous to use a word without qualification for a definition when you admit in another part of the book that it is complex. If then " 3 " tends to push its way into " 4 " you write instead of simply " 4 " the warning sign " 4 (3)". I submit that this takes the minimum of space, and I believe it would be a real innovation in dictionaries ; even the great N.E.D. is only prepared to make this kind of admission occasionally and as it were conversationally. Indeed, most of the time the N.E.D. goes recklessly to the opposite extreme, because it will number up to thirty meanings for a common word without showing the smallest interest in how anyone ever comes to pick out the right one, let alone whether they overlap.

These points seem to me to be covered if one writes (in Basic) :

ROUGH : 1D not smooth. Met. without enough care, feeling, " polish " (*r. soldier*). 2. violent, not quiet or kind. 3. (1). not complete, (*r. copy*, first attempt at a bit of writing ; incomplete copy.).
RUDE : 1P in natural first condition (without education, art) ; f. *rough* 3. 2D. Unpleasing in behaviour, probably on purpose. 3 (1, 2). *r. health*, strong, having force.

When there are two numbers in the bracket it is assumed that the first is more likely to appear. The method is only used for cases where the extra sense is dangerously likely to intrude ; a sense marked as " D " is any case likely to be in view unless the context makes it irrelevant, and this does not have to be shown separately by the bracket.

These two words give examples of dominant and primary meanings, but are not as puzzling as VULGAR, a word from the same group which is often used to hint at the speaker's aesthetic or even political opinions, and therefore made to carry an equation. The obvious equation between the primary and the later head meaning is " anything aimed at the crowd is in bad taste ", but this has become old-fashioned or even itself " vulgar ", and the modern equations are much harder to peg down. However, a short dictionary which merely sets out to warn you against traps need not attempt to do it.

The C.O.D. entry for VULGAR is :

> " Of, characteristic of, the common people, plebeian, coarse, low, as *v. expressions, mind, tastes, finery, an air of v. prosperity, the v. HERD*, (abs.) *the v.*, the common people ; in common use, generally prevalent, as *v. errors, superstitious, the v.* (national, esp. formerly as opp. to Latin) *tongue, v. fraction, the v.* (Christian) *era.*"

As usual, phrases are thrown in to give " life " without being correctly explained ; " which fractions are most generally prevalent in England ? " the foreigner is left to wonder. But the real difficulty about the word is hidden under the doublet " Of, characteristic of ", which a reader might well take for no more than the stutter of pomposity. " Characteristic of " is the only hint that there has been a Typifying process which has gone in an odd direction. The N.E.D., on the other hand, gives a final heading " 13 " which tries to isolate the modern use : " having a common and offensively mean character, coarsely common-place ; lacking in refinement and good taste ; uncultured, ill-bred ". The interest of this is that, though it seems clear if you know the language already, it depends on your putting just the right shade onto *mean*, which will then influence *coarse* and *common*. G. K. Chesterton has an essay on the word, arguing that it means a person who tries to seem generous, or intelligent, or refined, or in fact to have almost any virtue, and thereby shows that he has a low (especially a " mean ") idea of what that virtue may be. Chesterton therefore claims that it is not at all characteristic of the common people, and that he can regard it with disgust in spite of being a democrat. The definition is perhaps over-elaborate, but the practical claim seems to be true. All shades of Left-Wing politics in England feel that they can use the word without inconsistency, because the derivation is almost completely ignored. This makes the word a trap for foreigners, who expect the derivation to give the head meaning, and neither the C.O.D. nor the N.E.D. do anything to enlighten them. For example, I remember a Chinese student who put in an essay on the Scotch ballads " The ballad must be simple and vulgar ". Most of the essay was spent in laborious praise of the Scotch ballads, which he felt to be required of him, but I gathered that he felt they were like popular works in China which a proud scholar would despise. That is, he knew the word had two meanings, and wanted to use it to drop an insinuation. The mistake was, therefore, an extremely marginal one ; it was merely that he took " of the common people " to be the head sense, under which " coarse " could insinuate itself as an Implication (equated to the head sense, perhaps). But this is a definite mistake ; whatever the political or literary views of the reader, he will feel that there has been a ridiculous collapse of an attempt at tact. I submit that it is fatuous for the N.E.D. to number thirteen senses without attempting to make this point clear, and for the C.O.D. to hide it under " Of, characteristic of, the common people ". Very little extra space is required to mark " coarse " as the dominant present day meaning, and this seems to be enough. But I am not sure that any secondary meanings should be listed ; " of the common people " ought to be " of the lower middle classes " or the " petty bourgeoisie " or something confusing of that kind, and in any case never appears alone. If you put " coarse, flashy (Derivation : of the crowd)" that is the shortest way to give the right impression.

The interesting point about COMMON, to continue with this group, is that it seems to have no dominant ; whether the word means " frequent " or " low-class " depends purely on context and neither sense tends to recall the other. One can invent puzzles by taking sentences alone ; thus " That is a common way to talk " seems to be a low-class way, whereas " That is a common way of talking " seems only to be to a usual one. The first turn of grammar is only slightly more governessy and buttoned-up but even this touch of a thumb is enough to call out the change of meaning, because there is no other " context " to decide. The C.O.D. does fairly well here by putting both these meanings late in its list. Finally, ORDINARY is a neat contrast to VULGAR because it assumes that the good, sane, sensible thing is to do what the crowd does ; in class situations it assumes that your crowd is your own class. At least, this has been true in England since about the middle of the nineteenth-century, when snobbery became subtle, whereas the " ornery " of Huckleberry Finn meant something very low-class indeed. The point might be made in a dictionary if the words were collected to distinguish synonyms, but should not I suppose be made part of the definition.

The case of BROAD and WIDE is interesting, because Fowler treats it in *Modern English Usage* as well as in the *Concise Oxford*, and because it is particularly hard to see who wants a circular definition here. A foreigner who knows BROAD but does not know

WIDE surely needs an interlingual dictionary. The only occasion for looking either of them up is to get clear the rather subtle distinction between them. But Fowler's two dictionary articles seem to have the extraordinary ambition of writing down all the nouns with which the two adjectives are commonly used. Extraordinary, because in *Modern English Usage* he can state a clear and general distinction of meaning. To be sure, in the intervening thirteen years he may have discovered the distinction by working on the examples, and I would be sorry to talk as if collecting examples was not important ; but in the carefully revised second edition of the *Concise Oxford*, published three years after *Modern English Usage*, he still seems to feel that he is not allowed to tell the answer. It cannot have been kept out of the two long dictionary entries for the sake of space ; it can be quoted shortly enough :

" . . . *wide* refers to the distance that separates the limits, and *broad* to the amplitude of what connects them . . . *wide intervals* . . . *broad leaves*. . . some secondary notion such as generosity or downrightness or neglect of the petty (may be) the representative of the simple idea of amplitude . . . *broad jests*."

This is rather grandly phrased, but it goes into Basic clearly enough. WIDE is given with no puzzles—" with a great distance between the sides ; opposite of narrow " and BROAD is referred back to it— " *wide* when used with the idea that there is something solid between the two sides, or when the thing seems solid to our feelings—because full-hearted, not small-minded, straight-forward ". Of course, I am not saying that there is any harm in giving examples after the definition, only that they cannot take its place.

However, Fowler does not simply start the entry after WIDE with " broad, not narrow " and *vice versa*. There is no carelessness about the thing. BROAD he gives as " large across ", then of course " wide, not narrow " ; WIDE as " measuring as much or more than other things of the same kind across from side to side " (why not this *relative* aspect under BROAD as well ?), then of course, " broad, not narrow ". A lot of thought has gone into this process of evasion. BROAD is given " large " because both *broad* and *large* have a kind of body-feeling about them, though " large " in itself is a tricky enough word to appeal to. WIDE is given what appears to be a scientific definition, but the main purpose of this is to give a *feeling* of being scientific so as to cut out the body-feeling of BROAD. Once you know the answer you can see that the cross-word puzzle was set quite fairly. But why should we be given a guessing game at all—why can't he tell us ? The mood seems to be that of a professional man who must guard the interests of his client, and only one word is his client at a time. Or maybe the difference between the words is a kind of feeling, and a lexicographer must not chat frankly about emotions or he will appear unbalanced. Or again, the dictionary is a collection of senses presumed to be separate, because no dictionary admits that words are used in two senses at once ; the semi-colons are to mark off alternatives. But in *Modern Usage* his energies are flowing in the opposite direction ; the induction has been performed, and it is in order for the separate senses to be deducted from one principle as if they were only one sense. There is really a puzzle here ; you have continually to decide whether a word has a set of separable uses or whether these combine to give a " connotation " or feeling which is faintly present in all its uses ; and probably no dictionary technique could handle all the shades in between these alternatives. But still you don't measure a plank by seeing how many pieces you can cut it up into. I submit that the " living dictionary " idea led Fowler into very queer and unhelpful behaviour over BROAD.

EFFECT and RESULT are a similar pair, but there is a different moral to be drawn. The C.O.D. gives :

> EFFECT : Result, consequence (*cause and e.*, causation) ; efficacy, as *of no e. ;* combination of colour or form in picture etc., as *a pretty e. ;* (pl) property. . . ; *give e. to,* take e., make, become operative ; impression produced on spectator, hearer, &c., as calculated for e. ; *bring to, carry to, e.*, accomplish ; *in e.*, for practical purposes.
>
> RESULT : v.i. &c., n.   Arise as actual or follow as logical consequence (*from* conditions, causes, premises, etc., or abs.) ; have issue or end in specific manner, esp. in failure &c., (*resulted badly, in a large profit*). N. consequence, issue or outcome of something (*without r.*, in vain, fruitless).

Effect is explained by *result* and both by *consequence ;* does this mean that *effect* is the least fundamental and *consequence* the most ? Does it mean that " result, consequence " somehow cancels out the complexities of both words so that the phrase means only " effect " ? Can a consequence when used to define *effect* be both actual and logical, and anyway why does the distinction have to be made in one place and not another ? Why is an *effect* not an *issue* or an *outcome ?* None of these questions are rhetorical ; I do not at all understand what he thought he was doing. And yet the difference between the words is surely a simple result of derivation, which a classicist like Fowler might be trusted to use. EFFECT " what is caused or made or done, sometimes with an idea that it comes quickly or with clear knowledge ". RESULT " what comes back, as a ball may come back from the wall at a surprising angle ; it has gone through more stages than an EFFECT ".   Hence " result " is generally a summing-up of the whole situation, whereas " effect " tends to pick out one of the causes operating. CONSEQUENCE " what comes after, as an

EFFECT which was not designed ". By all means collect stock phrases, but the old pedantry of derivation is what you want for the definitions, and it goes into Basic all right.

In a concise dictionary, I think there would be hardly any need to worry about Moods or Equations, and on the rare occasion where an Emotion needs to be isolated one could use the exclamation mark as something immediately intelligible. It seems reasonable to use the term Mood and define it in the preface but not worry the reader with the symbol. Thus QUITE would appear as :

1. Completely. Not exciting ! (speaker cool). *I q. like him*, like him only moderately.
2. Used with turns of language implying excitement to produce Mood (a) *q. too delightful*, cosy : " you will understand me ", (b) *not q. good enough*, insolent : " I expect the best ".
3. Used alone for an answer, with either Mood : " I knew that already but you were right to say it ".

This does not look too fussy, surely, and it is no longer than the C.O.D. version :

" completely, wholly, entirely, altogether, to the utmost extent, nothing short of, in the fullest sense, positively, absolutely (*q. covers it; was q. by myself; q. other*, very different; *I q. like him; is q. too delightful* coll. i.e., to be done justice to by words ; *is q. the thing*, fashionable ; *not q. proper*, rather improper.

Here it seems to me that all the uses are covered by " completely " (without needing eight equivalents) except those which are wrongly explained. It is most curious that " I quite like him " could be written down as a " living " illustration of how *quite* means " to the utmost degree ". Under *just* the C.O.D. gives a head " exactly; barely; exactly at that moment " ; and then " colloq ; positively, quite, as *it is j. splendid, not j. a jest* ". The first example really is the same as *quite ;* it is a jocular emotional contradiction " exciting, and I feel cool and cosy about it " ; but *not just a jest* means " not merely " and has no connection with " positively, quite ".

To admit Emotions would perhaps look a bit odd, but one reason for the stuttering of the thesaurus-mongers is the usual reason for stuttering, viz. that they are shy ; they have been let in for explaining words, but they want to make the explanation look a bit less queer than it is. Many of us get our first experience of dictionaries from looking up mysterious improper words and finding them only related to still more mysterious improper words ; this device is far more widespread in dictionaries than we realise, or than it has any reason to be.

I want now to give some space to examining the practice of circular definition ; a tedious process, I am afraid, but without doing it in some detail one cannot show how dismal and misleading a practice it really is. The groups around *damage* and *scold* seem convenient ones to take, as the shades of meaning are sometimes subtle but there is a good deal of mere " wealth of synonyms ". The C.O.D. gives for the damage group (shortening a bit) :

damage	n.	harm (*to one's great d.*), injury impairing value or usefulness.
	v.	injure (usu. thing) so as to diminish value ; detract from reputation of (person, &c.)
harm	n.	and v. damage, hurt (out of H.'s way, in safety)
hurt	n.	wound, material injury ; harm, wrong.
	v.	cause bodily injury or pain to ; damage, distress. wound (person, his feelings &c.) ; (colloqu.) suffer injury or pain.
injury		wrongful action or treatment ; harm, damage.
injure		Do wrong to ; hurt, harm, impair.

The effect is of a stage army marching round and round, put a little out of order each time to make the repetition less obvious. One real point of distinction seems to be whether or not someone is blamed. *Injure* and *injury* are "wrong" before the semicolon and *hurt* (n. & v.) after it ; *damage* and *harm* are not wrong except at the second remove *via* hurt and injury. Surely there must be some process of literary tact in play by which we can make sense of this if we try. Let us concentrate on HURT n. " wound, material injury ; harm, wrong ". Now *injury* was " wrong " before its semi-colon, presumably in its head sense, therefore both halves of *hurt* are " wrong ", before and after its semicolon. Therefore, all hurts are the results of wrong actions. But this seems clearly wrong ; I was assuming that words separated only by commas can be taken together, and this must have been a mistake. Hurts may be material or not (the semicolon), and each type may or may not be due to a wrong act (the commas). But surely it is very hard for a reader to guess at first sight that some wounds are not material injuries—after all, we were told under *injury* that all injuries are due to wrong acts, and most *wounds* are inflicted by men, so that the opposition might actually be meant to go the other way. On the whole it seems clear that " wound, material injury " is meant to be two shots at one idea. But then so is " harm, wrong ", by symmetry, and if we cling to our meaning for the semicolon we have to deduce that all immaterial hurts are due to wrong acts, though not necessarily all material ones. And then we get a mysterious change from " material " to " bodily " when we go to the verb ; it seems that you can give the gear-box a hurt but you can't hurt it. Has this something to do with the rule that hurting a person isn't necessarily wrong but giving him an immaterial hurt is ? I am sorry to seem to be inventing trivial puzzles, but the learner *has* to invent reasons for these elaborate distinctions, which he is sure have been carefully prepared for him.

And yet the distinctions to be made here are not difficult ones. Nothing need be said about HURT n. at the " concise " level except that it is rare and literary ; the reader might need a warning against " Have you a hurt ? " instead of " Are you hurt ? ", and he doesn't get it. HARM is the most general one and covers any " bad effects " (with a reference number on " bad " to show that it needn't mean morally wrong). But *harm* tends to imply lasting bad effects, whereas *hurt* considers immediate ones, especially pain, hence it is extended to cover hurt feelings and almost confined to living beings. *Damage* is harm to inorganic objects. *Injury* really does bring up the puzzles we are guessing at under *hurt*. A bodily *injury* is harm done to the body, not necessarily external like a *wound*, and expected to be lasting, but given by a sudden event—you wouldn't get an injury from bad drains ; and it may come by accident, so that even the sentence " he injured me " need not impute blame if the injury is a bodily one. But if he injures *me* (not my body) or " does me an injury " (a phrase not used of bodily injuries) he is presumed to be in the wrong and conscious of what he is doing. The C.O.D. fails to make the distinction in the one case where it is needed. It can be done quite shortly :

INJURY : wrong and harmful behaviour to person (do him an i.) ; harm to body (give it an i.) from sudden event.
INJURE : do harm wrongly to person ; harm body by sudden event.

No doubt other points may need putting in ; but while you are making *this* point you only befuddle the reader if you throw in half the group of synonyms. Of course, you can " injure " a delicate piece of machinery too, but that is on the edge of metaphor and had better be absorbed as such. What is aimed at in a concise dictionary is to show the working sources of difference between the synonyms ; anybody ought to know that they will stretch to give special effects. The reason why you can " injure " a *delicate* piece of machinery is that it is thought of as tender like flesh ; if you put in a separate word *impair* to cover that you only muddle the reader, because it is very hard for him to guess that you were thinking of this metaphor. This group I suppose hardly needs collecting under HARM, because the distinctions are quite manageable once you have cleared away the stage army, but it would be a convenience to have them collected.

The scolding group is more of a nuisance, because English is very well provided with such words, and owing to their prevailing excitement there is no general colourless word under which they can all be collected. The living dictionary has endless opportunities here, and it is hard to see on what principle its babble was ever stopped.

SCOLD : v.i. and t., & n. Find fault noisily, rail ; rate, rebuke (chiefly of parent, employer, speaking to child, servant), whence scolding, railing or nagging woman.

The semicolon may mark the distinction (a) between the intransitive and the transitive verb, (b) between the sounds made and the intention of them, or (c) between " undignified noisy complaint " and " correcting an inferior ". There is, I think, such a distinction as "(c)", put in by a Mood ; " I suppose I shall have to try to scold my cook for this meal " arrives at the second meaning by a vaguely self-deprecating use of the first. It seems quite an interesting distinction, and the phrase in the bracket seems to point out the contrast intentionally. But then, looking up RAIL, one finds it to be " use abusive language ", and taking this with " noisily " it looks as if the distinction meant under scold was only the trivial one " b ". ABUSIVE is defined as " reviling ", REVILE as " call by ill names, abuse, rail at ; talk abusively, rail ". The semicolon here obviously means the same as " v. i. & t." and makes no distinction between the meanings of the grammatical forms, though it pretends to ; perhaps then the distinction meant under SCOLD was only " a ". No doubt one might argue that all three distinctions work together, but surely the reader cannot be meant to find this improbable theory obvious ? RATE is defined as " scold angrily, storm at ", so it is even more undignified than ordinary scolding ; this seems to refute the theory that " rate, rebuke " was intended to suggest a dignified form of scolding. But REBUKE supports it with " reprove, reprimand, censure authoritatively " ; and after all we have no reason to feel sure that the compilers were consistent about RATE. STORM AT (which was used to define it) yields " talk violently, rage, bluster, fume, scold ". This entry is perhaps the blankest piece of thesaurus-work so far, because the metaphor of " storm " is much clearer than the group of words supposed to define it. They are only separated by commas, so must be close together in meaning. Certainly the storm is still rising if you look up RAGE " rave, storm, speak madly or furiously, be full of anger ", or BLUSTER " storm boisterously ", but then after the next comma the thing peters out in pathos : FUME " be pettish, chafe ". It seems clear that this process will never tell anybody anything about RATE, and the purpose of the semicolon in the entry for SCOLD must therefore also remain a mystery.

Pursuing the words used to define REBUKE, we find that REPROVE is " rebuke, chide ", and CHIDE is " make complaints, speak scoldingly (esp. fig. of hounds, wind, etc.) ; scold, rebuke ". The idea that chiding makes a thin kind of noise is the first peep of real definition. REPRIMAND is sensible enough—" official(ly) rebuke ". This explains that when *reprimand* was used to define *rebuke* it meant to separate off one kind of rebuke. CENSURE gives "blame, criticise unfavourably, reprove". But REBUKE is "reprove, reprimand, censure authoritatively"; why can't we eliminate CENSURE and read "reprove either officially or not"? The noun CENSURE is "reprimand", which is "official rebuke", which is "official authoritative censure". This is quite a plausible view, because the nouns here tend to be stricter than the verbs, but can we be sure that the dictionary meant to say it? Must we not, on the contrary, be quite sure that all these words are shifting about all the time while the dictionary pretends to use them to explain each other?

Nor is the machine even sufficient as a thesaurus, which seems the only purpose it could have. That is, there are other words in the family, such as REPROACH, which don't get swept up into the eddy of mutual definition, and if you thumb the definitions over when you want to be reminded of " reproach " you won't be helped. Its definition is " Upbraid, scold (person, often *with* offense) ; (of look, &c.) convey protests or censure to ". This seems to me to miss the whole point about " reproach ", but BLAME is done well : " find fault with, fix the responsibility on ; *be to b.*, deserve censure ".

After all this nagging I must risk an attempt at doing the work better, and I shall do well to confess that it is not easy. The only thing I say with assurance is that the purpose must be to show why the words are different, why a man might reasonably choose one rather than other. The only purpose one can suppose the C.O.D. to have here is to show that the language is so much " alive " that it has heaps of indistinguishable synonyms. Now in trying to show why they are different one must ignore the large areas where they overlap ; it is agreed that they can all be stretched in special uses, and the question is where they start from before they are stretched. As to the words carried on living metaphors, all a definer can do is to point it out and say if it has some odd specialisation. If a learner doesn't know the source he is in danger of mixing metaphors and so on ; if he does know it he is to a great extent free to use it as he pleases. " Fume " is " betray repressed anger—met. from a smoking heap ". This is very different from " be pettish ", which is " show brief periods of anger about trifles repeatedly, like a spoiled child ". " Chafe " is " feel a long-continued irritation, like a prisoner with a feverish sore from leg-irons." " Storm at " is " talk like a storm at someone—violently angry but without much sense of direction ". " Bluster " is " act like a wind blowing in gusts—showing more force than it has, not steady". The C.O.D. version "storm boisterously " misses the idea of boasting and makes the word seem stronger than " storm ", let alone the nuisance of raising a new puzzle about BOISTER. To treat the metaphors directly perhaps makes them seem brighter than they are in practice, but one can put "(partly faded)" where necessary. They are a handsome group, I think, and it shows no respect to the living language to treat them as rubble. Going on now to the non-metaphorical words for abusiveness, the essential point seems to be the degree to which they are reflexive. We saw that SCOLD tends to make the person who scolds look comically low. If one person is REVILING another we tend to feel that he too is vile ; he is foul-mouthed. RAIL has the same effect in a less degree, and is anyway archaic. REBUKE is prim, apparently from the sound-effect ; a rebuker can easily appear fussy, and is not specifically a person in authority ; indeed, a strong use suggests the prophet rather than the priest. REPROVE is equally prim but milder, which makes it more open to irony ; it is rather more likely to be from a person in authority. RATE suggests to me an admiral scolding a rating ; it seems to be the only strong scolding word which does not imply loss of dignity. But it is now so rare that it hardly matters, and my associations about it may well be wrong. CHIDE is scolding that makes a high thin kind of noise (this is my first agreement with the C.O.D.) ; it is typical of the anxious but not masterful parent. ABUSE is from a simply low person, neither comically nor disgustingly low. REPRIMAND (I agree) is an official rebuke, severe but not involving the official's emotions or dignity, and probably brief. CENSURE seems to me a rebuke from public opinion in general, therefore not risking the dignity of the accuser. BLAME has the same coolness but from a different source ; it deals with placing the responsibility ; if you can put the blame on someone else you are free. And the tenderness of REPROACH comes from a different kind of mutual feeling ; " I am sorry about this, and you will be sorry when I have made you feel what you have done ". In short, the differences all come from the Moods.

Now this may seem very literary talk, but it is not lengthy as definitions go, and these are the reasons why a man chooses one such word and not another (the sort of reason, even if I have got some of them wrong); it is this kind of point, and not any flaunting of the thesaurus, that a man who looks such a word up in the dictionary wants to learn. Objections are sure to be raised that this kind of treatment is always " subjective ", a case where this misleading term must be supposed to mean that the work would be done badly. No doubt the lexicographer might only record his private associations with a word, but that would not be what he was trying to do. There is an obvious retort to this accusation of self-indulgence, and I hope I can give it without appearing unduly excited. It is better that he should try to do his work, however badly, than that he should cheat.

DICTIONARIES

At the same time, I cannot help realising that chat about the faults of existing dictionaries does not get very far. I could claim that it is necessary for the general plausibility of my thesis to show that the existing practice is inadequate, but perhaps there is not much point in doing it at such length without making the recommendations much more detailed. All I should claim for this chapter is that it gives a sort of final canter round the field.

THEORIES OF VALUE

THE most far-reaching, and apparently the oldest, suspicion about emotive language is that moral sentiments and the word " good " are merely emotive. Without pretending to settle such a question, I ought to try to show how my general theory stands with regard to it. It seems to me to make much less difference than has been supposed.

The emotive account has been obviously useful in the work of Westermarck, who was inspired by it to write world surveys of ethical ideas and thus give important information. But philosophically his point of view seems fairly innocent ; what he is really showing is that ethical ideas are " relational " (as was pointed out for instance by John Laird) ; that is, their particular form depends on a variety of factors in the society that holds them. The most prominent example of such a theory is the Marxist one, that the ideology of a society is caused by its means of production and distribution ; after accepting such a view it is still possible to judge that one ideology is better than another, and it seems clear that communists habitually do. As G. K. Chesterton remarked long ago, the fact that different noses are different shapes does not prove that noses are a delusion, nor yet the fact that, while some people use their noses and find the smell of incense nice, other people use their noses and find it nasty. Arguments on this level, it seems clear, need to be set aside.

The most important recent advocate of the Emotive view has been Mr. C. L. Stevenson, in " Ethics and Language ", a book which seems obviously right on many points of detail. He maintains a naturalist position, in which there are no absolute sanctions for ethics, without the effect of flippancy or intellectualism with which some previous advocates had alienated sober citizens ; indeed, with a touch of solid Victorian earnestness. So far as he interrupts the work of analysis to express any views of his own, he is anxious to make clear that science has done nothing to weaken human values.

It seems to me that he differs much less than he supposes from the absolutist theory of Professor Moore, and it is not surprising that Professor Moore could see no decisive argument against his position. We are told that " This is good " means " I approve of this ; do so as well " (i.e. " approve thou also "), and that this " first pattern " is normally present in all uses even when some other definition of good is imputed or used. The difference is said to be that " Moore has intellectualized this emotive meaning into an indefinable *quality*" (p. 272). Surely it is curious that Mr. Stevenson never attempts to define or explain "approval". "Desire" and "disapproval" are listed among "specific attitudes" (p. 60), and an attitude is :

> "a complicated conjunction of dispositional properties... marked by stimuli and responses which relate to hindering or assisting whatever it is that is the 'object' of the attitude."

This sounds rather altruistic, in a vague way, but I take it an amoeba can have an attitude as well as a man. There must, one would think, be something which makes an attitude of approval distinguishable from other attitudes, and if nothing at all is said about what this something may be it seems hard to be sure that Mr. Stevenson has not himself used a "non-natural" conception ; or at least a "unique" one, which is also forbidden.

"Approval" has the merit of being much narrower than "good". If somebody is said to approve of the plum-pudding it is a little joke ; the word is a specifically moral one. Mr. Stevenson does not *say* this ; he seems to take it for granted. Also he does not attempt to give a reason for the two parts of his analysis of "good" into a statement of approval and an imperative, which he admits to be a trifle artificial. Surely he needs to consider how this peculiar structure came into being. I take it that the man who says "this is good" feels "this is approvable ; I and you and *everybody* will approve"—he assumes a tribe around him in which all moral questions are settled and agreed. At least, of course he may not, but this is the presumption of the grammatical form, because it is "projective" and treats his feeling as something external. Indeed, he may be accepting an imperative rather than imposing one.* Now certainly the two parts of Mr. Stevenson's analysis draw attention to this element in the idea of "good", however roughly, but he seems to assume that "I approve" is simple, whereas surely the same element is in that too, though it is not made prominent by the grammar. A mere feeling of approval for something already implies that to approve it is good, and this implies that everyone should approve it. Whatever problem may arise about the nature of good, will also arise about the nature of approving ; the Emotive word is just as moral as the Cognitive one, indeed, rather more so. You do not solve any problem by favouring one bit of grammar rather than another.

However, the theory does say something definite in saying that approval is a tendency to action, being an attitude ; Mr. Stevenson sometimes also calls it an emotion or a feeling, but these are to be

*President Truman : "One of the worst things we are facing is the Presidential and Congressional Election this year. That is our system and it is good, but it is unfortunate that it comes at this moment ". (1948).

understood as signs that we have the attitude. But one must remember that the same kind of analysis has appeared to various philosophers (and eminently to the behaviourists, who are tacitly invoked by this linguistic approach) as the only way to deal with beliefs about historical facts. If they are put on the same footing we are left much where we were, and in both cases the difficulty is to see just *what* actions a tendency of this sort must be supposed to tend to. The belief that Julius Caesar was stabbed, as I understand the theory, must be resolved into a rather subtle class of expectations that future events will cohere with previous ones in that direction (but there may be no new evidence to discover) ; and the test of whether I sincerely hold the belief is whether or not I would act in accordance with it (but I seldom get an opportunity). No doubt the same test must be applied for the sincerity of a belief that the stabbing was a good action. But all these mental events are highly " projective " ; that is, they at least seem to be about something in the external world. Surely people can approve quite heartily of a martyr without having any tendency to get themselves tortured to death in their turn. Of course, the argument about both sorts of belief can be carried to very high points of subtlety ; it is plausible to say that the approval is insincere unless I would do something about it, however remote, and the unconscious mind can be brought in, to say that we have a frustrated and unobservable impulse to become a martyr whenever we approve of one. I should say that people often feel rather complacently " all right for him, but that's not the sort of thing I go in for ", and this excludes any feeling " if I wasn't a coward I would do the same". If they are quite sturdy about this we must at least say that the tendency has been repressed pretty deeply. But then again, if you plunge into the deep unconsciousness to find your tendency to action, you will find all kinds of tendencies which the " ego " does not approve at all. You may indeed say that the moral feeling is part of a logical structure, and that the test of its sincerity is how I would behave under quite different circumstances, such that my own principles were as deeply involved as those of the martyr in his circumstances. But then, the more you let my moral feelings form a coherent logical structure, the closer you draw the parallel to the structure of my feelings about historical fact. By the time you have put in the necessary reservations, it seems to me, the " emotive " account of ethical judgements is on exactly the same footing as the logical-positivist or behaviourist account of beliefs about the external world. It seems simpler, even in theory, to say that both a moral judgement and a historical belief are in themselves something different from the way they are tested, but no doubt this may be a delusion. Even so, the delusion really occurs ; the person who experiences these feelings does not take them to be primarily concerned with what he himself would do under circumstances which have not arisen. It seems to me that this is enough to make Approval an attitude of a peculiar kind, so that the mere classification of it as an attitude does not tell us everything about it. For instance it does not help to decide, to use common-sense language, whether a correct attitude of this kind has to correspond to something outside us, like the belief about Caesar.

The purpose of Mr. Stevenson's classification, as I understand him, is to refute any " non-naturalistic " theory about ethics, and these I think can be summed up as beliefs that our moral feelings correspond to something in the nature of the universe. Many people maintain a belief of this sort as part of a detailed theology, whereas Professor Moore seemed to toy with it in its barest possible form when he said that " good " had a meaning, like " yellow ", and that the meaning could not be resolved into anything else. Here if anywhere was his real difference from Mr. Stevenson ; the only point of his linguistic argument, however delicately it was insinuated, was to make moral judgements capable of corresponding with some subtle kind of external fact. Mr. Stevenson gets on very well without discussing this belief, because it does not thrust itself into the analyses of grammar and situation which are the point of his book. The only curious thing is that he believes he has refuted not only Professor Moore but anyone who holds beliefs of this sort, and he keeps coming back to the idea.

That he might be outflanked does indeed cross his mind on p. 108. " Perhaps some theorists may seek to accept the positive contentions of the present account and still remain ' non-naturalists '." He goes on to assume that they must do this by positing a unique quality of goodness, which is signalised by the emotion of approval, and says that " unless (this) can be defended on more positive grounds, it must be taken as an invisible shadow cast by confusion and emotive meaning ". Rather frankly emotive language from the author here. On p. 147 he says : " When the ethical terms are alleged to refer to a supersensible realm, the matter becomes too vital to be neglected. Here the charge of confusion will continue to be made, and will be provided it is hoped with an adequate defence. The constructive aim of this study, that of setting up a practicable analysis of ethics without departing from the world of experience, is itself a partial answer to those who claim that another course is necessary." But it is the *only* answer given in the book, and its force will depend on one's temperament and previous training. Since it was so large a part of the impulse behind the book to answer what may be called theological views of ethics, it would have been better to examine what they are. I understand it is an orthodox religious position in both Europe and Asia to say that " the basis of ethics is not itself ethical " ; heaven is not a scene of moral struggle ; doing one's duty on earth is only a tedious preliminary, required because conditions are so peculiar here. Now a man thinking on these lines is not likely to believe (as Professor Moore did) in a unique unanalysable quality as the cause of all feelings of approval ; he would probably wonder why such a thing was invented. He would be quite ready to agree that the ordinary moral feelings give only roundabout and confusing evidence for the Supreme Good which he believes in on other grounds; and it seems to me that he could very easily " accept the positive contentions of the present account " without changing any of the views which Mr. Stevenson really wants to change.

I do not want to prattle about this vast subject ; indeed, I do not see how a man can claim to know that a general ethical theory is true without claiming to have experienced all possible moral situations. But I think something can be said to make more definite the idea of a correspondence between a moral feeling and the universe or the outer world. It seems to be based on a sort of biological claim, that each kind of feeling of which a creature is capable must have a natural rudiment, and that the rudiment at least cannot be a mere delusion. There is a tacit analogy with the senses—we would not see yellow unless there really was such a thing. (This, I think, was the unacknowledged rhetorical force behind the analogy of Professor Moore, though the example is a subtle one because the colour sensations of other animals may be quite different from ours. Hence the analogy had another appeal for philosophers ; the scientists must not be allowed to jockey us into pretending that one such sensation is the same as another merely because it is caused by light of the same wavelength). Such at any rate was the main historical tradition which was to be refuted, but Mr. Stevenson does not even consider what the rudiment of the feeling was in the case of approval. I think that, if we follow up the analogy, the results are rather conflicting ; some of our sensations, as well as we can make out, give us much more direct or reliable evidence than others about the outside world. The pattern on the retina of the eye is the typical case of directness ; even an insect must be seeing the same shapes, whatever its colour sensations are, or it could not fly so accurately. At the other extreme, the sensation of sweetness is hardly more than a delusion ; I understand that you can have a balanced diet without ever tasting anything sweet, and there are chemicals with no food value which are sweeter than any food. It may have been evolved for some biological function ; for example, to make us eat fruit and thereby get vitamins or laxatives. But even if it is so far purposive (and not merely an accident of our constitution) it developed so as to have only a very insignificant correspondence with things in the outside world ; it correlates an inherently unconnected group of chemicals, and only gives useful information if you know a good deal about what you are eating already. Thus even if it be said that all sensations correspond to *something* in the outside world, and by analogy that all " intuitions " do as well, it is still possible that the feeling of approval may be a very unhelpful one like the sensation of sweetness, owing to the biological history of its development. On the other hand, reasons might be found tending to show that it is not, and that it is direct in the same way as the retina of the eye. I realise that this is a pretty flat piece of speculation ; all I want to show is that speculations of this kind can still go on after you have agreed that moral feelings are Merely Emotive.

No doubt as it stands the question has no practical importance. We know, in any case, from the variety of the actual moral judgements, that they can only reflect the nature of the universe in a very indirect way, and so a belief in the reflection cannot give any short cut in a particular case. One would still have to go through the patient consideration of consequences recommended by Mr. Stevenson. The only way to make it of practical importance is to make the specifically mystical claim that you have a technique for getting yourself to mirror the universe better, or that your leaders have had it, and used it. But the only example at all like this which Mr. Stevenson considers is a Nazi mystical assertion (p.145), which he can assume that his readers will disapprove. He is quite right to point out that suasion can be a valuable process, and that not all " emotive " uses of language are bad, but I think here he falls into rather too evasive a method of suasion. The Nazis were not the chief people he had to refute.

Mr. Stevenson's views, I take it, derive eventually from *The Meaning of Meaning* and its doctrine of the Emotive functions of language. However, there is an interesting footnote in that book on p. 125 (fourth edition) which raises new problems of its own.

" Of course, if we define ' the good ' as ' that of which we approve of approving ', or give any such definition when we say ' This is good ', we shall be making an assertion. It is only the undefinable ' good ' which we suggest to be merely an emotive sign."

This seems very reasonable, and would apply without difficulty to a definition like " the greatest happiness of the greatest number ". But with the definition about approving it is paradoxical ; whether or not you think, as I do, that approving a thing is already approving of approving it (because there is a regress inherent in the idea, as in knowing you know and choosing to choose), this is clearly an Emotive definition. So if this man wants his assertion to be emotive, or about emotions, this is precisely what stops it from being emotive. One might, no doubt, say that his mind is clear, he is not deluding himself about the process, and therefore is not in the despised condition of using Emotive language. But this view does not fit the supposed close connection between the Emotive use of language and the intention of exciting Attitudes, by which any piece of language which is "predominantly" concerned to excite an Attitude is called Emotive. We can hardly say that the language only becomes Emotive, or concerned to excite an Attitude, if the man does not know what he is predominantly concerned to do. No doubt poets are frequently inspired, but surely there are low uses of emotive language, by politicians perhaps, which are intended as such. It may seem that I am crowing ridiculously over a small slip, but the main point I have been trying to make is that this supposed close connection between the Emotive use of a word and the gist of a whole passage which includes it (the intention to excite an Attitude) is a delusively simple one. It may actually work backwards, as it is said to do here, so that the passage becomes more factual if you take the word to be more emotive.

I want now to say something about the Richards Theory of Value, expounded in *The Principles of Literary Criticism* and *Science and Poetry*. It has the great merit of getting away from the mere assertion that previously existing theories are Emotive, but I think it raises new puzzles about whether it is Emotive in its turn. A brief quotation from the *Principles* will, I take it, be sufficient to recall what the theory is about (an "appetency" is a positive impulse) :

> "Anything is valuable which will satisfy an appetency without involving the frustration of some equal or more important appetency . . . The importance of an impulse (is) the extent of the disturbance of other impulses in the individual's activities which the thwarting of the impulse involves . . . Thus morals become purely prudential."

I understand that we have about a million impulses a minute, so the calculation involved might be pretty heavy. But some estimate of the result is certainly envisaged :

> "The purpose of the theory is just to enable us to compare different experiences with respect to their value ; and their value, I suggest, is a quantitative matter."

There is also an "experimental test" of the truth of the theory, in that all men "when they can choose" choose to satisfy more appetencies rather than less. It seems clear that they might always do it and yet sometimes be ill-advised ; however, after saying that all men agree Professor Richards can reasonably take for granted that he agrees too. No doubt the choice must have an emotive basis, but this would equally be true of the choice to believe an absolutist ethic.

I do feel that something like this is probably true, but one must not take it to say very much. As regards the previous question, whether our moral sentiments correspond to something in the nature of the universe, I do not see that the Richards theory does anything to alter the state of doubt. It has the merit of making our judgements tolerably independent of theories about the universe, but one can still argue that, since the universe is such as to be able to produce us, it cannot be wholly alien to us. One can also still believe (to use a phrase of Professor J. B. S. Haldane's) that it is not only queerer than we know but queerer than we can know. Mr. T. S. Eliot, indeed, said that the Richards theory was " probably quite true ", but that he could believe a religious theory of value as well. The idea of measuring value has been objected to as such, but it is at least a traditional one, since the Christian God is to give us all marks on Judgement Day. No doubt there would be a free-will problem, in a practical form, if the scientists claimed to have worked out the calculation, but it would always be possible to claim that they had done it wrong. It may be that the human mind can recognise actually incommensurable values, and that the chief human value is to stand up between them ; but I do not see how we could know that they were incommensurable till the calculation had been attempted.

There is a separate group of objections about the technique proposed. You may doubt whether one impulse has a value at all, any more than an atom has a temperature ; but an extrapolation of this kind might still be a quite harmless fiction, as the basis for a method of calculating. Value seems to come into the sphere of fact of its own accord, rather like imaginary numbers into the solution of real equations ; but for rigorous logic you have then to go back and alter the definitions of the numbers in the equations— they were always complex numbers but with null imaginary parts. An inherent capacity for taking part in valuable situations can, I suppose, be imputed even to an electron. It is much more difficult, I think, to see why impulses should all have equal values, positive or negative ; this is not a peculiarity of the Richards theory, but a view which Bertrand Russell has also maintained. It seems to me an unconscious bit of politics ; democracy is invoked. But the point about democracy is not that people all really have equally good judgement ; no sane man believes this ; the claim is that the government or the constitution has no right to presume that some group of citizens has better judgement than the rest. People with better judgement must try to convince their neighbours, and not over-rule them. Now it may be said that a Theory of Value has itself a sort of political claim ; if it were seriously applied, it would be applied in politics as well as elsewhere ; and it would be no use telling people that some impulses were better than others, even if they actually are. It is not enough that there is justice ; there must be

" evident justice " ; and the only way to convince people (to dis-prove an idea that " push-pin is better than poetry " or what not) is to insist that you are starting fair. No doubt the falsity of the pretence that all *men* are equal entails a certain risk, and the same for *impulses*, but there is less risk in it than in any attempt to pre-judge their different values, because this is certain to be an " interested " one. On this view, it might be a duty to act in all public affairs as though the Theory of Value was true, even though everyone believed, correctly, that it was false. I remember long ago attending a lecture by Bertrand Russell at Cambridge, a dramatic affair, with the experts watching him keenly as some new paradox was expounded, and his own eyes shifting alertly and guardedly from one man whose theoretical toes were being trodden on to another whose turn was now coming. He brought out a coin, and the business about " me seeing my penny " was gone through with some new twist ; for quite a time, the eyes of everyone seemed to be shift-ing one way or another and back to this object. Then somebody at the back of the room began to laugh, and it turned out that what he had got was half-a-crown. I thought it a very neat symbol of the Whig aristocrat and his democratic views ; the actual value of his coin was a thing he would not have considered it polite to notice. Now on this view of the Theory of Value it is very definitely a " pseudo-statement ", a fiction adopted for good mental effects ; but the question whether the effects are really " good ", in some other sense of the term than that defined by the Theory of Value (that is whether the risk has been overcome), is sure to be a real one.

In any case, it is clear that a theory of value must itself be valued. I do not think there is any fallacy in calling this secondary process an emotive one ; what you do is to see whether your feelings can be made to accept the valuations given by the theory. When Professor Richards begins his sentence " Anything is valuable which . . ." the word may be supposed to be primarily emotive " Try to obtain anything which . . ." and secondarily redefinition " I will in future mean by ' valuable ' anything which . . .". Hence, when we have made the redefinition and given the word its new sense, it is no longer " merely emotive " (though still emotive) and can be used to make true or false assertions. This, I think, is clearly what was intended ; it would follow for instance from the footnote I have quoted from *The Meaning of Meaning*. Thus the moral or aesthetic judgements of a person who agrees with Professor Richards may all be regarded as factual, and I don't see why this should not be true if they are written in verse. It will be agreed that this is a tempting offer. But even though the word itself is not Emotive it seems likely that the whole passage in which the word occurs will be predomin-antly concerned to affect the reader's attitudes, and will therefore be Emotive by the other criterion. Thus, even if you agree that all impulses have equal value, it remains, I think, a question of great subtlety whether a statement of the Theory of Value is a " pseudo-statement " or not. One does not get clear from *Science and Poetry* what sort of pseudo-statements can still be valuable when they are recognised as such, and yet some of them must be of this sort because they are to save us from the collapse of the Magical View of Nature. I take it that the idea of God cannot healthily be used as a fiction on the mere ground that it does you good ; certainly an atheist can entertain it in his reading to good effect, but only because he is imagining some person who does believe in God, not because he is pretending that he himself does. And at the other extreme there seem to be fictions which are automatic. All the arts depend on empathy, something like "attributing feelings or impulses to objects of sense and then sympathising with them ". But this is instinctive ; it may have caused the Magical View of Nature, but would not collapse with it, and does not need to be viewed as a statement at all, whether pseudo or not. The difficulty is to see what beliefs form the class in between these two, for which the idea of a pseudo-statement is required ; you must be able to use them as statements for emotional effect without feeling that you are cheating yourself. To be sure, there are a great variety of verbal fictions, perhaps "the spirit of the age " will do as an example, which one should be able to use without fuss but with awareness that they may need analysing on occasion ; Vaihinger's *Philosophy of As If* presented a very mixed bag of these entities, as well as I remember, without constructing much of a philosophy of them. On the whole they seem of the nature of shorthand rather than of edification ; they are easily regarded as metaphors. Or it might be said that the good pseudo-statements are cases where you are expected to show tact in not pressing your deductions from the statement in unreasonable directions ; this would be unfair because the man could have stopped you if he had put in enough qualifications. But what the term is aiming at must be something more serious. And, of course, I don't deny, at the other extreme, that a good deal of firm ignoring of the facts around one may be positively heroic, or agreeably spirited ; there is the same general notion as the pseudo-statement theory when E. M. Forster writes (in *What I Believe*) " The people I respect must behave as if they were immortal and as if society were eternal." But surely this kind of thing is a matter of temperament or tradition, not of doctrine ; if it is taken quite seriously it becomes insane or factitious, and in either case disagreeable. I am looking for the pseudo-statements which are to be the basis for the arts of the future, which can be a reliable support for valuable attitudes. It seems a plausible view that the Theory of Value itself is the only important candidate.

I think it can be sincerely held after being regarded as a pseudo-statement (or after one has become a pragmatist) ; and after all what else is it intended to do but to support valuable attitudes ? Because of this peculiar staying power (under a process which makes so many beliefs wilt), it seems also to form the limiting case, at any rate within the Richards system, where the distinction between Emotive and Cognitive language breaks down.

On the other hand, some people would undoubtedly say that pragmatic grounds are what prove it false. For example, Mr. Michael Roberts in *The Recovery of the West* remarked : " The whole point about the self-conscious animal is that he becomes miserable if he is not convinced that his life is directed to some end beyond himself ; ethical philosophy attempts to reveal his end or to reinforce the conviction that there is such an end " ; and I take it that he and anyone who reasons like this would take it as refuting the Richards position. Of course, it is not to be assumed that this line of thought is necessarily encouraging. Pali Buddhism, unless it has been misunderstood, agreed fully with the first half of the sentence quoted but maintained that it was impossible to achieve the second, so that it made the aim of life an escape from all Being describable as such. Nor are views with scientific claims always in favour of " life " ; Mr. Money-Kyrle in *The Development of Sexual Impulses* (elaborating some hints of Freud) maintained that, since every reaction of an organism aimed at removing the stimulus which had caused it, all experience must be on balance painful, and if we could be psycho-analysed enough to realise this we would simply kill ourselves (so would all animals and plants). The same moral could not be drawn by the Buddhists because they regard suicide as useless for the purpose ; indeed, among people who are liable to act on their convictions, a stopper of this kind is necessary if such a theory is to be thought tolerable. The fallacy in the Money-Kyrle theory seems to me to arise simply from the behaviourist refusal to recognise consciousness and knowledge ; by his account a moderate appetite for dinner followed by a good dinner and digestion is on balance painful, and this might conceivably be true if the " reactions " appeared alone ; but if you are also sure that dinner is coming, and look forward to it, the whole process may be one round of pleasure with no need to strike a balance at all. The early Buddhist position, not offering an argument for its assertion that all existence is suffer-ing, cannot be refuted so easily ; and I understand that scholars in-creasingly suspect it (for all its unwillingness to say so) of an assump-tion that Nirvana is not merely a blowing-out of a flame but a re-absorption into the Absolute. This brings it into line with a mystical strain within all the great religions, one which has usually been at loggerheads with the offer of Heaven ; and there I think we find the great historical antagonist of anything like the Richards Theory of Value—that is, of any self-fulfilment theory. It is opposed to any such theory not because it is pessimistic but because it does not believe in the individual. I cannot pretend to feel I have any capacity to act as a go-between in this quarrel. It looks, however, as if there is one chink through which a Buddhist conclusion might creep into the arguments of Professor Richards ; his rather mysterious distinction between a deadlock (which is bad) and a balance (which is good). It seems that conflicting impulses may satisfy themselves very fully in a state of balance, although the apparent result may be mere passivity. This condition appears as most prominently created by the arts ; but after all, if the Theory of Value merely recommends the satisfaction of the human creature, whatever makes it really satisfied, Professor Richards need not be as secure against the religions as he intended to be. What satisfied the most impulses might turn out to be the same as what was to the glory of God or even as what tended to Nirvana. In any case, he would not deny (to come back to Mr. Michael Roberts) that some impulses not merely selfish are necessary for mental health and general content ; that would come into the calculation.

But all this assumes that the calculation can really be performed. As it cannot, and as the mathematics of summing up the impulses (supposing the general idea to be sound) is pretty sure to be vastly more complicated than the simple addition sum which he envisages, so that the answer is peculiarly hard to guess, we can only judge the value of the theory in terms of how it would be used prematurely ; that is, whether people would be likely to make good guesses with it or bad ones. This gives the theory another peculiar position, as the only belief which is inherently of a pragmatist type whether the believer in it is a pragmatist or not. It seems likely to make people take a narrow view. Professor Richards has sometimes said in passing that of course we ought to work for other people's satisfactions too, but it is not clear where this *ought* comes from, as long as the individual believes in his separate existence. So far as the one candidate for martyrdom is concerned, even the most miserable life of shame would seem likely to satisfy more impulses than death ; indeed, though I am very vague about impulses, I imagine that great numbers of them must get satisfied if life is carried on at all. This is not to say that the theory is *really* an egotistical one, which would be very hard to decide ; it may be, as the Buddhists would say, that even the existence of the individual is a delusion ; it may be, as the Freudians sometimes suggest, that the death-wishes are tyrannous and give the martyr an intense sum of satisfaction. But one can maintain that ordinary people are likely to misunderstand the theory as an egotistical one, and as we have seen the only effects it can have are from misunderstandings of it. Of course, the theory does not tend to make you ignore, what is evident, that you satisfy more impulses of your own if you have a general tendency to satisfy other people's ; the point is that if you are told to satisfy other people for that purpose alone, and to check the effects upon yourself by a pretence of calculation, you are likely not only to miss the crown of martyrdom but to over-reach yourself in common life. We are back in the familiar contradiction of pragmatism ; if the belief is held only because it does you good, it does not do you good. However, I feel that this could be got around somehow ; people are fairly well supplied with other-regarding impulses, if they are not actually taught to repress them ; and perhaps all that would be required would be a sufficiently firm statement by the Head Calculator that, supposing the calculation could ever be performed, it would work out just a little more in favour of altruism than you expect.

It is hard to write about the theory without facetiousness, because it seems to recommend a low view with so much pomp. But one needs, I think, to realise that Professor Richards became keenly aware of this ; the whole emotional stress behind *Science and Poetry* comes from his belief that, since the facts about our moral life are of this uninspiring kind, and since more and more people are bound to realise it, therefore it is going to become more and more hard to make them live well. I suspect that the necessity of egotism, not the mere loss of a heavenly reward, was what made him feel so horrified, and indeed, that he felt the egotism needed to be lumped along with other ideas and partially denied so as to give it a decent obscurity. (Of course, this may be my fancy, but otherwise the note of doom in the book seems hard to explain.) It is to get over this difficulty, much more than any other, I think, that the pseudo-statements are required, the inspiring lies told by the poets ; and they need not certainly be lies, because they are precisely in the position of the firm statement from the Head Calculator, who cannot really do the calculation. The theory is therefore a consistent and serious attempt to touch rockbottom in the matter, and so long as it is viewed as a painful truth I do not think it can be harmful. I do, on the other hand, think that believing more rosy things about the universe, on the specific ground that we will otherwise feel frustrated (and this is what the arguments that are proffered to us nowadays by nearly all religious leaders tend to make us do), is extremely harmful. What is put at the back of the mind of the convert, though it must not be pulled out and looked at, is the feeling " Men rot without lies, and the lies are rotting, and therefore it is my duty to tell half-rotten lies ". If the original purpose was to avoid feeling frustrated, it is clear that no course of action could have failed more dismally. Certainly, by comparison with that kind of thing, the glumness of the theory of Professor Richards is its most attractive feature.

Many other people (Unamuno, Santayana, J. M. Krutch) have expressed the same horror as Professor Richards does here, and suggested a similar way out of it ; I ought not to treat it as an oddity, and perhaps it is mere lack of self-knowledge which keeps me from feeling the same. But it seems to me that I worry about much more mundane things. I can, however, sympathise all right if what they were revolting against was a supposed necessity to believe in an ethic of pure egotism ; that would be a disgusting experience, and no wonder they seem to be talking about something else. But surely it is a delusion. The belief to be defended at all cost, by fiction if nothing else will serve, is " whatever is a good state of being is good in other people as well as me, so it is good to see that they get it ". It seems to me that anyone not insane will believe this by animal faith (however little he acts on it, unless properly encouraged) in exactly the same way as he believes in the existence of other people, or for that matter as he believes in his own existence in the immediate past or future. These beliefs are also impossible to prove against an arguer who adopts a radical scepticism, and the point to make is not so much that we are sure they are all true as that we can afford to play at doubting them because they are inborn. Not even the insidious drug of " believing them pragmatically " can make them rot away as it does the religions. And since they are beliefs, however peculiar the kind of external fact to which they must correspond, they would not be " merely emotive " even if they were false. No doubt they are believed because of feelings, which can be encouraged by suasion, and to this extent the behaviourist account of them is not simply off the point. But one needs, I think, to admit that such a feeling is of a peculiar kind, which the behaviourist account obscures; the idea that it is good to do good is parallel to the regress in the feeling of approval.

These flat little fundamental problems are wonderfully slippery, but it seems clear that the fundamental step here is not an emotive one. The creature must think " It is good, in general, to act so as to produce good effects. Good effects are the same when I am there as when I am not, like the rest of the external world, hence they are good in you as well as in me. Hence, it is good for me to produce good effects in you." Surely this simply follows from the intellectuality of the creature ; it does not depend on exciting emotions of fraternal love or what not, though no doubt they are needed if he is to act on the belief when under strain. It is part of the process of believing that there is a real world outside you, an idea which is built up by generalisation and analogy (however stupid the baby may appear), and the question whether I love you or hate you is logically a later one than the discovery that you are the same kind of thing as me, but outside me. Of course, the experiencing creature always starts in the middle of things, with an extremely rich confused experience which is gradually analysed and clarified ; we cannot say at what stage this notion begins to appear. But it is clear that a tendency to perform kind (or indeed cruel) actions involves a belief, in a sense in which a tendency to howl if there is no sugar in the feeding-bottle doesn't.

As to whether the universe recommends pure egotism, there is of course quite a strong case from evolution for saying that it recommends Mutual Aid, and that intra-specific competition only produces freaks like the giraffes. The trouble with a book like Julian Huxley's *Evolution and Ethics*, it seems to me, is merely that he cannot hold in mind the logical puzzles of his position, not even from the beginning of one sentence to the end of it, so that his prose style is an endless series of question-begging phrases. For instance, there is at least a difficulty in saying that you know things are getting better but don't know what good is ; one that might be got over if it were ever faced. What he aims at saying is, I should think, true. But anyway this line of argument would not prevent a pure egotist from deciding that it is worth his while to do things which would make his society collapse after he is dead ; the decision will depend partly on the effectiveness of his belief that other people exist and partly, I am not trying to deny, on his emotional equipment. It still seems quite possible to say that one decision would be *better* than another. And, on either count, the idea that there is a fundamental tragedy or scandal, a thing which (most dangerously) people are now finding out, viz. that the universe recommends pure egotism, is I think merely a result of taking a philosophical puzzle too seriously. Anyway people are not finding it out ; the typical products of our time are avid for self-sacrifice. No doubt this justifies a strong note of doom, but not because of any excessive individualism.

I therefore feel that though the Theory of Value is adequate, and indeed fruitful as giving insight, in the field for which it is supplied in the *Principles*, that of describing what happens when we get a valuable effect from a piece of artwork, still the darker puzzles about pseudo-statements were always unnecessary. Of course, if you say that a statement about the existence of other people is inherently meaningless, as I take it Professor Wittgenstein would do, then all statements about value are meaningless too ; but we need not bring these scruples into other branches of study. No doubt the position I am recommending is what the philosophers like to call naive realism, but I hope that need not be confused with religiosity. It seems to me that statements about value, though most of them are very rough, are capable of being true or false ; and the ultimate criterion though likely to remain obscure is, I should think, very much on the lines of the Richards Theory of Value. And so the idea that laying bare and outfacing the scandal about the universe was somehow the key to discovering and implementing the Emotive functions of language seems to me merely an unfortunate case of " making it all fit in ". I think it has only delayed the treatment of emotions in words on their own terms.

APPENDIX II

I ought also to say something about *Signs, Language and Behaviour* (1946) by Charles Morris, an important recent work on this kind of topic. He starts much further back than I do, and never reaches the kind of case I want to handle ; like most half-behaviourists he has practically nothing to say about double meanings. The Modes of signifying by language are divided into designation, appraisal, prescription, and formulization ; these roughly correspond to statements, expressions of emotion or preference, incitements to action (as in the imperative), and logical connectives or logical propositions. They are to be considered from the point of view of the hearer, who interprets the language ; from the point of view of the speaker, there is another set of four, very similar but with different names, which are described as the Usages of language. They are the informative, valuative, incitive, and systemic usages, and any Mode may be combined with any Usage. A piece of language is " expressive " if besides its ordinary function it gives the hearer information about the speaker, and this too (as I understand) is independent of the other eight. It certainly looks as if my set of terms is inadequate, and confuses a lot of these separate objects together.

However, I am not clear that there is much advantage in separating them, at any rate for dictionary purposes. Emotions Mr. Morris ties very firmly to preferences (because the behaviourist is not interested in what the organism may feel but what it would do) ; and establishing a preference in someone seems to me very hard to distinguish from inciting him to act in accordance with it. In the same way, there seems no great need to separate the informative from the systemic, except to grapple with the difficulties of a behaviourist theory of knowledge. Thus the four distinctions could be made to collapse into the old Ogden-Richards two. Then again, the case of an imperative which is treated as coming from nobody must be pretty rare ; when you are given an order (even if it comes from God or from tribal custom) you tend to have a pretty clear idea about who it comes from. It would then be " expressive " in Mr. Morris's system, but this seems a rather misleading term ; it need not express anything else about the speaker except that he had given you the order. I should say then that (at any rate in the ordinary way) those incitements which need to be separated from appraisals are also " expressive ", and I would call them Moods ; whereas the appraisals and the non-expressive incitements are my Emotions. The doubling of the class of four to distinguish speaker from hearer seems to me to under-rate the extent to which they imagine each other's mental processes ; they have to be trying to do this, however many mistakes they make, or they could not talk at all, and the effect is that both groups are represented in both of them.

However, I am glad to be able to claim support from Mr. Morris when he deals with the relations between the Modes. They can be independent ; signs in one mode can appear without there being signs in the other modes. But " when the situation itself does not supply the clues needed for the direction of behaviour", he says, and a variety of signs are produced, " prescriptions rest on appraisals and appraisals on statements in a way in which statements do not need to be followed by appraisals and appraisals by prescriptions." In my account, a Mood appears as normally based on an Emotion and an Emotion on a Sense, and the Moods partly overlap the prescriptions, so they pile up in the same order.

Mr. Morris then permutes the four modes and the four usages to describe sixteen types of discourse, a neat piece of work ; but rather a baffling one, because it is hard to be sure whether the distinction of speaker from hearer is really meant, or instead a distinction between the grammatical form (either of words or sentences, for the modes cover both) and the general purport of the piece of language. The purport of a script is clearly separate from the purpose of the author. Mr. Morris actually points out that the author may only be trying to earn money, but he still seems to feel that this is part of the meaning of the text ; whereas it is usual for a critic to assume that he can judge the purport as well as the author can, if not better. I think that this purport must have been in view when Mr. Morris gave Fiction (novels and so on) as examples of designative-valuative discourse ; the form makes statements, but the purport distinguishes good lives from bad ones. There is no need to suppose that a novel consists of true statements in the mind of a reader but of moral suasion in the mind of the author. Appraisive-informative discourse, when the pair is swapped round, is exemplified by myths ; they are emotive in form but they are telling you moral truths. I think this is a graceful and broadminded account of myths, and I would like to put a lot of poetry into this class ; but surely the idea that speaker is distinguished from hearer has become very dim here. Appraisive-valuative discourse, where both sides are concerned with preferences, is then exemplified by Poetry, and the only difficulty here is to remember how little the term *valuation* is allowed to mean. " It may appear that appraisive signifying, especially when metaphorical in character, is sufficient and that there is no further need to claim that the poet aims to excite valuations . . . But there is still the question of the criterion by which it is called poetic discourse, and I believe that this involves the aim of exciting valuative attitudes." *Valuation* seems to be different from *appraisal* because it deals with good and bad, not only with whether the organism will first eat the lettuce or the banana ; and I suspect that Mr. Morris himself, when he wrote these sentences, did not clearly remember what they have to mean. Presumably they have to mean something like : not only does the poem tend to make the organisms who read it start with the banana, but the author intended it to make them start with the banana. The phrases used by Mr. Morris certainly have an air of meaning more, and I think this shows (by the way) that the practice of extracting one's own technical terms from ordinary language on this profuse scale is a dangerous one. However, I take it the unmentioned alternative view of these terms is also in play ; the idea is that the general purport of a poem is Emotive as well as its individual words and sentences. I ought not to complain at Mr. Morris's insistence on this distinction (if that is what he means), because he has anticipated a point I have been trying to make myself; that the question whether the general purport is Emotive is very different from the question whether the individual words are. But if this is what is meant there is no point in distinguishing speaker from hearer, because the hearer too is expected to get the general purport ; and if we are considering single words (e.g. for a dictionary) there is no need for terms which only apply to whole passages. Apart from this, so far as I can see, Mr. Morris's treatment of poetry is only the old Emotive one over again.

His treatment of Value in general is interesting to follow, but I doubt whether it gets us anywhere different. Within the limitation of defining everything " behaviourally " it is meant to be as liberal as possible, and he insists that the term " good " is often not merely emotive (p. 81) ;

> " ' Good ' is an appraisor in so far as it disposes its interpreters to preferential behaviour, and is a designator in so far as it signifies merely that some organism has certain preferences or that something is preferable to something else in the sense that it more fully satisfies a certain need. . . . the term ' good ' does not signify an emotion and is no more ' expressive ' of its user than is any other sign. The appraisor simply signifies the preferential status of objects ; it determines which objects the organism is disposed to favour in its behaviour."

In the same way *preferable* may have " a strong and even dominant designative core ", saying that one thing " gives more complete satisfaction to some need or needs " than another, and in this sense of the term an animal may prefer objects which are not preferable. On the other hand (p. 107) " a T-appraisive ascriptor " (and " T-ascriptors which denote would ordinarily be called ' true ' ")

> " is an appraisive ascriptor such that what is identified evokes the responses in its interpreters which are signified as required."

That is, an Emotive term is used truly if the hearers agree with it, or perhaps if it succeeds in making them agree with it. This seems a very unnecessary immorality after the previous admission ; suppose an Emotive term makes you prefer what is not preferable—why must it be allowed the coy label " T " ?

The notion of right and wrong comes in under the head of " social control " (p. 207).

> " Through language signs and post-language symbols the individual internalises in himself the socially objective process of language communication, his thinking retaining the pattern of conversation, and his self-control through signs continuing in a new and subtle form the techniques of social control. It is in such ways that the phenomena of conscience and guilt arise . . . "

(Later it is admitted that the individual may change the culture in which he has appeared.) There is nothing to complain of in this account ; it is possible to put a moral belief and a preference for bananas into the same general class, even if you think them very different in themselves. Mr. Morris claims, indeed, that his " semiotic " is not concerned to give a " theory of value " and could be combined with any ; I should think this is true, though the holders of some theories of value would regard it as an attempt at boring from within. The real trouble is not so much the doctrine as what the language always appears to be hinting—here chiefly by the word *phenomena*. It hints that if I am walking down the road and find you, a stranger, screaming under a tree-trunk, and all I have to do is to push it up and let you out, then there is no meaning at all in saying that I have any obligation to let you out, or that it would be wrong not to let you out ; there is no sense in my doing such a thing unless it satisfies one of my own needs. The people who hold or toy with this view do seem to have a vague idea that it would be a bit unpopular if it was widely known, and that I imagine is why they use such very long words, all through each one of their sentences, at the beginning, middle, and end. I cannot see that they have any other skeleton in their cupboard.

I have been agreeing with Professor Richards, unless I misunderstood him, that egoist ethical theory needs to be escaped, by pseudo-statements if necessary, and merely adding that I don't think they are necessary. But I doubt whether the strict logical theory is what people have in mind when they are accepting this kind of talk. The logical argument is that it is meaningless to say you ought to help other people, because " good " can mean nothing to you except the satisfaction of your own impulses, and there can be no duty except to acquire this good. What people commonly feel, when they accept this argument with self-approval, is I believe something quite different ; it is the individualist tradition, which I have tried to illustrate by the phrases about dogs, and the tricks of the word *honest*, and in its corrupt form by Iago. Up to a point this is a very healthy thing, and in any case it is not felt to be " mean ", because you may need a good deal of altruism to put up with the activities of a rival individual. If you take a stylist who appears to be preaching pure egotism, for instance La Rochefoucauld, this is made fairly clear though in a subtle way. The charm of the system is to be like a working model, therefore somehow like a toy, and at the same time it is felt to be positively generous. Human pretensions need to be exposed because a great deal of cruelty is due to self-righteousness ; a noble mind will not assert that its good actions are truly generous, but will recognise the variety of its satisfactions ; and we under-rate our neighbours if we do not see the painful complexity of their position. The triumph of the style is that he can say a very long list of mean things without your ever eeling that he is himself mean ; it would not be good writing unless it was felt to carry a hint of paradox and therefore self-contradiction. Whereas consistent action in accordance with the pure theory, so far as I can see, would be quite recognisably insane ; for one thing, there is so much reciprocity needed to understand ordinary language that such a man would not be able to use it. There is perhaps a sign of this confusion in the language adopted by behaviourists themselves; they put out sentence after sentence implying " there is nothing in the world but knee-jerks " (to borrow a phrase from Mr. Wyndham Lewis), but all in a style of such pomposity as to imply " I'm not in the world myself, because I'm God ". The author himself, for example, is never compared to a chimpanzee, only the ordinary users of language. I do not mean that this is due to a moral weakness or a " psychic lesion " ; it is so hard to include the scientist himself in a behaviourist view of the world that he can hardly avoid presenting himself as outside it. But unless he can get himself into it we can be certain that his theory is wrong. And all classification of moral preferences together with the preference of the " organism " for the banana holds the confusion in reserve, ready to be hinted at by this insane literary style. However, I do not mean that one mustn't generalise in this way ; I have done it myself by accepting the class of " Emotions in words ".

It also seems to me that, if he claims all moral ideas as products of language, as Mr. Morris is doing in this passage, the semiot is over-playing his hand. What we really want to know is whether language affects our moral ideas in a much narrower and more obvious way, that is, whether we would alter our moral ideas if we realised what language was doing to us. It seems to me that most people, whether educated or not, are tolerably clear about " emotive " words ; if they don't feel as the word tells them to do they recognise a dis-agreement for which they feel they have grounds, and they " get round " the word by irony or something. But I think we do get deceived fairly often by " equations " in words, for example, by the now out-of-date one which I examined in *native;* and, if people were more aware of the process, I think that would sometimes be enough to save them from being deceived, though no doubt not very often.

APPENDIX III

(This was published in *Psyche* for 1935, and is perhaps rather remote from the present book. But I hope it makes clear my defence against a possible line of attack, one which if successful would reduce to nonsense the theory I have been putting forward).

The connection between theory and practice, where both are living and growing, need not be very tidy ; they may work best where there is some mutual irritation. Also the difference between any two conflicting theories is partly a matter of what they put first, that is, what they ask you to think of first ; by the time that you get hold of the refinements and exceptions the theories may come to much the same, and you may be too muddled to know how much. A man who has that active knowledge of a subject which it is so strangely hard to connect to theoretical knowledge may often safely use a theory for " telling the reader what to think of first " ; he has a " skill " which keeps it from misleading him ; on the other hand this will not tell him how other people might be misled. I want here to look at some remarks in Professor Bloomfield's excellent and learned *Language,* which support " mechanist " (behaviorist) psycho-logy or linguistic theory, and I think are misleading ; but the point is not that they mislead him—it is amusing to see how firmly he can prevent them. Nor indeed that the theory is wrong at bottom ; the bottom, to quote one of Mr. Eliot's solemn thoughts, is a great way down. The curious thing is that behaviorism can be used in such irrelevant ways, that its terms make battle-cries for any war on hand, that one is so little tempted here to leave linguistics and discuss philosophy.

For example, it is one thing to define linguistic meaning in terms of mechanism, quite another to assume that the makers of language handled it stupidly. I think it is fair to say he does this (p. 355) when he makes a stand on the word " cuckoo ". There are " advocates of sporadic sound-change " who wish to connect

" Sanskrit [ko:kilah], Greek ['kokkuks], Latin *cuculus* : English *cuckoo*. They admit that this leaves us no criterion of decision, but insist that our inability to draw a line does not prove anything . . . The neo-grammarian sees in this a grave violation of scientific method. The beginning of our science was made by a procedure which implied regularity of linguistic change . . ." and so on. There is a definite argument against them, that

" we should have to assume that in every case of sporadic sound-change, the discrepant sound has been reduced to some ordinary phonetic type in time to escape the ear of the observer."

Of course, he is right in refusing most irregular sound-changes for etymology, and right in demanding a " criterion of decision ". It is only in the choice of the example " cuckoo " that he shows a too firm preference of method to sense. The reason that *cuckoo* kept its sound was that everyone knew it was meant to sound like a cuckoo, and neither " guggoo " nor " huhoo " would have done this well. It is not true to say that no criterion of decision had been offered ; indeed, Jespersen had offered living evidence, in the shape of a lady who pronounced the first vowel of the word as in " but " and came from a part of Scotland lacking in cuckoos. As to the argument from gradualness, the discrepancy need *not* be supposed to " escape the ear of the observer ". " Cuckoo " would presumably shift its " k " normally along [kh—kx—x—h] (" x " as of " ich ") until the parallel scale [g—k] provided a better imitation of a cuckoo ; then there would be two versions in competition, exchanging across heaven knows what variety of dialects ; then the better one would win. You may of course say that the new version is a new word, though it has the same intention and effect as the old one and direct continuity with it, but this is not the claim. Professor Bloomfield gives no explanation of his own, and the presumption from his other examples is that there were two words for a cuckoo (one no doubt " guggoo ") in Primitive Aryan. I submit that this is a mistake due to blind following of " mechanist " theory ; what he denies or refuses to say is that the speakers had a reasonable intention and carried it out. I take this first because I think it is the only case where his theory has definitely misled him. Yet it is a quite irrelevant effect of mechanist theory. The tendency to echo the bird's song in its name can easily be described in non-mentalist terms, and the observable fact that there is such an echo gives a " criterion " for irregular sound-change (there is a force making for irregularity even if other forces are stronger). It is only not the sort of thing a mechanist likes ; he feels that when a machine has one rule it does not complicate its behaviour with another.

It looks, then, as if the mechanist attitude carries a tendency to over-simplify, and one could put this suspicion into any rule he gives. An irregular form (p. 399) is more likely to be kept up in a common word, because that gives a more frequent stimulus against the force of analogy. He does not deny that this is only one of the main factors at work ; a common word may be boiled down for convenience and a rare word treated with respect. But we need to remind ourselves that there may be such other factors at work ; I suggest that a good way to do this is to say "the speakers do what they think proper ". Similarly about "-ish:"*

> " The starting-point of semantic specialization is to be sought in forms where the underlying word has the special value ; thus the unpleasant flavour of -*ish* comes from words like *loutish*, *boorish*, *swinish*, *hoggish*."

This gives one of the crucial factors. But firstly, there is a typical hen-and-egg problem ; why do you not get " lordish " and " angelish " at the starting-point, unless " ish " had taken its line already ? Secondly, it is not inevitable that the factor described should win the day ; the kind of knowledge claimed here does not admit of prophecy. " Un- " commonly makes words that give a null or slack feeling, *unable*, *unemployed*, but in words where the meaning goes the other way it is not touched by this feeling : *undimmed*, *unwearying*, *unassailable*. The speakers hold on to the root meaning of " un- " " because they feel that is the sensible thing to do ". Now mentalist terms like " proper " and " sensible " may be mere conveniences of thought, things like " force " in dynamics, which is still used though it does not appear in the equations to which it leads ; or a mechanist psychology, once complete, might be able to calculate our future actions without using such terms at all. But neither view gives a reason for not using them at present ; they at least remind you of the complexity of the machine and may suggest what factors are working.

After backing the mechanist against the mentalist for several pages, Professor Bloomfield remarks (p. 143) that "the dispute has

---

*Prof. Bloomfield's " undesirably, inappropriately resembling " is an improvement on the N.E.D. " having the bad or undesirable qualities of," since *mannish* is essentially not used of men, and *hoggish* while used of hogs was not rude to them. On the whole, sixteenth century formations start as simple derived adjectives used of the hog or what-not itself, while seventeenth century ones start as rude and figurative. Cases like the admiring *waggish*, and *foolish* (less rude than *fool*), have got mixed up with the other sense " rather, partly ".

really very little to do with problems of linguistic meaning ". This is so true that one wonders how it is brought in. Then ". . . The mental processes or internal bodily processes "—the crucial distinction—" of other people are known to each one of us only from speech-utterances and other observable actions. Since these are all we have to work with, the mentalist in practice defines meanings exactly as does the mechanist ", etc. So the crux is the word *observable* ; what may a scientist claim to have observed—may he admit that he knows that ' cuckoo ' is an onomatopoeia ? Professor Bloomfield himself fairly insists that the scientist cannot even list the fundamental sounds (phonemes) of a language without admitting that he knows which differences of sound are significant, so the field of war is a marginal one. It is dealt with by means of hint and tautology. On p. 144 we have a " fundamental assumption ", admitted to be only partial truth, that " in certain communities (speech-communities) some utterances are alike as to form and meaning ". This only means that the scientist may admit one thing that he knows as a man, and its only use is to make the step a serious one. On p. 168 we stumble on another " necessary principle —perhaps we should call it an assumption "—" that a language can only convey such meanings as are attached to some formal feature ; the speakers can signal only by means of signals." Here we have a more complex trope. On pp. 162–67 ' tagmemes ' and ' morphemes ' (in grammar and lexicon) have been defined as the smallest meaningful units of signalling. Tagmemes come down to such things as ' exclamatory final pitch ', but it is not clear if they would be allowed further—e.g. avoiding what you would be expected to say, or calling a thing by an unusual name. On p. 244 we get definitely below morphemes. " Perhaps in most languages, most of the roots are morphemes . . . In other cases, however, we find . . . such roots as . . . [skr-] ' grating impact or sound ' : *scratch, scrape, scream* " ; they are not morphemes but he attaches signals to them. This would be a very unimportant looseness in the terms if it were not for the claim in the tautology about signals. You are meant to give the tautology sense by limiting the meaning of *signal* in its second occurrence— " they can only signal by the signals here defined ", and it is then wrong ; a more open sense is to be recommended— " it is certain that they can signal as they do, and any means that they use we must call a signal ". But to use this version you must admit that you can sometimes tell what they are signalling. Till you have decided what a piece of language conveys, like any literary critic, you cannot look round to see what ' formal features ' convey it ; you will then find that some features are of great subtlety, and perhaps fail to trace some at all. Nor will this process only work in your native language ; literature makes rigid requirements from individual words if a whole passage is to take effect, so it gives a powerful means of understanding the doubtful words of a foreign or ancient language. This whole notion of the scientist viewing language from outside and above is a fallacy; we would have no hope of dealing with the subject if we had not a rich obscure practical knowledge from which to extract the theoretical. There seems no fundamental reason why a mechanist should object. The reason one does not at once feel this about Professor Bloomfield's remarks is that they might only mean " guesses are often wrong, and one must aim at getting the thing tidy ", and with that one must heartily agree.

A few other suasive devices may be noted. We are frequently told that ' the linguist ' cannot deal with meanings, for they must be left to the psychologist (or some such figure). This is not quite settled ; on p. 146 the mathematician is " acting as a linguist " when he defines the numbers, given ' one ' and ' add ', but on p. 508 the linguist can only classify the forms for meanings that have been " determined by some other science ", and numbers appear again as an example. In any case, if only the title of this person keeps him from the study of language, he had better change it ; Professor Bloomfield himself is clearly larger than his linguist. The linguist, of course, is a worthy rhetorical device so far as he means that you must make an adequate collection of facts before you judge or generalize.

An odd introduction is used (p. 426) for the list of types of sense-change. " We can easily see today that a change in the meaning of a speech-form is merely the result of a change in the use of it and other, semantically related, speech-forms. Earlier students, however ", in their folly, ". . . set up such classes as the following ". They occupy a full page, making distinctions as to meaning in an untrammelled manner, and at the end we are told they are " useful ". Not that this is anything to complain about ; it is a fine thing that the book should be larger than its theory.

Also a mysterious remark about the Future is several times used to keep meanings at bay. " The statement of meaning is therefore the weak point in language study, and will remain so until human knowledge advances very far beyond its present state " (p. 140). Interesting and suggestive ; but this has become a sinister influence by p. 441, where a longish discussion of the sense-change of *meat* ends with the helpless remark " We may some day find out why *flesh* was disfavoured in culinary situations." At least, then, it is not impossible on philosophical grounds. Of course, any theory may be refuted in the future, but this is no reason for not giving the obvious theory about *flesh*—that people had a delicacy about words which insisted you were eating a dead animal. I had best try to show what kind of evidence there is.

Thou needst not, mistress cook, be told
That meat tomorrow will be cold
Which now is fresh and hot ;
Even so our flesh will, by and by,
Be cold as stone.   Cook, thou must die,
There's death within the pot.

There is nothing archaic about this, but it is a revival of the old
flesh (for cooking-meat) as an amusing challenge to the squeamishness.   Dr. Johnson's mildly archaic uses were meant to have at once
a solemn and a plain-man flavour (from dialect and Biblical influence), so give evidence of the same feeling.   However, one may
doubt whether this reason for the shift, implying a somewhat
anxious refinement, was likely to work before the eighteenth
century, still more whether it worked in the early settlement of
Norman words for each animal when cooked.   The origin of forms
like ' pig—pork ' was probably political only, and these might act
on *flesh* by mere analogy (" cooked flesh will have a special word like
cooked pig ") ; even so they would encourage the development of
this kind of squeamishness, and that would help the shift to *meat*.
There may well be too little evidence to decide.   My only point is
that evidence like the verse from Hood would be real ; Professor
Bloomfield seems to be treating it as ' non-linguistic '.   " The
methodical error which has held up this phase of our work, is our
habit of putting the question in non-linguistic terms—in terms of
meaning and not of form.   When we say that the word *meat* has
changed from the meaning ' food ' to the meaning ' edible flesh ',
we are merely stating the practical result of a linguistic process ",
etc.   He tends to avoid letting this way of treating the matter
interfere with his practice, but one can imagine its being used to
stop someone else's practice with very sturdy conviction.

Some examples should now be given to show that Professor
Bloomfield himself is not a strict mechanist, if you take the narrow
view of his phrases on the subject, and that the full weight of the grim
Puritan virtues of behaviorism is reserved for those without its
pale.   On p. 149, discussing the *mouth* of a bottle and so forth,
Professor Bloomfield can say :

" The remarkable thing about these transferred meanings is
our assurance and our agreement in viewing one of the meanings
as *normal* (or *central*) and the others are *marginal* (*metaphoric* or
transferred).   The central meaning is favoured in the sense that
we understand a form (that is, respond to it) in the central meaning
unless some factor of the practical situation forces us to look to a
transferred meaning."

On p. 435 :

" Wundt defines the central meaning as the *dominant element* of meaning, and shows how the dominant element may shift when a form occurs in new typical contexts. Thus, when *meat* had been heard predominantly in situations where fleshfood was concerned the dominant element became, for more and more speakers, not ' food ' but ' flesh-food '. This statement leaves the matter exactly where it was."

Exactly where it was after you had learned Professor Bloomfield's term ' central meaning ', but he has had to fix one such term before pointing out his ' remarkable thing '. No doubt, Professor Bloomfield would say that the metaphor of domination is where the ' mentalist ' position comes in, with its always useless explanation, but that is only a descriptive name ; he has argued from what we feel about the affair (*assurance*) no less than Wundt.

There is a special tone of triumph here because an advance in method had some correspondence to the behaviorist programme. The change from prayers to *beads* in that word went through phrases like ' telling his beads ', where it could satisfactorily mean either ; the German *kopf* ' head ', derived from ' pot ', is at least known to have changed in a special context, that of head-smashing in battle. It is true that you would be more likely to *think* of looking for these crucial contexts if you had (p. 139) " defined the meaning of a linguistic form as the situation in which the speaker utters it and the response which it calls forth in the hearer ". But whichever end you start from you have to work towards the other. This is not so clear in the shift of *bead*, which could be sometimes an irony, sometimes a convenience (I don't know what other word for *beads* they had), sometimes perhaps a poetical feeling that the prayers were inherent in the holy beads ; that is, different states of mind might work towards the shift in different speakers. But with *kopf* I think the feeling must have been one of two, because the two would conflict ; either a piece of tough humour, as in ' bashing his block ', or a solemn euphemism, perhaps imitating the Romance shift (French *tete*, Latin *testum*), anyhow meant to imply that head-smashing is correct here though not elsewhere. Now it may well be that we cannot discover which, and if so to know the context is at least something. But you cannot say that you have ' explained ' the shift till you have given the feeling or intention that pushed it through. Professor Bloomfield indeed admits this in his next example : " We can best understand the shift in modern cases, where the connotative values and the practical background are known " (p. 441), so he explains the feelings behind the advertiser's use of ' home ' for *house*. But to do this, to admit that he knows the advertiser's feelings, is to give up his first position (p. 38), that " we have no way of determining what the speakers may feel ". It may be said of course that this was only a practical truth, too often applicable, but not always. But he went on at once to say " it may be stated as a principle that in all sciences like linguistics, which observe some specific type of human activity, the worker must proceed exactly as if he held the materialistic view ". This is perhaps always true in some deep sense, but its natural sense, if you take it with the other, is one that he has been too sensible to maintain.

It is curious to compare the treatment of ' marginal meaning ' to that of ' connotation ', which follows at once.

> " The second important way in which meanings show instability, is the presence of supplementary values which we call connotations."

No doubt this, and not the gist of the subsequent remarks, is meant as the definition ; but the leap back to fundamental dogma which follows is I think actively confusing.

> " The meaning of a form for any one speaker is nothing more than a result of the situations in which he has heard the form. If he has not heard it very many times, or if he has heard it under very unusual circumstances, his use of the form may deviate from the conventional. We combat such personal deviations by giving explicit definitions of meaning ; this is a chief use of our dictionaries. In the case of scientific terms, we manage to keep the meaning nearly free from connotative factors, though even here we may be unsuccessful ; the number *thirteen*, for instance, has for many people a strong connotation."

Language is full of pitfalls, but I fancy I see a distinction here between ' we ', the scientists, ' combating ' the insane herd, and this herd itself, mere users of language, objects of behaviorist study ; there is at least no other clear distinction. As to dictionaries, the N.E.D. is good at listing what it sometimes calls connotations, and does not treat them as ' personal deviations'. Professor Bloomfield indeed proceeds to admit that " in the last analysis, every speech-form has its own connotative flavour for the entire speech-community and this, in turn " has personal deviations added to it ; an important difference between two things given the same name. The phrase about meaning being a ' result ' of situations is here a typical fallacy of pseudo-scientific discourse (like the ' signal ' tautology) ; irrefutable with a broad view of the causes at work, wrong with a narrow view such as would make it distinctive. It is really no use confusing the belief that thirteen is unlucky with a mistake in the sense of that term due to " not hearing it very many times ". Of course there is no harm in making ' connotation ' so general that it covers both. But there is no means of connecting a connotation so introduced to a marginal meaning (e.g. does a m.m., used sometimes, give rise to a c., present always ?) ; they belong to different degrees of generality and seem to belong to different philosophies. The effect of behaviorist language here is only to say that he does not think well of connotations, and when he gets interested in some he uses the term definitely.

We are told that Dodgson, after using new formations in *The Jabberwocky*, " later in the book, explains what connotative significance they had for him ". It is clear at least that their connotation cannot have been " nothing more than the result of the situations in which he had heard them," for he had not. Also it looks as if there is a muddle here, because what Humpty Dumpty gives is not the ' connotations ' but the ' central meaning ' and then the reason for the ' connotation ' ; " That'll do very well ", says Alice, who had the feeling already, as a person of taste, and only wanted the plain sense to fit in. But when Professor Bloomfield is prepared to be interested in such words he is quite at home with the distinction.

> " English is especially rich in another type of intense forms, the *symbolic* forms. Symbolic forms have a connotation of somehow illustrating the meaning more immediately than do ordinary speech-forms. The explanation is a matter of grammatical structure and will concern us later ; to the speaker it seems as if the sounds were specially suited to the meaning."

The explanation (p. 245), a brief but excellent treatment of these words, points out that e.g. ' flare ' combines ' flash, flicker etc.' with ' glare, blare etc.', so seems to carry its own explanation. This is just the Jabberwocky principle, but ' connotation ' is now used for a feeling, something quite different from the ' central meaning ' and not needing to be ' combated ' by a dictionary. Nor do such words get their connotation from being heard only in special contexts. One may add that the use of *connotation* here is unnecessary, if the main work of that term is for words with extra emotive colours and implications as to *milieu* ; he could say " symbolic forms somehow illustrate . . ." without more ado.

I brought in this passage before, to claim that it disturbed the ' morpheme ' system, and for that matter it involves a third step, an oblivion of the great principle " We have no means of determining what the speakers may feel "—luckily he had some means of determining what he felt about *flare*. There is something rather dismal about a whole laborious essay attempting only to nag at one good writer, and it is no more than fair to point out that Professor Bloomfield deserves a great deal of admiration for having been able to write this paragraph against such odds. But surely there is clear need to protest against the theory that imposed them.

I shall try finally to list some things that *might* be meant by a vague assumption that the linguist cannot observe meanings so must not use them. They might be like absolute space, and I fancy this analogy is somewhere in the behaviorist mind. On this view, not only are they deduced from what is observed instead of observed themselves, but they are so related to observation that there is no experiment to decide whether they are this or that, just as there is no experiment to decide which velocity is absolute rest. In such a case there is no use for the notion and it is better abandoned. But the analogy is not seriously maintained ; after abandoning oneself to 'mentalist' theory it is still often possible to decide whether a word means this or that. Or there might be no test to decide between mentalist and mechanist, which is probably true, but this gives no reason for refusing help from either. Professor Bloomfield's practical claim, that the mentalist never gives useful help, I hope to have refuted from his practice. Or meanings might be like point electrons, not observed as directly as common objects, faced with a theory that views them with suspicion, but still the only fiction that will sum up the results of a large group of experiments. On this analogy mentalist meanings might be not only unobservable but unreal, and yet it might be the business of the linguist to use them. Finally they might simply be out of reach, and Professor Bloomfield can hardly · take this as evidence of unreality ; he has no hope of observing the primitive Aryan language, but he treats it as real. That they are often gravely out of reach certainly needs underlining, or one may jump at the wrong conclusion in practice ; but the reason for that is that one wants the right one ; and to underline this with the other ideas is to seek confusion.

My own reason for complaining about this good book had best be explained at the end. I read it while trying to find some way of separating out the emotions, implications, personal suggestions and suchlike in our complex words, seeing how they are related, how a learner might pick them up more easily ; a region in which Dr. Richards has already done a good deal. Now supposing I did some useful work on this difficult topic I should feel sure of the understanding and goodwill of Professor Bloomfield. But, if you take at their face value these remarks that he lets drop, he is saying that such work would be beyond the pale of the exact sciences, impossible to understand, impossible to criticize.

INDEX

INDEX

446

INDEX

INDEX

INDEX

THE HOGARTH PRESS

A New Life For A Great Name

This is a paperback list for today's readers – but it holds to a tradition of adventurous and original publishing set by Leonard and Virginia Woolf when they founded The Hogarth Press in 1917 and started their first paperback series in 1924.

Now, after many years of partnership, Chatto & Windus · The Hogarth Press are proud to launch this new series. Our choice of books does not echo that of the Woolfs in every way – times have changed – but our aims are the same. Some sections of the list are light-hearted, some serious: all are rigorously chosen, excellently produced and energetically published, in the best Hogarth Press tradition. We hope that the new Hogarth Press paperback list will be as prized – and as avidly collected – as its illustrious forebear.

A list of our books already published, together with some of our forthcoming titles, follows. If you would like more information about Hogarth Press books, write to us for a catalogue:

40 William IV Street, London WC2N 4DF

Please send a large stamped addressed envelope

HOGARTH CRITICS

HOGARTH FICTION

Behind A Mask: The Unknown Thrillers of Louisa May Alcott
Edited and Introduced by Madeleine Stern

Death of a Hero by Richard Aldington
New Introduction by Christopher Ridgway

The Amazing Test Match Crime by Adrian Alington
New Introduction by Brian Johnston

Epitaph of a Small Winner by Machado de Assis
Translated and Introduced by William L. Grossman

Mrs Ames by E.F. Benson
Paying Guests by E.F. Benson
Secret Lives by E.F. Benson
New Introductions by Stephen Pile

Ballantyne's Folly by Claud Cockburn
New Introduction by Andrew Cockburn
Beat the Devil by Claud Cockburn
New Introduction by Alexander Cockburn

Chance by Joseph Conrad
New Introduction by Jane Miller

Lady Into Fox & A Man in the Zoo by David Garnett
New Introduction by Neil Jordan

The Whirlpool by George Gissing
New Introduction by Gillian Tindall

Morte D'Urban by J.F. Powers
Prince of Darkness and other stories by J.F. Powers
New Introductions by Mary Gordon

Mr Weston's Good Wine by T.F. Powys
New Introduction by Ronald Blythe

The Revolution in Tanner's Lane by Mark Rutherford
New Introduction by Claire Tomalin
Catharine Furze by Mark Rutherford
Clara Hopgood by Mark Rutherford
New Afterwords by Claire Tomalin

The Last Man by Mary Shelley
New Introduction by Brian Aldiss

The Island of Desire by Edith Templeton
Summer in the Country by Edith Templeton
New Introductions by Anita Brookner

Christina Alberta's Father by H.G. Wells
Mr Britling Sees It Through by H.G. Wells
New Introductions by Christopher Priest

Frank Burnet by Dorothy Vernon White
New Afterword by Irvin Stock

William Empson
Seven Types of Ambiguity

Chaucer, Milton, Marvell, Pope, Hopkins and T. S. Eliot are among the poets cited in this brilliant analysis of the effects which ambiguity, deliberate or unconscious, creates in English verse. Hailed as a masterpiece on its first publication in 1930, when Empson was twenty-four, *Seven Types of Ambiguity* is now acknowledged as a great work of modern criticism – theoretically daring and scholarly, yet witty, controversial and immensely readable.

Also by
William Empson
Collected Poems

William Empson is one of our most distinguished twen-
tieth-century poets; allusive, concentrated, challenging,
blending intellectual wit and elegance with powerful
feeling. His work helped to create the poetic climate of the
Forties and Fifties and the *Collected Poems*, published in
1955, established his eminence. The Hogarth Press now
reissues it for the first time in paperback.

Raymond Williams
The Country and the City

When this book was first published it was immediately
hailed as a masterpiece. By concentrating on changing
attitudes to the country and the city as they are portrayed
in English literature from the sixteenth to the twentieth
centuries, Raymond Williams shows the fascinating,
shifting associations of these two traditional poles of life,
and closely relates them to social developments. The
range of the analysis is as impressive as its depth: this is a
work which not only makes us look at the world afresh –
in fact and in literature – but also helps us to understand
why we see it as we do.